American Casino Guide

2012 Edition

Written and Edited By
Steve Bourie

Assistant Editor
Matt Bourie

Contributing Writers
Linda Boyd
John Grochowski
Dewey Hill
H. Scot Krause
Jean Scott
Henry Tamburin

This book is dedicated to the memory of Scott Barr.
A truly great guy who will forever be missed by his friends and family.

American Casino Guide - 2012 edition

Copyright ©2012, Casino Vacations Press, Inc.

Published By:
Casino Vacations Press, Inc.
P.O. Box 703
Dania, Florida 33004
(954) 989-2766

e-mail: info@americancasinoguide.com
website: americancasinoguide.com

ISBN-13: 978-1-883768-21-8
ISSN: 1086-9018

Table of Contents

About Your Guide

This guide has been written to help you plan your visit to casino gambling areas and also to help you save money once you are there. The first edition of this guide began 20 years ago as an eight-page newsletter and it has continued to grow each year as casino gambling has spread throughout the country. We have listed information on all of the states that offer any type of traditional casino table games or slot machines (including video lottery terminals). We have also included stories to help you understand how casinos operate; how video poker and slot machines work; how to make the best plays in blackjack, craps, roulette and baccarat; and how to take advantage of casino promotional programs. Additionally, we have included a casino coupon section that should save you many times the cost of this book.

Virtually every casino has a "comp" program whereby you can get free rooms, food, shows or gifts based upon your level of play at their table games. If you plan on gambling during your trip to the casino, you should call ahead and ask their marketing department for details on their programs. There are also stories in this book to help you understand how "comp" programs work and how to best take advantage of them.

One more suggestion to save you money when visiting a casino is to join their slot club. It doesn't cost anything and you would be surprised at how quickly those points can add up to earn you gifts, cash, food or other complimentaries. Also, as a slot club member you will usually receive periodic mailings from the casino with money-saving offers that are generally not available to the public.

When using this guide please remember that all of the listed room rates reflect the lowest and highest prices charged during the year. During holidays and peak periods, however, higher rates may apply. Also, since the gambling games offered at casinos vary from state to state, a listing of available games is found at the start of each state heading. We hope you enjoy your guide and we wish you good luck on your casino vacation!

Your Best Casino Bets - Part I

by Henry Tamburin

The majority of casino players leave too much to chance when playing in a casino. To put it bluntly, they don't have a clue as to how to play. They are literally throwing their money away with little chance of winning. Luck most certainly has a lot to do with your success in a casino but what really separates the winners from the losers is the skill of the players. Granted, there is no guarantee that you will win, but on the other hand, there is no guarantee that you must lose. My objective in this article is to educate you on the casino games so that at the very least, you'll be able to enjoy yourself in the casino with maximum play time and minimum risk to your bankroll.

Let's begin our understanding of casino gambling by learning how casinos win as much as they do. They don't charge admission, and they certainly don't depend on the luck of their dealers to generate the income they need to pay their overhead. In fact, they guarantee themselves a steady income by having a built in advantage, or house edge, on every bet. Think of it as a very efficient hidden tax that generates them a guaranteed daily profit.

Here's an example of how this works. Suppose we take a coin and play heads or tails. Every time you lose a flip of the coin you pay me $1. Every time you win a flip, I pay you 90¢. Would you play? I hope you said no. Here's why. In this simple game I would have an advantage over you and I created that advantage by not paying you at the true odds of one-to-one (or $1).

Casinos do this very same thing to create their advantage. They simply pay off winning bets at less than the true odds. For example, the true odds of winning a bet on number 7 on roulette are 37-to-1 (the latter means you have 37 chances to lose vs. one chance to win). If you get lucky and the roulette ball lands in the number seven slot, you'd expect the casino to pay you 37 chips as winnings for the one chip you bet on number 7 (37-to-1 payoff). If they did that, the casino's advantage would be zero. However, as I mentioned above, the casinos create their advantage by paying off winning bets at less than true odds. In the case of our bet on number 7, the winning payoff is 35 chips (instead of 37 chips). The two chips the casino quietly kept is what pays their bills. Mathematically, the casino advantage is 5.26% on this bet which simply means day in and day out, the casino expects to win (or keep) 5.26% of all money wagered in roulette.

The casino games with the lowest casino advantage (less than 1.25%), and your best bets, are blackjack, craps, baccarat, and video poker. Now don't sell the ranch and run over to your nearest casino just yet. These games, plus table poker, are your best bets but you must learn how to play these games properly to enhance your chances of winning. Here are some tips to get you started:

BLACKJACK - This is your best casino game, but you must learn how to play your hands (when to hit, stand, double-down, split, etc.). This is known as the basic strategy. Learn it and you can reduce the casino's advantage to virtually zero. And if you learn how to keep track of the cards as they are played (i.e. card counting) you can actually turn the tables on the casino and have the edge over them! Do not try to play blackjack if you haven't learned the correct basic strategy. If you do, your chances of winning are slim. Also, it's wise not to make any side bets that may be offered on your table and please stay away from any game which only pays 6-to-5 for an untied blackjack. Blackjack tournaments are also popular and here players compete against other players with the player with the most chips at the end of the round advancing. Tournament prizes can be substantial. Playing and betting strategy for blackjack tournaments, however, is different than playing blackjack in a casino so bone up on your tournament skills before considering playing in a tournament.

CRAPS - The game of craps intimidates most casino players because of the complicated playing layout and the multitude of bets. In fact craps is an easy game to play. And it also has some of the best bets in the casino (and also some of the worst). Your best bet is the pass line with odds and come with odds. Next best is a place bet on six or eight. Stay away from all other bets on the layout because the casino's advantage is too high. If you really enjoy the game of craps you might consider learning dice control – it's not an easy skill to learn and it requires a lot of practice but if you get good at it, you can have the edge over the casino.

ROULETTE - Every bet on the American roulette layout (with 0 and 00 on the wheel) has a high casino advantage. That goes for bets straight up on numbers that pay 35-to-1, as well as even money wagers on red or black. Atlantic City players get a break. If you bet on an even money payoff bet and 0 or 00 hits, you lose only half your wager. This cuts the casino's advantage in half. Also, some casinos offer a European layout with only one zero. This is a better bet than wheels with 0 and 00.

BACCARAT - Many casinos offer a low stakes version called mini-baccarat. Not a bad game to play. If you bet on the bank hand, the casino's edge is only 1.17%. And when you play baccarat, there are no playing decisions to make which makes the game very easy to play. However, this game is fast with many decisions per hour. It's best to play slowly. One way is to only bet on the bank hand after it wins (meaning you won't be betting on every hand which will slow down your play).

BIG SIX WHEEL - Stay away from spending a lot of time (and money) at this game. The casino's advantage is astronomical (11% to 26%). Its drawing card for the novice player is the low minimum bet ($1). Save your money for the better games.

CARIBBEAN STUD POKER - This popular cruise ship game has found its way to land-based and dockside casinos. Unlike regular table poker where players compete against each other, in this game the players play against the house. But the rules favor the casino and their advantage is about 5%. The part of this game that appeals to players is the progressive jackpot side bet. You should not make this side bet, however, unless the jackpot exceeds $280,000 for the $1 ante and the $1 jackpot bet.

PAI GOW POKER - Strange name for a casino game. The game is a cross between Pai Gow, a Chinese game of dominoes, and the American game of seven-card poker. Players are dealt seven cards and they must arrange (or set) their cards into a five-card poker hand and a two-card poker hand. Skill is involved in setting the two hands which can help reduce the casino's advantage.

SLOT MACHINES - Casinos earn more money from slot machines than all the table games combined. The casino's advantage varies from one machine to another. Typically the higher denomination machines ($1 and up) pay back more than the nickel, quarter and fifty-cent machines. Slots are not your best bet in the casino, but here are a few tips: It's wise to play one coin only in machines where all the payouts increase proportionally to the number of coins played (i.e, there is no jackpot for playing maximum coins). However, if the machine has a substantial jackpot when you play maximum coins, then you should play always play the maximum number of coins the machine will accept or you won't be eligible for a bonus payoff for the jackpot. Don't waste hours looking for a machine that's "ready to hit." Join the slot clubs, always use your slot club card when you play, and try to schedule your play time when the casino offers multiple points. Joining is free and you'll be rewarded with discounts and other freebies. Machines that have lower jackpots pay smaller amounts more frequently which means you normally get more playing time for your money. Playing machines that have bonus rounds and fancy graphics may be fun, but the house edge on these machines is usually higher than traditional reel spinning machines. Likewise, the house edge is higher for linked machines that have those life-changing mega jackpots. Some casinos now certify their machines to return 98% or more and these machines are your best bets. Also, consider playing in slot tournaments where you are competing against other players, rather than the house, and the prizes can be substantial.

VIDEO POKER - Your best bet if you enjoy playing slot machines. Skill is involved as well as learning to spot the better payoff machines. For example, on the classic jacks-or-better game, always check the full house and flush payoff schedule. The machines on jacks or better pay nine coins for a full house and six coins for a flush for each coin played. These machines are known as 9/6 machines. They are readily available; seek them out. The same analogy holds for bonus poker, double bonus, deuces wild, joker wild, etc., video poker games.

There are good pay schedules and bad ones, and it's up to you to know the difference and play only the higher paying schedules with the correct playing strategy (readily available on the Internet, in books, and on strategy cards).

KENO - This casino game has a very high casino advantage (usually 20% and up). Stay away if you are serious about winning.

RED DOG - This is the casino version of the old acey-deucey. The stakes are low, but the casino edge is a wee-bit steep (3.5%). If you play, only make the raise wager when the spread between the two cards is seven or more.

SIC BO - This is an oriental game in which players bet on the outcome of the roll of three dice. There are lots of bets on the layout, some that pay odds of 150-to-1. However, most have a very high casino advantage. Your best bet is a bet on the big or small wager.

LET IT RIDE - This casino table game is based on the all-American game of poker. Like Caribbean Stud Poker, players compete against the house rather than against each other. What makes this game so unique is that the players can remove up to two of their initial mandatory three bets if they don't think they can win. The objective is to end up with a five-card poker hand of at least 10's or higher. The higher the rank, the greater the payoff; up to 1,000-to-1 for the royal flush. The casino edge is about 3% and about 70% of the hands will be losing hands. If you are lucky enough to catch a high payoff hand, be smart, push your chair back, and take the money and run!

THREE CARD POKER - One of the more successful table games in recent years, you can wager on either the Ante/Play or Pair Plus. You win your Ante/Play bet if your three card poker hand beats the dealer's hand. If you wager Pair Plus, you win money if your three card hand contains at least a pair or higher (the higher the ranking hand, the greater the payout). There are different paytables – the best pays 4-1 for a flush rather than 3-1. The optimum playing strategy is to raise on Q-6-4 or higher and avoid playing the Pair Plus if the flush pays only 3-1.

Henry Tamburin has more than 30 years of experience as a casino player, author, columnist and instructor. More than 7,500 of his articles on casino gambling have been published in numerous national gaming publications including Casino Player magazine. He is also the author of numerous books and instructional videos, edits the popular Blackjack Insider newsletter (www.bjinsider.com), and is the Lead Instructor for the Golden Touch Blackjack course (www.goldentouchblackjack.com). You can visit his web site at http://www.smartgaming.com

Your Best Casino Bets - Part II

by Steve Bourie

In the previous story Henry gave you his choices for your best casino bets based on which ones offer you the best mathematical odds. Now, Henry is a great mathematician who is truly an expert at crunching numbers to figure out what the theoretical odds are, but what about real life? By this I mean - at the end of the week, or the month, or the year, how much does a casino really make from blackjack, or craps, or roulette? Sure, you can do the math to calculate the casino advantage on a bank hand in mini-baccarat as 1.17%, but at the end of the day what percent of those bets on mini-baccarat actually wind up in the hands of the casino? Is it precisely 1.17%? Or is it less? Or is it more? And, if you knew how much the casino truly averaged on all of the games it offered, which one would turn out to be your best bet based on that information?

To find the answer to this question I began my search by looking at the annual gaming revenue report issued by Nevada's State Gaming Control Board. It lists the win percentages, based on the *drop* (an explanation of this term is provided later), for all of the games offered by the casinos and, as Henry stated in his story, blackjack, baccarat and craps were among the best casino bets. The first column below lists the actual win percentages based on the "drop" (an explanation of "drop" follows shortly) for Nevada's various games for the fiscal year from July 1, 2010 through June 30, 2011:

GAME	WIN %	ADJUSTED WIN %
Keno	27.15	27.15
Race Book	15.49	15.49
Sports Pool	5.69	5.69
Slot Machines	6.26	6.26
3-Card Poker	29.16	5.83
Caribbean Stud Poker	26.32	5.26
Let It Ride	23.08	4.62
Pai Gow Poker	20.47	4.09
Roulette	17.06	3.41
Pai Gow	15.76	3.15
Craps	13.34	2.67
Bingo	2.60	2.60
Baccarat	11.61	2.32
Twenty-One	10.99	2.20
Mini-Baccarat	9.50	1.90

Casinos measure their take in table games by the drop and the win. The drop is the count of all of the receipts (including cash and credit markers) that go into the drop box located at the table. Later, an accounting is made to see how much more (or less) they have at that table than they started with. This amount is known as the win.

What the first column in the table shows you is how much the casinos won as a percentage of the drop. For example, on the roulette table for every $100 that went into the drop box the casino won $17.06 or 17.06%. What it doesn't tell you, however, is how much the casinos won as a percentage of all the bets that were made. In other words, the drop tells you how many chips were bought at that table, but it doesn't tell you how many bets were made with those chips.

For example, if you buy $100 worth of chips at a blackjack table and play $10 a hand you don't bet for exactly 10 hands and then leave the table, do you? Of course not. You win some hands and you lose some hands and if you counted all of the times you made a $10 bet before you left the table you would see that your original $100 in chips generated many times that amount in bets. In other words, there is a multiplier effect for the money that goes into the drop box. We know that for every dollar that goes into the drop box there is a corresponding number of bets made. To find out exactly what that number is I asked Henry for some help. He replied that there is no exact answer, but during a 1982 study of the roulette tables in Atlantic City it was discovered that the total amount bet was approximately five times the amount of the buy-in. This means that for every $100 worth of chips bought at the table it resulted in roughly $500 worth of bets being made.

The multiplier effect for the money that goes into the drop box is also dependent on the skill of the player. A blackjack player that loses his money quickly because he doesn't know good playing strategy will have a much lower multiplier than a player who uses a correct playing strategy. For purposes of this story, however, we'll assume that they balance each other out and we'll also assume that all games have the same multiplier of five. We can now return to our win percentage tables and divide by five the percentages for those games that have a multiplier effect. These new adjusted numbers let us know approximately how much the casinos actually won as a percentage of the amount bet on each of those games. Keep in mind, however, that there are four game categories that do not need to be adjusted: keno, bingo, race book and sports pool; plus slot machnes. All of these need no adjustment because there is no multiplier factor involved. The casinos know the exact total of the bets they take in and the exact total of the bets they pay out.

After calculating our adjusted win numbers we can now go back and take another look at which games are your best casino bets.

The worst game, by far, is keno with its 27.15% edge. Next comes the race book with 15.49%, followed by sports betting which has a casino win rate of 5.69%. However, that number actually deserves a closer look because there are really five different types of bets that make up that 5.69% figure: football at 4.05%; basketball at 6.48%; baseball at 5.27%; sports parlay cards at 33.19%; and other sports (golf, car racing, etc.) at 5.58%. As you can see, all sports bets carry a relatively low house edge, except for sports parlay cards.

Next on our list is slot machines at 6.26%, followed by three-card poker at 5.83%; Caribbean stud poker at 5.26%; let it ride at 4.62%; pai gow poker at 4.09%; roulette at 3.41%; and pai gow at 3.15%.

Finally, we come to four of the best casino bets that all have roughly the same edge of less than three percent, plus a fifth game that might surprise you. We have craps at 2.67%; bingo at 2.60%; baccarat at 2.32%; twenty-one (blackjack) at 2.20%; and mini-baccarat at 1.90%

Now, usually bingo would rank as one of the games with the worst odds, but not in Nevada where it's sometimes used as a "loss leader." Just like your local Kmart runs especially low prices on a couple of items to bring you into the store where they believe you'll buy some other items, Nevada casinos use bingo to bring people into their casinos, believing that while they're there they'll play other games and also develop a loyalty to that casino. Some years the casinos offering bingo actually lose money on the game rather than make money. So, if you're a bingo player Nevada casinos are the best places you'll ever find to play your game.

So there you have it. Mini-baccarat is your best casino bet! Henry said it was a good game to play and he was right. But didn't he also say that blackjack was your best casino bet? Was he wrong about that? Not really, because he prefaced it by saying "you must learn how to play your hands."

You have to remember that of all the table games offered in a casino (other than poker) only blackjack is a game of skill. This means that the better you are at playing your cards, the better you will be able to beat the house average. The 2.20% figure shown is just an average and if you learn proper basic strategy you can cut it down even more which would then make it your best bet. Good luck!

Casino Comps

by Steve Bourie

In the world of casino gambling a "comp" is short for complimentary and it refers to anything that the casino will give you for free in return for your play in their casino.

Naturally, the more you bet, the more the casino will be willing to give you back. For the truly "high roller" (those willing to bet thousands, tens of thousands or even hundreds of thousands on the turn of a card) there is no expense spared to cater to their every whim, including: private jet transportation, chauffeur-driven limousines, gourmet chef-prepared foods, the finest wines and champagnes, plus pampered butler and maid service in a $10 million penthouse suite. But what about the lower-limit bettor?

Well, it turns out that pretty much any gambler can qualify for comps no matter what their level of play and if you know you're going to be gambling anyway, you might as well ask to get rated to see what you can get on a comp basis.

When you sit down to play be sure to tell the dealer that you want to be rated and they'll call over the appropriate floorperson who will take down your name and put it on a card along with information on how long you play and how much you bet. The floorperson won't stand there and constantly watch you, instead they'll just glance over every once in awhile to see how much you're betting and note it on the card. If you change tables be sure to tell the floorperson so that they can continue to track your play at the new table.

Usually a casino will want you to play for at least three hours and virtually all casinos use the same formula to calculate your comp value. They simply take the size of your average bet and multiply it by: the casino's advantage on the game you're playing; the decisions per hour in your game; and the length of your play in hours. The end result is what the casino expects to win from you during your play and most casinos will return anywhere from 10% to 40% of that amount to you in the form of comps.

So, let's say you're a roulette player that averages $20 a spin and you play for four hours. What's that worth in comps? Well, just multiply your average bet ($20), by the casino's advantage in roulette (5.3%) to get $1.06, which is the average amount the casino expects to make on you on each spin of the wheel. You then multiply that by the number of decisions (or spins) per hour (40) to get $42.40, which is the average amount the casino expects to make on you after one hour. Then, multiply that by the total hours of play (4) to get $169.60, which is the average amount the casino expects to make on you during your four hours of play. Since the casinos will return 10% to 40% of that amount in comps, you should qualify for a minimum of $16.96 to a maximum of $67.84 in casino comps.

One thing to keep in mind about comps is that you don't have to lose in order to qualify. The casino only asks that you put in the time to play. So, in our example if, after four hours of gambling, our roulette player ended up winning $100, they would still be eligible for the same amount of comps.

The last thing to mention about comps is that some casino games require skill (blackjack and pai gow poker), or offer various bets that have different casino advantages (craps) so those factors are sometimes adjusted in the equation when determining the casino advantage in those games. Just take a look at the chart below to see how the average casino will adjust for skill in blackjack and pai gow poker as well as for the types of bets that are made in craps.

Game	Game Advantage	Decisions Per Hour
Blackjack	.0025 (Card Counter) .01 (Good Basic Strategy) .015 (Soft Player)	70
Roulette	.053	40
Craps	.005 (Pass Line/Full Odds) .01 (Knowledgeable) .04 (Soft)	144
Baccarat	.012	70
Mini-Baccarat	.012	110
Pai Gow Poker	.01 (Knowledgeable) .02 (Average)	25

Taking Advantage of Slot Clubs

by H. Scot Krause

Slot Clubs originated in Atlantic City over 25 years ago as a way to begin recognizing and rewarding the casino's good players. Today, slot clubs are the casino's most powerful marketing tool and the player's best benefit the casino has to offer. It's the best of both worlds for both the player and the casino.

To begin, perhaps the word "club" is a little misleading, since there are no dues to pay, meetings to attend or any of the usual aspects associated with joining a club. You do get a slot club membership card (also called a player's card) which is your key to unlocking the benefits and rewards of the casino you're playing in.

Typically, your slot club membership card is a plastic card, with your identifying number on it, that you will use while playing at any of the casino's slot or video poker machines or while playing table games. It resembles a credit card, but only in its appearance, and is in no way an actual credit card. I mention that because there are some people who actually, mistakenly believe they will be inserting a credit card into their slot machine and play on credit, and therefore they refuse to get their player's card and are basically denied any and all benefits they are entitled to!

So let's start at the beginning and walk through the slot card program, when and why to do it and discuss some benefits, rewards and perks.

When you enter any casino for the first time, ask someone immediately where you can find the slot club or players club booth before you put any money into a machine. At the booth, you should find a rather friendly group of employees who will get you started, signed up and get your card for you pronto.

You'll probably need to fill out a short application form or at least give your identification card to the clerk. It's simply a way to register the card in your name. You usually don't need to give your social security number if you don't want to, but always give your birthday and anniversary dates when asked. They help identify you with the casino in case others have your same name and many times the birthday benefits are nothing short of fantastic.

Always ask the slot club personnel about how to use the card and any other current promotions or benefits in addition to using your card. There will usually be a brochure or literature available that you can take explaining all the club benefits. There may also be a sign-up bonus such as a free gift or free points when you register. Be sure to ask. Sometimes an easily obtainable coupon may be required, and the clerks can tell you where or how to get one. Finally, I like to request two cards when I join, and you might like to do the same. You'll find that you may lose one, or want to play two machines at one time. That's it! You're on your way.

When you're out on the casino floor, you'll notice a slot on the machines that your card fits into. When you decide which machine you want to play, put your card in the slot and leave it in the entire time you play that machine. (Note: Take a moment to look for the card reader slot and not the bill acceptor. If you accidentally put your card in the bill acceptor you'll probably strip the magnetic reader off your card and it won't work).

Most machines will have some type of reader that will display your name, points earned or at least let you know your card has been accepted. It's not a swipe card, and you must leave it in the machine while you play. It's simply counting the coins, or credits, that go through the machine while you're playing and giving you credit in the form of points for the amount of money that cycles through the machine. (Some casinos consider time on the machine as well as money being cycled, but that is a little more rare than in years past). Now, while you're playing, you'll be earning valuable points that become redeemable for anything from cashback to restaurant complimentaries (refered to as "comps") show tickets, gifts, reduced room rates or free rooms, to almost any amenity you may want or require.

Be sure to keep your card in the machine until you have completed your play and cashed all coins out of the machine. Some clubs base their points on a coin-out system, rather than coin-in. Of course, these rewards are based on total play and your rewards may vary according to point formulas created exclusively for the casino at which you're playing. I do caution you not to continue to play beyond your comfortable gambling range and budget just to earn a point level or comp. Let the comps fall in place as you play or when you return again in the future. Which brings me to another interesting thought. I've heard players refuse to get a card because they believe they won't return to the casino again. First of all, you never know what your future plans may hold. Second, you may earn enough points while you're on this trip to at least earn a small comp or some cash back before you leave. You'll at least get on the casino's mailing list for future specials and events. You may win a jackpot that will allow you to return sooner that you originally thought was possible. And finally, with as many consolidations and buy-outs as there are in the casino business today, the casino you're playing at today may be owned by someone else tomorrow, who may in turn, be closer to your home, and you'll be able to use your points with them. There's just no good excuse not to get a player's card at any casino you visit.

Here are a couple other tips when you plan to visit a casino and need to get a slot club card. Sometimes you can apply or sign-up in advance by mail registration or visiting the casino's website on the Internet. They will often mail you the card in advance or have it already prepared for you when you get to the casino. Call and ask ahead of time for this service and you'll save time and won't have to stand in long lines when you hit the casino floor. Sometimes, when you receive your card by mail or Internet sign-up, you'll get additional offers, coupons, gifts and funbook offers along with it.

Many casinos now employ slot club ambassadors, cash hosts, or enrollment representatives who will sign you up on the casino floor, making it even easier for you to enroll in the club. They often have additional incentives or perks they can give you when you sign up with them. You might also check to see if a card you have from another casino might work where you're playing now. Many casino corporations are beginning to combine their clubs to offer you benefits at any of their respective properties. We're sure to see more of this as consolidations and mergers continue to take place.

Now, let's take a little closer look at the benefits and reasons why you want to belong to these slot clubs. Obviously, the casinos want your business and will go to great lengths to have you return. In addition to the points you're earning while playing, which will entitle you to various comps as mentioned previously, your most valuable asset from joining the slot club will be your mailing list advantage. Offers to slot club members are mailed often and repeatedly for room specials, many times even free room offers, meal discounts (two for ones), and often other free offers. We've been mailed match play offers, double and triple point coupons, show and movie theater tickets, spa specials, gifts and gift certificates, drawing tickets, and a myriad of other offers.

The casino offers are based on levels of play, and better offers including lavish parties, Superbowl and New Year's Eve invitations, free participation to invited guest slot tournaments, limousine services, and even free round-trip airfare, are offerd to the casino's best players. Don't rule yourself out just because you don't think you'll reach those levels of play to be awarded those opportunities. Everyone is rewarded in some way for even the most nominal play. Just wait until your birthday rolls around and I can almost guarantee you'll get some fabulous offers from the casinos to spend your celebration with them!

Finally, we'll now take a look at some of the myths regarding slot clubs and player's cards and dispose of them accordingly. Here are some of the arguments I've heard against slot club cards, or excuses as to why players don't use them...

"I never win when I play with my card." The truth is your results would be the same regardless if you had a card in or not. There is no relation between the card counting coins through the machine and what comes up on the screen when you push the button. The card just records how much money is wagered. It has no memory of whether you have won or lost and it doesn't care.

"I don't want to be tracked," or "I don't want the casino to know how much I'm playing," or "I don't want the IRS to have my records." In fact, you do want the casino to track you so you can be rewarded for your play. They have no way of knowing you, or how they can help and reward you unless they know who you are, what you're playing and how much you're spending. The IRS does not have access to your gambling activities, but you, in fact, do. The slot club can provide you with a year end win-loss record of your play that may help you offset wins with losses for tax purposes.

"I don't need a card, I'm a local," or "I'm a tourist." Basically, you're one or the other, but either way you still should have a card. The casino's computers usually separate locals from tourists and tailor their offers accordingly. If you're going to play anyway, get a card!

"I always lose those cards." You can always have another card made. Get extras made. Why play without it? It's like losing your wallet. The card has so much value for you, yet you leave it in the machine. You don't forget your airline frequent flier card at the airport, or your grocery savings card when you go shopping, do you?

"I don't need a card, I'm leaving in an hour." It doesn't matter how long you will be staying or how soon you will be leaving. Remember that all-important mailing list, and that you just might return some time in the future or play at a sister property somewhere else. (Don't worry. Most casinos do not sell their mailing list names. They want you for themselves and are very selfish!)

All-in-all, I've never heard of one good reason not to join a slot club. In fact, I hope I've given you enough good reasons to always join every slot club at every casino you ever visit. Good luck and happy slot clubbing!

H. Scot Krause is a freelance writer, gaming industry analyst and researcher. Scot reports, researches, and specializes in writing about casino games, events, attractions and promotions. His work is regularly featured in several gaming publications and he writes the popular Vegas Values" weekly column for the American Casino Guide website.

Slot Clubs And Comps

by Steve Bourie

Before you start playing any kind of electronic gaming machine in a casino, you should first join the casino's slot club to reap the rewards that your play will entitle you to. What is a slot club you ask? Well, it's similar to a frequent flyer club, except that in these clubs you will earn cash or comps (free food, rooms, shows, etc.) based on how much money you put through the machines.

Virtually all casinos in the U.S. have a slot club and joining is simple. Just go to the club's registration desk, present an ID, and you'll be issued a plastic card, similar to a credit card. When you walk up to a machine you'll see a small slot (usually at the top, or side) where you should insert your card before you start to play. The card will then record how much money you've played in that particular machine. Then, based on the amount you put through, you will be eligible to receive cash (sometimes) and comps (always) back from the casino. Naturally, the more you gamble, the more they will give back to you.

Some casinos will give you a free gift, or some other kind of bonus (extra slot club points, free buffet, etc.) just for joining and since there's no cost involved, it certainly makes sense to join even if you don't plan on playing that much. As a club member you'll also be on the casino's mailing list and you'll probably be receiving some good money-saving offers in the mail. Additionally, some casinos offer discounts to their club members on hotel rooms, meals and gift shop purchases.

While almost no casino will give you cashback for playing their table games, virtually all casinos will give you cashback for playing their machines. The amount returned is calculated as a percentage of the money you put through the machines and it basically varies from as low as .05% to as high as 1%. This means that for every $100 you put into a machine you will earn a cash rebate of anywhere from five cents to $1. This may not seem like a great deal of money but it can add up very quickly. Additionally, some casinos (usually the casinos with the lower rates) will periodically offer double, triple or quadruple point days when your points will accumulate much more rapidly.

One other point to make about cashback is that the vast majority of casinos (about 90%) offer a lower cash rebate on their video poker machines than they do on their slot machines. Generally, the rate is about one-half of what the casino normally pays on its slot machines. The reason for the reduced rate is that video poker is a game of skill and knowledgeable players can achieve a greater return on video poker games than they could on slots. Since the casino will make less money on video poker games they simply reduce their cash rebates accordingly. This is very important to keep in mind, especially if you're a bad video poker player, because you'll probably only be earning half the cash rebate you could be getting by just playing the slots.

Of course, the best situation is to be a smart video poker player in a casino that offers the same cash rebate to all of its player regardless of what kind of machine they play. This way you could be playing a good VP game, combined with a good rebate, and this will allow you to be playing at a near 100% level!

One final point to make about cash rebates is that not all clubs will allow you to get your cashback immediately. In Atlantic City, for example, all of the casinos will send a voucher to your home address which you must bring back to the casino (usually within 90 days) to receive your cash. You should always make it a point to ask if your cashback from the slot club is available immediately. If not, you may find yourself being mailed a voucher that is worthless to you.

While not every casino's slot club will give you back cash it is standard for every slot club to allow you to earn "comps" for your machine play. "Comps" is short for complimentaries and it means various things that you can get for free from the casino: rooms, meals, shows, gifts, etc.

Once again, the comp you will earn is based on the amount of money you put through the machines but it is usually at a higher level than you would earn for cashback. After all, the real cost to a casino for a $15 meal is much less than giving you back $15 in cash so the casinos can afford to be more generous.

When it comes to casino slot club comp policies they basically fall into one of three categories. Some casinos have clubs that allow you to redeem your points for either cash at one rate, or comps at a reduced rate that will cost you fewer points. In these clubs, for example, you might have a choice of redeeming your 1,000 points for either $10 in cash or $20 in comps.

Another option (one that is commonly used by many "locals" casinos in Las Vegas) is for the casino to set a redemption schedule for each particular restaurant, or meal. For example: breakfast is 800 points, lunch is 1,200 points and dinner is 1,600 points. These are popular programs because players know exactly what is required to earn their comp.

At the other extreme, many casinos base their comps on your total machine play but won't tell you exactly what's required to achieve it. At the MGM Resorts properties in Las Vegas, for example, you will earn cashback at a set schedule but you'll never quite know what you need to earn a food comp. You just have to go to the slot club booth, present your card, and ask if you can get a buffet or restaurant comp. The staff will then either give it to you or say you need some more play on your card before they can issue you a food comp.

And which casinos have the best slot clubs? Well, that would really be dependant on what's most important to you. If you're visiting from out of town you would probably want a slot club that's more generous with room comps so you could save money on your accomodations. However, if you're going to be playing at a casino near your home you would be more interested in which casino offers the best cashback rate and food comps. Whatever the situation, be sure to give most of your play to the casino that offers the best benefits for you and you'll soon be reaping the rewards of slot club membership!

Meet Max Rubin - Comp Hustler Extraordinaire

by Steve Bourie

I initially heard of Max Rubin in 1994 when his book, "Comp City," was first published. The book was revolutionary in that it gave gamblers an inside glimpse into how casinos rated players and how to take advantage of the casino comping system. Rubin's philosophy was that any gambler could learn how to play a break-even game of blackjack and still come out ahead simply by getting comps (free rooms, free food, free drinks, etc.) in return for their action at the tables. The book was an immediate best-seller and to this day it continues to sell well with many players considering it a "must have" for their gaming library. In the spring of 2006 I had the chance to interview him by phone from his home in Las Vegas and here's the story of one of gambling's more colorful characters.

At the age of 18 Max Rubin hitchhiked to Las Vegas from a little town called Borger, Texas where he had grown up. "It was an oil patch town of about 10,000," he says. "My parents had been divorced since I was two and my dad at the time was an "eye in the sky" at the Golden Nugget. He was also a bit of a crossroader (casino cheater). He did a little bit of mucking (switching cards) and marking cards; those sorts of things."

If his dad was a known cheater one might wonder why a casino would hire him, but Rubin explains that things were different back then. "In those days the crossroaders worked upstairs watching the tables," he says. "Keep in mind, the casinos had no cameras. My dad did what's typically called 'surveillance' now. He was one of the 'wise guys' that worked the catwalks on the top of the casinos and looked for cheaters. Nobody else knew what they were looking for, so they needed cheaters to look for cheaters."

Being new to the town, and trying to earn a few extra bucks, Rubin says he was used as a "rounder" a couple of times by professional teams. "Being a rounder," he explains, "meant I would stand outside of a blackjack pit or right outside on the street and have a fake fight with somebody so that everybody's heads would turn. Then the guys would go into the pits and actually take cards off the podium so that they could mark them and get them back into the games."

Rubin's life-style with the "guys" lasted only a short time because he says "I saw they lived in crappy day-by-day apartments and drove cars with bald tires, if they had cars at all. It just wasn't the kind of life that appealed to me."

He got a track scholarship to UNLV (University of Nevada, Las Vegas) where he went through the typical college stuff: going to school, doing college jobs, living in the dorms, and being broke at all times because he gambled almost every day, as did everybody else. "We all played blackjack and we didn't have a clue what we were doing," he says.

When he turned 21 the Selective Service System held a lottery for potential draftees for the Vietnam War and he won - meaning he had a very high number - so he dropped out of school and started breaking in at the Horseshoe in downtown Las Vegas as a dealer. Shortly after that he went up to Lake Tahoe where he worked for a year-and-a-half. It was during this stint in Tahoe that Rubin first learned about card counting. "I ran into some guys who were starting card counting teams and I got to know a little bit about it," he says. "I was dabbling in it, but not really doing much."

Rubin came back to Las Vegas to finish his degree in hotel administration at UNLV and upon graduation he became a casino manager in 1975 at the North Shore Club in Lake Tahoe. That only lasted for about one year, but while he was there it allowed him to renew his contacts with his card-counting friends and he started learning more about it.

Rubin moved back to Vegas to work at the Riviera while learning the real estate business. Within two years he quit his casino job and made his living as a broker. He did well and, once again, renewed his contacts with his card counting friends who were now playing in Vegas as well as Tahoe. "They were starting to use some very sophisticated plays," he says. "They were playing with computers and they were shuffle tracking before shuffle tracking was even known. They were doing a lot of really interesting things, so I went out and started playing a little bit. I did what was called BP'ing, where I was the Big Player (the player who makes big bets at the blackjack table after receiving a signal from a team member) and I played with them for a little bit."

Within four years, Rubin's real estate ventures hit troubled waters and he returned to work as a pit boss at the Sands. He did that for a year-and-a-half while playing blackjack on the side. During the next few years he dabbled in some other business ventures, while still playing blackjack, but then he came to a life-altering decision.

"It was time for me to figure out what I was going to do with my life," he says. "I thought to myself, well I can keep trying to start all of these businesses or I can do what I always wanted to do which was to be a writer and do some creative stuff." That was in 1989 and some of his friends were opening a new casino called the Mirage, so he asked them for a job, but not in management. He decided that he just wanted to be a dealer, play blackjack on the side and try his hand at writing.

Over the course of about a year-and-a-half Rubin wrote a screenplay that won the Nevada Screenwriters Award and, surprisingly, he ended up becoming a boss on the Mirage's graveyard shift. Because of his card counting background Rubin became the casino's "counter catcher," but he imposed limits on how he handled the situation. "Basically, I would never finger anybody," he explains. "I would just tell them: don't play on my shift, go play some place else.

I was very forthcoming with management at the Mirage because they were my friends. I said I know you want to keep these guys from playing in here, but it's not my job to put people in the Griffin book (the Griffin Detective Agency's record book with photos of suspected cheats and card counters) and do those sort of things. I will just nicely tell them there's a lot of soft spots in the world, but this isn't one of them. So I had a good reputation from both sides because I was always very up front with both sides and I've always been that way."

It was also at this time that Rubin was having his greatest success as a card counter. "I was playing a lot and I was playing with probably the biggest count team in the country," he says. "We were doing a lot of pretty sophisticated stuff: shuffle tracking and something called depth charging. I was making about as much money at the time playing blackjack on weekends as I was working."

Within another year-and-a-half, Rubin was doing so well playing blackjack that he retired from his casino job. "The last job I had was in 1992," he says. "After that all I did was play blackjack, manage teams, organize teams and do all sorts of team things until 1999 when other opportunities opened up for me."

As a professional player Rubin learned how to maximize his opportunities for casino comps. "I was getting all these marvelous comps as a big player for a big team," he says. "I was learning all the intricacies of what made the comp system work and I figured out a way to beat it. That's what "Comp City" is all about and why it really kind of revolutionized how blackjack players can approach the game. The basis of the book is how to play with an advantage against the casino without counting cards or doing anything else. Simply by being a basic strategy player, but instead of winning money you'll win stuff."

And what originally inspired him to write "Comp City"? "I wrote the book," he says, "because I was in Lake Tahoe and we were staying at Caesars. I had comp suites for my family and another family and there was a limo waiting for us at the bottom of our ski lift when we got stuck. My wife was sitting there and she said you know what? You ought to write a book about this comp thing. Tell people how they can really beat it. I was writing some things at the time, scripts and screenplays, and that was the direction I wanted to go in, so I said okay. I didn't know if anybody had ever written about comps, so I went over to my friend ("Las Vegas Advisor" publisher) Anthony Curtis' house to research the subject. It turned out that nobody had ever written anything on it so Anthony let me run with it.

"It took me close to two years to assemble the stuff and then I wrote about a 600-page rambling book which was edited into about 300 pages. It did very well for us and it was interesting because the casinos, as they typically do, overreacted and started changing some of the comp policies, but because of those knee-jerk reactions they opened up some other doors. The thing that made Comp City work as far as being able to "fool the bosses" still works. You bet big when the boss is watching, you bet small when he's not. You just learn how the systems work and take advantage of those systems. As a matter of fact I'm now in the process of finishing the third edition of Comp City. The new edition also covers video poker, plus it's going to somewhat cover slots and how you can beat the technologies, but primarily it's still a book about blackjack."

Since the introduction of "Comp City" in 1994 many casinos have introduced new blackjack games with a much higher casino advantage. Examples are Super Fun 21 which pays even-money on blackjack instead of the standard three-to-two, plus single-deck games that only pay six-to-five for blackjack. Rubin warns players that these games are more difficult to beat, but that they can still offer an advantage for some.

"Typically it's gotten more difficult in the tourist venues like Las Vegas," he says. "Most people in America are what we call day-trippers which means they sleep in their own beds after they gamble, which you can do now around most of the country. Most of those venues don't have six-to-five blackjack because it harvests the money too quickly from the players.

"In Vegas they have six-to-five games and frankly I think it's a great introductory game for someone who has never played before, simply because the people on the game will not intimidate you when you sit down to play because these other players don't know how to play themselves. I've been involved with a number of focus groups on why people, particularly ladies, will not play blackjack in a casino environment, and it's because they're intimidated by the dealers and the other players. So in order to get your chops and learn how to play the game, six-to-five is okay for players on a $10 game.

"But the reality is that a six-to-five game takes a lot of money out of people. It's kind of a safety net for the casinos that really don't know how to protect themselves and I think they've gone a little bit too far in spreading it too fast. There are so many gimmick games out there. The ones that I really find distasteful are all the side bets. Those little dollars that people throw out make the house a lot more money than the $10 and $15 wagers do and it just chews people up too much. I don't like those, I think the real value in a customer is their long-term lifetime value to a casino.

"I think Amarillo Slim said it best: 'you can shear a sheep many times, but you can only skin it once.' Some casinos try to skin everybody and I personally find it very distasteful. As a matter of fact, that's what I'm going to be speaking about at an upcoming Canadian Gaming Summit: how to nurture your customers and create long-term relationships. Using all those gimmick games is not the way to do it."

In mentioning the Gaming Summit Rubin alludes to the fact that his reputation has grown within the gaming industry and he credits it to when he quit gambling for a living in 1999. While he enjoyed it, he decided that it was "a young man's game" and it was time to put it behind him.

"You're on the road a lot and you can't make mistakes," he explains. "Plus, it's always kind of a hollow victory when you win because all you win is money and you don't get much of a sense of accomplishment when you're playing blackjack. Certainly if you've got financial needs it comes in handy. It was really fun tricking the comp systems and all those things, but it just got to the point it wasn't fun anymore and I try to never do anything if I don't have fun doing it. I'll go out and gamble a little bit to have some fun, but as far as being a pro? I just said that's enough.

"Fortunately, in 1999 other things started happening for me. I was helping a former business partner, acting as a consultant to him on how to run the best games possible at a casino in San Diego called Barona Valley Ranch. I taught customer service, marketing and game protection. I began doing that on a quasi-full time basis and I'm still doing it now.

"I also started getting TV work by helping some guys that were doing shows for the Travel and Discovery channels. At first I just volunteered to be a talking head on the show, but after a while I started getting recognized quite a bit and other opportunities came along. I wound up being host of "The World Series of Blackjack," host of "The Ultimate Blackjack Tour" and I've been on "Casino Diaries" and the "Breaking Vegas" series.

"It turns out that I really love doing those sort of things and I morphed into something else. I have literally been on scores of television shows, written hundreds of articles and now I'm getting real Hollywood dollars for shows I appear on. I've got the biggest agents in Hollywood and I'm getting offers everywhere.

"I've got a new series of DVDs called "Vegas Maximus"coming out soon. I've got a Master Blackjack DVD series on how to count cards and it's going to evolve to where I'm going to have a DVD on tournament play, gonna have a DVD on Comp City. I'm working on a thing called "The Road to Vegas" where people can listen to CDs with comical lessons on how to gamble. Then I've got agreements with other publishers of video poker software and we will have an entire arsenal of DVDs. We launch all this soon and it's going to follow that model where you get the first one free and then you get into a continuity program. So that's what I've been spending a lot of my time on now. I'm doing all of this and in the meantime I'm still training people at Barona."

Rubin's philosophy of offering good blackjack games with liberal rules for players is very apparent in his consulting work at Barona. "We offer the loosest blackjack game on planet Earth without question," he says. "$50,000 a hand, single-deck blackjack with surrender. It's a break-even game off the top. The fact that Barona has such a loose game means they win much more money than anybody else. A very interesting thing about blackjack that has still failed to dawn on so many casinos is that the more options you give players, such as surrender and doubling after split, it gives the players more opportunities to make mistakes. There are very few players than can actually beat blackjack, but there are tens of thousands that like to think they can. It's really created an enormous amount of business at Barona."

With such loose games it seems inevitable that professional players would be drawn to Barona and it's up to Rubin to keep the wolves at bay. "The pros don't really hold that against me," he says. "They understand that if I weren't part of Barona then the blackjack games would be just like everybody else. Although I'm really too busy to do it, I will help any casino with consulting as far as cheating is concerned, but I will not help any casino other than Barona when it comes to advantage play. If I did that then I would become persona non grata with all my friends. I know virtually every player in the world of professional blackjack and I host a party every year called the Blackjack Ball. I respect those people for what they do and they respect me for what I do. We also have a Blackjack Hall of Fame at Barona and anyone who is in the Blackjack Hall of Fame gets room, food and beverage for life simply by agreeing not to play there."

In looking to the future, some gaming suppliers are now beginning to offer RFID-enabled chips to the casinos. The RFID stands for Radio Frequency Identification and it means that each chip has its own identifiable radio signal which can be tracked by the casino to determine its location at any given time. It also means, however, that the casino can tell exactly how much a player is betting at any given time and they will no longer need to rely on the floorperson to estimate a player's average bet. Does this new technology mean that the end is near for players trying to hustle comps?

"The only casino in Las Vegas that is using RFID today to track your average bet is the Hard Rock, but they still can't tell what level of skill you have," says Rubin. "But I think it will probably be the end of times for comp hustlers within the next five to ten years because the technology is getting cheaper. Moore's Law says that every 18 months everything gets half as big and costs half as much so it's getting cheaper and cheaper. Casinos want to reduce their workforce and by embracing this technology they won't have to use floor supervisors to rate people.

"It's almost affordable for the casinos now and it's only a very short matter of time before we see the premier Vegas mega-resorts starting to put it in. Then it will slowly proliferate around the country to where almost all operations will find it necessary to have it because if they don't, what's going to happen is that the non-profitable people, such as me, and the other customers that don't make them money are going to leave the premier properties that invest in this technology and they're going to migrate to the competition that doesn't have the sophisticated technologies. Right now, there are terrible blackjack players that the house doesn't know are terrible players, and there are also extremely skilled players that the house doesn't know are skilled, yet they lump them all together and give them all the same bite of the pie. That isn't the way it should work. They should invest most of their money in the most profitable customers and let the unprofitable customers go down the street."

While acknowledging that these new technologies will give an added advantage to the casinos, Rubin believes that smart lower-limit players will always have an edge in the comp-hustling game.

"Typically the $5 and $10 player isn't getting rated so the casino doesn't know who they are anyway and they're going to have a slight advantage," he says. "For example, if you're a $10 blackjack player and you like to have a cocktail every hour, you're playing at an advantage over the casino. You're expected loss is $1 to $1.50 and you can have a drink or two which has a retail value of $6 or $7, so you're actually playing with a bit of an advantage over the casino. Most of these people we call the grazers, and they are always going to have a slight edge over the casino if they have the skill sets to do it. The problem is some grazers don't take the time to learn how to play basic strategy and if you don't know how to play the game properly the casino always has an edge over you. That's the biggest kind of conundrum there is that most low-end players won't take the hour or two to learn how to play the game right."

When asked for his best advice for players seeking to take advantage of casino comps, Rubin offers up a few of his favorites. "The best tip is to ask. You gotta ask because if you don't ask they won't give it to you," he says. Also, bet big when the bosses are watching; bet low when they're not watching; learn basic strategy; and be nice!"

Finally, Rubin gives some advice which may seem somewhat contrary to what he usually advocates, but it's something he believes all players should think about when deciding which games to play.

"There's something I want to say that all of the purist and the professionals just rail at me when I do it, but I believe if you want to play a game it doesn't matter about the math," he explains. "You come to Las Vegas to have a good time and yes, roulette has bad math, but it's still fun. I have guilty pleasures. I like Megabucks and I like roulette. I play the games for fun and if it's not fun you shouldn't play. If you want to play a game, play it anyway and don't let the math snots tell you not to play. If you go to New York City, you should go to a Yankees game, you should go to a play, you should eat at Tavern on the Green, you should do all those things. There's not a mathematical edge on any of those. If you come to Vegas you should go to the shows, you should play the games, you should play whatever you want to play and have a good time.

"But if you're going to play a long time and you're going to become a serious blackjack player, then take a few hours to study the game and learn how to take advantage of the comp system. Learn how to reduce your losses and maximize your fun by getting more free stuff."

Las Vegas Resort Fees

by Dewey Hill

What are resort fees? Resort fees are per night mandatory charges added to your hotel bill and collected by the hotel/casino. Ostensibly, for certain amenities, most of which traditionally have come free with any paid hotel, like free parking, or pool use. Sometimes there are some new amenities like free wifi, access to the fitness center, free water bottles in the room, a free daily newspaper, or a VIP line pass to avoid crowds at the buffet.

Generally, if resort fees appear in advertisements at all, they are hidden in the fine print. Websites that let us name our own room price do not include the resort fee in the mathematics of their comparative search.

Sometimes a property will impose resort fees on their less expensive options, but not on the upscale room or suite. Unlike sales taxes, resort fees work like a flat tax; they might add a mere 10-20% to the nightly charges of expensive hotels, but as much as 50% to inexpensive hotels.

Are these like the extra fees airlines charge? No, because those fees for extra baggage or a blanket and pillow are not mandatory. We do not have to check bags or use a blanket to fly; when those amenities are not used, we pay no additional fee. Casino resort fees are universally applied to every hotel bill whether we choose to use the amenities or not.

What about comped rooms? Policies vary. Some casinos automatically waive resort fees for comped rooms, some require that we ask them to be waived, and for others it depends upon how the room is comped. Many will use resort fees as another incentive for higher levels of play. Others charge everyone the same fee even if the room is comped.

Station Casinos and Boyd Casinos generally charge no resort fee on any comped room and do not limit amenities. This past year resort fees stopped being added to Mlife comped rooms at MGM Resorts properties. Some places allow us to pay the resort fee with Player's Card points.

Are there ways to book and avoid resort fees? Often there are. Booking Boyd casinos using the B-Connected website available to Player's Club card holders will often not incur a resort fee even when the booking paperwork says one will be charged. Some convention bookings negotiate a waive of resort fee. SEMA and AAPEX which attracts 120,000 participants annually in November negotiates waived fees for members booking through their site.

Condos at Signature MGM that are rented out directly by the condo owners, or through third-party companies they hire, can be booked without the usual resort fee.

Some casinos, like Tropicana, periodically drop resort fees as a come-on in advertised room rate specials. Call and ask if any such deal is available.

Caesars' Entertainment casinos, The Cosmopolitan and the Hilton openly advertise NO RESORT FEES as part of their marketing. Stay for more than five nights at the Stratosphere and the resort fee caps at $37.50, and yet you, and everyone in your room, will get free amenities like access to the Tower for your entire stay. 28 days is the maximum single booking.

Why would a casino use a resort fee rather than put all charges up front? Casinos charging resort fees appear less expensive until the fine print is examined, so that helps in advertisements. It also might trick the inexperienced Vegas traveler, or those who don't attend to the details of their bills, into believing that what they will be charged is much less than it actually is. And since most reporting of hotel room charges ignore resort fee numbers, media tends to be complicit in this bait and switch tactic. My experience with savvy travelers suggests that even they are often tricked. While in theory the resort fee could easily be mentally added to the posted hotel charge, in practice it is often mentally ignored, even by veteran visitors.

Discount brokers typically have search engines that arrange the hotels according to price, so that the customer can enter trip dates and make easy comparison based on cost. Because resort fees are not included in the programmed rankings of those searches, the casino hotel will see their rooms disingenuously ranked as cheaper than they actually are.

Resort fees also help casinos when discount brokers discount any rooms they have been unable to sell in order to liquidate an overstock. In a real sense, a discount broker, when selling any room in a casino hotel that charges a resort fee, can only sell or discount a percentage of that room. The casino still collects the resort fee.

Resort fees may attract customers who have been paying higher a la carte fees for fitness centers or in-room wifi. A resort fee charges every customer for these amenities. Few use them, but those who do are then subsidized by those who don't. If the resort fee itself is used as a comp for well bankrolled players, the cost of providing amenities is paid for by lower bankrolled guests. In some cases, however, comped rooms may not incur mandatory resort fees, but will also not provide resort fee amenities, unless customers opt to pay the fee.

Resort fees also may be a tool used by the casino hotel to discourage frugal travelers who want a cheap night on the road, but have no intention of gambling. The El Cortez added a $25 a night fee which is charged for every night a customer books beyond seven nights in any calendar month. Technically, this is not a resort fee, but since it is generally included in the fine print of the booking and collected on check-in, it works in a very similar way. It can be waived based on sufficient play.

In short, the resort fee structure adds an element of flexibility to room charges that the casino hotel can use to their advantage in renting rooms in a highly competitive market to a variety of customers. While customers lose the transparency and dependability of an agreed upon cost that is determined upfront at the time of booking, casino hotels are able to raise prices after the booking and to more fluidly flex the price of the hotel room to match the variegated profile of their customer.

How much are these fees? Fees change often. Ask what they are before you book. Further confusing cost comparisons is that some charge a tax on the fee. Red Rock advertises a fee of $24.99, but 12 % tax on that $25 adds $3 so the full amount presents the consumer with two levels of hidden fees.

Here is an overview (as of summer 2011):

Station Casinos all have resort fees from about $13 to the high rates of $28 at Red Rock and Green Valley Ranch. Wynn and Encore are $22.40 (tax included); Palazzo is $19.04.

Treasure Island and MGM Grand Signature ($22.40 each) are high as well.

Mandalay Bay is $16.80.

The Rumor suites across from the Hard Rock charge an untaxed fee of $9.95.

Boyd casinos, which were some of the first to try out this idea, are some of the cheapest: Orleans - $6; Gold Coast - $3; Sam's Town - $4.50; and Suncoast - $5.

All MGM properties installed a resort fee in 2010. Bellagio is $22.40

Orleans raised their resort fee from $5 to $6. Palms raised last year's token $1 fee to $12 and has the prize for the most unusual amenity: $20 in bar credit for each $12 resort fee. Aria now charges $22.40.

Harrah's, Cosmopolitan, and Hilton have announced that they will NOT charge a resort fee.

Las Vegas Hilton gets the prize for the best reverse resort fee promotion. They charge no resort fee; however, using the "Go Green" promotion, hotel guests can get a $10 daily voucher for food in the casino for each day that they hang a "Go Green" sign on the door to decline housekeeping. Environmentally conscious guests by declining one amenity, levy a fee on the resort.

Super 8 next to Ellis Island gets the prize for the most free amenities and NO resort fee: wifi in the room, parking, 24-hour heated pool, free airport pickup/delivery, a guest laundromat and television with twice the number of channels, including TCM and three HBO channels.

Downtown, only the Gold Spike charges a resort fee ($8.98) which often adds a huge percentage to room rates as low as $12 per night.

However, at $21 total with free wifi and a dawn to dusk pool, after the mathematics the Gold Spike still is generally the best downtown bargain.

Booking Gold Spike using Hotels.com wins the prize for the most confusing. They collect the amount of the resort fee, but call it a "service fee" and bundle it with sales tax. The Gold Spike says that they will not collect a resort fee on any rooms charged that "service fee" by Hotels.com. However, in the fine print and in letters asking for clarification, the hotels.com site says the "resort fee" is still owed and collected by the hotel.

On the Boulder Strip, Sam's Town and Boulder Station have fees, while Eastside Cannery and Arizona Charlie's do not.

First time visitors who wish to avoid resort fees might look in the area of Flamingo and Las Vegas Boulevard for a great Strip location and many fee-free options: Paris, Planet Hollywood, Bill's, Caesars, Bally's, Super 8(Ellis Island,) Terribles, Rio. And the Gold Coast at $3 has the lowest resort fee in Vegas. In contrast, almost all Strip hotels on and near the corner of NYNY and Las Vegas Boulevard and South to Mandalay Bay, or North of Harrah's charge resort fees.

Resort fees can change any day. To be certain of accurate, up to date information, call the casino hotel and ask before booking any location. Ask the amount of the resort fee and also ask if taxes are charged on the fee, or just on the room charge. Ask how it can be waived.

After booking, ask for an emailed, detailed description of your charges, and bring a printout to the hotel. If resort fees are implemented, or raised, after your booking, but before your check-in, a printout of the original booking will often save you the new costs.

Remember that the resort fees generally will not appear on a printout from a discount broker, except as a courtesy in fine print, because resort fees are collected directly by the casino hotel.

As often as you can, book directly with hotels rather than using a discount broker. Resort fees can then be made clear as you book.

In addition, cancellation or alteration of a reservation will not incur discount broker fees,(i4Vegas for example charges $15 for changes or cancellations) and paperwork will not get lost or misinterpreted. Many discount broker phone contacts are talking to you from far away in an English new to them. Only when booking directly with the hotel, rather with a broker, can you reduce the length of a booking without losing the original sale rate. Hotel discount brokers must cancel the entire first booking and rebook at newer, and generally higher, rates.

Also, your play may reduce the cost of your stay if you book directly. Hosts can rarely comp discount broker charges; they can, however, comp direct bookings.

However you make your reservation, be sure to make a confirmation phone call directly to the hotel a few days before you arrive. Carefully recheck dates and charges and resort fees. Reconfirm any changes or cancellations. This will save you any surprises at check-in when you are overtired from air travel, anxious to enjoy Vegas, and forced to stand in repeated lines between phone calls to a discounter, or while waiting for misinformation to be corrected.

Also pay attention to what you sign when you check in. Hotels with resort fees generally have you agree to the fees when you arrive, but sometimes that is in the fine print.

If you take advantage of Internet name-your-own-price offers or air-hotel package deals, resort fees will not be included in quoted charges, but added on by the hotel afterwards. This is especially frustrating when a discounter searches for a hotel using your set price, but will not tell you the name until you make the reservation, so you can't check on resort fees before booking. When naming your own price, it may be wise to just assume you will pay an additional $15 or so in resort fees.

For those of us who might like to splurge for a stay at some upscale suite or tower room, or who negotiate an upgrade, it is important in the mathematics of cost comparison that we consider the possibility of no resort fee on the upscale choice. The cost of the splurge may not be as high as it looks at first glance.

What methods are there of protest? Complain at the front desk in a calm, reasoned manner. Ask for a manager and be prepared to wait.

If you have been caught with an unexpected new fee, or a raised fee, argue that your original contract should be honored.

If you encounter resistance, tell the casino you will dispute the entire bill with your credit card. It is often more bother for them to go through that process than to waive the fee.

Actually dispute all charges when your credit card bill comes due, mentioning the fine print fee as your reason. The casino may waive it at that point.

Complain in writing to the casino, even if you lost the argument at the front desk. Casinos pay attention to letters. You may find you get an offer for a free upgrade or a future stay free of the resort fee.

Express your opinion here: http://forum.americancasinoguide.com. Casino representatives read this board to sample the feelings of the public. Encourage others to complain directly to the hotels and on American Casino Guide discussion boards. Also, check in to this forum when you are booking for news of resort fee changes, angles, as well as other Vegas tips and information.

Whenever you cancel a reservation, include the resort fee as one of the reasons for cancellation.

If you feel that the casino did not clearly inform you of this fee in enough time for you to change your reservation, and yet they are unwilling to waive the fee when you ask at check in, try this approach: "Fine, I'll pay this tricky resort fee that I feel has trapped me, but I'll not wager a dime in this casino. I'll go next door or down the street. While I'm here, I'll enjoy the amenities included in this mandatory fee. I'll go on the Internet in my room, use the fitness center, read the free newspaper. I'll enjoy the pool, and use up my current points on free food, but I won't gamble here this trip. That will more than save me the resort fee and give me a bankroll I can use to establish myself as a good customer in a casino free of resort fees, one who respects transparent booking rather than small print trickery. If you want me to treat you as a resort rather than a casino, I can do that."

Actually use a comped visit at a resort fee casino hotel to seed future offers with play in a nearby casino that does not charge a resort fee, and explain your decision in writing to both casinos.

Write to any casino that does not charge a resort fee. Thank them, and tell them you have decided to move your business to their casino.

Write or call to encourage casinos that charge exceptionally low and untaxed resort fees not to raise that expense. Each time we write to a casino and mention resort fees, we remind them that this issue is important to us.

Will it do any good? Customer complaints always are noted, even if they are not answered. Regular customers may expect an answer and perhaps, if the letter touches the right nerve, the answer may include a waived fee or a free room upgrade on your next visit.

M casino responded to customer complaints by dropping the practice altogether.

Cosmopolitan decided not to charge resort fees so as not to "irritate customers."

Harrah's responded to customers by promising to no longer impose resort fees on any of their properties in Las Vegas.

Even when the fees do not get dropped, your complaints may keep them from rising.

Casinos are balancing the extra money they might receive against the amount of anger the fees may incur. They like charging more than they are required to advertise, but they can't afford to lose their steady customers.

Hopefully, they will get the message that consumers like upfront charges and dislike being tricked.

You have probably heard the old expression, "Fool me once, shame on you; fool me twice, shame on me."

Our hope is that this American Casino Guide information has precluded even the initial deception.

Dewey Hill retired from teaching English to travel in the most frugal ways, play poker at the lowest limits, and fish bluegills. His love of Vegas, as well as his disdain for resort fees, keeps him on discussion boards and blogging daily. He collects Vegas experiences at vegasbirthdaybash.blogspot.com.

Slot Machines

by Steve Bourie

Virtually anyone who visits a casino, even for the first time, is familiar with a slot machine and how it operates: just put in your money, pull the handle and wait a few seconds to see if you win. It isn't intimidating like table games where you really need some knowledge of the rules before you play and it's this basic simplicity that accounts for much of the success of slot machines in the modern American casino.

As a matter of fact, the biggest money-maker for casinos is the slot machine with approximately 65 percent of the average casino's profits being generated by slot machine play. As an example, in Nevada's fiscal year ending June 30, 2011 the total win by all of the state's casinos was a little more than $10.63 billion. Of that amount, $6.68 billion, or slightly less than 63 percent, was from electronic machine winnings.

With this in mind, you must ask yourself, "can I really win money by playing slot machines?" The answer is a resounding yes...and no. First the "no" part: in simplest terms a slot machine makes money for the casino by paying out less money than it takes in. In some states, such as Nevada and New Jersey, the minimum amount to be returned is regulated. In Nevada the minimum is 75 percent and in New Jersey it's 83 percent. However, if you look at the slot payback percentages for those particular states in this book you will see that the actual average payback percentages are much higher. In New Jersey it's close to 92 percent and in Nevada it's slightly less than 94 percent. Even though the actual paybacks are higher than the law requires, you can still see that on average for every $1 you play in an Atlantic City slot machine you will lose 8¢ and in a Las Vegas slot machine you will lose 6¢. Therefore, it doesn't take a rocket scientist to see that if you stand in front of a slot machine and continue to pump in your money, eventually, you will lose it all. On average, it will take you longer to lose it in Las Vegas rather than Atlantic City, but the result is still the same: you will go broke.

Gee, sounds kind of depressing, doesn't it? Well, cheer up because now we go on to the "yes" part. But, before we talk about that, let's first try to understand how slot machines work. All modern slot machines contain a random number generator (RNG) which is used to control the payback percentage for each machine. When a casino orders a slot machine the manufacturer will have a list of percentage paybacks for each machine and the casino must choose one from that list. For example, a manufacturer may have 10 chips available for one machine that range from a high of 98% to as low as 85%. All of these chips have been inspected and approved by a gaming commission and the casino is free to choose whichever chip it wants for that particular brand of machine.

In almost all instances, the casino will place a higher denomination chip in a higher denomination machine. In other words, the nickel machines will get the chips programmed to pay back around 87% and the $25 machines will get the chips programmed to pay back around 98%. A casino can always change the payback percentage, but in order to do that it must go back to the manufacturer to get a new RNG that is programmed with the new percentage. For this reason, most casinos rarely change their payback percentages unless there is a major revision in their marketing philosophy. And what exactly is a random number generator? Well, it's a little computer chip that is constantly working (as its name implies) to generate number combinations on a random basis. It does this extremely fast and is capable of producing hundreds of combinations each second. When you pull the handle, or push the spin button, the RNG stops and the combination it stops at is used to determine where the reels will stop in the pay window. Unlike video poker machines, you have no way of knowing what a slot machine is programmed to pay back just by looking at it. The only way to tell is by knowing what is programmed into the RNG.

As an example of the differences in RNG payout percentages I have listed below some statistics concerning various slot manufacturers' payback percentages in their slot machines. Normally, this information isn't available to the public, but it is sometimes printed in various gaming industry publications and that is where I found it. The list shows the entire range of percentages that can be programmed into each machine:

Aruze Gaming
    Paradise Fishing   88.00% - 90.00%
    Chinese Phoenix   85.26% - 95.20%

A.C. Coin and Slot
    Chef's Daily Special Bonus   87.84% - 92.85%
    Slingo Deluxe   85.92% - 91.92%
    Slotto Double Gold   88.00% - 93.00%

Aristocrat
    African Storm   87.86% - 94.84%
    Boot Scootin' (20-line)   87.20% - 97.15%
    Jaws   88.70% - 92.00%
    Mr. Woo   90.63% - 92.17%
    Power Play   85.81% - 92.19%
    Wild Panda   88.00% - 95.00%

Atronic
    Deal or No Deal The Show   86.00% - 96.00%
    IC Money   85.20% - 97.02%
    Lion Queen   85.01% - 92.01%
    Three Stooges   86.00% - 96.00%
    Tropical Paradise   86.00% - 96.00%

Bally Gaming

Betty Boop's Love Meter	87.68% - 87.99%
Black & White 5 Times Pay	84.49% - 96.72%
Black & White Sevens	87.00% - 95.00%
Blazing 7's Double (reel)	88.00% - 95.98%
Cash Spin	85.72% - 88.38%
Code Red	85.41% - 96.04%
Hot Shot Progressive	86.06% - 96.03%
Hot Spin	87.59% - 89.99%
Poppit!	87.95% - 95.89%
Spin & Win (3-Reel)	83.24% - 94.00%

IGT

Diamond Jackpots	87.90% - 96.50%
Dirty Dancing	89.09% - 94.05%
Elephant King	85.03% - 98.04%
Enchanted Unicorn	85.00% - 98.00%
Fortune Cookie	85.03% - 98.01%
Imperial Dragon	88.00% - 94.99%
Neon Nights	87.53% - 98.03%
Pink Panther	88.00% - 95.00%
Price is Right - Cliffhangers	85.00% - 98.00%
Red White and Blue	85.03% - 97.45%
Sex and The City Multi-Play	89.90% - 94.90%
Southern Belle	85.00% - 97.40%
Texas Tea	87.00% - 97.00%
Viva Las Vegas	87.50% - 87.80%
Wheel of Fortune Secret Spins	89.00% - 93.50%
Wheel of Fortune Super Spin/Wild	87.50% - 89.40%

Konami Gaming

Heat Engine	90.75%
African Diamond	82.13% - 96.03%

WMS Gaming

Alice	87.00% - 96.00%	
Reel 'em in/Compete to Win	86.92% - 96.15%	
Bigger Bang Big Event Stand Alone	86.09% - 86.26%	
Cash Crop	86.36% - 94.92%	
Dirty Harry:Make My Day	85.98% - 86.01%	Progressive
Dirty Harry:Make My Day	86.04% - 94.02%	Non-Progressive
Great and Powerful Oz Stand Alone	86.00% - 96.00%	
Great and Powerful Oz Progressive	86.00%	
Monopoly Real Estate Tycoon	86.00% - 94.00%	
Star Trek	84.49% - 93.95%	
Wizard of Oz Progressive	86.05% - 86.15%	
Wizard of Oz Stand Alone	86.05% - 93.99%	

Once again, keep in mind that casinos generally set their slot paybacks based on each machine's denomination. Therefore, nickel machines will probably be set towards the lower number and $5-$25 machines will be set towards the higher number.

Okay, now let's get back to the "yes" part. Yes, you can win money on slot machines by using a little knowledge, practicing some money management and, mostly, having lots of luck. First, the knowledge part. You need to know what kind of player you are and how much risk you are willing to take. Do you want to go for the giant progressive jackpot that could make you a millionaire in an instant or would you be content walking away just a few dollars ahead?

An example of a wide-area progressive machine is Nevada's Megabucks where the jackpot starts at $10 million. These $1 machines are located at more than 125 Nevada casinos around the state and are linked together by a computer. It's fine if that's the kind of machine you want to play, but keep in mind that the odds are fairly astronomical of you hitting that big jackpot. Also, the payback percentage is lower on these machines than the average $1 machine. During Nevada's fiscal year ending June 30, 2011 Megabucks averaged a little more than 88% payback while the typical $1 machine averaged a little less than 95%. So, be aware that if you play these machines you'll win fewer small payouts and it will be very difficult to leave as a winner. Unless, of course, you hit that big one! If you really like to play the wide-area progressive machines your best bet is probably to set aside a small percentage of your bankroll (maybe 10 to 15 percent) for chasing that big jackpot and saving the rest for the regular machines.

One other thing you should know about playing these wide-area progressives is that on most of them, including Megabucks, you will receive your jackpot in equal payments over a period of years (usually 25). You can avoid this, however, by playing at one of the casinos that link slot machines at their own properties and will pay you in one lump sum. Be sure to look on the machine before playing to see how it says you will be paid for the jackpot.

Knowledge also comes into play when deciding how many coins to bet. You should always look at the payback schedule posted on the machine to see if a bonus is payed for playing the maximum number of coins that the machine will accept. For example, if it's a two-coin machine and the jackpot payout is 500 coins when you bet one coin, but it pays you 1,200 coins when you bet two coins, then that machine is paying you a 200-coin bonus for playing the maximum number of coins and you should always bet the maximum two coins to take advantage of that bonus. However, if it's a two-coin machine that will pay you 500 coins for a one-coin bet and 1,000 coins for a two-coin bet, then there is no advantage to making the maximum bet on that machine and you should only bet the minimum amount.

Knowledge of which casinos offer the best payback percentages is also helpful. When available, we print that information in this book to help you decide where to go for the best return on your slot machine dollar. You may want to go to the Las Vegas Strip to see the free pirate show at Treasure Island (TI), but take a look at the slot machine payback percentages for the Strip-area casinos in the Las Vegas section and you'll see that you can get better returns for your slot machine dollar by playing at the off-Strip area casinos.

The final bit of knowledge you need concerns slot clubs. Every major casino has a slot club and you should make it a point to join the slot club before you insert your first coin. It doesn't cost anything to join and as a member you will be able to earn complimentaries from the casinos in the form of cash, food, shows, drinks, rooms or other "freebies." When you first join the club you'll be issued a card (similar to a credit card) that you insert into the machine before you start to play and it will track how much you bet, as well as how long you play. Naturally, the more money you gamble, the more "freebies" you'll earn. Just make sure you don't get carried away and bet more than you're comfortable with just to earn some extra "comps." Ideally, you want to get "comps" for gambling that you were going to do anyway and not be pressured into betting more than you had planned.

Now let's talk about money management. The first thing you have to remember when playing slot machines is that there is no skill involved. Unlike blackjack or video poker, there are no decisions you can make that will affect whether you win or lose. It is strictly luck, or the lack of it, that will determine whether or not you win. However, when you are lucky enough to get ahead (even if it's just a little) that's where the money management factor comes in. As stated earlier, the longer you stand in front of a machine and put in your money, the more likely you are to go broke. Therefore, there is only one way you can walk away a winner and that's to make sure that when you do win, you don't put it all back in. You really need to set a "win goal" for yourself and to stop when you reach it. A realistic example would be a "win goal" of roughly 25 percent of your bankroll. If you started with $400, then you should stop if you win about $100. The "win goal" you decide on is up to you, but keep in mind that the higher your goal, the harder it will be to reach it, so be practical.

And what if you should happen to reach your goal? Take a break! Go have a meal, see a show, visit the lounge for a drink or even just take a walk around the casino. You may have the urge to keep playing, but if you can just take a break from the machines, even it's just for a short time, you'll have the satisfaction of leaving as a winner. If, later on, you get really bored and find that you just *have* to go back to the machines you can avoid a total loss by not risking more than half of your winnings and by playing on smaller denomination machines. If you made your winnings on $1 machines, move down to quarters. If you won on quarters, move down to nickels. The idea now is basically to kill some time and have a little fun knowing that no matter what happens you'll still leave as a winner.

And now, let's move on to luck. As stated previously, the ultimate decider in whether or not you win is how lucky you are. But, is there anything you can do to help you choose a "winning" machine? Not really, because there is no such thing. Remember, in the long run, no machine will pay out more than it takes in. There are, however, some things you could try to help you find the more generous machines and avoid the stingy ones. Keep in mind that all slot machine payback percentages shown in this book are averages. Some machines are programmed to pay back more and some machines are programmed to pay less. Also, like everything else in life, machines have good cycles where they pay out more than average and bad cycles where they pay out less than average. Ultimately, what you want to find is a high-paying machine in a good cycle. Of course if I knew how to find that machine I wouldn't be writing this story, instead I'd be standing in front of it with a $100 bill in my hand and looking for the change attendant. So, I guess you'll have to settle for my two recommendations as to how you *might* be able to find the better paying machines.

First, is the "accounting" method. With this method you start with a predetermined number of coins and after playing them you take an accounting of your results. If you have more than you started with you stay at that machine and start another cycle. Just keep doing this until the machine returns less than you started with. As an example, let's say you start with 20 coins. After playing those 20 coins you count how many you got back. If it's more than 20 you start over again with another 20 coins and then do another accounting. If, after any accounting, you get back less than the 20 you started with, stop playing and move on to a different machine. This is an especially good method because you have to slow down your play to take periodic accountings and you will always have an accurate idea of how well you are doing.

The other method is even simpler and requires no math. It's called the "baseball" method and is based on the principle of three strikes and you're out. Just play a machine until it loses three times in a row, then move on to another machine. Both of these methods will prevent you from losing a lot in a machine that is either set for a low payback or is going through a bad cycle; yet both can still allow you to take advantage of a high payback machine or one that is going through a good cycle. Good luck!

Slot Machine Trends - 2012

by John Grochowski

Slot machines have been the games of choice for casino players for a decades now, long since having shot past blackjack, craps and other table games.

As the games of choice, they also offer a huge choice in games. No matter what your desired play experience short of the machines just giving money way, slot manufacturers are working to bring it on. Do you like to just watch the reels spin, or do you want to make choices that influence the outcome? Do you want to push the buttons and let 'em roll, or do you want to interact via the touchscreen? Do you want to play on your own, of do you want a full-out community experience, winning together or competing with each other?

Well, have it your way.

The biggest trend in electronic gaming is to use new technology to give the players what they want. For some players that means just keeping some three-reel games on the floor --- no fancy bonuses, no free spins, just spin the reels and hope for the jackpots. For some players, that means free spins, pick'em bonuses, Sensory Immersion with sound and motion effects, play-together community bonus events and more, in ever more intricate combinations and entertainment packages.

Take WMS Gaming's **Monopoly Bigger Event Big Money Spin**, the first in what WMS calls its "Collaborative Gaming" line. In community bonus events on the twin 52-inch screens overhead, players make choices that affect the bonuses of others playing the game. Players collaborate to build a bonus. In the Play the Board Bonus --- the ever-popular trip around the Monopoly board --- players roll the dice by touching their own screen, dragging the dice and letting them fly up to the top. The token moves around the board, bonuses accumulate, and then it's the next player's turn to roll. A player who lands on on Boardwalk is very popular indeed. So is a player who lands on a railroad, initiating a Railroad Bonus game within the game before getting back to the main board.

It's a little extra wrinkle to make the games more fun for players. That's what manufacturers are after as slot technology continues to evolve.

Every slotmaker is trying to put its own spin on your spins. Here's what some of the major manufacturers are rolling out, with some games that made it to casino floors in 2011, and some things to watch in the year ahead.

Bally Technologies: The first U-Spin game, **Cash Spin**, was such a success in 2010 that Bally plans more in the line of games that coordinates spinning wheels on a video screen with wheels up top.

The designated follow-up game is **Hot Pick**, and it's a game with a difference. Like Cash Spin and all U-Spin games, it incorporates a video wheel that the player can spin by touching the screen, dragging, and releasing. Keep your finger on the wheel and you can drag the wheel up or down --- forward or backward, if you prefer. You can move it fast or slow, and when you finally release the wheel, the speed of its turn will reflect the speed with which you drag your finger.

That's the same game play we've seen in Cash Spin, but there's a difference.

"In Hot Pick, we're enabling players to choose their own volatility," said Laura Olson-Reyes, Bally's director of corporate communications. "If they want a lot of time on device and frequent small wins, they can choose that, or if they like to bet more for the opportunity for bigger wins, they have the opportunity to choose that too."

The "choose your volatility" feature applies to the frequency of the bonus event as well as the prizes available on the bonus wheel. There are six levels of volatility available, represented by different symbols. When you go to choose, you can touch a single bar for the lowest volatility, with the most frequent bonus events and the lowest totals on the wheel. Touch a Wild symbol instead, and watch the numbers on the wheel change as the game shifts into the highest volatility level. Or you can choose 5-bar or various 7 symbols to pick a level in between.

Do you want a lot of chances to spin the wheel, or do you want the chance at a really big jackpot when the wheel comes up? You get to choose.

Bally is giving a few different looks to the wheel. On Cash Spin and Hot Pick, you basically spin the wheel up or down. **Vegas Hits** brings two wheels to the game, stacked high on its Digital Tower cabinet. You drag your finger up or down on an on-screen wheel, and the spin high above in the top box reflects your speed and direction on the screen.

And then there's Golden Pharoah, a game with a wide-area progressive jackpot and a different kind of **U-Spin**. This time, you get a side view of a wheel, and instead of spinning up and down you're spinning left to right or right to left. Golden Pharoah also includes another innovative new feature, the Directional Wild. When a compass-like wild symbol turns up on the video reels, a pointer rotates around the symbol. When it stops, it indicates a direction, and all symbols in the indicated path turn wild, leading to extra wins.

It was by no means the only cool technology at Bally. The new **iDeck** turns the button panel into something extra. One physical button remains --- Bally developers figured slot players still would like to push that button to spin the reels. The rest of the panel is an extra video screen. During regular play, you get touch-screen buttons for choosing how many lines and credits to play, a help button and a cashout button.

At bonus time, the iDeck can be something else. It can bring its own randomly occurring bonus events --- a feature Bally calls U-Win. On games under the OK Jalapeno theme --- choose the Hot and Spicy game, or Mild and Wild --- U-Win was set up to let players rub a magic lamp on the iDeck for bonus credits, or to touch the iDeck and spin a wheel.

On Betty Boop's **Love Meter**, the iDeck becomes an integral part of a bonus event. In the How Hot Are You bonus, images of hands appear on the panel. You place your hands on the iDeck outlines, and the outlines change colors a la the mood ring fad of the 1970s. Then a meter in the top box rises, from lovable to romantic to sexy to wild to smokin' and beyond. The higher it rises, the hotter your bonus.

International Game Technology: The Center Stage series with its 103-inch screen for bonuses, and film clips over a bank of machines, continues to be IGT's way of saying "That's entertainment in a big, big way. One big winner on Center Stage is **The Dark Knight**, based on the Batman film.

With film clips from the movie, The Dark Knight is packed with action. In a bonus event played out on the top screen, you can choose to play as Batman on his Batcycle, or as the Joker, in his truck bearing the message "Slaughter is the best medicine." The Caped Crusader and his green-haired foe careen through the streets of Gotham, the Joker veering into Batman's lane, trying to force the Batcycle off the road. Along the way, there are targets to drive through for bonuses, and checkpoints where the first to pass collects a jackpot.

You have a choice when you get to the bonus event. If you're playing with a friend and you want to wait for him or her to get to the bonus so you can compete against each other, you can save your trip to the big round.
IGT also goes Hollywood with **The Hangover**. With a cry of "It's Vegas, baby!" from a film clip, this is a game in its element. It's a multilevel progressive, with levels named after movie characters Alan, Phil, Stu and Doug. Movie scenes help introduce the bonus events. In Stu's Game, movie dentist Stu notices he's missing a tooth. Then the player starts selecting teeth on a grid to collect bonuses.

There are bonuses within the bonuses. Each character-themed event starts with a pick-a-picture game. You choose squares, and a photograph is revealed.

When you collect enough matching photos, you win the corresponding award --- perhaps one of the progressives, or a **Stun Fun Bonus**, where you hold a button on the screen to fire a stun gun as bonus credits mount. Then there's the Villa Bonus, where you can wind your way from room to room, touching objects such as a sword or a TV to win credits or multipliers. But watch out. If you find a tiger, your round's over.

In its new Player Affinity Series, IGT goes to the big top with **Ringling Brothers Barnum & Bailey** Circus. There are two versions, one with five video reels in a four-deep configuration, one with a hexagon-type layout for 720 ways to win. The 3-D circus symbols really pop out at you while on video a real Ringling Brothers ringmaster guides you through the game. And when you visit Clown Alley and clown videos in place of reel symbols start mounting up the winnings, well, send in the clowns.

WMS Gaming: Over the last decade, WMS has stepped up as an innovator and technology leader. That now includes developing online resources, including social media such as Facebook, to build a slot players' community.

The main thrust is through **Players Life**, www.playerslife.com. The start of something that could be really big came with the introduction of **The Lord of the Rings**, a film-action enhanced journey through Middle Earth. The games bring players a quest storyline with unlockable graphics and bonus events. Players create identities on the game and pick up where they left off the next time they play.

Play doesn't stop in the casino. You can accumulate miles toward unlocking the next bonus level away from the casino by playing casual games at playerslife. com. And players can browse through new games, see screen shots and videos of WMS' latest and greatest, and interact with other players and game designers, and even take it to your phone with the Players Life mobile app.

It's a major point of emphasis for WMS, which includes Players Life extra in coming attractions including Aladdin --- wait till you get a load of the Sensory Immersion effects while flying the magic carpet --- **Alice, Battleship, Clue** and more.

Also new at WMS is a suite of Portal Applications, with bonus events and progressives that can be layered onto any WMS game. **Ultra Hit Progressive** layers a mystery bonus onto the base games, with initial themes including **Piggy Bankin** and **Jackpot Explosion**. In the **Winner's Share** application, a random secondary event allows one player at the bank to play a round worth anywhere from 1 percent to 200 percent of the progressive jackpot. At G2E, Winner's Share debuted with **PengWins**, a physics-based event across the Transmissive screen on mechanical slots in which penguins careen from cliff to ice floe to walrus, picking up bonuses until they stop.

MetaScreen, a Portal Application that is designed for competitive slot play, is being launched with **Pirate Battle**, with some players on the bank grouped as the Red Team, exchanging cannon fire with the Blue Team. And the fourth Portal Application, **Mega Multiplier**, powered by a real-time physics engine, allows players to shoot an animated pinball into the top box for a chance to multiply credits up to 100 times.

WMS has a new licensing deal with Hasbro, and one of the initial offerings will be **Yahtzee**, the iconic dice rolling game.

"Yahtzee's a pretty frequently hitting bonus, explained Allon Engleman, vice president of game design and strategy at WMS. "Accumulate 5 bonus triggers, then you're eligible for the progressives, or with a max bet, you're eligible for the progressive from the beginning. Basically, the player plays out a Yahtzee game, There's no skill involved, but you throw the dice into the top box. With any five of a kind, you win that level of progressive."

There are eight progressive levels, and with back-to-back Yahtzees, you could win 10,000 credits.

Aristocrat: Chances are you've seen video slots with four sets of reels on the same screen --- you're playing four games at once. Aristocrat is putting a couple of new takes on that concept. In a new line called **Mega Pay**, the initial releases are called **More Chilli** and **More Hearts**, which carved out a following quickly in 2011. Each starts you with two sets of reels. Collecting enough peppers on More Chilli or hearts on More Hearts brings a third set of reels, with the fourth reel wild. Collect even more of the bonus symbols, and you get another set, this time with both the fourth and fifth reels wild. That brings both anticipation as you near unlocking another set, but also some big wins with all those wild symbols.

Gazillions and **Fortune Fantasy** go about the multiplay category in an opposite way. Instead of expanding to four sets of reels, they contract to one. If you trigger a free game feature on any of the reel sets, that set of reels takes over the entire screen as the free games are played out.

And for something completely different, there's a new line of games called **Remix**, with **Don Quixote** and **Dragon Emperor** as the first games in the category. Don Quixote is a traditional-looking five-reel game, but in a bonus event it shuffles the symbols on the reels, landing them in new positions with the possibility of new winning combinations. Dragon Emperor is a Reel Power version --- the reels are shuffled, rather than the symbols. If you've ever thought,. "I'd have a winner there if only that symbol would move over a reel or down a payline."

Atronic: Atronic waited to join the community gaming trend until it had just the right product. That meant going to its most successful line with the latest Deal or No Deal game, **Deal or No Deal Join 'N' Play**. It has 45-inch LCD screens overhead for the big suitcase bonus event. The base game features 243 ways to win, and has three mystery bonuses for the individual player. As they play, customers collect suitcases, with 18 cases bringing eligibility for the community bonus. The more the player bets from a minimum of 50 cents to a maximum of $2.50, the more reels are activated with qualifier cases. A sixth reel can multiply cases collected on any spin.

The first of the Deal or No Deal games to feature TV host Howie Mandel, Join 'N' Play puts the big bonus on an 11-minute timer. Anyone who plays steadily should be able to accumulate enough suitcases to participate in the big event, but those who continue to collect cases can earn multipliers for their winnings.

Aruze: Paradise Fishing brings hands-on play to the slots. You get the full feel of landing a big fish through a joystick that represents the old fishing pole.

With six machines under three 60-inch high definition LCD games showing scenes from the deep sea or coral reef, the game looks beautiful. The community style bonuses --- trying to catch the most fish, or the biggest fish, or some combination thereof --- is reminiscent of WMS' Reel 'Em In: Compete to Win. But the hook here is the controller using Aruze's Reel Feel technology. Grab hold, and raise or lower your worm. And when that marlin strikes, you can really feel it. The fish struggles and fights while you try to land it --- and sometimes it gets away.

The ol' fishing pole is one more cool little piece of technology to add to the mix as slotmakers carve out their own niches, and try to give the players what they want.

John Grochowski writes a weekly syndicated newspaper column on gambling, and is author of the "Casino Answer Book" series from Bonus Books.

Video Poker

by Steve Bourie

Okay, who knows the main difference between video poker and slot machines? C'mon now, raise your hands if you think you know it. If you said "a slot machine is a game of luck and video poker is a game of skill" then you are correct! When you play a slot machine there is no decision you can make which will affect the outcome of the game. You put in your money; pull the handle; and hope for the best. In video poker, however, it is your skill in playing the cards which definitely affects the outcome of the game.

Okay, who knows the other major difference between video poker and slot machines? Well, you're right again if you said "you never know what percentage a slot machine is set to pay back, but you can tell a video poker machine's payback percentage just by looking at it." Of course if you knew that answer then you also knew that video poker machines almost always offer you better returns than slot machines (provided you make the right playing decisions).

Now for those of you who didn't know the answers to those two questions, please read on. You others can skip the rest of this story as I am sure you're eager to get back to your favorite video poker machine.

First, let's cover the basics. Video poker has virtually the same rules as a game of five card draw poker. The only difference is that you have no opponent to beat and you can't lose more than your initial bet. First, you deposit from one to five coins in the machine to make your bet. You are then shown five cards on the video screen and your goal is to try to make the best poker hand possible from those cards. Since it is a draw game, you are given one opportunity to improve your hand. This is done by allowing you to discard from one, up to all five cards from your original hand. Of course, you don't have to discard any if you don't want to. After choosing which cards you want to keep (by pushing the button below each card), you then push the deal button and the machine will replace all of the other cards with new cards. Based on the resulting final hand the machine will then pay you according to the pay schedule posted on the machine. Naturally, the better your hand, the higher the amount the machine will pay you back.

That's pretty much how a video poker machine works from the outside, but what about the inside? Well, I had a few questions about that so I visited International Game Technology, which is the world's largest manufacturer of video poker machines (as well as slot machines), in January 2001 and spoke to their chief software engineer, James Vasquez. Here's what Jim had to say in answer to some questions about how his company's machines work:

Let's talk about the difference between video poker and slot machines. It's my understanding that with video poker you can't control the number of winning and losing combinations programmed into the computer chip, instead its based on a 52-card deck with a fixed number of combinations. Is that correct?

Vasquez: Yes, assuming there are no wild cards.

When the cards are dealt is it done on a serial basis where it's similar to cards coming off the top of a deck? Or, parallel where there are five cards dealt face up and one card is unseen underneath each of the initial five cards?

Vasquez: It's serial and the five later cards aren't determined until there is more player interaction at the time of the draw.

They aren't determined at the time of the deal?

Vasquez: No. They're determined at the time of the draw. That varies with the jurisdictional regulation actually. Some lottery jurisdictions tell you that you have to draw all 10 at once. Different jurisdictions write into their rules how they want it done, specifically on poker, because it's a simpler game and they understand it. They say they either want all 10 done at once, or however they want.

How is it done in Nevada? All ten at once, or five and five?

IGT: In Nevada it's five and five.

The talk with Jim Vasquez confirmed that in most regulated jurisdictions video poker machines use a Random Number Generator to shuffle a 52-card deck and then choose five cards to display to the player. (By the way, when played without wild cards, there are exactly 2,598,960 unique five-card poker hands possible.) Then, when the deal button is pushed, the next group of cards is chosen and dealt to the player.

One point must be made here regarding random outcomes in video poker machines. Please note that *gaming regulations* always require video poker machines to have random outcomes. You should be aware that there are casinos operating in places that *do not* have gaming regulations. Examples are cruise ships which operate in international waters, some Indian reservations that are not subject to state regulations, and virtually all Internet casinos. You should also be aware that the technology exists for machines to be set so they do not act randomly. These machines can be actually programmed to avoid giving the players better hands and they wind up giving the house a much bigger advantage. These machines are illegal in Nevada, New Jersey, Colorado and all other states that pattern their gaming regulations after those states. You may, however, come across them in unregulated casinos.

One final point you should keep in mind - IGT is not the only manufacturer of video poker machines. There are quite a few others and they may engineer their machines to work in a different manner. Their RNG may not stop in the same way and their draw cards may be dealt differently. IGT, however, is by far the largest and it is the type of machine you will most often encounter in a casino.

Now that you understand how a video poker machine works let's learn how to pick out the best paying ones. In the beginning of this story it was mentioned that "you can tell a video poker machine's payback percentage just by looking at it." That's true, but it takes a little bit of knowledge to know the difference among all the different types of machines. An example of some of the different machines available are: Jacks or Better, Bonus, Double Bonus, Double Double Bonus, Joker Poker and Deuces Wild. To make it even more confusing, not only are there different machines, but each of those machines can have a different pay schedule for the same hand.

Fortunately, every video poker machine's payback percentage can be mathematically calculated. Not only does this let you know which machines offer you the best return, but it also tells you the best playing decisions to make on that particular machine based on the odds of that combination occurring. The bad news, however, is that it's fairly impossible to do on your own so you'll have to either buy a book that lists all of the percentages and strategies or buy a computer program that does the work for you. Take a look at the tables on the next few pages and you'll see some different types of video poker games and their payback percentages (when played with maximum coin and perfect strategy). For those of you with a computer there are several software programs on the market that can determine the exact payback percentage for any video poker machine. They retail for prices from $29.95 to $59.95, but can be purchased at discounted prices at http://www.americancasinoguide.com/video-poker-software Besides calculating percentages, they also allow you to play different types of machines and analyze hands to show you the expected return for each play. You can set these games to automatically show you the best decision, or to just warn you if you make a wrong decision.

If you have no desire to get quite that serious about learning video poker then I'll try to provide some general tips to help you out. First, you'll need to find the machines that offer you the highest returns. One of the best is the 9/6 Jacks or Better machine. Of course, you're probably wondering "what is a 9/6 Jacks or Better machine?" Well, the Jacks or Better part refers to the fact that you won't win anything from the machine unless you have at least a pair of Jacks. The 9/6 part refers to the payback schedule on this kind of machine.

As stated earlier, each machine can have a different payback schedule and there are at least 20 different kinds of payback schedules available on Jacks or Better machines. In Las Vegas the two most common Jacks or Better machines you will find are 8/5 and 9/6. Here's a comparison of their pay schedules (per coin, for five-coin play):

Hand	9/6	8/5
Royal Flush	800	800
Straight Flush	50	50
4-of-a-Kind	25	25
Full House	9	8
Flush	6	5
Straight	4	4
3-of-a-Kind	3	3
Two Pairs	2	2
One Pair J's	1	1

As you can see, the schedules are identical except for the better payoffs on the 9/6 machines for Flushes and Full Houses. The payback on a 9/6 machine is 99.5% with perfect play, while the 8/5 machines return 97.3% with perfect play. Of course, it doesn't make any sense to play an 8/5 machine if a 9/6 machine is available. Yet, you'll often see lots of people playing an 8/5 when a 9/6 can often be found in the same casino. The reason they do that is because they don't know any better; you do. Always look for the 9/6 machines. They can be usually found in most downtown Las Vegas casinos at the quarter level and in many Strip casinos at denominations of $1 and higher. In other states they won't be found as easily, and sometimes, not at all.

One other common machine you will come across is an 8/5 Jacks or Better progressive. These feature the same 8/5 pay table as above except for the royal flush which pays a jackpot amount that is displayed on a meter above the machine. The jackpot will continue to build until someone hits a royal flush; then it will reset and start to build again. When the progressive jackpot (for five coins) on a 25¢ machine first starts out at $1,000 the payback is only 97.30%, but when it reaches $2,166.50, the payback is 100%.

Another good tip is to restrict your play to the same kind of machine all the time. Each video poker machine has its own particular strategy and what works best on a Jacks or Better machine is definitely much different from what works best on a Deuces Wild machine. I usually only play 9/6 Jacks or Better machines because that is what I practice on and I automatically know the best decision to make all the time. Keep in mind that when you calculate the payback percentage for a video poker machine the number you arrive at is based on perfect play. As an example, a 9/6 Jacks or Better video poker machine has a 99.5% payback with perfect play. This means that, theoretically, it will return $99.50 for every $100 played in the machine, but only if the player makes the correct decision every time. If you make mistakes, and most players do,

Jacks or Better Pay Table Variations
(Per coin with maximum coin played and perfect strategy)

9/6		9/5	
Royal Flush	800	Royal Flush	800
Straight Flush	50	Straight Flush	50
4-of-a-kind	25	4-of-a-kind	25
Full House	*9*	*Full House*	*9*
Flush	*6*	*Flush*	*5*
Straight	4	Straight	4
3-of-a-kind	3	3-of-a-kind	3
2 Pair	2	2 Pair	2
Jacks or Better	1	Jacks or Better	1
Payback	**99.54%**	**Payback**	**98.45%**

8/6		8/5	
Royal Flush	800	Royal Flush	800
Straight Flush	50	Straight Flush	50
4-of-a-kind	25	4-of-a-kind	25
Full House	*8*	*Full House*	*8*
Flush	*6*	*Flush*	*5*
Straight	4	Straight	4
3-of-a-kind	3	3-of-a-kind	3
2 Pair	2	2 Pair	2
Jacks or Better	1	Jacks or Better	1
Payback	**98.39%**	**Payback**	**97.28%**

7/5		6/5	
Royal Flush	800	Royal Flush	800
Straight Flush	50	Straight Flush	50
4-of-a-kind	25	4-of-a-kind	25
Full House	*7*	*Full House*	*6*
Flush	*5*	*Flush*	*5*
Straight	4	Straight	4
3-of-a-kind	3	3-of-a-kind	3
2 Pair	2	2 Pair	2
Jacks or Better	1	Jacks or Better	1
Payback	**96.15%**	**Payback**	**95.00%**

Bonus Poker Pay Table Variations
(Per coin with maximum coin played and perfect strategy)

### 7/5 Bonus		### 8/5 Bonus	
Royal Flush	800	Royal Flush	800
Straight Flush	50	Straight Flush	50
Four Aces	80	Four Aces	80
Four 2s 3s 4s	40	Four 2s 3s 4s	40
Four 5s-Ks	25	Four 5s-Ks	25
Full House	*7*	*Full House*	*8*
Flush	*5*	*Flush*	*5*
Straight	4	Straight	4
3-of-a-kind	3	3-of-a-kind	3
2 Pair	2	2 Pair	2
Jacks or Better	1	Jacks or Better	1
Payback	**98.02%**	**Payback**	**99.17%**

### 10/7 Double Bonus		### 9/7 Double Bonus	
Royal Flush	800	Royal Flush	800
Straight Flush	50	Straight Flush	50
Four Aces	160	Four Aces	160
Four 2s 3s 4s	80	Four 2s 3s 4s	80
Four 5s-Ks	50	Four 5s-Ks	50
Full House	*10*	*Full House*	*9*
Flush	*7*	*Flush*	*7*
Straight	5	Straight	5
3-of-a-kind	3	3-of-a-kind	3
2 Pair	1	2 Pair	1
Jacks or Better	1	Jacks or Better	1
Payback	**100.17%**	**Payback**	**99.11%**

### 10/6 Double Double Bonus		### 9/6 Double Double Bonus	
Royal Flush	800	Royal Flush	800
Straight Flush	50	Straight Flush	50
Four Aces w/ 2, 3 or 4	400	Four Aces w/ 2, 3 or 4	400
Four 2, 3 or 4 w/A-4	160	Four 2, 3 or 4 w/A-4	160
Four Aces	160	Four Aces	160
Four 2,3 or 4	80	Four 2,3 or 4	80
Four 5-K	50	Four 5-K	50
Full House	*10*	*Full House*	*9*
Flush	*6*	*Flush*	*6*
Straight	4	Straight	4
3-of-a-kind	3	3-of-a-kind	3
2 Pair	1	2 Pair	1
Jacks or Better	1	Jacks or Better	1
Payback	**100.07%**	**Payback**	**98.98%**

Deuces Wild Pay Table Variations
(Per coin with maximum coin played and perfect strategy)

Short Pay		Full Pay	
Natural Royal Flush	800	Natural Royal Flush	800
Four Deuces	200	Four Deuces	200
Wild Royal Flush	25	Wild Royal Flush	25
5-of-a-kind	15	5-of-a-kind	15
Straight Flush	9	Straight Flush	9
4-of-a-kind	*4*	*4-of-a-kind*	*5*
Full House	3	Full House	3
Flush	2	Flush	2
Straight	2	Straight	2
3-of-a-kind	1	3-of-a-kind	1
Payback	**94.34%**	**Payback**	**100.76%**

Not So Ugly (NSU) Deuces		Deuces Deluxe	
Natural Royal Flush	800	Natural Royal Flush	800
Four Deuces	200	Four Deuces	200
Wild Royal Flush	25	Natural Straight Flush	50
5-of-a-kind	*16*	Wild Royal Flush	25
Straight Flush	*10*	5-of-a-kind	15
4-of-a-kind	*4*	Natural 4-of-a-kind	10
Full House	*4*	Wild Straight Flush	9
Flush	*3*	Wild 4-of-a-kind	4
Straight	2	Full House	4
3-of-a-kind	1	Flush	3
Payback	**99.73%**	Straight	2
		3-of-a-kind	1
		Payback	**100.34%**

the return to the casino will be higher. If you play several different kinds of machines it becomes increasingly harder to remember the correct play and you will make mistakes. Therefore, it only makes sense to memorize the correct decisions for one kind of machine and to always play on that same kind of machine (of course, in order to learn those proper strategies, you may want to buy that book or software).

Now that you've decided which machines to play, you'll need some help with strategy. On the next two pages are charts that will give you an excellent simple strategy for both 9/6 and 8/5 video poker machines. These charts were derived from calculations using a video poker software computer program and give you a near-perfect strategy. They aren't 100% perfect but they are close to it and will only be fractionally incorrect in some situations. The only difference between the two tables is shown in the poker hands that have been *italicized* in the 8/5 strategy tables.

Simple Strategy Table For 9/6 Jacks or Better

1.   Royal Flush
2.   Straight Flush
3.   4 of a kind
4.   4 card Royal Flush
5.   Full House
6.   Flush
7.   3 of a kind
8.   Straight
9.   4 card Straight Flush
10. Two Pairs
11. 4 card inside Straight Flush
12. High Pair (Jacks or higher)
13. 3 card Royal Flush
14. 4 card Flush
15. 4 card Straight with 3 high cards
16. Low Pair (2's through 10's)
17. 4 card Straight with 2 high cards
18. 4 card Straight with 1 high card
19. 3 card Inside Straight Flush with 2 high cards
20. 3 card Straight Flush with 1 high card
21. 4 card Straight with no high cards
22. 3 card Double Inside Straight Flush with 2 high cards
23. 3 card Inside Straight Flush with 1 high card
24. 3 card Straight Flush with no high cards
25. 4 card Inside Straight with 4 high cards
26. 2 card Royal Flush with no Ace or 10
27. 2 card Royal Flush with Ace and no 10
28. 3 card Double Inside Straight Flush with 1 high card
29. 3 card Inside Straight Flush with no high card
30. 4 card Inside Straight with 3 high cards
31. 3 high cards with no Ace
32. 2 high cards
33. 2 card Royal Flush with 10 and no Ace
34. 1 high card
35. 3 card Double Inside Straight Flush with no high card
36. All New Cards

Simple Strategy Table For 8/5 Jacks or Better

1.   Royal Flush
2.   Straight Flush
3.   4 of a kind
4.   4 card Royal Flush
5.   Full House
6.   Flush
7.   3 of a kind
8.   Straight
9.   4 card Straight Flush
10.   Two Pairs
11.   4 card inside Straight Flush
12.   High Pair (Jacks or higher)
13.   3 card Royal Flush
14.   4 card Flush
15.   4 card Straight with 3 high cards
16.   Low Pair (2's through 10's)
17.   4 card Straight with 2 high cards
18.   4 card Straight with 1 high card
19.   3 card Inside Straight Flush with 2 high cards
20.   3 card Straight Flush with 1 high card
21.   4 card Straight with no high cards
22.   3 card Double Inside Straight Flush with 2 high cards
23.   3 card Inside Straight Flush with 1 high card
24.   3 card Straight Flush with no high cards
25.   4 card Inside Straight with 4 high cards
26.   2 card Royal Flush with no Ace or 10
27.   2 card Royal Flush with Ace and no 10
28.   *3 high cards with no Ace*
29.   *4 card Inside Straight with 3 high cards*
30.   *3 card Double Inside Straight Flush with 1 high card*
31.   *2 high cards*
32.   *3 card Inside Straight Flush with no high card*
33.   2 card Royal Flush with 10 and no Ace
34.   1 high card
35.   3 card Double Inside Straight Flush with no high card
36.   All New Cards

To use any chart just look up your hand and play it in the manner that is closest to the top of the chart. For example: you are dealt (6♣,6♦,7♥,8♠,9♣). You keep (6♣,6♦) rather than (6♦,7♥,8♠,9♣) because a low pair (#16) is higher on the chart than a four-card straight with no high cards (#21). Remember to always look for the highest possible choice on the chart when there are multiple ways to play your hand. As another example: you are dealt (8♣,8♦, J♥,Q♥,K♥). You keep (J♥,Q♥,K♥) rather than (8♣,8♦) because a three-card royal flush (#13) is higher on the chart than a low pair (#16). As a final, but radical, example of how to play your hand by the chart what would you do if you're dealt (6♥,10♥,J♥,Q♥,K♥)? Yes, you have to break up your flush by discarding the 6♥ and go for the royal flush because the four-card royal flush (#4) is higher on the chart than the pat flush (#6). When looking at the 9/6 chart there are a few things that should seem rather obvious:

1) A low pair is relatively good. Of the 36 possible hands, a low pair is #16 which means there are 20 hands worse than a low pair. If you look at the 15 hands that are better than a low pair eight of them are pat hands that require no draw. Of the other seven hands, six of them are four card hands and the remaining hand is a three-card royal flush.

2) Don't hold three cards trying to get a straight or flush. Nowhere on the chart do you see that you should hold three cards to try for a straight or flush. In some instances you should hold three cards to try for a straight flush, but *never* a straight or flush.

3) Rarely draw to an inside straight. Inside straights (6,7,_,9,10) appear only twice on the chart and only in rather bad positions: #30 (with three high cards) and #25 (with four high cards). It is much easier to draw to an outside straight (_7,8,9,10_) where you can complete your straight by getting the card you need on either end. Open end straights appear four times on the chart and in much higher positions than inside straights: #21 (with no high cards), #18 (with one high card), #17 (with two high cards) and #15 (with three high cards).

4) Don't hold a kicker. A kicker is an unpaired card held with a pair. For example (8,8,K) or (K,K,9) are examples of hands where an extra card (the kicker) is held. *Never* hold a kicker because they add no value to your hand!

If you want to make your own video poker strategy charts there are some special video poker programs that can do this for you and they are included in some game playing software. For information on buying these programs, go to http://www.americancasinoguide.com/video-poker-software With these specialized video poker software programs you can then print out the strategy charts and bring them with you into the casino.

For your information there are exactly 2,598,960 unique poker hands possible on a video poker machine (when played without a joker). On a 9/6 Jacks or Better machine a royal flush will occur about once every 40,000 hands; a straight flush about every 9,000 hands; four-of-a-kind about every 425 hands; a full house about every 87 hands; a flush about every 91 hands; a straight about every 89

Other Video Poker Game Pay Tables
(Per coin with maximum coin played and perfect strategy)

Pick'Em Poker (five coin payout)		All American Poker	
Royal Flush	6,000	Royal Flush	800
Straight Flush	1,199	Straight Flush	200
4-of-a-kind	600	4-of-a-kind	40
Full House	90	Full House	8
Flush	75	Flush	8
Straight	55	Straight	8
3-of-a-kind	25	3-of-a-kind	3
Two Pair	15	Two Pair	1
Pair 9's or Better	10	Pair Jacks or Better	1
Payback	**99.95%**	**Payback**	**100.72%**

Double Joker Full-Pay		Double Joker Short-Pay	
Natural Royal Flush	800	Natural Royal Flush	800
Wild Royal Flush	100	Wild Royal Flush	100
5-of-a-kind	50	5-of-a-kind	50
Straight Flush	25	Straight Flush	25
4-of-a-kind	*9*	*4-of-a-kind*	*8*
Full House	5	Full House	5
Flush	4	Flush	4
Straight	3	Straight	3
3-of-a-kind	2	3-of-a-kind	2
2 Pair	1	2 Pair	1
Payback	**99.97%**	**Payback**	**98.10%**

hands; three-of-a-kind about every 14 hands; two pairs about every 8 hands; and a pair of Jacks or better about every 5 hands. The interesting thing to note here is that both a flush and a straight are harder to get than a full house, yet a full house always has a higher payback. The majority of the time, about 55% to be exact, you will wind up with a losing hand on a 9/6 machine.

The next bit of advice concerns how many coins you should bet. You should always bet the maximum amount (on machines returning 100% or more) because it will allow you to earn bonus coins when you hit the royal flush. Example: For a royal flush on a 9/6 machine with one coin played you receive 250 coins; for two coins you get 500; for three coins you get 750; for four coins you get 1,000 and for five (maximum) coins you get 4,000 coins! This translates into a bonus of 2,750 coins! A royal flush can be expected once every 40,400 hands on a 9/6 machine; once every 40,200 hands on an 8/5 machine; and once every 32,700 hands on an 8/5 progressive. The odds are high, but the added bonus makes it worthwhile. If you can't afford to play the maximum coins on a positive machine then move down to a lower denomination machine. And, if you absolutely insist on playing less than the maximum, be sure to play only one at a time. It doesn't make any sense to play two, three or four coins, because you still won't be eligible for the bonus.

One important thing to keep in mind when you look at the total payback on these video poker machines is that those numbers always include a royal flush and the royal flush plays a *very* big factor in the total return. As a matter of fact, the royal flush is such a big factor on video poker machines that you are actually expected to lose until you get that royal flush. Yes, even by restricting your play to video poker machines with a more than 100% payback you are *still* expected to lose money until you hit a royal flush. Once you hit that royal flush it will bring your cash back up to that 100% level but until it happens you should be fully aware that you are statistically expected to lose money.

According to video poker expert Bob Dancer, "on a 25¢ Jacks or Better 9/6 machine you will lose at a rate of 2.5% while you are waiting for the royal to happen. Another way to look at this is quarter players who play 600 hands per hour can expect to lose about $18.75 per hour, on average, on any hour they do not hit a royal." You really have to keep in mind that there are no guarantees when you play video poker. Yes, you are expected to get a royal flush about once every 40,000 hands but there are no guarantees that it will happen and if you don't get that royal flush it could cost you dearly.

A final tip about playing video poker concerns slot clubs. Every major casino has a slot club and you should make it a point to join the slot club before you insert your first coin. It doesn't cost anything to join and as a member you will have the opportunity to earn complimentaries from the casinos in the form of cash, food, shows, drinks, rooms or other "freebies." When you join the club you'll be issued a card (similar to a credit card) that you insert in the machine before you start to play and it will track how much you bet, as well as how long you play. Naturally, the more money you gamble, the more freebies you'll earn. Just make sure you don't get carried away and bet more than you're comfortable with just to earn some extra comps. Ideally, you want to get comps for gambling that you were going to do anyway and not be pressured into betting more than you had planned. Many clubs will also give you cash back for your play and that amount should be added into the payback percentage on the kind of machine you'll be playing. For example: at MGM Grand in Las Vegas, the slot club rebates .22% in cash for your video poker play (.67% for slots). By only playing 9/6 Jacks or Better machines with a return of 99.54% you can add the .22% rebate to get an adjusted figure of 99.76%. This means that you are, theoretically, playing an almost even game, *plus* you're still eligible for other room and food discounts on top of your cash rebate.

Be a Good Video Poker Scout

by Jean Scott

It used to be so easy in the '80s! Walk briskly up and down the aisles of a casino, quickly scan the names of the video poker machines, and look at the paytable right there on the glass front. Often there would be a whole row of the same game with the same name and the same paytable. The hardest it got was to peer over the shoulders of the drinkers who were hunkered down over the bartop games.

And even when casinos began springing up on riverboats all over the country and new variations of video poker were being developed for these new markets, there still weren't that many different games. As late as 1993, Lenny Frome, the grandfather of expert video poker play, published the book Winning Strategies for Video Poker, which included only 55 different pay schedules.

Well, as they say, "that was then and this is now."

For awhile the machine manufacturers just felt free to keep the same name on a game and change the paytable—usually downward, of course. Jacks or Better could pay 9/6 for full house/flush, or 8/5, or even 6/5. But then the public became savvier. So the casinos decided to play the word game to see if they could make the VP-playing population feel better about lower-paying games. If Bonus Poker was good, then Double Bonus would be better—and it was. But then came Bonus Poker Deluxe, Bonus Poker Plus, Triple Bonus, and Super Triple Bonus, even Ultra Bonus Poker.

Then the manufacturers decided this should be the Multi Millennium— multi-line, multi-game, multi-denomination. First, three lines, then five, then 10, then 50, and even One Hundred Play. And why should good casino customers only have the choice of playing one game on one machine? Why couldn't they just press buttons and go from Red, White and Blue to Keno Plus to Super Double Bonus Plus? Oh, and another terrific space-saver: They could play each game with a choice of denomination, from perhaps pennies to dollars. The casino floor has become a video poker scout's nightmare!

So to help players keep their sanity and find the best VP games in any casino, I offer this "Video Poker Scout's Guide to the Multi Millennium."

1. Ignore the name on the front of any VP machine and check the paytable. Sometimes casinos will change a game and not replace the name glass on the front of the machine. Or, a familiar game may be given a different name. Inexplicably, on many multi-game machines, the manufacturer chooses to label the machine with the name of just one of the games.

2. Check every machine in a row of look-alikes; they'll often have different pay tables for the same game, even on side-by-side machines. This is a good practice not only on the traditional single-game machines, but it's an excellent way to find a real gem in a row of multi-game machines that mostly look like costume jewelry. And since the paytables on the new multis are on a separate screen, expect a lot of time-consuming button pushing. No quick walk-by and a glance at the glass on the front for these new babies.

3. Check the paytable of every game AT EVERY DENOMINATION on a multi-denomination machine. Many casinos vary the paytables for the various denominations. Often a full-pay quarter game will be short pay at lower and/or higher levels. Therefore, if you have one machine that offers six different VP games at six different denominations, you will need to check 36 pay schedules!

4. Always be careful to check the COMPLETE paytable on one game. I don't know how many times someone has reported that they found a "good" deuces machine in a hitherto VP wasteland. They become so excited over finding a Deuces Wild machine that paid 5 for 4-of-a-kind that they failed to notice that the 5-of-a-kind and wild royal had both been cut. I don't want to accuse casinos of deliberately trying to fool the customer. But when I see a 9/6 Jacks or Better with a 2,500-coin royal instead of 4,000, or when a casino keeps the 9/6, then sneakily drop the trips from 3 to 2 for a wallet-emptying return, I have to wonder if they're hoping the customer won't notice. Another "fooler" for beginning players is a 9/6 schedule that they think is regular 9/6 Jacks or Better, when it's actually a short-pay Double Bonus machine.

5. Check the paytables for five-coin payoffs as well as for one coin. This bit of extra attention will sometimes reward you with a standard game that has a bonus for the fifth coin.

6. Check the maximum number of coins any machine takes. Most VP players have come across a machine that looked like it was one to die for, like a quarter machine that gives $2,000 for a royal instead of $1,000 --only to find they've run across a 10-coin machine. And don't be fooled like the player who reported putting a $100 bill in a $1 machine, planning to play for a while. She pressed the max-coin button and all the 100 credits were immediately eaten up. She'd met a 100-coin-max machine!

7. Don't forget to check VP machines at the bar. It's not an easy assignment in this Multi Millennium, especially on Friday and Saturday nights, since it takes quite a bit of time to check every game at every denomination. Try to pick a time when the bar isn't crowded and some of the barstools are empty, so you can get to some of the machines easily.

8. Although there's no substitute for checking every game at every denomination in each casino you visit, there are some scouting shortcuts that regular players in one casino can use. Since they're already familiar with the complete machine inventory, they're constantly alert for new machines

that come onto the floor. For example, here's a trick I learned from a pro who's very good at finding good VP plays that no one else knows about: Look for machines that have been reconfigured in any way, especially multi-games that have added or changed games, multi-denominations that have added or changed denominations/games, and multi-lines that have gone from, say, Triple Play to Triple/Five Play. The reason for this is that each change requires the slot technician to set the paytables for each combination of lines/games/denominations ONE AT A TIME on each machine. This often invites mistakes due to boredom or fatigue on the tech's part. And very often a casino mistake becomes a player's dream!

Scouting is never an easy job, but there's a tool to help you, The Frugal Video Poker Scouting Guide, the sturdy pocketsize booklet containing over 200 paytables with their EVs, including Multi-Strike and Super Times Pay, and the break-even point for many progressives. Don't leave home without it!

More and more casinos are springing up all over the country, and they're building them bigger and bigger—it's a jungle out there for VP players. However, before you say that there isn't any good video poker in one casino, be sure you sharpen your hunting skills. You never know when you will find video poker hidden treasure.

Jean Scott is one of the country's most renowned and successful gamblers. Her first book, The Frugal Gambler, has been a best-seller for many years. She also wrote a sequel, More Frugal Gambling, and a tax guide for gamblers. She provides a complete resource package for video poker players, from beginners to the experienced.

How to Keep Your Edge in Video Poker

by Linda Boyd

If you play table games in a casino then you already know a combination of skill and luck determines whether you walk away a winner or a loser. It makes for better bragging if you have a big win in blackjack or hold'em than if you hit a jackpot by pulling the handle on a slot machine. The problem for some is that they are intimidated by both the dealers and other players in live games, especially if they are beginners.

Video poker is an excellent alternative for those who shy away from live action, but want to wager on a game that rewards for skill. Of course you'll have to know how to select the best games and then play them mathematically correct.

Selecting a Game: Begin by reading the pay tables on the machine and choosing the one that pays the most for the same hand, say a full house or a flush. If this is the only thing you do you will be better off than just plopping down at the first open seat. To improve your odds even more, bring pay schedules with both the expected return (ER) and variance (risk to bankroll) along with you. Be aware that you will find the pay schedule right on the device by pressing the "see pays" button; however, you will not be given either the ER or variance.

Several Game Versions: There are several versions of games named by the manufacturer. We'll take a look at Jacks or Better (JOB), also called Draw Poker on some machines, to make this clear. Some versions of JOB return 45 coins for a full house when you bet 5 coins while others only pay 30 for the same hand, a full house. Of course you will want to play the version that pays more for a given hand. If anybody tells you "they are programmed" to pay the same, then they are mistaken. The probability of having a full house before the deal is identical on all machines with a random number generator, RNG. (There are a few jurisdictions with video lottery terminals, VLTs, that don't have RNGs but not in the Midwest, Nevada or New Jersey. A detailed explanation can be found in my book, "The Video Poker Edge".) If the only thing you do is select a JOB game that returns 9 for every coin bet on a full house and 6 for every coin bet on a flush instead of 8 for a full house and 5 for a flush, then you will be ahead over time. Make sure you're comparing the same game. For example, it will do you no good to compare the returns of a JOB game with a Bonus Poker (BP) game.

Understanding Pay Tables: When you first see a pay chart with the expected return for each version of the game it may appear confusing. Once you get used to using the charts, however, it won't be difficult at all. The paying hands will always be the same and so will the return for most of the winning combinations on the table. The few differences, however, can be very deceiving. If it's for a moderately frequent hand just one minor change can have a major impact on your final results. For example, using JOB, you'll notice that the only changes in Table 1.1 are for the return on a full house and a flush. All winning combination payouts are the same. In fact, that's why they have the same name, but may have significantly different theoretical returns. You'll also notice that the variance is similar for all versions of the game. You can use the same basic strategy for all variations as well. For those who want to be more precise you will need to practice at home on tutorial software and use strategy cards.

Hand: This column lists all the final hands that return money. For all versions of the same game the winning combinations will be identical, even though the amount paid may differ.

5-Coin Return: Here you'll find the number of coins returned when you wager 5-coins, usually the max bet. Make sure you look at the max bet carefully on the machine you've selected since sometimes 20 coins or more is the highest wager. Once you select the max coin button it's too late to change your mind.

Expected Return (ER): Assuming you play the game according to statistically accurate strategy this percentage represents the amount of your long term return. The higher the ER percentage the better the version is for the player. If the percentage is 100% then it pays "even money", meaning over time you will break even. This is an excellent play for casual gamblers since you can keep the comps and any extra cash or promotional gifts that come your way.

Variance: This figure represents the likelihood that your results will vary from the expected return (ER). The higher the variance the more risky or volatile the game; if the variance is high then you are more likely to lose your bankroll than if the variance is low. For example, 9/6 Double Double Bonus (DDB), has a variance of 41.98498, or almost 42. On the other hand 9/6 JOB (see Table 1.1) has a variance of 19.51468 or around 19.5. From a player's perspective DDB is around twice as risky as JOB, so you would need a larger bankroll to play the game for approximately the same amount of time.

Comparing Jacks or Better Variations: The following Table 1.1 gives you the return and variance for 5 different versions of JOB that can be found in casinos. Notice that the only differences are for the full house and the flush, but even seemingly minor differences in payment for these two hands dramatically changes the likely outcome. I've *italicized* and **bolded** the hands that will differ; a quick check and you'll see that all else is the same on JOB games. These changes may seem unimportant but notice the major differences in the payback percentages. That's why you should carefully check the tables before you decide whether or not you want to play.

Table 1.1: Versions of Jacks or Better

Hand: 5-Coin Return	9/6 JOB	9/5 JOB	8/5 JOB	7/5 JOB	6/5 JOB
Royal Flush	4000	4000	4000	4000	4000
Straight Flush	250	250	250	250	250
4 of a Kind	125	125	125	125	125
Full House	*45*	*45*	*40*	*35*	*30*
Flush	*30*	*25*	*25*	*25*	*25*
Straight	20	20	20	20	20
3 of a Kind	15	15	15	15	15
Two Pair	10	10	10	10	10
Jacks or Better	5	5	5	5	5
Expected Return (ER)	99.5439%	98.4498%	97.2984%	96.1472%	94.9961%
Variance *	19.51468	19.49564	19.32326	19.17190	19.04472

Comparing Deuces Wild Games: Table 1.2 gives you the return percentages for four different deuces wild games. Notice that there is only one version of each of these four games, unlike non-deuces choices. That's because they were named by players and not by manufacturers. (Some deuces wild games are named by manufacturers and then you will see several versions of the same game. An example is Loose Deuces.) The differences in returns are highlighted. Notice there are more differences in the returns for the same final hand then in JOB. This means there are more differences in game strategy as well. That's the reason why I had to write a separate strategy card for each game.

Table 1.2: Deuces Wild Games

Hand	5-Coin Return	5-Coin Return	5-Coin Return	5-Coin Return
Game Name	Full Pay Deuces	Not-So-Ugly Deuces	Illinois Deuces*	Colorado Deuces**
Royal Flush	4000	4000	4000	4000
4 Deuces	1000	1000	1000	1000
Wild Royal	125	125	125	125
5 of a Kind	*75*	*80*	*75*	*80*
Straight Flush	*45*	*50*	*45*	*65*
4 of a Kind	*25*	*20*	*20*	*20*
Full House	*15*	*20*	*20*	*15*
Flush	*10*	*15*	*15*	*10*
Straight	10	10	10	10
3 of a Kind	5	5	5	5
Expected Return	100.76%	99.72%	98.91%	96.76%
Variance	25.83462	25.78027	25.61744	25.42391

*Illinois Deuces, also called Airport Deuces, are often found on progressives. When the Royal Flush is 6,000 coins the expected return is 99.8819% and the variance is 47.78641.

** Colorado Deuces are also called Coyote Ugly Deuces due to their bad payback percentage.

Strategy: Selecting the game with the highest ER available within the casino is a big step in the right direction. After all, if you're playing baseball would you rather be paid $10 or $100 for every home run? To take a giant step towards maximizing your odds, though, you must play the game "according to Zamzow". He's the Hoyle for video poker and his pioneer computer-perfect software is a must-have for serious video poker players. While playing in the casino you're allowed to use strategy cards but not electronic devices. That's an excellent reason to bring your strategy cards along with you. Remember, the only way long term results will mirror the theoretical expectations (ER) is if your play is statistically accurate. That is, in fact, the reason casinos can offer a few excellent video poker plays.

Software: There are some good tutorial software products on the market, but one of the best in my opinion is Dean Zamzow's WinPoker, which can be purchased at americancasinoguide.com/video-poker-software. I come from a math background and gravitate towards computer-perfect practice. You can always choose to just learn the basic plays for the game. In other words you may only want to practice the correct holds for frequently dealt hands like one or two pairs. The fact that the options are up to the player is a big plus. Zamzow's software offers several teaching modes, indicates your accuracy percentage for each session, enables you to easily determine the game's ER, you can change the pay tables and much more. In addition, the graphics look like those on the devices inside the casino and there are plenty of whistles and bells. If you want to use correct game strategy then you should practice on your software at home before you go to the casino.

Strategy Cards: My strategy cards, free with my book "The Video Poker Edge", offer complete and easy to use playing instructions for each of several core games you'll find in virtually every casino. For those only interested in the basics you must still consider each game separately; that's because the holds change whenever the game changes. Although that may seem overwhelming it's tempered by the fact that different versions of the same game will use the same basic strategy. Given a deck of 52 cards there are 2,598,960 possible combinations on the deal; after the deal there are 32 hold possibilities. After conducting dozens of format trials, the easiest for players is a two matrix system that allows you to quickly locate your hand-type and then determine the correct holds. If you only refer to the card occasionally it will increase your odds. I suggest you use your strategy cards while practicing on the software so you can be comfortable with them inside the casino.

Publications/Products: There are several good publications and books that will keep you informed of the latest in video poker and other casino games. Whether you're a casual or regular player you'll quickly recover the price of the instructional material by improving your play.

Final Thoughts: The fact that you've decided to play a table game doesn't guarantee you an advantage over slot players. You have to select a game with a fair rake and rules and know mathematically correct strategy as well. The same is true for video poker players. The big advantage for video poker is there are still many games that have close to even odds and some give the player an advantage over the house. Casinos can afford to have a few excellent video poker options because you must play the games accurately and few people can.

Linda Boyd, a long-time table game player before turning to video poker, writes for " Midwest Gaming and Travel," "Arizona Player" and other gaming magazines. Her book, "The Video Poker Edge," includes free removable pay schedules and her free strategy cards for the eight most popular games. The 2010 Second Edition is available at amazon.com, Square One Publishers and major bookstores. www.squareonepublishers.com

Blackjack

by Steve Bourie

Blackjack is the most popular casino game in America and one of the biggest reasons for that is its relatively simple rules that are familiar to most casino visitors. Blackjack also has a reputation as being "beatable" and although that is true in some cases, the vast majority of players will always be playing the game with the house having a slight edge over them.

At most blackjack tables there are seven boxes, or betting areas, on the table. This means that up to seven people can play at that table and each player has their own box in front of them in which they'll place their bet. Now, before you take a seat at any blackjack table the first thing you should do is to take a look at the sign that's sitting on each table because it will tell you the minimum amount that you must bet on each hand. If you're a $5 player you certainly wouldn't want to sit at a table that has a $25 minimum so, once again, be sure to look before you sit down.

Once you're at the table you'll need chips to play with and you get them by giving your cash to the dealer who will exchange it for an equal amount of chips. Be careful, however, that you don't put your cash down into one of the betting boxes because the dealer might think you're playing it all on the next hand!

After everyone has placed their bets in their respective boxes the dealer will deal out two cards to each player. He will also deal two cards to himself; one of those cards will be face up and the other face down. Now, if you've ever read any brochures in a casino they'll tell you that the object of the game of blackjack is to get a total of cards as close to 21 as possible, without going over 21. However, that really isn't the object of the game. The true object is to beat the dealer and you do that by getting a total closer to 21 than the dealer, or by having the dealer bust by drawing cards that total more than 21.

The one thing that's strange about blackjack is that the rules can be slightly different at each casino and this is the only game where this happens. If you play baccarat, roulette or craps you'll find that the rules are virtually the same at every casino in the U.S. but that isn't the case with blackjack. For example, in most jurisdictions all of the casinos use six or eight decks that are always dealt from a rectangular box called a *shoe* and the cards are always dealt face up. In Las Vegas, some casinos will offer that same kind of game while others will offer games that use only one or two decks that are dealt directly from the dealer's hand and all of the cards will be dealt face down. To make it even stranger, some casinos in Las Vegas will offer both kinds of games in their casinos and the rules will probably change when you move from one table to

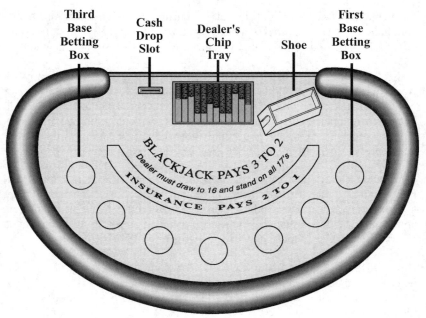

Typical Blackjack Table Layout

another. There can also be other rule variations concerning doubling down and splitting of pairs but we'll talk about those later. For now, just be aware that different casinos can have different blackjack rules and some of those rules will be good for you while others will be bad for you. Hopefully, after reading this story you'll know the good rules from the bad ones and which tables are the best ones to play at.

For our purposes, we'll assume we're playing in a casino that uses six decks of cards that are dealt out of a shoe and all of the player's cards are dealt face up. By the way, whenever you play blackjack in a casino where the cards are dealt face up don't touch the cards. In that kind of game the dealer is the only who is allowed to touch the cards and if you do happen to touch them they'll give you a warning not to do it again - so, don't touch the cards!

After the cards are dealt the players must determine the total of their hand by adding the value of their two cards together. All of the cards are counted at their face value except for the picture cards - jack, queen and king which all have a value of 10 - and the aces which can be counted as either 1 or 11. If you have an ace and any 10-value card you have a blackjack which is also called a natural and your hand is an automatic winner, unless the dealer also has a blackjack in which case the hands are tied. A tie is also called a *push* and when that happens it's a standoff and you neither win nor lose. All winning blackjacks should be paid at 3-to-2, so if you bet $5, you would be paid $7.50. You should avoid playing at any game that pays 6-to-5 (or even money) for blackjacks.

If the dealer has an ace as his up card the first thing he'll do is ask if anyone wants to buy *insurance*. When you buy insurance you're betting that the dealer has a blackjack by having a 10 as his face down card. To make an insurance bet you would place your bet in the area just above your betting box that says "insurance pays 2-to-1" and you're only allowed to make an insurance bet of up to one-half the amount of your original bet. So, if you originally bet $10 you could only bet a maximum of $5 as your insurance bet. After all the insurance bets are made the dealer will check his face down card and if it's a 10 he'll turn it over and all of the insurance bets will be paid off at 2-to-1. If he doesn't have a 10 underneath, the dealer will then take away all of the losing insurance bets and the game will continue. By the way, according to basic strategy, insurance is a bad bet and you should never make an insurance bet.

If the dealer has a 10 as his up card the first thing he'll do is check to see if he has an ace underneath which would give him a blackjack. If he does have an ace he'll turn it face up and start collecting the losing bets that are out on the table. If he doesn't have an ace underneath the game will continue. In some casinos, however, the dealer won't check his hole card until after all of the hands are played out.

If the dealer doesn't have an ace or a 10 as his up card the game continues and the dealer will start with the player to his immediate left to see if they want another card. If a player wants another card they indicate that with a hand signal by tapping or scratching the table with their finger to show they want another card. Taking a card is also known as *hitting* or taking a hit. If a player doesn't want another card they would just wave their hand palm down over their cards. Not taking another card is known as *standing*. The reason hand signals are used is because it eliminates any confusion on the part of the dealer as to exactly what the player wants and it also allows the security people to follow the game on the closed-circuit cameras that are hung from the ceiling throughout the casino.

Keep in mind that the hand signals will be slightly different if you're playing in a casino where the cards are dealt face down and you're allowed to pick them up. In that situation a player would signal that they wanted another card by scratching the table with the edges of the two cards they're holding. If they didn't want another card, they would simply place their two cards under the bet in their box.

In either case, if a player draws another card the value of that card is added to the total of the other cards and the player can continue to draw cards unless he gets a total of more than 21 in which case he busts and loses his bet.

When a player doesn't want any more cards, or stands, the dealer then moves on to the next player and after all of the players are finished then it's the dealer's turn to play. While each player can decide whether or not they want another card the dealer doesn't have that option and he must play by a fixed set of rules that require him to draw a card whenever his total is 16 or less and to stop when his total is 17 or more. If the dealer goes over 21 then he has busted and all of the players remaining in the game will be paid 1-to-1, or even money, on their bet.

If the dealer doesn't bust then each player's hand is compared to the dealer's. If the player's total is higher than the dealer's then they win and are paid even money. If the player's hand has a total that is lower than the dealer's hand then the player loses his bet. If the player and the dealer have the same total then it's a tie, or a push and neither hand wins. After all of the bets have been paid off, or taken by the dealer, a new round begins and new hands are dealt to all of the players.

When deciding how to play your hand there are also three other options available to you besides standing or hitting. The first is called *doubling down* and most casinos will allow a player to double their bet on their first two cards and draw only one more card. To do this you would place an amount equal to your original bet right next to it and then the dealer would give you one more card, sideways, to indicate that your bet was a double down. To double down in a game where the cards are dealt face down you would turn up your original two cards and tell the dealer you wanted to double down. Then, after you double your bet, the dealer would give you one more card face down. Some casinos may have restrictions on this bet and may only allow you to double down if the total of your two cards is 10 or 11, but it's always to your advantage if they allow you to double down on any two cards.

Another thing you can do is *split* your cards if you have a pair and then play each card as a separate hand. For example, if you had a pair of 8's you would place a bet equal to your original bet right next to it and tell the dealer you wanted to split your pair. The dealer would then separate your two 8's and give you one card on your first 8. Unlike doubling down, however, you are not limited to only getting one card and you can play your hand out normally. When you were finished with your first hand the dealer would then give you a card on your other 8 and you would play that hand out. Although you aren't usually limited to just one card on your splits, there is one instance where that will happen and that happens when you split aces. Almost all casinos will give you just one card on each ace when you split them. Also, if you get a 10-value card with your ace it will only count as 21 and not as a blackjack so you'll only get even money on that bet if you win. Besides splitting pairs you can also split all 10-value cards such as jack-king or 10-queen but it would be a very bad idea to do that because you would be breaking up a 20 which is a very strong hand and you should never split 10's. By the way, if you wanted to split a pair in a casino where the cards are dealt face down you would simply turn your original two cards face-up and tell the dealer that you wanted to split them.

The last option you have is not available in most casinos but you may come across it in some casinos and it's called *surrender*. With the surrender option you're allowed to lose half of your bet if you decide you don't want to play out your hand after looking at your first two cards. Let's say you're dealt a 10-6 for a total of 16 and the dealer has a 10 as his face-up card. A 16 is not a very strong hand, especially against a dealer's 10, so in this case it would be a good idea to surrender your hand and when the dealer came to your cards you would say "surrender." The dealer would then take half of your bet and remove your cards. Surrender is good for the player because in the long run you will lose less on the bad hands you're dealt and you should always try to play in a casino that offers the surrender option.

All right, we've covered the basics of how to play the game of blackjack and all of the possible options a player has, so the next question is how do you win? Well, the best way to win is to become a card counter, but for the average person that isn't always possible so let's start off by taking a look at basic blackjack strategy.

Computer studies have been done on the game of blackjack and millions of hands have been analyzed to come up with a basic formula for how to play your hand in any given situation. The main principle that these decisions are based on is the dealer's up card because, remember that the dealer has no say in whether or not he takes a card - he must play by the rules that require him to draw a card until he has a total of 17 or more. Now, according to these computer calculations the dealer will bust more often when his up card is a 2,3,4,5 or 6 and he will complete more hands when his up card is a 7,8,9,10-value card or an ace. Take a look at the following chart that shows how each up-card affects the dealer's chance of busting:

Chance The Dealer's Up Card Will Bust

2	35%
3	38%
4	40%
5	43%
6	42%
7	26%
8	24%
9	23%
10	21%
Ace	11%

As you can see, the dealer will bust most often when he has a 5 or 6 as his upcard and he will bust the least amount, approximately 11% of the time, when his upcard is an ace. This means it's to your advantage to stand more often when the dealer's upcard is a 2 through 6 and hope that the dealer will draw cards that make him bust. It also means that when the dealer's upcard is a 7 through ace he will complete more of his hands and in that situation you should draw cards until you have a total of 17 or more.

Now let's show you how to play your hands by using the basic strategy and we'll start off with the *hard hand* strategy and hard hand means a two-card total without an ace. A hand with an ace is known as a **soft hand** because the ace can be counted as either a 1 or an 11. So, if you had an ace-6 you would have a soft 17 hand and if you had a 10-6 you would have a hard 16 hand. Later on we'll take a look at how to play soft hands, but for now we'll concentrate on the hard hand totals. Oh yes, one more thing, the following basic strategy applies to casinos where they deal more than one deck at a time and the dealer stands on soft 17, which is the situation you'll find in the majority of casinos today. So, keep in mind that the strategy would be slightly different if you were playing against a single deck and it would also be slightly different if the dealer hit a soft 17.

Whenever your first two cards total 17 through 21, you should stand, no matter what the dealer's up card is.

If your cards total 16, you should stand if the dealer has a 2 through 6 as his upcard otherwise, draw a card. By the way, 16 is the worst hand you can have because you will bust more often with 16 than with any other hand. So, if that's the case then why would you want to ever hit a 16? Well, once again, those computer studies have shown that you should hit a 16 when the dealer has 7 through ace as his upcard because in the long run you will lose less often. This means that yes, 16 is a terrible hand, but you should hit it because if you don't you will lose even more often than when you do take a card.

If your cards total 15, you should also stand if the dealer has a 2 through 6 as his upcard otherwise, draw cards until your total is 17 or more.

The same rules from 15 and 16 also apply if your cards total 14. Stand if the dealer has a 2 through 6, otherwise draw cards until your total is 17 or more. The same rules also apply if your cards total 13. Stand if the dealer has a 2 through 6, otherwise draw cards until your total is 17 or more.

When your cards total 12 you should only stand when the dealer has a 4,5 or 6 as his upcard, remember - those are his three weakest cards and he will bust more often with those cards, so you don't want to take a chance on busting yourself. If the dealer's upcard is a 2 or a 3, then you should take just one card and stop on your total of 13 or more. Finally, if the dealer has a 7 through ace as his upcard then you should draw cards until your total is 17 or more.

When your cards total 11 you would always want to hit it because you can't bust, but before you ask for a card you should consider making a double down bet. If the casino allows you to double down then you should do that if the dealer has anything but an ace as his upcard. After you double down the dealer would give you just one additional card on that hand. If the dealer's upcard is an ace then you shouldn't double down. Instead, you should hit the hand and continue to draw until your total is 17 or more. If the casino doesn't allow you to double down then you should just hit your hand and then, depending on your total, play it by the rules you were given for the hands that totaled 12 through 21. Meaning, if you had an 11 and the dealer had a 5 as his upcard, you should take a card. Then let's say you draw an ace which gives you a total of 12. Well, as noted before, if you have a 12 against a dealer's 5 you should stand and that's how you should play that hand.

If your total is 10 you would, once again, want to double down unless the dealer showed an ace or a 10. If the dealer had an ace or a 10 as his upcard you should hit your hand and then use the standard rules for a hand valued at 12 through 21. Therefore, if you had a 10 and the dealer had an 8 as his up card you would want to double down and take one more card. If you weren't allowed to double, then you would take a hit and let's say you got a 4 for a total of 14. You should then continue to hit your hand until your total is 17 or more.

If your total is 9 you would want to double down whenever the dealer was showing a 3,4,5 or 6 as his upcard. If the dealer had a 2 as his upcard, or if he had a 7 through ace as his upcard, you should hit your hand and then use the standard playing rules as discussed before. So, let's say you had a 9 and the dealer had a 4 as his upcard you would want to double down and take one more card. If you weren't allowed to double then you should take a hit and let's say you got a 2 for a total of 11, you would then take another hit and let's say you got an ace. That would give you a total of 12 and, as mentioned previously, you should stand on 12 against a dealer's 4.

Finally, if your total is 8 or less you should always take a card and then use the standard playing rules that were already discussed.

Now, let's take a look at splitting pairs, but keep in mind that the rules for splitting will change slightly depending on whether or not the casino will allow you to double down after you split your cards. Most multiple-deck games allow you to double down after splitting so that's the situation we'll cover first and then we'll talk about the changes you need to make if you're not allowed to double down after splitting.

Basic Strategy - Single Deck

Dealer stands on soft 17 • Double on any 2 cards • Double allowed after split

Your Hand	Dealer's Upcard									
	2	3	4	5	6	7	8	9	10	A
17	ALWAYS STAND ON HARD 17 (OR MORE)									
16	-	-	-	-	-	H	H	H	H*	H
15	-	-	-	-	-	H	H	H	H*	H
14	-	-	-	-	-	H	H	H	H	H
13	-	-	-	-	-	H	H	H	H	H
12	H	H	-	-	-	H	H	H	H	H
11	ALWAYS DOUBLE									
10	D	D	D	D	D	D	D	D	H	H
9	D	D	D	D	D	H	H	H	H	H
8	H	H	H	D	D	H	H	H	H	H
A,8	-	-	-	-	D	-	-	-	-	-
A,7	-	D	D	D	D	-	-	H	H	-
A,6	D	D	D	D	D	H	H	H	H	H
A,5	H	H	D	D	D	H	H	H	H	H
A,4	H	H	D	D	D	H	H	H	H	H
A,3	H	H	D	D	D	H	H	H	H	H
A,2	H	H	D	D	D	H	H	H	H	H
A,A	ALWAYS SPLIT									
10,10	ALWAYS STAND (NEVER SPLIT)									
9,9	Sp	Sp	Sp	Sp	Sp	-	Sp	Sp	-	-
8,8	ALWAYS SPLIT									
7,7	Sp	Sp	Sp	Sp	Sp	Sp	Sp	H	-*	H
6,6	Sp	Sp	Sp	Sp	Sp	Sp	H	H	H	H
5,5	NEVER SPLIT (PLAY AS 10 HAND)									
4,4	H	H	Sp	Sp	Sp	H	H	H	H	H
3,3	Sp	Sp	Sp	Sp	Sp	Sp	Sp	H	H	H
2,2	Sp	H	Sp	Sp	Sp	Sp	H	H	H	H

- =Stand   H=Hit   D=Double   Sp=Split   *= Surrender if allowed

shaded boxes show strategy changes from chart on next page

Basic Strategy - Single Deck

Dealer stands on soft 17 • Double on any 2 cards • Double <u>NOT</u> allowed after split

Your Hand	Dealer's Upcard									
	2	3	4	5	6	7	8	9	10	A
17	ALWAYS STAND ON HARD 17 (OR MORE)									
16	-	-	-	-	-	H	H	H	H*	H*
15	-	-	-	-	-	H	H	H	H*	H
14	-	-	-	-	-	H	H	H	H	H
13	-	-	-	-	-	H	H	H	H	H
12	H	H	-	-	-	H	H	H	H	H
11	ALWAYS DOUBLE									
10	D	D	D	D	D	D	D	D	H	H
9	D	D	D	D	D	H	H	H	H	H
8	H	H	H	D	D	H	H	H	H	H
A,8	-	-	-	-	D	-	-	-	-	-
A,7	-	D	D	D	D	-	-	H	H	-
A,6	D	D	D	D	D	H	H	H	H	H
A,5	H	H	D	D	D	H	H	H	H	H
A,4	H	H	D	D	D	H	H	H	H	H
A,3	H	H	D	D	D	H	H	H	H	H
A,2	H	H	D	D	D	H	H	H	H	H
A,A	ALWAYS SPLIT									
10,10	NEVER SPLIT (ALWAYS STAND)									
9,9	Sp	Sp	Sp	Sp	Sp	-	Sp	Sp	-	-
8,8	ALWAYS SPLIT									
7,7	Sp	Sp	Sp	Sp	Sp	Sp	H	H	-*	H
6,6	Sp	Sp	Sp	Sp	Sp	H	H	H	H	H
5,5	NEVER SPLIT (PLAY AS 10 HAND)									
4,4	NEVER SPLIT (PLAY AS 8 HAND)									
3,3	H	H	Sp	Sp	Sp	Sp	H	H	H	H
2,2	H	Sp	Sp	Sp	Sp	Sp	H	H	H	H

- =Stand   H=Hit   D=Double   Sp=Split   *= Surrender if allowed

Basic Strategy - Multiple Decks

Dealer stands on soft 17 • Double on any 2 cards • Double allowed after split

Your Hand	Dealer's Upcard									
	2	3	4	5	6	7	8	9	10	A
17	ALWAYS STAND ON 17 (OR MORE)									
16	-	-	-	-	-	H	H	H*	H*	H*
15	-	-	-	-	-	H	H	H	H*	H
14	-	-	-	-	-	H	H	H	H	H
13	-	-	-	-	-	H	H	H	H	H
12	H	H	-	-	-	H	H	H	H	H
11	D	D	D	D	D	D	D	D	D	H
10	D	D	D	D	D	D	D	D	H	H
9	H	D	D	D	D	H	H	H	H	H
8	ALWAYS HIT 8 (OR LESS)									
A,8	ALWAYS STAND ON SOFT 19 (OR MORE)									
A,7	-	D	D	D	D	-	-	H	H	H
A,6	H	D	D	D	D	H	H	H	H	H
A,5	H	H	D	D	D	H	H	H	H	H
A,4	H	H	D	D	D	H	H	H	H	H
A,3	H	H	H	D	D	H	H	H	H	H
A,2	H	H	H	D	D	H	H	H	H	H
A,A	ALWAYS SPLIT									
10,10	ALWAYS STAND (NEVER SPLIT)									
9,9	Sp	Sp	Sp	Sp	Sp	-	Sp	Sp	-	-
8,8	ALWAYS SPLIT									
7,7	Sp	Sp	Sp	Sp	Sp	Sp	H	H	H	H
6,6	Sp	Sp	Sp	Sp	Sp	H	H	H	H	H
5,5	D	D	D	D	D	D	D	D	H	H
4,4	H	H	H	Sp	Sp	H	H	H	H	H
3,3	Sp	Sp	Sp	Sp	Sp	Sp	H	H	H	H
2,2	Sp	Sp	Sp	Sp	Sp	Sp	H	H	H	H

- =Stand   H=Hit   D=Double   Sp=Split   *= Surrender if allowed

Basic Strategy - Multiple Decks

Dealer stands on soft 17 • Double on any 2 cards • Double NOT allowed after split

Your Hand	Dealer's Upcard									
	2	3	4	5	6	7	8	9	10	A
17	ALWAYS STAND ON HARD 17 (OR MORE)									
16	-	-	-	-	-	H	H	H*	H*	H*
15	-	-	-	-	-	H	H	H	H*	H
14	-	-	-	-	-	H	H	H	H	H
13	-	-	-	-	-	H	H	H	H	H
12	H	H	-	-	-	H	H	H	H	H
11	D	D	D	D	D	D	D	D	D	H
10	D	D	D	D	D	D	D	D	H	H
9	H	D	D	D	D	H	H	H	H	H
8	ALWAYS HIT 8 (OR LESS)									
A,8	ALWAYS STAND ON SOFT 19 (OR MORE)									
A,7	-	D	D	D	D	-	-	H	H	H
A,6	H	D	D	D	D	H	H	H	H	H
A,5	H	H	D	D	D	H	H	H	H	H
A,4	H	H	D	D	D	H	H	H	H	H
A,3	H	H	H	D	D	H	H	H	H	H
A,2	H	H	H	D	D	H	H	H	H	H
A,A	ALWAYS SPLIT									
10,10	ALWAYS STAND (NEVER SPLIT)									
9,9	Sp	Sp	Sp	Sp	Sp	-	Sp	Sp	-	-
8,8	ALWAYS SPLIT									
7,7	Sp	Sp	Sp	Sp	Sp	Sp	H	H	H	H
6,6	H	Sp	Sp	Sp	Sp	H	H	H	H	H
5,5	NEVER SPLIT (PLAY AS 10 HAND)									
4,4	H	H	H	H	H	H	H	H	H	H
3,3	H	H	Sp	Sp	Sp	Sp	H	H	H	H
2,2	H	H	Sp	Sp	Sp	Sp	H	H	H	H

- =Stand   H=Hit   D=Double   Sp=Split   *= Surrender if allowed
shaded boxes show strategy changes from chart on previous page

As noted earlier, when your first two cards are the same most casinos will allow you to split them and play them as two separate hands so let's go over the basic strategy rules on when you should do this.

The first thing you should remember is that you always split aces and 8's. The reason you split aces is obvious because if you get a 10 on either hand you'll have a perfect 21, but remember that you won't get paid for a blackjack at 3-to-2, instead it'll be counted as a regular 21 and you'll be paid at even money. If you have a pair of 8's you have 16 which is a terrible hand and you can always improve it by splitting your 8's and playing them as separate hands.

The next thing to remember about splitting pairs is that you never split 5's or 10's. Once again, the reasons should be rather obvious, you don't want to split 10's because 20 is a great hand and you don't want to split 5's because 10 is a great hand to draw to. Instead, you would want to double down on that 10, unless the dealer was showing a 10 or an ace as his upcard.

2's, 3's and 7's should only be split when the dealer is showing a 2 through 7 as his upcard. Split 4's only when the dealer has a 5 or 6 as his upcard (remember 5 and 6 are his weakest cards!), 6's should be split whenever the dealer is showing a 2 through 6 and finally, you should always split 9's unless the dealer is showing a 7, 10 or ace. The reason you don't want to split 9's against a 10 or an ace should be rather obvious, but the reason you don't want to split them against a 7 is in case the dealer has a 10 as his hole card because in that case your 18 would beat out his 17.

If the casino will not allow you to double down after splitting then you should make the following three changes: For 2's and 3's only split them against a 4,5,6 or 7; never split 4's; and for a pair of 6's only split them against a 3,4,5 or 6. Everything else should be played the same.

Now, let's take a look at how to play *soft hands* and, remember, a soft hand is any hand that contains an ace that can be counted as 1 or 11. For a soft hand of 19 or more you should always stand.

For soft 18 against a 2,7 or 8 you should always stand. If the dealer shows a 9, 10 or an ace you should always take a hit and for a soft 18 against a 3,4,5 or 6 you should double down, but if the casino won't allow you to double then you should just hit.

For soft 17 you should always take a hit, but if the casino allows you to double down, then you should double against a dealer's 3,4,5 or 6.

For soft 16 or a soft 15 you should always take a hit, but if the casino allows you to double down then you should double against a dealer's 4,5 or 6.

For soft 14 you should always take a hit, but if the casino allows you to double down then you should double against a dealer's 5 or 6.

Finally, for a soft 13 you should always take a hit, but if the casino allows you to double down then you should double against a dealer's 5 or 6.

The last thing we need to cover is surrender which, as noted before, isn't offered in many casinos but it is an option that does work in your favor and if available, you should play in a casino that offers it. The surrender rules are very simple to remember and only apply to hard totals of 15 or 16. If you have a hard 16 you should surrender it whenever the dealer has a 9, 10 or ace as his upcard and if you have a hard 15 you should surrender it whenever the dealer has a 10 as his upcard. That's all there is to surrender.

Now that you know how to play the game and you have an understanding of the basic strategy let's take a quick look at how the rule variations can affect the game of blackjack. As noted before, various computer studies have been made on blackjack and these studies have shown that each rule change can either hurt or help the player by a certain amount. For example, a single-deck game where you can double on any first 2 cards (but not after splitting pairs), the dealer stands on soft 17 and no surrender is allowed has no advantage for the casino when using the basic strategy. That's right, in a game with those rules in effect the game is dead even and neither the casino nor the player has an edge!

Take a look at the following chart and you'll see how some rules changes can hurt you or help you as a player. Minus signs in front mean that the casino gains the edge by that particular amount while plus signs mean that you gain the edge by that amount.

RULES THAT HURT YOU		RULES THAT HELP YOU	
Two decks	-0.32%	Double after split	+0.13%
Four decks	-0.49%	Late surrender	+0.06%
Six decks	-0.54%	Resplit Aces	+0.14%
Eight decks	-0.57%	Double anytime	+0.20%
Dealer hits soft 17	-0.20%		
No soft doubling	-0.14%		
BJ pays 6-to-5	-1.40%		
BJ pays 1-to-1	-2.30%		

As you can see, it's always to your advantage to play against as few decks as possible. The house edge goes up substantially as you go from 1 deck to 2, but the change is less dramatic when you go from 2 to 4, or from 4 to 6, and it's barely noticeable when you go from 6 to 8. You can also see that you would prefer not to play in a casino where the dealer hits a soft 17 because that gives the dealer a slight edge. You would also want to play in a casino where you're allowed to double down on your soft hands or else you would be giving another added edge to the casino.

You can also see from these charts that you would want to play in a casino where you were allowed to double down after splitting cards and you would also want to play in a casino that offered surrender. The other two rules variations that help the player are somewhat rare but they were put in to show you how these rules changes can affect your odds in the game. Some casinos will allow you to resplit aces again if you draw an ace to one of your original aces and this works to your advantage. Also, some casinos will allow you to double down on any number of cards rather than just the first two. In other words, if you got 2-4-3-2 as your first four cards you would then be allowed to double down on your total of 11 before receiving your 5th card. If they allow you to do this then, once again, you have a rule that works in your favor.

The point of showing you these charts is to help you understand that when you have a choice of places to play you should always choose the casino that offers the best rules. So, if you find a single-deck game with good rules you could be playing an even game by using the basic strategy, or at worst be giving the casino an edge of less than one-half of 1%.

Now, there is one way that you can actually have the edge working in your favor when you play blackjack and that's by becoming a card counter. As mentioned before, card counting is not for the average person but it really is important that you understand the concept of card counting and if you think you'd like to learn more about counting cards then it's something you can follow up on later.

Many people think that to be a card counter you have to have a photographic memory and remember every single card that's been played. Fortunately, it's not quite that difficult. Actually, the main concept behind card counting is the assumption that the dealer will bust more often when there are a lot of 10's in the deck and that he will complete more hands when there are a lot of smaller cards in the deck. Now, if you stop to think about it, it makes sense doesn't it? After all, the dealer has to play by set rules that make him take a card until he has a total of 17 or more. If there are a lot of 2's, 3's and 4's in the deck the dealer won't bust very often when he draws cards, but if there are a lot of 10's in the deck then chances are he will bust more often when he is forced to draw cards.

The card counter tries to take advantage of this fact by keeping a running total of the cards that have been played to give him an idea of what kind of cards remain in the deck. If there are a lot of 10 cards remaining in the deck then the counter will bet more money because the odds are slightly in his favor. Of course, if there are a lot of small cards remaining then the counter would only make a small bet because the odds would be slightly in favor of the dealer. Another thing that the card counter can do is to change his basic strategy to take advantage of the differences in the deck.

There are at least a dozen different card counting systems but let's take a quick look at a relatively simple one (it's also the most popular) and it's called the *high-low* count. With this system you assign a value of +1 to all 2's, 3's, 4's, 5's and 6's, while all 10's, Jacks, Queens, Kings and Aces are assigned a value of -1. The remaining cards: 7, 8 and 9 have no value and are not counted.

$$+1 = 2, 3, 4, 5, 6$$
$$-1 = 10, J, Q, K, A$$

When you look at these numbers you'll see that there are an equal number of cards in each group: there are five cards valued at +1 and five cards valued at -1. This means that they balance each other out and if you go through the deck and add them all together the end result will always be a total of exactly zero.

What a card counter does is to keep a running total of all the cards as they're played out and whenever the total has a plus value he knows that a lot of small cards have appeared and the remaining deck is rich in 10's which is good for the player. But, if the total is a minus value then the counter knows that a lot of 10-value cards have appeared and the remaining deck must be rich in low cards which is bad for the player. To give you an example of how to count let's say the following cards have been dealt on the first hand from a single deck:

$$2, 3, 3, 4, 5, 5, 5, 6, = +8$$
$$J, K, Q, A, = -4$$
$$Total = +4$$

As you can see, there were eight plus-value cards and four minus-value cards which resulted in a total count of +4. This means that there are now four more 10-value cards than low cards remaining in the deck and the advantage is with the player. Naturally, the higher the plus count, the more advantageous it is for the player and counters would be proportionally increasing their bets as the count got higher. The card counter would also be using the same basic strategy we spoke about previously, except for certain instances where a slight change would be called for.

On the other hand, if the count is negative, a card counter will always bet the minimum amount. Of course, they would prefer not to bet at all, but the casinos don't like you to sit at their tables and not bet so the counter has to bet something and the minimum is the least they can get by with.

There is one more important thing to explain about card counting and it's called the ***true count***. The true count is a measure of the count per deck rather than a ***running count*** of all the cards that have been played and to get the true count you simply divide the running count by the number of decks remaining to be played. As an illustration, let's say you're playing in a six-deck game and the count is +9. You look at the shoe and estimate three decks remain to be played. You then divide the count of +9 by three to get +3 which is the true count. As another example, let's say you're in an eight-deck game with a count of +12 and there are six decks left to be played. You divide +12 by six to get +2 which is the true count. To put it another way, a +2 count in a double-deck game with one deck left to be played is the same as a +4 count in a four-deck game with two decks left to be played, which is the same as a +6 count is a six-deck game with three decks left to be played, which is the same as a +12 count in an eight-deck game with six decks left to be played.

For the card counter, it is crucial to always take the running count and then divide it by the number of decks remaining in order to get the true count because all betting and playing decisions are based on the true count rather than the running count.

Of course, if you're playing in a single-deck game the running count and the true count are initially the same. The more you get into the deck, however, the more weight is given to the running count because there is less than one deck remaining. So, if the running count was +3 and only a 1/2-deck remained you would calculate the true count by dividing +3 by 1/2 (which is the same as multiplying by 2/1, or 2) to get a true count of +6. As another example, if the running count was +2 and about 2/3 of the deck remained you would divide +2 by 2/3 (the same as multi-plying by 3/2 or, 1 and 1/2) to get +3.

As you can see, the count becomes much more meaningful as you get closer to the last cards in the deck and that's why casinos never deal down to the end. Instead, the dealer will insert a plastic card about 2/3 or 3/4 of the way in the deck and when that card is reached the dealer will finish that particular round and then shuffle the cards. How far into the deck(s) that plastic card is inserted is known as the ***penetration point*** and card counters always look for a dealer that offers good penetration. The card counter knows that the further into the deck(s) the plastic card is placed the more meaningful the true count will be and the more advantageous it will be for the card counter.

So, now that you know how those card counters keep track of the cards, what kind of advantage do you think they have over the casino? Well, not too much. Depending on the number of decks used, the rules in force, and the skill of the counter, it could be as much as 2% but that would be at the high end. Probably 1% would be closer to the actual truth. This means that for every $1,000 in bets that are made the card counter will win $10. Not exactly a huge amount but there are people out there who do make a living playing the game.

21 Mistakes Made By Blackjack Players

by Henry Tamburin

The casino game of blackjack has its procedures, codes of conduct, and playing strategies. The procedures are essential to ensure the security and integrity of the game. The codes of conduct encompass the playing etiquette so you don't attract the ire of your fellow players, or the dealer. The playing strategies help you win. When you don't follow any of the above, you are not going to play your best game. So avoid making these 21 common mistakes.

1. Handing money directly to the dealer. - All cash transactions must be visible to the security cameras, so always place your cash on the layout outside of your betting spot, and then tell the dealer what denomination chips you want.

2. Touching the cards when they are dealt face up. - When four or more decks of cards are used, they are dealt face up to each player from a dealing shoe. The reason is two-fold. First, it eliminates the potential for player cheating (by either marking or switching the cards), and secondly, it speeds up the game, because the dealer can quickly announce the total of each player's hand. There is no reason to touch the cards, so don't do it.

3. Holding the cards with two hands. - In games where the cards are dealt face down (usually single- and two-deck games), pick the cards up with one hand please, not two.

4. Removing the cards from the table. - Your cards must always be in full view of the dealer and the security cameras. Therefore, you should never hold them in your lap.

5. Placing objects on the table. - Purses, wallets, bags, and other items should be placed on your person or next to you (except women's purses, which should be held in the lap). It is OK to have a drink on the table, but use the drink holders provided by the casino to avoid spilling anything on the layout.

6. Telling the dealer that you want a "hit." - Saying "hit me" might be OK when you play blackjack with friends back home, but in the casinos, it won't fly. For security reasons, you must always use hand signals to signify whether you want to hit or stand.

7. Touching your chips after you have made your bet and the cards are dealt. - Your original bet must stay on the layout untouched until it either wins, losses, or ties. Once the dealer starts dealing the cards that is your cue to not touch your wager.

8. Placing a higher denomination chip on top of a lower denomination chip in your betting spot. - If you are wagering two or more different denomination chips, always place the higher denomination chip on the bottom of the stack and the lower on top.

9. Not betting double the table minimum if you decide to play two (or more) spots. - If it's a $5 minimum table and you decide to spread to two hands, most casinos require that you wager $10 on each spot. If you are not sure, ask the dealer. Also, if the cards are dealt face-down, do not look at the second hand until after you have completed playing your first hand.

10. Taking your bad luck out on the dealer or fellow players. - They are not the reason why you are losing; most likely, it is just a bad run of cards, which happens to all blackjack players.

11. Telling your fellow players how to play their hands. - It is their money and they have the right to play their hand any way they want to. However, if a fellow player asks you for advice, then it's OK to offer it.

12. Inserting the cut card a few cards from either end of the shuffled deck(s) of cards. - On six-deck games, most casinos require that players place the cut card at least a half-deck from either end of the stack (some require a full-deck). If you place it less than that, you will get a rebuke from the dealer and a request to cut again.

13. Sitting down and making a bet in the middle of a shoe. - In some casinos, this is forbidden and there will be a "No Mid-Shoe Entry" sign posted on the table. If you are not sure, ask the dealer.

14. Not using the basic playing strategy. - The basic playing strategy is the mathematically correct way to play every hand dealt to you. This playing strategy is readily available in books, on the Internet, and on strategy cards, which you can take with you when you play (they are legal to use in a casino). Even if you are a regular player, there really is no reason to guess how to play a hand when you can have the answers at your fingertip by using a strategy card.

15. Playing a 6-to-5 game. - Some blackjack tables will pay only 6-to-5 when you get an untied blackjack, rather than the traditional 3-to-2 payoff. Getting paid 6-to-5 is bad. How bad? The house edge in a single-deck, 6-to-5 game is increased as much as seven-fold! Usually there will be a sign on the table stating that blackjacks pay 6-to-5. Some casinos have it imprinted on the layout. If you are not sure, ask the dealer. By avoiding these awful 6-to-5 games, you will take a big step to improve your bottom line.

16. Playing on a table that uses a Continuous Shuffling Machine (CSM). - Don't confuse a CSM with a traditional automatic shuffling machine. A CSM is a device that randomly shuffles the discards after every round has been played. The net result is the game plays faster (no downtime for reshuffling) and you will play about 20% more hands per hour. Since the house has the edge on every hand, playing more hands dealt per hour will increase your theoretical loss by 20%. For average players, playing on a table that uses a CSM is bad news and should be avoided.

17. Never being rated when you play. - The casinos give away many comps to players in the hopes that they become loyal players. You will not get your fair share of these comps unless you ask to be rated when you play blackjack. If you do not know how to go about this, get the details at the Player's Club or ask a casino host (VIP or Marketing Department).

18. Asking arrogantly for a comp. - While playing recently, I overheard a fellow player, after less than 30 minutes of play, say to the floor supervisor, "Can you gimme a comp for four to the buffet." This is not the way to ask for a comp. First off, comps are not a God-given right to players. You must earn a comp by meeting a casino's play requirements (average bet and time of play). Check with a casino host or the Marketing Department to obtain this information, and then only after you have met their play requirements, asks the floor supervisor, "Have I played enough for a dinner comp?" You will be surprised how often you'll receive a no-hassle comp when you politely ask for one.

19. Using a progressive betting system. - I know, I know, many players use them and swear they work. However, trust me, they don't work. Never have, and never will, because your chance of winning the next hand is completely independent of whether or not you won (or lost) the previous hand. The secret to winning at blackjack (actually the secret has been known for about 50 years) is to bet more money only when the unplayed cards are rich in tens

and aces. Therefore, if you want to increase your bet, you would be wise to watch the cards as they are played and bet more only after you have seen a fair number of small vs. high cards played in previous rounds. Better yet, learn a simple card counting system, like Speed Count, which will tell you when it is the right time to increase your bet.

20. Never using a casino host. - This is a big mistake if you are a regular player. Casino hosts can do a lot for you and you don't necessarily have to be a high roller to use one. Read Jean Scott's book, *More Frugal Gambling*, for the low-down.

21. Never tipping the dealer. - You tip a waiter or waitress for good service, don't you? You should consider doing the same for a blackjack dealer. It is not mandatory to tip a dealer; however, if the dealer has been pleasant and helpful, it is customary to tip to show your appreciation for a job well done. Of course, tipping will not miraculously change the cards in your favor, but think of this - it might put you in a favorable light with the floor supervisor, who is the person that has some leeway in approving your comp and the amount (get the picture?).

Henry Tamburin is the editor of the Blackjack Insider newsletter (www.bjinsider.com), lead instructor for the Golden Touch Blackjack Course (www.goldentouchblackjack.com) and host of www.smartgaming.com. For a free three-month subscription to his blackjack newsletter, go to www.bjinsider.com/freetrial

Roulette

by Steve Bourie

Virtually all American casinos use a double-zero roulette wheel which has pockets numbered from 1 to 36, plus 0 and 00 for a total of 38 pockets. This is in contrast to Europe where a single-zero wheel is used and the game has always been the most popular in the casino.

There are usually six seats at the roulette table and to help the dealer differentiate what each player is betting every player is assigned a different color chip which they purchase right at the table. Each table has its own minimum chip values and that information is usually posted on a sign at the table. As an example let's say a table has a $1 minimum chip value. This means that when you give the dealer your money the colored chips he gives you in return must have a minimum value of $1 each. So, if you gave the dealer $50 he would ask what value you wanted on the chips and if you said $1 he would give you 50 colored chips.

If you prefer, you could say you wanted the chips valued at $2 each and he would just give you 25 chips rather than 50. You can make the value of your colored chips anything you want and you'll notice that when the dealer gives you your chips he'll put one of your chips on the railing near the wheel with a marker on top to let him know the value of your chips. Later on when you're done playing at that table you must exchange your colored chips for regular chips before leaving. The colored chips have no value anywhere else in the casino so don't leave the table with them.

Besides the minimum chip value, there is also a minimum amount that must be bet on each spin of the wheel. Once again, the minimums are probably posted on a sign at the table. If it says $2 minimum inside/$5 minimum outside this means that when betting on any of the 38 numbers that pay 35-to-1 the total of all your bets must be $2. You could make two different $1 bets or one $2 bet, it doesn't matter except that the total of all your bets on the numbers must be at least $2. The $5 minimum outside means that any of the outside bets that pay 2-to-1, or even money, require that you bet $5 each time. On the outside bets you can't make a $3 bet and a $2 bet to meet the minimums - you have to bet at least $5 every time. After you've exchanged your cash for colored chips you're ready to place your first bet so, let's see what your options are:

You can make a *straight* bet where you only bet on one number and if it comes in you'll be paid 35-to-1. The casino advantage on this bet is 5.26% and by the time you're done with this roulette section I'm sure you'll be very familiar with that number.

Another choice you have is to do a *split*. This is where you put a chip on the line that separates two numbers. If either number comes up you'll be paid at 17-to-1. The casino advantage on this bet is 5.26%.

If you put a chip in an area that splits 4 numbers this is called a *corner* bet and if any one of those 4 numbers comes in you will be paid off at 8-to-1. The casino advantage on this bet is 5.26%.

If you put a chip at the beginning of a row of 3 numbers, this is called a *street* bet and if any one of those 3 numbers shows up you will be paid off at 11-to-1. The casino advantage on this bet is 5.26%.

You can also put a chip on the line between two streets so that you have a *double street* covered and if any one of those 6 numbers come in you'll be paid off at 5-to-1. The casino advantage on this bet is?... you guessed it...5.26%.

The only other bet you can make on the inside numbers is the *5- number* bet where you place one chip in the upper left corner of the number 1 box. If any one of those 5 numbers comes in you'll be paid off at 6-to-1 and what do you think the casino advantage is on this bet? Nope, I gotcha... it's 7.89%. Actually, this is the worst possible bet on the roulette table and the only bet you'll come across that doesn't have a 5.26% house edge on the double-zero roulette wheel. You should never make this bet.

One quick word here about "to" and "for" when discussing odds. Whenever the odds are stated as "to" this means that in addition to the stated payoff you also receive your original bet back. In other words, if you won your single number bet in roulette you would receive 35-to-1, which is a 35-chip payoff, plus you'd still keep your original one-chip bet, so you end up with 36 chips. Now if the odds are stated as "for" that means you do not receive back your original bet. If the odds in your single number bet were 35-*for*-1 you would still receive a 35-chip payoff but the casino would keep your original one-chip bet so you would only end up with 35 chips. The only place in a casino where the odds are always stated as "for" is in video poker. You might also come across it on a couple of craps bets where the odds are stated as "for-one" rather than "to-one" in order to give the casino a slightly better edge.

Now, getting back to our roulette examples, let's look at all of the outside bets that you can make and keep in mind that the house edge on all of these outside bets is...do you remember the number?...that's right...5.26%.

There are three bets you can make that will pay you even money, or 1-to-1, which means that if you win, you will get back one dollar for every dollar you bet:

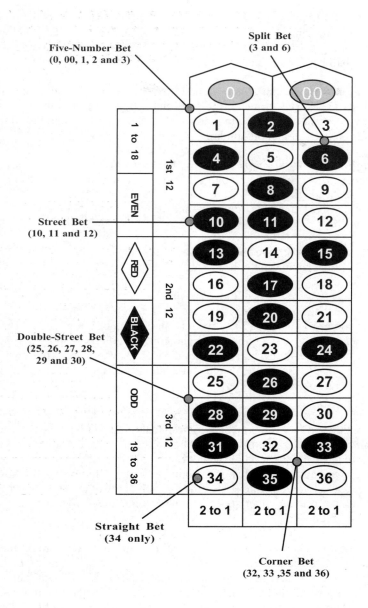

Typical felt layout for placing bets on
American double-zero roulette wheel

Red or black - If you put a chip on red then a red number must come up in order for you to win. If the ball lands on a black number, 0 or 00 - you lose. The same thing goes for black - you lose if it comes in red, 0 or 00 and you win if the ball lands on a black number.

Odd or even - If you put a chip on odd then the ball must land on an odd number in order for you to win. If it lands on 0, 00, or an even number - you lose. If you bet on even, you win if an even number shows up and lose if the ball lands on 0, 00 or an odd number.

1 through 18 and 19 through 36 - If you bet on 1 through 18, then you win if a number from 1 through 18 comes in and you lose if the ball lands on 0, 00 or a number higher than 18. Similarly, if you bet on 19 through 36, you win if one of those numbers comes in and you lose on 0, 00 or any number lower than 19.

The only other bets left are the *dozens* and columns bets. If you look at the roulette betting layout you can see three areas that each correspond to 12-number sections on the table. The one marked 1st 12 covers the numbers from 1 to 12, the one marked 2nd 12 covers the numbers from 13 to 24 and the other one that's marked 3rd 12 covers the last section of numbers from 25 to 36. If you bet on the 1st 12 you would win if a number from 1 to 12 came in and you would lose if anything else came in, including 0 or 00. The same principle holds true for each of the other dozen bets where you would win if a number in that section came in and you would lose if anything else showed up. All dozens bets pay 2-to-1.

The last bet to look at is the *column* bet and that is also a bet that pays 2-to-1. There are three possible column bets you can make and you'll notice that each area corresponds to the numbers in the column directly above it. So, if you put a chip under the first column you will win if any of the numbers in that column come in and you will lose if any other number, including 0 or 00 shows up. Once again, the same rule is in effect for each of the other columns where you would win if the number appears in the column above your bet and you would lose if it doesn't.

All right, now you know all the possible bets and you know how to make them at the table. So, the next question is "How do you win?" and the answer to that is very simple - You have to get lucky! And that's the ONLY way you can win at roulette. As you found out earlier, every bet, except for the 5-number bet, which I'm sure you'll never make, has a house edge of?...that's right...5.26%. So, feel free to put your chips all over the table and then just hope that you're lucky enough to have one of your numbers come up. You see, it just doesn't matter what you do because you'll always have that same house edge of 5.26% working against you on every bet you make.

Now, you may have heard of a system for roulette where you should place your bets only on the numbers that are evenly spaced out around the wheel. For example, if you wanted to play only four numbers, you could bet on 1,2,31 and 32 because when you looked at a roulette wheel, you would notice that if you divided it into four equal parts, you would have a number that appears in each of the four sections. So, is this a good system? Well, actually it's no better and no worse than any other roulette system. The fact is that it's purely a matter of chance where the ball happens to land and it makes no difference whether the numbers you choose are right next to each other or evenly spaced out on the wheel. Each number has an equal chance to occur on every spin of the wheel and the house edge always remains at 5.26%.

You can probably tell that I wouldn't recommend roulette as a good game to play because there are other games that offer much better odds, but if you really insist on playing the game I have three good suggestions for you. #1 - Go to Atlantic City! In Atlantic City if you make an even-money outside bet, like red or black, odd or even, 1 through 18 or 19 through 36 and if 0 or 00 come up, the state gaming regulations allow the casino to take only half of your bet. Because you only lose half of your bet this also lowers the casino edge on these outside bets in half to 2.63%. This rule is only in effect for even-money bets so keep in mind that on all other bets the house edge still remains at that very high 5.26%.

The second suggestion I have for you also involves some travel and here it is: Go to Europe! The game of roulette began in Europe and many casinos over there use a single-zero wheel which makes it a much better game because the house edge on a single-zero roulette wheel is only 2.70%. To make it even better, they have a rule called "en prison" which is similar to the Atlantic City casino rule. If you make an even-money outside bet and the ball lands on 0 you don't lose right away. Instead, your bet is "imprisoned" and you have to let it ride on the next spin. Then, if your bet wins, you can remove it from the table. Because of this rule, the casino edge on this bet is cut in half to 1.35% which makes it one of the best bets in the casino and almost four times better than the same bet when it's made on a standard double-zero roulette wheel in the United States.

Now, if you're not into traveling and you don't think you can make it to Atlantic City or Europe, then you'll just have to settle for suggestion #3 which is: Win quickly! Naturally, this is easier said than done, but in reality, if you want to win at roulette the best suggestion I can give you is that you try to win quickly and then walk away from the table because the longer you continue to bet the longer that big 5.26% house edge will keep eating away at your bankroll. One major principle of gambling is that in order to win you must only play the games that have the lowest casino edge and, unfortunately, roulette is not one of them.

Before closing out this look at roulette, let's take a minute to examine one of the most famous betting systems of all time and the one that many people frequently like to use on roulette. It's called the Martingale system and it is basically a simple system of doubling your bet whenever you lose. The theory behind it is that sooner or later you'll have to win and thus, you will always come out ahead. As an example, let's say you're playing roulette and you bet $1 on red, if you lose you double your next bet to $2 and if you lose that then you double your next bet to $4 and if you lose that you double your next bet to $8 and so forth until you eventually win. Now, when you finally do win you will end up with a profit equal to your original bet, which in this case is $1. If you started the same system with a $5 bet, you would have to bet $10 after your first loss, $20 after your second loss and so forth, but whenever you won you would end up with a $5 profit.

In theory, this sounds like a good idea but in reality it's a terrible system because eventually you will be forced to risk a great amount of money for a very small profit. Let's face it, even if you only wanted to make a $1 profit on each spin of the wheel, sooner or later you will hit a major losing streak where you will have to bet an awful lot of money just to make that $1 profit. For example, if you go eight spins without a winner, you would have to bet $256 on the next spin and if that lost then you'd have to bet $512. Would you really want to risk that kind of money just to make $1? I don't think so. You may think that the odds are highly unlikely that you would lose that many bets in a row, but eventually it will happen and when it does you will suffer some astronomical losses. One other problem with this system is that eventually you won't be able to double your bet because you will have reached the casino maximum, which in most casinos is $500 on roulette. Just keep in mind that the Martingale system works best when it's played for fun on paper and not for real money in a casino. If it was truly a winning system it would have bankrupted the world's casinos years ago.

Baccarat

by Steve Bourie

When you think of Baccarat you probably think of a game that's played by the casino's wealthiest players who sit at a private table and can afford to bet tens of thousands of dollars on the flip of a card and you know what? You're right! The game of Baccarat has always had a reputation as being for the richest gamblers and that usually scared off the average player, but nowadays more and more people are discovering that Baccarat is really a good game for the small stakes player because 1.-it has a relatively small advantage for the casino and 2.-it's very simple to play.

The mini-Baccarat table is the kind of Baccarat table you're most likely to find in the standard American casino and the game is played pretty much the same as regular Baccarat except that in the mini version all of the hands are dealt out by the dealer and the players never touch the cards. Other than that, the rules are virtually the same. Oh yes, one other difference you'll find is that the betting minimums will always be lower on mini-Baccarat and it's usually pretty easy to find a table with a $5 minimum.

Now, as noted before, the game of Baccarat is very simple to play and that's because the only decision you have to make is what bet you want to make from the three that are available: player, banker or tie. After the players make their bets the game begins and two 2-card hands are dealt from a shoe that contains 8 decks of cards. One hand is dealt for the banker and another hand is dealt for the player. The values of the two cards in each hand are added together and the object of the game is to have a total as close to 9 as possible. After the values of the first two cards in each hand are totaled, a third card can be drawn by either the player, the banker or both. But, the decision as to whether or not a third card should be drawn is not decided by the dealer or the players - it is only decided by the rules of the game.

Actually the name Baccarat comes from the Italian word for zero and as you'll see there are lots of zeros in this game because when you add the cards together all of the 10's and all of the face cards are counted as zeros, while all of the other cards from ace though 9 are counted at their face value. So, a hand of Jack, 6 has a total of 6; 10,4 has a total of 4; king, 7 has a total of 7; and ace, queen which would be a great hand in blackjack, only has a total of 1. The other thing about adding the cards together is that no total can be higher than 9. So, if a total is 10 or higher you have to subtract 10 to determine its value. For example, 8,8 totals 16 but you subtract 10 and your total is 6; 9,5 has a total of 4; 8,3 has a total of 1; and 5,5 has a total of 0.

Once again, the object of the game of Baccarat is to have a total as close to 9 as possible, so after the first two cards are dealt if either the player or banker hand has a total of 9 then that's called a "natural" and that hand is the winner. If neither hand has a total of 9 then the next best possible hand is a total of 8 (which is also called a "natural") and that hand would be the winner. If both the player and the banker end up with the same total then it's a tie and neither hand wins.

Now, if neither hand has an 8 or a 9 then the rules of the game have to be consulted to decide whether or not a third card is drawn. Once that's done, the values of the cards are added together again and whichever hand is closest to a total of 9 is the winner. If both hands end up with the same total then it's a tie and neither hand wins.

If you want to bet on the player hand just put your money in the area marked "player" and if you win you'll be paid off at even-money, or $1 for every $1 you bet. The casino advantage on the player bet is 1.36%. If you want to bet on the banker hand you would place your bet in the area marked "banker" and if you win, you'll also be paid off at even-money, but you'll have to pay a 5% commission on the amount you win. So, if you won $10 on your bet, you would owe a 50¢ commission to the house. The 5% commission is only required if you win and not if you lose. The dealer will keep track of the amount you owe by putting an equal amount in a small area on the table that corresponds to your seat number at the table. So, if you're sitting at seat #3 and won $10 on the bank hand the dealer would pay you $10 and then put 50¢ in the #3 box. This lets him know how much you owe the casino in commissions and when you get up to leave the table you'll have to pay the dealer whatever amount is in that box. After adjusting for that 5% commission the casino advantage on the banker bet is 1.17%

Finally, if you want to bet on a tie you would place your bet in the area marked "tie" and if you win you'll be paid off at 8-to-1, or $8 for every $1 you bet. The big payoff sounds nice but actually this is a terrible bet because the casino advantage is a very high 14.1% and this bet should never be made.

As you've seen, the casino advantage in Baccarat is very low (except for the tie bet) and the rules are set in advance so no decisions are made by either the players or the dealer about how to play the cards. This means that, unlike blackjack where you have to decide whether or not you want another card, you have no decisions to make and no skill is involved. This also means that Baccarat is purely a guessing game, so even if you've never played the game before you can sit at a table and play just as well as anyone who's played the game for 20 years! This is the only game in the casino where this can happen and that's why I tell people that Baccarat is an especially good game for the beginning player because you need no special knowledge to take advantage of those low casino edge bets.

The only part of Baccarat that gets a little confusing is trying to understand the rules concerning the draw of a third card, but remember, the rules are always the same at every table and they'll usually have a printed copy of the rules at

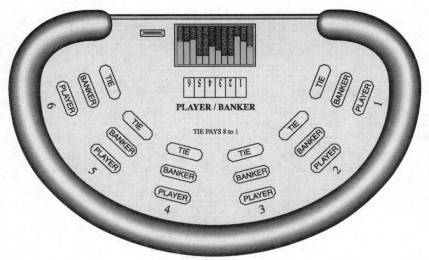

A Sample Mini-Baccarat Table Layout

the table and will give you a copy if you ask for it. After playing the game for awhile you'll start to remember the rules on your own, but until then here's a rundown on how it works:

As noted before, if the first two cards in either hand total 8 or 9, then the game is over and the highest total wins. If the totals are both 8 or both 9 then it's a tie and neither hand wins. For any other total the rules have to be consulted and it's always the player hand that goes first. If the player hand has a total of 6 or 7, it must stand. The only other totals it can possibly have are 0,1,2,3,4 or 5 and for all of those totals it must draw a card.

PLAYER HAND RULES

8,9	STANDS (Natural)
6,7	STANDS
0,1,2,3,4,5	DRAWS

There, that wasn't too hard to understand was it? If the player hand has a total of 6 or 7 it stands and for anything else it has to draw a card. Well, that was the easy part because now it gets a little complicated.

After the player hand is finished the banker hand must take its turn and if its first 2 cards total 0,1 or 2 it must draw a card. If its two cards total 7 it must stand and if the total is 6 it will stand, but only if the player hand did not take a card.

BANK HAND RULES

8,9	STANDS (Natural)
0,1,2	DRAWS
6	STANDS (If player took no card)
7	STANDS

The only other possible totals the bank can have are 3,4,5 or 6 and the decision as to whether or not a 3rd card is drawn depends on the 3rd card that was drawn by the player hand.

When the banker hand has a total of 3 it must stand if the player's 3rd card was an 8 and it must draw if the player's 3rd card was any other card.

IF BANK HAS 3 and
Player's third card is 8 - BANK STANDS
Player's third card is 1,2,3,4,5,6,7,9,10 - BANK DRAWS

When the banker hand has a total of 4 it must stand if the player's 3rd card was a 1,8,9, or 10 and it must draw if the player's 3rd card was any other card.

IF BANK HAS 4 and
Player's third card is 1,8,9,10 - BANK STANDS
Player's third card is 2,3,4,5,6,7 - BANK DRAWS

When the banker hand has a total of 5 it must draw if the player's 3rd card was a 4,5,6 or 7 and it must stand if the player's 3rd card was any other card.

IF BANK HAS 5 and
Player's third card is 1,2,3,8,9,10 - BANK STANDS
Player's third card is 4,5,6,7 - BANK DRAWS

When the banker hand has a total of 6 it must draw if the player's 3rd card was a 6 or 7 and it must stand if the player's 3rd card was any other card.

IF BANK HAS 6 and
Player's third card is 1,2,3,4,5,8,9,10 - BANK STANDS
Player's third card is 6 or 7 - BANK DRAWS

There you have it - those are the rules of Baccarat concerning the draw of a third card. As you saw they were a little complicated, but remember that you don't have to memorize the rules yourself because the dealer will know them and play each hand by those rules, but you can always ask for a copy of the rules at the table to follow along.

Now let's try some sample hands: The player hand has queen,9 for a total of 9 and the banker hand has 4,4 for a total of 8. Which hand wins? Both hands are naturals, but the player hand total of 9 is higher than the banker hand total of 8, so the player hand is the winner.

If the player hand has 4,2 for a total of 6 and the banker hand has ace, jack which totals 1, what happens? The player hand must stand on its 6 and the banker hand must always draw when it has a total of 0,1 or 2. Let's say the bank draws a 7 and wins 7 to 6.

What happens when the player hand has king, 5 and the bank hand has 2,4? The player hand must draw and let's say it gets a 7 for a total of 2. The banker hand has a total of 6 and if it could stand on that total it would win because its 6 is higher than the 2 held by the player. Of course, if you were betting on banker that's exactly what you would want to happen but, unfortunately for you, the rules require the bank hand to draw another card whenever its first two cards total 6 and the third card drawn by the player is a 7. So now, instead of having a winning hand you have to hope that the card you draw isn't a 5, which would give you a total of 1 making you a loser. You also wouldn't want to draw a 6 because that would give you a total of 2 which would give you a tie. In this case let's say that the bank hand goes on to draw an 8 which gives it a total of 3 and it wins 3 to 2.

Baccarat Rules Summary

Player Hand
**When the first
two cards total**

0-1-2-3-4-5	**Draws**
6-7	**Stands**
8-9	**Natural (Banker cannot draw)**

Banker Hand

When the first player's two cards total	DRAWS when player's third card is	STANDS when third card is
0-1-2	**Always Draws**	
3	1-2-3-4-5-6-7-9-0	8
4	2-3-4-5-6-7	1-8-9-0
5	4-5-6-7	1-2-3-8-9-0
6	6-7	1-2-3-4-5-8-9-0
7		**Stands**
8-9		**Stands (Natural)**

If the Player's hand does not draw a third card, then the Banker's hand stands on a total of 6 or more.

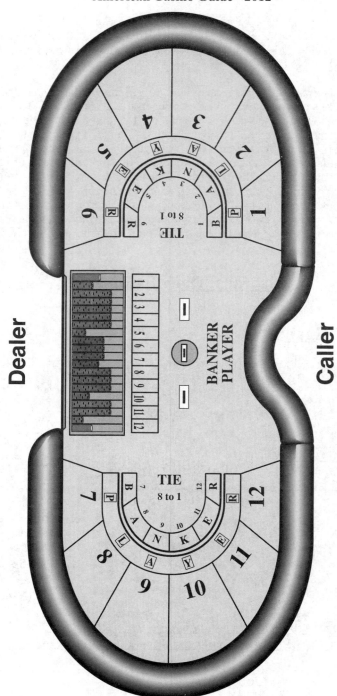

A 12-Seat Baccarat Table Layout

If the player hand has 3,ace for a total of 4 and the banker hand has 8,7 for a total of 5, what happens? The player hand must draw and say it gets a 9 for a total of 3. Once again, the banker hand would like to stand on its total because it would win, but the rules have to be consulted first and in this case when the banker's first 2 cards total 5 and the player's third card drawn is a 9 the banker hand must stand, so the banker hand wins 5 to 3.

Finally, let's say the player hand has 4,3 for a total of 7 and the banker hand has 6,10 for a total of 6. The player hand must always stand on totals of 6 or 7 and the banker hand must also stand on its total of 6 because the player hand didn't take a third card. The player hand wins this one 7 to 6.

All right, now that you know how to play Baccarat we come to the important question which is - how do you win? Well, as I said before, if you bet on player you'll only be giving the casino a 1.36% edge and if you bet on banker you'll be giving the casino an even more modest edge of just 1.17%. While both of these are pretty low edges to give the casino you're still stuck with the fact that the casino will always have an edge over you and in the long run the game of Baccarat is unbeatable. So, if that's the case then how do you win? Well, the answer to that is very simple - You have to get lucky! And that's the ONLY way you can win at Baccarat. Of course, this is easier said than done, but fortunately, in the game of Baccarat, you have the option of making two bets that require no skill and both offer the casino a very low edge especially when you compare them to roulette where the house has a 5.26% advantage on a double-zero wheel and slot machines where the edge is about 5% to 15% I always stress the point that when you gamble in a casino you have to play the games that have the lowest casino edge in order to have the best chance of winning and with that in mind you can see that Baccarat is not that bad a game to play for the recreational gambler.

Now let's take a quick look at one of the most common systems for betting on Baccarat. One thing that many Baccarat players seem to have in common is a belief in streaks and the casinos accommodate these players by providing scorecards at the table that can be used to track the results of each hand. Many players like to bet on whatever won the last hand in the belief that it will continue to come in and they hope for a long streak.

The thinking for these players is that since Baccarat is purely a guessing game it's just like guessing the outcome of a coin toss and chances are that a coin won't alternately come up heads, tails, heads, tails, heads, tails but rather that there will be streaks where the same result will come in for awhile. So, is this a good system? Well, actually, it's no better and no worse than any other system because no matter what you do you'll still have the same casino edge going against you on every bet you make: 1.36% on the player and 1.17% on the banker. The one good thing about a system like this though is that you don't have to sit there and guess what you want to play each time. Instead, you go into the game knowing how you're going to play and you don't have to blame yourself if your guess is wrong, instead you get to blame it on your system!

Craps

by Steve Bourie

At first glance the game of craps looks a little intimidating because of all the various bets you can make but actually the game itself is very simple, so first let me explain the game without any reference to the betting.

Everyone at the craps table gets a turn to roll the dice, but you don't have to roll if you don't want to. The dice are passed around the table clockwise and if it's your turn to roll you simply take two dice and roll them to the opposite end of the table. This is your first roll of the dice which is also called the "come-out" roll. If you roll a 7 or 11 that's called a "natural" and you win, plus you get to roll again. If you roll a 2,3 or 12 those are all called "craps" and you lose, but you still get to roll again. The only other possible numbers you can roll are 4,5,6,8,9 or 10 and if one of those numbers shows up, then that number becomes your "point" and the object of the game is to roll that number again before you roll a 7.

If a 7 shows up before your "point" number does then you lose and the dice move on to the next shooter. If your "point" number shows up before a 7 does, then you have made a "pass." You then win your bet and you get to roll again. That's all there is to the game of craps.

Now that you know how to play the game, let's find out about the different kinds of bets you can make. Two of the best bets you'll find on the craps table are in the areas marked "pass" and "don't pass". When you bet on the "pass" line you're betting that the shooter will win. To make a pass line bet you put your bet right in front of you on the pass line. Pass line bets are paid even-money and the house edge on a pass line bet is 1.41% You can also bet on the "don't pass" line in which case you're betting that the shooter will lose. To make a don't pass bet you put your bet in front of you in the don't pass area. Don't pass bets are also paid even-money and the house edge on them is 1.40%

In reality, the odds are always 1.41% against the shooter and in favor of the "don't pass" bettor by that same amount. Of course, if you're a "don't pass" bettor the casinos don't want to give you a bet where you have an edge so they have a rule in effect on "don't pass" bets where on the come out roll if the shooter throws a 12, you don't win. You don't lose either, the bet is just considered a "push," or tie, and nothing happens. In some casinos they may make 2 instead of 12 the number that's a push. Just look on the don't pass line and you'll you see the word "bar" and then the number that the casino considers a push. In our illustration it says bar 12, so in this casino your bet on the don't pass line will be a push if the come-out roll is a 12. This rule is what gives the casino its advantage on don't pass bets and it doesn't matter whether the casino bars the 2 or 12 the result is the same 1.40% advantage for the house.

All right, let's say you put $10 on the pass line and you roll the dice. If you roll 7 or 11 you win $10 and if you roll 2,3 or 12 you lose $10. So, what happens if you roll any of the other numbers? Well, as I said before, that number becomes your point and you have to roll that number again before you roll a 7 in order to win your pass line bet.

Once your point is established the dealer at each end of the table will move a marker into the box that corresponds to your point number to let everyone at the table know what your point is. The marker that's used has two different sides. One side is black with the word "off" and the other side is white with the word "on." Before any point is established the marker is kept in the Don't Come box with the black side facing up until you roll a point number and then the dealer turns it over to the white side and moves it inside the box that contains your point number.

For example let's say your come-out roll is a 4. The dealer simply turns the marker over to the white side that says "on" and places it in the 4 box. This lets everyone know that 4 is your point and that you will continue to roll the dice, no matter how long it takes, until you roll a 4, which will make you a winner, or a 7, which will make you a loser.

Now, keep in mind that once your point is established you can't remove your pass line bet until you either win, by throwing your point, or lose, by rolling a 7. The reason for this is that on the come out roll the pass line bettor has the advantage because there are 8 ways to win (by rolling a 7 or 11) and only 4 ways to lose (by rolling a 2, 3 or 12). If a point number is rolled, no matter what number it is, there are then more ways to lose than to win and that's why the bet can't be removed. If you were allowed to remove your bet everyone would just wait for the come-out roll and if they didn't win they would take their bet back which would give them a big advantage over the house and, as you know, casinos don't like that, so that's why you can't remove your bet.

As previously noted, the pass line is one of the best bets you'll find, but there is a way to make it even better because once your point number is established the casino will allow you to make another bet that will be paid off at the true odds. This is a very good bet to make because the casino has no advantage on this bet.

In this instance, since your point was 4, the true odds are 2-to-1 and that's what your bet will be paid off at: $2 for every $1 you bet. This is called an "odds bet," "taking the free odds" or "betting behind the line" and to make this bet you simply put your chips directly behind your pass line bet. There is a limit to how much you're allowed to bet and for many years most casinos allowed a maximum of 2 times the amount of your pass line bet. Nowadays, however, many casinos offer 5 times odds and some casinos are even allowing up to 100 times odds. In Las Vegas, Casino Royale is one casino that offers 100 times odds.

Because the casino has no advantage on these bets you are effectively lowering the house edge on your total pass line bet by taking advantage of these free odds bets. For example, the normal house edge on a pass line bet is 1.41% but if you also make a single odds bet along with your pass line bet you will lower the house edge on your total pass line bets to .85%. If the casino offers double odds then the edge on your bets is lowered to .61%. With triple odds the edge is lowered to .47% and if you were to play in a casino that allowed 10 times odds the edge would be lowered to only .18% which means that, statistically speaking, over time, that casino would only make 18¢ out of every $100 you bet on that table. As you can see, the more the casino allows you to bet behind the line, the more it lowers their edge, so it's always a good idea to take advantage of this bet. By the way, free odds bets, unlike regular pass line bets, can be removed or reduced, at any time.

All right, let's make our free odds bet on our point number of 4 by putting $20 behind the line. Then we continue to roll until we either roll a 4 or a 7. If a 4 came up we would get even money on the pass line bet, plus 2-to-1 on the free odds bet, for a total win of $50. But, if we rolled a 7, we would lose both the pass line bet and the free odds bet for a total loss of $30.

In this example we used 4 as our point number, but there are 5 other numbers that could appear and here are the true odds for all of the possible point numbers: the 4 and 10 are 2-to-1; the 5 and 9 are 3-to-2; and the 6 and 8 are 6-to-5. You'll notice that the numbers appear in pairs and that's because each paired combination has the same probability of occurring.

7 = 6 ways	1+6,6+1,2+5,5+2,3+4,4+3
6 = 5 ways	1+5,5+1,2+4,4+2,3+3
8 = 5 ways	2+6,6+2,3+5,5+3,4+4

As you can see there are 6 ways to make a 7 and only 5 ways to make a 6 or 8. Therefore, the true odds are 6-to-5.

7 = 6 ways	1+6,6+1,2+5,5+2,3+4,4+3
4 = 3 ways	1+3,3+1,2+2
10 = 3 ways	4+6,6+4,5+5

There are 6 ways to make a 7 and only 3 ways to make a 4 or 10, so the true odds are 6-to-3, which is the same as 2-to-1;

7 = 6 ways	1+6,6+1,2+5,5+2,3+4,4+3
5 = 4 ways	1+4,4+1,2+3,3+2
9 = 4 ways	3+6,6+3,4+5,5+4

and finally, there are 6 ways to make a 7, but just 4 ways to make a 5 or 9, so the true odds here are 6-to-4 which is the same as 3-to-2.

Typical craps table layout

It's important that you remember these numbers, because 1.- you want to make sure that you're paid the right amount when you do win and 2.- you want to make sure that when you make your odds bets you make them in amounts that are paid off evenly.

As an example, if your point is 5 and you have $5 on the pass line, you wouldn't want to bet $5 behind the line because at 3-to-2 odds the casino would have to pay you $7.50 and they don't deal in change. When making the odds bet on the 5 or 9 you should always bet in even amounts and in the situation just mentioned most casinos would allow you to add an extra $1 so you would have $6 out and they could pay you $9, if you won. The only other situation where this occurs is on the 6 and 8 where the payoff is 6-to-5. So, in that instance you want to make your bets in multiples of $5. Also, if your pass line bet is $15, most casinos will allow you to bet $25 behind the line because, if you win, it's quicker for them to pay you $30, rather than dealing in $1 chips to give you $18 for $15. When situations like this exist, it's good to take advantage of them and bet the full amount you're allowed because that helps to lower the casino edge even more.

We've spent all this time talking about pass line betting, so what about don't pass betting? Well, everything applied to pass line betting works pretty much just the opposite for don't pass betting. If you put $10 on don't pass you would win on the come out roll if the shooter rolled a 2 or 3, you would tie if the shooter rolled a 12, and you would lose if the shooter rolled a 7 or 11. If any other number comes up then that becomes the shooter's point number and if he rolls a 7 before he rolls that same point number, you will win. If he rolls his point number before he rolls a 7, you will lose.

Don't pass bettors are also allowed to make free odds bets to back up their original bets, however, because the odds are in their favor they must lay odds rather than take odds. This means that if the point is 4 or 10, the don't pass bettor must lay 2-to-1, or bet $10 to win $5; on 5 or 9 he must lay 3-to-2, or bet $6 to win $4; and on 6 or 8 he must lay 6-to-5, or bet $6 to win $5. By taking advantage of these free odds bets the casino advantage is slightly lowered on the total don't pass bets to .68% with single odds; .46% with double odds; .34% with triple odds and .12% with 10 times odds. If you want to you can remove, or reduce the amount of your free odds, bet at any time. To make a free odds bet on don't pass you should place your odds bet right next to your original bet and then put a chip on top to connect the two bets. Keep in mind that when you make a free odds bet on don't pass the casino will allow you to make your bet based on the payoff, rather than the original amount of your don't pass bet. In other words, if the casino offered double odds, the point was 4 and you had $10 on don't pass, you would be allowed to bet $40 because you would only win $20 which was double the amount of your original $10 bet. Since you have to put out more money than you'll be getting back, laying odds is not very popular at the craps table and you'll find that the vast majority of craps players would rather bet with the shooter and take the odds. Statistically speaking, it makes no difference whether you are laying or taking the odds because they both have a zero advantage for the house.

One last point about don't pass betting is that once the point is established, the casino will allow you to remove your don't pass bet if you want to - but don't do it! As noted before, on the come out roll the pass line bettor has the advantage because there are 8 rolls that can win and only 4 that can lose, but once the point is established, there are more ways the shooter can lose than win, so at that point the don't pass bettor has the advantage and it would be foolish to remove your bet.

Now, let's take a look at the area marked come and don't come. Since you already know how to bet pass and don't pass, you should easily understand come and don't come because they're the exact same bets as pass and don't pass, except for the fact that you bet them after the point has already been established.

Let's say that the shooter's point is 6 and you make a come bet by putting a $5 chip anywhere in the come box. Well, that's just like making a pass line bet, except that the shooter's next roll becomes the come-out roll for your bet. If the shooter rolls a 7 or 11, you win. If a 2,3, or 12 is rolled you lose, and if anything else comes up then that becomes your point and the shooter must roll that number again before rolling a 7 in order for you to win. In this example if the shooter rolled a 4 the dealer would move your $5 come bet up into the center of the 4 box and it would stay there until either a 4 was rolled, which would make you a winner, or a 7 was rolled which would make you a loser. The house edge on a come bet is the same 1.41% as on a pass line bet. You are allowed free odds on your come bet and you make that bet by giving your chips to the dealer and telling him you want to take the odds. The dealer will then place those chips slightly off center on top of your come bet to show that it's a free odds bet. By the way, if you win, the dealer will put your winnings back in the come bet area so be sure to pick them up off the table or else it will be considered a new come bet.

One other point to note here is that when you make a come bet your bet is always working on every roll, even a come-out roll. However, when you take the odds on your come bets they are never working on the come-out roll. That may sound a little confusing, but here's what it means. In our example the shooter's initial point was 6 and then we made a $5 come bet. The shooter then rolled a 4 which became the point for our come bet. The dealer then moved our $5 come bet to the middle of the 4 box at the top of the table. We then gave $10 to the dealer and said we wanted to take the odds on the 4. On the next roll the shooter rolls a 6 which means he made a pass by rolling his original point number. The next roll will then become the shooter's come-out roll and the odds bet on our 4 will not be working. If the shooter rolls a 7 the pass line bettors will win and we will lose our $5 come bet because he rolled a 7 before rolling a 4. The dealer will then return our $10 odds bet because it wasn't working on the come-out roll. Now, if you want to, you can request that your odds bet be working on the come-out roll by telling the dealer. Then he'll put a marker on top of your bet to show that your odds bet is in effect on the come-out roll.

Naturally, don't come betting is the same as don't pass betting, except again for the fact that the bet isn't made until after the point is established. In this case let's say the point is 5 and you make a don't come bet by placing a $5 chip in the don't come box. Well, once again, that's just like making a don't pass bet except that the shooter's next roll becomes the come-out roll for your bet. If the shooter rolls a 2 or 3, you win. If a 7 or 11 is rolled, you lose. If a 12 is rolled it's a standoff and if anything else comes up then that becomes your point and the shooter must seven-out, or roll a 7, before rolling that point number again in order for you to win. In this example if the shooter rolled a 10 the dealer would move your $5 don't come bet into the upper part of the 10 box and it would stay there until either a 7 was rolled, which would make you a winner, or a 10 was rolled which would make you a loser. The house edge on a don't come bet is the same 1.40% as on a don't pass bet and you can make a free odds bet on your don't come bet by giving your chips to the dealer and telling him you want to lay the odds. The dealer will then place those chips next to and on top of your don't come bet to show that it's a free odds bet. The final point to note here is that don't come bets, as well as the free odds bets on them, are always working - even on the come-out roll.

Now let's talk about place betting and that refers to the 6 numbers you see in the area at the top of the table: 4,5,6,8,9 and 10. Anytime during a roll you can make a bet that one of those numbers will appear before a 7 and if it does you will receive a payoff that is slightly less than the true odds. For example: the true odds are 2-to-1 that a 4 or 10 will appear before a 7. However, if you make a place bet on the 4 or 10 you will only be paid off at 9-to-5 and that works out to a casino advantage of 6.67%

The true odds of a 5 or 9 appearing before a 7 are 3-to-2, but on a place bet you would only receive a payoff of 7-to-5 which works out to a casino edge of 4.0%. Finally, on the 6 and 8 the true odds are 6-to-5 that one of those numbers will appear before a 7, but on a place bet you would only be paid off at 7-to-6 which means the casino would have an edge of 1.52% on this bet.

As you can see, making a place bet on the 6 or 8 gives the casino its lowest edge and this means that a place bet on the 6 or 8 is one of the best bets you will find on the craps table.

When you want to make a place bet you aren't allowed to put the bet down yourself, you have to let the dealer do it for you. To do this you would just drop your chips down onto the table and tell the dealer what bet you wanted to make. For example you could put three $5 chips down and say "Place the 4,5 and 9." The dealer would then put $5 on the edge of the 4 box, $5 on the edge of the 5 box and $5 on the edge of the 9 box. You'll notice that when the dealer puts your bets on the edge of the boxes they will always be placed in an area that corresponds to where you're standing at the table and this helps the dealer to remember who placed that bet.

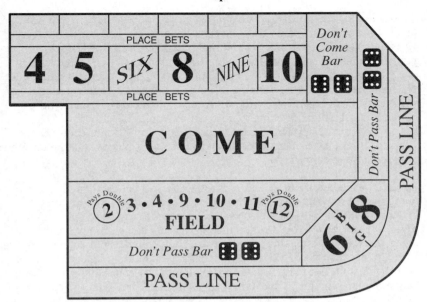

Enlargement of right side of craps layout

When making a place bet you don't have to bet more than one number and you don't have to bet the same amount on each number. You should, however, make sure that you always bet in multiples of $5 whenever you bet on the 4,5,9 or 10 and in multiples of $6 whenever you bet the 6 and 8. This will allow you to always get the full payoff on your bet. If, for example, you bet $3 on the 6 and you won you would only get back even-money, or $3, rather than the $3.50 which your bet should have paid and this results in an even bigger advantage for the casino. Another thing about place bets is that, unlike pass line bets, you can remove your place bets at any time and you do that by telling the dealer you want your bet down and he will take your chips off the table and return them to you. You could also tell the dealer that you didn't want your bet to be working on any particular roll or rolls and you do this by saying for example "off on the 5." The dealer would then put a little button on top of your bet that said "off" and he would remove it when you told him you wanted that number working again.

When we spoke about come bets before I mentioned that come bets are always working on every roll, but that's not the case with place bets because place bets are never working on the come-out roll. If you wanted to, however, you could ask for your place bet to be working on the come out roll by telling the dealer you wanted it working and he would place a button on top of your bet that said "on" to show that your bet was working on the come-out roll.

One last point about place bets is that when you win the dealer will want to know what you want to do for your next bet and you have three choices: if you want to make the same bet just say "same bet" and the dealer will give you your winning chips and leave your original place bet on the table. If you don't want to bet again, just say "take it down" and the dealer will return your place bet along with your winnings. And if you want to double your bet just say "press it" and the dealer will add your winning chips to your other place bet and return any extra chips to you. For example, if you won a $10 place bet on the 5 the dealer would have to give you back $14 in winning chips. If you said "press it" the dealer would add $10 to your place bet and return the remaining $4 in chips to you.

Besides, place betting there is also another way to bet that one of the point numbers will show up before a 7 does and that's called buying a number. A buy bet is basically the same as a place bet except you have to pay a commission of 5% of the amount of your bet and then if you win, the casino will pay you at the true odds. When making a buy bet you should always remember to bet at least $20 because 5% of $20 is $1 and that's the minimum amount the casino will charge you. The reason for the $1 minimum is because that's the smallest denomination chip they have at the craps table and they won't make change for anything under $1. The casino edge on any buy bet for $20 works out to 4.76% so let's take a look at a chart that shows the difference between buying and placing the point numbers.

Point Number	Casino Edge Buy Bet	Casino Edge Place Bet
4 or 10	4.76%	6.67%
5 or 9	4.76%	4.00%
6 or 8	4.76%	1.52%

As you can see the only numbers that you would want to buy rather than place are the 4 and 10 because the 4.76% edge on a buy bet is lower than the 6.67% edge on a place bet. For 5 and 9 the 4.76% edge on a buy bet is slightly worse than the 4.00% edge on a place bet and for the 6 and 8 the 4.76% is a hefty three times higher than the 1.52% edge on the place bet.

To buy the 4 or 10 you would just put your chips down on the layout and tell the dealer what bet you wanted to make. For example, if you put down $21 and said "buy the 10." The dealer will then keep the $1 chip for the house and put your $20 in the same area as the place bets but he'll put a button on top that says "buy" to let him know that you bought the number rather than placed it. Buy bets, just like place bets, can be removed at any time and are always off on the come-out roll. Also, if you do remove your buy bet you will get your 5% commission back.

Besides buy bets where you're betting with the shooter and hoping that a point number will appear before a 7 does, there are also lay bets where you're doing just the opposite - you're betting against the shooter and hoping that a 7 will appear before a point number does.

Lay bets are also paid at the true odds and you have to pay a 5% a commission of the amount you will win rather than the amount you're betting. Once again, when making a lay bet you should always remember to make them based on a minimum payoff of $20 because 5% of $20 is $1 and that's the minimum amount the casino will charge you.

Lay Number	Payoff	Casino Edge
4 or 10	$40 for $20	2.44%
5 or 9	$30 for $20	3.23%
6 or 8	$24 for $20	4.00%

For 4 and 10 you'll have to lay $40 to win $20 and the casino edge is 2.44%; for the 5 and 9 you'll have to lay $30 to win $20 and the casino edge is 3.23%; and for the 6 and 8 you'll have to lay $24 to win $20. The casino edge on that bet is 4.00%.

To make a lay bet you would just put your chips down on the layout and tell the dealer what you wanted to bet. For example, if you put down $41 and said "lay the 10." The dealer would then keep the $1 chip for the house and put your $40 in the same area as the don't come bets but he'll put a button on top that says "buy" to let him know that it's a lay bet. Lay bets, unlike buy bets, are always working on come-out rolls. Lay bets are, however, similar to buy bets in that they can be removed at any time and if you do remove your lay bet you will also receive your 5% commission back.

There are only a few other bets left located on the ends of the table to discuss and two of them are the big 6 and the big 8 which are both very bad bets. To bet the big 6 you place a chip in the big 6 box and then if the shooter rolls a 6 before rolling a 7 you win even money, or $1 for every $1 you bet. To bet the big 8 the same rules would apply: you put your bet in the box and then hope that the shooter rolls an 8 before rolling a 7 so you could win even money on your bet. The big 6 and big 8 can both be bet at any time and both are always working, even on the come-out roll. The casino edge on both the big 6 and the big 8 is 9.1%, which is the biggest edge we've seen so far. But, if you think back about some of the other bets we discussed doesn't this bet sound familiar? It should. This bet is the exact same as a place bet on the 6 or 8, but instead of getting paid off at 7-to-6 we're only getting paid off at even-money! Why would you want to bet the big 6 or big 8 at a house edge of more than 9% instead of making a place bet on the 6 or 8 at a house edge of only 1.5%? The answer is you wouldn't - so don't ever make this bet because it's a sucker bet that's only for people who don't know what they're doing.

The last bet we have to discuss on the player's side of the table is the field bet which is a one-roll bet that will pay even money if a 3,4,9,10 or 11 is rolled and 2-to-1 if a 2 or 12 is rolled. To make a field bet you would just place your chip anywhere in the field box and at first glance it doesn't seem like a bad bet. After all, there are 7 numbers you can win on and only 4 numbers you can lose on! The only problem is that there are 20 ways to roll the 4 losing numbers and only 16 ways to roll the 7 winning numbers and even after factoring in the double payoff for the 2 and 12 the casino winds up with a hefty 5.6% advantage. In some casinos they pay 3-to-1 on the 2 (or the 12) which cuts the casino edge in half to a more manageable 2.8%, but as you've seen there are still much better bets you can make. By the way, if you win on a field bet the dealer will put your winning chips right next to your bet so it's your responsibility to pick them up, or else they'll be considered a new bet!

Now, let's take a look at some of the long-shots, or proposition bets in the center of the table. When you look at these bets one of the first things you'll notice is that, unlike the bets on the other side of the table, the winning payoffs are clearly labeled. The reason they do that is so you can see those big payoffs and want to bet them, but as you'll see, although the payoffs are high, so are the casino advantages.

All of the proposition bets are controlled by the stickman and he is the person who must make those bets for you. So, if you wanted to make a $1 bet on "any craps" you would throw a $1 chip to the center of the table and say "$1 any craps" and the stickmen would place that bet in the proper area for you. Then if you won, the stickman would tell the dealer at your end of the table to pay you. You should also be aware that they will only pay you your winnings and keep your original bet in place. If you don't want to make the same bet again, you should tell the stickman that you want your bet down and it will be returned to you.

There are only four proposition bets that are not one-roll bets and they are known as the "hardways." They are the hard 4, hard 6, hard 8 and hard 10. To roll a number the hardway means that the number must be rolled as doubles. For example 3 and 3 is a hard 6, but a roll of 4-2, or 5-1 are both called an easy 6, because they are easier to roll than double 3's.

To win a bet on hard 10 the shooter has to roll two 5's before rolling a 7 or an easy 10 such as 6-4 or 4-6. To win a bet on hard 4 the shooter has to roll two 2's before rolling a 7 or an easy 4 such as 3-1 or 1-3. The true odds of rolling a hard 4 or hard 10 are 8-to-1, but the casino will only pay you 7-to-1 which works out to a casino advantage of 11.1% on both of these bets.

To win a bet on hard 6 the shooter must roll two 3's before rolling a 7 or an easy 6 such as 5-1, 1-5; or 4-2, 2-4. To win a bet on hard 8 the shooter must roll two 4's before rolling a 7 or an easy 8 such as 6-2, 2-6 or 5-3, 3-5. The true odds of rolling a hard 6 or hard 8 are 10-to-1, but the casino will only pay you 9-to-1 which works out to a casino advantage of 9.1% on both of these bets.

Two different types of proposition bets layouts

As noted before, all of the other proposition bets are one-roll bets which means that the next roll of the dice will decide whether you win or lose. As you'll see, the house edge on all of these bets is very high and they should all be avoided.

For the any craps bet you will win if a 2,3,or 12 is thrown on the next roll and lose if any other number comes up. The true odds are 8-to-1 but the casino will only pay you at 7-to-1 which gives them an edge of 11.1% on this bet and you'll notice that the stickman can put your bet either in the any craps box or, more likely, he'll put it on the circled marked "C" which stands for craps. The reason your bet will be placed in the "C" circle is that it's put in the circle that corresponds to where you're standing at the table and it makes it easier for the stickman to know who that bet belongs to.

For a craps 2 bet you win if the next roll is a 2 and lose if any other number shows up. The true odds are 35-to-1 but the casino will only pay you 30-to-1 which means that the edge on this bet is 13.9% In some casinos the odds for this bet will be shown as 30-for-1 which is actually the same as 29-to-1 and this results in an even bigger edge of 16.7% for the casino

A craps 12 bet works the same as a craps 2 bet, except that now you will only win if a 12 is thrown. Again, the true odds are 35-to-1 but you will only be paid at 30-to-1 which means the casino edge on this bet is the same 13.9% as in the last craps 2 bet. Also if the bet is shown on the layout as 30-for-1 the casino edge is raised to 16.7%

For a craps 3 bet you will only win if the next throw is a 3. The true odds are 17-to-1, but the casino will only pay you 15-to-1 which results in a casino advantage of 11.1% Once again, in some casinos the payoff will be shown as 15-for-1 which is the same as 14-to-1 and the house edge in that casino is an even higher 16.7%

The 11 bet is similar to the craps 3 bet, except that now the only number you can win on is 11. The true odds of rolling an 11 are 17-to-1, but the casino will only pay you 15-to-1 which gives them an 11.1% advantage. Additionally, if the payoff is shown on the layout as 15-for-1 rather than 15-to-1 the casino edge will be even higher at 16.7% By the way, because 11 sounds so much like 7 you will always hear 11 referred to at the table as "yo" or "yo-leven" to eliminate any confusion as to what number you are referring to. So, if you wanted to bet $5 on 11 you would throw a $5 chip to the stickman and say "$5 yo" and then he will either place it in the 11 box or place it on top of the "E" circle that corresponds to where you're standing at the table.

With a horn bet you are betting on the 2,3,11 and 12 all at once. A horn bet has to be made in multiples of $4 because you're making 4 bets at one time and you'll win if any one of those 4 numbers shows up on the next roll. You'll be paid off at the odds for the number that came in and you'll lose the rest of your chips. For example, if you make an $8 horn bet, this is the same as betting $2 on the 2, $2 on the 3, $2 on the 11 and $2 on the 12. If the number 2 came in you would get paid off at 30-to-1 so you would get back $60 in winnings and the casino would keep the $6 that you lost for the three $2 bets on the 3,11 and 12. The only advantage of a horn bet is that it allows you to make 4 bad bets at once rather than one at a time.

The last proposition bet we have to look at is also the worst bet on the craps table and it's the any 7 bet. With this bet you win if a 7 is rolled and lose if any other number comes up. The true odds are 5-to-1, but the casino will only pay you at 4-to-1 which gives them an edge of 16.7%

So there you have it! We've gone over all the possible bets you can make and now it's time to tell you how to win at the game of craps. Unfortunately, as you've seen, craps is a negative expectation game which means that every bet you make has a built-in advantage for the house. Actually, there is one bet that the casino has no advantage on and do you remember the name of that one? That's right it's the free odds bet and it's great that the casino has no advantage on that bet but the only way you're allowed to make that bet is to first make a negative expectation bet on pass/don't pass or come/don't come, so in essence, there are no bets you can make where you have an advantage over the house and in the long run the game of craps is unbeatable.

So, if that's the case then how do you win? Well, in reality there is only one way to win in craps and that way is to get lucky! Of course, this is easier said than done, but you will find it much easier to come out a winner if you only stick to the bets that offer the casino its lowest edge and those are the only bets you should ever make.

If you want to bet with the shooter I suggest you make a pass line bet, back it up with the free odds and then make a maximum of two come bets that are also both backed up with free odds. For example if double odds are allowed, you could start with a $5 pass line bet and say a 4 is rolled. You would then put $10 behind the line on your 4 and make a $5 come bet. If the shooter then rolled an 8 you would take $10 in odds on your come bet on the 8 and make another $5 come bet. If the shooter then rolled a 5 you would take $10 in odds on your come bet on the 5 and then stop betting. The idea here is that you always want to have a maximum of three numbers working and once you do, you shouldn't make anymore bets until one of your come numbers hits, in which case you would make another come bet, or if your pass line bet wins and then you would follow that up with another pass line bet. The important thing to remember is not to make more than two come bets because you don't want to have too much out on the table if the shooter rolls a 7. By using this betting system you'll only be giving the casino an edge of around .60% on all of your bets and with just a little bit of luck you can easily walk away a winner.

If you wanted to be a little more aggressive with this betting system there are some modifications you could make such as making a maximum of three come bets rather than two, or you could add place bets on the 6 and 8. Remember that a place bet on either the 6 or 8 only gives the casino a 1.52% advantage and that makes them both the next best bets after pass/don't pass and come/don't come. To add the place bets you would start off the same as before, but after you've made your second come bet you would look at the 6 and 8 and if they weren't covered you would then make a $6 place bet on whichever one was open or on both. By adding the place bets on the 6 and 8 you would always have at least three numbers in action and you could have as many as five covered at one time.

One final option with this system is to gradually increase the amount of your pass line and come bets by 50%, or by doubling them, and then backing them up with full odds, but I would only suggest you do this if you've been winning for a while because it could get very expensive if the table was cold and no one was rolling many numbers. Of course, if the table got real cold you could always change your strategy by betting against the shooter and the strategy for that is basically just the opposite of the one I just told you about.

To bet against the shooter you would start with a $5 don't pass bet which you would back up with single free odds and then bet a maximum of two don't come bets that are both backed up with single odds. The reason you don't want to back up your bets with double odds is because when you're betting against the shooter you have to lay the odds which means you're putting up more money than you'll be getting back and, once again, it could get very expensive if a shooter got on a hot roll and made quite a few passes.

For an example of this system let's say you start with a $5 don't pass bet and a 4 is rolled. You would then lay the odds by putting $10 next to your $5 don't pass bet and then make a $5 don't come bet. If the shooter then rolled an 8 you would lay $6 in odds on your don't come bet on the 8 and make another $5 don't come bet. If the shooter then rolled a 5 you would lay $9 in odds on your come bet on the 5 and then stop betting. The idea here is that you always want to have a maximum of three numbers working and once you do that, you shouldn't make anymore bets until, hopefully, the shooter sevens out and all of your bets win. If that does happen, then you would start all over again with a new don't pass bet. Once again, the important thing to remember is not to make more than two don't come bets because you don't want to have too much out on the table if the shooter gets hot and starts to roll a lot of numbers. With this system you'll always have a maximum of three numbers in action and you'll only be giving the casino an edge of about .80% on all of your bets. Some options to bet more aggressively with this system are to increase your free odds bets to double odds rather than single odds and also to make three don't come bets, rather than stopping at two. The choice is up to you but remember that because you must lay the odds and put out more money than you'll be getting back you could lose a substantial amount rather quickly if the roller got hot and made a lot of point numbers.

Now, one last point I want to make about betting craps is that the bankroll you'll need is going to be much bigger than the bankroll you'll need for playing any other casino game. If you're betting with the shooter you'll have one $5 pass line bet with double odds and two come bets with double odds which means that you could have as much as $45 on the table that could be wiped out with the roll of a 7. If you're betting against the shooter you'll have $5 on don't pass with single odds and two don't come bets with single odds which means you could have as much as $44 on the table that could be wiped out if the shooter got on a "hot" roll and made a lot of numbers. As I said before, you need to have an adequate bankroll to be able to ride out the losing streaks that will eventually occur and you need to be able to hold on until things turn around and you start to win.

So how much of a bankroll is enough? Well, I would say about 7 times the maximum amount of money you'll have out on the table is adequate and 10 times would be even better. In both of our examples then you should have a bankroll of at least $300. If you don't have that much money to put out on the table then you might want to consider having less money out on the table by making only one come or don't come bet rather than two or maybe even just limiting your bets to pass and don't pass along with the free odds.

Just remember that it doesn't matter whether you want to bet with the shooter or against the shooter - both of these systems will give you the best chance of winning because they allow the casino only the slightest edge and with a little bit of luck you can easily come out a winner. Good luck!

A Few Last Words

by Steve Bourie

When I sit down to put this book together each year I try to make sure that everything in here will help to make you a better and more knowledgeable gambler when you go to a casino.

I try to include stories that will help you understand how casinos operate, how to choose the best casino games and also how to play those games in the best way possible.

My philosophy with this book is that gambling in a casino is a fun activity and, according to research studies, for about 98% of the people who visit casinos this statement is true. The vast majority of people who gamble in casinos are recreational players who enjoy the fun and excitement of gambling. They know that they won't always win and they also realize that over the long term they will most likely have more losing sessions than winning ones. They also understand that any losses they incur will be the price they pay for their fun and they only gamble with money they can afford to lose. In other words, they realize that casino gambling is a form of entertainment, just like going to a movie or an amusement park, and they are willing to pay a price for that entertainment. Unfortunately, there are also some people who go to casinos and become problem gamblers.

According to Gamblers Anonymous you may be a problem gambler if you answer yes to at least seven of the following 20 questions:

1. Do you lose time from work due to gambling?
2. Does gambling make your home life unhappy?
3. Does gambling affect your reputation?
4. Do you ever feel remorse after gambling?
5. Do you ever gamble to get money with which to pay debts or to otherwise solve financial difficulties?
6. Does gambling cause a decrease in your ambition or efficiency?
7. After losing, do you feel you must return as soon as possible and win back your losses?
8. After a win, do you have a strong urge to return and win more?
9. Do you often gamble until your last dollar is gone?
10. Do you ever borrow to finance your gambling?
11. Do you ever sell anything to finance your gambling?
12. Are you reluctant to use your "gambling money" for other expenses?
13. Does gambling make you careless about the welfare of your family?
14. Do you ever gamble longer than you planned?

15. Do you ever gamble to escape worry or trouble?
16. Do you ever commit, or consider committing, an illegal act to finance your gambling?
17. Does gambling cause you to have difficulty sleeping?
18. Do arguments, disappointments, or frustrations create within you an urge to gamble?
19. Do you have an urge to celebrate good fortune by a few hours of gambling?
20. Do you ever consider self-destruction as a result of your gambling?

If you believe you might have a gambling problem you should be aware that help is available from The National Council on Problem Gambling, Inc. It is the foremost advocacy organization in the country for problem gamblers and is headquartered in Washington, D.C. It was formed in 1972 as a non-profit agency to promote public education and awareness about gambling problems and operates a 24-hour nationwide help line at (800) 522-4700, plus a website at www.ncpgambling.org. Anyone contacting that organization will be provided with the appropriate referral resources for help with their gambling problem.

Another good source for anyone seeking help with a gambling problem is Gambler's Anonymous. They have chapters in many cities throughout the U.S. as well as in most major cities throughout the world. You can see a list of all those cities on their website at www.gamblersanonymous.org or contact them by telephone at (213) 386-8789.

A third program, Gam-Anon, specializes in helping the spouse, family and close friends of compulsive gamblers rather than the gamblers themselves.If you are adversely affected by a loved one who is a compulsive gambler, then Gam-Anon is an organization that may benefit you. They have a website at www.gam-anon.org that lists the cities which host meetings. They can also be contacted by telephone at (718) 352-1671.

I sincerely hope that none of you reading this book will ever have a need to contact any of these worthwhile organizations, but it was an issue that I felt should be addressed.

ALABAMA

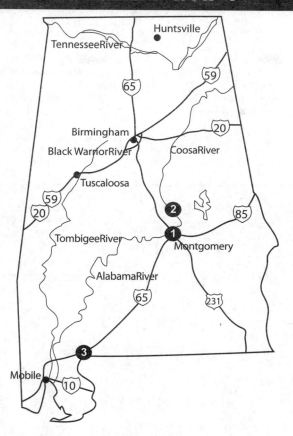

Alabama has three Class II indian casinos.

Class II video gaming devices look like slot machines, but are actually bingo games and the spinning reels are for "entertainment purposes only." No public information is available concerning the payback percentages on any gaming machines in Alabama.

The minimum gambling age is 21 at the Indian casinos. All three casinos are open 24 hours. For Alabama tourism information call (800) ALABAMA, or go to: www.alabama.travel

Creek Casino Montgomery
1801 Eddie Tullis Drive
Montgomery, Alabama 36117
(334) 273-9003
Website: www.pcigaming.com
Map: **#1**

Toll Free: (800) 958-9003
21,000 Square feet
Restaurants: 1 snack bar
Overnight RV Parking: Free

Creek Casino Wetumpka
100 River Oaks Drive
Wetumpka, Alabama 36092-3084
(334) 514-0469
Website: www.pcigaming.com
Map: **#2** (20 miles N. of Montgomery)

Toll Free: (800) 897-7198
Restaurants: 2
Buffet: L-$7.00 D-$12.00
Overnight RV Parking: Free
Senior discount: Free breakfast Mon-Fri 7-10am

Wind Creek Casino & Hotel
303 Poarch Road
Atmore, Alabama 36502
(251) 446-4200
Website: www.windcreekcasino.com
Map: **#3** (55 miles NE. of Mobile)

Room Reservations: (866) WIND-360
Rooms: 236 Price Range: $99-$139
Restaurants: 4 (1 open 24 hours) Valet: Free
Buffet: B- $10/$14.95 (Sun) L-$9.95
          D- $12.95/ $19.95 (Fri/Sat)
Casino Size: 50,000 Square Feet
Overnight RV Parking: Free

ARIZONA

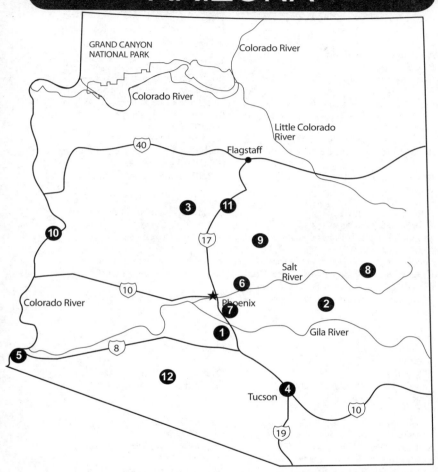

In mid-1993 Arizona's Governor Symington signed a compact with the state's tribes that allowed them to offer slot machines on their reservations.

The compact originally didn't allow for any table games but in early 2003 blackjack was added as a permissible table game.

Arizona tribes aren't required to release information on their slot machine percentage paybacks, however, according to the Arizona Department of Gaming, the terms of the compact require each tribes' machines to return the following minimum and maximum paybacks: video poker and video blackjack - 83% to 100%, slot machines - 80% to 100%, keno - 75% to 100%. Each tribe is free to set its machines to pay back anywhere within those limits.

All Arizona casinos have slots, video poker and video keno. Optional games include: blackjack (BJ), Spanish 21 (S21), let it ride (LIR), poker (P), live keno (K), and bingo (BG).

The minimum gambling age is 21 and all casinos are open 24 hours. For more information on visiting Arizona call the state's Office of Tourism at (866) 275-5816 or visit their website at: www.azot.com

Apache Gold Casino Resort

P.O. Box 1210
San Carlos, Arizona 85550
(928) 475-7800
Map: **#2** (90 miles E. of Phoenix)
Website: www.apachegoldcasinoresort.com

Toll-Free Number: (800) APACHE-8
Rooms: 146 Price Range: $79-$109
Suites: 10   Price Range: $89-$149
Restaurants: 2 Liquor: Yes
Buffets: L/D-$7.00
Casino Size: 10,000 Square Feet
Other Games: BJ, BG, P
Overnight RV Parking: Yes
Senior Discount: 15% Food and room
　　discount if 55+
Special Features: Hotel is off-property and is Best Western. 18-hole golf course. Convenience store. 60-space RV Park ($20 per night) w/full hookups and dump station.

Blue Water Casino

11300 Resort Drive
Parker, Arizona 85344
(928) 669-7000
Website: www.bluewaterfun.com
Map: **#10** (160 miles W. of Phoenix)

Toll-Free Number: (888) 243-3360
Rooms: 200 Price Range: $79-$109
Suites: 25 Price Range: $99-$199
Restaurants: 4 Liquor: Yes
Buffet: B- $8.95/$9.95 (Fri-Sun)
　　L-$10.95/$11.95(Fri-Sun)
　　D-$10.95/$15.95 (Fri-Sun)
Other Games: BJ, P, BG
Overnight RV Parking: Free (only 1 night)
　　　　　　　　RV Dump: No
Senior Discount: Various buffet discounts

Bucky's Casino & Resort

530 E. Merritt
Prescott, Arizona 86301
(928) 776-1666
Website: www.buckyscasino.com
Map: **#3** (91 miles S.W. of Flagstaff, Junction of Hwy. 69 & Hwy. 89)

Toll-Free Number: (800) SLOTS-44
Room Reservations: (800) 967-4637
Rooms: 81 Price Range: $89-$209
Suites: 80 Price Range: $129-$239
Restaurants: 3 Liquor: Yes
Other Games: BJ, P
Overnight RV Parking: No
Special Features: Located in Prescott Resort Hotel. Free on-site shuttle service. Gas station with RV dump and mini-mart.

Casino Arizona 101 & McKellips

524 N. 92nd Street
Scottsdale, Arizona 85256
(480) 850-7777
Website: www.casinoaz.com
Map: **#6** (15 miles N.E. of Phoenix)

Toll-Free Number: (877) 724-4687
Restaurants: 5 Liquor: Yes
Buffets: B-$9.95(Sat) L-$9.95
　　　　D-$14.50/$19.50 (Fri/Sat)
Casino Size: 40,000 Square Feet
Other Games: P, BJ, LIR, TCP, K
Overnight RV Parking: Free/RV Dump: No
Special Features: 500-seat showroom.

Casino Del Sol

5655 W. Valencia
Tucson, Arizona 85757
(520) 883-1700
Website: www.casinodelsol.com
Map: **#4**

Hotel to open Early 2012.
Toll-Free Number: (800) 344-9435
Restaurants: 2 Liquor: Yes
Casino Size: 22,500 Square Feet
Other Games: BJ, P, BG, TCP, S21, PGP
Overnight RV Parking: Free/RV Dump: No
Special Features: 4,400-seat amphitheater.

Casino of the Sun
7406 S. Camino De Oeste
Tucson, Arizona 85757
(520) 883-1700
Website: http://solcasinos.com/
Map: **#4**

Toll-Free Number: (800) 344-9435
Restaurants: 2 Liquor: No
Buffets: L/D $8.30/ $15.95 (Fri/Sat)/
$13.25 (Sun)
Overnight RV Parking: Free/RV Dump: No
Special Features: Smoke shop. Gift shop. 50%
food discount on Tuesdays.

Cliff Castle Casino Hotel
555 Middle Verde Road
Camp Verde, Arizona 86322
(928) 567-7999
Website: www.cliffcastlecasino.net
Map: **#11** (50 miles S. of Flagstaff)

Toll-Free Number: (800) 381-SLOT
Room Reservation Number: (800) 524-6343
Rooms: 82 Price Range: $80-$100
Suites: 2 Price Range: $105-$135
Restaurants: 7 Liquor: Yes
Casino Size: 14,000 Square Feet
Other Games: BJ, P
Overnight RV Parking: Free/RV Dump: No
Special Features: Casino is in Cliff Castle
Lodge. Bowling alley. Kid's Quest childcare
facility.

Cocopah Resort
15136 S. Avenue B
Somerton, Arizona 85350
(928) 726-8066
Map: **#5** (13 miles S.W. of Yuma)
Website: www.cocopahresort.com

Toll-Free Number: (800) 23-SLOTS
Rooms: 101 Price Range: $87- $107
Suites: 7 Price Range: $127-$187
Restaurants: 2 Liquor: Yes
Buffets: B- $8.00 L-$9.95 D-$12.95
/ $24.95 (Fri)/ $14.95 (Sat-Sun)
Other Games: BJ, BG
Overnight RV Parking: No
Special Features: 18-hole golf course. $3 off
lunch buffet for slot club members.

Desert Diamond Casino - I-19
1100 West Pima Mine Road
Sahuarita, Arizona 85629
(520) 294-7777
Website: www.desertdiamondcasino.com
Map: **#4**

Toll-Free Number: (866) 332-9467
Restaurants: 2 Liquor: Yes
Buffets: L-$6.85/$13.95 (Sun)
D-$8.85/ $15.95 (Mon)
Casino Size: 15,000 Square Feet
Other Games: , BJ, P
Overnight RV Parking: Free/RV Dump: No
Special Features: 2,500-seat event center.

Desert Diamond Casino - Nogales
7350 S. Nogales Highway
Tucson, Arizona 85706
(520) 294-7777
Website: www.desertdiamondcasino.com
Map: **#4**

Toll-Free Number: (866) 332-9467
Rooms: 140 Rates: $86-$196
Suites: 8 Rates: $266-$350
Restaurants: 2 Liquor: Yes
Buffets: L-$6.85/$13.95 (Sun)
D-$8.85/ $15 .95 (Mon)
Casino Size: 15,000 Square Feet
Other Games: BJ, P, K, BG
Overnight RV Parking: Free/RV Dump: No

Desert Diamond Casino - Why
PO Box 10
Ajo, Arizona 85321
(520) 547-4306
Website: www.desertdiamondcasino.com
Map: **#12** (125 miles S.W. of Phoenix)

Toll-Free Number: (866) 332-9467
Restaurants: 1 Snack Bar
Hours: 10am-12am Daily
Other Games: Only machines
Overnight RV Parking: No
Special Features: Located on State Highway
86 at mile post 55 near Why, Arizona

Fort McDowell Casino
P.O. Box 18359
Fountain Hills, Arizona 85269
(480) 837-1424
Website: www.fortmcdowellcasino.com
Map: **#6** (25 miles N.E. of Phoenix)

Toll-Free Number: (800) THE-FORT
Restaurants: 6　Liquor: Yes
Buffets: L/D-$9.50 (Mon-Thu)
　　　　L/D-$9.99 (Fri/Sat)/$14.50 (Sun)
Other Games: BJ, P, K, BG
Overnight RV Parking: No
Special Features: Free local shuttle. Gift shop.

Harrah's Ak Chin Casino Resort
15406 Maricopa Road
Maricopa, Arizona 85239
(480) 802-5000
Website: www.harrahs.com
Map: **#1** (25 miles S. of Phoenix)

Toll-Free Number: (800) HARRAHS
Rooms: 142　Price Range: $109-$299
Suites: 4　Price Range: Casino Use Only
Restaurants: 4　Liquor: Yes
Buffets: L-$11.99/$17.99 (Sun)
　　　　D-$14.99/$21.99 (Fri/Sat)
Casino Size: 43,000 Square Feet
Other Games: BJ, P, K, BG, TCP, LIR, PGP
Overnight RV Parking: Free/RV Dump: No
Senior Discount: Various Mon/Thu if 50+
Special Features: Free local shuttle.

Hon-Dah Resort Casino
777 Highway 260
Pinetop, Arizona 85935
(928) 369-0299
Website: www.hon-dah.com
Map: **#8** (190 miles N.E. of Phoenix)

Toll-Free Number: (800) 929-8744
Rooms: 126　Price Range: $99-$119
Suites: 2　Price Range: $160-$190
Restaurants: 1　Liquor: Yes
Buffets: B/L-$7.95
　　　　D-$8.95/$19.95 (Sat/Sun)
Casino Size: 20,000 Square Feet
Overnight RV Parking: Must use RV park
Other Games: BJ, P
Special Features: 258-space RV park ($27.81 per night). Convenience store. Gas station.

Lone Butte Casino
1200 S. 56th Street
Chandler, Arizona 85226
(520) 796-7777
Website: www.wingilariver.com
Map: **#7** (10 miles S.W. of Phoenix)

Toll-Free Number: (800) WIN-GILA
Restaurants: 3　Liquor: Yes
Casino Size: 10,000 Square Feet
Other Games: BJ, BG, PGP, LIR, TCP
Overnight RV Parking: Free 4 day max/RV
　　　Dump: No

Mazatzal Hotel & Casino
P.O. Box 1820
Hwy. 87, Milemarker 251
Payson, Arizona 85547
(928) 474-6044
Website: www.777play.com
Map: **#9** (90 miles N.E. of Phoenix)

Toll-Free Number: (800) 777-7529
Suites: 40 Prices: $112-$165
Restaurants: 2　Liquor: Yes
Buffets: L-$8.95 (Mon-Sat)
　　　　D-$10.95(Fri)
　　　　Brunch$16.95 (Sun Only)
Casino Size: 35,000 Square Feet
Other Games: BJ, P, K, BG (Mon-Thu)
Overnight RV Parking: Free/RV Dump: No
Senior Discount: 10% off food if 55 or older
Special Features: Offers Stay & Play packages (Sun-Thu) with local motels. Free shuttle.

Paradise Casino Arizona
450 Quechan Drive
Yuma, Arizona 85364
(760) 572-7777
Website: www.paradise-casinos.com
Map: **#5** (244 miles W. of Tucson)

Toll-Free Number: (888) 777-4946
Restaurants: 1　Liquor: Yes
Buffets: B-$5.99　L-$7.99
　　　　D-$9.99/$11.99 (Fri)
Other Games: BG
Overnight RV Parking: Free/RV Dump: No
Special Features: Part of casino is located across the state border in California. Poker offered in CA casino. 10% food discount with slot club card.

Spirit Mountain Casino
8555 South Highway 95
Mohave Valley, Arizona 86440
(928) 346-2000
Map: **#12** (15 miles S. of Bullhead City)

Toll-Free Number: (888) 837-4030
RV Reservations: (928) 346-1225
Restaurants: 1 Snack Bar Liquor: Yes
Casino Size: 12,000 Square Feet
Other Games: Only Machines
Overnight RV Parking: Must use RV park
Special Features: Adjacent to 82-space Spirit
Mountain RV park ($25 per night). Convenience store. Gas station.

Talking Stick Resort
9700 E. Indian Bend
Scottsdale, Arizona 85256
(480) 850-7777
Website: www.talkingstickresort.com
Map: **#6** (15 miles N.E. of Phoenix)

Toll-Free Number: (866) 877-9897
Rooms: 470 Prices: $100-$189
Suites: 27   Prices: $449-$799
Restaurants: 2 Liquor: Yes
Buffet Prices: B-$9.95/(Sun) $26
           L-$12.95 D-$19.95/(Fri/Sat) $24.95
Other Games: BJ, P, TCP, LIR, CW, K
Overnight RV Parking: Free 3 day max/RV Dump: No

Vee Quiva Casino
6443 N. Komatke Lane
Laveen, Arizona 85339
(520) 796-7777
Website: www.wingilariver.com
Map: **#7** (10 miles S.W. of Phoenix)

Toll-Free Number: (800) WIN-GILA
Restaurants: 2   Liquor: Yes
Casino Size: 15,000 Square Feet
Other Games: BJ, P, BG, TCP, PGP
Overnight RV Parking: Free 4 day max/
           RV Dump: No

Wild Horse Pass Hotel & Casino
5040 Wild Horse Pass Blvd
Chandler, Arizona 85226
(520) 796-7727
Website: www.wingilariver.com
Map: **#7** (25 miles S.E. of Phoenix)

Toll-Free Number: (800) 946-4452
Rooms: 223 Rates: $99-$299
Suites: 19 Rates: $169-$369
Restaurants: 2   Liquor: Yes
Casino Size: 100,000 Square Feet
Other Games: BJ, P
Overnight RV Parking: Free 4 day max/
           RV Dump: No
Senior Discount: Various Mon if 50+
Special Features: 1400-seat showroom.

Yavapai Casino
1501 E. Highway 69
Prescott, Arizona 86301
(928) 445-5767
Website: www.buckyscasino.com
Map: **#3** (91 miles S.W. of Flagstaff)

Toll-Free Number: (800) SLOTS-44
Restaurants: 1 Snack Bar Liquor: Yes
Overnight RV Parking: No
Special Features: Located across the street
from Bucky's Casino. Free local-area shuttle
bus.

ARKANSAS

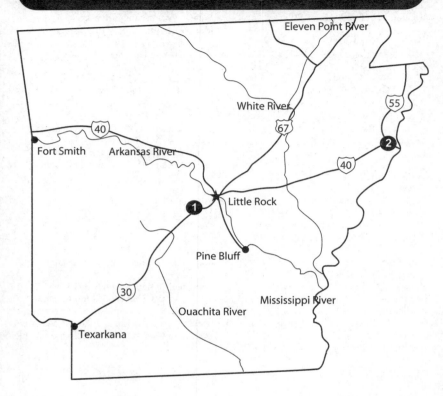

Arkansas has two pari-mutuel facilities featuring "electronic games of skill," which are defined as "games played through any electronic device or machine that affords an opportunity for the exercise of skill or judgment where the outcome is not completely controlled by chance alone."

The games offered are video poker, video blackjack, and "skill" slots where you have two opportunities to spin the reels. The "skill" factor comes into play because after seeing the results of your first spin you then have to decide whether to keep none, one, two, or all three of the symbols on each reel before you spin them again.

Gaming regulations require that all of the electronic games of skill must return a minimum of 83%.

For the one year period from July 2010 through June 2011, the average gaming machine's return at Oaklawn was 93.66% and at Southland it was 94.41%

The minimum gambling age is 21 for slots and 18 for pari-mutuel wagering. For more information on visiting Arkansas call the state's tourism office at (800) 628-8725 or visit their web site at: www.arkansas.com.

Oaklawn Jockey Club
2705 Central Avenue
Hot Springs, Arkansas 71901
(302) 674-4600
Website: www.oaklawn.com
Map: **#1** (55 miles S.W.. of Little Rock)

Toll-Free Number: (800) 625-5296
Restaurants: 3
Buffets: L-$10.50 D-$15.50
Hours: 10am-2am /4am(Fri/Sat)
Other Games: P
Admission: Free Parking: Free
Overnight RV Parking: No
Special Features: Live throroughbred racing Mid-January through Mid-April. Daily simulcasting of horse racing.

Southland Park Gaming & Racing
1550 North Ingram Boulevard
West Memphis, Arkansas 72301
(870) 735-3670
Website: www.southlandgreyhound.com
Map: **#2** (130 miles E. of Little Rock)

Toll-Free Number: (800) 467-6182
Restaurants: 4
Hours: 8am-4am (Sun-Thu)
       Open 24 hours (Fri/Sat)
Other Games: P, LIR, TCP
Admission: Free Parking: Free
Preferred Parking: $3/Valet Parking: $5
Buffets: B- $4.99/$11.99 (Sat)
       L/D-$19.99/$10.99 (Mon)/
       $12.99 (Fri)/$19.99(Sat)
Overnight RV Parking: No
Special Features: Live greyhound racing Mon/Wed-Sat. Daily simulcasting of greyhound and horse racing. Buffet Discount for Player's Club members.

CALIFORNIA

California's Indian casinos are legally allowed to offer electronic gaming machines, blackjack, and other house-banked card games. The games of craps and roulette are not permitted. However, some casinos do offer modified versions of craps and roulette that are played with cards rather than dice or roulette wheels.

Most California card rooms also offer some form of player-banked blackjack, but because they are prohibited by law from playing blackjack, the game is usually played to 22 rather than 21. Additionally, players must pay a commission to the house on every hand they play. The amount will vary depending on the rules of the house but, generally, it's about two to five percent of the total amount bet. There are about 90 card rooms in California and you can see a listing of them on the Internet at: http://www.cgcc.ca.gov

California's tribes aren't required to release information on their slot machine percentage paybacks and the state of California does not require any minimum returns.

Unless otherwise noted, all California casinos are open 24 hours and offer: slots, video poker, and video keno. Optional games offered include: baccarat (B), blackjack (BJ), Spanish 21 (S21), mini-baccarat (MB), poker (P), pai gow poker (PGP), Caribbean stud poker (CSP), let it ride (LIR), three card poker (TCP), four card poker (FCP) bingo (BG), casino war (CW) and off track betting (OTB).

The minimum gambling age is not uniform at all casinos; it is 21 at some casinos and 18 at others. Unless noted otherwise, all casino are open 24 hours.

Although most of the casinos have toll-free numbers be aware that many of those numbers will only work for calls made within California. Also, many of the casinos are in out-of-the-way locations, so it is advisable to call ahead for directions, especially if you will be driving at night.

For more information on visiting California contact the state's department of tourism at (800) 862-2543 or www.visitcalifornia.com.

Agua Caliente Casino
32-250 Bob Hope Drive
Rancho Mirage, California 92270
(760) 321-2000
Website: www.hotwatercasino.com
Map: **#3** (115 miles E. of L. A.)

Toll-Free Number: (888) 999-1995
Gambling Age: 21
Rooms: 340 Price Range: $89-$250
Suites: 22 Price Range $329-$429
Restaurants: 4 Liquor: Yes
Buffets: B/L-$9.99/$23.99 (Sun)
          D-$14.99/$23.99 (Fri-Sat)
Other Games: BJ, MB, CSP, TCP, S21, LIR P, PGP
Overnight RV Parking: Only offered at adjacent Flying J truck stop
Special Features: Associated with Spa Casino. Offers card version of craps.

Augustine Casino
84001 Avenue 54
Coachella, California 92236
(760) 391-9500
Website: www.augustinecasino.com
Map: **#8** (125 miles E. of L. A.)

Toll-Free Number: (888) 752-9294
Gambling Age: 21
Restaurants: 2 Liquor: Yes
Buffets: B-$7.50
          L-$8.95
          D-$11.75/19.95 (Fri) $27.50 (Sat)
Other Games: BJ, TCP, S21
Overnight RV Parking: No

Barona Valley Ranch Resort and Casino
1932 Wildcat Canyon Road
Lakeside, California 92040
(619) 443-2300
Website: www.barona.com
Map: **#1** (15 miles N.E. of San Diego)

Toll-Free Number: (888) 7-BARONA
Room Reservations: (877) 287-2624
Gambling Age: 18
Rooms: 397 Price Range: $129-$279

Suites: 9 Price Range: Private Use Only
Restaurants: 8   Liquor: Yes
Buffets: B/L/D-$20.99
Other Games: BJ, B, MB, P, CSP, PGP,
               TCP, LIR, CW, OTB, FCP
Overnight RV Parking: Free 3 day Max
/RV Dump: No
Special Features: Offers card versions of
roulette and craps. Food court. Wedding
chapel. 18-hole golf course. Buffet discounts
for slot club members.

Bear River Casino
11 Bear Paws Way
Loleta, California 95551
(707) 733-9644
Website: www.bearrivercasino.com
Map: **#38** (10 miles S. of Eureka)

Toll-Free Number: (800) 761-BEAR
Gambling Age: 21
Hours: 9am-5am/ 24 hours (Fri/Sat)
Restaurants: 2 Liquor: Yes
Buffet: D- $15.95 (Wed)
Casino Size: 31,000 Square Feet
Other Games: BJ, S21, P, PGP, TCP
Overnight RV Parking: Yes check in with
security first

Black Oak Casino
19400 Tuolumne Road North
Tuolumne, California 95379
(209) 928-9300
Website: www.blackoakcasino.com
Map: **#5** (100 miles S.E. of Sacramento)

Toll-Free Number: (877) 747-8777
Gambling Age: 21
Restaurants: 6 Liquor: Yes
Buffet: Brunch-$12.95 (Sat)/ $14.95 (Sun)
    L- $7.99(Mon-Fri)
    D-$12.99/$21.99 (Fri)/$18.99 (Sat)
Casino Size: 22,000 Square Feet
Other Games: BJ, TCP, LIR, PGP, S21, FCP
Overnight RV Parking: Free/RV Dump: No

Blue Lake Casino & Hotel
777 Casino Way
Blue Lake, California 95525
(707) 668-9770
Website: www.bluelakecasino.com
Map: **#34** (10 miles N. of Eureka)

Toll-Free Number: (877) BLC-2WIN
Gambling Age: 21
Rooms: 102 Rates: $95-$105
Suites: 12 Rates: $175-$295
Restaurants: 2 Liquor: Yes
Other Games: BJ, S21, P, TCP, FCP,
    PGP, BG (Mon/Tue)
Overnight RV Parking: Free/RV Dump: No

Cache Creek Indian Bingo & Casino
14455 Highway 16
Brooks, California 95606
(530) 796-3118
Website: www.cachecreek.com
Map: **#2** (35 miles N.W. of Sacramento)

Toll-Free Number: (800) 452-8181
Gambling Age: 21
Room Reservations: (888) 772-2243
Rooms: 173 Prices: $139-$285
Suites: 27 Prices: $159-$349
Restaurants: 9 Liquor: Yes
Buffets: L/D-$9.99/$19.99 (Sat)
Casino Size: 18,000 Square Feet
Other Games: BJ, P, CSP, LIR, PGP,
             TCP, B, MB, FCP, CW
Overnight RV Parking: Free/RV Dump: No
Senior Discount: $2 off buffet if 55 or older
Special Features: Offers card versions of craps
and roulette. Full-service spa. No buffet Wed
or Thu.

Cahuilla Casino
52702 Highway 371
Anza, California 92539
(951) 763-1200
Website: www.cahuillacasino.com
Map: **#19** (30 miles S. of Palm Springs)

Toll-Free Number: (888) 371-2692
Restaurants: 2 Liquor: Yes
Other Games: BJ
Overnight RV Parking: Free/RV Dump: No

Casino Pauma
777 Pauma Reservation Road
Pauma Valley, California 92061
(760) 742-2177
Website: www.casinopauma.com
Map: **#20** (35 miles N.E. of San Diego)

Toll-Free Number: (877) 687-2862
Gambling Age: 18
Restaurants: 1 Liquor: Yes
Buffets: L-$9.00
Casino Size: 35,000 Square Feet
Other Games: BJ, P, PGP, TCP, LIR
Overnight RV Parking: Free/RV Dump: No
Senior Discount: 50% off lunch buffet if 55+
Special Features: Offers card versions of craps
and roulette.

Cherae Heights Casino
P.O. Box 635
Trinidad, California 95570
(707) 677-3611
Website: www.cheraeheightscasino.com
Map: **#4** (25 miles N. of Eureka)

Toll-Free Number: (800) 684-BINGO
Gambling Age: 21
Restaurants: 3 Liquor: Yes
Other Games: BJ, S21, P, PGP, TCP,
          BG (Wed-Sun)
Overnight RV Parking: Free/RV Dump: No

Chicken Ranch Bingo
16929 Chicken Ranch Road
Jamestown, California 95327
(209) 984-3000
Map: **#5** (100 miles S.E. of Sacramento)

Toll-Free Number: (800) 752-4646
Gambling Age: 18
Restaurants: 1 Snack Bar Liquor: No
Hours: 10am-12am (Mon-Thu)
       9am-1am (Fri-Sun)
Casino Size: 30,000 Square Feet
Other Games: Slots only, BG (Thu-Sun)
Overnight RV Parking: No

Chukchansi Gold Resort & Casino
711 Lucky Lane
Coarsegold, California 93614
(559) 692-5200
Website: www.chukchansigold.com
Map: **#25** (35 miles N. of Fresno)

Toll-Free Number: (866) 794-6946
Gambling Age: 21
Rooms: 190 Prices: $99-$199
Suites: 6 Prices: Casino Use Only
Restaurants: 7 Liquor: Yes
Buffets: B- $8.99/ $10.99 (Sun)
        L-$12.00/$14.00 (Sun)
        D-$12.00/$14.00 (Wed)/$20.00(Fri/Sat)
Other Games: BJ, S21, TCP, PGP, LIR
Overnight RV Parking: Free/RV Dump: No
Senior Discount: $5.99 lunch buffet if 55+

Chumash Casino Resort
3400 East Highway 246
Santa Ynez, California 93460
(805) 686-0855
Website: www.chumashcasino.com
Map: **#13** (40 miles N.W. of Santa Barbara)

Toll-Free Number: (800) 728-9997
Gambling Age: 18
Room Reservations: (800) 248-6274
Rooms: 89 Prices: $195-$350
Suites: 17 Prices: $380-$550
Restaurants: 3 Liquor: No
Buffets: L-$14.99 (Mon-Fri)/ $19.95 (Sun)
         D-$14.95(Mon)/19.95(Tue/Wed)
         $24.95 (Fri-Sun)
Casino Size: 94,000 Square Feet
Other Games: S21, BJ, P, CW, BG (Sun-Wed),
         TCP, FCP, LIR, MB
Overnight RV Parking: No
Special Features: Spa.

Colusa Casino Resort
3770 Highway 45
Colusa, California 95932
(530) 458-8844
Website: www.colusacasino.com
Map: **#6** (75 miles N. of Sacramento)

Toll-Free Recording: (800) 655-8946
Gambling Age: 21
Room Reservations: (877) 869-7829
Rooms: 50 Prices: $119-$139
Suites: 10 Prices: $199-$219
Restaurants: 3 Liquor: Yes
Buffets: B- $7.95 L-$8.95
          D-$10.95/ $19.95 (Fri/Sat)
Other Games: BJ, MB, P, TCP, PGP,
          BG (Sat-Wed)
Overnight RV Parking: Free/RV Dump: No

Coyote Valley Casino
7751 N. State Street
Redwood Valley, California 95470
(707) 485-0700
Website: www.coyotevalleycasino.com
Map: **#23** (115 miles N. of San Francisco)

Toll-Free Number: (800) 332-9683
Gambling Age: 21
Restaurants: 1 Cafe Liquor: Yes
Other Games: BJ, TCP, PGP, P
Overnight RV Parking: Free/RV Dump: No

Desert Rose Casino
901 County Road 56
Alturas, California 96101
(530) 233-3141
Map: **#27** (250 miles N.E. of Sacramento)

Gambling Age: 21
Restaurants: 1 Snack Bar Liquor: Yes
Hours: 9am-12am/2am (Fri/Sat)
Casino Size: 5,000 Square Feet
Other Games: BJ
Overnight RV Parking: Free/RV Dump: No
Senior Discount: Monday specials from
10am to 6pm if 55 +

Diamond Mountain Casino and Hotel
900 Skyline Drive
Susanville, California 96130
(530) 252-1100
Website: www.diamondmountaincasino.com
Map: **#31** (160 Miles N.E. of Sacramento)

Toll-Free Number: (877) 319-8514
Gambling Age: 21
Rooms: 63 Prices: $79-$109
Suites: 7 Prices: $119-$189
Restaurants: 2 Liquor: Yes
Buffets: B-$9.95 D-$15.95 (Sun)
Casino Size: 26,000 Square Feet
Other Games: BJ, P BG (Tue/Sun)
Overnight RV Parking: Free/RV Dump: No
Senior Discount: 50% off in lava cafe for 55+
from 3-5 pm

Eagle Mountain Casino
P.O. Box 1659
Porterville, California 93258
(559) 788-6220
Website: www.eaglemtncasino.com
Map: **#21** (60 miles S.E. of Fresno)

Toll-Free Number: (800) 903-3353
Gambling Age: 18
Hours: 11am-4am/ 24 hours (Fri/Sat)
Restaurants: 2 Liquor: No
Buffets: L-$10.50 D-$11.50/$13.00 (Fri/Sat)
Casino Size: 9,600 Square Feet
Other Games: BJ, P, PGP, TCP
Overnight RV Parking: Free/RV Dump: No
Special Features: Food Court with four fast
food stations.

Elk Valley Casino
2500 Howland Hill Road
Crescent City, California 95531
(707) 464-1020
Website: www.elkvalleycasino.com
Map: **#7** (84 miles N. of Eureka)

Toll-Free Number: (888) 574-2744
Gambling Age: 21
Restaurants: 1 Liquor: Yes
Buffets: L-$7.95 (Tue)
        D-$14.99 (Wed)
Casino Size: 23,000 Square Feet
Other Games: BJ, P, BG (Sun/Mon/Tue/Fri)
Overnight RV Parking: No
Senior Discount: $3.95 lunches on Tuesdays.
Buffet discount for slot club members.

Fantasy Springs Casino
82-245 Indio Springs Drive
Indio, California 92203
(760) 342-5000
Website: www.fantasyspringsresort.com
Map: **#8** (125 miles E. of Los Angeles)

Toll-Free Number: (800) 827-2WIN
Gambling Age: 21
Rooms: 250 Prices: $129-$209
Suites: 11 Prices: $299-$399
Restaurants: 6 Liquor: Yes
Buffets: L-$12.99 D-$17.99/$22.99 (Fri-Sat)
        Brunch-$21.99 (Sun)
Casino Size: 95,000 Square Feet
Other Games: BJ, S21, MB, P, LIR, PGP,
        TCP, FCP, BG, OTB
Overnight RV Parking: Free/RV Dump: No
Special Features: 24-lane bowling center.
5,000-seat special events center. Card version
of craps. Golf course.

Feather Falls Casino
3 Alverda Drive
Oroville, California 95966
(530) 533-3885
Website: www.featherfallscasino.com
Map: **#22** (100 miles N. of Sacramento)

Toll-Free Number: (877) OK-BINGO
Gambling Age: 21
Rooms: 74 Prices: $79-$89
Suites: 10 Prices: $180-$280
Restaurants: 2 Liquor: Yes
Buffets: L-$7.95/$9.50 (Sat/Sun)
　　　　D-$10.95/$16.95 (Fri/Sat)
Casino Size: 38,000 Square Feet
Other Games: BJ, P
Overnight RV Parking: No
Senior Discount: Various on Mon/Wed if 55+

Gold Country Casino
4020 Olive Highway
Oroville, California 95966
(530) 538-4560
Website: www.goldcountrycasino.com
Map: **#22** (100 miles N. of Sacramento)

Toll-Free Number: (800) 334-9400
Gambling Age: 21
Rooms: 87 Prices: $59-$139
Restaurants: 3 Liquor: Yes
Buffets: L-$8.49(Wed-Fri)/$10.99 (Sat/Sun)
　　　　D-$10.49/$17.99 (Fri/Sat)
Other Games: BJ, P, TCP, MB
　　　　PGP, FCP, BG (Wed-Sun)
Overnight RV Parking: Free/RV Dump: No
Senior discount: 10% off buffet if 55+
Special Features: 1,200-seat showroom.

Golden Acorn Casino and Travel Center
1800 Golden Acorn Way
Campo, CA 91906
(619) 938-6000
Website: www.goldenacorncasino.com
Map: **#33** (40 miles S.E. of San Diego)

Toll-Free Number: (866) 794-6244
Gambling Age: 18
Restaurants: 2 Liquor: Yes
Other Games: BJ, TCP
Overnight RV Parking: Free/RV Dump: No
Special Features: 33-acre auto/truck stop and convenience store.

Harrah's Rincon Casino & Resort
33750 Valley Center Road
Valley Center, California 92082
(760) 751-3100
Website: www.harrahs.com
Map: **#20** (35 miles N.E. of San Diego)

Toll-Free Number: (877) 777-2457
Gambling Age: 21
Rooms: 552 Prices: $89-$409
Suites: 101 Prices: $129-$609
Restaurants: 7 Liquor: Yes
Buffets: B-$20.99 (Sat/Sun) L-$17.99
　　　　D-$23.99/$28.99 (Fri/Sat)
Casino Size: 55,000 Square Feet
Other Games: BJ, PGP, MB, P, TCP, LIR
Overnight RV Parking: Free/RV Dump: No
Special Features: Card version of craps and roulette.

Havasu Landing Resort & Casino
5 Main Street
Havasu Lake, California 92363
(760) 858-4593
Website: www.havasulanding.com
Map: **#18** (200 miles E. of L. A.)

Toll Free Number: (800) 307-3610
Gambling Age: 21
Restaurants: 1 Liquor: Yes
Hours: 8:30am-12:30am/2:30am (Fri/Sat)
Other Games: BJ, TCP
Overnight RV Parking: Must use RV park
Casino Size: 6,000 Square Feet
Special Features: Tables open 11:30 am/
2:30 pm (Mon-Thu). Marina, RV park ($25 per night), campground rentals. Mobile homes available for daily rental.

Hopland Sho-Ka-Wah Casino
13101 Nakomis Road
Hopland, California 95449
(707) 744-1395
Website: www.shokawah.com
Map: **#23** (100 miles N. of San Francisco)

Toll Free Number: (888) 746-5292
Gambling Age: 21
Restaurants: 2 Liquor: Yes
Other Games: BJ, PGP
Overnight RV Parking: Free/RV Dump: No

Jackson Rancheria Casino & Hotel
12222 New York Ranch Road
Jackson, California 95642
(209) 223-1677
Website: www.jacksoncasino.com
Map: **#9** (60 miles S.E. of Sacramento)

Toll-Free Number: (800) 822-WINN
Gambling Age: 18
Rooms: 126 Price Range: $99-$149
Suites: 20 Price Range: $199-$399
Restaurants: 6 Liquor: No (only with dinner)
Buffets: B-$8.00/$15.00 (Sun)
         L-$10.00 (Mon-Fri)
         D-$7.00/$19.95 (Fri)
Other Games: BJ, PGP, LIR, TCP, CW,
         FCP, MB, P
Overnight RV Parking: Must use RV park
/RV Dump: No
Senior Discount: 10% off buffet if 55 or older
Special Features: 1,500-seat showroom. 100
space RV park ($40 per night) .

Konocti Vista Casino Resort & Marina
2755 Mission Rancheria Road
Lakeport, California 95453
(707) 262-1900
Website: www.kvcasino.com
Map: **#23** (120 miles N. of San Francisco)

Toll-Free Number: (800) 386-1950
Gambling Age: 21
Rooms: 80 Prices: $79-$139
Restaurants: 1 Liquor: Yes
Other Games: BJ, PGP
Overnight RV Parking: Must use RV park
RV Dump: Free
Special Features: Marina with 80 slips.
74-space RV park ($25 per night).

La Posta Casino
777 Crestwood Road
Boulevard, California 91905
(619) 824-4100
Website: www.lapostacasino.com
Map: **#33** (60 miles E. of San Diego)

Gambling Age: 21
Restaurants: 1 Liquor: No
Hours: 6am-2am/ 24hrs (Fri-Sun)
Other Games: Only Machines
Overnight RV Parking: Yes/RV Dump: No

Lucky Bear Casino
P.O. Box 729
Hoopa, California 95546
(530) 625-5198
Map: **#24** (30 miles N.E. of Eureka)

Gambling Age: 18
Restaurants: 1 Snack Bar Liquor: No
Hours: 10am-Mid/1am (Fri/Sat)
Other Games: BJ
Overnight RV Parking: No
Special Features: Non-smoking casino.

Lucky 7 Casino
350 N. Indian Road
Smith River, California 95567
(707) 487-7777
Website: www.lucky7casino.com
Map: **#7** (100 miles N. of Eureka)

Toll-Free Number: (866) 777-7170
Gambling Age: 21
Restaurants: 1 Liquor: Yes
Other Games: BJ, BG (Sun/Tue/Wed), P
Overnight RV Parking: Free/RV Dump: No
Casino Size: 24,000 Square Feet

Mono Wind Casino
37302 Rancheria Lane
Auberry, California 93602
(559) 855-4350
Website: www.monowind.com
Map: **#25** (30 miles N.E. of Fresno)

Gambling Age: 18
Restaurants: 1 Liquor: Yes
Overnight RV Parking: Free/RV Dump: No
Casino Size: 10,000 Square Feet

Morongo Casino Resort and Spa
49750 Seminole Drive
Cabazon, California 92230
(951) 849-3080
Website: www.morongocasinoresort.com
Map: **#3** (90 miles E. of L. A.)

Toll-Free Number: (800) 252-4499
Gambling Age: 18
Rooms: 310 Prices: $89-$269
Suites: 32 Prices: $269-$499
Restaurants: 5 Liquor: Yes
Buffets: B $19.95 (Sun) L-$10.95
　　　D-$14.95/$19.95 (Fri)/
　　　$18.95 (Sat/Sun)
Casino Size: 145,000 Square Feet
Other Games: BJ, P, TCP, FCP, MB, PGP, BG
Overnight RV Parking: Free/RV Dump: No
Special Features: Card version of craps.

Paiute Palace Casino
2742 N. Sierra Highway
Bishop, California 93514
(760) 873-4150
Website: www.paiutepalace.com
Map: **#26** (130 miles N.E. of Fresno)

Toll-Free Number: (888) 3-PAIUTE
Gambling Age: 18
Restaurants: 1 Liquor: No
Other Games: BJ, P
Overnight RV Parking: Free/RV Dump: No
Senior Discount: 10% off in restaurant if 55+
Special Features: 24-hour gas station and convenience store.

Pala Casino Spa and Resort
11154 Highway 76
Pala, California 92059
(760) 510-5100
Website: www.palacasino.com
Map: **#20** (35 miles N.E. of San Diego)

Toll-Free Number: (877) 946-7252
Gambling Age: 21
Room Reservations: (877) 725-2766
Rooms: 425 Prices: $129-$209
Suites: 82 Prices: $139-$360
Restaurants: 8 Liquor: Yes
Buffets: B-$21.99 (Sat/Sun)
　　　L-$18.99
　　　D-$24.99/$29.99 (Fri-Sun)
Other Games: BJ, B, MB, TCP, PGP,
　　　LIR
Overnight RV Parking: Free (park in west lot)
RV Dump: No
Special Features: Offers card versions of craps and roulette. Fitness center and spa. Discount on buffet if player's club member.

Pechanga Resort and Casino
45000 Pechanga Parkway
Temecula, California 92592
(951) 693-1819
Website: www.pechanga.com
Map: **#28** (50 miles N. of San Diego)

Toll-Free Number: (877) 711-2946
Gambling Age: 21
Room Reservations: (888) PECHANGA
Rooms: 458 Price Range: $109-$349
Suites: 64 Price Range: $179-$750
Restaurants: 8 Liquor: Yes
Buffets: B-$19.99 (Sat/Sun) L-$16.99
　　　D- $21.99/$26.99 (Fri/Sat)
Other Games: BJ, MB, P, PGP, LIR, TCP
Overnight RV Parking: Must use RV park
RV Dump: $14.00 charge to use
Casino Size: 88,000 Square Feet
Special Features: 168-space RV park ($42 per night/$52 Fri-Sat). Offers card version of craps.

Pit River Casino
20265 Tamarack Avenue
Burney, California 96013
(530) 335-2334
Website: www.pitrivercasino.com
Map: **#29** (190 miles N. of Sacramento)

Toll-Free Number: (888) 245-2992
Gambling Age: 18
Restaurants: 1 Snack Bar Liquor: No
Casino Hours: 9am-12am/2am (Fri/Sat)
Other Games: BJ, P
Overnight RV Parking: Free/RV Dump: No
Senior Discount: $5 match play and lunch
special on Mondays if 55 or older.
Special Features: Tables open at 6pm/2pm
(Sat/Sun)

Quechan Casino Resort
525 Algodones Road
WinterHaven, California 92283
(760) 572-3900
Website: www.playqcr.net
Map: **#37** (170 miles E. of San Diego)

Toll-Free Number: (877) 783-2426
Rooms: 158 Price Range: $109-$129
Suites: 8 Price Range: $225-$750
Gambling Age: 21
Restaurants: 2 Liquor: Yes
Buffet:B-$6.99 L-$9.99
        D-$11.99/$16.99(Fri-Sat)
Other Games: BJ, P, PGP, TCP
Overnight RV Parking: Free/RV Dump: No
Special Features: Part of casino is located
across the state border in Arizona. Offers video
versions of craps and roulette. 10% off food
with slot club card. $1.99 breakfast special.

Red Earth Casino
3089 Norm Niver Road
Salton City, California 92274
(760) 395-1700
Website: www.redearthcasino.com
Map: **#39** (114 miles S.E. of Riverside)

Gambling Age: 21
Restaurants: 1 Liquor: Yes
Casino Size: 10,000 Square Feet
Other Games: BJ
Overnight RV Parking: Free/RV Dump: No

Red Fox Casino
300 Cahto Drive
Laytonville, California 95454
(707) 984-6800
Website: www.redfoxcasino.net
Map: **#30** (150 miles N.W. of Sacramento)

Toll-Free Number: (888) 4-RED-FOX
Gambling Age: 18
Restaurants: 1 Snack Bar Liquor: No
Hours: 10am-Mid
Overnight RV Parking: Free/RV Dump: No

Red Hawk Casino
5250 Honpie Road
Placerville, California 95667
(530) 677-7000
Website: Redhawkcasino.com
Map: **#40** (40 miles E of Sacramento)

Toll-Free Number: (888) 573-3495
Gambling Age: 21
Restaurants: 6 Liquor: Yes
Buffets: B- $8.99/$18.99 (Sun)
        L-$9.99/$11.99 (Sat)
        D-$13.99/$19.99 (Fri/Sat)/$15.99 (Sun)
Other Games: BJ, P, PGP, TCP, LIR, MB
Special Features: Childcare facility.
Shopping arcade. Offers a card version of
craps.

River Rock Casino
3250 Hwy 128 East
Geyserville, California 95441
(707) 857-2777
Website: www.riverrockcasino.com
Map: **#32** (75 miles N. of San Fran.)

Gambling Age: 21
Restaurants: 2 Liquor: Yes
Buffets: B-$13.99 L-$9.99
        D-$12.99
Other Games: BJ, MB, P, PGP
Overnight RV Parking: No

Robinson Rancheria Resort & Casino
1545 E. Highway 20
Nice, California 95464
(707)275-9000
Website: www.robinsonrancheria.biz
Map: **#11** (100 miles N.W. of Sacramento)

Toll-Free Number: (800) 809-3636
Gambling Age: 21
Rooms: 49 Price Range: $69-$129
Suites: 2 Price Range: $175-$295
Restaurants: 2 Liquor: Yes
Buffets: B-$9.95 (Sun)
　　　　D-$11.95//$16.95 (Thu)/
　　　　$17.95 (Fri/Sat)
Casino Size: 37,500 Square Feet
Other Games: BJ, P, PGP, LIR, TCP,
　　　　MB, BG (Sun-Wed)
Overnight RV Parking: Free (one night only)
RV Dump: No
Senior Discount: Various on Wed if 55+
Special Features: 60-site RV park ($18/$25
per night), 2.5 miles from casino.

Rolling Hills Casino
2655 Barham Avenue
Corning, California 96021
(530) 528-3500
Website: www.rollinghillscasino.com
Map: **#36** (115 miles N. of Sacramento)

Toll-Free Number: (888) 331-6400
Gambling Age: 21
Rooms: 90 Price Range: $99-$169
Suites: 21 Price Range: $159-$210
Restaurants: 2 Liquor: Yes
Buffet: B-$8.95 L-$10.95
　　　　D-$15.95/$19.95(Fri/Sat)
Casino Size: 60,000 Square Feet
Other Games: BJ, PGP, TCP
Overnight RV Parking: Free in truck lot
RV Dump: Only for those staying in RV Park
Senior Discount: Various Tue/Thu if 50+
Special Features: 48-space RV park ($25 per
night).

San Manuel Indian Bingo & Casino
5797 North Victoria Avenue
Highland, California 92346
(909) 864-5050
Website: www.sanmanuel.com
Map: **#12** (65 miles E. of L. A.)

Toll-Free Number: (800) 359-2464
Gambling Age: 21
Restaurants: 5 Liquor: Yes
Buffet: L-$11.95/ $15.95 (Sun)
　　　　D-$15.95/$22.95(Fri-Sat)
Casino Size: 75,000 Square Feet
Other Games: BJ, MB, P, PGP, LIR, TCP,
　　　　FCP, BG
Overnight RV Parking: Free/RV Dump: No
Senior Discount: Special bingo price Fri if 55+
Special Features: Food Court with 3 fast food
dining stations. Offers a card version of Craps.

San Pablo Lytton Casino
13255 San Pablo Ave
San Pablo, CA 94806
(510) 215-7888

Gambling Age: 21
Restaurants: 2
Other Games: BJ, TCP, B, PG
Special Features: All machines are Class-II
gaming machines based on bingo. All table
game players must place $1 ante for every
$100 bet.

Santa Ysabel Resort and Casino
25575 Highway 79
Santa Ysabel, California 92070
(760) 782-0909
Website: santaysabelresortandcasino.com
Map: **#1** (52 miles N.E. of San Diego)

Restaurants: 1 Liquor: Yes
Gambling Age: 21
Casino hours: 6:30am-2am/24 hours (Fri/Sat)
Other Games: BJ, B, P
Overnight RV Parking: Free/RV Dump: No

Sherwood Valley Rancheria Casino
100 Kawi Place
Willits, California 95490
(707) 459-7330
Website: blackbartcasino.com
Map: **#11** (130 miles N. of San Francisco)

Restaurants: 1 Deli Liquor: No
Casino Size: 6,000 Square Feet
Other Games: Slots Only
Overnight RV Parking: Free/RV Dump: No

Soboba Casino
23333 Soboba Road
San Jacinto, California 92583
(909) 654-2883
Website: www.soboba.net
Map: **#3** (90 miles E. of L. A.)

Toll-Free Number: (866) 4-SOBOBA
Gambling Age: 21
Restaurants: 1 Liquor: Yes
Casino Size: 52,000 Square Feet
Other Games: BJ, S21, MB, P, PGP, LIR,
TCP, FCP, BG
Overnight RV Parking: Free/RV Dump: No

Spa Resort Casino
140 N. Indian Canyon Drive
Palm Springs, California 92262
(760) 323-5865
Website: www.sparesortcasino.com
Map: **#3** (115 miles E. of L. A.)

Toll-Free Number: (800) 258-2WIN
Gambling Age: 21
Room Reservations: (800) 854-1279
Rooms: 213 Price Range: $109-$329
Suites: 15 Price Range: $199-$1,700
Restaurants: 5 (1 open 24 hours) Liquor: Yes
Buffets: B-$9.99/$23.99 (Sun) L-$14.99
D-$19.99/$23.99 (Fri-Sat)
Casino Size: 15,000 Square Feet
Other Games: BJ, MB, P, PGP, TCP, FCP, LIR
Overnight RV Parking: No
Special Features: Hotel offers hot mineral spa
with massages and facials.

Spotlight 29 Casino
46200 Harrison Place
Coachella, California 92236
(760) 775-5566
Website: www.spotlight29.com
Map: **#8** (130 miles E. of L. A.)

Toll-Free Number: (866) 377-6829
Gambling Age: 21
Restaurants: 2 Liquor: Yes
Buffets: L-$9.95 D-$14.95/$18.95 (Fri)
Other Games: BJ, MB, P, PGP, TCP
Overnight RV Parking: Free/RV Dump: No
Special Features: Three fast-food outlets
including McDonald's. 2,200-seat showroom.
Special Breakfast buffet for slot club members.

Sycuan Resort & Casino
5469 Casino Way
El Cajon, California 92019
(619) 445-6002
Website: www.sycuan.com
Map: **#14** (10 miles E. of San Diego)

Toll-Free Number: (800) 279-2826
Gambling Age: 21
Room Reservations: (800) 457-5568
Rooms: 103 Price Range: $125-$185
Suites: 14 Price Range: $150-$3550
Restaurants: 4 Liquor: Yes
Buffets: L/D-$19.95
Casino Size: 73,000 Square Feet
Other Games: BJ, S21, P, BG, CW, TCP,
CSP, FCP, OTB, PGP
Overnight RV Parking: Free/RV Dump: No
Senior Discount: Various Wed 7-11am if 55+
Special Features: Offers card/tile versions of
roulette and craps. Hotel is three miles from
casino with free shuttle service. Three 18-hole
golf courses. 500-seat showroom.

Table Mountain Casino & Bingo
8184 Table Mountain Road
Friant, California 93626
(559) 822-2485
Website: www.tmcasino.com
Map: **#15** (15 miles N. of Fresno)

Toll-Free Number: (800) 541-3637
Gambling Age: 18
Restaurants: 3 Liquor: No
Buffets: B- $12.00 (Sat/Sun)
    L-$12.00/$14.00 (Sat/Sun)
    D-$12.00/$19.00 (Fri/Sat)
Other Games: BJ, S21, P, PGP, TCP,
    BG, CW
Overnight RV Parking: Free/RV Dump: No
Senior Discount: Buffet discount Mon-Fri
if 55+

Tachi Palace Hotel and Casino
17225 Jersey Avenue
Lemoore, California 93245
(559) 924-7751
Website: www.tachipalace.com
Map: **#10** (50 miles S. of Fresno)

Toll-Free Number: (800) 942-6886
Gambling Age: 18
Room Reservations: (800) 615-8030
Rooms: 215 Price Range: $89-$209
Suites: 40 Price Range: $149-$250
Restaurants: 2 Liquor: Yes
Buffets: B-$10.99 (Sat/Sun)
    L-$7.99 (Mon-Thurs)/$8.99 (Fri)/
    $10.99 (Sat-Sun)
    D-$11.99/ $12.99 (Fri-Sat)
Casino Size: 50,000 Square Feet
Other Games: BJ, P, PGP, TCP,
    FCP, MB, BG
Overnight RV Parking: Free/RV Dump: No
Senior Discount: $5.99 lunch buffet if 55+
Special Features: Offers a card-based version
of roulette.

Thunder Valley Casino
1200 Athens Ave
Lincoln, California 95648
(916) 408-7777
Website: www.thundervalleyresort.com
Map: **#35** (35 miles N.E. of Sacramento)

Toll-Free Number: (877) 468-8777
Gambling Age: 21
Rooms: 297 Price Range: $115-$189
Suites: 40 Price Range: $300-$399
Restaurants: 4 Liquor: Yes
Buffets: B-$16.95 (Sun)
    L-$10.95
    D-$14.95/$26.95 (Fri)/ $25.95 (Sat)
Other Games: BJ, MB, PGP, P, LIR, TCP, FCP
Overnight RV Parking: No
Special Features: Affiliated with Station
Casinos of Las Vegas. Five fast-food outlets.
Buffet discount with player's card.

Twin Pine Casino
22223 Highway 29 at Rancheria Road
Middletown, California 95461
(707) 987-0197
Website: www.twinpine.com
Map: **#32** (70 miles W. of Sacramento)

Toll-Free Number: (800) 564-4872
Rooms: 60 Price Range: $89-$109
Suites: 3 Price Range: $149-$250
Gambling Age: 21
Restaurants: 1 Liquor: No
Other Games: BJ, PGP, TCP
Overnight RV Parking: No/RV Dump: No
Senior Discount: Various Tue/Thu mornings
8:30 am-12:00 pm if 55+.

Valley View Casino Resort
16300 Nyemii Pass Road
Valley Center, California 92082
(760) 291-5500
Website: www.valleyviewcasino.com
Map: **#20** (35 miles N.E. of San Diego)

Toll-Free Number: (866) 843-9946
Gambling Age: 21
Restaurants: 2   Liquor: Yes
Buffets:B- $22.99 (Sat-Sun)
          L-$19.99
          D-$27.99
Other Games: BJ, PGP, TCP, B
Overnight RV Parking: Free/RV Dump: No
Special Features: Slot club members receive
$3 off buffets. Offers card-based version of
Roulette.

Viejas Casino
5000 Willows Road
Alpine, California 91901
(619) 445-5400
Website: www.viejas.com
Map: **#16** (25 miles E. of San Diego)

Toll-Free Number: (800) 84-POKER
Gambling Age: 18
Restaurants: 6   Liquor: Yes
Buffets: Brunch- $12.95 (Sat-Sun)
          L-$9.95/$15.95(Sun)
          D-$14.95
Other Games: BJ, B, MB, P, CSP, LIR, TCP
          FCP, CW, PGP, BG, OTB
Overnight RV Parking: Free/RV Dump: No
Special Features: 51-store factory outlet
shopping center. Buffet discounts for slot
club members. Card-based versions of craps
and roulette.

Win-River Casino
2100 Redding Rancheria Road
Redding, California 96001
(530) 243-3377
Website: www.winrivercasino.com
Map: **#17** (163 miles N. of Sacramento)

Toll-Free Number: (800) 280-8946
Gambling Age: 21
Restaurants: 1   Liquor: Yes
Buffets: B- $17.99 (Sun) D- $7.99 (Sun)
Casino Size: 37,000 Square Feet
Other Games: BJ,TCP, PGP, FCP,
          P, BG (Sun-Wed)
Overnight RV Parking: Free/RV Dump: No
Special Features: Comedy club. Food
discounts for slot club members. 1,000-seat
showroom.

COLORADO

Colorado casinos can be found in the mountain towns of Black Hawk, Central City and Cripple Creek. There are also two Indian casinos (which abide by Colorado's limited gaming rules) in Ignacio and Towaoc.

When casino gambling was initally introduced in 1991 it was limited in that only electronic games (including slots, video poker, video blackjack and video keno) and the table games of poker, blackjack, let it ride and three-card poker were allowed. Plus, a single wager could not exceed $5.

All that changed, however, on July 2, 2009 when the maximum bet was raised to $100, plus the games of craps and roulette were added to the mix. Additonally, the casinos were allowed to stay open for 24 hours, rather than having to be closed between 2 a.m. and 8 a.m.

Here's information, as supplied by Colorado's Division of Gaming, showing the slot machine payback percentages for each city's casinos for the one-year period from July 1, 2010 through June 30, 2011:

	Black Hawk	Central City	Cripple Creek
1¢ Slots	90.12%	91.32%	**91.75%**
5¢ Slots	93.26%	**93.99%**	93.28%
25¢ Slots	93.84%	94.14%	**95.35%**
$1 Slots	94.54%	**95.73%**	95.07%
$5 Slots	95.22%	94.30%	**95.31%**
All	92.89%	93.52%	**93.75%**

These numbers reflect the percentage of money returned on each denomination of machine and encompass all electronic machines including video poker and video keno. The best returns for each category are highlighted in bold print.

The minimum gambling age at all Colorado casinos is 21, including indian casinos.

The major gaming-oriented magazine in Colorado is *The Gambler*. It is free, and available in most casinos. Look in it for ads for casino coupons or fun books. The *Denver Post* Weekend section (published every Friday) also contains coupons and fun book offers for the casinos in Black Hawk and Central City.

For information on visiting Black Hawk or Central City, call (877) 282-8804, or visit their web site at: www.visitbhcc.com. For Cripple Creek information call (877) 858-GOLD.

For general information on Colorado contact the state's tourism board at (800) 433-2656 or www.colorado.com.

Black Hawk

Map Location: **#1** (35 miles west of Denver. Take U.S. 6 through Golden to Hwy 119. Take Hwy 119 to Black Hawk. Another route is I-70 West to exit 244. Turn right onto Hwy. 6. Take Hwy 6 to 119 and into Black Hawk.)

The Lodge at Black Hawk, Colorado Central Station and the Isle of Capri are the only casinos with hotel rooms. The next closest lodging is at Fortune Valley Casino, 3/4-mile up Gregory St. in Central City (see Central City listings for particulars). Another alternative is the Gold Dust Lodge, located on Hwy. 119 about 1.5 miles from the Black Hawk casinos. The Gold Dust features 23 rooms with private baths.

The casinos in Black Hawk and Central City are located one mile apart. The Black Hawk Shuttle Service provides free transportation throughout Black Hawk and Central City.

There are a few bus tour programs operating between the metropolitan Denver area and Black Hawk/Central City. These programs are priced around $15 and usually affiliated with a few casinos that will reimburse a portion of the transportation charge. Check the "Weekend" section of the Friday *Denver Post* and *Rocky Mountain News* for bus tour ads.

All casinos offer electronic games (slots, video poker, video blackjack and video keno). Some casinos also offer: blackjack (BJ), poker (P), let it ride (LIR) and three card poker (TCP).

Ameristar Black Hawk
111 Richman Street
Black Hawk, Colorado 80422
(720) 946-4000
Web Site:www.ameristar.com/blackhawk

Toll-Free Number (866) 667-3386
Rooms: 472 Price Range: $99-$189
Suites: 64 Price Range: $259-$429
Restaurants: 4
Buffets: B- $17.99 (Sat/Sun)
          L-$12.99
          D-$15.99/$21.99 (Fri/Sat)
Casino Size: 46,534 Square feet
Other Games: BJ, P, C, R

Black Hawk Station
141 Gregory Street
Black Hawk, Colorado 80422
(303) 582-5582

Casino Size: 1,827 Square feet
Restaurants: 1 (snack bar)
Casino Hours: 8am-2am/4am (Fri/Sat)
Special Features: Includes **Sasquatch Casino**.

Bull Durham Saloon & Casino
110 Main Street
Black Hawk, Colorado 80422
(303) 582-0810
Website: www.bulldurhamcasino.com

Restaurants: 1 (snack bar)
Casino Size: 2,579 Square Feet

Bullwhackers Casino
101 Gregory Street
Black Hawk, Colorado 80422
(303) 271-2500
Website: www.bullwhackers.com

Toll-Free Number: (800) GAM-BULL
Restaurants: 2
Casino Size: 10,471 Square Feet
  (Bullwhackers)
Senior Discount: Specials on Tue/Wed if 55+
Special Features: Bakery.

Canyon Casino
131 Main Street
Black Hawk, Colorado 80422
(303) 777-1111
Website: www.canyoncasino.com

Restaurants: 1
Casino Size: 8,456 Square Feet (Canyon)
Casino Size: 2,428 Sq Ft (Grand Plateau)
Other Games: BJ, C, R
Special Features: Connected to **Grand Plateau Casino**.

Fitzgeralds Casino
101 Main Street
Black Hawk, Colorado 80422
(303) 582-6162
Website: www.fitzgeraldsbh.com

Toll-Free Number: (800) 538-5825
Restaurants: 1
Casino Size: 17,129 Square Feet
Other Games: BJ, C, R, TCP, LIR

Gilpin Hotel Casino
111 Main Street
Black Hawk, Colorado 80422
(303) 582-1133
Website: www.thegilpincasino.com

Restaurants: 2
Other Games: BJ, C, R
Casino Size: 11,087 Square Feet
Senior Discount: Specials on Tue if 50+

Golden Gates Casino
261 Main Street
Black Hawk, Colorado 80422
(303) 582-1650
Website: www.goldencasinogroup.com

Casino Size: 8,004 Square Feet (Golden Gates)
Casino Size: 3,440 Square Feet (Golden Gulch)
Other Games: P, BJ
Special Features: Connected to **Golden Gulch Casino**.

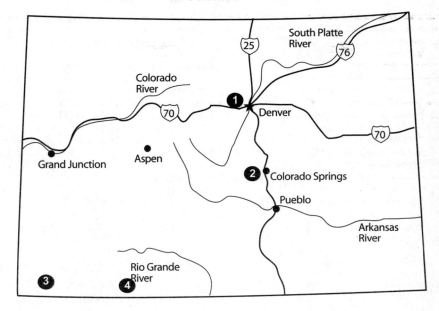

Golden Mardi Gras Casino
333 Main Street
Black Hawk, Colorado 80422
(303) 582-5600
Website: www.goldenmardigras.com

Restaurants: 1
Casino Size: 17,888 Square Feet
Other Games: BJ, P, C, R, TCP
Special Features: Skybridge to **The Lodge Casino.**

Isle of Capri Casino - Black Hawk
401 Main Street
Black Hawk, Colorado 80422
(303) 998-7777
Website: www.isleofcapricasino.com

Toll-Free Number (800) 843-4753
Rooms: 107 Price Range: $99-$229
Suites: 130 Price Range: $129-$179
Restaurants: 3
Buffets: B-$7.99/$15.99 (Sat/Sun) L-$10.99
    D-$15.99/$17.99 (Fri/Sat)
Casino Size: 27,611 Square Feet
Other Games: BJ, TCP, LIR, C, R

Lady Lucky Casino
340 Main Street
Black Hawk, Colorado 80422
(303) 582-3000
Website: www.coloradocentralstation.com

Toll-Free Number (888) LadyLuck
Rooms: 140 Price Range: $79-$206
Suites: 24 Price Range: $174-$215
Restaurants: 2   Valet parking: Free
Casino Size: 17,726 Square Feet
Other Games: BJ, P, C, R, TCP
Senior Discount: Various Wed/Fri if 50+
Special Features: Affiliated with Isle of Capri.

The Lodge Casino at Black Hawk
240 Main Street
Black Hawk, Colorado 80422
(303) 582-1771
Website: www.thelodgecasino.com

Rooms: 47 Price Range: $119-$165
Suites: 3 Price Range: Casino Use Only
Restaurants: 3
Buffets: B-$7.49 L-$10.49$13.99 (Sun)
    D-$16.99/$18.99 (Fri/Sat)
Casino Size: 23,951 Square Feet
OtherGames: BJ, P, C, R
Special Features: Skybridge to **Golden Mardi Gras Casino**. Free valet parking.

Red Dolly Casino
530 Gregory Street
Black Hawk, Colorado 80422
Website: Reddollycasino.net
(303) 582-1100

Restaurants: 1 (snack bar)
Other Games: BJ, TCP
Casino Size: 1,992 Square Feet

Riviera Black Hawk Casino
444 Main Street
Black Hawk, Colorado 80422
(303) 582-1000
Website: www.rivierablackhawk.com

Restaurants: 1
Buffet: B-$5.99 L-$9.99/$12.99 (Sat-Sun)
       D-$14.99/$16.99 (Fri-Sun)
Casino Size: 25,860 Square Feet
Other Games: BJ, TCP, R
Senior Discount: 50% off buffet Mon if 50+

Wild Card Saloon & Casino
112 Main Street
Black Hawk, Colorado 80422
Website: thewildcardsaloon.com
(303) 582-3412

Restaurants: 1
Casino Size: 2,750 Square Feet
Special Features: Grocery store.

Central City

Map location: **#1** (same as Black Hawk).
Central City is located one mile from Black
Hawk. Turn left at the third stoplight on Hwy.
119 and proceed up Gregory Street.

Besides the two casino hotels in Central City
that have rooms, there are also several bed
& breakfasts: Gregory Inn (303-582-5561),
Chateau L'Acadienne (303-582-5209) and
Skye Cottage (303-582-0622).

Century Casino & Hotel - Central City
102 Main Street
Central City, Colorado 80427
(303) 582-5050
Website: Cnty.com

Toll-Free Number: (888) 507-5050
Rooms: 22 Price Range $119-$159
Restaurants: 2
Casino Size: 13,899 Square Feet
Other Games: BJ, P, TCP, C, R

Doc Holliday Casino
101 Main Street
Central City, Colorado 80427
(303) 582-1400
Website: Docholidaycasino.net

Restaurants: 1 Snack Bar
Casino Size: 5,066 Square Feet

Dostal Alley Saloon & Gaming Emporium
1 Dostal Alley
Central City, Colorado 80427
(303) 582-1610
Website: Dostalalley.net

Restaurants: 1 Snack Bar
Casino Size: 1,041 Square Feet

Famous Bonanza/Easy Street
107 Main Street
Central City, Colorado 80427
(303) 582-5914
Website: www.famousbonanza.com

Toll-Free Number: (866) 339-5825
Restaurants: 1
Casino Size: 5,056 Square Feet (F. Bonanza)
Casino Size: 4,289 Square Feet (Easy Street)
Other Games: BJ, TCP, R

Fortune Valley Hotel & Casino
321 Gregory Street
Central City, Colorado 80427
(303) 582-0800
Website: www.fortunevalleycasino.com

Toll-Free Number: (800) 924-6646
Room Reservations: (866) 924-6646
Rooms: 118 Price Range $119-$169
Suites: 6 Price Range $159-$219
Restaurants: 2
Casino Size: 31,695 Square Feet
Other Games: BJ, P, TCP, C, R
Special Features: Tony Roma's restaurant. Covered parking garage.

Cripple Creek

Map Location: **#2** (47 miles west of Colorado Springs. Take exit 141 at Colorado Springs off I-25. Go west on Hwy. 24 to the town of Divide. Turn left onto Hwy. 67 and go 18 miles to Cripple Creek.)

Cripple Creek has several hotel/casinos the largest of which is the Double Eagle Hotel & Casino. There is also a 67-room motel, Gold King Mountain Inn, located 1/8-mile from the casinos with free shuttle service. For room reservations, call (800) 445-3607.

Many Cripple Creek casinos hand out coupons and Fun Books at their doors. Also check the ads in the *Colorado Springs Gazette*, the *Pueblo Chieftain* and the free tourist magazines. For Cripple Creek tourism information call (877) 858-GOLD or go to www. visitcripplecreek.com

All casinos offer electronic games (slots, video poker, video blackjack and video keno). Some casinos also offer: blackjack (BJ), poker (P), let it ride (LIR) and three card poker (TCP).

Big Jim's Casino
279 E Bennett Ave
Cripple Creek, CO 80813
(719) 689-2601
Website: bigjimscasino.com

Restaurants: 1 snack bar
Hours: 8am-4am daily
Other Games: BJ

Brass Ass Casino
264 E. Bennett Avenue
Cripple Creek, Colorado 80813
(719) 689-2104
Website: www.triplecrowncasinos.com

Restaurants: 1 (snack bar)
Casino Size: 7,486 Square Feet
Other Games: BJ, TCP, C, R
Special Features: Free hot dogs and popcorn for players. Connected to **Midnight Rose** and **J.P McGill's**. Covered parking garage.

Bronco Billy's Casino
233 E. Bennett Avenue
Cripple Creek, Colorado 80813
(719) 689-2142
Website: www.broncobillyscasino.com

Toll Free Number: (877) 989-2142
Restaurants: 3
Other Games: BJ, P, TCP, C, R
Casino Size: 6,086 Square Feet (Bronco's)
Casino Size: 5,991 Square Feet (Buffalo's)
Casino Size: 1,300 Square Feet (Billy's)
Senior Discount: Specials Mon/Fri 8am-6pm
Special Features: Includes **Buffalo Billy's Casino & Billy's Casino**. Free popcorn. Free cookies on weekends. Free donuts Mon-Thu. 49¢ breakfast.

Century Casino - Cripple Creek
200-220 E. Bennett Avenue
Cripple Creek, Colorado 80813
(719) 689-0333
Website: cnty.com

Toll-Free Number: (888) 966-2257
Rooms: 21 Price Range: $79-$99
Suites: 3 Price Range: $119
Restaurants: 1
Casino Size: 5,609 Square Feet (Womacks)
Casino Size: 4,189 Square Feet (Legends)
Other Games: BJ, P, C, R
Special Features: Rooms for club members only.

Colorado Grande Casino
300 E. Bennett Avenue
Cripple Creek, Colorado 80813
(719) 689-3517
Website: www.coloradogrande.com

Toll Free Number: (877) 244-9469
Rooms: 7 Prices: $59-$119
Restaurants: 1
Casino Size: 2,569 Square Feet
Other Games: TCP, BJ
Senior Discount: Dining discounts if 50+
Special Features: Free cookies on weekends.
Covered parking garage.

Double Eagle Hotel & Casino
442 E. Bennett Avenue
Cripple Creek, Colorado 80813
(719) 689-5000
Website: www.decasino.com

Toll-Free Reservations: (800) 711-7234
Rooms: 146 Price Range: $69-$139
Suites: 12 Price Range: $159-$500
Restaurants: 3
Buffets: B-$5.99
          D-$22.99 (Fri)
Casino Size: 14,631 Sq Ft (Double Eagle)
Casino Size: 6,018 Square Feet (Gold Creek)
Other Games: BJ, P, C, R, TCP
Special Features: Connected to **Gold Creek**
casino. Starbucks. Slot club members get
room discount. Covered parking garage.
48-space RV park ($20/$30 with hookups)

Johnny Nolon's Casino
301 E. Bennett Avenue
Cripple Creek, Colorado 80813
(719) 689-2080
Website: www.johnnynolons.com

Restaurants: 2
Casino Size: 3,505 Square Feet

J.P. McGill's Hotel & Casino
232 E. Bennett Avenue
Cripple Creek, Colorado 80813
(719) 689-2446
Website: www.triplecrowncasinos.com

Toll-Free Number: (888) 461-7529
Rooms: 36 Price Range: $80-$115
Suites: 5 Price Range: $180-$240
Restaurants: 1
Casino Size: 7,386 Square Feet
Special Features: Connected to **Midnight
Rose** and **Brass Ass**. 10% room/food discount
for slot club members. Free popcorn for
players. Covered parking garage.

Midnight Rose Hotel & Casino
256 E. Bennett Avenue
Cripple Creek, Colorado 80813
(719) 689-2865
Website: www.triplecrowncasinos.com

Toll-Free Number: (800) 635-5825
Rooms: 19 Price Range: $90-$120
Restaurants: 2
Casino Size: 9,590 Square Feet
Other Games: P
Special Features: Connected to **Brass Ass** and
J.P McGill's. 10% room/food discount for
slot club members. Covered parking garage.

Wildwood Casino At Cripple Creek
119 Carbonate Sreet
Cripple Creek, CO 80813
(719) 689-2814
Website: Playwildwood.com

Toll-Free Number: (877) 945-3963
Valet Parking: Free
Restaurants: 3
Casino Size: 18,965 Square Feet
Other Games: BJ, P, TCP, C, R
Senior Discount: Various Thu if 50+
Special Features: Covered parking garage.

Indian Casinos

Sky Ute Casino and Lodge
14826 Highway 172 N.
Ignacio, Colorado 81137
(970) 563-3000
Website: www.skyutecasino.com
Map Location: **#4** (345 miles S.W. of Denver, 20 miles S.E. of Durango)

Toll-Free Number: (888) 842-4180
Room Reservations: (800) 876-7017
Rooms: 36 Price Range: $90-$150
Restaurants: 2 Liquor: No
Hours: 24 Hours Daily
Other Games: BJ, TCP, LIR, C, R
                Bingo (Wed/Thu/Fri/Sun)
Overnight RV Parking: Must use RV Park $45/$55 (Fri-Sat)
Senior Discount: 10% off room/food if 55+
Special Features: 24-space RV park on property ($30 per night). Southern Ute Cultural Center and Museum. Free local shuttle.

Ute Mountain Casino & RV Park
3 Weeminuche Drive/P.O. Drawer V
Towaoc, Colorado 81334
(970) 565-8800
Website: www.utemountaincasino.com
Map Location: **#3** (425 miles S.W. of Denver, 11 miles S. of Cortez on Hwys. 160/166)

Toll-Free Number: (800) 258-8007
Hotel Reservations: (888) 565-8837
RV Reservations: (800) 889-5072
Rooms: 70 Price Range: $75-$109
Suites: 20 Price Range: $126-$155
Restaurants: 1 Liquor: No
Buffets: B-$7.95 L-$8.95
        D-$11.95/$19.95 (Fri)
Casino Size: 32,000 Square Feet
Other Games: BJ, P
                Keno, Bingo (Fri-Tue)
Overnight RV Parking: Must use RV park
Senior Discount: 15% off non-buffet food if 55+
Special Features: 84-space RV Park ($23-$25 per night). Ute Tribal Park tours available.

CONNECTICUT

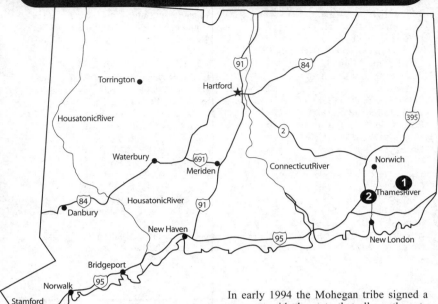

Foxwoods was New England's first casino and it is now the second largest casino in the world.

The Mashantucket Pequot Tribe which operates Foxwoods had to sue the state to allow the casino to open. They argued that since the state legally permitted "Las Vegas Nights," where low-stakes casino games were operated to benefit charities, then the tribe should be entitled to do the same. Eventually, they won their case before the U.S. Supreme Court and began construction of their casino which was financed by a Malaysian conglomerate (after 22 U.S. lenders turned down their loan requests).

When the casino first opened in February 1992, slot machines were not permitted. In January 1993 a deal was made between Governor Weicker and the Pequots which gave the tribe the exclusive right to offer slot machines in return for a yearly payment of 25% of the gross slot revenue. The agreement was subject to cancellation, however, if the state allowed slot machines anywhere else in Connecticut.

In early 1994 the Mohegan tribe signed a compact with the state that allows them to offer casino gambling at their reservation in Uncasville (map location #2). The Pequots gave permission for the Mohegans to have slot machines in their casino. The same 25% of the gross slot revenue payment schedule also applies to the Mohegans. The payment schedules are subject to cancellation, however, if the state legalizes any other form of casino gambling. The Mohegan casino opened in October 1996.

The minimum gambling age at both properties is 18 for bingo and 21 for the casino. Both casinos are open 24 hours. For information on visiting Connecticut call the state's Vacation Center at (800) 282-6863 or visit their website at www.ctbound.org

The games offered at Foxwoods are: blackjack, craps, roulette, baccarat, mini-baccarat, midi baccarat, big six (money wheel), pai gow poker, pai gow tiles, Caribbean stud poker, sic bo, let it ride, casino war, Spanish 21, three-card poker, Crazy 4 poker and poker; in addition to bingo, keno and pull tabs. There is also a Race Book offering off-track betting on horses, greyhounds and jai-alai.

Foxwoods Resort Casino, North America's largest casino, has over 300,000 square feet of gaming space. The property features three hotels, over 30 food and beverage outlets, 24 retail shops, 6 casinos, Ultimate Race Book, various high limit gaming areas, a 3,200-seat bingo room, a state of the art smoke free World Poker Room™ and more than 6,800 electronic gaming machines.

Foxwoods Resort Casino
Route 2
Mashantucket, Connecticut 06338
(860) 312-3000
Website: www.foxwoods.com
Map Location: **#1** (45 miles S.E. of Hartford; 12 miles N. of I-95 at Mystic). From I-95 take exit 92 to Rt. 2-West, casino is 7 miles ahead. From I-395 take exit 79A to Rt. 2A follow to Rt. 2-East, casino is 2 miles ahead.

Toll-Free Number: (800) FOXWOODS
Hotel Reservations: (800) FOXWOODS
Rooms: 1,398 Price Range: $125-$585
Suites: 209 Price Range: $175-$1,500
Restaurants: 26 (3 open 24 hours)
Buffets: B-$10.50 L/D-$16.95/$19.95 (Fri/Sat)
Casino Size: 323,376 Square Feet
Casino Marketing: (800) 99-SLOTS
Overnight RV Parking: Free (self-contained only) RV Dump: No
Special Features: Three hotels with pool, Grand Pequot Tower hotel spa and beauty salon, golf. Headliner entertainment, The Club and Atrium Lounge. Gift shops. Dream Card Mega Store. Hard Rock Cafe. Dream Card members earn complimentaries at table games, slots, poker and race book. 10% room discount for AAA and AARP members. Two Rees Jones designed golf courses. $1 buffet discount for Dream Card members.

In May 2008, a new casino resort was opened at Foxwoods. The MGM Grand at Foxwoods is a partnership between MGM Mirage and Foxwoods. It is connected to the Foxwoods Casino Resort by a covered, moving, walkway.

The property has its own casino offering electronic gaming machines, plus the following games: blackjack, craps, roulette, Spanish 21, and three-card Poker.

MGM Grand at Foxwoods
240 MGM Grand Drive
Mashantucket, Connecticut 06338
Website: www.mgmatfoxwoods.com
Map Location: **#1**

Toll-Free Number: (866) MGM-0050
Rooms: 590 Price Range: $199-$349
Suites: 235 Price Range: $315-$555
Restaurants: 5
Casino Size: 50,000 Square Feet
Overnight RV Parking: Must use Foxwoods lot.
Special Features: 4,000-seat theater. Spa, hair and nail salon. Fast food court with six restaurants. Shopping arcade with five retail stores and boutiques. Lake of Isles Golf Course is adjacent to property. 115,000-square-foot convention space. Outdoor pool and patio area.

The following information is from Connecticut's Division of Special Revenue regarding MGM Grand and Foxwoods' slot payback percentages:

Denomination	Payback %
1¢	89.24
2¢	90.35
5¢	89.84
25¢	91.74
50¢	90.67
$1.00	94.13
$5.00	94.57
$10.00	95.74
$25.00	95.50
$100.00	96.41
Average	**91.71**

These figures reflect the total percentages returned by each denomination of slot machine from July 1, 2010 through June 30, 2011.

The games offered at Mohegan Sun are: blackjack, craps, roulette, baccarat, mini-baccarat, pai gow, wheel of fortune, bingo, pai gow poker, Caribbean stud poker, let it ride, Spanish 21, casino war, sic bo and keno. There is also a Race Book offering off-track betting on horses, greyhounds and jai-alai.

Mohegan Sun Casino
1 Mohegan Sun Boulevard
Uncasville, Connecticut 06382
(860) 862-8000
Website: www.mohegansun.com
Map Location: **#2** (Take I-95 Exit 76/I-395 North. Take Exit 79A (Route 2A) East. Less than 1 mile to Mohegan Sun Boulevard)

Toll-Free Number: (888) 226-7711
Room Reservations: (888) 777-7922
Rooms: 1,020 Price Range: $209-$599
Suites: 180 Price Range: $309-$1,000
Restaurants: 29 (3 open 24 hours)
Buffets (Seasons): B-$12.50 L-$21.00
                          D-$25.00
Buffets (Sunburst): B- $9.95 L-$17.99
                          D-$21.99
Casino Size: 295,000 Square Feet
Overnight RV Parking: Free/RV Dump: No
Special Features: Food court with specialty food outlets. Kid's Quest supervised children's activity center. On-site gas station. 30-store shopping arcade.

Here's information from Connecticut's Division of Special Revenue regarding Mohegan Sun's slot payback percentages:

Denomination	Payback %
1/4¢	86.11
1/2¢	85.94
1¢	89.04
2¢	89.45
5¢	88.34
25¢	91.42
50¢	92.11
$1.00	93.51
$5.00	93.87
$10.00	96.10
$25.00	95.66
$100.00	94.46
Average	**92.02**

These figures reflect the total percentages returned by each denomination of slot machine from July 1, 2010 through June 30, 2011.

DELAWARE

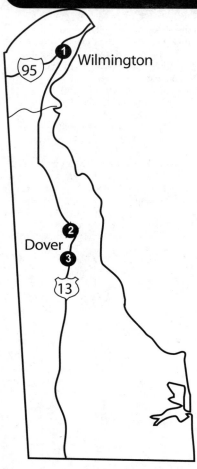

According to figures from the Delaware Lottery for the one-year period from July 25, 2010 through June 26, 2011 the average VLT return at Delaware Park was 92.62%, at Dover Downs it was 91.84% and at Harrington Raceway it was 91.88%.

In mid-2009 the state legalized sports betting for Delaware's three casinos. You can bet on professional and college sporting events, but not on single games-only on multiple games as seen on parlay cards.

In January 2010 the Delaware legislature approved the addition of table games for the state's casinos. All Delaware casinos offer: blackjack, roulette, craps, slots and video poker. Some casinos also offer: mini-baccarat (MB), poker (P), pai gow poker (PGP), Caribbean stud poker (CSP), let it ride (LIR), big 6 (B6), bingo (BG), keno (K), three card poker (TCP), casino war (CW), four card poker (FCP) and Spanish 21 (S21).

All casinos are open 24 hours. They are also closed on Easter and Christmas.

The minimum gambling age is 21 for slots and 18 for horse racing. For more information on visiting Delaware call the state's tourism office at (800) 441-8846 or visit their web site at: www.visitdelaware.com.

Delaware's three pari-mutuel facilities all feature slot machines. Technically, the machines are video lottery terminals (VLT's) because they are operated in conjunction with the Delaware Lottery. Unlike VLT's in other states, however, Delaware's machines pay out in cash. The VLT's also play other games including: video poker, video keno and video blackjack.

By law, all video lottery games must return between 87% and 95% of all wagers on an annual basis. Games can return above 95% but only with the Lottery Director's approval.

Delaware Park Racetrack & Slots
777 Delaware Park Boulevard
Wilmington, Delaware 19804
(302) 994-2521
Website: www.delawarepark.com
Map: **#1**

Toll-Free Number: (800) 41-SLOTS
Restaurants: 8
Admission: Free Parking: Free
Valet Parking: $4
Other Games: P
Overnight RV Parking: Free/RV Dump: No
Special Features: Live thoroughbred
racing late-April to early-November. Daily
simulcasting of horse racing. Ask for Delaware
Park discounted hotel rate at Christiana Hilton
(800-348-3133).

Dover Downs Hotel And Casino
1131 N. DuPont Highway
Dover, Delaware 19901
(302) 674-4600
Website: www.doverdowns.com
Map: **#2**

Toll-Free Number: (800) 711-5882
Rooms: 206 Price Range: $125-$250
Suites: 26 Price Range: $195-$805
Restaurants: 4
Buffets: B-$10.50/$14.50 (Sun)
        L-$14.50 D-$17.50
Admission: Free Parking: Free
Valet Parking: $4
Casino Size: 91,000 Square Feet
Other Games: S21, TCP, PGP, B, LIR
Overnight RV Parking: Free/RV Dump: Free
        (Not free during NASCAR events)
Special Features: Casino is non-smoking. Live
harness racing November through April. Daily
simulcasting of horse racing. Comedy Club.
Motorsports speedway with NASCAR racing.
$2 buffet discount for slot club members.

Harrington Raceway & Casino
Delaware State Fairgrounds
U.S. 13 South
Harrington, Delaware 19952
(302) 398-4920
Website: www.Harringtonraceway.com
Map: **#3** (20 miles S. of Dover)

Toll-Free Number: (888) 88-SLOTS
Restaurants: 3
Buffets: L-$13.95/$16.95 (Sun)
        D- $16.95/$21.95 (Wed)
Admission: Free
Parking: Free Valet Parking: $2
Other Games: MB, P, PGP, TCP,
        FCP, LIR, CW
Overnight RV Parking: Free/RV Dump: No
Special Features: Live harness racing April-
June and August-October. Daily simulcasting
of horse racing.

FLORIDA

Florida has three forms of casinos: casino boats, Indian casinos and gaming machines at pari-mutuels in two south Florida counties.

The casino boats offer gamblers the opportunity to board ships that cruise offshore where casino gambling is legal. From the west coast the boats travel nine miles out into the Gulf of Mexico. From the East coast they travel 3 miles out into the Atlantic Ocean.

Unless otherwise noted, all Florida casino boats offer: blackjack, craps, roulette, slots and video poker. Some casinos also offer: mini-baccarat (MB), poker (P), pai gow poker (PGP), three-card poker (TCP), Caribbean stud poker (CSP), let it ride (LIR), big 6 wheel (B6) bingo (BG) and sports book (SB).

The minimum drinking age on all boats is 21. Due to security restrictions, you must present a photo ID at all casino boats or you will not be allowed to board.

For Florida visitor information call (888) 735-2872 or visit their website at: www. visitflorida.com.

Atlantic Beach

Map: **#8** (15 miles E of Jacksonville)

Jacks or Better Casino
4378 Ocean Street
Atlantic Beach, FL 32233
Website: www.jacksorbettercasino.com

Toll-Free Number: (877)605-6673
Gambling Age: 18
Food Service: A la Carte
Schedule:
    11am-4pm (Wed-Fri)
    11am-4:30pm (Sat)
    1pm-6pm (Sun)
    7pm-12am (Wed-Sun)
    7pm-12:30am (Fri/Sat)
Price: $10 (Wed/Thurs/Fri matinee/sun eve)
    $15 (Fri eve/Sat/Sun matinee)
Port Charges: $3
Other games: B
Special Features: 155-foot ship with 181 gaming machines, table games and a virtual sports book.

Fort Myers Beach

Map: **#5** (40 miles N. of Naples)

Big "M" Casino
450 Harbor Court
Fort Myers Beach, Florida 33931
(239) 765-7529
Website: www.bigmcasino.com

Toll-Free Number: (888) 373-3521
Gambling Age: 21   Ship's Registry: U.S.A.
Schedule:
    10:30am - 4:30pm (Wed-Sun)
    6:00pm - 11:45pm (Thu-Sun)
Prices: $10
With Buffet: $20.55/$25.85 night cuise
Port Charges: Included
Parking: Free (Valet also free)
Other Games: LIR, TCP
Special Features: 400-passenger *Big M* sails from Moss Marina next to Snug Harbor on Fort Myers Beach. Closed Mondays unless a major holiday. Must be 21 or older to board. A la carte menu also available. Cashback for slot play.

Cape Canaveral

Map: **#9** (60 miles S.E. of Orlando)

Victory Casino Cruises
180 Christopher Columbus Drive
Cape Canaveral, Florida 32920
(321) 799-0021
Website: www.victorycasinocruises.com

Toll-Free Number: (855) 468-4286
Gambling Age: 18
Food Service: A la Carte
Schedule: 11am-4pm (Mon-Sat)
    12pm-6pm (Sun)
    7pm-12am (Mon-Sat)
Price: $10
Buffet Price: $15/$20 (Fri-Sun)
Port Charges: Included   Parking: Free
Other Games: MB, TCP, SB
Special Features: 1,200-passenger *Victory I* departs from Port Canaveral. 6-hour cruise on Sundays

Port Richey

Map: **#6** (37 miles N.W. of Tampa)

SunCruz Casino - Port Richey
7917 Bayview Street
Port Richey, Florida 34668
(727) 848-3423
Website: www.portricheycasino.com

Toll-Free Number: (800) 464-3423
Gambling Age: 18
Food Service: A la Carte
Shuttle Schedule:
Departs: 11am/3:30pm/7pm
Returns: 5:30pm/9pm/12:00am
Price: Free
Port Charges: Included   Parking: Free
Other Games: LIR, TCP
Special Features: 465-passenger *Royal Casino 1* stays offshore and a water taxi shuttles passengers back and forth according to above schedule. Shuttle departs from dock on Pithlachascotee River off of US 19 in Port Richey.

Indian Casinos

Florida has eight Indian gaming locations. The Seminole Tribe has seven and the eighth is on the Miccosukee Tribe's reservation.

The Seminoles signed a compact with the state that allows them to offer both Class II and traditional Class III gaming machines. As part of their compact, five Seminole casinos are also allowed to offer blackjack (BJ), baccarat (B), mini-baccarat (MB), three card poker (TCP), let it ride (LIR) and pai gow poker (PGP).

The Miccosukee Tribe has not signed a compact and they only offer Class II gaming machines at their casino.

Class II video gaming devices look like slot machines, but are actually bingo games and the spinning reels are for "entertainment purposes only." No public information is available concerning the payback percentages on any gaming machines in Florida's Indian casinos.

The other games allowed in all Indian casinos are: high-stakes bingo, video pull tabs and poker. All of the casinos are open 24 hours (except Big Cypress) and all offer bingo except for both Seminole Hard Rock Casinos and the Seminole Casino Coconut Creek. The minimum gambling age is 18 at all Indian casinos for bingo or poker and 21 for electronic gaming machines.

Big Cypress Casino
30013 Josie Billie Highway
Clewiston, Florida 33440
(863) 983-7245
Website: www.seminolebigcypresscasino.com

Map: **#7** (75 miles W. of Palm Beach)

Hours: Noon-1am
Restaurants: Snack Bar
Games: Only Class II Gaming Machines

Brighton Seminole Bingo and Casino
17735 Reservation Road
Okeechobee, Florida 34974
(863) 467-9998
Website: www.seminolecasinobrighton.com
Map: **#7** (75 miles N.W. of West Palm Beach)

Toll-Free Number: (866) 2-CASINO
Hours: 24 hours
Restaurants: 1   Liquor: Yes
Casino Size: 24,400 Square Feet
Overnight RV Parking: No

Seminole Casino Hollywood
4150 N. State Road 7
Hollywood, Florida 33021
(954) 961-3220
 www.seminolehollywoodcasino.com
Map: **#2** (1 miles S. of Fort Lauderdale)

Toll-Free Number: (800) 323-5452
Restaurants: 3   Liquor: Yes
Buffets: B- $2.99 L-$5.99 D-$7.99
Casino Size: 73,500 Square Feet
Other Games: BJ, MB, TCP, PGP, LIR
Overnight RV Parking: Free/RV Dump: No
Special Features: Located one block south of Hard Rock Hotel & Casino. Must have Player's Club card for buffet.

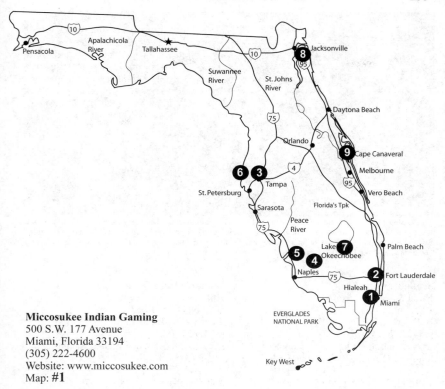

Miccosukee Indian Gaming
500 S.W. 177 Avenue
Miami, Florida 33194
(305) 222-4600
Website: www.miccosukee.com
Map: **#1**

Toll-Free Number: (800) 741-4600
Room Reservations: (877) 242-6464
Rooms: 256 Price Range: $129-$149
Suites: 46 Price Range: $149-$189
Restaurants: 4 Liquor: Yes
Buffets: B-$7.95 L/D-$10.95
Overnight RV Parking: Free/RV Dump: No

Seminole Casino Coconut Creek
5550 NW 40th Street
Coconut Creek, Florida 33073
(954) 977-6700
Website: www.seminolecoconutcreekcasino.
com
Map: **#2**

Toll-Free Number: (866) 2-CASINO
Restaurants: 2 Liquor: Yes
L-$12.95 (Wed-Thu)
Casino Size: 30,000 Square Feet
Other Games: BJ, MB, TCP, PGP, LIR
Overnight RV Parking: Call Ahead
Special Features: Free valet parking.

Seminole Casino Immokalee
506 South 1st Street
Immokalee, Florida 33934
(941) 658-1313
Website: www.theseminolecasino.com
Map: **#4** (35 miles N.E. of Naples)

Toll-Free Number: (800) 218-0007
Restaurants: 1 Liquor: Yes
Casino Size: 22,000 Square Feet
Other Games: BJ, MB, TCP, PGP, LIR
Overnight RV Parking: Yes

The Seminole Hard Rock Hotel & Casino in Hollywood is South Florida's leading entertainment destination. It features a 130,000-square-foot casino, including a poker room, plus a 4-Diamond rated 500-room hotel with a European-style spa. There is also an adjacent complex featuring 24 retail shops, 17 restaurants, 10 nightclubs and a state-of-the-art 6,400-seat Hard Rock Live entertainment venue.

Seminole Hard Rock
Hotel & Casino - Hollywood
1 Seminole Way
Hollywood, Florida 33314
(954) 327-7625
www.seminolehardrockhollywood.com
Map: #2 (1 mile S. of Fort Lauderdale)

Toll-Free Number: (866) 502-7529
Room Reservations: (800) 937-0010
Rooms: 437 Price Range: $149-$399
Suites: 63 Price Range: $299-$449
Valet Parking: $7 ($4 with players Card)
Restaurants: 4 Liquor: Yes
Buffets: Brunch-$49.95 (Sun)
Casino Size: 130,000 Square Feet
Other Games: BJ, MB, TCP, PGP, LIR
Overnight RV Parking: No
Special Features: Food court. Lagoon-style pool. Health spa. Shopping mall with 20 stores.

Seminole Hard Rock
Hotel & Casino - Tampa
5223 N. Orient Road
Tampa, Florida 33610
(813) 627-7625
www.hardrockhotelcasinotampa.com
Map: #3

Toll-Free Number: (800) 282-7016
Room Reservations: (800) 937-0010
Rooms: 204 Price Range: $189-$379
Suites: 46 Price Range: $195-$395
Restaurants: 2 (1 open 24 hours) Liquor: Yes
Buffets: B-$35 (Sun) L-$20 D- $27/$35 (Fri)
Casino Size: 90,000 Square Feet
Other Games: BJ, MB, TCP, PGP, LIR
Overnight RV Parking: Call ahead
Special Features: Food court. Health club.

Pari-Mutuels

In early 2005 voters in Broward County (home county of Fort Lauderdale) passed a referendum to allow slot machines at four pari-mutuel facilities within that county.

The first slot facility opened in late 2006 and two others followed within six months. The fourth facility, Dania Jai-Alai, has indefinitely postponed the installation of its slot machines.

In January 2008 voters in Miami-Dade County also passed a referendum permitting slot machines at three pari-mutuel facilities. Two facilities have opened and the third, Miami Jai-Alai, is not expected to begin offering slots until mid 2012 at the earliest.

Florida gaming regulations require a minimum payback of 85% on all gaming machines. From July 1, 2010 through June 30, 2011, the gaming machines at Gulfstream returned 92.08%, the return was 91.76% at Mardi Gras Gaming, 92.70% at The Isle, 92.76% at Magic City and 91.20% at Calder.

South Florida's pari-mutuel facilities (as well as most pari-mutuels throughout the state), also offer poker. Admission to all casinos is free and they are allowed to be open a maximum of 18 hours per day during the week and 24 hours on the weekends and some holidays.

If you want to order a drink while playing, be aware that Florida gaming regulations do not allow pari-mutuel casinos to provide free alcoholic beverages.

The minimum gambling age is 18 for pari-mutuel betting or poker and 21 for gaming machines.

Calder Casino & Race Course
21001 N. W. 27th Avenue
Miami Gardens, Florida 33056
(305) 625-1311
Website: www.calderracecourse.com
Map: #1

Toll Free - (800) 333-3227
Parking: Free Valet: $5
Hours 9am-3am/ 24 hours (Fri/Sat)
Restaurants: 3
Buffets B-$9.99 (Sun) L/D-$9.99
Other Games: P
Special Features: Live horse racing Thu-Sun at 12:40pm from late April through early Jan. Daily simulcasting of thoroughbred racing.

Dania Jai-Alai
301 E. Dania Beach Boulevard
Dania Beach, Florida 33004
(954) 920-1511
Website: www.dania-jai-alai.com
Map: #2

Self-Parking: Free Valet: $3
Restaurants: 1
Other Games: P
Overnight RV Parking: No
Special Features: Live jai-alai games Tue-Sat eves and Tue/Sat/Sun afternoons. Daily simulcasting of thoroughbred/harness racing and jai-alai. **The installation of slot machines has been postponed until late 2012.**

Gulfstream Park Racing & Casino
901 S. Federal Highway
Hallandale Beach, Florida 33009
(954) 454-7000
Website: www.gulfstreampark.com
Map: #2

Toll-Free Number: (800) 771-TURF
Track Admission: $3/$5 (Fri-Sat)
Parking: Free Valet: $6
Hours 9am-3am/ 24 Hours (Fri/Sat)
Restaurants: 3
Overnight RV Parking: No
Special Features: Live thoroughbred racing Wed-Sun from January through April. Daily simulcasting of thoroughbred racing. Outdoor shopping area with over 20 shops and restaurants.

Magic City Casino
401 NW 38th Court
Miami, Florida 33126
305-649-3000
Website: www.magiccitycasino.com
Map: #**1**

Toll-free Number: (888) 566-2442
Parking: Free
Hours 10am-4am Daily Restaurants: 2
Other Games: P
Buffet: L$10.95 (Sat/Sun) D- $15.95 (Sat/Sun)
Special Features: Live dog racing Tue/Thu-Sun at 1pm . Daily simulcasting of dog and harness racing. $2 off buffet with slot club card.

Mardi Gras Racetrack and Gaming Center
831 N. Federal Highway
Hallandale Beach, Florida 33009
(954) 924-3200
Website: www.playmardigras.com
Map: #**2**

Toll-Free Number: (877) 557-5687
Track Admission: Free
Parking: Free   Valet: $7
Hours 9am-3:30am/24 Hours (Fri/Sat)
Restaurants: 1
Overnight RV Parking: No
Special Features: Live dog racing daily November through May. Daily simulcasting of dog, thoroughbred and harness races. Poker room is open 24 hours.

Miami Jai-Alai
3500 N.W. 37th Avenue
Miami Florida 33142
(305) 633-6400
Website: www.fla-gaming.com/miami/
Map: #**1**

General Admission: $1
Parking: Free Valet: $3
Restaurants: 1
Special Features: Live jai-alai Wed-Mon at noon and Fri/Sat at 7pm. Daily simulcasting of jai-alai and harness racing. Slot machines expected to begin operating in mid-2012.

Isle Casino Racing Pompano Park
777 Isle of Capri Circle
Pompano Beach, Florida 33069
(954) 972-2000
Website: www.theislepompanopark.com
Map: #**2**

Toll-Free Number: (800) 843-4753
Track Admission: Free
Self-Parking: Free Valet: Free
Hours 9am-3am/24 hours (Fri/Sat)
Restaurants: 4
Buffet: B- $15.99 (Sat/Sun) L- $11.99
        D- $19.99/ $24.99 (Fri-Sat)
Overnight RV Parking: No
Special Features: Live harness racing various evenings (see website for schedules). Daily simulcasting of thoroughbred/harness racing and jai-alai.

GEORGIA

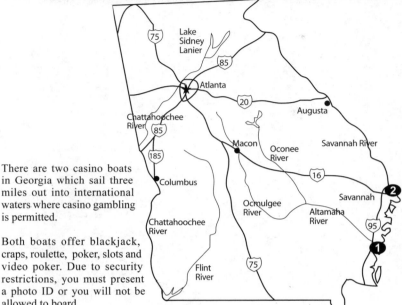

There are two casino boats in Georgia which sail three miles out into international waters where casino gambling is permitted.

Both boats offer blackjack, craps, roulette, poker, slots and video poker. Due to security restrictions, you must present a photo ID or you will not be allowed to board.

For information on visiting Georgia call the state's tourism department at (800) 847-4842 or visit their web site at www.georgia.org.

Diamond Casino
8010 US Highway 80 East
Wilmington Island
Savannah, Georgia 31410
(912) 897-3005
Website: www.diamondcasinosavannah.com
Map Location: **#2**

Reservation Number: (877) 758-2597
Gambling Age: 18   Parking: Free
Food: A la carte menu
Schedule
 12:00pm - 5:00pm (Wed-Sun)
 7:00pm - 12:00am (Sun-Thu)
 7:00pm - 1:00am (Fri/Sat)
Price: $5   Port Charges: Included
Other Games: TCP, MB
Special Features: 500-passenger *Midnight Gambler II* sails from Wilmington Island across from Bull River Marina.

Emerald Princess II Casino
1 Gisco Point Drive
Brunswick, Georgia 31523
(912) 265-3558
Website: www.emeraldprincesscasino.com
Map Location: **#1** (75 miles S. of Savannah)

Reservation Number: (800) 842-0115
Gambling Age: 18   Parking: Free
Schedule
 11:00am - 4:00pm (Fri/Sat)
 1:00pm - 6:00pm (Sun)
 7:00pm - 12:00am (Mon-Thu)
 7:00pm - 1:00am (Fri/Sat)
Price: $10   Port Charges: Included
Special Features: 400-passenger *Emerald Princess II* sails from Gisco Point, at the southern end of the Sidney Lanier Bridge. Soup, salad and sandwich included with cruise. Reservations are required for all cruises. Packages with hotel accommodations are available. No one under 18 permitted to board.

IDAHO

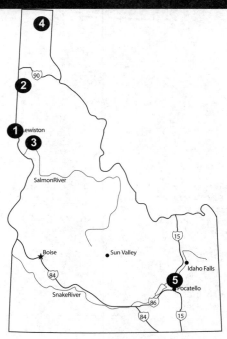

Idaho has six Indian casinos that offer electronic pull-tab machines and other video games. The machines don't pay out in cash. Instead they print out a receipt which must be cashed by a floor attendant or taken to the cashier's cage. Some casinos also offer bingo (BG) and off-track betting (OTB).

The terms of the compact between the tribes and the state do not require any minimum payback percentage that the gaming machines must return to the public.

The minimum gambling age at all casinos is 18 and they are all open 24 hours. For Idaho tourism information call (800) 635-7820 or visit their web site: www.visitid.org

Bannock Peak Casino
1707 W. Country Road
Pocatello, Idaho 83204
(208) 235-1308
Web site: www.sho-ban.com
Map: **#5** (5 miles N. of Pocatello)

Restaurants: 1 Snack Bar Liquor: No
Hours: 10am-12am/1am (Fri/Sat)
Casino Size: 5,000 Square Feet
Other Games: Only gaming machines
Overnight RV Parking: Free/RV Dump: No

Clearwater River Casino
17500 Nez Perce Road
Lewiston, Idaho 83501
(208) 746-5733
Web site: www.crcasino.com
Map: #1 (250 miles N. of Boise)

Toll-Free Number: (877) 678-7423
Restaurants: 1 Liquor: No
Buffets: B- $12.95 (Sun)
      D-$24.95 (Fri)/$18.95 (Sat)
Casino Size: 30,000 Square Feet
Other Games: BG (Sun-Wed)
Overnight RV Parking: Free/RV Dump: No
Special Features: 33-space RV park ($27 per night).

Coeur D'Alene Casino Resort Hotel
U.S. Highway 95/P.O. Box 236
Worley, Idaho 83876
(208) 686-5106
Web site: www.cdacasino.com
Map: #2 (350 miles N. of Boise)

Toll-Free Number: (800) 523-2464
Rooms: 202 Price Range: $70-$125
Suites: 8 Price Range $150-$400
Restaurants: 7 Liquor: Yes Valet: Free
Buffet: B-$7.99$11.99 (Sat/Sun) L-$10.99
      D-$15.99/$18.99(Fri/Sat)
Casino Size: 30,000 Square Feet
Other Games: BG (Fri-Sun), OTB
Overnight RV Parking: Free/RV Dump: No
Special Features: 18-hole golf course.

Fort Hall Casino
I-15 Exit 80, PO Box 868
Fort Hall, Idaho 83203
(208) 237-8778
Web site: www.shobangaming.com
Map: #5 (14 miles N. of Pocatello)

Toll-Free Number: (800) 497-4231
Restaurants: 1 Snack Bar Liquor: No
Casino Size: 15,000 Square Feet
Other Games: BG (Wed-Sun)
Overnight RV Parking: Must use RV Park
Special Features: 47-space RV park ($20 per night).

It'Se-Ye-Ye Casino
419 Third Street
Kamiah, Idaho 83536
(208) 935-7860
Web site: www.crcasino.com
Map: #3 (225 miles N. of Boise)

Restaurants: 1 Liquor: No
Hours: 6am-2am
Casino Size: 2,300 Square Feet
Overnight RV Parking: Free/RV Dump: No

Kootenai River Inn Casino and Spa
Kootenai River Plaza
Bonners Ferry, Idaho 83805
(208 267 8511
Web site: www.kootenairiverinn.com
Map: #4 (450 miles N. of Boise)

Toll-Free Number: (800) 346-5668
Rooms: 47 Price Range: $99-$139
Suites: 4 Price Range $124-$350
Restaurants: 2 Liquor: Yes
Buffets: B-$10.99 (Sun)
Casino Size: 30,000 Square Feet
Other Games: BG (1st and 3rd Wed)
Overnight RV Parking: Free/RV Dump: No
Special Features: Hotel is Best Western. Spa.

Sage Hill Casino
Interstate 15 Exit 89
Blackfoot, Idaho 83221
Map: #5 (14 miles N. of Pocatello)
(208) 237-4998

Restaurants: 1
Casino Hours: 6:30am-5am
Casino Size: 13,200 Square Feet
Other Games: Only gaming machines

ILLINOIS

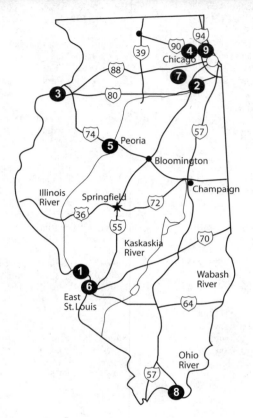

Illinois was the second state to legalize riverboat casinos. Riverboat casinos began operating there in September 1991 with the launching of the first boat: the Alton Belle.

All Illinois riverboats remain dockside and do not cruise. Unlike Mississippi, however, the casinos are not open 24 hours and state law limits the number of gaming licenses to 10.

Here's information from the Illinois Gaming Board showing each casino's average slot payback percentage for the one-year period from July 1, 2010 through June 30, 2011:

CASINO	PAYBACK %
Casino Queen	94.28
Alton Belle	92.85
Grand Victoria	92.68
Rock Island	91.90
Par-A-Dice	91.58
Harrah's Joliet	91.58
Hollywood	91.30
Empress	91.07
Harrah's Metropolis	89.48

These figures reflect the total percentages returned by each casino for all of their electronic machines.

The Best Places To Play In The Chicago Area

by John Grochowski

The Chicago area market has never been short on change. Casinos have moved from small river-cruising boats to stationary barges as regulations requiring excursions on the water and maintenance of full maritime crews were eliminated. They've been sold, branded and re-branded, as Empress in Joliet became Hollywood Joliet, Empress in Hammond became Horseshoe, Trump in Gary became Majestic Star II and Showboat Mardi Gras in East Chicago had a whole string of ownership and name changes before settling in as Ameristar .

One thing the market hadn't seen since 1997 was a whole new operation. That changed in July 2011, when the Rivers Casino in northwest suburban Des Plaines became the first new Illinois casino since Grand Victoria in Elgin launched in 1994, and the first in the Chicago area since Showboat Mardi Gras

The new casino is designed as a premium property, with table limits up to $100,000 on baccarat, $25,000 on blackjack (or $50,000 for approved players), and $20,000 on line bets with up to $30,000 in free odds on craps. It's the first casino in the Chicago area to turn to the outside for its high-end restaurant, Hugo's Frog Bar and Chop House. Hugo's, with restaurants in Chicago and Naperville, is part of Chicago's famed Gibson's steak house group.

Will a casino designed for premium play make it big in suburbia? Des Plaines is right next door to Rosemont, with its Convention Center and meeting spaces at hotels that attract business travelers. There are 16,000 hotel rooms within five miles of the casino, which is why Rivers didn't build its own hotel, choosing instead to run shuttles for after-hours meeting and convention trade. Des Plaines is right next door to O'Hare Airport. And 3.7 million people live within 20 miles of the casino. It's no wonder operators are thinking big.

A limiting factor is Illinois' legal maximum of 1,200 gaming positions per license, making Rivers and other casinos on the Illinois side of the border much smaller than their competitors in northwest Indiana. There is no maximum in Indiana and the Chicago area is really two markets in one. In Illinois, there are five casinos within about a 45-minute to 1-hour drive of the city --- Hollywood and Harrah's in Joliet, Hollywood in Aurora, Grand Victoria in Elgin and Rivers.

There has been plenty of turmoil with the state driving operators and players alike to distraction with its ever-shifting gaming tax laws and their consequences. The state has shifted from free admission to charges to back again as the gaming tax has soared and rolled back. And the state's 2008 ban on smoking in public places sent at least some casino players across state lines, looking for establishments where they could have their tobacco and blackjack too.

It's been a wild ride across the border in Indiana, where Horseshoe in Hammond, Ameristar in East Chicago, Majestic Star and Majestic Star II in Gary all are closer to the city than any of the Illinois casinos. Horseshoe opened its new half-billion dollar facility in the summer of 2008, with 100,000 square feet of gaming space on one floor. That's a far different --- and more pleasant --- experience than negotiating crowded stairways, up and down four flights to reach the small gaming decks at the vessel that was known as Empress Hammond before Jack Binion bought it, rechristened it Horseshoe Hammond, and in turn sold it to Harrah's Entertainment, now Caesars Entertainment.

A few miles down the road, in East Chicago, the casino originally known as Showboat Mardi Gras before morphing into Harrah's Mardi Gras, Harrah's East Chicago and Resorts East Chicago, morphed once again with its fourth owner. Now Ameristar East Chicago, its changes were mainly seen in revamped restaurants and players club.

In Gary, where founder Don Barden passed on in 2011, Majestic Star and Majestic Star II, share a common boarding area. Their locations just across a corridor from each other was a perpetual marketing problem until Barden bought out the former Trump Casino at the end of 2005 and rechristened it Majestic Star II. Even under one owner, the Gary boats have been far less successful than neighbors in Hammond and East Chicago. .

A little farther away, in Michigan City, Indiana, about an hour's drive from Chicago, Blue Chip opened its luxury hotel late in 2008. The casino was badly in need of a boost, with business having slipped after a nearby competitor, Four Winds, opened its land-based tribal casino in New Buffalo, Michigan in 2007.

There remain differences in the markets, though the riverboat cruises that once were required in Illinois and the simulated cruise times on the stationary Indiana vessels are a thing of the past. Players used to pay up to $28 for the privilege of boarding a boat and risking their money. The boarding fees are gone with the times, thank goodness.

In Illinois, the typical mix consists of about 1,100 slots and video poker machines, along with about 30 table games. Rivers is an exception, with 48 tables and 1,050 slots as it caters to big players. The only limit in Indiana is that the games must fit on one boat, so the casinos there are much larger --- the largest facility, Horseshoe Hammond's barge, has more than 3,000 electronic games and 140-plus table games.

In Indiana, casinos are permitted to remain open 24 hours a day, and they do. In Illinois, 24-hour gaming has never been approved. And Illinois has its smoking ban, while Indiana does not.

As for the games, Chicago area players have little these days that resembles its video poker hey-day of the mid-2000s. Then, Chicagoans used to the volume of 99-percenters close to home were often shocked to find pay tables that didn't match up when they visited the Las Vegas Strip. Alas, the video poker oasis has dried up, though there remain some good plays on high-denomination and multi-hand games.

VIDEO POKER: There are no 100 percent-plus games in the Chicago area, the last having disappeared in 2003 when Empress moved from its old boats onto the current Hollywood barge. For nearly a decade, Empress had 10-7 Double Bonus poker, a 100.17-percent game with expert play, and even added a progressive jackpot on dollar games.. Empress bought new gaming equipment for the barge, and in putting video poker on IGT's new game platform, Empress had to get each game re-approved by the Illinois Gaming Board. The board found that 10-7 Double Bonus did not meet its standard that no game may pay more than 100 percent in the long run.

Poof! The best deal in the Chicago area was gone.

The scenario repeated itself in 2009 when Jumer's Casino Rock Island, on the Mississippi River in northwest Illinois, moved onto its new boat. Long a staple on the old Jumer's boat, quarter 10-7 Double Bonus had to be scaled back for the move to meet state licensing standards. With five-coins wagered, the 250-coin pays on four 5s through Kings or on straight flushes have been scaled back to 239 coins. That leaves a 99.8 percent game with expert play.

The closest to a 100-percent games in the Chicago market today are the 10-6 Double Double Bonus Poker and a version of Deuces Wild version that both check in at 99.96 percent. The Deuces game is recognizable by paying 15-for-1 payoff on five of a kind, a big 11-for-1 on straight flushes, 4-for-1 on both four of a kind and full houses, and 3-for-1 on flushes. It'll take a big bankroll to play either game. The 99.6 percent version of Deuces is available at Horseshoe in Hammond on 50 Play games at dollar level, at on Triple Play/Five Play games at $2, $5 and $10 levels, and on single-hand games at $25, $50 and $100.

The 10-6 version of Double Double Bonus, paying 10-for-1 on full houses and 9-for1 on flushes, is also for big shooters, with single-hand games at $5 on up at Horseshoe and multi-hand games at $2 and up at Grand Victoria in Elgin.

What about games for those of more modest means? There's not much for quarter single-hand players. Rivers even opened without any single-hand 25-cent games. Single-hand play is reserved for dollar-and-up players, while the only quarter play is on multihand games such as Triple Play/Five Play Poker, Super Times Pay, and Multi-Strike Poker.

Majestic Star and Majestic Star II, once the home of a video poker room that could fit right into a Las Vegas locals joint, has a few remaining quarter games that approach 99-percent payback with expert play. The Deuces Wild version the late video poker guru Lenny Frome called "Illinois Deuces," a 98.9 percent game with expert play, is easy to find. Quarter players also can choose from 9-6 Double Double Bonus Poker (99.0) and 9-7-5 Double Bonus (99.1). Watch the Double Bonus pay tables, though. Some pay only 239 coins instead of 250 for straight flushes and for four of a kind, 5s through Kings. That drops the return to 98.7 percent, though some up the stakes with a progressive jackpot on royal flushes.

One go-to game for Chicago area operators is 9-6 Double Double Bonus Poker (98.98 percent), with a progressive jackpot. Hollywood (nee Empress) Joliet, Harrah's Joliet and Ameristar East Chicago all have $1 progressives, with the two Joliet casinos both offering three-way progressives --- progressive jackpots on royal flushes, four Aces with a low card kicker, and four Aces without the kicker.

Other than that, most high-paying games on the Illinois side of the border either are at $5 denomination on up, or multihand machines of at least $1 denomination. An exception is at Grand Victoria in Elgin, which has the game the late Lenny Frome called Illinois Deuces Wild (98.9) on Triple Play/Five Play games at quarter level. Other high-payers in Elgin are on high-denomination, multihand games, such as the NSU Deuces on $1 and up Multi-Strike.

Hollywood Aurora has 9-6 Double Double Bonus and Illinois Deuces Wild on single-hand games in multigame, multidenomination machines at the $1-$2-$5-$10 level and in the high-limit room in $5-$10-$25 machines, but like Grand Victoria, puts most of its best payers on high denomination, multihand games.

Craps: The addition of Rivers gave the Chicago area a second casino catering to big craps players. Rivers offers 100x odds --- the same as Horseshoe in Hammond. Horseshoe had dramatically changed the face of Chicago area craps after Jack Binion bought the former Empress in 1999. Bringing in 100x odds and $10,000 maximums was a radical change for Chicago, which had been a double-odds kind of town through the mid-1990s.

Now 20x odds have become common among competitors, while Rivers, which hired many of its key gaming personnel from Horseshoe, makes it a 100x odds duo.

Blackjack: Most games in the Chicago area use either six or eight decks. Table minimums are high, especially in Illinois where anything under $15 a hand is rare treat for a midweek morning. In Indiana, you can still find $5 tables at Majestic Star, which also offers the area's only double-deck game. However, Majestic Star has a tough set of rules, with dealers hitting soft 17; double downs allowed on 10 or 11 only; no doubling after splits; pairs permitted to be split only once, and no splitting Aces. That's a tough game, with a house edge against a basic strategy player upwards of eight-tenths of a percent.

Rules can be a mixed bag through the rest of the area. At Harrah's Joliet, high-limit six-deck games have the dealer standing on all 17s, you may double after splits and resplit Aces. House edge against a basic strategy player is 0.34 percent. But on low limit games, starting at $10, the dealer hits soft 17, taking the house edge up to 0.59 percent. Rivers has that same dichotomy, with the dealer hitting soft 17 on machine-shuffled games in the main pit, but standing on all 17s on hand-shuffled games in the high-limit room..

In Indiana, Horseshoe, Resorts and Blue Chip have the same basic game: Six decks, double after splits allowed, no resplitting of Aces, dealer stands on all 17s for a 0.41 percent house edge. All but Blue Chip have eight-deck tables, too, increasing the house edge to 0.43 percent. Horseshoe also has tables where the dealer hits soft 17. Watch out --- that one rule adds about two-tenths of a percent to the house edge.

Hollywood in Aurora has some six deck tables with $25 minimums that have the same rules as the Indiana boats, but lower-minimum tables have eight decks and call for the dealer to hit soft 17. House edge on that game is 0.66 percent. Grand Victoria has the dealer hit soft 17 on its six-deck games, leaving a 0.63 percent house edge on Grand Victoria's six-deck game. North of the border, in Milwaukee, Potawatomi has a six-deck game with the dealer hitting soft 17, double after splits permitted and resplitting pairs restricted so that you can wind up with a total of only three hands. The house edge against a basic strategy player is 0.64 percent.

OTHER TABLE GAMES: You'll find the highest maxiums and lowest minimum bets in Indiana. At Majestic Star, $5 tables remain a big part of the mix. But if you're a big-money baccarat player, then you can wager $100,000 a hand at Horseshoe or Rivers.

With bigger table pits, Indiana casinos offer much more variety than the Illinois competition. In addition to blackjack and craps, Illinois operations tend to stick with roulette and Caribbean Stud, with a little mini-baccarat, Let It Ride or Three Card Poker in the mix at some casinos. In Indiana, most operators have all those games, and also pick and choose from among pai-gow poker, Spanish 21, 3-5-7 Poker, Four Card Poker, Boston Stud, Bonus Six, Play Four --- if there's a promising new game, someone in Indiana is likely to try it.

SLOT MACHINES: Along with the rest of the country, Chicago has seen a great expansion in video bonusing slot games, with the hottest trend being toward lower and lower coin denominations. All Chicago area casinos now have penny slots. Horseshoe had been reluctant to join the penny trend, but the nationwide growth and popularity of the games have even casinos that cater to big players clamoring for copper.

Traditional three-reel games remain a big part of the mix at dollars and above, with Majestic Star having the largest selection of quarter three-reelers.

All slot machines in the area have gone TITO --- ticket in, ticket out for easy payouts with no delays for hopper fills or hopper jams.

One thing you'll not find in Illinois or Indiana is million-dollar jackpots. Wide-area progressives such as Megabucks that link several different properties to the same jackpot are illegal in Illinois and Indiana. If you're a jackpot chaser, you'll need to go to Potawatomi in Milwaukee or Four Winds in New Buffalo, which both are on the national Native American link.

Slot payouts tend to be higher in Illinois than in Indiana, from quarters on up, but the Indiana casinos pay as much or more than the Illinois operations in nickels and below. Illinois averages tend to hover around 95 percent on dollars, 93 percent on quarters and 88 percent on nickels, 85 percent on pennies while Indiana returns, are around 94 percent on dollars, 92 percent on quarters and 89 percent on nickels and 86 percent on pennies --- with variations from casino to casino, of course.

Admission is free to all Illinois casinos and, unless otherwise noted, all casinos offer: slots, video poker, blackjack, craps, roulette, Caribbean stud poker and three card poker. Some casinos also offer: let it ride (LIR), baccarat (B), mini-baccarat (MB), poker (P), Texas hold em bonus (THB), pai gow poker (PGP) and four card poker (FCP).

If you want to order a drink while playing, be aware that Illinois gaming regulations do not allow casinos to provide free alcoholic beverages. The minimum gambling age is 21.

For more information on visiting Illinois contact the state's Bureau of Tourism at (800) 226-6632 or www.enjoyillinois.com

Argosy Alton Casino
1 Front Street
Alton, Illinois 62002
(618) 474-7500
Web site: www.argosy.com/stlouis
Map: **#1** (260 miles S.W. of Chicago. 25 miles N. of St. Louis, MO)

Toll-Free Number: (800) 711-4263
Restaurants: 3
Buffets: L-$12.99/$15.99 (Sun)
　　　　D-$15.99/$26.99 (Thu)
Valet Parking: $5 (Free for slot club members)
Casino Hours: 8am-6am Daily
Casino Size: 23,000 Square Feet
Overnight RV Parking: Yes
Special Features: Casino features a 1,200-passenger modern yacht and a barge docked on the Mississippi River. 10% off buffets for slot club members.

Casino Queen
200 S. Front Street
E. St. Louis, Illinois 62201
(618) 874-5000
Web site: www.casinoqueen.com
Map: **#6** (290 miles S.W. of Chicago)

Toll-Free Number: (800) 777-0777
Rooms: 150 Price Range: $89-$149
Suites: 7 Price Range: $159-$499
Buffets: B-$6.95/$9.95 (Sun) L-$10.95
　　　　D-$13.95/$23.95(Mon)
Valet Parking: $4
Casino Hours: 8am-6am Daily
Casino Size: 40,000 Square Feet
Other Games: MB
Senior Discount: Various Wed 9am-Mid. if 50+
Overnight RV Parking: Must use RV park
Special Features: Land-based casino. 140-space RV park ($25-$39 per night). Sports Bar. MetroLink light-rail station at doorstep. $1 off buffets for slot club members.

Grand Victoria Casino
250 S. Grove Avenue
Elgin, Illinois 60120
(847) 468-7000
Web site: www.grandvictoriacasino.com
Map: **#4** (41 miles N.W. of Chicago)

Toll Free Number: (888) 508-1900
Restaurants: 4
Buffets: L-$11.99/$16.99 (Sun)
　　　　D-$16.99/$29.99 (Wed)/
　　　　$19.99(Sat)/$17.99(Sun)
Valet Parking: $5
Casino Hours: 8:30am-6:30am Daily
Casino Size: 29,850 Square Feet
Other Games: B, P
Overnight RV Parking: Yes
Senior Discount: $1 off buffets if 65+
Special Features: 1,200-passenger paddle wheeler-replica docked on the Fox River.

Harrah's Joliet
150 N. Joliet Street
Joliet, Illinois 60432
(815) 740-7800
Web site: www.harrahs.com
Map: **#2** (43 miles S.W. of Chicago)

Toll-Free Number: (800) HARRAHS
Rooms: 200 Price Range: $99-$199
Suites: 4 Price Range: Casino Use Only
Restaurants: 3
Buffets: B- $8.99 (Sun) L-$12.99/$17.99 (Sun)
D-$16.99/$28.99 (Fri)/ $22.99 (Sat)
Valet Parking: $5/Free if hotel guest
Casino Hours: 8am-6am Daily
Casino Size: 39,000 Square Feet
Other Games: MB, THB, LIR, No CSP
Overnight RV Parking: No
Special Features: Casino is on a barge docked on the Des Plaines River.

Harrah's Metropolis
100 E. Front Street
Metropolis, Illinois 62960
(618) 524-2628
Web site: www.harrahs.com
Map: **#8** (Across from Paducah, KY. Take exit 37 on I-24)

Toll-Free Number: (800) 929-5905
Rooms: 252 Price Range: $89-$299
Suites: 6 Price Range: Casino Use Only
Restaurants: 4
Buffets: L-$10.99/$15.99 (Sat/Sun)
D-$13.99/$17.99 (Sat/Sun)
Hours: 9am-5am/7am (Fri/Sat)
Valet Parking: $5
Other Games: P, LIR, MB, No CSP
Casino Size: 30,985 Square Feet
Overnight RV Parking: Free/RV Dump: No
Special Features: 1,300-passenger sidewheeler-replica docked on the Ohio River.

Hollywood Casino - Aurora
1 New York Street Bridge
Aurora, Illinois 60506
(630) 801-7000
Web site: www.hollywoodcasinoaurora.com
Map: **#7** (41 miles W. of Chicago)

Toll Free Number: (800) 888-7777
Restaurants: 3
Buffets: L-$12.99
D-$16.99/$22.99 (Fri)/
$18.99(Sat/Sun)
Valet Parking: $5
Casino Hours: 9:30am-4:30am/5:30 (Fri/Sat)
Casino Size: 41,384 Square Feet
Other Games: THB
Overnight RV Parking: No
Special Features: Casino is on a barge docked on the Fox River. $3 buffet discount for slot club members.

Hollywood Casino - Joliet
777 Hollywood Blvd
Joliet, Illinois 60436
(815) 744-9400
Web site: www.hollywoodcasinojoliet.com
Map: **#2** (43 miles S.W. of Chicago)

Toll-Free Number: (888) 436-7737
Rooms: 85 Price Range: $79-$120
Suites: 17 Price Range: $109-$129
Casino Hours: 8:30am-6:30am Daily
Restaurants: 3
Buffets: B-$16.99 (Sun)
L-$13.99
D-$17.99/$26.99 (Fri)/$19.99 (Sat)
Valet Parking: Free
Casino Size: 50,000 square feet
Other Games: MB, P
Overnight RV Parking: Must use RV park
Special Features: 2,500-passenger barge docked on the Des Plaines River. Rooms are at on-property Empress Hotel. 80-space RV park ($24-$30 per night).

Jumer's Casino & Hotel Rock Island
777 Jumer Drive
Rock Island, Illinois 61201
(309) 756-4600
Web site: www.jumerscri.com
Map: **#3** (170 miles W. of Chicago)

Toll-Free Number: (800) 477-7747
Rooms: 205 Price Range: $89-$250
Suites: 7 Price Range: For Casino Use Only
Restaurants: 4
Buffets: B-$13.99 (Sat/Sun)
     L-$9.99 D-$14.99/$9.99 (Wed)/
     $17.99 (Thu)
Valet Parking: Free
Casino Hours: 7am-5am Daily
Casino Size: 42,000 Square Feet
Other games: THB, PGP
Overnight RV Parking: No

Par-A-Dice Hotel Casino
21 Blackjack Boulevard
East Peoria, Illinois 61611
(309) 698-7711
Web site: www.par-a-dice.com
Map: **#5** (170 miles S.W. of Chicago)

Toll-Free Number: (800) 727-2342
Room Reservations: (800) 547-0711
Rooms: 195 Price Range: $105-$155
Suites 13 Price Range: $175-$500
Restaurants: 4
Buffets: B-$6.95 L-$9.99/$12.99 Sat/Sun)
D-$12.99/$9.99 (Tue/Sun)/$16.99 (Fri/Sat)
Valet Parking: $5
Casino Hours: 8am-5am/6am (Fri/Sat)
Casino Size: 26,116 Square Feet
Other Games: MB, LIR
Overnight RV Parking: Free/RV Dump: No
Senior Discount: Various Wed 9:30-3:30 if 55+
Special Features: 1,600-passenger modern
boat docked on the Illinois River.

Rivers Casino
3000 S River Road
Des Plaines, Illinois 60018
(847) 795-0777
Web site: www.playrivers.com
Map: **#9** (20 miles N.W. of Chicago)

Toll Free Number: (888) 307-0777
Restaurants: 6
Buffet Prices: L-$19/$21 (Fri-Sun)
              D-$24/$26 (Fri-Sun)
Casino Hours: 9am-7am Daily
Casino Size: 147,000-square-feet
Special features: Entire casino is non-smoking. Closest casino to O'Hare airport.
Free lounge entertainment nightly.
Other Games: MB
Overnight RV Parking: No

INDIANA

In June 1993 Indiana became the sixth state to legalize riverboat gambling. All of the state's riverboat casinos offer dockside gambling and, unless otherwise noted, are open 24 hours. The minimum gambling age is 21.

Following is information from the Indiana Gaming Commission regarding average slot payout percentages for the one-year period from July 1, 2010 through June 30, 2011:

CASINO	PAYBACK %
Hoosier Park	91.98
Indiana Live!	91.75
Grand Victoria	91.71
Blue Chip	91.62
French Lick	91.54
Belterra	91.40
Hollywood	91.16
Horseshoe SI	90.51
Casino Aztar	90.48
Majestic Star	90.38
Majestic Star II	90.38
Ameristar	90.19
Horseshoe Hammond	90.04

These figures reflect the average percentage returned by each casino for all of their electronic machines including slot machines, video poker, video keno, etc.

Unless otherwise noted, all casinos offer: blackjack, craps, roulette, slots, video poker, video keno and Caribbean stud poker. Optional games include: baccarat (B), mini-baccarat (MB), poker (P), pai gow poker (PGP), three card poker (TCP), four card poker (FCP), Spanish 21 (S21), big 6 wheel (B6) and let it ride (LIR).

If you want to order a drink while playing, be aware that Indiana gaming regulations do not allow casinos to provide free alcoholic beverages.

NOTE: If you happen to win a jackpot of $1,200 or more in Indiana, the casino will withhold 3.4% of your winnings for the Indiana Department of Revenue. You may, however, be able to get *some* of that money refunded by filing a state income tax return.

The $1,200 threshold also applies to any cash prizes won in casino drawings or tournaments.

For more information on visiting Indiana call (800) 289-6646 or visit their web site at www.enjoyindiana.com

Ameristar East Chicago
777 Ameristar Boulevard
East Chicago, Indiana 46312
(219) 378-3000
Web site: www.ameristarcasinos.com
Map: **#9** (12 miles E. of Chicago)

Toll-Free Number: (877) 496-1777
Hotel Reservations: (866) 711-7799
Rooms: 286 Prices: $149-$199
Suites: 7 Prices: Casino Use Only
Restaurants: 5
Buffets: B-$9.99 (Sat/Sun) L-$12.99
    D-$13.99/$24.99 (Fri)/$19.99 (Sat)
Valet Parking: $5/ Discounted for club members
Casino Size: 53,000 Square Feet
Other Games: S21, B, MB, P, PGP, TCP, LIR
Overnight RV Parking: No
Special Features: 3,750-passenger modern yacht docked on Lake Michigan.

Belterra Casino Resort and Spa
777 Belterra Drive
Florence, IN 47020
(812) 427-7777
Web site: www.belterracasino.com
Map: **#1** (35 miles S.W. of Cincinnati, Ohio)

Toll-Free Number: (888) 235-8377
Rooms: 608 Price Range: $99-$220
Suites: Casino use only
Restaurants: 7   Valet Parking: Free
Buffets: B-$9.95/$15.95 (Sun) L-$12.95
    D-$17.95/$23.95(Fri/Sat)
Casino Size: 38,000 Square Feet
Other Games: P, PGP, TCP, LIR
Overnight RV Parking: Free (must park in back rows of parking lot)/RV Dump: No
Special Features: 2,600-passenger sidewheeler docked on the Ohio River. Health club and spa. 18-hole golf course. 1,500-seat showroom. 10x odds on craps.

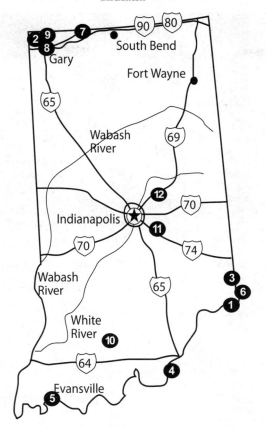

Blue Chip Casino & Hotel
2 Easy Street
Michigan City, Indiana 46360
(219) 879-7711
Web site: www.bluechip-casino.com
Map: **#7** (40 miles E. of Chicago)

Toll-Free Number: (888) 879-7711
Rooms: 180 Price Range: $75-$190
Suites: Casino Use Only
Restaurants: 4   Valet Parking: Free
Buffets: B-$10.99 L-$13.99
          D- $19.99/$22.99 (Tue)/
          $23.99 (Thu/Fri)/$24.99 (Sat/Sun)
Casino Size: 25,000 Square Feet
Other Games: MB, LIR, P, TCP, FCP
Overnight RV Parking: Free/RV Dump: No
Senior Discount: Various Wed if 55+
Special Features: 2,000-passenger modern yacht docked in a man-made canal.

Casino Aztar
421 N.W. Riverside Drive
Evansville, Indiana 47708
(812) 433-4000
Web site: www.casinoaztar.com
Map: **#5** (168 miles S.W. of Indianapolis)

Toll-Free Number: (800) DIAL-FUN
Rooms: 240 Price Range: $99-$149
Suites: 10 Price Range: $149-$225
Restaurants: 6   Valet Parking: Free
Buffets: B/L-$8.95
          D-$12.95
Hours: 8am-5am/24 Hours (Fri/Sat/Holidays)
Casino Size: 47,863 Square Feet
Other Games: S21, P, TCP, LIR
Overnight RV Parking: No
Senior Discount: Join Club 55, if 55+
Special Features: 2,700-passenger old fashioned paddlewheeler docked on the Ohio River.

The 5,000-passenger *Horseshoe Southern Indiana* is the world's largest riverboat casino.

French Lick Springs Resort & Casino
8670 West State Road 56
French Lick, Indiana 47432
(812) 936-9300
Web site: www.frenchlick.com
Map: **#10** (108 miles S. of Indianapolis)

Toll-Free Number: (800) 457-4042
Rooms: 442 Price Range: $169-$269
Restaurants: 7 Valet Parking: Free
Buffets: B-$12/$15 (Sat/Sun) L-$12
      D-$20/ $24.95 (Fri)
Casino Size: 84,000 Square Feet
Other Games: MB, TCP
Overnight RV Parking: Free/RV Dump: No
Special Features: Two 18-hole golf courses. Full-service spa. Six-lane bowling alley. Located on a 3,500-passenger barge in a man-made moat.

Grand Victoria Casino & Resort
600 Grand Victoria Drive
Rising Sun, Indiana 47040
(812) 438-1234
Web site: www.grandvictoria.com
Map: **#6** (40 miles S.W. of Cincinnati)

Toll-Free Number: (800) GRAND-11
Rooms: 201 Price Range: $69-$199
Restaurants: 5 Valet Parking: Free
Buffets: B-$16.95 (Sun) L-$11.99
      D-$16.99/$29.99 (Wed)/
      $26.99(Fri)/$17.99(Sun)
Hours: 8:30am-6:30am
Casino Size: 40,000 Square Feet
Other Games: TCP, B6
Overnight RV Parking: Free/RV Dump: No
Senior Discount: Various discounts Tue if 55+
Special Features: 3,000-passenger paddle wheeler docked on Ohio River. Hotel is Hyatt. 18-hole golf course. 1,100-seat showroom. 10x odds on craps.

Hollywood Casino & Hotel - Lawrenceburg
777 Hollywood Blvd
Lawrenceburg, Indiana 47025
(812) 539-8000
Web site: www.hollywoodindiana.com
Map: **#3** (95 miles S.E. of Indianapolis)

Toll-Free Number: (888) ARGOSY-7
Rooms: 440 Price Range: $59-$299
Restaurants: 5   Valet Parking: $3
Buffets: B-$15.95 (Sat/Sun) L-$15.95
       D-$18.95/$24.95 (Wed)/
       $19.95(Thu)/$27.95(Sat/Sun)
Casino Size: 80,000 Square Feet
Other Games: B6, MB, LIR, P, TCP, PGP,
       FCP, B
Overnight RV Parking: Free (only in lot across
    the street from the casino)/RV Dump: No
Special Features: 4,000-passenger modern
yacht docked on the Ohio River. Closest
casino to Cincinnati.

Horseshoe Casino Hotel Southern Indiana
11999 Casino Center Drive SE
Elizabeth, Indiana 47117
(812) 969-6000
Web site: www.horseshoe-indiana.com
Map: **#4** (20 miles S. of New Albany)

Toll-Free Number: (866) 676-SHOE
Toll-Free Number: (877) 237-6626
Reservation Number: (877) 766-2671
Rooms: 503 Prices: Price Range: $99-$299
Restaurants: 9   Valet Parking: Free
Buffets: B-$11.99/$19.99 (Sun)
       L-$15.95 D-$19.99/
       $27.99 (Fri)/$24.99 (Sat)
Casino Size: 93,000 Square Feet
Other Games: S21, B, MB, P, PGP, LIR, TCP
Overnight RV Parking: Free/RV Dump: No
Special Features: 5,000-passenger sidewheeler
docked on the Ohio River. 18-hole golf course.

Horseshoe Casino Hammond
777 Casino Center Drive
Hammond, Indiana 46320
(219) 473-7000
Web site: www.chicagohorseshoe.com
Map: **#2** (10 miles E. of Chicago)

Toll-Free Number: (866) 711-7463
Restaurants: 4
Buffets: B-$9.99/$19.99 (Sat/Sun)
       L-$15.99 D-$19.99
Valet Parking: $5/$3 with Total Rewards Card
Casino Size: 43,000 Square Feet
Other Games: MB, TCP, LIR, P
Overnight RV Parking: Free/RV Dump: No
Special Features: 4,000-passenger barge
docked on Lake Michigan.

Majestic Star Casinos & Hotel
1 Buffington Harbor Drive
Gary, Indiana 46406
(219) 977-7777
Web site: www.majesticstar.com
Map: **#8** (15 miles E. of Chicago)

Toll-Free Number: (888) 2B-LUCKY
Toll-Free Number: (888) 218-7867
Rooms: 300 Price Range: $99-$139
Restaurants: 6
Buffets: B-$6.99 L-$9.99
       D-$12.99/$9.99 (Tue)/$19.99 (Fri-Sun)
Valet Parking: Free/$5 (Fri-Sun)/$3 for
       slot club members
Casino Size: 43,000 Square Feet
Other Games: S21, B, MB, PGP, TCP, LIR, P
Overnight RV Parking: Free/RV Dump: No
Special Features: Two boats: 1,300-passenger
and 2,300-passenger modern yachts docked on
Lake Michigan.

Pari-Mutuels

In April 2007, the Indiana state legislature authorized the state's two horse tracks to have up to 2,000 electronic gaming machines.

Both casinos are open 24 hours and the minimum gambling age is 21. The minimum age for pari-mutuel betting is 18.

Hoosier Park
4500 Dan Patch Circle
Anderson, Indiana 46013
(765) 642-7223
Web site: www.hoosierpark.com
Map: **#12** (45 miles N.E. of Indianapolis)

Toll-Free Number: (800) 526-7223
Restaurants: 7
Buffets: B-$21.95 (Sun)
        L-$9.95
        D-$15.95/$23.95 (Fri/Sat)
Other Games: Only Gaming Machines
Casino Size: 92,000 Square Feet
Special Features: Thoroughbred horse racing August through October. Harness racing Late March through May. Year-round simulcasting of thoroughbred and harness racing.

Indiana Live! Casino
4200 N. Michigan Road
Shelbyville, Indiana 46176
(317) 421-0000
Web site: www.indianalivecasino.com
Map: **#11** (32 miles S.E. of Indianapolis)

Toll-Free Number: (877) 386-4463
Restaurants: 4
Buffets: B-$8.95/ $15.95 (Sun) L-$9.95
        D- $15.95/$23.95 (Fri)
Casino Size: 70,000 Square Feet
Other Games: Only Gaming Machines
Special Features: Thoroughbred horse racing late April through early July. Harness racing mid-July through early November. Year-round simulcasting of thoroughbred and harness racing.

IOWA

Iowa was the first state to legalize riverboat gambling. The boats began operating on April Fools Day in 1991 and passengers were originally limited to $5 per bet with a maximum loss of $200 per person, per cruise.

In early 1994 the Iowa legislature voted to eliminate the gambling restrictions. Additionally, gaming machines were legalized at three of the state's four pari-mutuel facilities. In mid-2004 a provision was added to allow table games at those three tracks. That same year the state also legalized casinos on moored barges that float in man-made basins of water and no longer required the casinos to be on boats. Iowa also has three Indian casinos.

Here's information, as supplied by the Iowa Racing and Gaming Commission, showing the electronic gaming machine payback percentages for all non-Indian locations for the one-year period from July 1, 2010 through June 30, 2011:

LOCATION	PAYBACK%
Isle of Capri - Waterloo	91.81
Prairie Meadows	91.74
Rhythm City	91.62
Isle of Capri - Bettendorf	91.67
Wild Rose - Emmetsburg	91.67
Isle of Capri - Marquette	91.60
Riverside	91.11
Wild Rose - Clinton	90.95
Mystique Casino	90.86
Catfish Bend	90.79
Diamond Jo Dubuque	90.72
Terrible's Lakeside	90.71
Diamond Jo Worth	90.59
Ameristar	90.56
Argosy Sioux City	90.44
Harrah's	89.54
Horsehoe Council Bluffs	89.77

These figures reflect the total percentages returned by each riverboat casino or pari-mutuel facility for all of its electronic machines including: slots, video poker, video keno, etc.

Admission to all Iowa casinos is free and, unless otherwise noted, all casinos are open 24 hours.

All Iowa casinos offer: blackjack, roulette, craps, slots and video poker. Some casinos also offer: mini-baccarat (MB), poker (P), pai gow poker (PGP), Caribbean stud poker (CSP), let it ride (LIR), big 6 (B6), bingo (BG), keno (K), three card poker (TCP), four card poker (FCP) and Spanish 21 (S21). The minimum gambling age is 21.

NOTE: If you happen to win a jackpot of $1,200 or more in Iowa, the casino will withhold 5% of your winnings for the Iowa Department of Revenue. If you want to try and get that money refunded, you will be required to file a state income tax return and, depending on the details of your return, you *may* get some of the money returned to you. The $1,200 threshold would also apply to any cash prizes won in casino drawings or tournaments.

For more information on visiting Iowa call the state's tourism department at (800) 345-4692 or visit their web site at www.traveliowa.com.

Ameristar Casino Council Bluffs
2200 River Road
Council Bluffs, Iowa 51501
(712) 328-8888
Website: www.ameristarcasinos.com
Map: **#8**

Toll-Free Number: (877) 462-7827
Rooms: 152 Price Range: $109-$299
Suites: 8 Price Range: $225-$375
Restaurants: 4 Valet Parking: Free
Buffets: B-$12.99 (Sat)/$15.99 (Sun)
L-$11.99
D-$15.99/$24.99 (Fri)/$17.99 (Sat/Sun)
Casino Size: 38,500 Square Feet
Other Games: S21, PGP, CSP, LIR, TCP
Overnight RV Parking: Free/RV Dump: No
Senior Discount: Various discounts if 55+
Special Features: 2,700-passenger sidewheeler replica on the Missouri River. Kids Quest supervised children's center.

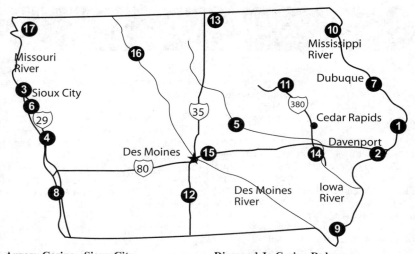

Argosy Casino - Sioux City
100 Larsen Park Road
Sioux City, Iowa 51101
(712) 294-5600
Website: www.argosy.com/siouxcity
Map: **#3**

Toll-Free Number: (800) 424-0080
Restaurants: 2   Valet Parking: Free
Casino Size: 20,498 Square Feet
Other Games: P, PGP, FCP
Overnight RV Parking: Free/RV Dump: No
Special Features: 1,200-passenger old-
fashioned stern wheeler on the Missouri River.
Comedy Club.

Catfish Bend Casino - Burlington
3001 Wine Gard Ave
Burlington, Iowa 52601
(319) 753-2946
Website: www.catfishbendcasino.com
Map: **#9** (180 miles S.E. of Des Moines)

Toll Free Number: (800) 372-2946
Rooms: 20 Price Range: $99-$119
Suites: 20 Price Range: $169-$259
Restaurants: 5 (1 open 24 hours)
Buffets: B-$5.95 L-$7.95/$12.95 (Sun)
     D-$15.95 (/$15.95(Thu)/$14.95(Fri/Sat)
Hours: 8am-3am/24 hours (Fri/Sat)
Casino Size: 23,000 Square Feet
Other Games: S21, P, PGP, TCP, FCP, MB
Overnight RV Parking: Free/RV Dump: No
Special features: Land-based casino.

Diamond Jo Casino Dubuque
400 E. Third Street
Dubuque, Iowa 52001
(563) 690-2100
Website: www.diamondjo.com
Map: **#7**

Toll-Free Number: (800) LUCKY-JO
Restaurants: 3   Valet Parking: Free
Buffets: B-$12.95 (Sun) L-$9.95
      D-$14.95
Hours: 8am-3am/24 Hours (Fri/Sat)
Casino Size: 37,500 Square Feet
Other Games: P, PGP, TCP
Overnight RV Parking: Free RV Dump: No
Special features: Land-based casino.

Diamond Jo Casino Worth
777 Diamond Jo Lane
Northwood, Iowa 50459
(641) 323-7777
Website: www.diamondjo.com
Map: **#13** (140 miles N. of Des Moines)

Toll-Free Number: (877) 323-5566
Rooms: 100 Price Range: $90-$150
Restaurants: 2   Valet Parking: Free
Buffets: B-$13.95 (Sun) L-$9.99/
      D-$13.99/$17.99 (Fri)
Casino Size: 36,363 Square Feet
Other Games: TCP, P, PGP
Overnight RV Parking: Free/RV Dump: No
Special features: Land-based casino. Burger
King and Starbucks.

Grand Falls Casino Resort
1415 Grand Falls Blvd
Larchwood, Iowa 51241
(712) 777-7777
Website: www.grandfallscasinoresort.com
Map: **#17** (17 Miles SE of Sioux Falls, SD)

Toll-Free number: (877)511-4FUN
Rooms: 88 Price Range: $84-$160
Suites: 10 Price Range: $108-$212
Restaurants: 3 Valet Parking: Free
Buffets: B-$8.99 L-$10.99/$16.99 (Sun)
         D-$16.99
Casino Size: 37,810
Other Games: P,FCP, PGP
Overnight RV Parking: No
Special features: 1,200-seat event center.

Harrah's Council Bluffs
One Harrah's Boulevard
Council Bluffs, Iowa 51501
(712) 329-6000
Website: www.harrahs.com
Map: **#8**

Toll Free Number: (800) HARRAHS
Rooms: 240 Price Range: $99-$279
Suites: 11 Price Range Casino Use Only
Restaurants: 4 Valet Parking: Free
Buffets: Brunch-$14.99 (Sat-Sun)
         L-$11.99 D-$14.99
Casino Size: 33,406 Square Feet
Other Games: S21, TCP, LIR, PGP, P
Overnight RV Parking: Free/RV Dump: No
Special Features: 2,365-passenger paddle
wheel-replica on the Missouri River.

Isle Casino Hotel - Bettendorf
1821 State Street
Bettendorf, Iowa 52722
(563) 359-7280
Website: www.isleofcapricasino.com
Map: **#2**

Toll-Free Number: (800) 724-5825
Rooms: 220 Price Range: $59-$129
Suites: 36 Price Range $109-$199
Restaurants: 5 Valet Parking: Free
Buffets: B-$5.99/$7.99 (Sat/Sun) L-$9.99
         D-$12.99/$14.99(Thu/Sun)/
         $16.99(Fri/Sat)
Other Games: P, PGP, TCP
Casino Size: 28,750 Square Feet
Overnight RV Parking: Free/RV Dump: No
Senior Discount: Various on Tue if 50+
Special Features: 2,500-passenger old-
fashioned paddle wheeler on the Mississippi
River. 53-slip marina.

Isle Casino Hotel - Waterloo
777 Isle of Capri Boulevard
Waterloo, Iowa 52701
(319)833-4753
Website: www.theislewaterloo.com
Map: **#11** (90 miles W. of Dubuque)

Toll-Free Number: (800) THE ISLE
Rooms: 170 Price Range: $89-$149
Suites: 27 Price Range: $149-$289
Restaurants: 3
Buffets: B-$7.95 L-$9.95
         Brunch-$14.95 (Sun)
         D-$12.95/$17.95 (Fri/Sat)
Other Games: P, TCP, PGP
Casino Size: 43,142 Square Feet
Overnight RV Parking: Free/RV Dump: No
Senior Discount: Various Tue/Thu if 50+
         always $1 off buffet if 50 or older
Special features: Land-based casino.

Lady Luck Casino - Marquette
100 Anti Monopoly Street
Marquette, Iowa 52158
(563) 873-3531
Website: www.isleofcapricasino.com
Map: **#10** (60 miles N. of Dubuque)

Toll-Free Number: (800) 4-YOU-BET
Rooms: 22 Price Range: $89-$109
Suites: 3 Price Range: $125
Restaurants: 2   Valet Parking: Free
Buffets: B-$5.99/$11.99 (Sun)
        L-$8.49 D-$11.99/$15.99 (Fri/Sat)
Hours: 9am-2am/24 Hours (Fri/Sat)
Other Games: P, TCP
Casino Size: 18,747 Square Feet
Overnight RV Parking: Free/RV Dump: No
Senior Discount: Various Tue/Thu if 50+
        always 10% off buffet if 50 or older
Special Features: 1,200-passenger paddle
wheeler on the Mississippi River.

Rhythm City Casino
101 West River Drive
Davenport, Iowa 52801
(319) 328-8000
Website: www.rhythmcitycasino.com
Map: **#2** (80 miles S.E. of Cedar Rapids)

Toll-Free Number: (800) BOAT-711
Restaurants: 2   Valet Parking: Free
Buffets: B-$3.99/$5.99 (Sat/Sun)
        L-$8.99/$12.99 (Sun) D-$12.99
Casino Size: 29,062 Square Feet
Other Games: PGP, TCP, P
Overnight RV Parking: Free/RV Dump: No
Senior Discount: Various Tue if 40+
Special Features: 2,200-passenger riverboat
on the Mississippi River. Affiliated with Isle
of Capri Casinos.

Riverside Casino & Golf Resort
3184 Highway 22
Riverside, Iowa 52327
(319) 648-1234
Website: www.riversidecasinoandresort.com
Map: **#14** (81 miles W. of Davenport)

Toll-Free Number: (877) 677-3456
Rooms: 200 Price Range: $110-$230
Restaurants: 2   Valet Parking: Free
Buffets: B-$8.99 L-$10.99/$16.99 (Sat/Sun)
        D-$16.99
Casino Size: 56,400 Square Feet
Overnight RV Parking: Free/RV Dump: No
Other Games: P, PGP, CSP, TCP
Special features: Land-based casino.18-hole
golf course. 20-space RV park. 1,200-seat
showroom.

Terrible's Lakeside Casino
777 Casino Drive
Osceola, Iowa 50213
(641) 342-9511
Website: www.herbstgaming.com
Map: **#12** (50 miles S. of Des Moines)

Toll-Free Number: (877) 477-5253
Suites: 63   Price: $79-$159
Restaurants: 2   Valet Parking: Free
Buffets: B-$5.99/$6.99 (Sat/Sun)
        L-$7.99/$8.99 (Sat)/ $11.99 (Sun)
        D-$10.99/$14.99 (Tue/Fri)/ $12.99 (Sat)
Casino Size: 36,200 Square Feet
Other Games: P, PGP, TCP
Overnight RV Parking: Free/RV Dump: No
Senior Discount: Various on Mon/Wed if 50+
Special Features: Casino is on a barge.
47-space RV park ($20 per night). Fishing/
boating dock.

Wild Rose Casino - Clinton
777 Wild Rose Drive
Clinton, Iowa 52733
(563) 243-9000
Website: www.wildroseresorts.com
Map: **#1** (90 miles E. of Cedar Rapids)

Toll-Free Number: (800) 457-9975
Rooms: 60 Price Range: $79-$119
Suites: 6 Price Range: $149-$179
Restaurants: 2
Valet Parking: Not Offered
Buffets: B-$6.99/ $12.99 (Sun) L-$6.99
        D-$12.99/ $15.99 (Sat)
Hours: 8am-2am/4am (Fri/Sat)
Casino Size: 19,681 Square Feet
Additional Games: PGP, LIR
Overnight RV Parking: Free/RV Dump: No
Special Features: Land-based casino.

Wild Rose Casino - Emmetsberg
777 Main Street
Emmetsburg, Iowa 50536
(712) 852-3400
Website: www.wildroseresorts.com
Map: **#16** (120 miles N.E. of Sioux City)

Toll-Free Number: (877) 720-7673
Rooms: 62 Price Range: $69-$99
Suites: 8 Price Range: $99-$129
Restaurants: 2 Valet Parking: Free
Buffets: B-$3.99 L-$8.99
        Brunch -$10.99 (Sun)
        D-$8.99(Sun)/$10.95 (Mon/Tue)
$10.99 (Tue)/$12.95 (Fri)/$13.95(Sat)
Hours: 8am-2am/24 Hours (Fri/Sat)
Casino Size: 16,270 Square Feet
Other Games: P, PGP
Senior Discount: Various Tue if 55+
Overnight RV Parking: Must use RV park
Special features: Land-based casino. $2 off
buffets for slot club members. 68-space RV
park ($15 per night).

Indian Casinos

Meskwaki Bingo Casino Hotel
1504 305th Street
Tama, Iowa 52339
(641) 484-2108
Website: www.meskwaki.com
Map: **#5** (40 miles W. of Cedar Rapids)

Toll-Free Number: (800) 728-4263
Rooms: 390 Price Range: $65-$105
Suites: 14 Price Range: $185-$250
Restaurants: 4 Liquor: Yes Valet Park: Free
Buffets: B-$6.95/$10.95 (Sun) L-$8.95
        D-$10.95/$17.25 (Fri)/$14.95 (Sat)
Other Games: S21, MB, P, PGP, LIR, TCP
        K, BG, Off-Track Betting
Overnight RV Parking: Must Use RV Park
Senior Discount: $1 off buffet if 55+
Special Features: 50-space RV park ($15-$20
per night). Spa.

WinnaVegas Casino
1500 330th Street
Sloan, Iowa 51055
(712) 428-9466
Website: www.winnavegas.biz
Map: **#6** (20 miles S. of Sioux City)

Toll-Free Number: (800) 468-9466
Restaurants: 1 Liquor: Yes Valet Park: Free
Buffets: B- $8.99 (Sun) L-$8.99
        D-$11.99/$14.99 (Thu/Sat)
Other Games: P, BG, TCP
Overnight RV Parking: Free/RV Dump: No
Special Features: 20-space RV park ($7 per
night).

Pari-Mutuels

Horseshoe Casino - Council Bluffs
2701 23rd Avenue
Council Bluffs, Iowa 51501
(712) 323-2500
Website: www.horseshoe.com/councilbluffs
Map: **#8** (102 miles S. of Sioux City)

Toll-Free Number: (877) 771-7463
Rooms: 158   Price Range: $119-$269
Restaurants: 3   Valet Parking: Free
Buffets: L-$11.99/$15.99 (Sun)
               D-$16.99/$17.99 (Fri/Sat)
Casino Size: 78,811 Square Feet
Other Games: P, PGP, LIR, MB, S21, TCP, FCP
Overnight RV Parking: Free/RV Dump: No
Special Features: Live dog racing (Tue-Sun). Daily horse and greyhound race simulcasting. Free shuttle service from local hotels. Affiliated with Harrah's. 100x odds on craps.

Mystique Casino
1855 Greyhound Park Road
Dubuque, Iowa 52001
(563) 582-3647
Website: www.mystiquedbq.com
Map: **#7**

Toll-Free Number: (800) 373-3647
Restaurants: 2   Valet Parking: Free
Hours: 8am-3am/24 Hours (Fri/Sat)
Casino Size: 44,200 Square Feet
Other Games: TCP, FCP, P, PGP
Overnight RV Parking: Free/RV Dump: No
Senior Discount: Various specials Wed if 55+
Special Features: Live greyhound racing (Wed-Sun) from late-April through October. Greyhound, harness and thoroughbred simulcasting all year.

Prairie Meadows Racetrack & Casino
1 Prairie Meadows Drive
Altoona, Iowa 50009
(515) 967-1000
Website: www.prairiemeadows.com
Map: **#15** (5 miles E. of Des Moines)

Toll-Free Number: (800) 325-9015
Restaurants: 3   Valet Parking: Free
Buffets: B- $8.95/ $11.95 (Sun) L- $8.95
D-$10.95/$8.95 (Mon/Tue)/ $15.95 (Fri/Sat)
Casino Size: 83,930 Square Feet
Other Games: MB, P, PGP, TCP
Overnight RV Parking: Yes
Senior Discount: Various specials if 55+
Special Features: Live thoroughbred and quarter-horse racing April through October. Daily simulcasting of dog and horse racing
.

KANSAS

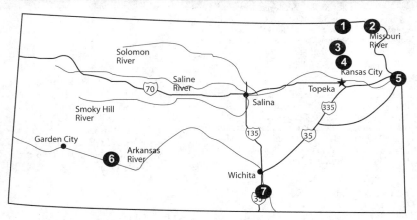

In April 2007 the Kansas legislature authorized local referendums to allow state-run casinos in four counties.

Casinos were approved for Wyandotte County (home to Kansas City), Ford County, Sumner County and Cherokee County. The Boot Hill Casino in Ford County was the first to open in December 2009.

The Hollywood Casino at Kansas Speedway is expected to open in Kansas City (Wyandotte County) by mid-2012, while in the city of Mulvane (Sumner County) the Kansas Star Casino is expected to open by February 2012.

As of August 2011, no company had applied for the remaining casino license for Cherokee country.

The Kansas Racing & Gaming Commission does not release information about the payback percentages on electronic gaming machines in Kansas. However, gaming regulations require that all machines return no less than 87%.

Unless otherwise noted, all Kansas casinos are open 24 hours and offer the following games: blackjack, craps, roulette, slots and video poker. Other games include: poker (P), Caribbean stud poker (CSP), let it ride (LIR), three card poker (TCP) and bingo (BG). The minimum gambling age is 21.

Boot Hill Casino & Resort
4000 W Comanche Street
Dodge City, Kansas 67801
(620) 225-0374
Website: www.boothillcasino.com
Map: **#6** (155 miles W of Wichita)

Toll-free Number: (877) 906-0777
Restaurants: 1
Other Games: P, TCP
Overnight RV Parking: Free/RV Dump: No
Special Features: Hotel expected to open December 2011.

Hollywood Casino at Kansas Speedway
777 Hollywood Casino Blvd
Kansas City, Kansas 66111
Web site: hollywoodcasinokansas.com
Map: **#5**
EXPECTED TO OPEN MID-2012

Kansas Star Casino
108 West Main St.
Mulvane, Kansas 67110
(316) 558-5710
Map: **#7** (25 miles S. of Wichita)
EXPECTED TO OPEN EARLY 2012

Pari-Mutuels

There are five Indian casinos in Kansas and they are not required to release information on their slot machine payback percentages. However, according to officials at the Kansas State Gaming Agency, which is responsible for overseeing the tribal-state compacts, "the minimum payback percentage for electronic gaming devices is 80%."

Unless otherwise noted, all Kansas Indian casinos are open 24 hours and offer the following games: blackjack, craps, roulette, slots and video poker. Other games include: poker (P), Caribbean stud poker (CSP), let it ride (LIR), three card poker (TCP) and bingo (BG). The minimum gambling age is 21.

Casino White Cloud
777 Jackpot Drive
White Cloud, Kansas 66094
(785) 595-3430
Website: www.casinowhitecloud.org
Map: **#2** (70 miles N.E. of Topeka)

Toll-Free Number: (877) 652-6115
Restaurants: 2 Liquor: Yes Valet Parking: No
Buffets: L-$8.00 D-$10.00
Casino Size: 21,000 Square Feet
Casino Hours: 9am-1am/3am (Fri/Sat)
Other Games: BG, No Roulette
Overnight RV Parking: Free/RV Dump: No

Golden Eagle Casino
1121 Goldfinch Road
Horton, Kansas 66439
(785) 486-6601
Map: **#3** (45 miles N. of Topeka)
Website: www.goldeneaglecasino.com

Toll-Free Number: (888) 464-5825
Restaurants: 2 Liquor: No Valet Parking: No
Buffets: L-$7.95/$10.95 (Sun)
        D-$10.95/$14.95 (Tue/Thu/Sat)
Other Games: P, TCP, BG (Wed-Sun)
Overnight RV Parking: Free/RV Dump: No
Senior Discount: Various Tue if 50+
Special Features: RV hookups available ($10 per night).

Prairie Band Casino & Resort
12305 150th Road
Mayetta, Kansas 66509
(785) 966-7777
Website: www.pbpgaming.com
Map: **#4** (17 miles N. of Topeka)

Toll-Free Number: (888) 727-4946
Rooms: 297 Price Range: $79-$219
Suites: 8 Price Range: Casino Use Only
Restaurants: 3 Liquor: Yes Valet Parking: Free
Buffets: B-$6.99 L-$8.99/$11.99 (Sun)
        D-$14.99/$20.95 (Mon)/
                $17.99 (Thu)/$21.95 (Fri)
Casino Size: 33,000 Square Feet
Other Games: MB, P, PGP, LIR, TCP
Overnight RV Parking: Must use RV park
Special Features: 67-space RV park ($20-$30 per night).

Sac & Fox Casino
1322 U.S. Highway 75
Powhattan, Kansas 66527
(785)-467-8000
Map: **#1** (60 miles N. of Topeka)
Website: www.sacandfoxcasino.com

Toll-Free Number: (800) 990-2946
Restaurant: 3 Liquor: Yes Valet Parking: No
Buffets: B-$7.99/$11.99 (Sun)
        L-$8.99/$3.99 (Mon/Tue)
        D-$11.99/$17.99 (Fri)/$9.99 (Wed/Sat)
Casino Size: 40,000 Square Feet
Other Games: TCP
Overnight RV Parking: Free/RV Dump: No
Senior Discount: $1 off meals if 55 or older
Special Features: 24-hour truck stop. Golf driving range. 12-space RV park ($10 per night).

7th Street Casino
803 North 7th Street
Kansas City, Kansas 66101
(913) 371-7500
Website: www.7th-streetcasino.com
Map: **#5**

Restaurant: 2 Liquor: Yes Valet Parking: No
Casino Size: 20,000 Square Feet
Other Games: Only Gaming Machines
Overnight RV Parking: No/RV Dump: No

LOUISIANA

Louisiana was the fourth state to approve riverboat casino gambling and its 1991 gambling law allows a maximum of 15 boats statewide. In 1992 a provision was added for one land-based casino in New Orleans.

The state also has three land-based Indian casinos and four gaming machines-only casinos located at pari-mutuel facilities. Additionally, video poker is permitted at Louisiana truck stops, OTB's and bars/taverns in 31 of the state's 64 parishes (counties). All riverboat casinos in Louisiana are required to remain dockside and all are open 24 hours.

Gaming regulations require that gaming machines in casinos be programmed to pay back no less than 80% and no more than 99.9%. For video gaming machines at locations other than casinos the law requires a minimum return of 80% and a maximum return of 94%.

Louisiana gaming statistics are not broken down by individual properties. Rather, they are classified by region: Baton Rouge (BR), Lake Charles (LC), New Orleans (NO) and Shreveport/Bossier City (SB).

The Baton Rouge casinos consist of the Belle of Baton Rouge, Hollywood Casino and Evangeline Downs. The Lake Charles casinos include: Isle of Capri, L'Auberge du Lac and Delta Downs. New Orleans area casinos are: Amelia Belle, Boomtown, Harrah's (landbased), Treasure Chest and Fairgrounds Raceway. The Shreveport/Bossier city casinos include: Boomtown, Diamond Jack's, Sam's Town, Eldorado, Horseshoe and Harrah's Louisiana Downs.

Here's information, as supplied by the Louisiana State Police-Riverboat Gaming Section, showing the average electronic machine payback percentages for each area's casinos for the 12-month period from June, 2010 through May, 2011:

	BR	LC	NO	SB
1¢	88.7%	89.1%	88.6%	88.9%
5¢	90.7%	90.5%	91.1%	90.4%
25¢	93.5%	91.9%	92.7%	92.0%
$1	93.6%	93.7%	93.4%	93.2%
$5	94.4%	94.6%	94.5%	93.8%
All	90.7%	91.3%	90.5%	91.0%

These numbers reflect the percentage of money returned on each denomination of machine and encompass all electronic machines including video poker and video keno. The best returns for each category are highlighted in bold print.

NOTE: If you happen to win a jackpot of $1,200 or more in Louisiana, the casino will withhold 6% of your winnings for the Louisiana Department of Revenue. If you want to try and get that money refunded, you will be required to file a state income tax return and, depending on the details of your return, you *may* get some of the money returned to you. The $1,200 threshold would also apply to any cash prizes won in casino drawings or tournaments.

All casinos offer: blackjack, craps, roulette, slots and video poker. Optional games include: Spanish 21 (S21), baccarat (B), mini-baccarat (MB), poker (P), Caribbean stud poker (CSP), pai gow poker (PGP), let it ride (LIR), casino war (CW), three-card poker (TCP), four card (FCP), big 6 wheel (B6), keno (K), Texas hold 'em Bonus (THB) and bingo (BG). The minimum gambling age is 21 for casino gaming and 18 for pari-mutuel betting.

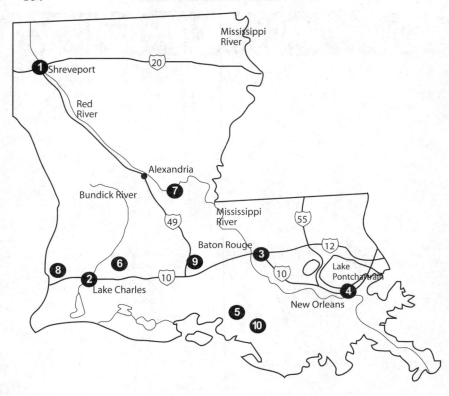

For more information on visiting Louisiana call the state's tourism department at (800) 633-6970 or visit www.louisianatravel.com

Amelia Belle Casino
500 Lake Palourde Rd
Amelia, Louisiana 70340
(985) 631-1777
Website: www.ameliabellecasino.com
Map: **#10** (75 miles S. of Baton Rouge)

Restaurants: 2
Buffets: L- $7.95/$10.95 (Sat/Sun) D- $10.95
Casino Size: 29,745 Square Feet
Other Games: P, MB, TCP
Overnight RV Parking: No
Special Features: 1,200-passenger paddle wheeler on Bayou Boeuf.

Belle of Baton Rouge
103 France Street
Baton Rouge, Louisiana 70802
(225) 378-6000
Website: www.belleofbatonrouge.com
Map: **#3**

Toll-Free Number: (800) 676-4847
Restaurants: 4   Valet Parking: $10
Casino Size: 28,500 Square Feet
Other Games: MB, P, PGP, TCP, FCP
Overnight RV Parking: No
Special Features: 1,500-passenger paddle wheeler on the Mississippi River. 300-room Sheraton Hotel is adjacent to casino (800-325-3535). 10% off food/drink for slot club members.

Boomtown Casino & Hotel Bossier City
300 Riverside Drive
Bossier City, Louisiana 71171
(318) 746-0711
Website: www.boomtownbossier.com
Map: **#1** (across the Red River From Shreveport)

Toll-Free Number: (866) 462-8696
Rooms: 100 Price Range: $89-$129
Suites: 88 Price Range: $119-$209
Restaurants: 4   Valet Parking: Free
Buffets: B-$7.99 L-$11.99
          D-$19.99/26.99 (Fri/Sat)
Casino Size: 29,649 Square Feet
Other Games: MB, TCP, FCP
Overnight RV Parking: No
Senior Discount: $4.99 breakfast if 55+
Special Features: 1,925-passenger paddle wheeler on the Red River. $1 off buffets for slot club members.

Boomtown Casino New Orleans
4132 Peters Road
Harvey, Louisiana 70058
(504) 366-7711
Website: www.boomtownneworleans.com
Map: **#4** (a suburb of New Orleans)

Toll-Free Number: (800) 366-7711
Restaurants: 4   Valet Parking: Free
Buffets: B- $9.78 (Sat/Sun)
          L-$7.99/$16.99 (Sun)
          D-$12.99/$29.99 (Thu)/
          $19.99 (Wed/Fri)/$29.99 (Sat)
Casino Size: 29,745 Square Feet
Other Games: MB, P, PGP, TCP
Overnight RV Parking: Free/RV Dump: No
Senior Discount: $2 off buffets if slot club memberSpecial Features: 1,600-passenger paddle wheeler on the Harvey Canal. Family arcade.

DiamondJacks Casino - Bossier City
711 DiamondJacks Blvd
Bossier City, Louisiana 71111
(318) 678-7777
Website: www.diamondjacks.com
Map: **#1** (across the Red River from Shreveport)

Toll-Free Number: (866) 552-9629
Suites: 570 Price Range: $109-$199
Restaurants: 3   Valet Parking: Free
Buffets: B-$9.99 L-$12.99
          D-$16.95/$20.95(Mon/Fri/Sat)
Casino Size: 29,921 Square Feet
Other Games: S21, MB, TCP, FCP, LIR, PGP
Overnight RV Parking: Must use RV park
Senior Discount: 50% off buffet if 50+
Special Features: 1,650-passenger paddle wheeler on the Red River. 32-space RV park ($30/$35 Fri-Sat). Supervised childcare center. 1,200-seat showroom. Buffet discount if slot club member.

Eldorado Casino Shreveport
451 Clyde Fant Parkway
Shreveport, Louisiana 71101
(318) 220-0981
Website: www.eldoradoshreveport.com
Map: **#1**

Hotel Reservations: (877) 602-0711
Suites: 403 Price Range: $95-$175
Restaurants: 4   Valet Parking: Free
Buffet: B-$14.99 (Sat-Sun) L-$11.99
          D-$16.99/$19.99 (Thu)/$21.99 (Fri)
Casino Size: 28,226 Square Feet
Other Games: CW, CSP, LIR, TCP, PGP
Overnight RV Parking: No
Special Features: 1,500-passenger paddle wheeler on the Red River.

Harrah's New Orleans
Canal at the River
New Orleans, Louisiana 70130
(504) 533-6000
Website: www.harrahs.com
Map: **#4**

Toll-Free Number: (800) 847-5299
Toll-Free Number: (800) HARRAHS
Suites: 450　Price Range: $160-$389
Restaurants: 4
Buffet: B-$11.99　L-$11.99/$29.99 (Sun)
　　　　D-$29.99/$19.99 (Mon-Wed)
Valet Parking: $10 first two hours/$5 for each
additional two hours/$25 maximum
　(Free for Diamond and Platinum members)
Casino Size: 125,119 Square Feet
Other Games: MB, P, PGP, CSP, LIR,
　　　　TCP, FCP, B6
Overnight RV Parking: No
Special Features: Landbased casino. Five
themed gaming areas. Fast food court. Daily
live jazz music. Self-parking costs $5 to
$25 depending on length of stay. Slot club
members playing for minimum of 30 minutes
can get validated for up to 24 hours of free
parking.

Hollywood Casino - Baton Rouge
1717 River Road North
Baton Rouge, Louisiana 70802
(225) 381-7777
Website: www.casinorouge.com
Map: **#3**

Toll-Free Number: (800) 44-ROUGE
Restaurants: 3　Valet Parking: Free
Buffets: L-$10.95/$17.95 (Sun)
　　　　D-$24.95 (Wed/Thu)/
　　　　$12.95(Mon)/$22.95(Fri)/
　　　　$19.95(Sat)/$13.95 (Sun)
Casino Size: 27,317 Square Feet
Other Games: TCP, FCP
Overnight RV Parking: Free/RV Dump: No
Special Features: 1,500-passenger paddle
wheeler on the Mississippi River.

Horseshoe Casino Hotel - Bossier City
711 Horseshoe Boulevard
Bossier City, Louisiana 71111
(318) 742-0711
Website: www.horseshoe.com
Map: **#1** (across the Red River from
　Shreveport)

Toll-Free Number: (800) 895-0711
Suites: 606　Price Range: $170-$550
Restaurants: 4　Valet Parking: Free
Buffets: L-$12.95/$20.95(Fri)
　　　　D-$17.95/$22.95 (Fri)
Casino Size: 25,540 Square Feet
Other Games: MB, P, CSP, TCP,
　　　　FCP, LIR, THB, PGP
Overnight RV Parking: Free/RV Dump: No
Senior Discount: 10% buffet discount if 55+
Special Features: 2,930-passenger paddle
wheeler on the Red River. Affiliated with
Harrah's.

Isle of Capri - Lake Charles
100 Westlake Avenue
Westlake, Louisiana 70669
(337) 430-0711
Website: www.isleofcapricasino.com
Map: **#2** (220 miles W. of New Orleans)

Toll-Free Number: (800) THE-ISLE
Inn Rooms: 241　Price Range: $89-$199
Suite Rooms: 252　Price Range: $139-$299
Restaurants: 5　Valet Parking: Free
Buffets: B-$6.99　L-$10.99
　　　　D-$16.99/$25.99 (Fri/Sat)
Casino Size: 51,569 Square Feet
Other Games: MB, TCP, LIR, PGP,
　　　　FCP, B6, P, THB
Overnight RV Parking: Must use RV park
Senior Discount: Various Tue if 50+
Special Features: Two 1,200-passenger paddle
wheelers on Lake Charles. 8-space RV park
($10 per night).

L'auberge du Lac Hotel & Casino
3202 Nelson Road
Lake Charles, Louisiana 70601
(337) 475-2900
Website: www.ldlcasino.com
Map: **#2** (220 miles W. of New Orleans)

Toll-Free Number: (866) 580-7444
Rooms: 636 Price Range: $109-$329
Suites: 99 Price Range: $199-$750
Restaurants: 5 Valet Parking: Free
Buffet: L-$13.50/$21.99 (Sat/Sun)
    D-$16.99/$22.99 (Tue/Wed)/
        $24.99 (Thu)/$25.99 (Fri/Sat)
Casino Size: 27,000 Square Feet
Other Games: MB, PGP, CSP, LIR,
    TCP, FCP, THB
Overnight RV Parking: Must use RV park.
Special Features: 18-hole golf course. Spa.
Pool with lazy river ride. 1,500-seat event
center. 13-space RV park ($25 per night).

Sam's Town Hotel & Casino Shreveport
315 Clyde Fant Parkway
Shreveport, Louisiana 71101
(318) 424-7777
Website: www.samstownshreveport.com
Map: **#1**

Toll-Free Number: (866) 861-0711
Rooms: 514 Price Range: $66-$195
Restaurants: 3 Valet Parking: Free
Buffet: B-$14.99 (Sat/Sun) L-$11.99
    D-$15.99/$17.99 (Thu)/ $19.99 (Fri/Sat)
Casino Size: 29,234 Square Feet
Other Games: MB, LIR, TCP, FCP, THB
Overnight RV Parking: No
Special Features: 1,650-passenger paddle
wheeler on the Red River.

Treasure Chest Casino
5050 Williams Boulevard
Kenner, Louisiana 70065
(504) 443-8000
Website: www.treasurechest.com
Map: **#4** (a suburb of New Orleans)

Toll-Free Number: (800) 298-0711
Restaurants: 2 Valet Parking: $5
Buffet: L-$10.99/$21.99 (Sun)
    D- $17.99/$19.99 (Thu)/$23.99 (Fri/Sat)
Casino Hours: 11am-3am/5am (Fri/Sat)
Casino Size: 23,680 Square Feet
Other Games: MB, PGP, TCP, LIR, FCP, P
Overnight RV Parking: No
Senior Special: 50% off buffet if 50+
Special Features: 1,900-passenger paddle
wheeler on Lake Pontchartrain. Hilton Garden
Inn located next to casino (504-712-0504).

Indian Casinos

Coushatta Casino Resort
777 Coushatta Drive
Kinder, Louisiana 70648
(318) 738-7300
Website: www.coushattacasinoresort.com
Map: **#6** (35 miles N.E. of Lake Charles)

Toll-Free Number: (800) 584-7263
Room Reservations: (888) 774-7263
Hotel Rooms: 118 Price Range: $149-$189
Suites: 90 Price Range: Casino Use Only
Inn Rooms: 195 Price Range: $89-$109
Lodge Rooms: 92 Price Range: $89-$109
Restaurants: 6 Liquor: Yes Valet Park: Free
Buffets: L-$12.00/$15.00 (Sat/Sun)
    D-$16.00/$25.00 (Wed)/
        $28.00 (Fri/Sat)
Casino Size: 105,000 Square Feet
Other Games: MB, P, PGP, LIR,
    TCP, FCP, THB
Overnight RV Parking: No
Special Features: Land-based casino.
100-space RV park ($19/$24 Fri-Sat). Video
arcade. Kids Quest childcare center. 18-hole
golf course.

Cypress Bayou Casino
P.O. Box 519
Charenton, Louisiana 70523
(318) 923-7284
Website: www.cypressbayou.com
Map: **#5** (75 miles S. of Baton Rouge)

Toll-Free Number: (800) 284-4386
Restaurants: 6 Liquor: Yes Valet : Free
Casino Size: 65,000 Square Feet
Other Games: PGP, LIR, P, OTB,
                          TCP, FCP, THB
Overnight RV Parking: Free/RV Dump: No
Special Features: Land-based casino. Gift
shop. Cigar bar. 12-space RV park ($10 per
night).

Paragon Casino Resort
711 Paragon Place
Marksville, Louisiana 71351
(318) 253-1946
Website: www.paragoncasinoresort.com
Map: **#7** (30 miles S.E. of Alexandria)

Toll-Free Number: (800) 946-1946
Rooms: 335 Price Range: $99-$179
Suites: 57 Price Range: $155-$345
Restaurants: 6 Liquor: Yes Valet Parking: Free
Buffets: B-$7.99 L-$9.99/$12.99 (Sat/Sun)
               D-$14.99/ $16.99 (Tue)/
                        $18.99 (Wed/Fri/Sat)
Casino Size: 103,520 Square Feet
Other Games: MB, P, LIR, OTB,
                          TCP, FCP, THB, PGP
Overnight RV Parking: Must use RV park
Special Features: Land-based casino.
185-space RV Park ($17/$22 Fri-Sat). Video
arcade. Kids Quest childcare center. 18-hole
golf course.

Pari-Mutuels

Delta Downs Racetrack & Casino
2717 Highway 3063
Vinton, Louisiana 70668
(337) 589-7441
Website: www.deltadowns.com
Map: **#8** (20 miles W. of Lake Charles)

Toll-Free Number: (800) 589-7441
Room Reservations: (888) 332-7829
Rooms: 203 Price Range: $94-$234
Suites: 33 Price Range: Casino use only
Restaurants: 7   Valet Parking: Free
Buffets: B- $14.99 (Sat/Sun)
               L-$11.99
               D-$15.99/$21.99 (Fri/Sat)
Casino Size: 14,825 Square Feet
Other Games: Only machines
Overnight RV Parking: Free/RV Dump: No
Special Features: Live thoroughbred and
quarter-horse racing (Wed-Sat) early October
through mid-July. Daily simulcasting of horse
racing.

Evangeline Downs Racetrack & Casino
2235 Creswell Lane Extension
Opelousas, Louisiana 70570
(337) 896-7223
Website: www.evangelinedowns.com
Map: **#9** (30 miles W. of Baton Rouge)

Toll-Free Number: (866) 472-2466
Restaurants: 3   Valet Parking: Free
Buffets: L-$16.99 (Sun)
               D-$12.99/$20.99 (Fri/Sat)/$13.99 (Sun)
Casino Size: 14,619 Square Feet
Other Games: Only machines
Overnight RV Parking: Free/RV Dump: No
Senior Discount: Various Tue if 50 or older
Special Features: Live thoroughbred and
quarter-horse racing (Wed-Sat) April through
November. Daily simulcasting of horse racing.

Fair Grounds Racecourse & Slots
1751 Gentilly Boulevard
New Orleans, Louisiana 70119
(504) 944-5515
Website: www.fairgroundsracecourse.com
Map: **#4**

Restaurants: 1   Valet Parking: $5
Other Size: 15,000 Square Feet
Other Games: Only Slots, No video poker
Overnight RV Parking: Free/RV Dump: No
Special Features: Live thoroughbred racing
November through March.

Harrah's Louisiana Downs
8000 E. Texas Street
Bossier City, Louisiana 71111
(318) 742-5555
Website: www.harrahs.com
Map: **#1**

Toll-Free Number: (800) HARRAHS
Restaurants: 5   Valet Parking: Free
Buffets: B-$10.99
         L-$12.99/$18.99 (Sat)/$12.99 (Sun)
         D-$15.99/ $21.99 (Sat)
Casino Size: 12,855 Square Feet
Other Games: Only machines
Overnight RV Parking: Free/RV Dump: No
Senior Discount: Various Tue if 50 or older
Special Features: Live thoroughbred racing
(Thu-Sun) May through early October.
Live quarter-horse racing racing (Sat-Wed)
late October through November. Daily
simulcasting of horse racing.

MAINE

In early 2004 the Maine legislature authorized slot machines to be placed at Bangor Raceway and that facility opened in November 2005.

Gaming regulations require a minimum return of 89% on all machines and the games offered include: slots, video poker and video blackjack.

During the 12-month period from July 2010 through June 2011, the average return on gaming machines was 91.20%

The minimum gambling age is 21 for slots and 18 for pari-mutuel wagering.

For more information on visiting Maine call their Office of Tourism at (888) 624-6345 or visit their website at www.visitmaine.com.

Hollywood Slots Hotel & Raceway
500 Main Street
Bangor, Maine 04402
(207) 262-6146
Website: www.hollywoodslotsatbangor.com
Map: **#1**

Toll-Free Number: (877) 779-7771
Rooms: 90 Price Range: $129-$189
Admission: Free   Parking: Free
Restaurants: 1
Buffets: B-$8.99 L-$9.99
         D-$13.99/$15.99 (Fri/Sat)
Hours: 8am-1am/2am (Sat/Sun)
Special Features: Live harness racing day and evenings from early May through late July and mid-October through mid-November. Daily simulcasting of horse and harness racing.

MARYLAND

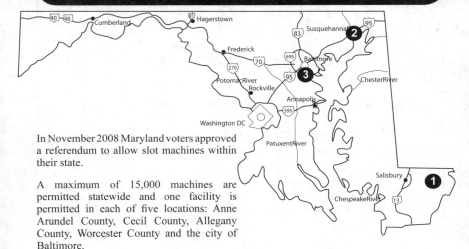

In November 2008 Maryland voters approved a referendum to allow slot machines within their state.

A maximum of 15,000 machines are permitted statewide and one facility is permitted in each of five locations: Anne Arundel County, Cecil County, Allegany County, Worcester County and the city of Baltimore.

The Ocean Downs Racetrack in Worchester county and Hollywood Casino Perryville in Cecil county opened in 2010 and 2011 respectively. Maryland Live! in Anne Arundel County is expected to open in June 2012.

The other two locations have not been licensed and no casinos are expected to open in those areas before the end of 2012.

No public information is available about the actual payback percentages on gaming machines in Maryland. However, gaming regulations require a minimum payback of 87%

For Maryland tourism information, call (800) 543-1036, or visit their web site at www.visitmaryland.com

Hollywood Casino - Perryville
1201 Chesapeake Overlook Parkway
Perryville, MD 29103
Website: hollywoodcasinoperryville.com

Map: **#2** (30 miles NE of Baltimore)

Restaurants: 2
Overnight RV Parking: No
Buffets: L- $13.95 D- $13.95/$17.95 (Fri/Sat)
Casino Size: 35,000 Square Feet

Ocean Downs Racetrack
10218 Racetrack Road
Berlin MD 21811
(410) 641-0600
Website: www.oceandowns.com

Map: **#1** (110 miles SE of Annapolis)

Track Admission: Free
Self-Parking: Free Valet: $6
Restaurants: 2
Overnight RV Parking: No
Special Features: Live harness racing Sun/Wed/Thu/Sat eves mid-June through late August. Daily simulcasting of thoroughbred and harness racing.

Maryland Live!
7000 Arundel Mills Blvd
Handover, MD 21076
Website: ppecasinoresortsmd.com

Map: **#3** (10 miles SW of Baltimore)
EXPECTED TO OPEN JUNE 2012

MICHIGAN

One of Michigan's most popular casinos is actually in Canada. It's Casino Windsor in Ontario which is just across the river from downtown Detroit.

All winnings are paid in Canadian currency and the minimum gambling age is 19. The casino is open 24 hours and offers the following games: blackjack, Spanish 21, craps, roulette, poker, baccarat, mini-baccarat, big six wheel, pai-gow poker, Caribbean stud poker, three-card poker and let it ride.

Caesars Windsor
377 Riverside Drive East
Windsor, Ontario N9A 7H7
(519) 258-7878
Website: www.caesarswindsor.com
Map: **#12**

PRICES ARE IN CANADIAN DOLLARS
Toll-Free Number: (800) 991-7777
Room Reservations: (800) 991-8888
Rooms: 349 Price Range: $99-$349
Suites: 40 Price Range: $229-$1,000
Restaurants: 4 (1 open 24 hours)
Buffets: L-$17.99/$19.99 (Sun)
            D-$22.99/$29.99(Fri)/$25.99 (Sat)
Valet Parking: Free
Casino Size: 100,000 Square Feet
Overnight RV Parking: Free/RV Dump: No
Special Features: Entire casino is non-smoking.

The only casinos in Michigan not on indian reservations are located in downtown Detroit. All three are open 24 hours and offer the following games: blackjack, craps, roulette, baccarat, mini-baccarat, Caribbean stud poker, three-card poker, pai gow poker, let it ride, big 6 wheel and casino war. No public information is available about the payback percentages on Detroit's gaming machines.

The minimum gambling age at all Detroit casinos is 21 and all three casinos offer free valet parking.

Greektown Casino
555 E. Lafayette Boulevard
Detroit, Michigan 48226
(313) 223-2999
Website: www.greektowncasino.com
Map: **#12**

Toll free Number: (888) 771-4386
Rooms: 400 Price Range: $99-$169
Restaurants: 2
Buffets: L/D- $17.99
Casino Size: 75,000 Square Feet
Other Games: Poker

MGM Grand Detroit Casino
1777 Third Avenue
Detroit, Michigan 48226
(313) 393-7777
Website: www.mgmgranddetroit.com
Map: **#12**

Toll-Free Number: (877) 888-2121
Room Reservations: (800) 991-8888
Rooms: 335 Price Range: $259-$459
Suites: 65 Price Range: $499-$3,000
Restaurants: 6 (1 open 24 hours)
Buffets: B-$18.00
            L-$22.00/$28.00 (Sun)
            D-$28.00/$32.00 (Wed/Fri)
Casino Size: 75,000 Square Feet
Other Games: Spanish 21
Overnight RV Parking: No

MotorCity Casino and Hotel
2901 Grand River Avenue
Detroit, Michigan 48201
(313) 237-7711
Website: www.motorcitycasino.com
Map: **#12**

Toll-Free Number: (877) 777-0711
Rooms: 359 Price Range: $169-$399
Suites: 41 Price Range: $319-$499
Restaurants: 4 (1 open 24 hours)
Buffets: B-$13.00 L-$19.00
            D-$24.00/$32.00 (Mon/Fri)
Casino Size: 75,000 Square Feet
Other Games: Spanish 21
Overnight RV Parking: Free/RV Dump: No

Indian casinos in Michigan are not required to release information on their slot machine payback percentages. However, according to officials at the Michigan Gaming Control Board, which is responsible for overseeing the tribal-state compacts, "the machines must meet the minimum standards for machines in Nevada or New Jersey." In Nevada the minimum return is 75% and in New Jersey it's 83%. Therefore, Michigan's Indian casinos must return at least 75% in order to comply with the law.

Unless otherwise noted, all Indian casinos in Michigan are open 24 hours and offer the following games: blackjack, craps, roulette, slots and video poker. Other games offered include: Spanish 21 (S21), craps (C), roulette (R), baccarat (B), mini-baccarat (MB), poker (P), Caribbean stud poker (CSP), let it ride (LIR), three-card poker (TCP), four-card poker (FCP), keno (K) and bingo (BG).

The minimum gambling age is 19 at all five Kewadin casinos. plus the odawa casino resort in Petoskey. It is 21 at all other Indian casinos except for the following seven where it's 18: Leelanau Sands, Turtle Creek, Island Resort, Ojibwa, Ojibwa II, Lac Vieux and Soaring Eagle. Valet parking is free at all casinos.

For more information on visiting Michigan call the state's department of tourism at (800) 543-2937 or go to www.michigan.org.

Bay Mills Resort & Casino
11386 Lakeshore Drive
Brimley, Michigan 49715
(906) 248-3715
Website: www.4baymills.com
Map: **#3** (12 miles S.W. of Sault Ste. Marie)

Toll-Free Number: (888) 422-9645
Rooms: 142 Price Range: $69-$119
Suites: 4 Price Range: $150-$200
Restaurants: 5 (1 open 24 hours) Liquor: Yes
Casino Size: 15,000 Square Feet
Other Games: P, CSP, LIR, TCP
Overnight RV Parking: Must use RV park
Senior Discount: Various Tue/Wed if 50+
Special Features: Free shuttle to King's Club and Kewadin casinos. 76-space RV park ($21/$29 with hookups). 18-hole golf course.

FireKeepers Casino
11 Mile Road
Battle Creek, Michigan 48022
(269) 962-0000
Website: www.firekeeperscasino.com
Map: **#18**

Toll-Free Number: (877) 352-8777
Valet Parking: $3/Free for slot club members
Restaurants: 5 Liquor: Yes
Buffets: L-$14.95 D-$18.95/$23.95 (Fri/Sun)
Casino Size: 107,000 Square Feet
Other Games: MB, TCP, LIR, PGP, P, BG
Overnight RV Parking: Free/RV Dump: No
Special Features: Sports bar. Dance club. Food court.

Four Winds Casino Resort
11111 Wilson Road
New Buffalo, MI 49117
(269) 926-4500
Website: www.fourwindscasino.com
Map: **#19** (75 miles E. of Chicago)

Toll-Free Number: (866) 494-6371
Rooms: 129 Price Range: $129-$259
Suites: 36 Price Range: $249-$949
Restaurants: 6 Liquor: Yes
Buffets: B-$18.00 (Sat/Sun)
          L- $14.00 D-$16.00/$24.00 (Fri)/$28 (Sat)
Casino Size: 130,000 Square Feet
Other Games: B, MB, P, LIR, TCP, FCP, PGP
Overnight RV Parking: Free/RV Dump: No

Four Winds Casino - Hartford
68600 Red Arrow Highway
Hartford, MI 49057
(269) 926-4500
Website: www.fourwindscasino.com
Map: **#21** (75 miles E. of Chicago)

Toll-Free Number: (866) 494-6371
Restaurants: 6 Liquor: Yes
Casino Size: 52,000 Square Feet
Other Games: No craps, MB, TCP
Overnight RV Parking: Free/RV Dump: No

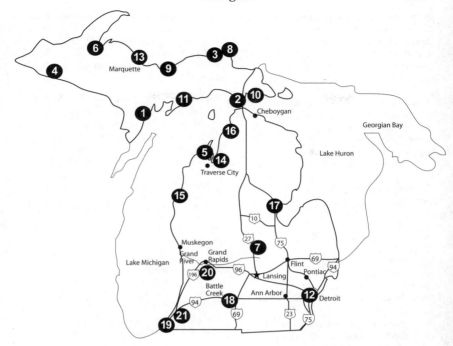

Gun Lake Casino
1123 129th Ave
Bradley, MI 49311
Website: Gunlakecasino.com

Map: **#20** (23 miles S of Grand Rapids)

Toll-free Number: (866) 398-7111
Restaurants: 1 Liquor: Yes
Casino Size: 30,000 Square Feet
Other Games: B, LIR
Special Features: Food court with three fast food outlets.

Island Resort & Casino
P.O. Box 351
Harris, Michigan 49845
(906) 466-2941
Website: www.islandresortandcasino.com
Map: **#1** (13 miles W. of Escanaba on Hwy. 41)

Toll-Free Number: (800) 682-6040
Rooms: 102 Price Range: $65-$89
Suites: 11 Price Range: $95-$500
Restaurants: 3   Liquor: Yes
Casino Size: 135,000 Square Feet
Overnight RV Parking: Must use RV park
Other Games: S21, P, TCP, FCP, LIR, BG
Special Features: 53-space RV park ($15 per night).

Kewadin Casino - Christmas
N7761 Candy Cane Lane
Munising, Michigan 49862
(906) 387-5475
Website: www.kewadin.com
Map: **#9** (40 miles E. of Marquette)

Toll-Free Number: (800) KEWADIN
Restaurants: 1   Liquor: Yes
Hours: 8am-3am Daily
Valet Parking: Not offered
Casino Size: 3,060 Square Feet
Other Games: LIR, TCP, No craps/roulette
Overnight RV Parking: Free/RV Dump: No
Special Features: Free local-area shuttle
service.

Kewadin Casino - Hessel
3 Mile Road, Box 789
Hessel, Michigan 49745
(906) 484-2903
Website: www.kewadin.com
Map: **#10** (20 miles N.E. of St. Ignace)

Toll-Free Number: (800) KEWADIN
Restaurants: 1 Deli   Liquor: Yes
Valet Parking: Not offered
Hours: 9am-11pm/Midnight (Fri/Sat)
Casino Size: 6,500 Square Feet
Other Games: Only gaming machines
Overnight RV Parking: Must use RV Park
Special Features: 40-space RV park open
May-October ($5/$10 with hook-ups per
night).

Kewadin Casino - Manistique
US 2 East, Rte 1, Box 1533D
Manistique, Michigan 49854
(906) 341-5510
Website: www.kewadin.com
Map: **#11** (95 miles S.E. of Marquette)

Toll-Free Number: (800) KEWADIN
Restaurants: 1 Deli   Liquor: Yes
Valet Parking: Not offered
Hours: 8am-3am Daily
Casino Size: 25,000 Square Feet
Other Games: LIR, TCP, No Craps
Overnight RV Parking: Free/RV Dump: No
Special Features: Free shuttle service from
local motels.

Kewadin Casino Hotel - Sault Ste. Marie
2186 Shunk Road
Sault Ste. Marie, Michigan 49783
(906) 632-0530
Website: www.kewadin.com
Map: **#8**

Toll-Free Number: (800) KEWADIN
Rooms: 300 Price Range: $69-$105
Suites: 20 Price Range: $95-$145
Restaurants: 2   Liquor: Yes
Buffets: B-$8.49/$11.99 (Sun) L-$9.99
          D-$13.49/$19.99 (Fri/Sat)
Casino Size: 85,123 Square Feet
Other Games: P, LIR, TCP, K, BG
Overnight RV Parking: Must use RV park
Senior Discount: Various Thu 7am-7pm if 50+
Special Features: Free shuttle service to local
motels and airport. 75-space RV park ($10
per night).

Kewadin Casino - St. Ignace
3039 Mackinaw Trail
St. Ignace, Michigan 49781
(906) 643-7071
Website: www.kewadin.com
Map: **#2** (50 miles S. of Sault Ste. Marie)

Toll-Free Number: (800) KEWADIN
Rooms: 81 Prices: $81-$101
Suites: 11 Prices: $111-$131
Restaurants: 1 Deli Liquor: Yes
Buffets: B-$8.49/$11.99 (Sun) L-$9.99
          D-$13.49/$19.99 (Fri/Sat)
Casino Size: 56,168 Square Feet
Other Games: P, LIR, TCP, FCP, K
Overnight RV Parking: Free/RV Dump: No
Senior Discount: Various Thu 7am-7pm if 50+
Special Features: Local motels/hotels offer
packages with free shuttle service. Sports bar.

Kings Club Casino
12140 W. Lakeshore Drive
Brimley, Michigan 49715
(906) 248-3700
Website: www.4baymills.com
Map: **#3** (12 miles S.W. of Sault Ste. Marie)

Toll-Free Number: (888) 422-9645
Restaurants: 3 Liquor: Yes
Valet Parking: Not offered
Casino Size: 6,500 Square Feet
Other Games: Only gaming machines
Overnight RV Parking: Must use RV park
Special Features: Two miles from, and
affiliated with, Bay Mills Resort & Casino.
75-space RV park ($17/$25 w/hookup) at
Bay Mills.

Lac Vieux Desert Casino
N 5384 US 45 North
Watersmeet, Michigan 49969
(906) 358-4226
Website: www.lvdcasino.com
Map: **#4** (49 miles S.E. of Ironwood)

Toll-Free Number: (800) 583-3599
Room Reservations: (800) 895-2505
Rooms: 107 Price Range: $49-$89
Suites: 25 Price Range: $79-$159
Restaurants: 1 Liquor: Yes
Buffets: B-$9.99 (Sun) L-$8.95 (Fri)
    D-$21.99 (Fri)/$19.99 (Sat)
Valet Parking: Not offered
Casino Size: 25,000 Square Feet
Other Games: P, BG
Overnight RV Parking: Must use RV park
Senior Discount: Various Tuesdays if 55+
Special Features: 9-hole golf course. 14-space RV park ($15 per night).

Leelanau Sands Casino
2521 N.W. Bayshore Drive
Sutton's Bay, Michigan 49682
(231) 271-4104
Website: www.casino2win.com
Map: **#5** (4 miles N. of Sutton's Bay)

Toll-Free Number: (800) 922-2946
Room Reservations: (800) 930-3008
Rooms: 51 Price Range: $79-$109
Suites: 2 Price Range: $109-$129
Restaurants: 1 Liquor: Yes
Buffets: Brunch-$11.95 (Sun)
Casino Size: 29,000 Square Feet
Hours: 8am-2am/4am (Fri/Sat)
Other Games: TCP, LIR, BG (Sun-Fri)
Overnight RV Parking: Free/RV Dump: No
Senior Discount: Various on Thu if 55+
Special Features: RV hook-ups available for $7 per night.

Little River Casino
2700 Orchard Drive
Manistee, Michigan 49660
(231) 723-1535
Website: www.littlerivercasinos.com
Map: **#15** (60 miles S.W of Traverse City)

Toll-Free Number: (888) 568-2244
Toll-Free Number: (866) 466-7338
Rooms: 271 Price Range: $89-$169
Suites: 20 Price Range: $199-$279
Restaurants: 3 Liquor: Yes
Buffets: B-$7.99 L-$9.99
    D-$14.99/$24.99 (Fri/Sat)
Casino Size: 75,000 Square Feet
Other Games: LIR, TCP, BG (Sun-Wed)
Senior Discount: Various if you sign up for
    Senior Slot Club. Must be 55+.
Overnight RV Parking: Free/RV Dump: Free
Special Features: 95-space RV park open April-November ($20-$38 per night).

Odawa Casino Resort
1760 Lears Road
Petoskey, Michigan 49770
(231) 439-9100
Website: www.odawacasino.com
Map: **#16** (50 miles S.W of Cheboygan)

Toll-Free Number: (877) 442-6464
Rooms: 127 Price Range: $69-$129
Suites: 10 Price Range- $109-$159
Restaurants: 4 Liquor: Yes
Buffets: B-$8.95 L-$8.95/$12.95 (Sun)
    D-$15.95/$23.95 (Thu)
Casino Size: 33,000 Square Feet
Other Games: LIR, P, TCP
Overnight RV Parking: Free/RV Dump: No
Senior Discount: Various Wed/Sun if 55+
Special Features: Hotel is 1/4-mile from casino and rooms offer views of Little Traverse Bay. Free shuttle service to/from local hotels.

Ojibwa Casino Resort - Baraga
797 Michigan Avenue
Baraga, Michigan 49908
(906) 353-6333
Website: www.ojibwacasino.com
Map: **#6** (30 miles S. of Houghton)

Toll-Free Number: (800) 323-8045
Rooms: 78 Price Range: $69-$89
Suites: 2 Price Range: $79-$99
Restaurants: 1 Liquor: Yes
Casino Size: 17,000 Square Feet
Other Games: TCP, BG (Tue/Thu)
Overnight RV Parking: Must use RV park
Senior Discount: Various Mon 10-5 if 55+
Special Features: 12-space RV Park ($20 per night). 8-lane bowling alley. Table games open Friday-Sunday.

Ojibwa Casino - Marquette
105 Acre Trail
Marquette, Michigan 49855
(906) 249-4200
Website: www.ojibwacasino.com
Map: **#13**

Toll-Free Number: (888) 560-9905
Restaurants: 1 Snack Bar Liquor: Yes
Valet Parking: Not offered
Other Games: P
Overnight RV Parking: Free/RV Dump: No
Senior Discount: Various Mon 10-5 if 55+
Special features: 7-space RV Park (Free).
Table games open 2pm-2am/4am (Fri/Sat).

Saganing Eagles Landing Casino
2690 Worth Road
Standish, Michigan 48658
(888) 732-4532
Website: www.saganing-eagleslanding.com
Map: ##**17**

Casino Size: 32,000 square feet
Restaurants: 2
Overnight RV Parking: Must stay in RV park
Special Features: Subway restaurant. Electronic versions of blackjack and roulette. 50-spot RV park ($15 per night).

Soaring Eagle Casino & Resort
6800 E Soaring Eagle Boulevard
Mount Pleasant, Michigan 48858
(517) 775-5777
Website: www.soaringeaglecasino.com
Map: **#7** (65 miles N. of Lansing)

Toll-Free Number: (888) 7-EAGLE-7
Room Reservations: (877) 2-EAGLE-2
Rooms: 491 Price Range: $149-$219
Suites: 21 Price Range: $199-$399
Restaurants: 5 Liquor: Yes
Buffets: B-$9.25 L-$15.75
    D-$18.75/$24.75 (Mon/Wed)
Casino Size: 150,000 Square Feet
Other Games: P, MB, CSP, LIR, TCP, FCP, BG (Wed-Mon), B6, K
Overnight RV Parking: Free/RV Dump: No
Special Features: Casino is in two separate buildings. Kid's Quest childcare center. Video arcade. Gift shop. Art gallery.

Turtle Creek Casino
7741 M-72 East
Williamsburg, Michigan 49690
(231) 534-8888
Website: www.turtlecreekcasino.com
Map: **#14** (8 miles E. of Traverse City)

Toll-Free Number: (888) 777-8946
Rooms: 127 Price Range: $105-$175
Suites: 10 Price Range: $125-$195
Restaurants: 2 Liquor: Yes
Buffets: B-$7.95 (Sun) L-$9.95
    D-$14.95/$19.95 (Fri)
Casino Size: 72,000 Square Feet
Other Games: CSP, LIR, P, TCP, FCP, BG (Wed/Thu/Fri/Sun)
Overnight RV Parking: Free/RV Dump: No

MINNESOTA

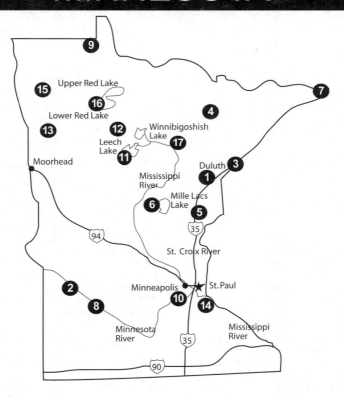

All Minnesota casinos are located on Indian reservations and under a compact reached with the state the only table games permitted are card games such as blackjack and poker. Additionally, the only kind of slot machines allowed are the electronic video variety. Therefore, you will not find any mechanical slots that have traditional reels - only video screens.

According to the terms of the compact between the state and the tribes, however, the minimum and maximum payouts are regulated as follows: video poker and video blackjack - 83% to 98%, slot machines - 80% to 95%, keno - 75% to 95%. Each tribe is free to set its machines to pay back anywhere within those limits and the tribes do not not release any information regarding their slot machine percentage paybacks.

The hours of operation are listed for those casinos that are not open on a 24-hour basis. Unless otherwise noted, all casinos offer: video slots, video poker, video keno and blackjack. Optional games include: poker (P), Caribbean stud poker (CSP), pai gow poker (PGP), three-card poker (TCP), let it ride (LIR) and bingo (BG).

The minimum gambling age is 18 at all casinos except Fon Du Luth where it is 21. Valet parking is free at all casinos except Jackpot Junction and Mystic Lake.

For more information on visiting Minnesota call the state's office of tourism at (800) 657-3700 or go to www.exploreminnesota.com.

Black Bear Casino Resort
1785 Highway 210
Carlton, Minnesota 55718
(218) 878-2327
Website: www.blackbearcasinoresort.com
Map: **#1** (130 miles N. of Twin Cities)

Toll-Free Number: (888) 771-0777
Reservation Number: (800) 553-0022
Rooms: 158 Price Range: $45-$74
Suites: 60 Price Range: $55-$99
Restaurants: 2 (open 24 hours) Liquor: Yes
Buffets: B-$5.99 /$8.99(Sat/Sun)
        L-$7.99 D-$11.99/
        $17.99/(Thu)/$14.99(Fri)/$12.99(Sat)
Casino Size: 65,000 Square Feet
Other Games: P, BG
Overnight RV Parking: Free/RV Dump: No
Senior Discount: Various Mon if 52+
Special Features: Golf Course. Arcade.

Fond-du-Luth Casino
129 E. Superior Street
Duluth, Minnesota 55802
(218) 722-0280
Website: www.fondduluthcasino.com
Map: **#3** (150 miles N.E. of Twin Cities)

Toll-Free Number: (800) 873-0280
Restaurants: 2 Snack Bars Liquor: Yes
Casino Size: 20,000 Square Feet
Other Games: Only Blackjack and Slots
Overnight RV Parking: No
Senior Discount: Various Tue 10am-5pm if 55+
Special Features: One hour free parking in
lot adjacent to casino (must be validated
in casino). Free shuttle to/from Black Bear
Casino.

Fortune Bay Resort/Casino
1430 Bois Forte Road
Tower, Minnesota 55790
(218) 753-6400
Website: www.fortunebay.com
Map: **#4** (150 miles N.E. of Twin Cities. 24
miles N.E. of Virginia, MN on the S. shore of
Lake Vermilion)

Toll-Free Number: (800) 992-7529
Hotel Reservations: (800) 555-1714
Rooms: 83 Price Range: $79-$109
Suites: 33 Price Range: $89-$159
Restaurants: 4 Liquor: Yes Valet: Free
Buffets: B-$6.95 (Fri/Sat)/$7.95 (Sun)
        D-$13.95/$15.95(Fri)/$17.95(Sat)
Casino Size: 17,000 Square Feet
Other Games: BG (Wed/Fri-Sun)
Overnight RV Parking: Must use RV park
Senior Discount: Specials Mon/Thu if 55+
Special Features: Located on S.E. shore of
Lake Vermilion. 84-slip marina. 36-space RV
Park ($25/$30 w/hookup). Snowmobile and
hiking trails. 18-hole golf course.

Grand Casino Hinckley
777 Lady Luck Drive
Hinckley, Minnesota 55037
(320) 384-7777
Website: www.grandcasinomn.com
Map: **#5** (75 miles N. of Twin Cities. One
mile E. of I-35's Hinckley exit on Hwy. 48)

Toll-Free Number: (800) 472-6321
Hotel/RV/Chalet Reservations: (800) 995-4726
Rooms: 485 Price Range: $69-$126 (Hotel)
        Price Range: $54-$103 (Inn)
        Price Range: $64-$116 (Chalet)
Suites: 52 Price Range: $99-$202
Restaurants: 5 Liquor: Yes Valet: Free
Buffets: B-$10.99 (Sat/Sun) L-$8.99
        D-$12.99/$22.99 (Tue)/$14.99 (Wed)/
        $15.99(Fri/Sat)
Casino Size: 54,800 Square Feet
Other Games: P, BG (Thu-Mon)
Overnight RV Parking: Must use RV park
Special Features: 222-space RV park ($23
per night/$28 Fri/Sat). Kid's Quest childcare
center. 18-hole golf course. Free pet kennel.

Grand Casino Mille Lacs
777 Grand Avenue
Onamia, Minnesota 56359
(320) 532-7777
Website: www.grandcasinomn.com
Map: **#6** (90 miles N. of Twin Cities. On Highway 169 on the W. shore of Lake Mille Lacs)

Toll-Free Number: (800) 626-5825
Room Reservations: (800) HOTEL-17
Rooms: 284 Price Range: $49-$129
Suites: 14 Price Range: $89-$379
Restaurants: 4 Liquor: No
Buffets: L-$8.99 Brunch-$10.49 (Sat/Sun)
D-$12.99/$14.99 (Wed)/ $22.99 (Fri)
$15.99(Sat)
Casino Size: 42,000 Square Feet
Other Games: P, BG
Overnight RV Parking: Free/RV Dump: No
Special Features: Resort has two hotels (one is off-property). Kid's Quest childcare center. Free pet kennel.

Grand Portage Lodge & Casino
P.O. Box 233
Grand Portage, Minnesota 55605
(218) 475-2441
Website: www.grandportage.com
Map: **#7** (N.E. tip of Minnesota. 300 miles N. of Twin Cities. On Highway 61, five miles from the Canadian border)

Reservation Number: (800) 543-1384
Rooms: 90 Price Range: $95-$115
Suites: 10 Price Range: $175-$195
Restaurants: 2 Liquor: Yes
Valet Parking: Not Offered
Casino Size: 15,268 Square Feet
Other Games: BG, No Blackjack
Overnight RV Parking: Must use RV park
Special Features: On shore of Lake Superior. Hiking, skiing and snowmobile trails. Gift shop. Marina. 10-space RV park open June-Sept ($30 per night). Free shuttle service to/from Thunder Bay, Ontario.

Jackpot Junction Casino Hotel
P.O. Box 420
Morton, Minnesota 56270
(507) 694-8000
Website: www.jackpotjunction.com
Map: **#8** (110 miles S.W. of Twin Cities)

Toll-Free Number: (800) WIN-CASH
Rooms: 253 Price Range: $65-$89
Suites: 23 Price Range: $105-$190
Restaurants: 4 (1 open 24 hours) Liquor: Yes
Buffets: B-$8.99/$13.25(Sun) L-$10.25
D-$12.25
Valet Parking: Not Offered
Other Games: P, TCP, BG
Senior Discount: Various Wed if 50+
Overnight RV Parking: Must use RV park
Special Features: 40-space RV park ($10-$20 per night). Kids Quest childcare center. 18-hole golf course. Gift shop.

Little Six Casino
2354 Sioux Trail N.W.
Prior Lake, Minnesota 55372
(952) 445-9000 (Mystic Lake)
Website: www.littlesixcasino.com
Map: **#10** (25 miles S.W. of Twin Cities. On County Road 83)

Toll-Free: (800) 262-7799 (Mystic Lake)
Restaurants: 1 Liquor: No
Special Features: 1/4-mile north of Mystic Lake Casino.

Mystic Lake Casino Hotel
2400 Mystic Lake Boulevard
Prior Lake, Minnesota 55372
(952) 445-9000
Website: www.mysticlake.com
Map: **#10** (25 miles S.W. of Twin Cities. On County Road 83, 3 miles S. of Hwy 169)

Toll-Free Number: (800) 262-7799
Hotel Reservations: (800) 813-7349
RV Reservations: (800) 653-2267
Rooms: 400 Price Range: $89-$159
Suites: 16 Price Range: $119-$349
Restaurants: 6 Liquor: No
Buffets: L-$9.95/$13.95 (Sat/Sun)
    D-$12.95/$22.95 (Wed)/$16.95(Sat/Sun)
Valet Parking: $3
Casino Size: 102,000 Square Feet
Other Games: BG
Overnight RV Parking: Free/RV Dump: No
Senior Discount: Various Tue 8-11am if 55+
Special Features: Free shuttle bus service from Twin Cities area. Also has a second casino - Dakota Country with 45,000-square-feet of gaming space. 122-space RV park ($30 per night spring/summer, $21 fall/winter). Health club. Childcare facility.

Northern Lights Casino & Hotel
6800 Y Frontage Rd NW
Walker, Minnesota 56484
(218) 547-2744
Website: www.northernlightscasino.com
Map: **#11** (175 miles N. of the Twin Cities. Near the S. shore of Lake Leech four miles S. of Walker, MN at the junction of Highways 371 & 200)

Toll-Free Number: (800) 252-7529
Toll-Free Number: (877) 544-4879
Room Reservations: (866) 652-4683
Rooms: 105 Price Range: $70-$135
Suites: 4 Price Range: $120-$165
Restaurants: 3 Liquor: Yes
Buffets: L-$8.50/$9.95 (Sat/Sun)
    D-$11.50/$21.50 (Thu)/$16.50(Fri)/
       $12.50 (Sun)
Casino Size: 40,000 Square Feet
Other Games: P
Overnight RV Parking: Free/RV Dump: No
Senior Discount: Various Mon 8am-mid if 50+
Special Features: 90-foot dome simulates star constellations. 20% room discount for slot club members.

Palace Casino & Hotel
6280 Upper Cass Frontage Rd NW
Cass Lake, Minnesota 56633
(218) 335-7000
Website: www.palacecasinohotel.com
Map: **#12** (220 miles N.W. of Twin Cities)

Toll-Free Number: (877) 9-PALACE
Room Reservations: (800) 442-3910
Rooms: 64 Price Range: $55-$85
Suites: 16 Price Range $70-$95
Restaurants: 2 Liquor: No
Buffet: B-$9.99 (Sun)
Casino Size: 30,000 Square Feet
Other Games: BG
Overnight RV Parking: Free/RV Dump: Free
Senior Discount: Various Wed 8am-mid if 50+
Special Features: 15-space RV park offers free parking and hookup.

Prairie's Edge Casino Resort
5616 Prairie's Edge Lane
Granite Falls, Minnesota 56241
(320) 564-2121
Website: www.prairiesedgecasino.com
Map: **#2** (110 miles W. of Twin Cities. Five miles S.E. of Granite Falls on Highway 67 E.)

Toll-Free Number: (866) 293-2121
Rooms: 79 Price Range: $59-$99
Suites: 10 Price Range: $129-$169
Restaurants: 2 Liquor: Yes
Buffets: Brunch-$10.95 (Sun)
    D-$9.95 (Wed-Thu)/$10.95 (Fri/Sat)
Valet Parking: Not Offered
Casino Size: 36,000 Square Feet
Other Games: P
Overnight RV Parking: Free/RV Dump: No
Special Features: 55-space RV park ($16 per night/$24 w/hookups). Convenience store. Non-smoking slot area.

Seven Clans Casino Red Lake

Highway 1 East
Red Lake, MN 56671
(218) 679-2500
Web: www.sevenclanscasino.com
Map: #16 (31 miles N. of Bemidji)

Toll-Free Number: (888) 679-2501
Rooms: 40 Prices: $79-$159
Restaurants: 1 Liquor: No
Casino Size: 40,000 Square Feet
Other Games: P
Overnight RV Parking: Free/RV Dump: No
Senior Discount: Special Mon 10am-7pm
if 55+

Seven Clans Casino Thief River Falls

Rt 3, Box 168A
Thief River Falls, Minnesota 56701
(218) 681-4062
Website: www.sevenclanscasino.com/trf.html
Map: #15 (275 miles N.W. of Minneapolis)

Toll-Free Number: (800) 881-0712
Room Reservations: (866) 255-7848
Suites: 151 Price Range: $79-$99
Restaurants: 1 Liquor: No
Buffets: B-$7.95 L-$9.95 D-$10.95
Valet Parking: Not Offered
Casino Size: 16,000 Square Feet
Other Games: P
Overnight RV Parking: Free/RV Dump: No
Senior Discount: 10% off food if 55+
Special features: Indoor water park. Malt shop.

Seven Clans Casino Warroad

1012 E. Lake Street
Warroad, MN 56763
(218) 386-3381
Website: www.sevenclanscasino.com
Map: #9 (400 miles N.W. of Twin Cities)

Toll-Free Number: (800) 815-8293
Room Reservations: (888) 714-5514
Rooms: 34 Price Range: $59-$75
Suites: 7 Price Range: $85-$110
Restaurants: 1 Liquor: No
Casino Size: 13,608 Square Feet
Other Games: P
Overnight RV Parking: Free/RV Dump: No
Senior Discount: Various Thu 8am-6pm if 55+
Special Features: Hotel is Super 8 located
one mile from casino with free shuttle service
provided.

Shooting Star Casino Hotel

777 Casino Boulevard
Mahnomen, Minnesota 56557
(218) 935-2701
Website: www.starcasino.com
Map: #13 (250 miles N.W. of Twin Cities)

Room Reservations: (800) 453-STAR
Rooms: 360 Price Range: $69-$109
Suites: 30 Price Range: $99-$259
Restaurants: 4 Liquor: Yes
Buffets: B-$5.99 L-$6.99/$11.49 (Sun)
   D-$9.99/$14.99 (Wed)/$16.50(Fri)/
   $22.95 (Sat)/$12.95 (Sun)
Other Games: P, BG
Overnight RV Parking: Must use RV park
Senior Discount: Various 1st Thu of month if 50+
Special Features: 47-space RV park ($19 per
night). Childcare facility for children up to
12 years of age.

Treasure Island Resort & Casino

5734 Sturgeon Lake Road
Red Wing, Minnesota 55066
(651) 388-6300
Website: www.treasureislandcasino.com
Map: #14 (40 miles S.E. of Twin Cities.
Halfway between Hastings and Red Wing, off
Highway 61 on County Road 18)

Toll-Free Number: (800) 222-7077
Room/RV Reservations: (888) 867-7829
Restaurants: 4 Liquor: Yes
Rooms: 250 Price Range: $89-$149
Suites: 28 Price Range: $179-$249
Buffets: B-$13.75 (Sat-Sun) L-$9.99
   D-$13.49/$24.99 (Thu)/$16.95 (Fri/Sat)
Valet Parking: $3
Casino Size: 110,000 Square Feet
Other Games: P, PGP, TCP, FCP, BG
Overnight RV Parking: Must use RV Park
Senior Discount: First Wednesday of each
   month 10am-2pm get coupon book if 55+
Special Features: 95-space RV park open
April-October ($20 per night/13 amp $22 per
night/50amp). 137-slip marina. Dinner and
sightseeing cruises. Childcare facility for
children up to 12 years of age.

White Oak Casino
45830 US Hwy 2
Deer River, MN 56636
(218) 246-9600
Website: www.whiteoakcasino.com
Map: **#17** (5 miles N.W. of Grand Rapids)

Toll-Free Number: (800) 653-2412
Restaurants: 1 Snack Bar Liquor: Yes
Casino Size: 11,000 Square Feet
Overnight RV Parking: Free/RV Dump: No
Senior Discount: Various Tue 10am-6pm if 50+

Pari-Mutuels

Minnesota has two racetracks that offer the card games of blackjack, poker, pai gow poker, let it ride, Caribbean stud poker, three card poker and four card poker.

The completely nonsmoking card rooms are open 24 hours and admission is free. Players must pay a commission to the card room on each hand played for all games except regular poker, where a rake is taken from each pot. The minimum gambling age is 18.

Canterbury Park
1100 Canterbury Road
Shakopee, Minnesota 55379
(952) 445-7223
Website: www.canterburypark.com
Map: **#10** (22 miles S.W. of Twin Cities)

Horse Track Toll-Free: (800) 340-6361
Card Room Toll-Free: (866) 667-6537
Admission: $5 (for horse racing)
Admission: Free (for card room)
Self-Parking: Free   Valet Parking: $6
Restaurants: 2
Casino Size: 18,000 Square Feet
Overnight RV Parking: No
Special Features: Live horse racing Mid-May through August. Daily simulcasting. Free shuttle service to/from Mall of America.

Running Aces
15201 Zurich St NE
Columbus, Minnesota 55372
(651) 925-4600
Website: www.littlesixcasino.com
Map: **#10** (25 miles S.W. of Twin Cities. On County Road 83)

Toll-Free: (877) RUN-ACES
Admission: Free
Self Parking: Free   Valet: $6 (Fri-Sun)
Restaurants: 1
Buffets: B-$8.95 (Sun) D-$23.95 (Thu)
Other Games: No Caribbean Stud Poker or Let it Ride
Special Features: 15-Space RV Park ($25 per night). Live Horse racing mid-May-mid-August.

MISSISSIPPI

Mississippi was the third state to legalize riverboat gambling when it was approved by that state's legislature in 1990. The law restricts casinos to coast waters (including the Bay of St. Louis and the Back Bay of Biloxi) along the Mississippi River and in navigable waters of counties that border the river.

Mississippi law also requires that riverboats be permanently moored at the dock and they are not permitted to cruise. This allows the riverboats to offer 24-hour dockside gambling. The Isle of Capri in Biloxi was the first casino to open on August 1, 1992 followed one month later by The President.

Since the law does not require that the floating vessel actually resemble a boat, almost all of the casinos are built on barges. This gives them the appearance of a land-based building, rather than a riverboat.

Due to the destruction caused by Hurricane Katrina in August 2005, the Mississippi legislature allowed the state's gulf coast casinos to be rebuilt on land within 800-feet of the shoreline and some casinos have been rebuilt in that manner.

The Mississippi Gaming Commission does not break down its slot statistics by individual properties. Rather, they are classified by region. The **Coastal** region includes Biloxi, Gulfport and Bay Saint Louis. The **North** region includes Tunica, Greenville and Lula. The **Central** region includes Vicksburg and Natchez.

With that in mind here's information, as supplied by the Mississippi Gaming Commission, showing the machine payback percentages for each area's casinos for the one-year period from June 1, 2010 through May 31, 2011:

These numbers reflect the percentage of money returned on each denomination of machine and encompass all electronic machines including video poker and video keno. The best returns for each category are highlighted in bold print and you can see that all of the gaming areas offer rather similar returns on their machines.

Mississippi is one of the few states that breaks down its progressive machine statistics separately and you can see that the return is almost always less on machines with progressive jackpots.

Unless otherwise noted, all casinos are open 24 hours and offer: slots, video poker, blackjack, craps, roulette and three card poker. Other game listings include: Spanish 21 (S21), baccarat (B), mini-baccarat (MB), poker (P), pai gow poker (PGP), let it ride (LIR), Caribbean stud poker (CSP), big six wheel (B6), casino war (CW) and keno (K). The minimum gambling age is 21.

NOTE: If you happen to win a jackpot of $1,200 or more in Mississippi, the casino will deduct 3% of your winnings and pay it to the Mississippi Tax Commission as a gambling tax. The tax is nonrefundable and the $1,200 threshold would also apply to any cash prizes won in casino drawings or tournaments.

For more information on visiting Mississippi call the state's tourism department at (866) SEE-MISS or go to: www.visitmisissippi.org

For Biloxi tourism information call (800) 237-9493 or go to: www.gulfcoast.org. For Tunica tourism information call (888) 4-TUNICA or go to: www.tunicamiss.com

	Coastal	North	Central
5¢ Slots	93.91%	92.93%	**95.55%**
5¢ Prog.	**95.55%**	88.95%	N/A
25¢ Slots	**94.47%**	93.30%	93.64%
25¢ Prog.	**95.16%**	91.35%	90.80%
$1 Slots	94.49%	**94.69%**	94.00%
$1 Prog.	**93.74%**	92.92%	90.52%
$5 Slots	94.67%	95.35%	**95.54%**
All	**92.84%**	92.28%	92.46%

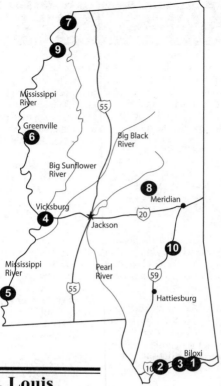

Bay St. Louis

Map: **#2** (on St. Louis Bay, 60 miles E. of New Orleans)

Hollywood Casino Bay St. Louis
711 Hollywood Boulevard
Bay St. Louis, Mississippi 39520
(228) 467-9257
Website: www.hollywoodcasinobsl.com

Toll-Free Number: (866) 758-2591
Rooms: 498 Price Range: $99-$179
Suites: 78 Price Range: Casino Use Only
Restaurants: 4 (1 open 24 hours)
Buffets: B- $9.99/ $22.99 (Sun)
          L-$11.99
          D-$17.99/$19.99 (Fri/Sat)
Casino Size: 58,500 Square Feet
Other games: PGP, P
Overnight RV Parking: Must use RV park
Special Features: 100 hookup RV Park ($35 per night). 18-hole golf course.

Silver Slipper Casino
5000 South Beach Boulevard
Bay St. Louis, Mississippi 39520
(228) 396-5943
Website: www.silverslipper-ms.com

Toll-Free Number: (866) 775-4773
Restaurants: 3 (1 open 24 hours)
Buffets: L-$10.95/ $21.95 (Sun)
          D-$19.95/$21.95 (Thu/Sun)/
          $23.95 (Fri/Sat)
Casino Size: 36,826 Square Feet
Other Games: K, P, PGP
Overnight RV Parking: Must use RV park.
Special Features: Land-based casino. 24-space RV park ($26-$37 per night) $2 buffet discount for slot club members.

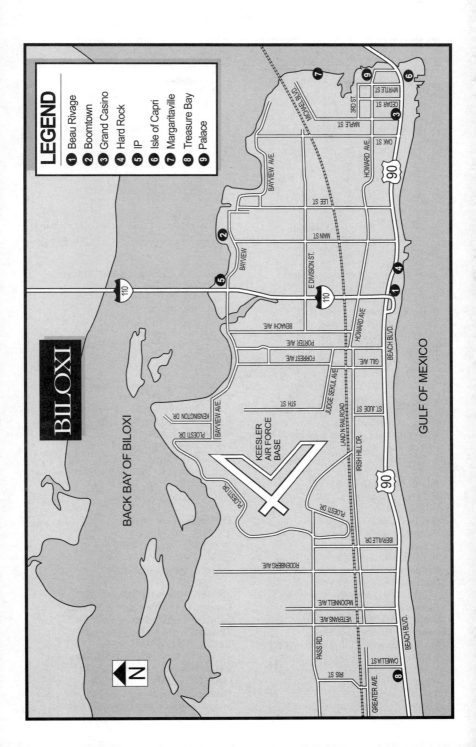

Biloxi

Map: #1 (On the Gulf of Mexico, 90 miles E. of New Orleans)

A new $48 million Margaritaville Casino is being built on Biloxi's back bay. The casino, which is part owned by musician Jimmy Buffet, will have a 68,000-square-foot casino and a restaurant, along with retail stores, an events center and a 27-slip marina. The property is expected to open by the early summer of 2012.

Beau Rivage Resort & Casino
875 Beach Boulevard
Biloxi, Mississippi 39530
(228) 386-7111
Website: www.beaurivageresort.com

Toll-Free Number: (888) 750-7111
Room Reservations: (888) 56-ROOMS
Rooms: 1,740 Price Range: $99-$299
Suites: 95 Price Range: $295-$375
Restaurants: 4 (1 open 24 hours)
Buffets: B- $9.99 L-$12.99/$19.99(Sat/Sun)
     D- $19.99/$23.99 (Thu)/$28.99 (Fri/Sat)
Casino Size: 76,715 Square Feet
Other Games: MB, PGP, P, CSP, LIR, CW
Overnight RV Parking: Free/RV Dunp: No
Special Features:Casino is on a barge. 18-hole golf course. Spa. Beauty salon. 13-store shopping arcade.

Boomtown Casino - Biloxi
676 Bayview Avenue
Biloxi, Mississippi 39530
(228) 435-7000
Website: www.boomtownbiloxi.com

Toll-Free Number: (800) 627-0777
Restaurants: 3 (1 open 24 hours)
Buffets: L-$10.99/$21.99 (Sun)
     D-$17.99/$21.99 (Fri/Sun)
Casino Size: 51,665 Square Feet
Other Games: P, PGP
Overnight RV Parking: Free/RV Dump: No
Special Features: Casino is on a barge.

Grand Biloxi Casino Resort
265 Beach Boulevard
Biloxi, Mississippi 39530
(228) 436-2946
Website: www.grandbiloxi.com

Toll-Free Number: (800) 946-2946
Rooms: 500 Price Range: $119-$229
Suites: 40 Price Range: Casino Use Only
Restaurants: 3 (1 open 24 hours)
Buffets: B-$7.99/$12.99 (Sat/Sun) L-$11.99
     D-$17.99/$19.99 (Thu)/$21.99 (Sat/Sun)
Casino Size: 28,785 Square Feet
Other Games: MB, PGP, LIR
Overnight RV Parking: Free/RV Dump: No
Special Features: Land-based casino. 18-hole golf course. Spa. Beauty salon. Starbucks.

Hard Rock Hotel & Casino - Biloxi
777 Beach Boulevard
Biloxi, Mississippi 39530
(228) 374-7625
Website: www.hardrockbiloxi.com

Toll-Free Number: (877) 877-6256
Rooms: 306 Prices: $139-$319
Suites: 64 Prices: $229-$529
Restaurants: 4 (1 open 24 hours)
Buffets: B-$10.99 L-$11.99
     D-$18.99/$22.99 (Fri/Sat)
Casino Size: 53,800 Square Feet
Other Games: MB, P, PGP
Overnight RV Parking: No
Special Features: Casino is on a barge. Spa. Nightclub. Collection of rock and roll memorabilia on display.

IP Casino Resort Spa
850 Bayview Avenue
Biloxi, Mississippi 39530
(228) 436-3000
Website: www.ipbiloxi.com

Toll-Free Number: (888) 946-2847
Rooms: 1,088 Price Range: $99-$229
Suites: 14 Price Range: $199-$475
Restaurants: 3 (1 open 24 hours)
Buffets: B-$12.00 L-$15.00
     D-$24.00/$29.00 (Fri-Sat)
Casino Size: 75,790 Square Feet
Other Games: MB, P, PGP, LIR, FCP
Overnight RV Parking: Free/RV Dump: No
Special Features: Casino is on a barge.

The Best Places To Play On The Gulf Coast
(Biloxi and Gulfport Only)

Roulette - The house edge on a single-zero wheel cuts the house edge from 5.26% down to a more reasonable 2.70%. Unfortunately, there are no casinos on the Gulf Coast that offer single-zero roulette.

Craps - IP and Boomtown are the most liberal of all gulf coast casinos by offering 20X odds on their crap games. All other casinos offer 10X odds.

Blackjack - Gulf Coast casinos offer some good blackjack games and not all casinos hit soft 17. This rule is advantageous for the player by .20%. All of the recommendations in this section apply to players using perfect basic strategy for each particular game.

The best single-deck game can be found at the Isle of Capri where the dealer stands on soft 17 and doubling down is only allowed totals of 10 or more. The casino advantage in this game is .29%. Six other casinos also offer a single-deck game, but all should be avoided because they all pay 6-to-5 rather than the standard 3-to-2 for winning blackjacks. The casino edge in all of these games is more than 1.20%.

Treasure Bay is the best double-deck game, with the following rules: stand on soft 17, double down on any first two cards, re-split any pair (including aces) and doubling allowed after splitting. This works out to a casino edge of just .14%. Next best is the Isle of Capri which has similar rules, except they don't allow the resplitting of aces which brings the casino edge up to .19%. Beau Rivage, Boomtown, Hard Rock, IP and Island View have the same rules, but they hit soft 17 and that brings the casino edge up to .40%. A similar game is offered at the Grand and Palace with one advantageous rule change: aces can be resplit. This rule makes the casino edge slightly lower at .35%. This same game is also offered at the Palace, except they only allow doubling on first two-card totals of 9, 10 or 11 and that brings the casino edge up to .47%.

For six-deck shoe games the best places to play are Treasure Bay and Hard Rock which both stand on soft 17, allow doubling down on any first two cards, doubling after splitting and resplitting of aces. The casino advantage in this game is .34%.

The Grand, IP, Island View and Palace offer an identical game, except they hit soft 17 and that brings the casino edge up to .56% Beau Rivage has a similar game, except they add late surrender to the mix and that lowers the edge slightly to .46%

Only the Grand and Hard Rock casinos have eight-deck games. It's best to avoid them, however, because the six-deck games offer lower casino advantages.

Video Poker - Some of the best video poker games on the Gulf Coast for lower limit players are 9/6 Double Double Bonus (98.98%), 9/6 Jacks or Better (99.54%) and 8/5 Bonus Poker (99.17%) and a version of Deuces Wild called Illinois Deuces (98.9%).

Island View has 9/6 Jacks or Better for quarters, 50-cents and $1 denominations, all with progressive jackpots. They also have the same denominations of games, including progressive jackpots, for 9/6 Double Double Bonus.

Grand Casino quarter 8/5 Bonus in single-line, 3-play, 5-play and 10-play versions. 9/6 Double Double Bonus is also offered in both 50-cent and $1 games with a progressive jackpot. Plus, Illinois Deuces is available in 50-cent games.

For quarter players The Isle offers 9/6 Jacks and 8/5 Bonus. They also have a $1 version of 8/5 Bonus, plus 50-cent and $1 9/6 Double Double Bonus games and some 25-cent and $1 Illinois Deuces games.

The Palace has 8/5 Bonus for quarters in 10-play.

The IP offers 50-cent and $1 9/6 Jacks, as well as 50-cent 8/5 Bonus Poker and $1/$2 versions with a progressive. Illinois Deuces is also offered in denominations ranging from 25-cents through $25.

The only decent game at Treasure Bay is $1 8/5 Bonus, plus a $5 9/6 Jacks or Better game with a progressive jackpot.

Isle Casino Hotel - Biloxi
151 Beach Boulevard
Biloxi, Mississippi 39530
(228) 436-4753
Website: www.isleofcapricasino.com/Biloxi

Toll-Free Number: (800) 843-4753
Rooms: 541 Price Range: $59-$219
Suites: 200 Price Range: $119-$279
Restaurants: 4 (1 open 24 hours)
Buffets: B-$5.99 L-$7.00/$8.99 (Fri/Sat)
      D-$11.00/$14.99(Fri/Sat)
Casino Size: 57,252 Square Feet
Other Games: P
Overnight RV Parking: No
Senior Discount: Various on Tue/Thu if 50+
Special Features: Land-based casino. Spa. Beauty salon. Golf packages offered.

Palace Casino Resort
158 Howard Avenue
Biloxi, Mississippi 39530
(228) 432-8888
Website: www.palacecasinoresort.com

Toll-Free Number: (800) PALACE-9
Rooms: 234 Price Range: $89-$179
Suites: 14 Price Range: $500
Restaurants: 2 (1 open 24 hours)
Buffets: B-$7.99 L-$10.99/$19.99 (Sun)
      D-$18.99
Casino Size: 26,260 Square Feet
Other Games: PGP
Overnight RV Parking: No
Special Features: Land-based casino. 10-slip marina. 100% smoke-free casino.

Treasure Bay Casino and Hotel
1980 Beach Boulevard
Biloxi, Mississippi 39531
(228) 385-6000
Website: www.treasurebay.com

Toll-Free Number: (800) 747-2839
Rooms: 234 Price Range: $89-$179
Suites: 14 Price Range: $229-$259
Restaurants: 5 (1 open 24 hours)
Buffets: B-$8.49 L-$9.99 D-$19.99
Casino Size: 24,557 Square Feet
Other Games: PGP, CSP, LIR
Overnight RV Parking: No
Special Features: Land-based casino.

Lighthouse Point Casino
199 N. Lakefront Road
Greenville, Mississippi 38701
(662) 334-7711
Website: www.lighthouse-casino.com

Toll-Free Number: (800) 878-1777
Hotel Reservations: (800) 228-2800
Restaurants: 1 Valet Parking: No
Casino Size: 22,000 Square Feet
Other Games: No table games
Overnight RV Parking: Free/RV Dump: No
Senior Discount: Various Thursdays if 50+
Special Features: Casino is on an actual paddlewheel boat.

Greenville

Map: **#6** (On the Mississippi River, 121 miles N.W. of Jackson)

Bayou Caddy's Jubilee Casino
211 N. Lakefront Road
Greenville, Mississippi 38701
(662) 335-1111
Website: www.bayoucaddyjubilee.com

Restaurants: 3 Valet Parking: No
Casino Size: 28,000 Square Feet
Other Games: No roulette
Senior Discount: Various Wed if 50+
Overnight RV Parking: Free/RV Dump: No

Harlow's Casino Resort
4250 Highway 82 West
Greenville, Mississippi 38701
(228) 436-4753
Website: www.harlowscasino.com

Toll-Free Number: (866) 524-LUCK
Rooms: 105 Price Range: $89-$119
Suites: 45 Price Range: $149-$199
Restaurants: 4 (1 open 24 hours)
Buffets: L-$9.95
        D-$12.95/$21.95 (Fri/Sat)
Casino Size: 33,000 Square Feet
Other Games: P, no Three Card Poker
Overnight RV Parking: Free/RV Dump: No
Special Features: Land-based casino.

Gulfport

Map: **#3** (On the Gulf of Mexico, 80 miles E. of New Orleans)

Island View Casino Resort
3300 W. Beach Boulevard
Gulfport, Mississippi 39501
(228) 314-2100
Website: www.islandviewcasino.com

Toll-Free Number: (800) 817-9089
Rooms: 600 Price Range: $109-$199
Restaurants: 3 (1 open 24 hours) Valet: Free
Buffets: B-$9.99 L-$11.99/$13.99(Sun)
        D-$21.99
Casino Size: 82,935 Square Feet
Other Games: MB, LIR, PGP
Overnight RV Parking: Free/RV Dump: No
Special Features: Land-based casino.

Lula

Map #9 (On the Mississippi River, 70 miles S. of Memphis, TN)

Isle of Capri Casino & Hotel - Lula
777 Isle of Capri Parkway
Lula, Mississippi 38644
(662) 363-4600
Website: www.isleofcapricasino.com

Toll-Free Number: (800) 789-5825
Toll-Free Number: (800) THE-ISLE
Rooms: 485 Price Range: $59-$299
Suites: 40 Price Range: Casino Use Only
Restaurants: 3
Buffets: B-$8.00/$12.50 (Sun) L-$10.00
      D-$12.00/$17.50 (Fri/Sat)
Casino Size: 63,500 Square Feet
Overnight RV Parking: $16.30 per night
Senior Discount: Various on Wed if 50+
Special Features: 28-space RV Park ($15 per night) Video arcade. Fitness center.

Natchez

Map: #5 (on the Mississippi River, 102 miles S.W. of Jackson)

Isle of Capri Casino & Hotel - Natchez
53 Silver Street
Natchez, Mississippi 39120
(601) 445-0605
Website: www.isleofcapricasino.com

Toll-Free Number: (800) 722-LUCK
Toll-Free Number: (800) THE-ISLE
Rooms: 138 Price Range: $69-$129
Suites: 5 Price Range: Casino Use Only
Restaurants: 1
Buffets: B: $13.99 (Sat/Sun) L-$9.99
      D-$11.99/$17.99 (Fri/Sat)
Casino Size: 17,634 Square Feet
Other Games: no roulette
Overnight RV Parking: No
Senior Discount: Various if 50+
Special Features: Casino is built on barge that resembles 1860s paddlewheeler. Hotel is across street with free shuttle service to/from casino.

Tunica

Map: #7 (on the Mississippi River, 28 miles S. of Memphis, TN)

The Sportsman Casino and Lodge is expected to open in Tunica by late 2012.

The $75 million resort will open at the site of the former Isle of Capri casino near Sam's Town on Casino Strip Boulevard. It will feature a 220-room hotel, plus a 50,000-square-foot casino.

Bally's Tunica
1450 Bally's Boulevard
Robinsonville, Mississippi 38664
(662) 357-1500
Website: www.ballystunica.com

Toll-Free Number: (800) 382-2559
Rooms: 235 Price Range: $49-$119
Suites: 8 Price Range: Casino Use Only
Restaurants: 3
Buffets: B-$7.99 L-$8.99 D-$12.99
Casino Size: 46,536 Square Feet
Overnight RV Parking: Free/RV Dump: No
Special Features: Refrigerators in every room.

Fitz Casino/Hotel
711 Lucky Lane
Robinsonville, Mississippi 38664
(662) 363-5825
Website: www.fitzgeraldstunica.com

Toll-Free Number: (800) 766-LUCK
Room Reservations: (888) 766-LUCK
Rooms: 507 Price Range: $59-$139
Suites: 70 Price Range: Casino Use Only
Restaurants: 3   Valet Parking: Free
Buffets: B-$6.95 L-$8.95/$13.95 (Sun)
      D-$14.95/$18.95 (Fri)/$16.95 (Sat)
Casino Size: 38,088 Square Feet
Overnight RV Parking: Free/RV Dump: No
Special Features: Indoor pool and spa. Sports pub.

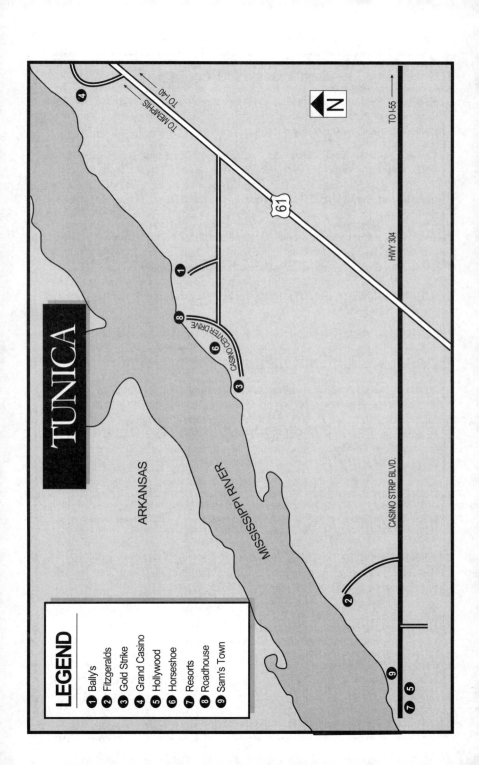

The Best Places To Play in Tunica

Roulette - The house edge on a single-zero wheel cuts the house edge from 5.26% down to a more reasonable 2.70%. Unfortunately, there are no casinos in Tunica that offer single-zero roulette

Craps - All casinos offer 20X odds, except for the Horseshoe which offers 100X odds. Four casinos pay triple (rather than double) on 12 in the field, which cuts the house edge on this bet in half from 5.6 percent to 2.8 percent. The casinos offering this slightly better field bet are: Hollywood, Horseshoe, Gold Strike and Sam's Town.

Blackjack - The blackjack games in Tunica are most similar to those offered in downtown Las Vegas. Most casinos offer both single and double-deck games, as well as six-deck shoe games. That's good. The bad part, however, is that dealers hit soft 17 at all games. This results in an extra advantage for the house of .20%. All of the following recommendations apply to players using perfect basic strategy for each particular game.

The best one-deck games can be found at Fitzgeralds, Harrah's and Horseshoe. They all allow doubling down on any two cards and resplitting any pair (including aces) which results in a casino advantage of just .15%

At Gold Strike, Roadhouse and Sam's Town they offer a game identical to the above except they won't allow you to resplit aces and this results in a slightly higher house edge of .18%. Be aware that there are some tables at Harrah's and Roadhouse offering single-deck games that pay 6-to-5 for blackjack rather than the standard 3-to-2. These games should be avoided as they have a casino advantage of greater than 1.40%.

Bally's, Fitzgeralds, Gold Strike, Harrah's, Hollywood, Horseshoe and Roadhouse are the best places to play double-deck because their games have the following rules: double down on any first two cards, resplit any pair (including aces), and double down after split. This works out to a casino edge of .35%.

Tunica's remaining two casinos: Resorts and Sam's Town, both offer the next best game. The only rule change from the previous one is that you aren't allowed to resplit aces and the casino edge in this game is .40%.

The best six-deck games can be found at Bally's, Fitzgeralds, Gold Strike, Harrah's, Hollywood, Horseshoe and Roadhouse which all have rules identical to their two-deck games. The casino advantage in this game is .56%.

The two remaining six-deck games are those offered at Resorts and Sam's Town. Both offer a game with a slightly higher casino edge of .63% because they won't allow you to resplit aces.

Video Poker - Some of the best video poker games in Tunica for lower limit players are 9/7 Double Bonus (99.1%), 9/6 Jacks or Better (99.5%), 8/5 Bonus Poker (99.2%) and a version of Deuces Wild called Illinois Deuces (98.9%).

Roadhouse has the best video poker in Tunica with 9/6 Jacks for quarters through dollars, plus hundred coin penny games with a progressive. There are also some 8/5 Bonus for quarters only. However, an even better version of 8/5 Bonus Poker is offered at Roadhouse which returns 99.7% rather than 99.2% To find them, look for games that pay 35-for-1 on all four-of-a-kinds rather than 25 (5-K), 40 (2-4) and 80 (aces). Roadhouse has these games in quarter, 50-cent and $1 denominations.

Roadhouse also has some other games in quarter through dollar denominations that return just under 100%: Double Double Bonus 99.96%), Super Aces (99.94%), Triple Deuces Wild (99.92%) and 2 Pair Joker Wild (99.92%).

Fitzgeralds has 9/6 Jacks for quarters, plus 8/5 Bonus from $1 through $5.

Harrah's has 9/6 Jacks for 50-cents up to $25, 9/7 Double Bonus beginning at quarters and ending at $25.

Resorts only offers $1 8/5 Bonus, while Sam's Town has 9/6 Jacks for quarters, 50-cents and $1.

Gold Strike Casino Resort
100 Casino Center Drive
Robinsonville, Mississippi 38664
(662) 357-1111
Website: www.goldstrikemississippi.com

Toll-Free Number: (888) 24K-PLAY
Room Reservations: (866) 245-7511
Rooms: 1,130 Price Range: $64-$244
Suites: 70 Price Range: $175-$229
Restaurants: 3
Buffets: B-$7.99 L-$9.99
          Brunch-$15.99 (Sat/Sun)
          D-$15.99/$21.99 (Fri/Sat)
Casino Size: 50,486 Square Feet
Other Games: MB, P, CSP, LIR, FCP
Overnight RV Parking: Free/RV Dump: No
Special Features: Food court with three fast-food restaurants. Health spa. Starbucks. Suites only available through casino host on Fri/Sat.

Harrah's Tunica
13615 Old Highway 61 N.
Robinsonville, Mississippi 38664
(662) 363-2788
Website: www.harrahstunica.com

Toll-Free Number: (800) 946-4946
Rooms: 1,356 Price Range: $39-$215
Suites: 117 Price Range: $149-$999
Restaurants: 8
Buffets: B-$8.99 L-$12.99
          D-$17.99/$22.99 (Fri)
Casino Size: 136,000 Square Feet
Other Games: MB, P, LIR, PGP
Overnight RV Parking: Must use RV park
Special Features: Kid's Quest childcare center. 18-hole golf course. 200-space RV park ($22 to $32 per night). Spa. Sport shooting range.

Hollywood Casino Tunica
1150 Casino Strip Boulevard
Robinsonville, Mississippi 38664
(662) 357-7700
Website: www.hollywoodtunica.com

Toll-Free Number: (800) 871-0711
Rooms: 437 Price Range: $59-$199
Suites: 57 Price Range: $149-$369
Restaurants: 3
Buffets: B-$7.50 L-$8.95/$12.95 (Sun)
　　　　　D-$15.95/$21.95 (Fri/Sat)
Casino Size: 54,000 Square Feet
Other Games: P
Overnight RV Parking: Must use RV park
Special Features: Casino features a collection of Hollywood memorabilia. 123-space RV park ($18 per night). Indoor pool and jacuzzi. 18-hole golf course.

Horseshoe Casino & Hotel
1021 Casino Center Drive
Robinsonville, Mississippi 38664
(662) 357-5500
Website: www.horseshoe.com

Toll-Free Number: (800) 303-7463
Rooms: 200 Price Range: $50-$32580
Suites: 311 Price Range: $129-$479
Restaurants: 5
Buffets: B-$9.99 L-$10.99/$16.49 (Sun)
　　　　　D-$19.99/$24.99 (Fri/Sat)
Casino Size: 63,000 Square Feet
Other Games: P, LIR, PGP, MB
Overnight RV Parking: Free/RV Dump: No
Special Features: Bluesville Nightclub.

Resorts Casino Tunica
1100 Casino Strip Boulevard
Tunica Resorts, Mississippi 38664
(662) 363-7777
Website: www.resortstunica.com

Reservation Number: (866) 676-7070
Rooms: 182 Price Range: $49-$149
Suites: 19 Price Range: Casino Use Only
Restaurants: 4
Buffets: B-$8.95 L-$9.99
　　　　　D-$14.99/$19.99 (Fri/Sat)
Casino Size: 35,000 Square Feet
Overnight RV Parking: Free/RV Dump: Free
Special Features: 18-hole River Bend Links golf course is adjacent to property.

Roadhouse Casino and Hotel
1107 Casino Center Drive
Robinsonville, Mississippi 38664
(662) 363-4900
Website: www.tunica-roadhouse.com

Toll-Free Number: (800) 391-3777
Suites: 140 Price Range: $65-$350
Restaurants: 3
Buffets: L-$8.99/$10.99 (Sun)
　　　　　D-$13.99/$18.99 (Fri)
Casino Size: 32,800 Square Feet
Other Games: P
Overnight RV Parking: Free/RV Dump: No
Special Features: All suite hotel with jacuzzi in every room. Spa and fitness center.

Sam's Town Tunica
1477 Casino Strip Boulevard
Robinsonville, Mississippi 38664
(662) 363-0711
Website: www.samstowntunica.com

Toll-Free Number: (800) 456-0711
Room Reservations: (800) 946-0711
Rooms: 850 Price Range: $59-$149
Suites: 44 Price Range: $99-$199
Restaurants: 4
Buffets: B-$7.99/$8.99(Sat/Sun)
　　　　　L-$8.99/$9.95 (Sat/Sun)
　　　　　D-$15.99/$19.99 (Fri/Sat)
Casino Size: 66,000 Square Feet
Other Games: P, LIR, K
Overnight RV Parking: Free/RV Dump: No
Special Features: 18-hole golf course. 100-space RV park ($15.99 per night).

Vicksburg

Map: **#4** (on the Mississippi River, 44 miles W. of Jackson)

Vicksburg is one of the most historic cities in the South and is most famous for its National Military Park where 17,000 Union soldiers are buried. The Park is America's best-preserved Civil War battlefield and you can take a 16-mile drive through the 1,858-acre Park on a self-guided tour. In the Park you can also see the U.S.S. Cairo, the only salvaged Union Ironclad. Admission to the Park is $8 per car and allows unlimited returns for seven days.

There are about 12 historic homes in Vicksburg that are open to the public for narrated tours. Admission prices are $6 for adults and $4 for children 12 and under. Some of the homes also function as Bed and Breakfasts and rooms can be rented for overnight stays.

For more information on visiting Vicksburg call the city's Convention and Visitors Bureau at (800) 221-3536, or visit their web site at: www.vicksburgcvb.org

Ameristar Casino Hotel - Vicksburg
4146 Washington Street
Vicksburg, Mississippi 39180
(601) 638-1000
Website: www.ameristarcasino.com

Reservation Number: (800) 700-7770
Rooms: 146 Price Range: $79-$169
Suites: 4   Price Range: $131-$209
Restaurants: 3
Buffets: B-$15.99 (Sun) L-$10.99
    D-$13.99/$24.99 (Fri/Sat)
Casino Size: 72,210 Square Feet
Other Games: P, LIR
Overnight RV Parking: Must use RV park
Special features: 67 space RV park ($22.50-$27 per night.)

DiamondJacks Casino - Vicksburg
3990 Washington Street
Vicksburg, Mississippi 39180
(601) 636-5700
Website: www.diamondjacks.com

Toll-Free Number: (877) 711-0677
Rooms: 60 Price Range: $79-$100
Suites: 62 Price Range: $160-$200
Restaurants: 3
Buffets: L-$8.99
    D-$11.99/$20.99 (Fri/Sat)
Casino Size: 32,000 Square Feet
Overnight RV Parking: No

Grand Station Hotel & Casino
1310 Mulberry Street
Vicksburg, Mississippi 39180
(601) 636-3423
Website: www.grandstationcasino.com

Toll-Free Number: (800) 843-2343
Rooms: 101 Price Range: $39-$119
Suites: 16 Price Range: $69-$149
Restaurants: 3
Buffets: B-$5.99 L-$6.99
    D-$13.99/$16.99 (Thu)/$19.99 (Fri/Sat)
Casino Size: 12,613 Square Feet
Other Games: P
Overnight RV Parking: Free/RV Dump: No
Special Features: Casino is on 1,200-passenger paddlewheel riverboat.

Rainbow Hotel Casino
1380 Warrenton Road
Vicksburg, Mississippi 39182
(601) 636-7575
Website: www.rainbowcasino.com

Toll-Free Number: (800) 503-3777
Room Reservations: (800) 434-5800
Rooms: 82 Price Range: $89-$120
Suites: 7 Price Range: $149-$219
Restaurants: 1
Buffets: L-$7.99 D-$11.99/$18.99 (Fri/Sat)
Casino Size: 25,000 Square Feet
Other Games: No Roulette, no TCP
Overnight RV Parking: Yes
Special Features: Hotel is Amerihost Inn. Affiliated with Isle of Capri Casinos

Riverwalk Casino & Hotel
1046 Warrington Road
Vicksburg, Mississippi 39180
(601) 634-0100
Website: www.riverwalkvicksburg.com

Toll-Free Number: (866) 615-9125
Room Reservations: (601) 634-0100
Rooms: 80 Price Range: $49-$99
Suites: 4 Price Range: $109-$129
Restaurants: 2
Buffets: L- $9.99/$14.99 (Sun)
    D- $13.99/$14.99(Thu)/$23.99 (Fri/Sat)
Casino Size: 25,000 square feet

Indian Casinos

Bok Homa Casino
1 Choctaw Rd
Heidelberg, Mississippi 39439
Website: www.bokhomacasino.com
Map: **#10** (42 miles S. of Meridian)

Toll-Free Number: (866) 447-3275
Restaurants: 1 (open 24 hours)
Casino Size: 27,000 Square Feet
Overnight RV Parking: Free/RV Dump: No

Pearl River Resort
Highway 16 West
Philadelphia, Mississippi 39350
(601) 650-1234
Website: www.pearlriverresort.com
Map: **#8** (81 miles N.E. of Jackson)

Toll-Free Number: (800) 557-0711
Room Reservations (866) 44-PEARL
Silver Star Rooms: 420 Prices: $89-$259
Silver Star Suites: 75 Prices: $189-$780
Golden Moon Rooms: 427 Prices: $99-$299
Golden Moon Suites: 145 Prices: $329-$879
Restaurants: 12 Liquor: Yes
Silver Star Buffet: L-$9.99/$14.99 (Sat/Sun)
    D-$13.99/$14.99(Thu)/$19.99 (Fri/Sat)
Silver Star Casino Size: 90,000 Square Feet
Other Games: MB, P, CSP, B6
Overnight RV Parking: Free/RV Dump: No
Special Features: Two separate hotels across the street from each other. Golden Moon has a 9,000-seat events arena, plus a slots-only casino that is only open Fridays and Saturdays. 18-hole golf course. 15-acre water park. Health spa. Beauty salon. Shopping arcade with nine stores.

MISSOURI

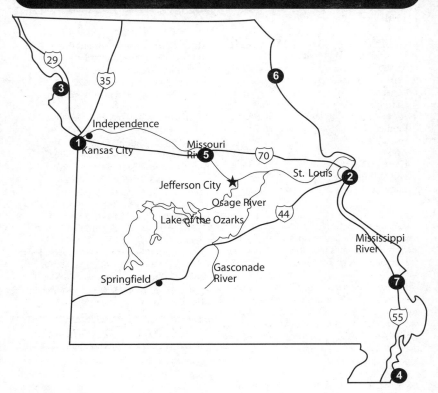

In November, 1992 Missouri voters approved a state-wide referendum to allow riverboat gambling. That made Missouri the fifth state to approve this form of gambling.

Since Missouri riverboats are not required to cruise, almost all casinos are built on a barge which gives them the appearance of a land-based building, rather than a riverboat.

When Missouri's riverboat casinos first began operating they were required to cruise and they all conducted two-hour gaming sessions with a $500 loss-limit on each session. In early 2000 the law was changed to allow continuous boardings and cruising was no longer required. In November 2008 the state's $500 loss limit provision was eliminated as the result of a state-wide referendum.

Unlike dockside gaming in Mississippi, most Missouri casinos are not open 24 hours and the hours of operation are listed for each casino.

Here's information from the Missouri Gaming Commission regarding the payback percentages for each casino's electronic machines for the 12-month period from July 1, 2010 through June 30, 2011:

CASINO	PAYBACK %
Isle of Capri - Boonville	91.66
River City	91.31
Terrible's Mark Twain	91.21
Terrible's St. Jo	91.20
Harrah's M.H.	90.99
Ameristar-St. Charles	90.94
Lumiere Place	90.77
Ameristar-K.C.	90.69
Argosy	90.68
Harrah's N.K.C.	90.68
Isle of Capri K.C.	90.47
Lady Luck	89.52

These figures reflect the total percentages returned by each casino for all of their electronic machines including slot machines, video poker, video keno, etc.

Unless otherwise noted, all casinos offer: slots, video poker, craps, blackjack, roulette, and three card poker. Optional games include: baccarat (B), mini-baccarat (MB), caribbean stud poker (CSP), poker (P), pai gow poker (PGP), let it ride (LIR), Spanish 21 (S21), and four card poker (FCP).

If you want to order a drink while playing, be aware that Missouri gaming regulations do not allow casinos to provide free alcoholic beverages. The minimum gambling age is 21.

NOTE: If you happen to win a jackpot of $1,200 or more in Missouri, the casino will withhold 4% of your winnings for the Missouri Department of Revenue. If you want to try and get that money refunded, you will be required to file a state income tax return and, depending on the details of your return, you may get some of the money returned to you. The $1,200 threshold would also apply to any cash prizes won in casino drawings or tournaments.

For more information on visiting Missouri call the state's Travel Center at (800) 877-1234 or go to: www.visitmo.com

Boonville

Map: **#5** (100 miles E. of Kansas City)

Isle of Capri Casino - Boonville
100 Isle of Capri Boulevard
Boonville, Missouri 65233
(660) 882-1200
Website: www.isleofcapricasino.com

Toll-Free Number: (800) 843-4753
Rooms: 113 Price Range: $69-$149
Suites: 27 Price Range: $109-$189
Restaurants: 3 Valet Parking: Free
Buffets: B-$6.99/$10.99 (Sat/Sun)
    L-$8.99 Brunch-$10.99
    D-$12.99/$16.99 (Wed)/
       $17.99 (Fri/Sat)/ $15.99 (Sun)
Hours: 8am-5am/24 Hours (Fri/Sat)
Casino Size: 28,000 Square Feet
Other Games: LIR
Overnight RV Parking: Free (In west lot.)
             /RV Dump: No
Senior Discount: Various on Tue/Thu if 50+
Special Features: 600-passenger barge on the Missouri River.

Cape Girardeau

Map: **#7** (115 miles S. of St. Louis)

Isle of Capri Casino - Cape Girardeau
Website: www.isleofcapricasino.com

Toll-Free Number (800) THE-ISLE
EXPECTED TO OPEN LATE 2012

The Best Places To Play Blackjack in Kansas City

All Missouri casinos "hit" soft 17. This is slightly more advantageous for the casino than "standing" on soft 17 and it adds an extra .20% to the casino's mathematical edge in all blackjack games.

The only single-deck blackjack games in Kansas City are offered at the Isle of Capri and Harrah's, but since blackjacks pay 6-to-5, rather than the traditional 3-to-2 (7.5-to-5), this results in an overall casino advantage of almost 1.5% and it's best to avoid these games.

The Isle of Capri offers the best two-deck game. It has a .35% casino advantage against a basic strategy player and the rules are: dealer hits soft 17 (ace and six), double down on any two cards, split and re-split any pair (including aces), and double allowed after splitting. Next best are Argosy, Ameristar and Harrah's which all offer the same game, with the exception of allowing aces to be re-split. The casino advantage in this game is .40%

Ameristar, Argosy, Harrah's and The Isle all offer an identical six-deck blackjack game with the following rules: dealer hits soft 17 (ace and six), double down on any two cards, split and re-split any pair (including aces), and double allowed after splitting. The casino's mathematical edge against a perfect basic strategy player in this game is .56%.

Caruthersville

Map: **#4** (200 miles S. of St. Louis)

Lady Luck Caruthersville
777 East Third Street
Caruthersville, Missouri 63830
(573) 333-6000
Website: www.ladyluckcaruthersville.com

Toll-Free Number (800) 679-4945
Restaurants: 1   Valet Parking: $2
Hours: 9am-3am/ 24 hours (Fri/Sat)
Casino Size: 21,400 Square Feet
Other Games: LIR, P
Overnight RV Parking: Free/RV Dump: Free
Senior Discount: Free valet parking if 55+
Special Features: 875-passenger sternwheeler on the Mississippi River. 27-space RV park ($20 per night). 1,000-seat amphitheater.

Kansas Cty

Map: **#1**

Ameristar Casino Hotel Kansas City
3200 North Ameristar Drive
Kansas City, Missouri 64161
(816) 414-7000
Website: www.ameristar.com/kansas_city.aspx

Toll-Free Number: (800) 499-4961
Rooms: 142 Price Range: $109-$269
Suites: 42 Price Range: $169-$529
Restaurants: 14   Valet Parking: $5
Buffets: L-$12.49/$15.99 (Sat/Sun)
    D-$14.99/$24.99 (Fri)/$18.99 (Sat/Sun)
Casino Size: 140,000 Square Feet
Other Games: MB, B, P, PGP, LIR, FCP
Overnight RV Parking: Free/RV Dump: No
Special Features: 4,000-passenger barge adjacent to the Missouri River. 41-screen Sports Pub. 18-screen movie theater complex. Burger King. 1,384-seat event center.

Argosy Casino Hotel & Spa
777 N.W. Argosy Parkway
Riverside, Missouri 64150
(816) 746-3100
Website: www.stayargosy.com

Toll-Free Number: (800) 270-7711
Rooms: 250 Price Range: $139-$199
Suites: 8 Price Range: $650
Restaurants: 5 Valet Parking: $4
Buffets: B-$9.99/$16.99 (Sat/Sun)
        L-$12.99/$15.99 (Sun)
        D-$15.99/$27.99 (Wed/Thu)/
        $23.99 (Fri/Sat)
Hours: 8am-5am/24 Hours (Sat/Sun)
Casino Size: 62,000 Square Feet
Other Games: S21, MB, PGP, LIR, CSP
Overnight RV Parking: No
Special Features: 4,675-passenger single-deck
Mediterranean-themed barge adjacent to the
Missouri River.

Harrah's North Kansas City
One Riverboat Drive
N. Kansas City, Missouri 64116
(816) 472-7777
Website: www.harrahs.com

Toll-Free Number: (800) HARRAHS
Rooms: 350 Price Range: $89-$249
Suites: 42 Price Range: $119-$279
Restaurants: 5 Valet Parking: $5
Buffets: B-$8.99/$16.99 (Sun)
        D-$16.99/$21.99(Fri)/
        $25.99(Sat)/$17.99 (Sun)
Casino Size: 63,300 Square Feet
Other Games: MB, P, PGP, LIR
Senior Discount: Various if 50 or older
Overnight RV Parking: Free/RV Dump: No
Special Features: 1,700-passenger two-deck
barge adjacent to the Missouri River. Closed
5am-8am Wednesdays.

Isle of Capri Casino - Kansas City
1800 E. Front Street
Kansas City, Missouri 64120
(816) 855-7777
Website: www.isleofcapricasino.com

Toll-Free Number: (800) 843-4753
Restaurants: 4 Valet Parking: Free
Buffets: B-$7.99 L-$10.99
        D-$13.99/$20.99 (Fri/Sat)
Casino Size: 30,000 Square Feet
Other Games: PGP, no Three card poker
Overnight RV Parking: Free/RV Dump: No
Senior Discount: Various Tue/Thu if 50+
Special Features: 2,000-passenger two-deck
Caribbean-themed barge docked in a man-
made lake fed by the Missouri River. Closed
5am-6am Wednesdays.

La Grange

Map: **#6** (150 miles N.W. of St. Louis)

Terrible's Mark Twain Casino
104 Pierce Street
La Grange, Missouri 63448
(573) 655-4770
Website: www.herbstgaming.com

Toll-Free Number: (866) 454-5825
Restaurants: 1 Valet Parking: Not Offered
Hours: 8am-2am/4am (Fri/Sat)
Casino Size: 18,000 Square Feet
Overnight RV Parking: Must use RV park
Special Features: 600-passenger barge on the
Mississippi River. 8-space RV park ($5 per
night). Gift shop.

The Best Places To Play Blackjack in St. Louis

All Missouri casinos "hit" soft 17. This is slightly more advantageous for the casino than "standing" on soft 17 and it adds an extra .20% to the casino's mathematical edge in all blackjack games.

The best two-deck game is offered at Ameristar with these rules: double down on any two cards, split and re-split any pair (except aces), and double allowed after splitting. The casino advantage is .40%. A similar game is offered by Harrah's with two rule changes: no doubling after splitting and doubling down is limited to two-card totals of 9 or more. The casino advantage is .65%. Lumiere Place and River City have a game similar to Harrah's, but they don't allow re-splits and the advantage there is .68%

All four St. Louis casinos: Ameristar, Harrah's Lumiere Place and River City offer an identical six-deck blackjack game with the following rules: double down on any two cards, split and re-split any pair (including aces), and double allowed after splitting. The casino's mathematical edge against a perfect basic strategy player in these games is .56%.

St. Joseph

Map: **#3** (55 miles N. of Kansas City)

Terrible's St. Jo Frontier Casino
77 Francis Street
St. Joseph, Missouri 64501
(816) 279-5514
Website: www.herbstgaming.com

Toll-Free Number: (800) 888-2946
Restaurants: 3   Valet Parking: Not Offered
Buffets: B-$7.49/$10.99 (Sun) L-$8.49
          D-$10.99/$18.99 (Tue)/
          $13.99(Wed)/$12.99 (Thu)
Hours: 8am-1:30am/3:30am (Fri/Sat)
Casino Size: 18,000 Square Feet
Overnight RV Parking: Free/RV Dump: No
Senior Discount: 50% off breakfast buffet
                 Tue/Thu if 55+
Special Features: 1,146-passenger
paddlewheel boat adjacent to the Missouri
River. Gift shop.

St. Louis

Map: **#2**

In addition to the five St. Louis-area casinos listed below, the Casino Queen in E. St. Louis, Illinois is also a nearby casino. It is located on the other side of the Mississippi river from downtown St. Louis. Additionally, the Alton Belle in Alton, Illinois is about 25 miles north of St. Louis.

Ameristar Casino St. Charles
P.O. Box 720
St. Charles, Missouri 63302
(314) 949-4300
Website: www.ameristarcasinos.com/stcharles

Toll-Free Number: (800) 325-7777
Rooms: 400 Price Range: $129-$249
Restaurants: 7   Valet Parking: $5
Buffets: L-$13.99/$17.99 (Sat/Sun)
          D-$15.99/$20.99 (Fri)/$25.99 (Sat)
Casino Size: 130,000 Square Feet
Other Games: P, LIR, PGP, FCP
Overnight RV Parking: No
Senior Discount: Various Mon-Thu if 55+
Special Features: 2,000-passenger barge on the Missouri River.

Harrah's St. Louis
777 Casino Center Drive
Maryland Heights, Missouri 63043
(314) 770-8100
Website: www.harrahs.com

Toll-Free Number: (800) HARRAHS
Rooms: 455 Price Range: $89-$320
Suites: 47 Price Range: $219-$529
Restaurants: 7 Valet Parking: $5
Buffets: B-$8.99 L-$12.99/$17.99 (Sun)
          D-$16.99/$27.50 (Fri)/
          $19.99 (Sat)/$18.99 (Sun)
Hours: 8am-5am/24 Hours (Fri-Sun)
Casino Size: 120,000 Square Feet Total
Other Games: MB, P, PGP, LIR, FCP, CSP
Overnight RV Parking: Free/RV Dump: No
Senior Discount: Various Tue/Fri if 50+
Special Features: Two 3,200-passenger
barges on the Missouri River. Ben & Jerry's
Ice cream.

Lumière Place Casino Resort
999 North Second Street
St. Louis, Missouri 63102
(314) 450-5000
Website: www.lumiereplace.com

Toll-Free Number: (877) 450-7711
Suites: 300 Price Range: $159-$299
Restaurants: 5   Valet Parking: Free
Buffets: B-$10.99/$22.99 (Sun)
          L-$13.99
          D-$17.99/$26.99 (Fri/Sat)
Hours: 8am-5am/24 Hours (Fri/Sat)
Casino Size: 75,000 Square Feet
Other Games: MB, PGP, P, LIR, FCP
Special Features: 2,500-passenger barge
floating in a man-made canal 700 feet from
the Mississippi River. Property also features
200-room Four Seasons Hotel.

River City Casino
777 River City Casino Boulevard
St. Louis, MO 63125
(314)388-7777
Website: www.rivercity.com

Toll-Free Number: (888)578-7289
Restaurants: 4 Liquor: Yes
Buffets:B-$17.99 (Sat)/$19.99 (Sun)
          L-$12.99 D-$15.99/$28.99(Fri/Sat)
Casino Size: 90,000 Square Feet
Hours: 8am-4:30am/24 hours (Fri-Sun)
Other Games:P, FCP, LIR, MB, PGP
Overnight RV Parking: No

MONTANA

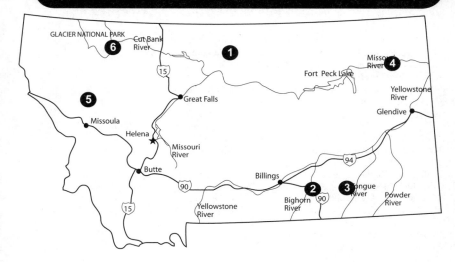

Montana law permits bars and taverns to have up to 20 video gaming devices that play video poker, video keno, or video bingo. These machines are operated in partnership with the state and are not permitted to pay out in cash; instead, they print out a receipt which must be taken to a cashier.

The maximum bet on these machines is $2 and the maximum payout is limited to $800. Montana gaming regulations require these machines to return a minimum of 80%.

All of Montana's Indian casinos offer Class II video gaming devices that look like slot machines, but are actually bingo games and the spinning reels are for "entertainment purposes only."

The maximum bet on the machines in Indian casinos is $5 and the maximum payout is capped at $1,500. According to Montana's Gambling Control Division, there are no minimum payback percentages required for gaming machines on Indian reservations. The minimum gambling age is 18.

For Montana tourism information call (800) VISIT-MT or go to: www.visitmt.com

Charging Horse Casino
P.O. Box 1259
Lame Deer, Montana 59043
(406) 477-6677
Website: www.charginghorse.com
Map: **#3** (90 miles S.E. of Billings on Hwy. 212)

Restaurants: 1 Liquor: No
Hours: 8am-2am Daily
Other Games: Bingo (Thu-Sat)
Overnight RV Parking: Free/RV Dump: No

Four C's Cafe & Casino
Rocky Boy Route, Box 544
Box Elder, Montana 59521
(406) 395-4863
Map: **#1** (75 miles N.E. of Great Falls)

Restaurants: 1 Liquor: No
Hours: 10am-12am/2am (Fri/Sat)
Overnight RV Parking: No/RV Dump: No

Glacier Peaks Casino
416 W Central Ave
Browning, Montana 59417
(406) 338-2274
Website: www.glaciercash.com
Map: **#6** (140 miles N.W of Great Falls)

Toll-Free: (877) 238-9946
Restaurants: 1 Snack Bar Liquor: No
Hours: 9am-2am Daily
Other Games: Bingo (Wed-Fri), P
Overnight RV Parking: Free, check in with
security first/RV Dump: Free

KwaTaqNuk Casino Resort
303 Highway 93
E. Polson, Montana 59860
(406) 883-3636
Website: www.kwataqnuk.com
Map: **#5** (65 miles N. Of Missoula)

Room Reservations: (800) 882-6363
Rooms: 112 Price Range: $54-$145
Restaurants: 1 Liquor: Yes
Hours: 24 Hours Daily
Overnight RV Parking: Free/RV Dump: Free
Special Features: Hotel is Best Western. Two
casinos, one is nonsmoking.

Little Big Horn Casino
P.O. Box 580
Crow Agency, Montana 59022
(406) 638-4000
Website: littlebighorncasino.biz
Map: **#2** (65 miles S.E. of Billings)

Restaurants: 1 Liquor: No
Hours: 8am-2am/4am (Thurs-/Sat)
Other Games: P, BG (Thu/Fri/Sun)
Overnight RV Parking: Free/RV Dump: No

Northern Winz Casino
11275 US Highway 87
Box Elder, Montana 59521
(406) 395-5420
Map: **#1** (75 miles N.E. of Great Falls)

Restaurants: 2 Liquor: No
Overnight RV Parking: No

Silver Wolf Casino
Highway 25 East
P.O. Box 726
Wolf Point, Montana 59201
(406) 653-3476
Map: **#4** (180 miles N.E of Billings)

Restaurants: 1 Snack Bar Liquor: No
Hours: 10am-12am/2am (Fri/Sat)
Other Games: Bingo
Overnight RV Parking: Free/RV Dump: No

NEVADA

All Nevada casinos are open 24 hours and, unless otherwise noted, offer: slots, video poker, craps, blackjack, and roulette. The minimum gambling age is 21.

For Nevada tourism information call (800) 237-0774 or go to: www.travelnevada.com.

Other games in the casino listings include: sports book (SB), race book (RB), Spanish 21 (S21), baccarat (B), mini-baccarat (MB), pai gow (PG), poker (P), pai gow poker (PGP), Caribbean stud poker (CSP), let it ride (LIR), three-card poker (TCP), four card poker (FCP), sic bo (SIC), keno (K), big 6 wheel (B6) and bingo (BG).

Amargosa Valley

Map Location: **#8** (91 miles N.W. of Las Vegas on Hwy. 95)

Longstreet Inn Casino & RV Resort
Route 373, HCR 70
Amargosa Valley, Nevada 89020
(775) 372-1777
Website: www.longstreetcasino.com

Rooms: 59 Price Range: $69-$119
Restaurants: 1
Other Games: No table games
Overnight RV Parking: No
Senior Discount: 10% off food if 55 or older
Special Features: 51-space RV Park ($19 per night). 24-hour convenience store.

Battle Mountain

Map Location: **#9** (215 mile N.E. of Reno on I-80)

Nevada Hotel & Casino
8 E. Front Street
Battle Mountain, Nevada 89820
(775) 635-2453

Restaurants: 1
Casino Size: 840 Square Feet
Other Games: No craps or roulette
Overnight RV Parking: No

Beatty

Map Location: **#10** (120 miles N.W. of Las Vegas on Hwy. 95)

Stagecoach Hotel & Casino
P.O. Box 836
Beatty, Nevada 89003
(775) 553-2419
Website: www.stagecoachhotelcasino.com

Reservation Number: (800) 4-BIG-WIN
Rooms: 50 Price Range: $35-$59
Restaurants: 2 (1 open 24 hours)
Casino Size: 8,810 Square Feet
Other Games: SB, RB, P, B6, no roulette
Overnight RV Parking: Free/RV Dump: No
Special Features: Swimming pool and Jacuzzi. Seven miles from Rhyolite ghost town.

Boulder City

Map Location: **#11** (22 miles S.E. of Las Vegas on Hwy. 93)

Hacienda Hotel & Casino
U.S. Highway 93
Boulder City, Nevada 89005
(702) 293-5000
Website: www.haciendaonline.com

Reservation Number: (800) 245-6380
Rooms: 360 Price Range: $40-$100
Suites: 18 Price Range: $90-$160
Restaurants: 3 (1 open 24 hours)
Buffets: L-$6.95
        D-$8.95/ $10.95(Fri-Sun)
Casino Size: 19,300 Square Feet
Other Games: SB, RB, P, TCP
Senior Discount: $6.95 Thu Buffet if 55+
Overnight RV Parking: No

Carson City

Map Location: **#7** (32 miles S. of Reno on Hwy. 395)

Carson Nugget
507 N. Carson Street
Carson City, Nevada 89701
(775) 882-1626
Website: www.ccnugget.com

Toll-Free Number: (800) 426-5239
Reservation Number: (800) 338-7760
Rooms: 82 Price Range: $40
Restaurants: 5 (1 open 24 hours)
Casino Size: 28,930 Square Feet
Other Games: SB, RB, P, TCP, BG, K
Overnight RV Parking: Free/RV Dump: No
Senior Discount: 15-20% off food if 50+
Special Features: Rare gold display. Free supervised childcare center. Rooms are one block away from casino.

Carson Station Hotel Casino
900 S. Carson Street
Carson City, Nevada 89702
(775) 883-0900
Website: www.carsonstation.com

Toll-Free Number: (800) 501-2929
Rooms: 92   Price Range: $64-$84
Suites: 3   Price Range: $99-$119
Restaurants: 2 (1 open 24 hours)
Casino Size: 12,750 Square Feet
Other Games: SB, RB, TCP,
                K, No Roulette or craps
Overnight RV Parking: No
Special Features: Hotel is Best Western.

Casino Fandango
3800 S. Carson Street
Carson City, Nevada 89005
(775) 885-7000
Website: www.casinofandango.com

Restaurants: 3
Casino Size: 42,943 Square Feet
Buffets: L-$11.99 (Wed-Fri)/$15.99 (Sat/Sun)
    D-$14.99 (Wed/Thu/Sun)/$22.99 (Fri/Sat)
Other Games: SB, RB, P, PGP, TCP, K
Overnight RV Parking: Free/RV Dump: No

Gold Dust West
2171 Highway 50 East
Carson City, Nevada 89701
(775) 885-9000
Website: www.gdwcasino.com

Toll-Free Number: (877) 519-5567
Rooms: 148 Price Range: $65-$100
Suites: 22 Price Range: $100-$175
Restaurants: 2 (1 open 24 hours)
Casino Size: 18,100 Square Feet
Other Games: SB, RB, TCP, P, no roulette
Overnight RV Parking: Must use RV park
Senior Discount: Various Mon if 50+
Special Features: Hotel is Best Western. 48-space RV park ($20-$33). 32-lane bowling center.

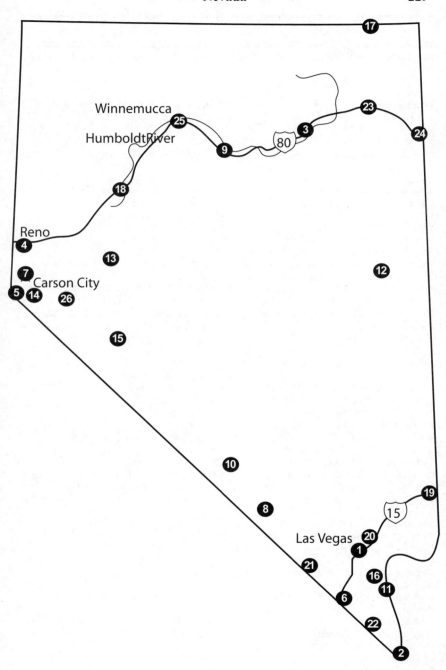

Winnemucca

HumboldtRiver

Reno

Carson City

Las Vegas

Elko

Map Location: **#3** (289 miles N.E. of Reno on I-80)

Commercial Casino
345 4th Street
Elko, Nevada 89801
(775) 738-3181
Website: www.commercialcasinos.com

Toll-Free Number: (800) 648-2345
Restaurants: 2 (1 open 24 hours)
Casino Size: 8,441 Square Feet
Other Games: No table games
Overnight RV Parking: Yes/RV Dump: No
Senior Discount: Various Tue if 55+
Special Features: Oldest continually operating casino in Nevada. 10-foot-tall stuffed polar bear in casino. Large gunfighter art collection.

Red Lion Hotel & Casino
2065 Idaho Street
Elko, Nevada 89801
(775) 738-2111
Website: www.redlioncasino.com

Reservation Number: (800) 545-0044
Rooms: 223 Price Range: $75-$119
Suites: 2 Price Range: $259
Restaurants: 3 (1 open 24 hours)
Buffets: L-$9.95/$11.95 (Sat/Sun)
D-$12.95/$15.95 (Fri/Sat)
Casino Size: 17,850 Square Feet
Other Games: P, TCP, K, SB, RB
Overnight RV Parking: No

Stockmen's Hotel & Casino
340 Commercial Street
Elko, Nevada 89801
(775) 738-5141
Website: www.stockmenscasinos.com

Reservation Number: (800) 648-2345
Rooms: 141 Price Range: $45-$75
Restaurants: 2
Casino Size: 6,914 Square Feet
Other Games: SB, RB, TCP, No roulette
Overnight RV Parking: Free/RV Dump: No
Special Features: 24-hour shuttle service.

Ely

Map Location: **#12** (317 miles E. of Reno on Hwy. 50)

Hotel Nevada & Gambling Hall
501 Aultman Street
Ely, Nevada 89301
(775) 289-6665
Website: www.hotelnevada.com

Reservation Number: (888) 406-3055
Rooms: 45 Price Range: $35-$125
Restaurants: 1 (open 24 hours)
Casino Size: 3,730 Square Feet
Other Games: SB, RB, P, TCP,
No craps or roulette
Overnight RV Parking: Free RV Dump: No
Special Features: Historical display of mining, ranching and railroad artifacts.

Fallon

Map Location: **#13** (61 miles E. of Reno on Hwy. 50)

Bonanza Inn & Casino
855 W. Williams Avenue
Fallon, Nevada 89406
(775) 423-6031

Rooms: 74 Price Range: $50-$65
Restaurants: 1
Casino Size: 5,830 Square Feet
Other Games: SB, RB, K, No Table Games
Overnight RV Parking: $15 per night

Stockman's Casino
1560 W. Williams Avenue
Fallon, Nevada 89406
(775) 423-2117
Website: www.stockmanscasino.com

Holiday Inn Reservations: (888) 465-4329
Rooms: 98 Price Range: $79-$99
Suites: 8 Price Range: $99-$139
Restaurants: 2 (1 open 24 hours)
Casino Size: 8,614 Square Feet
Other Games: SB, RB, K, No roulette or craps
Senior Discount: 1st/3rd Tue free lunch if 55+
Overnight RV Parking: No
Special Features: Hotel is Holiday Inn Express.

Gardnerville

Map Location: **#14** (45 miles S. of Reno on Hwy. 395)

Sharkey's Nugget
1440 Highway 395N
Gardnerville, Nevada 89410
(775) 782-3133

Restaurants: 1
Casino Size: 4,650 Square Feet
Other Games: SB, RB, No table games
Overnight RV Parking: No
Senior Discount: 10% off food if 50 or older

Topaz Lodge & Casino
1979 Highway 395 South
Gardnerville, Nevada 89410
(775) 266-3338
Website: www.topazlodge.com

RV/Room Reservations: (800) 962-0732
Rooms: 59 Price Range: $72-$85
Restaurants: 3 (1 open 24 hours)
Casino Size: 12,800 Square Feet
Other Games: SB, RB, BG, P , K
            TCP, No roulette
Overnight RV Parking: Must use RV park
Special Features: 60-space RV park ($35 per night).

Hawthorne

Map Location: **#15** (138 miles S.E. of Reno on Hwy. 95)

El Capitan Resort Casino
540 F Street
Hawthorne, Nevada 89415
(775) 945-3321
Website: www.elcapitanresortcasino.com

Toll Free: (800) 922-2311
Rooms: 103 Price Range: $50-$78
Restaurants: 1 (open 24 hours)
Casino Size: 12,860 Square Feet
Other Games: SB, RB, No table Games
Overnight RV Parking: Free/RV Dump: Free

Henderson

Map Location: **#16** (15 miles S.E. of Las Vegas on Hwy. 93)

Eldorado Casino
140 Water Street
Henderson, Nevada 89015
(702) 564-1811
Website: www.eldoradocasino.com

Restaurants: 3
Casino Size: 17,756 Square Feet
Other Games: SB, K, BG, No craps
Overnight RV Parking: No

Emerald Island Casino
120 Market street
Henderson, NV 89015
(702) 567-9160
Website: www.emeraldislandcasino.com

Restaurants: 1
Casino Size: 8,500 Square Feet
Other Games: No table games
Overnight RV Parking: No.

Fiesta Henderson Casino Hotel
777 West Lake Mead Drive
Henderson, Nevada 89015
(702) 558-7000
Website: www.fiestahendersonlasvegas.com

Toll-Free Number: (866) 469-7666
Rooms: 224 Price Range: $20-$100
Suites: 8 Price Range: $135-$259
Restaurants: 4 (1 open 24 hours)
Buffets: B-$11.99 (Sun) L-$7.99
   D-$10.99
Casino Size: 73,450 Square Feet
Other Games: SB, RB, P, PGP, K, BG
Overnight RV Parking: No
Senior Discount: Join Fun Club if 50+
Special Features: Buffet Discount with player's club card.

Green Valley Ranch Resort Spa Casino
2300 Paseo Verde Drive
Henderson, Nevada 89012
(702) 617-7777
Website: www.greenvalleyranchresort.com

Room Reservations: (866) 782-9487
Rooms: 200 Price Range: $128-$330
Suites: 45 Price Range: $310-$3,000
Restaurants: 8 (1 open 24 hours)
Buffets: B-$8.99/$18.99 (Sun) L-$10.99
   D-$18.99
Casino Size: 134,681 Square Feet
Other Games: SB, RB, B, MB, P,
   CSP, PGP, LIR, TCP
Overnight RV Parking: No

Jokers Wild
920 N. Boulder Highway
Henderson, Nevada 89015
(702) 564-8100
Website: www.jokerswildcasino.com

Restaurants: 2 (1 open 24 hours)
Casino Size: 23,698 Square Feet
Other Games: SB, P, K
Overnight RV Parking: No
Senior Discount: Various Tue/Wed if 55+

Klondike Sunset Casino
444 West Sunset
Henderson, Nevada 89015
(702) 568-7575

Restaurants: 1
Casino Size: 7,700 Square Feet
Other Games: SB, RB, No craps
Overnight RV Parking: No

M Resort • Spa • Casino
12300 Las Vegas Blvd South
Henderson, Nevada 89044
Phone: (702) 797-1000
Website: www.themresort.com

Toll-free Number: (877) 673-7678
Rooms: 355 Price Range: $89-$199
Suites: 35 Price Range: $129-$409
Restaurants: 7 (1 open 24 hours)
Buffet: B- $10.99/ $33.99 (Sat-Sun) L- $15.99
   D- $23.99/$33.99 (Fri-Sun)
Casino Size: 97,357 Square Feet
Games offered: RB, SB, P, PGP,
     MB, LIR, TCP

Railroad Pass Hotel & Casino
2800 S. Boulder Highway
Henderson, Nevada 89015
(702) 294-5000
Website: www.railroadpass.com

Toll-Free Number: (800) 654-0877
Rooms: 100 Price Range: $39-$69
Suites: 20 Price Range: $59-$99
Restaurants: 3 (1 open 24 hours)
Buffets: B-$6.99/$8.99 (Sun) L-$6.99
   D-$8.49/$10.99 (Fri/Sat)
Casino Size: 12,803 Square Feet
Other Games: SB, RB, PGP
Overnight RV Parking: No
Senior Discount: Various Tue if 55+

Skyline Restaurant & Casino
1741 N. Boulder Highway
Henderson, Nevada 89015
(702) 565-9116
Website:www.skylinerestaurantandcasino.com

Restaurants: 1
Casino Size: 4,200 Square Feet
Other Games: SB, RB, No craps or roulette
Overnight RV Parking: No

Sunset Station Hotel and Casino
1301 W. Sunset Road
Henderson, Nevada 89014
(702) 547-7777
Website: www.sunsetstation.com

Toll-Free Number: (888) 319-4655
Reservation Number: (888) 786-7389
Rooms: 448 Price Range: $39-$149
Suites: 18 Price Range: $69-$189
Restaurants: 7 (1 open 24 hours)
Buffets: B-$8.99/$14.99 (Sun) L-$10.99
        D-$14.99
Casino Size: 133,409 Square Feet
Other Games: SB, RB, MB, P, PGP,
        LIR, TCP, K, BG
Overnight RV Parking: No
Senior Discount: Various Wed if 55+
Special Features: 13-screen movie theater.
Kid's Quest childcare center. Hooter's sports
bar. Food Court with eight fast food stations.
Bowling Alley.

Jackpot

Map Location: **#17** (Just S. of the Idaho
border on Hwy. 93)

Barton's Club 93
Highway 93
Jackpot, Nevada 89825
(775) 755-2341
Website: www.bartonsclub93.com

Toll-Free Number: (800) 258-2937
Rooms: 98 Price Range: $35-$85
Suites: 4 Price Range: $81-$151
Restaurants: 2
Buffets: B-$9.99 (Sat)/$10.99 (Sun)
        D-$16.99 (Fri/Sat)
Casino Size: 12,550 Square Feet
Other Games: PGP, LIR
Overnight RV Parking: No

Cactus Pete's Resort Casino
1385 Highway 93
Jackpot, Nevada 89825
(775) 755-2321
Website: www.ameristarcasinos.com

Reservation Number: (800) 821-1103
Rooms: 272 Price Range: $79-$129
Suites: 28 Price Range: $159-$209
Restaurants: 4 (1 open 24 hours)
Buffets: Brunch-$16.99 (Sun)
        D-$13.99/$21.99 (Fri/Sat)
Casino Size: 24,727 Square Feet
Other Games: SB, RB, P, PGP, TCP, LIR, K
Overnight RV Parking: Must use RV park
Special Features: 91-space RV park ($18-
$24 per night). Every Wed 5pm-11pm two
restaurants are 2-for-1. 18-hole golf course.
Beauty Salon. Ampitheatre, and Tennis
Courts.

Horseshu Hotel & Casino
Highway 93
Jackpot, Nevada 89825
(702) 755-7777
Website: www.ameristarcasinos.com

Reservation Number: (800) 432-0051
Rooms: 110 Price Range: $59-$99
Suites: 10 Price Range: $79-$129
Restaurants: 1
Casino Size: 3,377 Square Feet
Other Games: No roulette or craps
Overnight RV Parking: No

Jean

Map Location: **#6** (22 miles S.W. of Las Vegas
on I-15; 12 miles from the California border)

Gold Strike Hotel & Gambling Hall
1 Main Street/P.O. Box 19278
Jean, Nevada 89019
(702) 477-5000
Website: www.stopatjean.com

Reservation Number: (800) 634-1359
Rooms: 800 Price Range: $30-$66
Suites: 13 Price Range: $59-$119
Restaurants: 3 (1 open 24 hours)
Buffets: B-$10.95 (Sat/Sun) L-$6.99
        D-$10.99/$11.95 (Sat/Sun)
Casino Size: 37,006 Square Feet
Other Games: SB, RB, P
Overnight RV Parking: No
Special Features: Burger King.

Lake Tahoe

Map Location: **#5** (directly on the Nevada/California border; 98 miles northeast of Sacramento and 58 miles southwest of Reno).

The area is best known for its many recreational activities with skiing in the winter and water sports in the summer. Lake Tahoe Airport is located at the south end of the basin. The next closest airport is in Reno with regularly scheduled shuttle service by bus. Incline Village and Crystal Bay are on the north shore of Lake Tahoe, while Stateline is located on the south shore. For South Lake Tahoe information call the Lake Tahoe Visitors Authority at (800) AT-TAHOE and for North Lake Tahoe information call the Incline Village/Crystal Bay Convention & Visitors Authority at (800) GO-TAHOE.

Here's information, as supplied by Nevada's State Gaming Control Board, showing the slot machine payback percentages for all of the south shore casinos for the fiscal year beginning July 1, 2010 and ending June 30, 2011:

Denomination	Payback %
1¢ Slots	89.07
5¢ Slots	N/A
25¢ Slots	91.26
$1 Slots	93.61
All Slots	93.24

And here's that same information for the north shore casinos:

Denomination	Payback %
1¢ Slots	92.13
5¢ Slots	89.73
25¢ Slots	90.63
$1 Slots	94.39
$1 Megabucks	87.25
$5 Slots	95.93
All Slots	94.50

These numbers reflect the percentage of money returned to the players on each denomination of machine. All electronic machines including slots, video poker and video keno are included in these numbers. Optional games in the casino listings include: sports book (SB), race book (RB), Spanish 21 (S21), baccarat (B), mini-baccarat (MB), poker (P), pai gow poker (PGP), Caribbean stud poker (CSP), let it ride (LIR), three-card poker (TCP), four card poker (FCP), keno (K) and bingo (BG).

Cal-Neva Resort Spa & Casino
2 Stateline Road
Crystal Bay, Nevada 89402
(775) 832-4000
Website: www.calnevaresort.com

Reservation Number: (800) CAL-NEVA
Rooms: 199 Price Range: $108-$179
Suites: 18 Price Range: $243-$269
Restaurants: 1
Casino Size: 500 Square Feet
Other Games: Gaming Machines Only
Overnight RV Parking: No
Special Features: Straddles California/Nevada state line on north shore of Lake Tahoe. European Spa. Three wedding chapels. Florist. Photo studio. Bridal boutique. Gift shop. Airport shuttle. Internet cafe.

Crystal Bay Club Casino
14 State Route 28
Crystal Bay, Nevada 89402
(775) 833-6333
Website: www.crystalbaycasino.com

Restaurants 2 (1 open 24 hours)
Casino Size: 14,020 Square Feet
Other Games: RB, SB, P
Overnight RV Parking: No

Harrah's Lake Tahoe
Highway 50/P.O. Box 8
Stateline, Nevada 89449
(775) 588-6611
Website: www.harrahs.com

Reservation Number: (800) HARRAHS
Rooms: 463 Price Range: $109-$359
Suites: 62 Price Range: $199-$800
Restaurants: 9
Buffets: Brunch-$15.99 (Sat)/$18.99 (Sun)
D-$18.99/$26.99 (Fri)/$28.99 (Sat)
Casino Size: 89,244 Sq Ft (including Harvey's)
Other Games: SB, B, MB, P, PG, PGP,
CSP, LIR, TCP, B6, K
Overnight RV Parking: No
Special Features: On south shore of Lake
Tahoe. Health club. Pet kennel.

Harveys Resort Hotel/Casino - Lake Tahoe
Highway 50
Stateline, Nevada 89449
(775) 588-2411
Website: www.harveys.com

Toll-Free Number: (800) 553-1022
Reservation Number: (800) HARVEYS
Rooms: 704 Price Range: $79-$249
Suites: 36 Price Range: $199-$679
Restaurants: 5 (1 open 24 hours)
Casino Size: 89,244 Sq Ft (including Harrah's)
Other Games: SB, B, MB, P, PG, PGP,
CSP, LIR, TCP, B6, K
Overnight RV Parking: No
Special Features: On south shore of Lake
Tahoe. 2,000-seat amphitheater. Hard Rock
Cafe. Owned by Harrah's. Lake cruises.

Hyatt Regency Lake Tahoe
Resort & Casino
P.O. Box 3239
Incline Village, Nevada 89450
(775) 832-1234
Website: www.laketahoehyatt.com

Toll-Free Number: (800) 553-3288
Hyatt Reservations: (800) 233-1234
Rooms: 412 Price Range: $190-$335
Suites: 48 Price Range: $540-$1,400
Restaurants: 4 (1 open 24 hours)
Buffets: B-$21 (Sat/Sun) D-$32 (Fri)/$28 (Sat)
Casino Size: 18,900 Square Feet
Other Games: SB, RB, P, LIR, TCP
Overnight RV Parking: No
Senior Discount: Food/room discounts if 62+
Special Features: On north shore of Lake
Tahoe. Two Robert Trent Jones golf courses.

Lakeside Inn and Casino
Highway 50 at Kingsbury Grade
Stateline, Nevada 89449
(775) 588-7777
Website: www.lakesideinn.com

Toll-Free Number: (800) 523-1291
Room Reservations: (800) 624-7980
Rooms: 124 Price Range: $69-$159
Suites: 8 Price Range: $109-$299
Restaurants: 4 (1 open 24 hours)
Casino Size: 17,852 Square Feet
Other Games: SB, RB, P, K, no roulette
Overnight RV Parking: No
Senior Discount: Various if 55 or older
Special Features: On south shore of Lake
Tahoe. $3.99 breakfast 11pm-11am. $10.50
prime rib dinner 4pm-10pm. Numerous
specials for birthday celebrants. $2 drinks at
all times.

**See page 271 for a
story on "The Best
Places to Gamble
in Reno/Tahoe"**

Montbleu Resort Casino & Spa
55 Highway 50
Stateline, Nevada 89449
(775) 588-3515
Website: www.montbleuresort.com

Toll-Free Number: (888) 829-7630
Reservation Number: (800) 648-3353
Rooms: 403 Price Range: $69-$299
Suites: 37 Price Range: $139-$999
Restaurants: 6 (1 open 24 hours)
Buffets: B- $12.99 (Sat/Sun)
       D-$17.99/$19.95(Thu-Sat)
Casino Size: 45,000 Square Feet
Other Games: SB, RB, P, LIR, TCP, PGP
Overnight RV Parking: No
Special Features: On south shore of Lake Tahoe. Health spa.

Tahoe Biltmore Lodge & Casino
#5 Highway 28/P.O. Box 115
Crystal Bay, Nevada 89402
(775) 831-0660
Website: www.tahoebiltmore.com

Reservation Number: (800) BILTMOR
Rooms: 92 Price Range: $69-$129
Suites: 7 Price Range: $139-$189
Restaurants: 2 (1 open 24 hours)
Casino Size: 10,480 Square Feet
Other Games: SB, RB
Overnight RV Parking: Free/RV Dump: No
Senior Discount: Various if 55 or older
Special Features: On north shore of Lake Tahoe. $2.99 breakfast special. $9.95 prime rib dinner.

Las Vegas

Map Location: **#1**

Las Vegas is truly the casino capital of the world! While many years ago the city may have had a reputation as an "adult playground" run by "shady characters," today's Las Vegas features many world-class facilities run by some of America's most familiar corporate names.

Las Vegas has more motel/hotel rooms - 148,000 - than any other city in the U.S. and it attracts more than 37 million visitors each year. The abundance of casinos in Las Vegas forces them to compete for customers in a variety of ways and thus, there are always great bargains to be had, but only if you know where to look.

H. Scot Krause is a freelance writer, gaming industry analyst and researcher who writes the weekly Vegas Values column that appears on the American Casino Guide website.

Here are Scot's picks for the best deals available to the Las Vegas visitor.

Best Appetizer Bargain
Golden Gate Shrimp Cocktail, $1.99

Hands down still the best bargain in Las Vegas, you can't beat downtown's Golden Gate Shrimp Cocktail for $1.99. Las Vegas' Original Shrimp Cocktail is featured in the Shrimp Bar & Deli and boasts a heap of ocean shrimp in a classic "tulip" sundae glass, served with their "secret cocktail sauce" and a wedge of fresh lemon.

Best Steak Deal
Ellis Island, $7.99

Mentioned elsewhere, you may find other steak deals in Las Vegas, but the steak special at Ellis Island Casino & Brewery still remains the leader in steak specials. It's not on the menu but available for the asking 24 hours a day, 7 days a week. For $7.99 you get a generous cut of tenderloin cooked to your liking, bread, salad, vegetable of the day, choice of potato and a beer (or root beer) from the microbrewery.

Best Place to Play Slots
Palms

Subjective, of course, but the Palms openly shares/shared and boasted the payback percentages on all of their slot machines. Numbers are among the best paybacks in Las Vegas, if not the best. Few seem to have challenged them or the numbers, but luck can happen anywhere. Your mileage may vary, but if you're a slot player, I'd try the Palms. For a little less noise and commotion hit the casino during the daytime rather than evenings when it fills up with the "younger" bar crowds. (Unless you like that sort of thing!)

Best Video Poker
South Point

South Point's gaming amenities include more than 2,563 of the most popular slot and video poker machines featuring ticket-in, ticket-out technology. They (arguably) offer the most video poker machines with paybacks over 99% of any casino in the city. Combine that with slot club benefits and promotions and you've got a winning play!

Best Bargain Show(s)
Mac King, Harrah's
Nathan Burton, Flamingo

The plaid-suited magician is hilarious and talented and cheap enough to take the whole family. Normally priced around $27, tickets can usually be found for far less using coupons, including FREE tickets (usually with the price of a drink.) Great afternoon bargain show! See him again for the first time!

Another "best bargain show" is Nathan Burton's Comedy Magic show performing at the Flamingo, daily at 4 pm. It's a unique and comedic approach to magic that leaves audiences of all ages in complete amazement. Tickets are currently available from $34 - $44, plus fees but again, look for those coupons and discounts. You can get this one close to or even free!

Best Free Attraction
Bellagio Fountains and Conservatory

Everyone has their favorite free attraction but the water show at Bellagio is by far a fan favorite for tourists as well as locals. It's quite a dazzling display. Some call it "romantic." While you're there, don't miss the Conservatory inside the hotel. Beautiful displays of flowers, gardens and scenery are changed four times a year depicting the seasons. Often breathtaking and definitely aromatic!

My personal favorite? I really enjoy the artifacts, photographs and showcases of various rock and rollers from years past and present at the Hard Rock Hotel & Casino.

Best Buffet(s)

Generally, the "best buffets" are not exactly bargains. Usually considered to be among the best by popular opinion are Wynn, Bellagio and Planet Hollywood. And although they all seem to be constantly changes prices and food selections, for good value, variety, consistency and quality, I would give Main Street Station and M Resort a try.

Scot's weekly Vegas Values column is updated every Sunday and you can read it at americancasinoguide.com/vegas-values.

The report is free and on that page you can also subscribe to have the report emailed directly to you each week.

Unlike New Jersey, the Nevada Gaming Control Board does not break down its slot statistics by individual properties. Rather, they are classified by area.

The annual gaming revenue report breaks the Las Vegas market down into two major tourist areas: the Strip and downtown. There is also a very large locals market in Las Vegas and those casinos are shown in the gaming revenue report as the Boulder Strip and North Las Vegas areas.

When choosing where to do your slot gambling, you may want to keep in mind the following slot payback percentages for Nevada's fiscal year beginning July 1, 2010 and ending June 30, 2011:

1¢ Slot Machines
The Strip - 88.40%
Downtown - 89.02%
Boulder Strip - 90.72%
N. Las Vegas - 90.73%

5¢ Slot Machines
The Strip - 91.57%
Downtown - 91.19%
Boulder Strip - 95.66%
N. Las Vegas - 95.31%

25¢ Slot Machines
The Strip - 91.78%
Downtown - 94.83%
Boulder Strip - 97.07%
N. Las Vegas - 96.48%

$1 Slot Machines
The Strip - 93.49%
Downtown - 95.26%
Boulder Strip - 96.37%
N. Las Vegas - 96.84%

$1 Megabucks Machines
The Strip - 88.18%
Downtown - 90.13%
Boulder Strip - 88.29%
N. Las Vegas - 86.25%

$5 Slot Machines
The Strip - 94.83%
Downtown - 94.21%
Boulder Strip - 96.38%
N. Las Vegas - 95.27%

$25 Slot Machines
The Strip - 96.66%
Downtown - 95.49%
Boulder Strip - N/A
N. Las Vegas - N/A

All Slot Machines
The Strip - 92.65%
Downtown - 93.57%
Boulder Strip - 94.76%
N. Las Vegas - 94.03%

These numbers reflect the percentage of money returned to the players on each denomination of machine. All electronic machines including slots, video poker and video keno are included in these numbers and the highest-paying returns are shown in bold print.

As you can see, the machines in downtown Las Vegas pay out more than those located on the Las Vegas Strip.

Returns even better than the downtown casinos can be found at some of the other locals casinos along Boulder Highway such as Boulder Station and Sam's Town and also in the North Las Vegas area which would include the Fiesta, Santa Fe and Texas Station casinos. Not only are those numbers among the best returns in the Las Vegas area, they are among the best payback percentages for anywhere in the United States.

This information is pretty well known by the locals and that's why most of them do their slot gambling away from the Strip unless they are drawn by a special slot club benefit or promotion.

If you are driving an RV to Las Vegas and want to stay overnight for free in a casino parking lot the only casino that will allow you to do that is Bally's.

For Nevada tourism information call (800) NEVADA-8. For Las Vegas information call the city's Convention & Visitors Authority at (702) 892-0711, or visit their web site at: www.lasvegas24hours.com.

Other games in the casino listings include: sports book (SB), race book (RB), Spanish 21 (S21), baccarat (B), mini-baccarat (MB), pai gow (PG), poker (P), pai gow poker (PGP), Caribbean stud poker (CSP), let it ride (LIR), three-card poker (TCP), four card poker (FCP), big 6 wheel (B6), sic bo (SIC), keno (K) and bingo (BG).

Aria Resort & Casino
3730 Las Vegas Boulevard South
Las Vegas, Nevada 89109
(702) 590-7757
Website: www.arialasvegas.com

Reservation Number: (866) 359-7757
Rooms: 3,436 Price Range: $179-$799
Suites: 568 Price Range: $500-$7,500
Restaurants: 10
Buffet B-$14.95/$24.95 (Sat/Sun) L- $19.95
         D-$29.95/$36.95 (Fri/Sat)
Casino Size: 150,000 Square Feet
Other Games: SB, RB, B, MB, P, PG, PGP,
         LIR, TCP, B6
Special Features: Located within 76-acre City Center project. Adjacent to 500,000-square-foot Crystals shopping/entertainment complex. *Viva Elvis* Cirque du Soleil stage show. 80,000-square-foot Spa.

Arizona Charlie's - Boulder
4575 Boulder Highway
Las Vegas, Nevada 89121
(702) 951-9000
Website: www.arizonacharliesboulder.com

Reservation Number: (888) 236-9066
RV Reservations: (800) 970-7280
Rooms: 300 Price Range: $31-$85
Restaurants: 3 (1 open 24 hours)
Buffets: B-$5.49/$8.99 (Sun) L-$6.99
         D-$8.99/$9.99 (Tue/Fri-Sun)
Casino Size: 47,541 Square Feet
Other Games: SB, RB, PGP, BG
Special Features: 239-space RV park ($32 per night).

Arizona Charlie's - Decatur
740 S. Decatur Boulevard
Las Vegas, Nevada 89107
(702) 258-5200
Website: www.arizonacharliesdecatur.com

Reservation Number: (800) 342-2695
Rooms: 245 Price Range: $65-$99
Suites: 10 Price Range: $119-$169
Restaurants: 5 (1 open 24 hours)
Buffets: B-$5.99 (Fri/Sat)
         L-$7.79/$8.99 (Sun) D-$11.99
Casino Size: 55,227 Square Feet
Other Games: SB, RB, P, PGP, K, BG
Special Features: Buffet discount with slot club card. 25% discount on buffet with player's club card.

Bally's Las Vegas
3645 Las Vegas Blvd. South
Las Vegas, Nevada 89109
(702) 739-4111
Website: www.ballyslv.com

Toll-Free Number: (800) 7-BALLYS
Reservation Number: (888) 215-1078
Rooms: 2,814 Price Range: $79-$219
Suites: 265 Price Range: $129-$449
Restaurants: 11 (1 open 24 hours)
Buffets: Brunch-$85.00 (Sun)
Casino Size: 66,187 Square Feet
Other Games: SB, RB, B, MB, P,
         PGP, CSP, LIR, TCP, K, B6
Overnight RV Parking: Free/RV Dump: No
Senior Discount: Various if 55+
Special Features: 20 retail stores. *Jubilee* stage show.

See page 29 to read a story about Las Vegas hotel Resort Fees; what they are, which hotels charge them and how you can sometimes avoid them.

Bellagio
3600 Las Vegas Blvd. South
Las Vegas, Nevada 89109
(702) 693-7111
Website: www.bellagioresort.com

Reservation Number: (888) 987-6667
Rooms: 2,688 Price Range: $149-$499
Suites: 308 Price Range: $575-$5,500
Restaurants: 13 (2 open 24 hours)
Buffets: B-$15.95/$24.95 (Sat/Sun)
   L-$19.95 D-$29.95/$36.95 (Fri/Sat)
Casino Size: 159,760 Square Feet
Other Games: SB, RB, B, MB, P, PG, PGP,
   CSP, LIR, TCP, K, B6
Special Features: Lake with nightly light and water show. Shopping mall. Two wedding chapels. Beauty salon and spa. Cirque du Soleil's "O" stage show.

Bill's Gamblin' Hall & Saloon
3595 Las Vegas Blvd. South
Las Vegas, Nevada 89109
(702) 737-2100
Website: www.billslasvegas.com

Reservation Number: (866) 245-5745
Rooms: 200 Price Range: $49-$125
Suites: 12 Price Range: $165-$255
Restaurants: 2 (1 open 24 hours)
Casino Size: 17,947 Square Feet
Other Games: SB, RB, TCP, LIR, P, PGP, B6

Binion's Gambling Hall and Hotel
128 E. Fremont Street
Las Vegas, Nevada 89101
(702) 382-1600
Website: www.binions.com

Toll-Free Number: (800) 937-6537
Restaurants: 4 (1 open 24 hours)
Casino Size: 79,800 Square Feet
Other Games: SB, RB, P, PGP, LIR,
   TCP, B6, B6
Special Features: Steak House on 24th floor offers panoramic views of Las Vegas. Free souvenir photo taken in front of $1,000,000 cash.

Boulder Station Hotel & Casino
4111 Boulder Highway
Las Vegas, Nevada 89121
(702) 432-7777
Website: www.boulderstation.com

Toll-Free Number: (800) 981-5577
Reservation Number: (800) 683-7777
Rooms: 300 Price Range: $29-$139
Restaurants: 6 (1 open 24 hours)
Buffets: B-$7.99 L-$10.99/$14.99 (Sat/Sun)
   D-$14.99
Casino Size: 89,443 Square Feet
Other Games: SB, RB, MB, P, PGP,
   TCP, K, BG
Special Features: 11-screen movie complex. Kid Quest childcare center. Buffet discount for slot club members.

Caesars Palace
3570 Las Vegas Blvd. South
Las Vegas, Nevada 89109
(702) 731-7110
Website: www.caesarspalace.com

Toll-Free Number: (800) 634-6001
Reservation Number: (800) 634-6661
Rooms: 3,349 Price Range: $99-$500
Petite Suites: 242 Price Range: $300-$600
Suites: 157 Price Range: $750-$4,400
Restaurants: 12 (1 open 24 hours)
Buffets: B-$17.95
   L-$19.95/$26.95 (Sat/Sun)
   D-$26.95
Casino Size: 131,095 Square Feet
Other Games: SB, RB, B, MB, PG, P, S21
   PGP, CSP, LIR, TCP, B6, K
Special Features: Health spa. Beauty salon. Shopping mall with 125 stores and interactive attractions. *Celine Dion* stage show.

The Best Places To Play In Las Vegas

Roulette - There are 15 casinos in Las Vegas that offer single-zero roulette: Aria, Bellagio, Caesars Palace, Encore, Luxor, M, Mandalay Bay, MGM Grand, Mirage, Monte Carlo, Palazzo, Riviera, Cosmopolitian, Venetian and Wynn. This game has a 2.70% edge as compared to the usual 5.26% edge on a double-zero roulette wheel. Be aware that all of these casinos offer single-zero wheels at just some of their roulette games and not all of them. The minimum bet is $25 at Aria, M, MGM Grand, Mirage, Monte Carlo and Venetian/Palazzo. It's $50 at Bellagio and $100 at all of the other casinos.

Craps - Only one casino allows up to 100x odds on its craps tables: Casino Royale (minimum bet is $3). Next best are Sam's Town and Main Street Station at 20X odds.

Blackjack- All recommendations in this section apply to basic strategy players. For single-deck games you should always look for casinos that pay the standard 3-to-2 for blackjacks. Many casinos only pay 6-to-5 for blackjack and this increases the casino edge to around 1.5% and they should be avoided. Many casinos also offer a blackjack game called Super Fun 21. This is another game that should be avoided as the casino advantage is around 1%.

The best single-deck games can be found at the El Cortez which offers the following rules: dealer hits soft 17, double down on any first two cards, split any pair, re-split any pair (except aces), and no doubling after splitting. The casino edge in this game is .18% and the minimum bet is $5. It's also offered at the Hacienda in Boulder City near Hoover Dam.

There are 12 casinos with two-deck games offering the following rules: dealer stands on soft 17, double down on any first two cards, re-split any pair (except aces) and doubling allowed after splitting. The casinos that offer it are: Aria, Bellagio, Cosmopolitan, Hard Rock, Luxor, MGM Grand, Mandalay Bay, Mirage, Monte Carlo, New York New York, Treasure Island and Venetian (not at Palazzo). The casino edge in these games is .19% with minimum bets of $50 and up.

The best double-deck games, however, are offered at both the Tropicana and M Resort. Those games have the same rules as the above games except they allow the re-splitting of aces and that brings the casino edge down to .14% The minimum bets at those games is $100.

The remaining best two-deckers in Las Vegas can be found at some "locals" casinos that have the same rules as above, with one exception: the dealer hits soft 17. The casino advantage is .35% and the game can be found at all of the Station casinos, plus Arizona Charlie's Boulder, the Plaza, Silverton and the M Resort. The minimum bet at these casinos is usually $5.

For six-deck shoe games the best casinos have these rules: dealer stands on soft 17, double after split allowed, late surrender offered and resplitting of aces allowed. The casino edge in this game works out to .26% and you can find it at many major casinos: Aria, Bellagio, Caesars Palace, Cosmopolitan, Hard Rock, M Resort, Mandalay Bay, MGM Grand, Monte Carlo, NYNY, Palms, Planet Hollywood, Red Rock, Wynn and the Venetian/Palazzo. The minimum bet at these casinos is at least $25.

Almost all of these casinos also offer this same game with identical rules except that they will hit soft 17. The minimums in this game are lower ($5 or $10) but the casino's mathematical edge is raised to .46%.

Cosmopolitan, MGM Grand, Mirage, Monte Carlo and Venetian/Palazzo offer the best eight deck games. They have the same rules as the .26% six-deck game and the casino advantage is .49% with minimum bets of $5 or $10.

Video Poker- Smart video poker players know that some of the best machines to look for are: 9/6 Jacks or Better (99.54% return), 8/5 Bonus Poker (99.17% return), 10/7 Double Bonus (100.17% return), full-pay Deuces Wild (100.76% return) and Not So Ugly Deuces (99.73% return). These games are very hard to find at Las Vegas Strip casinos, but they are usually widely available at "locals" casinos along Boulder Highway, or in Henderson or North Las Vegas.

Following is a list of casinos offering some of these better paying video poker games. The abbreviations used for each listing are JB (9/6 jacks or better), BP (8/5 bonus poker), DB (10/7 Double Bonus), FPDW (full-pay deuces wild) and NSUD (not so ugly deuces).

Strip-area Casinos
Casino Royale: BP - quarter to $5
Circus Circus: BP - quarter to $1
Clarion: JB - nickel
Ellis Island: JB - nickel to $5; NSUD - quarter; BP - nickel to quarter
Gold Coast: JB - quarter to $5; NSUD - quarter to $2; BP - quarter to $5
Hard Rock: BP - quarter to $25
Hooters: JB - quarter to $1
Las Vegas Hilton: JB - penny to $1; NSUD - quarter to $1
NYNY: JB - quarter to $25; BP quarter to $25 (note - these machines do not have a players club card reader on them so you will not be able to earn any comps or cashback).
Orleans: BP - quarter to $1; NSUD - quarter
Palms: JB -penny to $2; BP - quarter; FPDW with a progressive - quarter; NSUD - quarter to $5
Sahara: BP - quarter
Stratosphere: BP - nickel to $2
Terrible's: JB - quarter to fifty cents; BP - quarter to $5
Tuscany: BP - quarter to $1

One of the best upper-tier casinos offering good video poker, coupled with a good players club offer, is the Las Vegas Hilton. As a new player with a minimal amount of action you will probably receive a mailer for a discounted 3-day room package, including some free/discounted food deals. It's a very nice property and they don't charge resort fees, so that adds even more value to their room package offer.

Downtown Casinos
California: JB - quarter to $1; DB - quarter to $1; NSUD - nickel to fifty cents
El Cortez: JB - dime to quarter; DB - quarter to fifty cents; Double Deuces Wild (100.92% return) - quarter
Fitz: DB: quarter; NSUD - quarter to $1; BP - nickel to $2; Loose Deuces (101.60% return) - nickel
Four Queens: JB - nickel to $1; DB - quarter to $1; BP - nickel to $1
Fremont: JB - quarter to $1; NSUD - quarter to $1; BP - quarter to $1
Golden Nugget: BP - quarter
Las Vegas Club: JB and BP - quarter to $1
Main Street: JB - quarter to $1; DB - quarter to $1; NSUD - quarter; BP - quarter to $5
Plaza: JB and BP - quarter to fifty-cents
Western: JB - quarter; DB - quarter; BP - quarter

Locals Casinos - If you are looking for the best video poker in Las Vegas then you may want to make a side trip to some of the casinos along Boulder Highway, as well as in Henderson or North Las Vegas. Most of these casinos offer all of the games listed above in a variety of denominations. We especially like Sam's Town on Boulder Highway. They offer: JB - quarter to $1; DB - quarter to $1; FPDW - nickel to quarter; and 10/6 Double Double Bonus (100.07% return) - quarter to $1. With the B Connected Players Club at Sam's Town, you will also be able to redeem your points at any of their other major casinos around town including: Gold Coast, Orleans, Suncoast, California, Fremont and Main Street Station.

Free Things To See In Las Vegas!

Masquerade Village

The Masquerade Show in the Sky is a $25-million extravaganza in the sky and on the stage at the Rio Hotel & Casino.

Five floats travel on an overhead track above the casino, while dancers and musicians perform on stage, or from attractions that drop from the ceiling or from circular lifts rising from the floor.

There are three differently themed shows on a rotating schedule Thursday through Saturday evenings on the hour from 6-11pm.

California Hotel & Casino
12 Ogden Avenue
Las Vegas, Nevada 89101
(702) 385-1222
Website: www.thecal.com

Reservation Number: (800) 634-6505
Rooms: 781 Price Range: $36-$105
Suites: 74 Price Range: Casino Use Only
Restaurants: 4 (1 open 24 hours)
Casino Size: 35,848 Square Feet
Other Games: SB, PGP, LIR, TCP, K
Special Features: 93-space RV park ($14/$17 per night). Offers charter packages from Hawaii.

Casino Royale & Hotel
3411 Las Vegas Blvd. South
Las Vegas, Nevada 89109
(702) 737-3500
Website: www.casinoroyalehotel.com

Toll-Free Number: (800) 854-7666
Rooms: 151 Price Range: $69-$89
Suites: 3 Price Range: $149-$189
Restaurants: 4 (1 open 24 hours)
Casino Size: 22,000 Square Feet
Other Games: TCP
Special Features: Outback, Denny's and Subway. Refrigerator in every room. 100x odds on craps.

Circus Circus Hotel & Casino
2880 Las Vegas Blvd. South
Las Vegas, Nevada 89109
(702) 734-0410
Website: www.circuscircus.com

Room Reservations: (877) 224-7287
RV Reservations: (800) 562-7270
Rooms: 3,770 Price Range: $39-$119
Suites: 122   Price Range: $89-$269
Restaurants: 9 (2 open 24 hours)
Buffets: B-$11.99 L-$13.99 D-$14.99
Casino Size: 123,928 Square Feet
Other Games: SB, RB, P, PGP,
                    LIR, TCP, B6
Special Features: Free circus acts 11 am-midnight. 399-space KOA RV park ($39 to $85 per night). Wedding chapel. Midway and arcade games. Indoor theme park.

Clarion Hotel and Casino
305 Convention Center Drive
Las Vegas, NV 89109
(702)952-8000
Website: www.clarionhotelvegas.com

Reservations Number: (800) 633-1777
Rooms: 202 Price Range: $59-$170
Casino Size: 123,928 Square Feet
Restaurants: 1
Other Games: Slots Only

The Cosmopolitan of Las Vegas
3708 Las Vegas Boulevard South
Las Vegas, NV 89109
(702) 698-7000
Website: www.cosmopolitanlasvegas.com

Toll-free Number: (877) 551-7778
Rooms: 2,600 Price Range: $180-$480
Suites: 395 Price Range: $450-$1,500
Restaurants: 13
Casino Size: 100,000 Square Feet
Other games: LIR, B, MB, PGP,
  TCP, S21, B6

Eastside Cannery
5255 Boulder Highway
Las Vegas, Nevada 89122
(702) 458-8810
Website: www.eastsidecannery.com

Reservation Number: (866) 999-4899
Rooms: 190 Price Range: $39-$99
Rooms: 20 Price Range: $90-$199
Restaurants: 5 (1 open 24 hours)
Buffets: L-$8.99/$11.99 (Sat/Sun)
  D-$11.99/$17.99 (Thu)
Casino Size: 62,479 Square Feet
Other Games: SB, RB, P, PGP, BG
Senior Discount: Food discounts if 55+
Special features: $2 buffet discount with
player's club card.

El Cortez Hotel & Casino
600 E. Fremont Street
Las Vegas, Nevada 89101
(702) 385-5200
Website: www.elcortezhotelcasino.com

Reservation Number: (800) 634-6703
Rooms: 299 Price Range: $29-$109
Suites: 10 Price Range: $60-$159
Restaurants: 2 (1 open 24 hours)
Casino Size: 45,300 Square Feet
Other Games: SB ,RB, MB, P, PGP, TCP, K
Special Features: Video arcade. Gift shop and
ice cream parlor. Barber shop. Beauty salon.

Ellis Island Casino & Brewery
4178 Koval Lane
Las Vegas, Nevada 89109
(702) 733-8901
Website: www.ellisislandcasino.com

Restaurants: 1 (open 24 hours)
Casino Size: 13,916 Square Feet
Other Games: SB, RB
Special Features: Super 8 Motel next door.
$7.99 steak dinner (not on menu, must ask
for it). #1 Microbrewery in Nevada as voted
by the state's Brewers Association.

Encore Las Vegas
3131 Las Vegas Boulevard South
Las Vegas, Nevada 89109
(702) 770-7800
Website: www.encorelasvegas.com

Reservations Number: (888) 320-7125
Suites: 1,800 Price Range: $239-$769
Tower Suites: 234 Price Range $299-$2,500
Restaurants: 9 (1 open 24 hours)
Casino Size: 93,094 Square Feet
Other Games: SB, RB, B, MB, P, PG, CW,
  PGP, CSP, LIR, TCP, B6
Special Features: *Le Reve* and *Garth Brooks*
stage show. Attached to Wynn Las Vegas.

Excalibur Hotel/Casino
3850 Las Vegas Blvd. South
Las Vegas, Nevada 89109
(702) 597-7777
Website: www.excaliburcasino.com

Reservation Number: (800) 937-7777
Rooms: 4,008 Price Range: $33-$141
Suites: 46 Price Range: $160-$390
Restaurants: 5 (1 open 24 hours)
Buffets: B-$14.99 L-$15.99 D-$19.99
Casino Size: 99,960 Square Feet
Other Games: SB, RB, MB, P, PGP,
  CSP, LIR, CW, TCP, B6, K
Special Features: Canterbury wedding
chapel. Strolling Renaissance entertainers.
Video arcade and midway games. Nightly
Tournament of Kings dinner show. Food Court
with fast food outlets.

The Best Vegas Values

By H. Scot Krause

Welcome to "Vegas Values!" It's an exclusive weekly column found only at: Americancasinoguide.com, the companion website to this book. The column is updated weekly with some of the best entertainment, gambling, dining values, and promotions throughout Las Vegas. Below are examples from the "Vegas Values" column. Remember, promotions are subject to change and may be cancelled at anytime. Call ahead to verify before making a special trip.

Ellis Island Casino & Brewery: Best steak deal in Las Vegas! $7.99 complete steak dinner including a free beer available 24/7. The meal includes a 10-ounce filet-cut steak, salad, vegetable, potato, dinner rolls and an Ellis Island brewed draft beer. It's not on the menu. Ask your server for it!

Excalibur: Offers $30 for $20 Win Cards. Buy in for $20 and get a set of Win Cards (basic explanation/strategy for table games) and $30 in non-negotiable chips. Offer is available once per year. The $30 for $20 Win Cards are also offered at Luxor, Mandalay Bay, Circus Circus, Four Queens, Planet Hollywood, and Tropicana.

Four Queens: New members signing up for the Royal Player's Club receive a FREE t-shirt or canvas tote bag after earning 40 points within the first 24 hours of enrolling.

Gold Coast: Birthday Promotion: During your birth month, earn 1 point and swipe for a prize at a kiosk near slot club booth (see players club for details).

Golden Gate: New member sign-up promotion: $5 in FREE slot play for new members who earn 20 points.

Hard Rock: Mr. Lucky's 24/7 coffee shop features two new graveyard specials available from midnight to 6 am, daily. Guests can enjoy New York Steak & Eggs, complete with an 8 oz NY Steak, two eggs, hash browns and toast, all for $4.99. In addition, the classic old-school burger and French fries is now available as a Burger Basket Special for $3.99.

Harrah's: Take a stroll through the Carnaval Court area located outside between Harrah's and the Imperial Palace to pick up FREE coupons from representatives for valuable discounts to use at Harrah's Las Vegas properties.

M Resort: New members signing up for the Imagine Rewards slot club have a choice of a FREE M logo T-Shirt or $5 in FREE Slot Play.

Main Street Station: "Score with Four" promotion. Hit any 4-of-a-kind, straight flush, royal flush or 300-coin slot win and receive a scratch card for additional cash. Most cards are of the $2 to $5 variety, but they do offer cards valued at $20, $50 and $100, as well as rare $5,000 cards.

Orleans: Birthday Promotion: During your birth month, earn 1 point and swipe for a prize at a kiosk near slot club booth (see players club for details).

Riviera: New player's club sign-ups receive a FREE Buffet. (Note: this promotion is always subject to change but new members signing up almost always receive some type of FREE gift upon enrollment.)

Sam's Town: Willy & Jose's birthday special is a FREE T-Shirt, FREE Margarita and a FREE Desert with a minimum $9.99 entrée purchase on your birthday.

Santa Fe Station: Birthday Promotion: FREE $25 table games bet if you stop in and play on your birthday! (Must show a valid I.D.) Not a matchplay…just a FREE $25 bet!

South Point: Birthday Promotion: Offers birthday guests 2,500 FREE points after earning your first point during your birthday month. A $6+ value.

Luck, royals, good food and jackpots to all...

The Fitz Las Vegas
301 Fremont Street
Las Vegas, Nevada 89101
(702) 388-2400
Website: www.fitzgeralds.com

Reservation Number: (800) 274-5825
Rooms: 624 Price Range: $29-$99
Suites: 14 Price Range: $109-$239
Restaurants: 2 (1 open 24 hours)
Casino Size: 42,251 Square Feet
Other Games: SB, S21, LIR, PGP, P, TCP, K
Special Features: Fast food court with
McDonald's and Krispy Kreme.

Flamingo Las Vegas
3555 Las Vegas Blvd. South
Las Vegas, Nevada 89109
(702) 733-3111
Website: www.flamingolasvegas.com

Reservation Number: (800) 732-2111
Rooms: 3,545 Price Range: $50-$205
Suites: 215   Price Range: $205-$855
Restaurants: 8 (1 open 24 hours)
Buffets: B-$14.99 L-$15.99/$19.99 (Sat/Sun)
       D-$19.99
Casino Size: 76,763 Sq Ft (includes O'Shea's)
Other Games: SB, RB, MB, P, PG, PGP,
            LIR, TCP, B6, K
Special Features: Health Spa. Shopping
arcade.   Jimmy Buffet's Margaritaville
restaurant.

Four Queens Hotel/Casino
202 Fremont Street
Las Vegas, Nevada 89101
(702) 385-4011
Website: www.fourqueens.com

Reservation Number: (800) 634-6045
Rooms: 690 Price Range: $39-$119
Suites: 48 Price Range: $149-$240
Restaurants: 3 (1 open 24 hours)
Casino Size: 27,389 Square Feet
Other Games: SB, RB, PGP, LIR, TCP, K

Fremont Hotel & Casino
200 E. Fremont Street
Las Vegas, Nevada 89101
(702) 385-3232
Website: www.fremontcasino.com

Toll-Free Number: (800) 634-6460
Reservation Number: (800) 634-6182
Rooms: 428 Price Range: $36-$115
Suites: 24 Price Range: Casino Use Only
Restaurants: 4 (1 open 24 hours)
Buffets: B-$6.99 L-$7.99/$10.99 (Sat/Sun)
       D-$13.99/$17.99 (Tue/Fri)
Casino Size: 30,244 Square Feet
Other Games: SB, RB, PGP, LIR, TCP, K
Special Features: 99¢ shrimp cocktail at snack
bar. Tony Roma's restaurant.

Gold Coast Hotel & Casino
4000 W. Flamingo Road
Las Vegas, Nevada 89103
(702) 367-7111
Website: www.goldcoastcasino.com

Toll-Free Number: (888) 402-6278
Rooms: 750 Price Range: $34-$114
Suites: 27 Price Range: $165-$245
Restaurants: 6 (1 open 24 hours)
Buffets: B-$7.99/$12.99 (Sun) L-$9.99
       D-$13.99/$14.99 (Thu)/ $18.99 (Fri)
Casino Size: 88,915 Square Feet
Other Games: SB, RB, MB, PGP, TCP,
            K, BG
Special Features: 70-lane bowling center.
Showroom. Buffet discount with player's
club card.

Gold Spike Hotel & Casino
400 E. Ogden Avenue
Las Vegas, Nevada 89101
(702) 384-8444
Website: www.goldspike.com

Toll-Free Number: (866) 600-8600
Rooms: 102 Price Range: $40-80
Suites: 7 Price Range: $49-$250
Restaurants: 1 (open 24 hours)
Casino Size: 7,575 Square Feet
Other Games: No Craps or Roulette
Special Features: $5.99 prime rib dinner 4-11P.M..

Free Things To See In Las Vegas!

Sirens of TI Show

The front of the Treasure Island (TI) Resort features the Sirens of TI live-action show, where sexy females battle it out with a band of renegade male pirates in a modern interpretation of the Battle of Buccaneer Bay.

Shows nightly at 5:30 (fall/winter only),7, 8:30, 10 and 11:30 (spring/summer only). Lines start forming in front about 45 minutes before showtime. VIP viewing is offered in the front area for TI hotel guests who show their room key. The show is always subject to cancellation due to weather conditions. If it's a windy day, you may want to call ahead to verify that the show hasn't been canceled.

Golden Gate Hotel & Casino
One Fremont Street
Las Vegas, Nevada 89101
(702) 385-1906
Website: www.goldengatecasino.com

Reservation Number: (800) 426-1906
Rooms: 106 Price Range: $31-$84
Restaurants: 2 (2 open 24 hours)
Casino Size: 9,090 Square Feet
Other Games: SB, TCP
Special Features: $1.99 shrimp cocktail.
Oldest hotel in Vegas (opened 1906).

The Golden Nugget
129 E. Fremont Street
Las Vegas, Nevada 89101
(702) 385-7111
Website: www.goldennugget.com

Toll-Free Number: (800) 634-3403
Reservation Number: (800) 634-3454
Rooms: 1,805 Price Range: $59-$149
Suites: 102 Price Range: $149-$750
Restaurants: 8 (1 open 24 hours)
Buffets: B-$10.99 L-$11.99/$19.99 (Sat/Sun)
      D-$18.99/$21.99 (Fri-Sun)
Casino Size: 47,796 Square Feet
Other Games: SB, RB, MB, P, PGP,
            LIR, TCP, B6, K
Special Features: World's largest gold nugget (61 pounds) on display. Health spa. Swimming pool with shark tank.

Hard Rock Hotel & Casino
4455 Paradise Road
Las Vegas, Nevada 89109
(702) 693-5000
Website: www.hardrockhotel.com

Toll-Free Number: (800) HRD-ROCK
Rooms: 1,130   Price Range: $69-$420
Suites: 387   Price Range: $179-$529
Restaurants: 2 (1 open 24 hours)
Casino Size: 65,084 Square Feet
Other Games: SB, RB, B, MB, PGP,
            LIR, TCP, B6
Special Features: Rock and Roll memorabilia display. Beach Club with cabanas and sandy beaches. Lagoon with underwater music.

See page 29 to read a story about Las Vegas Hotel Resort Fees; what they are, which hotels charge them and how you can sometimes avoid them.

Harrah's Las Vegas
3475 Las Vegas Blvd. South
Las Vegas, Nevada 89109
(702) 369-5000
Website: www.harrahslasvegas.com

Toll-Free Number: (800) 392-9002
Reservation Number: (800) HARRAHS
Rooms: 2,672 Price Range: $35-$255
Suites: 94 Price Range: $110-$595
Restaurants: 10 (1 open 24 hours)
Buffets: B-$14.99/$19.99 (Sat/Sun)
        L-$15.99 D-$19.99/$21.99 (Fri/Sat)
Casino Size: 90,637 Square Feet
Other Games: SB, RB, MB, P, PG, PGP,
        LIR, TCP, B6, K
Special Features: Mardi Gras-themed casino.
Improv Comedy Club. *Mac King, Legends in
Concert* and *Defending the Caveman* stage
shows.

Hooters Casino Hotel
115 East Tropicana Avenue
Las Vegas, Nevada 89109
(702) 739-9000
Website: www.hooterscasinohotel.com

Toll-Free Number: (866) LV-HOOTS
Rooms: 694 Price Range: $55-$195
Suites: 17 Price Range: $205-$500
Restaurants: 4 (1 open 24 hours)
Casino Size: 27,528 Square Feet
Other Games: SB, LIR, P, PGP, TCP, B6
Special Features: *Men of X* stage show.

Imperial Palace Hotel & Casino
3535 Las Vegas Blvd. South
Las Vegas, Nevada 89109
(702) 731-3311
Website: www.imperialpalace.com

Toll-Free Number: (800) 351-7400
Reservation Number: (800) 634-6441
Rooms: 1,088 Price Range: $40-$125
Suites: 225 Price Range: $110-$285
Restaurants: 10 (1 open 24 hours)
Buffets: Brunch-$12.99 D-$18.99 (Tue-Sat)
Casino Size: 118,000 Square Feet
Other Games: SB, RB, P, PGP, LIR,
        TCP, B6, K
Special Features: Auto museum (admission
charge). Video arcade. Wedding chapel.

Jerry's Nugget
See North Las Vegas section

Las Vegas Club Hotel & Casino
18 E. Fremont Street
Las Vegas, Nevada 89101
(702) 385-1664
Website: www.vegasclubcasino.net

Reservation Number: (800) 634-6532
Rooms: 410 Price Range: $25-$110
Restaurants: 4 (1 open 24 hours)
Buffets: D-$11.88/$15.99 (Fri)
Casino Size: 22,778 Square Feet
Other Games: PGP, TCP, K, B6
Special Features: Sports themed-casino with
large collection of sports memorabilia.

Las Vegas Hilton
3000 Paradise Road
Las Vegas, Nevada 89109
(702) 732-5111
Website: www.lvhilton.com

Reservation Number: (800) 732-7117
Rooms: 2,956 Price Range: $69-$129
Suites: 305 Price Range: $130-$1,750
Restaurants: 11 (1 open 24 hours)
Buffets: B-$13.99/$18.99 (Sat/Sun)
        L-$14.99 D-$19.99
Casino Size: 74,676 Square Feet
Other Games: SB, RB, B, MB, PGP,
        LIR, TCP, B6
Special Features: World's largest race and
sports book. Health club. Jogging track.

Longhorn Casino
5288 Boulder Highway
Las Vegas, Nevada 89122
(702) 435-9170

Restaurants: 1 (open 24 hours)
Casino Size: 4,825 Square Feet
Other Games: SB, RB, No craps or roulette

Free Things To See In Las Vegas!

Fremont Street Experience

This $70 million computer-generated sound and light show takes place 90 feet in the sky over a pedestrian mall stretching four city blocks in downtown Las Vegas and in mid-2004 the entire system was upgraded with new LED modules to provide even crisper and clearer images. It's like watching the world's largest plasma TV with larger-than-life animations, integrated live video feeds, and synchronized music.

There are five differently themed shows nightly. Starting times vary, beginning at dusk, but then begin on the start of each hour through midnight.

Luxor Las Vegas
3900 Las Vegas Blvd. South
Las Vegas, Nevada 89119
(702) 262-4000
Website: www.luxor.com

Reservation Number (800) 288-1000
Pyramid Rooms: 1,948 Price Range: $59-$249
Pyramid Suites 237 Price Range: $165-$375
Tower Rooms: 2,256 Price Range: $79-$269
Tower Suites 236 Price Range: $179-$509
Restaurants: 6 (1 open 24 hours)
Buffets: B-$14.99 L-$15.99 D-$19.99
Casino Size: 100,090 Square Feet
Other Games: SB, RB, MB, P, PGP,
                     LIR, TCP, B6
Special Features: 30-story pyramid-shaped hotel with Egyptian theme. "Carrot Top" comedy show. Cirque Du soleil "Believe" Stage show. IMAX theater.

Main Street Station Hotel & Casino
200 N. Main Street
Las Vegas, Nevada 89101
(702) 387-1896
Website: www.mainstreetcasino.com

Toll-Free Number: (800) 713-8933
Reservation Number: (800) 465-0711
Rooms: 406 Price Range: $36-$109
Suites: 14 Price Range: Casino Use Only
Restaurants: 4 (1 open 24 hours)
Buffets: B-$7.99/$11.99 (Sat/Sun) L-$8.99
    D- $11.99/$14.99(Tue/Thu/Sat)/$18.99 (Fri)
Casino Size: 26,918 Square Feet
Other Games: PGP, LIR, TCP
Special Features: 99-space RV park ($14/$17 per night). Buffet discount for slot club members.

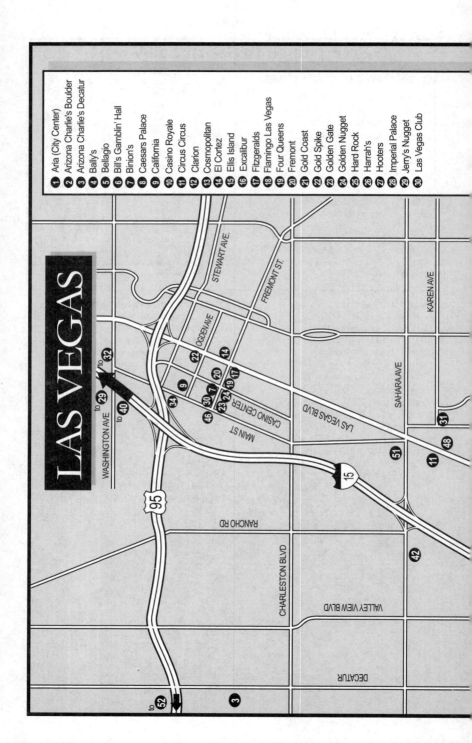

LAS VEGAS

1. Aria (City Center)
2. Arizona Charlie's Boulder
3. Arizona Charlie's Decatur
4. Bally's
5. Bellagio
6. Bill's Gamblin' Hall
7. Binion's
8. Caesars Palace
9. California
10. Casino Royale
11. Circus Circus
12. Clarion
13. Cosmopolitan
14. El Cortez
15. Ellis Island
16. Excalibur
17. Fitzgeralds
18. Flamingo Las Vegas
19. Four Queens
20. Fremont
21. Gold Coast
22. Gold Spike
23. Golden Gate
24. Golden Nugget
25. Hard Rock
26. Harrah's
27. Hooters
28. Imperial Palace
29. Jerry's Nugget
30. Las Vegas Club

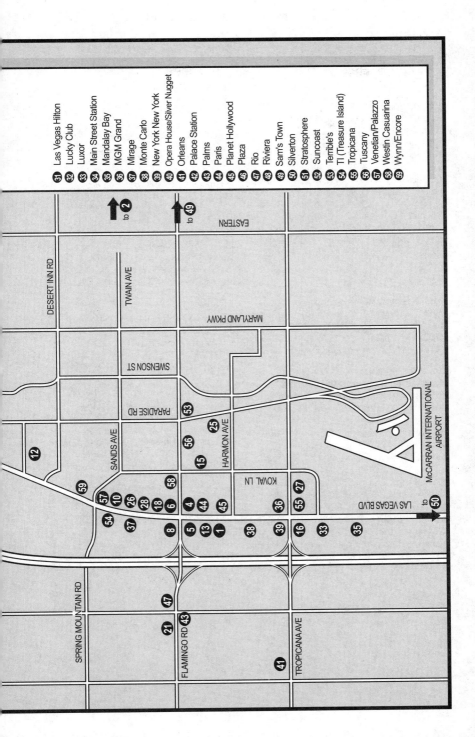

31 Las Vegas Hilton
32 Lucky Club
33 Luxor
34 Main Street Station
35 Mandalay Bay
36 MGM Grand
37 Mirage
38 Monte Carlo
39 New York New York
40 Opera House/Silver Nugget
41 Orleans
42 Palace Station
43 Palms
44 Paris
45 Planet Hollywood
46 Plaza
47 Rio
48 Riviera
49 Sam's Town
50 Silverton
51 Stratosphere
52 Suncoast
53 Terrible's
54 TI (Treasure Island)
55 Tropicana
56 Tuscany
57 Venetian/Palazzo
58 Westin Casuarina
59 Wynn/Encore

DESERT INN RD
TWAIN AVE
EASTERN
MARYLAND PKWY
SWENSON ST
PARADISE RD
SANDS AVE
HARMON AVE
KOVAL LN
LAS VEGAS BLVD
SPRING MOUNTAIN RD
FLAMINGO RD
TROPICANA AVE
McCARRAN INTERNATIONAL AIRPORT

to 2
to 49
to 50

Mandalay Bay
3950 Las Vegas Blvd. South
Las Vegas, Nevada 89109
(702) 632-7777
Web Site: www.mandalaybay.com

Reservation Number: (877) 632-7000
Rooms: 3,220 Price Range: $89-$360
Suites: 424 Price Range: $130-$600
Restaurants: 16 (1 open 24 hours)
Buffets: B-$15.99/$26.99 (Sun)
          L-$19.99 D-$26.99
Casino Size: 160,344 Square Feet
Other Games: SB, RB, B, MB, P, PG, PGP,
          LIR, TCP, B6
Special Features: 424-room Four Seasons
Hotel on 35th-39th floors. *House of Blues*
restaurant. Sand and surf beach with lazy
river ride. Shark Reef exhibit (admission
charge). Spa.

MGM Grand Hotel Casino
3799 Las Vegas Blvd. South
Las Vegas, Nevada 89109
(702) 891-1111
Web-Site: www.mgmgrand.com

Toll-Free Number: (800) 929-1111
Reservation Number: (800) 646-7787
Skyloft Reservations: (877) 646-5638
Rooms: 5,005 Price Range: $80-$280
Suites: 752 Price Range: $159-$899
Skylofts: 51 Price Range: $800-$10,000
Restaurants: 15 (1 open 24 hours)
Buffets: B-$17.25 L-$19.99/$24.99 (Sun)
          D-$29.99/$35.99 (Fri/Sat)
Casino Size: 156,023 Square Feet
Other Games: SB, RB, B, MB, PG, PGP,
          P, LIR, TCP, B6, CW
Special Features: Largest hotel in America.
Comedy Club. Rainforest Cafe. Midway
games and arcade. Free lion habitat exhibit.
Cirque du Soleil "Ka" stage show. *Crazy Horse* stage show.

The Mirage
3400 Las Vegas Blvd. South
Las Vegas, Nevada 89109
(702) 791-7111
Website: www.themirage.com

Reservation Number: (800) 627-6667
Rooms: 3,044 Price Range: $89-$450
Suites: 281 Price Range: $299-$1,500
Restaurants: 12 (1 open 24 hours)
Buffets: B-$15.99/$24.99 (Sat/Sun)
          L-$19.99   D-$26.99
Casino Size: 97,550 Square Feet
Other Games: SB, RB, B, MB, PG, P, CW
          PGP, LIR, TCP, B6
Special Features: Siegfried & Roy's Secret
Garden and Dolphin Habitat (admission
charge). Aquarium display at check-in desk.
Simulated volcano with periodic "eruptions."
Terry Fator and " Cirque du Soleil's *Love*
stage shows. B.B King's Blues Club.

Monte Carlo Resort & Casino
3770 Las Vegas Blvd. South
Las Vegas, Nevada 89109
(702) 730-7777
Website: www.montecarlo.com

Reservation Number: (800) 311-8999
Rooms: 3,002 Price Range: $60-$190
Suites: 259 Price Range: $139-$499
Restaurants: 7 (1 open 24 hours)
Buffets: Brunch-$16.95/$19.95 (Fri-Sun)
          D-$19.95/$24.95 (Fri-Sun)
Casino Size: 102,197 Square Feet
Other Games: SB, RB, MB, B, P, PGP,
          CSP, LIR, TCP, B6
Special Features: Food court. Microbrewery.
Pool with lazy river ride. Health spa.

Free Things To See In Las Vegas!

MGM Grand Lion Habitat

MGM Grand's $9 million Lion Habitat is located inside the property near the entertainment dome and it showcases up to five lions daily.

The Habitat is open 11 a.m. to 7 p.m. daily and features four separate waterfalls, overhangs, a pond and Acacia trees. There are numerous viewing areas that allow you to get an upclose view of the lions, including overhead and beneath you on the walkway.

For more information on the Lion Habitat, call the MGM Grand at (800) 929-1111, or visit their web site at www.mgmgrand.com

New York-New York Hotel & Casino
3790 Las Vegas Blvd. South
Las Vegas, Nevada 89109
(702) 740-6969
Website: www.nynyhotelcasino.com

Reservation Number: (800) 693-6763
Rooms: 2,024 Price Range: $60-$260
Suites: 12 Price Range: Casino Use Only
Restaurants: 8 (1 open 24 hours)
Casino Size: 64,269 Square Feet
Other Games: SB, RB, MB, PGP, SIC
                CSP, LIR, TCP, B6
Special Features: Replica Statue of Liberty and Empire State Building. *Manhattan Express* roller coaster. Cirque du Soleil's *Zumanity* stage show.

The Orleans Hotel & Casino
4500 W. Tropicana Avenue
Las Vegas, Nevada 89103
(702) 365-7111
Website: www.orleanscasino.com

Reservation Number: (800) ORLEANS
Rooms: 1,828 Price Range: $38-$165
Suites: 58 Price Range: $199-$499
Restaurants: 9 (1 open 24 hours)
Buffets: B-$7.99/$13.99 (Sun) L-$8.99
          D- $13.99/$15.99 (Wed)/$18.99 (Fri)
Casino Size: 137,000 Square Feet
Other Games: SB, RB, MB, P,
                PGP, LIR, TCP, K
Special Features: 70-lane bowling center. 18-screen movie theater. Kids Tyme childcare. 9,000-seat arena. Free shuttle to Gold Coast and Bills Gamblin' Hall.

O'Sheas Casino
3555 Las Vegas Blvd. South
Las Vegas, Nevada 89109
(702) 697-2767
Website: www.osheaslasvegas.com

Toll-Free: (800) 329-3232 ask for O'Shea's
Other Games: LIR
Special Features: Property is part of the Flamingo. Burger King.

Palace Station Hotel & Casino
2411 West Sahara Avenue
Las Vegas, Nevada 89102
(702) 367-2411
Website: www.palacestation.com

Reservation Number: (800) 544-2411
Rooms: 949 Price Range: $25-$109
Suites: 82 Price Range: $75-$159
Restaurants: 6 (1 open 24 hours)
Buffets: B-$7.99/$14.99 (Sun) L-$9.99
        D-$14.99
Casino Size: 84,000 Square Feet
Other Games: SB, RB, B, MB, PG, P, PGP,
        LIR, TCP, K, BG
Special Features: Buffet discount with slot club card. *Louie Anderson* Comedy Show.

The Palms
4321 Flamingo Road
Las Vegas, Nevada 89103
(702) 942-7777
Website: www.palms.com

Toll Free Number: (866) 942-7777
Reservation Number: (866) 942-7770
Rooms: 447 Price Range: $109-$359
Suites: 60 Price Range: $149-$750
Specialty Suites: 9 Prices: $2,500-$40,000
Restaurants: 10 (1 open 24 hours)
Buffets: B-$7.99/$18.99 (Sun) L-$11.99
        D-$19.99/$24.99 (Fri/Sat)
Casino Size: 94,136 Square Feet
Other Games: SB, RB, B, MB, P, PGP,
        LIR, TCP, B6
Special Features: 14-theater cineplex. IMAX theater. Tattoo shop. Kid's Quest childcare center. Recording studio. Playboy store.

Paris Casino Resort
3655 Las Vegas Blvd. South
Las Vegas, Nevada 89109
(702) 946-7000
Website: www.parislasvegas.com

Reservation Number: (888) BON-JOUR
Rooms: 2,916 Price Range: $90-$340
Suites: 300 Price Range: $285-$870
Restaurants: 11 (1 open 24 hours)
Buffets: B-$15.99/$27.99 (Sun)
        L-$18.99 D-$24.99
Casino Size: 95,263 Square Feet
Other Games: SB, RB, B, MB, TCP, CSP,
        PG, PGP, LIR, K, B6
Special Features: Replicas of Paris landmarks. 50-story Eiffel Tower with restaurant/ observation deck. *Barry Manilow* stage show.

Planet Hollywood Casino & Resort
3667 Las Vegas Boulevard S.
Las Vegas, Nevada 89109
(702) 785-5555
Website: www.planethollywoodresort.com

Reservation Number: (877) 333-9474
Rooms: 1,878 Price Range: $89-$269
Parlor Rooms: 466 Price Range: $259-$369
Suites: 223   Price Range: $229-$689
Restaurants: 5 (1 open 24 hours)
Buffets: B-$15.99/$24.99 (Sat/Sun)
        L-$18.99 D-$27.99
Casino Size: 90,425 Square Feet
Other Games: SB, RB, B, MB, P, PGP,
        LIR, TCP, B6
Special Features: 130-store retail mall. 7,000-seat Theater of the Performing Arts. Health spa and salon. *Peepshow* stage show. V-theater located in the Miracle Mile Shops offers a variety of stage shows.

Free Things To See In Las Vegas!

The Fountains at Bellagio

More than one thousand fountains dance in front of the Bellagio hotel, creating a union of water, music and light. The display spans more than 1,000 feet, with water soaring as high as 240 feet. The fountains are choreographed to music ranging from classical and operatic pieces to songs from Broadway shows.

Showtimes are every 30 minutes from 3 p.m (noon on Sat/Sun) until 8 p.m. After 8p.m. the shows start every 15 minutes until midnight. A list of all musical selections is available on the Bellagio web site at: www.bellagio.com

Plaza Hotel & Casino
1 Main Street
Las Vegas, Nevada 89101
(702) 386-2110
Website: www.plazahotelcasino.com

Reservation Number: (800) 634-6575
Rooms: 1,037 Price Range: $49-$139
Suites: 60   Price Range: $69-$189
Restaurants: 5 (1 open 24 hours)
Buffets: B-$7.77/$9.99 (Sat/Sun)
          L-$7.77 D-$12.99/$15.99 (Fri)
Casino Size: 57,436 Square Feet
Other Games: SB, RB, P, PGP,
          LIR, TCP, BG, K
Special Features: Firefly Restaurant offers full view of Fremont Street Experience. Buffet discount with slot club card.

Rampart Casino
221 N. Rampart Boulevard
Las Vegas, Nevada 89128
(702) 507-5900
Website: www.rampartcasino.com

Toll-Free Number: (866) 999-4899
Reservation Number: (877) 869-8777
Rooms: 440 Price Range: $139-$229
Suites: 70 Price Range: $209-$399
Restaurants: 6 (1 open 24 hours)
Buffets: L-$9.99/$14.99 (Sun)
   D-$13.99/$18.99 (Thu)/$15.99 (Sat)
Casino Size: 56,750 Square Feet
Other Games: SB, RB, PGP, TCP
Special Features: Hotel is JW Marriott. Golf course. Spa.

Red Rock Resort Spa Casino
10973 W. Charleston Boulevard
Las Vegas, Nevada 89135
(702) 797-7777
Website: www.redrocklasvegas.com

Rooms: 366 Price Range: $125-$360
Suites: 48 Price Range: $285-$520
Restaurants: 10 (1 open 24 hours)
Buffets: B-$8.99/$20.99 (Sun)
          L-$10.99 D-$20.99
Casino Size: 119,309 Square Feet
Other Games: SB, RB, MB, P, PGP,
          TCP, LIR, K, BG
Special Features: 16-screen movie complex. Childcare center. Full-service spa.

Rio Suites Hotel & Casino
3700 W. Flamingo Road
Las Vegas, Nevada 89103
(702) 252-7777
Website: www.playrio.com

Reservation Number: (800) PLAY RIO
Suites: 2,563 Price Range: $55-$230
Restaurants: 18 (1 open 24 hours)
Buffets: B-$14.99/$23.99 (Sat/Sun)
          L-$16.99 D-$23.99
Seafood Buffet: D-$38.00 (opens 4pm)
Casino Size: 117,330 Square Feet
Other Games: SB, RB, B, MB, P, PG,
          PGP, LIR, TCP, K
Overnight RV Parking: Free/RV Dump: No
Special Features: Masquerade Village area offers free "Masquerade Show in the Sky". 20-store shopping mall. Three wedding chapels. "Penn and Teller" stage show.

Riviera Hotel & Casino
2901 Las Vegas Blvd. South
Las Vegas, Nevada 89109
(702) 734-5110
Website: www.rivierahotel.com

Toll-Free Number: (800) 634-3420
Reservation Number: (800) 634-6753
Rooms: 2,100 Price Range: $69-$199
Suites: 154 Price Range: $269-$420
Restaurants: 5 (1 open 24 hours)
Buffets: B-$10.99/$14.99 (Sat/Sun)
    L-$12.99 D-$18.99
Casino Size: 103,800 Square Feet
Other Games: SB, RB, MB, P,
    PGP, LIR, TCP
Special Features: Burger King, Pizza Hut,
Panda Express and Quizno's Subs. *Crazy Girls*
stage show. Comedy Club.

Sam's Town Hotel & Gambling Hall
5111 Boulder Highway
Las Vegas, Nevada 89122
(702) 456-7777
Website: www.samstown.com

Toll-Free Number: (800) 897-8696
Reservation Number: (800) 634-6371
Rooms: 620 Price Range: $39-$109
Suites: 30 Price Range: $120-$240
Restaurants: 6 (1 open 24 hours)
Buffets: B-$7.49/$11.49 (Sat/Sun) L-$8.49
    D-$11.99/$18.99 (Fri)/
        $13.99 (Sat/Sun)
Casino Size: 120,681 Square Feet
Other Games: SB, RB, P, LIR, TCP, K, BG
Special Features: 500-space RV park ($20 to
$24 per night). Indoor promenade with free
laser-light show. 24-hour 56-lane bowling
center. 18-theater cinema complex. Childcare
center. $1 buffet discount for slot club
members.

Santa Fe Station Hotel & Casino
4949 North Rancho Drive
Las Vegas, Nevada 89130
(702) 658-4900
Website: www.santafestationlasvegas.com

Toll Free Number: (866) 767-7770
Reservation Number: (866) 767-7771
Rooms: 200 Price Range: $39-$129
Restaurants: 3 (1 open 24 hours)
Buffets: B-$7.99 L-$10.99/$14.99 (Sat/Sun)
    D-$14.99
Casino Size: 156,401 Square Feet
Other Games: SB, RB, MB, P, PGP,
    LIR, TCP, K, BG
Special Features: 60-lane bowling center.
16-screen cinema. Live entertainment. Kid's
Quest childcare center.

Silver Saddle Saloon
2501 E. Charleston Boulevard
Las Vegas, Nevada 89104
(702) 474-2900

Restaurants: 1
Other Games: No craps or roulette. Blackjack
only played 4pm-4am (Fri)/9am-6am (Sat)

Silverton Casino Hotel Lodge
3333 Blue Diamond Road
Las Vegas, Nevada 89139
(702) 263-7777
Website: www.silvertoncasino.com

Toll-Free Number: (800) 588-7711
Room/RV Reservations: (866) 946-4373
Rooms: 292 Price Range: $34-$94
Suites: 8 Price Range: $175-$365
Restaurants: 8 (1 open 24 hours)
Buffets: L- $8.99/$18.99 (Sat/Sun)
    D- $13.99/$19.99 (Thu/Sat/Sun)/
        $21.99 (Fri)
Casino Size: 66,463 Square Feet
Other Games: SB, RB, P, PG,
    PGP, TCP, K
Special Features: Starbucks coffee house.

More FREE Things to See in Las Vegas

By H. Scot Krause

Las Vegas attracts over 37 million visitors every year and seeing the sights and free attractions are still some of the "best bets" anywhere in the world. While "old Vegas" and the lure of cheap buffets is disappearing, since the mid 90's, the grandeur of the attractions is the new lure that entices guests to visit the city and enjoy its splendor---much of it for FREE!

In no particular order, we start at The Bellagio Hotel and Casino, one of the largest premier megaresorts on the Strip. From the outside, Bellagio's world-famous fountains entertain guests with a dazzling water and light show that combines opera, classical and whimsical music with carefully choreographed movements.

Once inside, just beyond Bellagio's gracious lobby, which in itself is another sight to behold with sculptures and marble galore, lies the Conservatory & Botanical Gardens, a kaleidoscope for your senses. Each season these magnificent gardens take on an entirely new look, abounding in fragrance, texture and color. Row upon row of exotic plants and flowers weave a glorious tapestry displaying the unique highlights of every season and holiday. The display is open 24 hours a day.

With its amazing columns and pillars, just strolling the grounds at Caesars Palace is an awesome sight, but the Forum Shops and shows are a huge attraction. The Fall of Atlantis fountain show features animatronic figures fighting for control of Atlantis in this exciting production. An amazing salt water aquarium comprises the show's platform and you can watch as a diver feeds the tropical puffers, flounder, sharks and the rest of the aquarium's inhabitants at various times each day. On the west end of the mall is the Festival Fountain show where visitors are entertained by the Greek gods Bacchus, Venus, Apollo and Plutus in animatronic form, holding the audience spellbound with a fantastic laser, water and light show.

Every fifteen minutes from usually starting around 8:00 p.m. (depending on the time of year) to 11 p.m, the earth shakes and flames shoot into the night sky spewing smoke and fire 100 feet above the waters below, transforming a tranquil waterfall into spectacular streams of molten lava. The volcano at The Mirage has been a Las Vegas signature attraction since the resort opened in 1989, mesmerizing spectators with it thunderous, fiery display. The volcano, situated on three water-covered acres, is 54 feet high and circulates 119,000 gallons of water per minute. The show may be cancelled during times of high winds or inclement weather.

Bringing the kids? Or just feel like a kid again yourself? How about free high wire and live circus acts all for free? Billed as the "World's Largest Permanent Circus" a variety of world renowned live circus acts perform every half hour from 11:00 a.m. to midnight on the carnival midway at Circus Circus Hotel and Casino.

The Auto Collections at the Imperial Palace Hotel & Casino is the world's largest and finest selection of antique, classic, muscle and special interest automobiles on display. Additionally, all vehicles (unless otherwise noted) are for sale. The collection is located on the fifth floor of the self-parking garage and is open daily from 10 a.m. to 6 p.m.

While, technically, the attraction is not free (general admission is $8.95 for adults and $5.00 for seniors or children 12 and under, children 3 and under free with an adult) it is a great low-cost bargain and there are usually 2-for-1 or discount coupons found in many of the tourist publications around town.

Be part of the free "Piano Bar" show at Harrah's Las Vegas nightly. Keyboarding extraordinaires battle it out for the best-played piano music as judged by you, the audience. It's always a good time atmosphere.

And just outside the doors of the lounge is Harrah's Carnival Court featuring entertainment and some of the world's finest flair bartenders. Masterful mixologists create colorful and potent concoctions while they entertain the thirsty crowds.

Other flair bartenders can be seen at the Ghost Bar at The Palms Hotel & Casino, Kahunaville at TI, Studio 54 at the MGM Grand and the Voodoo Lounge at the Rio Hotel & Casino.

The aquarium in the lobby of the Mandalay Bay Hotel is a sight to behold. The 12,200-gallon saltwater tank is a preview to what can be seen in the 1 million gallon Shark Reef at Mandalay Bay exhibit located near the South convention center.

Luck, royals, good food and jackpots to all...

Slots-A-Fun Casino
2890 Las Vegas Blvd. South
Las Vegas, Nevada 89109
(702) 734-0410

Toll-Free Number: (800) 354-1232
Restaurants: 1 Subway Sandwich Shop
Casino Size: 16,733 Square Feet
Other Games: Machines only.

South Point Hotel and Casino
9777 Las Vegas Blvd. South
Las Vegas, Nevada 89123
(702) 796-7111
Website: www.southpointcasino.com

Toll-Free Number: (866) 796-7111
Rooms: 1,325 Price Range: $79-$160
Suites: 25 Price Range: $209-$950
Restaurants: 12 (1 open 24 hours)
Buffets: B-$7.95 L-$9.95/$17.95 (Sat/Sun)
        D-$16.95/$18.95 (Mon)/$22.95 (Fri)
Casino Size: 96,433 Square Feet
Other Games: SB, RB, MB, P,
        PGP, TCP, BG
Special Features: 16-screen movie complex.
Equestrian center with 4,400-seat arena and
1,200 stalls. 64-lane bowling center. Kid's
Tyme childcare facility. Health spa.

Stratosphere Hotel & Casino
2000 Las Vegas Blvd. South
Las Vegas, Nevada 89104
(702) 380-7777
Website: www.stratospherehotel.com

Reservation Number: (800) 99-TOWER
Rooms: 2,444 Price Range: $35-$149
Suites: 250 Price Range: $95-$219
Restaurants: 8 (1 open 24 hours)
Buffets: B/L/D-$14.99/$19.99 (Sat/Sun)
Casino Size: 80,000 Square Feet
Other Games: SB, RB, MB, P,
        PGP, LIR, TCP
Senior Discount: Tower discount if 55+
Special Features: 135-story observation tower
(admission charge). Revolving restaurant at
top of tower. 50 retail stores. *Bite* stage show.

Suncoast Hotel and Casino
9090 Alta Drive
Las Vegas, Nevada 89145
(702) 636-7111
Website: www.suncoastcasino.com

Toll-Free Number: (866) 636-7111
Rooms: 432 Price Range: $49-$150
Suites: 40 Price Range: $165-$265
Restaurants: 9 (1 open 24 hours)
Buffets: B-$8.99/ $14.99 (Sun) L-$10.99
        D-$14.99
Casino Size: 95,898 Square Feet
Other Games: SB, RB, MB, P, PGP, TCP, BG
Special Features: 64-lane bowling center.
16-screen movie theater. Kids Tyme childcare.
Seattle's Best Coffee. Free shuttles to airport,
Strip and other Coast properties.

Terrible's Hotel and Casino
4100 Paradise Road
Las Vegas, Nevada 89156
(702) 733-7000
Website: www.herbstgaming.com

Reservation Number: (800) 640-9777
Rooms: 370 Price Range: $45-$140
Restaurants: 2 (1 open 24 hours)
Buffets: B: $5.99/$10.99 (Sat/Sun)
        L-$8.99 D-$10.99
Casino Size: 27,225 Square Feet
Other Games: SB, RB, P, BG
Special features: 24-hour $9.99 Dinner
specials.

Treasure Island (TI)
3300 Las Vegas Blvd. South
Las Vegas, Nevada 89109
(702) 894-7111
Website: www.terriblescasinos.com

Reservation Number: (800) 944-7444
Rooms: 2,665 Price Range: $79-$299
Suites: 220 Price Range: $125-$999
Restaurants: 9 (2 open 24 hours)
Buffets: B-$14.95/$23.95 (Sat/Sun)
        L-$17.95 D-$22.95/$26.95 (Fri-Sun)
Casino Size: 55,680 Square Feet
Other Games: SB, RB, B, MB, P, PG,
        PGP, LIR, TCP, B6, K
Special Features: *Sirens of TI* live-action show
every 90 minutes from 7:00pm until 11:30pm.
Health spa/salon. Two wedding chapels. Ben
&Jerry's. Starbucks. Krispy Kreme. Cirque
du Soleil's *Mystere* stage show.

Tropicana Resort & Casino
3801 Las Vegas Blvd. South
Las Vegas, Nevada 89109
(702) 739-2222
Website: www.troplv.com

Reservation Number: (888) 826-8767
Rooms: 1,877 Price Range: $89-$139
Suites: 115 Price Range: $229-$329
Restaurants: 5 (1 open 24 hours)
Buffets: B-$24.99 (Sat/Sun)
Casino Size: 60,700 Square Feet
Other Games: SB, RB, MB, PGP,
        LIR, TCP
Senior Discount: Various if 65+
Special Features: Wedding chapel. Brad
Garrett's Comedy club.

Tuscany Suites & Casino
255 East Flamingo Road
Las Vegas, Nevada 89109
(702) 893-8933
Website: www.tuscanylasvegas.com

Reservation Number: (877) 887-2261
Suites: 760 Price Range: $21-$199
Restaurants: 4 (1 open 24 hours)
Casino Size: 53,680 Square Feet
Other Games: SB, RB, P
Special Features: All suite hotel. Wedding
chapel.

The Venetian Resort Hotel Casino
3355 Las Vegas Blvd. South
Las Vegas, Nevada 89109
(702) 414-1000
Website: www.venetian.com

Reservation Number: (888) 283-6423
Suites: 4,046 Price Range: $179-$2,500
Restaurants: 17 (1 open 24 hours)
Casino Size: 138,684 Square Feet
Other Games: SB, RB, B, MB, P, PG, CW,
        PGP, CSP, LIR, TCP, B6, S21
Special Features: Recreates city of Venice
with canals, gondoliers and replica Campanile
Tower, St. Mark's Square, Doge's Palace
and Rialto Bridge. 90 retail stores. Madame
Tussaud's Wax Museum. Canyon Ranch Spa.
Blue Man Group and *Phantom* stage shows.

Western Hotel & Casino
899 East Fremont Street
Las Vegas, Nevada 89101
(702) 384-4620
Website: www.westernhotelcasino.com

RV/Room Reservations: (800) 634-6703
Restaurants: 2 (open 24 hours)
Casino Size: 9,207
Other Games: No roulette, K, P
Special Features: 69-space RV park ($15 per
night).

Westin Casuarina Hotel & Casino
160 East Flamingo Road
Las Vegas, Nevada 89109
(702) 836-5900
Website: www.starwood.com

Westin Reservations: (800) 228-3000
Rooms: 816 Price Range: $129-$219
Suites: 10 Price Range: $199-$439
Restaurants: 1 (open 24 hours)
Buffets: B-$18.00
Casino Size: 13,500 Square Feet
Other Games: RB, SB, TCP,

Wild Wild West Casino
3330 West Tropicana Avenue
Las Vegas, Nevada 89103
(702) 740-0000
Website: www.wwwesthotelcasino.com

Reservation Number: (800) 634-3488
Rooms: 262 Price Range: $39-$119
Restaurants: 1 (open 24 hours)
Casino Size: 11,250 Square Feet
Other Games: SB
Special Features: Part of Station Casinos
group. Discount smoke shop. 15-acre truck
plaza.

Wynn Las Vegas
3145 Las Vegas Blvd. South
Las Vegas, Nevada 89109
(702) 770-7000
Website: www.wynnlasvegas.com

Toll-Free Number: (888) 320-WYNN
Rooms: 2,359 Prices: $199-$639
Suites: 351 Prices: $450-$1,300
Restaurants: 18 (2 open 24 hours)
Buffets: B-$19.95/$38.95 (Sat/Sun) L-$22.95
       D-$34.95/$38.95 (Fri/Sat)
Casino Size: 93,094 Square Feet
Other Games: SB, RB, B, MB, P, PG,
         PGP, LIR, TCP, B6
Special Features: 150-foot man-made
mountain with five-story waterfall. 18-hole
golf course. Full-service Ferrari and Maserati
dealership. *Le Reve* stage show. Spa and salon.

Laughlin

Map location: **#2** (on the Colorado River, 100
miles south of Las Vegas and directly across
the river from Bullhead City, Arizona)

Laughlin is named after Don Laughlin, who
owns the Riverside Hotel & Casino and
originally settled there in 1966. The area offers
many water sport activities on the Colorado
River as well as at nearby Lake Mojave.

For Laughlin tourism information call: (800)
4-LAUGHLIN. You can also visit their
Website at: www.visitlaughlin.com.

Here's information, as supplied by Nevada's
State Gaming Control Board, showing the
slot machine payback percentages for all
of Laughlin's casinos for the fiscal year
beginning July 1, 2010 and ending June 30,
2011:

Denomination	Payback %
1¢ Slots	88.87
5¢ Slots	93.23
25¢ Slots	94.82
$1 Slots	95.25
$1 Megabucks	87.83
$5 Slots	94.54
All Slots	92.84

These numbers reflect the percentage of
money returned to the players on each
denomination of machine. All electronic
machines including slots, video poker and
video keno are included in these numbers.

Optional games in the casino listings include:
sports book (SB), race book (RB), Spanish
21 (S21), baccarat (B), mini-baccarat (MB),
poker (P), pai gow poker (PGP), Caribbean
stud poker (CSP), let it ride (LIR), three-card
poker (TCP), four card poker (FCP), keno (K),
sic bo (SIC), big 6 wheel (B6) and bingo (BG).

Aquarius Casino Resort
1900 S. Casino Drive
Laughlin, Nevada 89029
(702) 298-5111
Website: www.aquariuscasinoresort.com

Reservation Number: (800) 435-8469
Rooms: 1,900 Price Range: $39-$89
Suites: 90   Price Range: $109-$299
Restaurants: 6 (1 open 24 hours)
Buffets: Brunch-$9.99/$11.95 (Sun)
       D-$15.99/$23.99 (Fri)/$19.99 (Sat)
Casino Size: 57,070 Square Feet
Other Games: SB, RB, MB, P,
         LIR, TCP, B6, K
Overnight RV Parking: No
Special Features: Fast Food court. Outback
Steakhouse. 3,300-seat amphitheater.

**Colorado Belle Hotel Casino &
Microbrewery**
2100 S. Casino Drive
Laughlin, Nevada 89029
(702) 298-4000
Website: www.coloradobelle.com

Reservation Number: (800) 477-4837
Rooms: 1,124 Price Range: $19-$70
Suites: 49   Price Range: $105-$175
Restaurants: 6 (1 opened 24 hours)
Buffets: B-$3.99/$9.99 (Fri)/$11.99 (Sat/Sun)
       L-$9.99 D-$8.99/$17.99 (Fri/Sat)/
         $13.99 (Sun)
Casino Size: 47,968 Square Feet
Other Games: SB, P, PGP,
         TCP, LIR, K
Overnight RV Parking: No
Special Features: Video arcade. Microbrewery.
Spa.

Don Laughlin's
Riverside Resort Hotel & Casino
1650 S. Casino Drive
Laughlin, Nevada 89029
(702) 298-2535
Website: www.riversideresort.com

Reservation Number: (800) 227-3849
Rooms: 1,405 Price Range: $45-$89
Executive Rooms: 93 Price Range: $79-$699
Restaurants: 7 (2 open 24 hours)
Buffets: B-$7.99 L-$8.49/$12.99 (Sun)
        D-$12.99/$15.99 (Fri)
Casino Size: 89,106 Square Feet
Other Games: SB, RB, P, LIR,
            TCP, FCP, K, BG
Overnight RV Parking: Must use RV park
Special Features: 740-space RV park ($23-$27
per night). Six-screen cinema. Free classic car
exhibit. 34-lane bowling center. Childcare
center.

Edgewater Hotel Casino
2020 S. Casino Drive
Laughlin, Nevada 89029
(702) 298-2453
Website: www.edgewater-casino.com

Toll-Free Number: (800) 289-8777
Reservation Number: (800) 677-4837
Rooms: 1,420 Price Range: $20-$75
Suites: 23 Price Range: $95-$195
Restaurants: 3 (1 opened 24 hours)
Buffets: B-$3.99/$9.99 (Fri)/$11.99 (Sat/Sun)
        L-$9.99 D-$8.99/$17.99 (Fri/Sat)/
        $13.99 (Sun)
Casino Size: 47,386 Square Feet
Other Games: SB, RB, P, PGP,
            TCP, LIR, K, BG
Overnight RV Parking: No

Golden Nugget Laughlin
2300 S. Casino Drive
Laughlin, Nevada 89029
(702) 298-7111
Website: www.goldennugget.com

Reservation Number: (800) 237-1739
Rooms: 300 Price Range: $24-$89
Suites: 4 Price Range: $150-$300
Restaurants: 5 (1 open 24 hours)
Casino Size: 32,600 Square Feet
Other Games: SB, RB, PGP, TCP, K
Overnight RV Parking: Free/RV Dump: No
Special Features: Suites must be booked
through casino marketing. Gift shop.

Harrah's Laughlin Casino & Hotel
2900 S. Casino Drive
Laughlin, Nevada 89029
(702) 298-4600
Website: www.harrahslaughlin.com

Reservation Number: (800) HARRAHS
Rooms: 1,451 Price Range: $19-$139
Suites: 115 Price Range: $114-$249
Restaurants: 4 (1 open 24 hours)
Buffets: B-$11.99/$13.99 (Sun) L-$11.99
        D-$14.99/$19.99 (Fri)/$16.99 (Sat)
Casino Size: 56,357 Square Feet
Other Games: SB, RB, P, PGP,
            TCP, LIR, K
Overnight RV Parking: No
Special Features: Salon and day spa. Beach
and pools. 300-seat showroom. 3,000-seat
amphitheater. McDonald's. Baskin-Robbins.
Cinnabon. Starbucks.

Pioneer Hotel & Gambling Hall
2200 S. Casino Drive
Laughlin, Nevada 89029
(702) 298-2442
Website: www.pioneerlaughlin.com

Reservation Number: (800) 634-3469
Rooms: 416 Price Range: $25-$85
Suites: 20 Price Range: $60-$90
Restaurants: 2 (1 open 24 hours)
Buffets: B-$5.95
        L-$6.95/$12.95 (Fri)/$8.95 (Sun)
        D-$8.95/$12.95 (Fri)/$8.95 (Sun)
Casino Size: 16,300 Square Feet
Other Games: SB, RB, LIR, P, TCP, K
Overnight RV Parking: Free/RV Dump: No
Special Features: Western-themed casino.
Western wear store. Liquor/cigarette store.

River Palms Resort Casino
2700 S. Casino Drive
Laughlin, Nevada 89029
(702) 298-2242
Website: www.river-palms.com

Toll-Free Number: (800) 835-7904
Reservation Number: (800) 835-7903
Rooms: 995 Price Range: $30-$65
Suites: 8 Price Range: $55-$295
Restaurants: 7 (1 open 24 hours)
Buffets: B-$7.99 (Sat/Sun)
D-$8.99/$11.99 (Fri/Sat)
Casino Size: 58,000 Square Feet
Other Games: SB, P, LIR, BG
Overnight RV Parking: Free/RV Dump: No
Special Features: Health spa.

Tropicana Laughlin
2121 S. Casino Drive
Laughlin, Nevada 89029
(702) 298-4200
Website: www.tropicanax.com

Toll-Free Number: (800) 243-6846
Rooms: 1,501 Price Range: $39-$69
Suites: 55 Price Range: $79-$119
Restaurants: 5 (1 open 24 hours)
Buffets: B-$9.99 D-$7.99/$9.99 (Fri/Sat)
Casino Size: 53,000 Square Feet
Other Games: SB, RB, P, PGP, TCP, LIR
Overnight RV Parking: Free/RV Dump: No
Special Features: Display of railroad antiques
and memorabilia. Free train rides (Noon-10pm
Fri/Sat). Train-shaped swimming pool.

Lovelock

Map Location: **#18** (92 miles N.E. of Reno
on I-80)

Sturgeon's Casino
1420 Cornell Avenue
Lovelock, Nevada 89419
(775) 273-2971
Website: www.ramada.com

Toll-Free Number: (888) 234-6835
Rooms: 74 Price Range: $59-$70
Spa Rooms: 2 Price Range: $89-$100
Restaurants: 1
Casino Size: 7,000 Square Feet
Other Games: SB, RB, No Table Games
Overnight RV Parking: Free/RV Dump: No
Special Features: Hotel is Ramada Inn.

Mesquite

Map Location: **#19** (77 miles N.E. of Las
Vegas on I-15 at the Arizona border)

Here's information, as supplied by Nevada's
State Gaming Control Board, showing the
slot machine payback percentages for all of
the Mesquite area casinos for the fiscal year
beginning July 1, 2010 and ending June 30,
2011:

Denomination	Payback %
1¢ Slots	91.33
5¢ Slots	95.45
25¢ Slots	94.35
$1 Slots	95.51
$1 Megabucks	86.56
$5 Slots	95.14
All Slots	94.34

These numbers reflect the percentage of
money returned on each denomination
of machine and encompass all electronic
machines including slots, video poker and
video keno.

CasaBlanca Hotel-Casino-Golf-Spa
950 W. Mesquite Boulevard
Mesquite, Nevada 89027
(702) 346-7259
Website: www.casablancaresort.com

Reservation Number: (800) 459-7529
Rooms: 500 Price Range: $39-$109
Suites: 18 Price Range: $69-$229
Restaurants: 3 (1 open 24 hours)
Buffets: B-$7.99 (Sat/Sun)
          D-$15.99 (Fri)/$14.99 (Sat)
Casino Size: 27,000 Square Feet
Other Games: SB, RB, PGP, TCP, LIR
Overnight RV Parking: Must use RV park
Special Features: 45-space RV park ($19 per night). 18-hole golf course. Health spa.

Eureka Casino & Hotel
275 Mesa Boulevard
Mesquite, Nevada 89027
(702) 346-4600
Website: www.eurekamesquite.com

Reservation Number: (800) 346-4611
Rooms: 192 Price Range: $49-$109
Suites: 18 Price Range: $99-$249
Restaurants: 2 (1 open 24 hours)
Buffets: B-$6.99/$11.99 (Sat)/$14.99 (Sun)
          L-$8.99 D-$13.99 /$18.99 (Fri)/
          $16.99 (Sat)
Casino Size: 40,285 Square Feet
Other Games: SB, RB, P, PGP, TCP, LIR, BG
Overnight RV Parking: No
Special Features: $2 off buffet with player's club card.

Virgin River Hotel/Casino/Bingo
100 Pioneer Boulevard
Mesquite, Nevada 89027
(702) 346-7777
Website: www.virginriver.com

Reservation Number: (800) 346-7721
Rooms: 720 Price Range: $25-$60
Suites: 2 Price Range: $250
Restaurants: 2 (1 open 24 hours)
Buffets: B-$6.50 L-$7.50
          D-$9.99 /$11.99 (Tue/Sat)/
          $15.99 (Fri)/$11.50 (Sun)
Casino Size: 37,000 Square Feet
Other Games: SB, RB, PGP, TCP, K, BG
Overnight RV Parking: Must use RV park
Special Features: 24-lane bowling center. Four movie theaters.

Minden

Map Location: **#14** (42 miles S. of Reno on Hwy. 395)

Carson Valley Inn
1627 Highway 395 N.
Minden, Nevada 89423
(775) 782-9711
Website: www.cvinn.com

Reservation Number: (800) 321-6983
Hotel Rooms: 146 Price Range: $75-$115
Hotel Suites: 7 Price Range: $129-$189
Lodge Rooms: 75 Price Range: $59-$99
Lodge Suites: 5 Price Range: $89-$119
Restaurants: 4 (1 open 24 hours)
Casino Size: 22,300 Square Feet
Other Games: SB, RB, P,
               TCP, no roulette
Overnight RV Parking: Free/Dump; $5
Senior Discount: Various discounts if 50+
Special Features: 59-space RV park ($25-$36 per night). 24-hour convenience store. Wedding chapel. Childcare center.

N. Las Vegas

Map Location: **#20** (5 miles N.E. of the Las Vegas Strip on Las Vegas Blvd. N.)

Aliante Station Casino & Hotel
7300 Aliante Parkway
North Las Vegas, NV 89084
(702) 692-7777
Website: www.aliantecasinohotel.com

Toll-Free Number: (877) 477-7627
Rooms: 202 Price Range: $59-$129
Restaurants: 6
Buffets: B-$8.99/$14.99 (Sun) L-$10.99
          D-$14.99
Casino Size: 125,000 Square Feet
Other Games: SB, RB, B, MB, P,
               TCP, PGP, BG
Overnight RV Parking: No
Special Features: 16-screen Regal Theater. Arcade.

Bighorn Casino
3016 E. Lake Mead Boulevard
N. Las Vegas, Nevada 89030
(702) 642-1940

Restaurants: 1
Casino Size: 3,740 Square Feet
Other Games: SB, RB, No craps or roulette
Overnight RV Parking: No

Cannery Hotel & Casino
2121 E Craig Road
N. Las Vegas, Nevada 89030
(702) 507-5700
Website: www.cannerycasino.com

Toll-Free Number: (866) 999-4899
Rooms: 201 Price Range: $39-$119
Restaurants: 5 (1 open 24 hours)
Buffets: B- $11.99 (Sat-Sun)
        L- $8.99 (Mon-Fri)
        D-$13.99
Casino Size: 80,375 Square Feet
Other Games: RB, SB, P, PGP, BG
Overnight RV Parking: No
Special Features: Property is themed to resemble a 1940's canning factory. Buffet discount for player's club members.

Fiesta Casino Hotel
2400 N. Rancho Drive
N. Las Vegas, Nevada 89130
(702) 631-7000
Website: fiestarancholasvegas.com

Reservation Number: (800) 731-7333
Rooms: 100 Price Range: $29-$119
Restaurants: 4 (1 open 24 hours)
Buffets: Brunch-$11.99 (Sun) L-$7.99
        D-$10.99
Casino Size: 59,951 Square Feet
Other Games: SB, RB, PGP, K, BG
Overnight RV Parking: Yes/Dump: No
Senior Discount: Join Fiesta 50 for discounts
Special Features: Ice skating arena. Coffee bar. Smoke shop. Buffet discount for slot club members.

Jerry's Nugget
1821 Las Vegas Blvd. North
N. Las Vegas, Nevada 89030
(702) 399-3000
Website: www.jerrysnugget.com

Restaurants: 2
Casino Size: 24,511 Square Feet
Other Games: SB, RB, K,
Overnight RV Parking: No
Senior Discount: Various if 55+
Special Features: Bakery.

Lucky Club Casino
3227 Civic Center Drive
N. Las Vegas, Nevada 89030
(702) 399-3297
Website: luckyclublv.com

Reservation Number: (877) 333-9291
Rooms: 92 Price Range: $49-$99
Suites: 3 Price Range: $119-$129
Restaurants: 1 (open 24 hours)
Casino Size: 16,000 Square Feet
Other Games: SB, RB
Overnight RV Parking: No
Special Features: Closest hotel/casino to Las Vegas Motor Speedway.

Opera House Saloon & Casino
2542 Las Vegas Blvd. North
N. Las Vegas, Nevada 89030
(702) 649-8801
Website: Operahousecasino.com

Restaurants: 1
Casino Size: 15,000 Square Feet
Other Games: No table Games, SB, RB, BG
Overnight RV Parking: No

The Poker Palace
2757 Las Vegas Blvd. North
N. Las Vegas, Nevada 89030
(702) 649-3799
Website: www.pokerpalace.net

Restaurants: 1
Casino Size: 25,900 Square Feet
Other Games: SB, RB, P, BG,
                No craps or roulette
Overnight RV Parking: No

Silver Nugget
2140 Las Vegas Blvd. North
N. Las Vegas, Nevada 89030
(702) 399-1111
Website: www.silvernuggetcasino.net

Restaurants: 1
Casino Size: 22,395 Square Feet
Other Games: SB, RB, BG, No roulette/craps
Overnight RV Parking: Must use RV park
Senior Discount: 10% off food if 55+
Special Features: 24-lane bowling center.

Texas Station
2101 Texas Star Lane
N. Las Vegas, Nevada 89032
(702) 631-1000
Website: www.texasstation.com

Toll-Free Number: (800) 654-8804
Reservation Number: (800) 654-8888
Rooms: 200 Price Range: $34-$194
Restaurants: 8 (1 open 24 hours)
Buffets: B-$8.99/$14.99 (Sat/Sun)
    L-$10.99 D-$14.99
Casino Size: 123,045 Square Feet
Other Games: SB, RB, P, PGP,
        TCP, K, BG
Overnight RV Parking: No
Senior Discount: Various if 50+
Special Features: 18-screen movie theater.
60-lane bowling center. Kids Quest childcare
center. Food court. Wedding chapels. Video
arcade. 2,000-seat events center. Buffet
discount for slot club members.

Pahrump

Map Location: **#21** (59 miles W. of Las Vegas
on Hwy. 160)

Pahrump Nugget Hotel & Gambling Hall
681 S. Highway 160
Pahrump, Nevada 89048
(775) 751-6500
Website: www.pahrumpnugget.com

Toll Free Number: (866) 751-6500
Rooms: 70 Price Range: $69-$89
Suites: 5 Price Range: $110-$213
Restaurants: 3 (1 open 24 hours)
Buffets: Brunch-$6.99 (Sat/Sun)
        D-$9.99/$11.99 (Fri)
Casino Size: 19,259 Square Feet
Other Games: SB, RB, P, TCP, BG
Overnight RV Parking: No
Senior Discount: $6.49 Dinner Buffet (Sun-Thu)
Special Features: 24-lane bowling center.
Video arcade. Supervised childcare center.
Food court with Dairy Queen and sub shop.

Saddle West Hotel/Casino & RV Park
1220 S. Highway 160
Pahrump, Nevada 89048
(775) 727-1111
Website: www.saddlewest.com

Reservation Number: (800) 433-3987
Rooms: 148 Price Range: $49-$115
Suites: 10 Price Range: $89-$129
Restaurants: 2 (1 open 24 hours)
Buffets: B-$5.95 L-$7.95
        D-$8.95/$15.95 (Fri)
Casino Size: 16,115 Square Feet
Other Games: SB, RB, BG, No roulette
Overnight RV Parking: Free/RV Dump: No
Special Features: 80-space RV park ($20 per
night). Closest casino to Death Valley Park.

Terrible's Town Casino
771 Frontage Road
Pahrump, Nevada 89048
(775) 751-7777
Website: www.terriblestownpahrump.com/

Toll Free Number: (888) 837-7425
Restaurants: 1
Buffets: B-$8.99 (Sat/Sun)
D-$8.99 (Tue/Thu)/$10.99 (Sat/Sun)
Casino Size: 15,057 Square Feet
Other Games: SB, RB, P, BG, No craps
Overnight RV Parking: Free/RV Dump: No
Special Features: Fast food court. General store and gas station.

Primm

Map Location: #6 (25 miles S.W. of Las Vegas on I-15; 9 miles from the California border)

Buffalo Bill's Resort & Casino
31700 Las Vegas Blvd S.
Primm, Nevada 89019
(702) 382-1212
Website: www.primmvalleyresorts.com

Toll-Free Number: (800) FUN-STOP
Rooms: 1,242 Price Range: $20-$85
Suites: 15 Price Range: $89-$125
Restaurants: 3 (1 open 24 hours)
Buffets: B-$10.99 L-$12.99 D-$13.99
Casino Size: 62,130 Square Feet
Other Games: SB, RB, P, PGP, LIR,
            TCP, B6, K, BG
Overnight RV Parking: Free/RV Dump: No
Special Features: 3 Roller coasters. Flume ride. Two water slides. Movie theater. Video Arcade. 6,500-seat arena. Train shuttle connects to Whiskey Pete's and Primm Valley. Fast Food Court.

Primm Valley Resort & Casino
31900 Las Vegas Blvd S.
Primm, Nevada 89019
(702) 382-1212
Website: www.primmvalleyresorts.com

Reservation Number: (800) FUN-STOP
Rooms: 661 Price Range: $34-$99
Suites: 31 Price Range: $113-$178
Restaurants: 2 (1 open 24 hours)
Buffets: L-$11.99 D-$10.95
Casino Size: 38,049 Square Feet
Other Games: SB, RB, PGP, LIR,
            TCP
Overnight RV Parking: Free/RV Dump: No
Special Features: Free monorail to Whiskey Pete's. Al Capone's car and Bonnie & Clyde's "death" car on display. Free monorail service to Primm Valley.

Whiskey Pete's Hotel & Casino
100 W. Primm Boulevard
Primm, Nevada 89019
(702) 382-1212
Website: www.primmvalleyresorts.com

Reservation Number: (800) FUN-STOP
Rooms: 777 Price Range: $40-$99
Suites: 4 Price Range: $139-$219
Restaurants: 2 (1 open 24 hours)
Casino Size: 36,400 Square Feet
Other Games: SB, RB
Overnight RV Parking: Free/RV Dump: No

See page 29 to read a story about Las Vegas Casino Hotel Resort Fees; what they are, which hotels charge them and how you can sometimes avoid them.

Reno

Map Location: **#4** (near the California border, 58 miles N.E. of Lake Tahoe and 32 miles N. of Carson City).

Reno may be best known for its neon arch on Virginia Street which welcomes visitors to "The Biggest Little City in the World." The current arch is actually the fourth one since the original arch was built in 1927. The area also houses the nation's largest car collection at the National Automobile Museum.

For Reno information call the Reno/Sparks Convention & Visitors Authority at (800) FOR-RENO or go to: www.renolaketahoe.com.

Overnight parking of an RV in a casino parking lot is prohibited in Reno.

Here's information, as supplied by Nevada's State Gaming Control Board, showing the slot machine payback percentages for all of the Reno area casinos for the fiscal year beginning July 1, 2010 and ending June 30, 2011:

Denomination	Payback %
1¢ Slots	92.17
5¢ Slots	94.93
25¢ Slots	93.92
$1 Slots	96.01
$1 Megabucks	89.21
$5 Slots	96.31
$25 Slots	96.92
All Slots	95.09

These numbers reflect the percentage of money returned on each denomination of machine and encompass all electronic machines including slots, video poker and video keno.

Optional games in the casino listings include: sports book (SB), race book (RB), Spanish 21 (S21), baccarat (B), mini-baccarat (MB), pai gow (PG), poker (P), pai gow poker (PGP), Caribbean stud poker (CSP), let it ride (LIR), three-card poker (TCP), four card poker (FCP), big 6 wheel (B6), keno (K) and bingo (BG).

Atlantis Casino Resort
3800 S. Virginia Street
Reno, Nevada 89502
(775) 825-4700
Website: www.atlantiscasino.com

Reservation Number: (800) 723-6500
Rooms: 975 Price Range: $49-$299
Suites: 120 Price Range: $79-$325
Restaurants: 8 (1 open 24 hours)
Buffets: B-$10.99/$11.99 (Sat)/$18.99 (Sun)
    L-$11.99/$12.99 (Sat) D-$16.99
    $27.99 (Fri) $26.99 (Sat)/
    $19.99 (Wed)/$17.99 (Sun)
Casino Size: 64,814 Square Feet
Other Games: SB, RB, MB, P,
    PGP, LIR, TCP, K
Senior Discount: 10% off buffet if 55+
Special Features: Health spa and salon.

Bonanza Casino
4720 N. Virginia Street
Reno, Nevada 89506
(775) 323-2724
Website: www.bonanzacasino.com

Restaurants: 2 (1 open 24 hours)
Buffets: Brunch-$9.95 (Sat/Sun)
    D-$9.95 (Fri/Sat)
Casino Size: 12,484 Square Feet
Other Games: SB, RB, TCP, no Roulette

Circus Circus Hotel Casino/Reno
500 N. Sierra Street
Reno, Nevada 89503
(775) 329-0711
Website: www.circusreno.com

Toll-Free Number: (888) 682-0147
Reservation Number: (800) 648-5010
Rooms: 1,464 Price Range: $35-$109
Suites: 108   Price Range: $70-$210
Restaurants: 6 (1 open 24 hours)
Buffets: B/L-$8.99/$9.99 (Sat)
    D-$12.99/$16.99 (Fri/Sat)
Casino Size: 65,959 Square Feet
Other Games: SB, RB, MB, P, PGP,
    TCP, FCP, B6, K
Special Features: Free circus acts. Carnival games. 24-hour gift shop/liquor store. Buffet discount for player's club members.

The Best Places To Play in Reno/Tahoe

Roulette- The house edge on a single-zero wheel cuts the house edge from 5.26% down to a more reasonable 2.70%. Unfortunately, there are no casinos in Reno/Tahoe that offer single-zero roulette

Craps- Almost all Reno/Tahoe area casino offer double odds on their crap games. The casinos offering the highest odds are The Sands Regency in Reno and the Lakeside Inn in Lake Tahoe which all offer 10X odds.

Blackjack - There's good news and bad news for blackjack players in Northern Nevada. The good news is that there is an abundance of single-deck and double-deck games available. The bad news is that all casinos in the Reno/Tahoe area hit soft 17. This results in a slightly higher advantage (.20%) for the casinos. Additionally, some casinos may also restrict your double-downs to two-card totals of 10 or 11 only. The following recommendations apply to basic strategy players.

For single-deck games you should always look for casinos that pay the standard 3-to-2 for blackjacks. A few casinos only pay 6-to-5 for blackjack and this increases the casino edge tremendously. The casino advantage in these games is around 1.5% and they should be avoided.

The best single-deck game is at the Alamo Travel Center in Sparks which has the following rules: double down on any first two cards, split any pair, resplit any pair, late surrender, and they will count a "six-card Charlie" as an automatic winner. The casino edge here is .10%.

Next best are five casinos that offer single-deck with the basic Northern Nevada rules: double down on any first two cards, split any pair and resplit any pair (except aces): Boomtown, John Ascuaga's Nugget, Rail City, Siena and Western Village. The casino edge here is .18%. (NOTE: There are numerous casinos that offer a game similar to this one except they will only allow you to double down on totals of 10 or more. This raises the casino edge in this game to .44%)

There are nine casinos that tie for best place to play double-deck blackjack: Atlantis, Boomtown, Club Cal-Neva, Eldorado, Grand Sierra, John Ascuaga's Nugget, Peppermill, Siena and Silver Legacy. Their two-deck games have the following rules: double down on any first two cards, split any pair, and resplit any pair (except aces). This works out to a casino edge of .53%

The best six-deck game can be found in Reno at the Silver Legacy The game's edge is .39% with these rules: double down on any two or more cards, split any pair, resplit any pair (except aces) and double allowed after split.

Next best is a game found at five Lake Tahoe casinos: Crystal Bay Club, Harrah's, Harvey's, Hyatt Regency and Lakeside Inn. The casino edge here is .56% with the following rules: double down on any two cards, split any pair, resplit any pair (including aces) and double allowed after split.

If you take away resplitting of aces from the previous game then you have a game with a casino edge of .63% which is offered in Reno at Atlantis, Circus Circus, Eldorado, Grand Sierra, John Ascuaga's Nugget, the Peppermill and Sands Regency.

Video Poker - Smart video poker players know that the three best varieties of machines to look for are: 9/6 Jacks or Better (99.54% return), 10/7 Double Bonus (100.17% return) and full-pay Deuces Wild (100.76% return).

All of these games are available in Northern Nevada, with the exception of full-pay Deuces Wild, which is hard to find. A slightly lesser-paying version, known as Not So Ugly Deuces (NSUD), which returns 99.73%, however, is widely available.

Following is a list of casinos offering the better paying video poker games. The abbreviations used for each listing are JB (9/6 jacks or better), DB (10/7 Double Bonus), FPDW (full-pay deuces wild) and NSUD (not so ugly deuces).

Atlantis: JB - penny to quarter; DB - nickel to $2 (some with progressives); Loose Deuces (100.15%) - nickel and dime

Boomtown: FPDW - nickel and quarter

Circus Circus: JB - nickel to $5 (quarter has progressive jackpot)

Club Cal Neva: JB - fifty cent and $1

Eldorado: JB - quarter to $5 ($1 has progressive jackpot)

Harrah's Reno: JB - quarter to $10

John Ascuaga's Nugget: JB - penny to $2 (10-cent and 25-cent in 3-play and 5-play); DB - nickel to quarter; NSUD - penny to $1

Peppermill: JB - penny to $100; NSUD - two-cents to $100; DB - nickel to quarter

Silver Legacy: JB - nickel to $2; DB - nickel to quarter; FPDW - quarter; NSUD - quarter to $1

Western Village: JB - penny to $1; DB - nickel to $1; NSUD penny to $1

Harrah's Lake Tahoe: JB - $1 to $100

Harvey's: JB - $5 to $100

Montbleu: JB - quarter to $1

Siena and Tahoe Biltmore: JB - $1

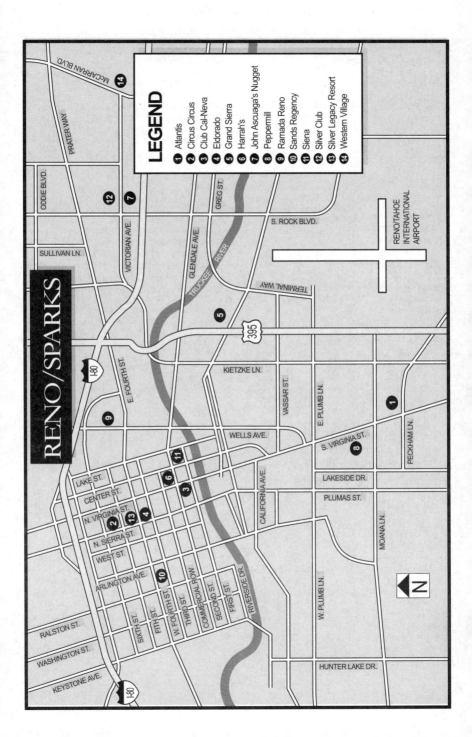

Club Cal-Neva/Virginian Hotel and Casino
38 E. Second Street
Reno, Nevada 89505
(775) 323-1046
Website: www.clubcalneva.com

Toll-Free Number (877) 777-7303
Rooms: 303 Price Range: $29-$129
Suites: 6 Price Range: $104-$194
Restaurants: 5 (1 open 24 hours)
Casino Size: 40,140 Square Feet
Other Games: SB, RB, P, PGP, LIR, TCP, K
Special Features: Hot dog and a beer for $3.75.

Eldorado Hotel Casino
345 N. Virginia Street
Reno, Nevada 89501
(775) 786-5700
Website: www.eldoradoreno.com

Toll-Free Number: (800) 648-4597
Reservation Number: (800) 648-5966
Rooms: 817 Price Range: $44-$129
Suites: 127 Price Range: $125-$399
Restaurants: 8 (1 open 24 hours)
Buffets: B-$9.99
      L-$10.99/$12.99 (Sat)/$13.99 (Sun)
      D-$15.99/$20.99 (Fri/Sat)
Casino Size: 76,500 Square Feet
Other Games: SB, RB, MB, PG, P, PGP,
      LIR, TCP, K
Senior Discount: Food discounts if 60+
Special Features: In-house coffee roasting.
Pasta shop. Microbrewery. Bakery. Butcher
shop. Gelato factory. Buffet discount for
player's club members.

Grand Sierra Resort & Casino
2500 E. Second Street
Reno, Nevada 89595
(775) 789-2000
Website: www.grandsierraresort.com

Room Reservations: (800) 501-2651
RV Reservations: (888) 562-5698
Rooms: 1,847 Price Range: $79-$255
Suites: 154 Price Range: $149-$899
Restaurants: 10 (1 open 24 hours)
Buffets: B-$9.99 L-$10.99
      D-$15.99/$17.99 (Fri/Sat)
Casino Size: 64,688 Square Feet
Other Games: SB, RB, MB, P, PG, PGP,
      LIR, TCP, K
Senior Discount: Various if 55 or older
Special Features: Two movie theaters. 50-lane
bowling center. 174-space RV park ($40-$52
summer/$25-$35 winter). 50-lane bowling
center. Health club. Shopping mall. Family
amusement center. Laketop golf driving range.
Indoor simulated golf.

Harrah's Reno
219 N. Center Street
Reno, Nevada 89501
(775) 786-3232
Website: www.harrahsreno.com

Toll-Free Number: (800) 423-1121
Reservation Number: (800) HARRAHS
Rooms: 886 Price Range: $55-$200
Suites: 60 Price Range: Casino use only
Restaurants: 7 (1 open 24 hours)
Buffets: B/L-$12.99/$13.99 (Sat)
      D-$15.99/$20.99 (Fri/Sat)
Casino Size: 41,600 Square Feet
Other Games: SB, RB, MB, P, PG,
      PGP, LIR, TCP, K
Special Features: Improv Comedy Club. No
dinner buffet Mon/Tue.

The arch in downtown Reno that welcomes visitors to
"The Biggest Little City in the World" is the city's most famous landmark.

Peppermill Hotel Casino Reno
2707 S. Virginia Street
Reno, Nevada 89502
(775) 826-2121
Website: www.peppermillreno.com

Toll-Free Number: (800) 648-6992
Reservation Number: (800) 282-2444
Rooms: 1,070 Price Range: $55-$135
Suites: 185 Price Range: $149-$209
Restaurants: 6 (1 open 24 hours)
Buffets: B-$12.99/$13.99 (Sat)/$20.99 (Sun)
   L-$13.99/$14.99 (Sat)
   D-$17.99/$28.99 (Fri)/$27.99 (Sat)/
   $18.99 (Sun)
Casino Size: 76,685 Square Feet
Other Games: SB, RB, MB, PG, P, PGP,
   LIR, TCP, K, FCP
Senior Discount: Various discounts if 55+

Ramada Reno Hotel & Casino
1000 E. 6th Street
Reno, Nevada 89512
(775) 786-5151

Ramada Reservations: (888) 288-4982
Rooms: 280 Price Range: $69-$109
Suites: 6 Price Range: $89-$199
Restaurants: 2 (1 open 24 hours)
Casino Size: 8,000 Square Feet
Other Games: SB, RB, No roulette or craps

The Sands Regency Hotel Casino
345 North Arlington Avenue
Reno, Nevada 89501
(775) 348-2200
Website: www.sandsregency.com

Reservation Number: (800) 648-3553
Rooms: 811 Price Range: $39-$139
Suites: 27 Price Range: $99-$249
Restaurants: 4 (1 open 24 hours)
Buffets: L/D-$9.99/$11.99 (Fri/Sat)
Casino Size: 25,791 Square Feet
Other Games: SB, RB, P, LIR,
   PGP, TCP, BG
Special Features: Arby's restaurant.

Siena Hotel Spa Casino
1 S. Lake Street
Reno, Nevada 89501
(775) 337-6260
Website: www.sienareno.com

Toll-Free Number: (877) 743-6233
Rooms: 214 Price Range: $109-$259
Suites: 27 Price Range: $139-$649
Restaurants: 5 (1 open 24 hours)
Buffets: B-$24.95 (Sun)
Casino Size: 20,900 Square Feet
Other Games: B, SB
Special Features: Health spa.

Silver Legacy Resort Casino
407 N. Virginia Street
Reno, Nevada 89501
(775) 325-7401
Website: www.silverlegacy.com

Toll-Free Number: (800) 687-7733
Reservation Number: (800) 687-8733
Rooms: 1,720 Price Range: $49-$175
Suites: 150 Price Range: $89-$200
Restaurants: 5 (1 open 24 hours)
Buffets: B-$8.99/$12.99 (Sat/Sun)
　　　　L-$9.99 D-$14.99/$19.99 (Fri/Sat)
Casino Size: 89,200 Square Feet
Other Games: SB, RB, B, PG, PGP,
　　　　LIR, TCP, B6, K
Special Features: Simulated mining machine
above casino floor. Comedy club. Rum bar.

Searchlight

Map Location: **#22** (58 miles S. of Las Vegas
on Hwy. 95)

Searchlight Nugget Casino
100 N. Highway 95
Searchlight, Nevada 89046
(702) 297-1201
Website: www.searchlightnugget.com

Casino Size: 3,260 Square Feet
Other Games: P, No craps or roulette
Overnight RV Parking: Free/RV Dump: No

Sparks

Map Location: **#4** (Sparks is a suburb of Reno
and is located one mile east of Reno on I-80)

Here's information, as supplied by Nevada's
State Gaming Control Board, showing the
slot machine payback percentages for all of
the Sparks area casinos for the fiscal year
beginning July 1, 2010 and ending June 30,
2011:

Denomination	Payback %
1¢ Slots	93.72
5¢ Slots	95.55
25¢ Slots	95.28
$1 Slots	96.39
$1 Megabucks	98.46
$5 Slots	95.87
All Slots	95.43

These numbers reflect the percentage of
money returned on each denomination
of machine and encompass all electronic
machines including slots, video poker and
video keno.

Alamo Casino & Travel Center
1959 East Greg Street
Sparks, Nevada 89431
(775) 355-8888
Website: www.thealamo.com

Super 8 Room Reservations: (800) 800-8000
Rooms: 64 Price Range: $79-$129
Suites: 7 Price Range: $104-$159
Restaurants: 1 (open 24 hours)
Casino Size: 7,150 Square Feet
Other Games: SB, RB, P, No roulette
Overnight RV Parking: Free/RV Dump: No
Special Features: Motel is Super 8. Truck
stop. Video arcade. Post office and gas station.

John Ascuaga's Nugget
1100 Nugget Avenue
Sparks, Nevada 89431
(775) 356-3300
Website: www.janugget.com

Toll-Free Number: (800) 648-1177
Rooms: 1,450 Price Range: $85-$189
Suites: 150 Price Range: $109-$295
Restaurants: 8 (1 open 24 hours)
Buffets: B-$11.50 (Thu/Fri)/14.95 (Sat/Sun)
D-$16.95 (Thu)/$22.95 (Fri/Sat)/$19.95 (Sun)
Casino Size: 82,600 Square Feet
Overnight RV Parking: Free (3 day maximum)
                         RV Dump: No
Other Games: SB, RB, P, PGP,
                 LIR, TCP, K, BG
Special Features: Wedding chapel. Health club.

Western Village Inn & Casino
815 Nichols Boulevard
Sparks, Nevada 89432
(775) 331-1069
Website: www.westernvillagesparks.com

Reservation Number: (800) 648-1170
Rooms: 147 Price Range: $55-$65
Suites: 4 Price Range: $155-$175
Restaurants: 3 (1 open 24 hours)
Casino Size: 26,452 Square Feet
Other Games: SB
Overnight RV Parking: No/RV Dump: No
Senior Discount: Room discount if 55 or older

Verdi

Map Location: **#4** (4 miles W. of Reno on I-80 at the California border)

Boomtown Hotel & Casino
P.O. Box 399
Verdi, Nevada 89439
(775) 345-6000
Website: www.boomtownreno.com

Toll-Free Number: (800) 648-3790
Room/RV Reservations: (877) 626-6686
Rooms: 318 Price Range: $69-$149
Suites: 20 Price Range: $105-$265
Restaurants: 4 (1 open 24 hours)
Buffets: Brunch-$14.99(Sun)
           D-$31.99 (Fri-Mon)
Casino Size: 38,675 Square Feet
Other Games: SB, RB, P, PGP, TCP, LIR, K
Overnight RV Parking: Free (1 night only)/
                         RV Dump: No
Special Features: 203-space RV park ($42 per night). 24-hour mini-mart. Indoor family fun center with rides and arcade games. Free shuttle to/from Reno. Buffet discount for slot club members.

Terrible's Gold Ranch Casino & RV Resort
350 Gold Ranch Road
Verdi, Nevada 89439
(775) 345-6789
Website: www.goldranchrvcasino.com

RV Reservations: (877) 927-6789
Restaurants: 2
Casino Size: 8,000 Square Feet
Other Games: SB, RB No Table Games
Overnight RV Parking: Must use RV park
Special Features: 105-space RV park ($40-$70 per night). 24-hour mini-mart.

Wells

Map Location: **#23** (338 miles N.E. of Reno on I-80)

Four Way Bar/Cafe & Casino
U.S. 93 & Interstate 80
Wells, Nevada 89835
(775) 752-3344

Restaurants: 1
Casino Size: 6,100 Square Feet
Other Games: No table games
Overnight RV Parking: Free/RV Dump: No

W. Wendover

Map Location: **#24** (Just W. of the Utah border on I-80)

Here's information, as supplied by Nevada's State Gaming Control Board, showing the slot machine payback percentages for all of the Wendover area casinos for the fiscal year beginning July 1, 2010 and ending June 30, 2011:

Denomination	Payback %
1¢ Slots	92.80
5¢ Slots	N/A
25¢ Slots	93.79
$1 Slots	96.43
$5 Slots	96.41
All Slots	94.40

These numbers reflect the percentage of money returned on each denomination of machine and encompass all electronic machines including slots, video poker and video keno.

Montego Bay Casino Resort
100 Wendover Boulevard
W. Wendover, Nevada 89883
(775) 664-9100
Website: www.montegobaywendover.com

Toll-Free Number: (877) 666-8346
Reservation Number: (800) 537-0207
Rooms: 437 Price Range: $54-$109
Suites: 75 Price Range: $94-$179
Restaurants: 2 (1 open 24 hours)
Buffets: L-$12.95
    Brunch-$14.95 (Sat/Sun)
    D-$15.95/$24.95 (Fri)/$19.95 (Sat)
Casino Size: 49,400 Square Feet
Other Games: SB, RB, P, PGP, LIR,TCP
Overnight RV Parking: Free/RV Dump: No
Senior Discount: $2 buffet discount at 55+
Special Features: Connected by sky bridge to Wendover Nugget. Liquor Store. Golf packages.

Peppermill Inn & Casino
680 Wendover Boulevard
W. Wendover, Nevada 89883
(775) 664-2255
Website: www.peppermillwendover.com

Reservation Number: (800) 648-9660
Rooms: 302 Price Range: $50-$170
Suites: 42 Price Range: $60-$205
Restaurants: 2 (1 open 24 hours)
Buffets: L-$12.95
    Brunch-$14.95 (Sat/Sun)
    D-$15.95/$24.95 (Fri)/$19.95 (Sat)
Casino Size: 30,577 Square Feet
Other Games: SB, RB, PGP, LIR, TCP
Overnight RV Parking: Free/RV Dump: No
Senior Discount: $2 buffet discount if 55+

Rainbow Hotel Casino
1045 Wendover Boulevard
W. Wendover, Nevada 89883
(775) 664-4000
Website: www.rainbowwendover.com

Toll-Free Number: (800) 217-0049
Rooms: 379 Price Range: $50-$150
Suites: 50 Price Range: $70-$205
Restaurants: 3 (1 open 24 hours)
Buffets: L-$12.95
          Brunch-$14.95 (Sat/Sun)
          D-$15.95/$24.95 (Fri)/$19.95 (Sat)
Casino Size: 51,060 Square Feet
Other Games: SB, RB, P, PGP, LIR, TCP
Overnight RV Parking: Free/RV Dump: No
Senior Discount: $2 buffet discount if 55+

Red Garter Hotel & Casino
1225 Wendover Boulevard
W. Wendover, Nevada 89883
(775) 664-2111
Website: www.redgartercasino.com

Toll-Free Number: (800) 982-2111
Rooms: 46 Price Range: $27-$65
Restaurants: 1 (open 24 hours)
Casino Size: 13,520 Square Feet
Other Games: SB, P
Overnight RV Parking: No

Wendover Nugget Hotel & Casino
101 Wendover Boulevard
W. Wendover, Nevada 89883
(775) 664-2221
Website: www.wendovernugget.com

Toll-Free Number: (800) 848-7300
Rooms: 500 Price Range: $50-$109
Suites: 60 Price Range: $75-$205
Restaurants: 3 (1 open 24 hours)
Buffets: Brunch-$14.95 (Sat/Sun) L-$12.95
          D-$15.95/$24.95 (Fri)/$19.95 (Sat)
Casino Size: 40,089 Square Feet
Other Games: SB, RB, P, TCP,
                LIR, PGP, K,
Overnight RV Parking: Must use RV park
Senior Discount: Room/food discounts if 55+
Special Features: 56-space RV park ($35 per
night). Sky bridge to Montego Bay.

Winnemucca

Map Location: **#25** (164 miles N.E. of Reno
on I-80)

Model T Hotel/Casino/RV Park
1130 W. Winnemucca Blvd.
Winnemucca, Nevada 89446
(775) 623-2588
Website: www.modelt.com

Reservation Number: (800) 645-5658
Rooms: 75 Price Range: $80-$90
Restaurants: 2 (1 open 24 hours)
Casino Size: 7,053 Square Feet
Other Games: SB, RB, TCP, No table games
Overnight RV Parking: Free/RV Dump: No
Special Features: Hotel is Quality Inn.
58-space RV park ($30 per night).

Winnemucca Inn
741 W. Winnemucca Boulevard
Winnemucca, Nevada 89445
(775) 623-2565
Website: www.winnemuccainn.com

Reservation Number: (800) 633-6435
Rooms: 105 Price Range: $69-$115
Suites: 6 Price Range: $109-$170
Restaurants: 1 (open 24 hours)
Casino Size: 2,853 Square Feet
Other Games: SB, RB, No craps or roulette
Overnight RV Parking: No

Winners Hotel/Casino
185 W. Winnemucca Boulevard
Winnemucca, Nevada 89445
(775) 623-2511
Website: www.winnerscasino.com

Reservation Number: (800) 648-4770
Rooms: 123 Price Range: $49-$70
Suites: 3 Price Range: $69-$99
Restaurants: 2 (1 open 24 hours)
Casino Size: 10,340 Square Feet
Other Games: SB, RB, P, TCP, no roulette
Overnight RV Parking: Free/ Dump: No
Senior Discount: Room discount if 55+

Yerington

Map Location: **#26** (60 miles S.E. of Reno on Hwy. Alt. 95)

Casino West
11 N. Main Street
Yerington, Nevada 89447
(775) 463-2481

Reservation Number: (800) 227-4661
Rooms: 49 Price Range: $46-$50
Suites: 29 Price Range: $55-59
Restaurants: 1 (open 24 hours)
Buffets: D- $9.95/$13.95 (Fri)
Casino Size: 4,950 Square Feet
Other Games: No craps or roulette
Overnight RV Parking: Must use RV park
Senior Discount: Room discounts if 55+
Special Features: Hotel is Best Western. 5-space RV park ($15 per night). Movie theater. 12-lane bowling alley.

Indian Casino

Avi Resort & Casino
10000 Aha Macav Parkway
Laughlin, Nevada 89029
(702) 535-5555
Website: www.avicasino.com
Map Location: **#2**

Toll-Free Number: (800) AVI-2-WIN
Rooms: 426 Price Range: $35-$110
Suites: 29 Price Range: $51-$135
Restaurants: 4 (1 open 24 hours)
Buffets: B-$6.99/$7.99 (Sun)
        L-$7.99 (Thu/Sat/Sun)
        D-$10.99/$13.49 (Fri)/$11.49 (Sat)
Casino Size: 25,000 Square Feet
Other Games: SB, RB, P, TCP, PGP,
        LIR, K, BG
Overnight RV Parking: Free/RV Dump: No
Special Features: 260-space RV park ($19 May-Oct/$23 Nov-April). On Colorado River with boat dock, launch and private beach. Fast Food Court. 8-screen cinema. Smoke shop. Kid's Quest childcare center.

NEW JERSEY

Map Location: **#1** (on the Atlantic Ocean in southeast New Jersey, 130 miles south of New York City and 60 miles southeast of Philadelphia)

Once a major tourist destination that was world-famous for its steel pier and boardwalk attractions, Atlantic City gradually fell into decline and casino gambling was seen as its salvation when voters approved it there in 1976.

The first casino (Resorts International) opened to "standing-room-only" crowds in 1978. Since then 11 more casinos have opened and all but three are located along the boardwalk. Those three, Borgata, Harrah's and Golden Nugget, are located in the marina section.

In mid-1997 Bally's Wild Wild West casino (Atlantic City's first themed casino) opened, but due to a quirk in the licensing law, this casino is only considered part of Bally's and not a separate casino. Additionally, in late 2002, the Claridge Casino Hotel formally joined Bally's as "The Claridge Tower" and it is no longer considered a separate casino.

A new $2 billion casino/resort is being built in Atlantic City on the Boardwalk just north of the Showboat Hotel and Casino.

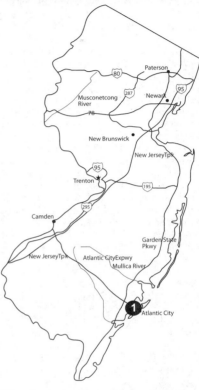

The Revel Resort and Casino will be the city's tallest structure with a 47-story-tall hotel tower housing 1,900 rooms. There will also be a two-story 150,000-square-foot casino, 20 restaurants, a 40-store retail mall, a 5,000-seat theater, a spa, a waterfall and pools. The property is expected to open May 15, 2012.

If you fly into Atlantic City it's a 14-mile drive from the airport to the casinos and there are only two choices of transportation. The taxi charges are regulated and it's a flat $27 to any casino. That price includes all tolls and luggage.

The other option is a rental car and there are three rental car companies at the airport: Hertz, Avis and Budget. Rental rates are in the range of $45-$70 per day but you can usually get a discount on those rates by booking online or using a coupon. In addition to the rental cost there's about another 22% in taxes and fees.

There is a charge of $3 to $5 per 24 hours (6 a.m. to 6 a.m.) for parking in a garage at any casino in Atlantic City. Whenever you pay the fee you are issued a receipt which you can then use to park for free at *one* other casino. When you leave the second garage you have to give them the receipt from the first garage.

For transportation among the casinos there are two options, besides taxis. A 24-hour jitney service makes stops along Pacific Avenue and will drop you off by any casino including those in the Marina. The jitneys are very efficient and you will probably never have a wait of more than five minutes for one to arrive.

The cost for one ride is $2.25 per person. Frequent rider tickets are offered for $20.00 per 10 rides and senior citizens, 65 or older, can buy 10 rides for $7.50. For jitney information call (877) 92-TRAIN.

On the Atlantic City Boardwalk itself, there are the famous rolling chairs. These are covered two-seater wicker chairs on wheels that are pushed by an attendant as he walks you to your destination. The posted rates are the same for all chairs, but some of the drivers are willing negotiate a better price, The charges are: $5 for up to five blocks; $10 for six to 12 blocks; $15 for 13 to 21 blocks; and $20 for 22 to 32 blocks. For more information on rolling chairs call (609) 347-7500 or (609) 344-1702.

Following is information from the New Jersey Casino Control Commission regarding average slot payout percentages for the 12-month period from July 1, 2010 through June 30, 2011:

CASINO	PAYBACK %
Borgata	91.67
Trump Taj Mahal	91.55
Trump Plaza	91.40
Resorts	91.38
A.C.H.	91.34
Harrah's	91.28
Tropicana	91.15
Golden Nugget	91.06*
Bally's A.C.	90.91
Caesars	90.64
Showboat	89.71

* Please note this includes period when casino was formerly known as .Trump Marina

These figures reflect the total percentages returned by each casino for all of their electronic machines which include slot machines, video poker, etc.

All Atlantic City casinos are open 24 hours and, unless otherwise noted, the games offered at every casino are: slots, video poker, craps, blackjack, Spanish 21, roulette, baccarat, mini-baccarat, poker, Caribbean stud poker, three card poker, four card poker, Texas hold'em bonus poker, let it ride, pai gow tiles and pai gow poker. Additional games offered include: sic bo (SB), keno (K), off-track betting (OTB), and big six wheel (B6). The minimum gambling age is 21.

For more information on visiting New Jersey you can contact the state's Travel & Tourism Department at (800) 537-7397 or go to: www.visitnj.com.

For information only on Atlantic City call (800) VISIT-NJ or go to: www.atlanticcitynj.com.

ACH Casino Resort
Boston Avenue & The Boardwalk
Atlantic City, New Jersey 08401
(609) 347-7111
Website: www.hiltonac.com

Reservation Number: (800) 257-8677
Rooms: 604 Price Range: $79-$365
Suites: 200 Price Range: $220-$600
Restaurants: 8   Valet Parking: $5
Buffets: L/D-$18.95
Casino Size: 75,416 Square Feet
Other Games: SB, B6
Special Features: 1,200-seat theater. Unisex salon. Spa. Beach bar. Free Valet parking with Hilton card.

Bally's Atlantic City
Park Place and the Boardwalk
Atlantic City, New Jersey 08401
(609) 340-2000
Website: www.ballysac.com

Toll-Free Number: (800) 772-7777
Reservation Number: (800) 225-5977
Rooms: 1,611 Price Range: $119-$389
Suites: 146   Price Range: $210-$620
Restaurants: 18   Valet Parking: $5
Buffets (Bally's): Brunch-$39.99 (Sun)
Buffets (W.W. West): B-$15.99
            L-$16.99 D-$21.99/$25.99(Fri)
Casino Size 225,940 Square Feet
Other Games: B6, K, SB
Special Features: Southern walkway connects to Wild Wild West casino. Northern walkway connects to Claridge casino and hotel.

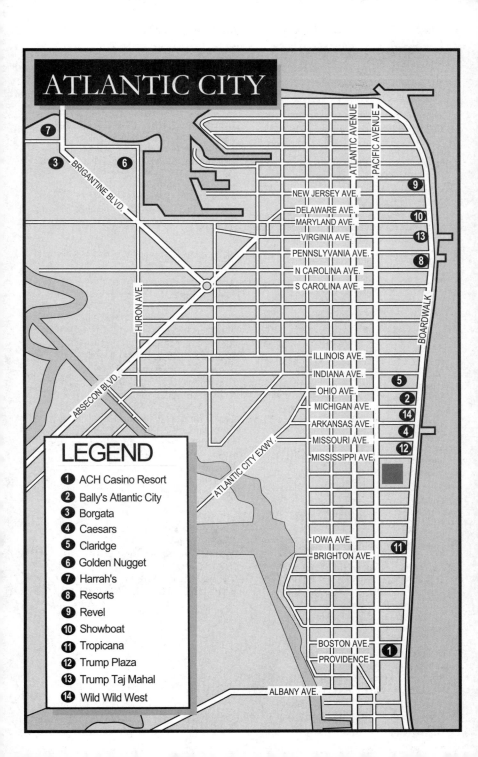

Borgata Hotel Casino and Spa
One Borgata Way
Atlantic City, NJ 08401
(609) 317-1000
Website: www.theborgata.com

Toll-Free Number: (866) 692-6742
Rooms: 2,200 Prices Range: $119-$519
Suites: 600 Price Range: $299-$1,000
Restaurants: 13 Valet Parking: $5
Buffets: B-$15.95/$27.95 (Sat/Sun)
          L-$18.95 D-$30.95
Casino Size: 160,287 Square Feet
Other Games: B6, SB
Special Features: 3,700-seat events center.
1,000-seat music theater. Comedy club. Health
spa. Barbershop. Hair and nail salon.

Caesars Atlantic City
2100 Pacific Avenue
Atlantic City, New Jersey 08401
(609) 348-4411
Website: www.caesarsac.com

Toll-Free Number: (800) 443-0104
Reservation Number: (800) 524-2867
Rooms: 979 Price Range: $125-$450
Suites: 198 Price Range: $195-$800
Restaurants: 12 Valet Park: $10/$20 (Fri-Sun)
Buffets: Brunch-$44.95
          L-$18.99 D-$24.95/$27.95 (Wed)
Casino Size: 140,775 Square Feet
Other Games: SB, B6
Special Features: Roman themed hotel
and casino. Planet Hollywood. Health spa.
Shopping arcade. Unisex beauty salon.

Golden Nugget Hotel Casino
Huron Avenue & Brigantine Boulevard
Atlantic City, New Jersey 08401
(609) 441-2000
Website: goldennugget.com/atlanticcity

Reservation Number: (800) 365-8786
Toll-Free Number (800) 777-8477
Rooms: 568 Price Range: $89-$359
Suites: 160 Price Range: $175-$650
Restaurants: 9 Valet Parking: $5
Buffets: B-$12.99
          L/D-$16.99/$25.99 (Fri-Sun)
Casino Size: 78,535 Square Feet
Other Games: No poker
Special Features: Adjacent to marina with
640 slips. 3-acre recreation deck with pools,
jogging track, tennis courts, miniature golf
course and health club. 1,500-seat event
center.

Harrah's Resort
777 Harrah's Boulevard
Atlantic City, New Jersey 08401
(609) 441-5000
Website: www.harrahs.com

Reservation Number: (800) 2-HARRAH
Rooms: 2,010 Price Range: $89-$439
Suites: 616 Price Range: Casino Use Only
Restaurants: 8 Valet Parking: $5
Buffets: L/D-$29.99
Casino Size: 177,570 Square Feet
Other Games: B6, K
Special Features: 65-slip marina. Beauty
salon. Miniature golf course (in season).

Resorts Atlantic City
1133 Boardwalk
Atlantic City, New Jersey 08401
(609) 344-6000
Website: www.resortsac.com

Toll-Free Number: (800) 334-6378
Reservation Number: (800) 334-6378
Rooms: 879 Price Range: $79-$375
Suites: 79 Price Range: $250-$1,000
Restaurants: 10 Valet Park: $5/$15(fri-Sat)
Buffets: B- $11.99 (Sat/Sun)
          L-$18.95 D-$24.95
Casino Size: 99,030 Square Feet
Other games: B6, no poker or Off track betting
Special Features: Indoor/outdoor pools.
Health spa. 1,350-seat theater. Comedy club.
Beachfront bar. Various buffet discounts for
slot club members. $5 valet discount with
players club card.

Revel Casino Resort
500 Boardwalk
Atlantic City, New Jersey 08401
(609) 344-6000
Website: www.revelresorts.com
EXPECTED TO OPEN MAY 15, 2012

The Best Places To Play in Atlantic City

Blackjack: Some Atlantic City casinos offer a single-deck blackjack game. The problem is that these single-deck games only pay 6-to-5 when you get a blackjack rather than the standard 3-to-2 and this raises the casino advantage in this game to 1.58%, Don't play this game!

In mid-2010 some casinos began offering low-limit games starting at $1. However, in order to play, you must pay a 25-cent fee for each hand you play. Avoid this game too because you are paying up to a 25% commission!

Other than those single-deck variations, the blackjack games offered at Atlantic City casinos are pretty much all the same: eight-deck shoe games with double down on any first two cards, dealer hits soft 17, pairs can be split up to three times and doubling after splitting is allowed. This works out to a casino edge of .67% against a player using perfect basic strategy and every casino in Atlantic City offers this game, except for Borgata where the dealers stand on soft 17. This is the best eight-deck game in the city and thew casino advantage advantage is .42%.

If you're willing to make higher minimum bets you can find slightly better games. All casinos offer six-deck games with minimum bets of $25, $50 or $100 per hand (Borgata has $10 minimums during the day). In those games the dealers also stand on soft 17 and the casino edge in these games is lowered to .42%. It is offered at every casino in the city, except for Wild Wild West which only offers eight-deck games. Additionally, the Golden Nugget offers the city's best six-deck game because they add late surrender to the above rules, which brings their house advantage down to .34%. The minimum bet on this game is $50.

Roulette: When choosing roulette games it's usually best to play in a casino offering a single-zero wheel because the casino advantage is 2.70% versus a double-zero wheel which has a 5.26% advantage. However, that situation is somewhat different in Atlantic City because of certain gaming regulations. On double-zero wheels the casinos can only take one-half of a wager on even money bets (odd/even, red/black, 1-18/19-36) when zero or double-zero is the winning number. This lowers the casino edge on these particular bets to 2.63%, while the edge on all other bets remains at 5.26%. This rule is not in effect on single-zero wheels and virtually all bets on that game have a 2.70% house edge. There are six casinos that have single-zero roulette wheels: Harrah's, Bally's, Borgata, Trump Taj Mahal, Tropicana and Caesars. You should be aware, however, that almost all of these games are only open on weekends (or by special request) and they require $25-$100 minimum bets.

Craps: Bally's and the Hilton offer 10x odds, all other Atlantic City casinos offer 5x odds.

Video Poker: Several casinos tightened their video poker in the last year, but there are still good plays available. There are no true advantage video-poker plays in Atlantic City. But with a little luck, using promotional offers, and scouting out computer glitches, a skilled and disciplined player can probably come out ahead by sticking to the 99-plus percent games.

The best commonly found game in Atlantic City is 9/6 Jacks or Better (99.54%), which is available in some form at many casinos. The Borgata is the best place to find it in multiple denominations, but check out a machine before you play it, as they also have short-pay games.

Quarter Games – The Showboat has eight full-pay machines in a non-smoking section of the main casino across the hall from the Carousel high-limit slot area. These multi-game, multi-denomination machines range from 25 cents to $2. Choices include 9/6 Jacks or Better, 8/5 Bonus Poker (99.16%), 9/7 Double Bonus Poker (99.11%) and 8/6/4 Double Joker Poker. It is usually not hard to find a seat at these games.

The Borgata has 9/6 Jacks or Better in the B-bar (a smoking section with drinks comped for players) and several banks of machines scattered around the casino. Also in the Borgata are a few Multi Strike Machines with 9/6 Jacks or Better, located near the buffet entrance. Caesars has a bank of six slow-moving slant-top progressive 9/6 Jacks or Better machines in the smoking section behind the Toga Bar. You can also find three multi-game, multi-denomination machines with 9/6 Jacks or Better in a triangle at Harrah's, by following the tile pathway from the entrance to the parking garage. Bally's has a bank of multi-game, multi-denomination machines with 9/6 Jacks or Better in the Park Place Poker section, which allows smoking, but you have to play 10 coins per hand to be eligible for the jackpot. There are also four machines in the non-smoking section with 10-coin 9/6 Jacks or Better, 8/5 Bonus Poker, and 9/7 Double Bonus Poker. The Tropicana has a bank of eight full-pay (99.59%) Five- Joker games in an alcove just outside the Slot City Estates area, but they're almost always in use so it's likely to have to wait for a seat. Look for Sigma games next to the entrance to the women's restroom. You have to play 10 coins per hand, or a royal flush pays only 500 per coin rather than 800. There are also a few games with 9/6 Jacks or Better at the Rumba bar near the table-games section, mixed in with short-pay games.

The best place for 8/5 Bonus Poker is Resorts, scattered in multi-game machines throughout the casino. As this is written, Resorts offers some of the most generous cash back and comps for video-poker players in Atlantic City. For more action, Bally's has two rows, back-to-back, of 8/5 Bonus triple-play progressives in the non-smoking section of the Park Place casino. The Hilton also has one bank of six triple-play Bonus Poker progressives near the main casino cage. These are also in non-smoking, and the jackpots for the three individual lines top off at $1,1199.99

Dollar Games - Dollar players may want to check out Bally's, with a bank of dollar progressive 9/6 Jacks or Better in its Park Place video-poker section, which allows smoking. There are three dollar 8/5 Bonus Poker games in the non-smoking section. Bally's also has three multi-game machines in dollars with triple-play Jacks or Better and Bonus Poker in the high-limit area off the hotel lobby. But players earn one Total Rewards credit for each $20 of play, instead of one point for $10 as in other video poker games at the Caesars Entertainment properties, so you'll earn comps at a slower rate.

Dollar players can find 9/6 Jacks or Better at most Atlantic city casinos, with the largest number at the Borgata. If you like to smoke or drink while you play, head for the B-bar. In other casinos, look in or near the high-limit area, except at the Tropicana, where the full-pay dollar machines are in a walkway between the two main playing areas. Check carefully, because the 50-cent version on these multi-game, multi-denomination machines is short-pay.

Dollar 8/5 Bonus players will find the best pickings at Resorts, in the high-limit smoking section toward the Boardwalk end. A few machines near the Boardwalk end offer dollar 8/5 Bonus Poker in the non-smoking section.

Trump Plaza has two 9/7 Double Bonus in the raised area near the hotel elevators. You can also play it at the eight multi-game machines in the Showboat House of Blues area.

If you want to play 9/6 Jacks or Better at the $5 or higher level, it's in almost every high-limit slot room in town.

Showboat Casino-Hotel
801 Boardwalk
Atlantic City, New Jersey 08401
(609) 343-4000
Website: www.showboatac.com

Reservation Number: (800) 621-0200
Rooms: 1,181 Price Range: $79-$379
Suites: 128 Price Range: Casino Use Only
Restaurants: 7 Valet Park: $5/$10 (Fri-Sun)
Buffets: L-$18.99
          D-$24.99/$27.99 (Sat)
Casino Size: 139,540 Square Feet
Other Games: B6
Special Features: New Orleans-themed casino.
Various buffet discounts for Total Rewards
Card members.

Tropicana Casino & Resort
Brighton Avenue and the Boardwalk
Atlantic City, New Jersey 08401
(609) 340-4000
Website: www.tropicana.net

Toll-Free Number: (800) THE-TROP
Reservation Number: (800) 338-5553
Rooms: 1,426 Price Range: $79-$409
Suites: 340 Price Range: $155-$675
Restaurants: 16 Valet Park: $5/$10 (Fri-Sun)
Buffets: B/L-$19.95 D-$26.95
Casino Size: 138,130 Square Feet
Other Games: B6
Special Features: Features "The Quarter," a
dining/entertainment complex with 30 stores.

Trump Plaza Hotel and Casino
The Boardwalk at Mississippi Avenue
Atlantic City, New Jersey 08401
(609) 441-6000
Website: www.trumpplaza.com

Reservation Number: (800) 677-7378
Rooms: 762 Price Range: $129-$329
Suites: 142 Price Range: $250-$575
Restaurants: 9 Valet Parking: $5
Buffets: L/D-$16.95
Casino Size: 86,923 Square Feet
Other Games: No poker, no off-track betting
Special Features: Health spa. Indoor pool.
Rainforest Cafe. Beach bar.

Trump Taj Mahal Casino Resort
1000 Boardwalk at Virginia Avenue
Atlantic City, New Jersey 08401
(609) 449-1000
Website: www.trumptaj.com

Reservation Number: (800) 825-8888
Rooms: 1,795 Price Range: $150-$450
Suites: 311 Price Range: $350-$600
Restaurants: 11 Valet Parking: $5
Buffets: B-$14.95
          L/D- $22.47/$29.99 (Fri-Sun)
Casino Size: 161,722 Square Feet
Other Games: SB, B6, K
Special Features: Health spa. Hard Rock cafe.
5,000-seat event center. 1,400-seat showroom.

NEW MEXICO

New Mexico's Indian casinos offer an assortment of table games and electronic gaming machines. Additionally, slot machines are allowed at the state's racetracks as well as at about 40 various fraternal and veterans clubs.

New Mexico gaming regulations require that electronic machines at racetracks and fraternal/veterans organizations return a minimum of 80% to a maximum of 96%.

New Mexico's Indian tribes do not make their slot machine payback percentages a matter of public record but the terms of the compact between the state and the tribes require all electronic gaming machines to return a minimum of 80%.

Unless otherwise noted, all New Mexico Indian casinos are open 24 hours and offer: blackjack, craps, roulette, video slots and video poker. Some casinos also offer: Spanish 21 (S21), mini-baccarat (MB), poker (P), pai gow poker (PGP), three card poker (TCP), four card poker (FCP), Caribbean stud poker (CSP), let it ride (LIR), casino war (CW), big 6 wheel (B6), keno (K), bingo (BG) and off track betting (OTB). The minimum gambling age is 21 for the casinos and 18 for bingo or pari-mutuel betting.

Please note that all New Mexico casinos are prohibited from serving alcohol on the casino floor. If a casino serves alcohol it can only be consumed at the bar and not in the casino itself.

For information on visiting New Mexico call the state's tourism department at (800) 733-6396 or go to: www.newmexico.org.

Apache Nugget Casino
PO Box 650
Dulce, New Mexico 87528
(575) 289-2486
Map: **#15** (on Jicarilla reservation at intersection of Hwys 550 and 537 near Cuba)

Restaurants: 1 Liquor: No
Other Games: Only gaming machines
Casino Size: 12,000 Square Feet
Overnight RV Parking: Free (check in with security first)/RV Dump: No

Best Western Jicarilla Inn and Casino
U.S. Highway 64
Dulce, New Mexico 87529
(575) 759-3663
Map: **#12** (95 miles N.W. of Santa Fe)

Room Reservations: (800) 428-2627
Rooms: 43 Price Range: $75-$95
Restaurants: 1 Liquor: Yes
Hours: 11am-1am/2am (Fri/Sat)

Buffalo Thunder Resort & Casino
30 Buffalo Thunder Trail
Santa Fe, New Mexico 87506
(505) 455-5555
Website: www.buffalothunderresort.com
Map: **#2**

Room Reservations: (800) HILTONS
Rooms: 350 Price Range: $179-$229
Suites: 45 Price Range: $229-$279
Restaurants: 6 Liquor: Yes
Buffets: B-$9.99 (Mon) L-$16.95 (Fri/Sat)
         D-$15.95/$21.95 (Fri)
Other Games: P, TCP
Casino Size: 61,000 Square Feet
Special Features: Hotel is Hilton. Health Spa. Retail shopping area. Native American art gallery. 2-for-1 buffet on Tue for player's club members.

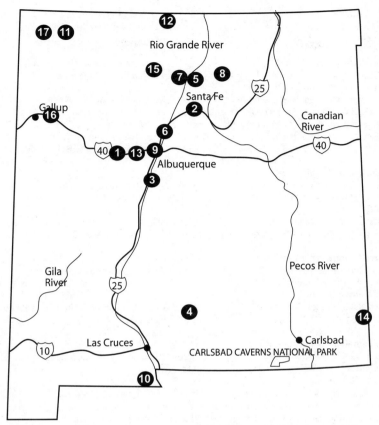

Camel Rock Casino
17486-A Highway 84/285
Santa Fe, New Mexico 87504
(505) 984-8414
Website: www.camelrockcasino.com
Map: **#2**

Toll-Free Number: (800) GO-CAMEL
Restaurants: 1   Liquor: No
Hours: 8am-2am/24 Hours (Thurs-Sat)
Casino Size: 60,000 Square Feet
Other Games: TCP,
Overnight RV Parking: Free/RV Dump: No
Senior Discount: Various on Thursday if 55+

Casino Apache Travel Center
25845 U.S. Highway 70
Ruidoso, New Mexico 88340
(575) 464-7777
Map: **#4** (90 miles N.E. of Las Cruces)

Restaurants: 1 Liquor: Yes
Hours: 8am-4am/24 Hours (Thurs-Sun)
Other Games: No Craps
Casino Size: 10,000 Square Feet
Overnight RV Parking: Free/RV Dump: No
Special Features: Free shuttle service to Inn
of the Mountain Gods Casino. Truck stop.
Discount smoke shop.

Casino Express
14500 Central Avenue
Albuquerque, New Mexico 87120
(505) 552-7777
Map: **#3** (I-40 at exit 140)

Toll-Free Number: (866) 352-7866
Other Games: Only gaming machines
Overnight RV Parking: Free/RV Dump: No
Special Features: Adjacent to, and affiliated with, Route 66 Casino.

Cities of Gold Casino Hotel
10-B Cities of Gold Road
Santa Fe, New Mexico 87501
(505) 455-3313
Website: www.citiesofgold.com
Map: **#2 (**Intersection of Hwys 84/285/502)

Toll-Free Number: (800) 455-3313
Room Reservations: (877) 455-0515
Rooms: 122 Price Range: $65-$109
Suites: 2 Price Range: $136
Restaurants: 3 Liquor: Yes
Buffets: B-$7.95/$10.95 (Sun)
          L-$8.95 D-$13.95/$19.95 (Fri/Sat)
Hours: 8am-4am/24 hours (Fri/Sat)
Casino Size: 40,000 Square Feet
Other Games: TCP, BG
Overnight RV Parking: No
Special Features: They also operate the Cities of Gold Sports Bar which is one block away from main casino. Liquor is served there but they only have slots and OTB - no table games. 27-hole golf course.

Dancing Eagle Casino and RV Park
Interstate 40, Exit 108
Casa Blanca, New Mexico 87007
(505) 552-1111
Website: www.dancingeaglecasino.com
Map: **#1** (40 miles W. of Albuquerque)

Toll-Free Number: (877) 440-9969
Restaurants: 1 Liquor: No
Casino Size: 21,266 Square Feet
Other Games: No craps
Senior Discount: Various Mon-Thu if 50+
Overnight RV Parking: Free/RV Dump: No
Special Features: Located on I-40 at exit 108. Truck stop. 35-space RV park ($20 per night/$10 for slot club members).

Fire Rock Navajo Casino
249 State Highway 118
Church Rock, New Mexico 87313
(505) 905-7100
Website: www.firerocknavajocasino.com
Map: **#16** (8 miles E of Gallup)

Toll-Free Number: (866) 941-2444
Restaurants: 1
Buffet: B- $6.99 (Sun)
Casino Size: 64,000 square Feet
Other Games: P, No Craps, BG (Wed-Sun)

Flowing Water Navajo Casino
2710 US highway 64
Waterflow, New Mexico 87421
(505) 368-2300
Map: **#17** (105 miles N of Gallup)

Restaurants:1
Casino Size: 11,000 square Feet

Hard Rock Hotel and Casino Albuquerque
11000 Broadway S.E.
Albuquerque, New Mexico 87105
(505) 724-3800
Website: www.hardrockcasinoabq.com
Map: **#3**

Toll-Free Number: (877) 475-3827
Restaurants: 6 Liquor: Yes
Buffets: B-$7.95/$10.95 (Sun)
          L-$8.95
          D-$13.95/$19.95 (Fri/Sat)
Hours: 8am-5am/24 Hours (Thu-Sun)
Casino Size: 30,000 Square Feet
Other Games: P, LIR, TCP, BG
Overnight RV Parking: Free/RV Dump: No
Special Features: Convenience store. Gas station. Three nine-hole golf courses. Alcohol is only served at sports bar in casino.

Inn of the Mountain Gods Resort & Casino
277 Carrizo Canyon Road
Mescalero, New Mexico 88340
(575) 464-7777
Website: www.innofthemountaingods.com
Map: **#4** (90 miles N.E. of Las Cruces)

Toll-Free Number: (800) 545-9011
Rooms: 250 Price Range: $149-$199
Suites: 23 Price Range: $269-$399
Restaurants: 4 Liquor: Yes
Buffets: Brunch-$15.95 (Sat/Sun) B-$9.95
    L-$12.50 D-$16.95/
    $25.00 (Wed)/$18.95 (Fri/Sat)
Hours: 8am-4am/24 Hours (Fri/Sat)
Casino Size: 38,000 Square Feet
Other Games: MB, P, PGP, LIR, TCP, FCP
Overnight RV Parking: Free/RV Dump: No
Senior Discount: 20% off buffet if 55+
Special Features: 18-hole golf course.

Ohkay Casino Resort
P.O. Box 1270
San Juan Pueblo, New Mexico 87566
(575) 747-1668
Website: www.ohkay.com
Map: **#5** (24 miles N. of Santa Fe)

Toll-Free Number: (800) PLAY-AT-OK
Room Reservation (877) 829-2865
Rooms: 101 Price Range: $84-$104
Suites: 24 Price Range: $114-$134
Restaurants: 2 Liquor: Yes
Buffets: B- $9.99 (Sun)
    D-$6.99/$9.99 (Sun)
Hours: 7am-3am/24 hrs (Fri-Sun)
Casino Size: 30,000 Square Feet
Overnight RV Parking: Free/RV Dump: No
Special Features: Hotel is Best Western.
Sporting clays club.

Palace West Casino
State Road 45
Albuquerque, New Mexico 87105
(505) 869-4102
Map: **#3** (at Coors & Isleta Road)

Hours: 8am-Midnight Daily
Other Games: Only gaming machines
Overnight RV Parking: Free/RV Dump: No
Special Features: Completely nonsmoking.

Route 66 Casino Hotel
14500 Central Avenue
Albuquerque, New Mexico 87121
(505) 352-7866
Website: www.rt66casino.com
Map: **#13** (20 miles W. of Albuquerque)

Toll-Free Number: (866) 352-7866
Rooms: 154 Rates: $79-$109
Restaurants: 2 Liquor: No
Buffets: L-$9.99/$12.99 (Sun)
    D-$9.99/$11.99 (Sun)
Hours: 8am-4am/24 Hours (Fri-Sun)
Other Games: P, PGP, TCP, BG
Overnight RV Parking: Free/RV Dump: No
Special Features: Johnny Rockets restaurant.
Adjacent to, and affiliated with, Casino
Express.

San Felipe Casino Hollywood
25 Hagan Road
Algodones, New Mexico 87001
(505) 867-6700
Website: www.sanfelipecasino.com
Map: **#6** (17 miles N. of Albuquerque)

Toll-Free Number: (877) 529-2946
Restaurants: 1 Liquor: No
Buffets: B-$11.95(Sun) L-$9.95.25 D-$9.95
Hours: 8am-4am/24 Hours (Fri-Sat)
Other Games: P, TCP
Overnight RV Parking: Must use RV park
Special Features: 100-space RV park ($10
per night). Adjacent to Hollywood Hills
Speedway

Sandia Resort & Casino
30 Rainbow Road NE
Albuquerque, New Mexico 87113
(505) 796-7500
Website: www.sandiacasino.com
Map: **#9**

Toll-Free Number: (800) 526-9366
Rooms: 198 Price Range: $188-$226
Suites: 30 Price Range: $269-$339
Restaurants: 4   Liquor: Yes
Buffets: B-$7.95 L-$9.95/$14.95 (Sun)
    D-$12.25/$25.95 (Fri)
Hours: 8am-4am/24 Hours (Fri-Sun)
Casino Size: 65,000 Square feet
Other Games: P, CSP, LIR, TCP,
    PGP, BG, K, MB
Overnight RV Parking: Free/RV Dump: No
Senior Discount: Various Wed 10-6pm if 50+
Special Features: 4,200-seat amphitheater.
18-hole golf course, smoke-free slot room.

Santa Ana Star Casino
54 Jemez Dam Canyon Road
Bernalillo, New Mexico 87004
(505) 867-0000
Website: www.santaanastar.com
Map: **#6** (17 miles N. of Albuquerque)

Restaurants: 5   Liquor: No
Buffets: B-$13.95 (Sun) L-$9.95
    D-$15.95/$19.95 (Thu/Fri)/$14.95 (Sat/Sun)
Hours: 8am-4am/24 Hours (Thurs-Sat)
Casino Size: 19,000 Square Feet
Other Games: P, LIR, FCP
Overnight RV Parking: Free/RV Dump: No
Senior Discount: Various Mondays if 50+
Special Features: 36-lane bowling alley. 18-
hole golf course. Spa. Smoke shop. 3,000-seat
event center.

Santa Claran Hotel Casino
460 North Riverside Drive
Espanola, New Mexico 87532-3470
(505) 367-4500
Website: www.santaclaran.com
Map: **#7** (25 miles N of Sante Fe)

Rooms: 124 Price Range: $89-$209
Restaurants: 4 Liquor: Yes
Hours:8am-4am/24 hours (Fri/Sat)
Casino Size: 36,000 square feet
Other Games: TCP, P
Overnight RV Parking: No
Special Features: 24 lane bowling alley

Sky City Casino Hotel
Interstate 40, Exit 102
Acoma, New Mexico 87034
(505) 552-6017
Website: www.skycitycasino.com
Map: **#1** (50 miles W. of Albuquerque)

Toll-Free Number: (888) 759-2489
Rooms: 132 Price Range: $79-$99
Suites: 15 Price Range: $109-$129
Restaurants: 4 Liquor: No
Buffets: L-$9.95 D-$12.95/$18.99 (Fri)/
    $23.50 (Sat)
Hours: 8am-4am/24 Hours (Fri/Sat)
Casino Size: 30,000 Square Feet
Other Games: TCP, BG
Overnight RV Parking: Free/RV Dump: No
Senior Discount: 10% off buffet if 55 or older
Special Features: 42-space RV park ($25 per
night).

Taos Mountain Casino
P.O. Box 1477
Taos, New Mexico 87571
(575) 737-0777
Website: www.taosmountaincasino.com
Map: **#8** (50 miles N.E. of Santa Fe)

Toll-Free Number: (888) 946-8267
Restaurants: 1 Deli   Liquor: No
Hours: 8am-1am/2am (Thu-Sat)
Other Games: No Roulette, TCP
Overnight RV Parking: No
Special Features: Entire casino is nonsmoking.

Pari-Mutuels

**The Downs Racetrack and Casino
at Albuquerque**
201 California Northeast
Albuquerque, New Mexico 87108
(505) 266-5555
Website: www.abqdowns.com
Map: **#9**

Restaurants: 1
Hours: 10am-1am/3am (Fri)/2am(Sat/Sun)
Other Games: Only gaming machines
Overnight RV Parking: No
Senior Discount: $2 off buffets if 55+
Special Features: Live horse racing August
through October. Daily simulcasting of horse
racing.

Ruidoso Downs & Billy The Kid Casino
1461 Highway 70 West
Ruidoso Downs, New Mexico 88346
(575) 378-4431
Website: www.ruidownsracing.com
Map: **#4** (90 miles N.E. of Las Cruces)

Restaurants: 2
Hours: 10am-Midnight/1am (Fri/Sat)
Other Games: Only gaming machines
Overnight RV Parking: No
Senior Discount: Various Wed 2-9pm if 55+
Special Features: Live horse racing (Thu-Sun)
late May through early September. Daily
simulcasting of horse racing.

Sunland Park Racetrack & Casino
1200 Futurity Drive
Sunland Park, New Mexico 88063
(575) 874-5200
Website: www.sunland-park.com
Map: **#10** (5 miles W. of El Paso, TX)

Restaurants: 5
Buffets: L-$9.00/$10 (Sat/Sun)
         D-$10.00/$19.95 (Fri)
Hours: 9:30am-1am/2am (Fri/Sat)
Other Games: Only gaming machines
Overnight RV Parking: Free/$5 w/hookups
Senior Discount: $1 off lunch buffet and
                 special coupon book if 55+
Special Features: Live thoroughbred and
quarter-horse racing December through April.
Daily simulcasting of horse racing.

SunRay Park and Casino
#39 Road 5568
Farmington, New Mexico 87401
(575) 566-1200
Website: www.sunraygaming.com
Map: **#11** (150 miles N.W. of Santa Fe)

Restaurants: 1
Hours: 11am-2am/3am (Thu)/4am (Fri)
        10-am-4am (Sat)/10am-2am (Sun)
Other Games: Only gaming machines
Overnight RV Parking: No
Special Features: Live horse racing (Thu-
Sun) from mid-April through June. Daily
simulcasting of horse racing.

Zia Park Race Track & Black Gold Casino
3901 W. Millen Drive
Hobbs, New Mexico 88240
(575) 492-7000
Website: www.blackgoldcasino.net
Map: **#14** (70 miles N.E. of Carlsbad)

Toll-Free Number: 888-942-7275
Restaurants: 3
Buffets: D-$14.99 (Fri)/$19.99 (Sat/Sun)
Hours: 9am-12:30am/2am (Fri)/ 2:30am (Sat)
Other Games: Only gaming machines
Overnight RV Parking: Free/RV Dump: No
Special Features: Live horse racing mid-
September through early December. Daily
simulcasting of horse racing. Buffet Discount
with Slot club card.

NEW YORK

Indian Casinos (Class III)

There are five Indian casinos located in upstate New York which offer traditional Class III casino gambling.

The terms of the compact between the tribes and the state allow table games and slot machines, including video keno and video poker. These machines do not pay out in cash. Instead, they print out a receipt which must be exchanged for cash.

All casinos also offer a cashless system whereby you have to go to a cashier cage, or a kiosk, get a "smart" card and deposit money to that card's account. The machines will then deduct losses from, or credit wins to, your account.

All of these casinos are open 24 hours and offer the following games: blackjack, craps, roulette and Caribbean stud poker. Some casinos also offer: Spanish 21 (S21), baccarat (B), mini-baccarat (MB), big six wheel (B6), keno (K), poker (P), pai gow poker (PGP), let it ride (LIR), three-card poker (TCP), four-card poker (FCP) and casino war (CW).

The minimum gambling age is 21 at the three Seneca casinos and 18 at the other two casinos. For more information on visiting New York call the state's travel information center at (800) 225-5697 or go to: www.iloveny.com.

Akwesasne Mohawk Casino
873 State Route 37
Hogansburg, New York 13655
(518) 358-2222
Website: www.mohawkcasino.com
Map: **#2** (65 miles W. of Champlain)

Toll-Free Number: (888) 622-1155
Restaurants: 2 Liquor: Yes Valet Park: Free
Buffets: B-$5.95/$10.95 (Sat/Sun)
        L-$9.95 D-$16.95
Casino Size: 40,000 Square Feet
Other Games: S21, P, LIR, TCP,
        PGP, FCP, MB
Overnight RV Parking: Free/RV Dump: No

Seneca Allegany Casino & Hotel
777 Seneca Allegany Boulevard
Salamanca, New York 14779
(716) 945-9300
Web Site: www.senecaalleganycasino.com
Map: **#12** (65 miles S. of Buffalo)

Toll-Free Number: (877) 553-9500
Rooms: 189 Price Range: $115-$345
Suites: 23 Price Range: $215-$445
Restaurants: 6 (1 open 24 hours)
Liquor: Yes Valet Park: Free
Buffets: L-$15.95 D-$18.95
Casino Size: 48,000 Square Feet
Other Games: TCP, LIR, S21, B6
Overnight RV Parking: No
Special Features: Buffet discount for slot club members.

Seneca Buffalo Creek Casino
1 Fulton Street
Buffalo, New York 14204
(716) 853-7576
www.senecagamingcorporation.com/sbcc
Map: **#3**

Restaurants: 1 Snack Bar Liquor: Yes
Valet Park: Free
Casino Size: 5,000 Square Feet
Other Games: Only Gaming Machines
Overnight RV Parking: No

Seneca Niagara Casino
310 Fourth Street
Niagara Falls, New York 14303
(716) 299-1100
Web Site: www.senecaniagaracasino.com
Map: **#4**

Toll-Free Number: (877) 873-6322
Rooms: 574 Price Range: $139-$265
Suites: 30 Price Range: $239-$305
Restaurants: 4 Liquor: Yes Valet Park: Free
Buffets: B-$11.99 (Sat/Sun) L- $15.95
        D-$20.99/ $24.99 (Fri/Sun)
Other Games: S21, B, MB, P, PGP,
        TCP, LIR, FCP, K
Overnight RV Parking: No
Special Features: Buffet discount for slot club members.

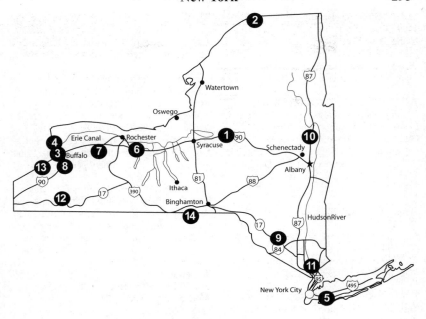

Turning Stone Casino Resort
5218 Patrick Road
Verona, New York 13478
(315) 361-7711
Web Site: www.turning-stone.com
Map: **#1** (adjacent to NY State Thruway exit 33 at Verona, off Route 365, 30 miles E. of Syracuse)

Toll-Free Number: (800) 771-7711
Rooms: 572 Price Range: $130-$229
Suites: 143 Price Range: $179-$595
Restaurants: 14 Liquor: No Valet Park: $5
Buffets: B-$8.95/$10.95 (Sat/Sun)
      L-$12.95/ $14.95 (Fri/Sat)/$16.95 (Sun)
      D-$16.95/ $24.95 (Thu)/
          $21.95 (Fri/Sat)/$19.95 (Sun)
Casino Size: 122,000 Square Feet
Other Games: B, MB, P, LIR, PGP, BG,
         TCP, FCP, K, CW, B6
Overnight RV Parking: No
Special Features: Three golf courses. Gift shop. Discount smoke shop. 800-seat showroom. 175-space RV park ($45 per night/$55 weekends).

Indian Casinos (Class II)

There are some Indian casinos that offer Class II gambling which consist of electronic gaming machines which look like slot machines, but are actually games of bingo and the spinning video reels are for "entertainment purposes only." No public information is available concerning the payback percentages on the video gaming machines.

Some of these casinos also offer high-stakes bingo and poker, as shown in the "Other Games" listings.

Mohawk Bingo Palace
202 State Route 37
Akwesasne, New York 13655
(518) 358-2246
Web Site: www.mohawkpalace.com
Map: **#2** (65 miles W. of Champlain)

Toll-Free Number: (866) 452-5768
Restaurants: 1 Liquor: No Valet Park: No
Other Games: Bingo
Overnight RV Parking: Free/RV Dump: No

Seneca Gaming - Irving
11099 Route 5
Irving, New York 14081
(716) 549-6356
Web Site: www.senecagames.com
Map: **#13** (38 miles S.W. of Buffalo)

Toll-Free Number: (800) 421-BINGO
Restaurants: 1 Liquor: No Valet Park: No
Hours: 9:30am-2am/4:30am (Fri/Sat)
Other Games: Bingo, Poker
Overnight RV Parking: Free (must check in
          with security first)/RV Dump: No
Special Features: Discount smoke shop.

Seneca Gaming - Salamanca
768 Broad Street
Salamanca, New York 14779
(716) 945-4080
Web Site: www.senecagames.com
Map: **#12** (65 miles S. of Buffalo)

Toll-Free Number: (877) 860-5130
Restaurants: 1 Liquor: No Valet Park: No
Hours: 9:30am-1am/2am (Fri/Sat)
Other Games: Bingo, Poker
Overnight RV Parking: Free (must check in
          with security first)/RV Dump: No

Pari-Mutuels

In October 2001, legislation was passed to
allow for the introduction of slot machine-
type video lottery machines at New York
racetracks. Officially referred to as *Video
Gaming Machines* (VGM's), they are
regulated by the New York State Lottery
Division.

All VGM's offer standard slot machine-type
games, plus keno in denominations from five
cents to $10. The machines all accept cash but
do not pay out in cash. They print a receipt
which must be taken to a cashier.

The VGM's do not operate like regular slot
machines. Instead, they are similar to scratch-
off-type lottery tickets with a pre-determined
number of winners.

According to a spokesperson at the Lottery's
headquarters, "no public information is
available concerning the actual payback
percentages on the machines." However, the
legislation authorizing the VGM's states, "the
specifications for video lottery gaming shall be
designed in such a manner as to pay prizes that
average no less than ninety percent of sales."

All Video Gaming Machine facilities are
open from 9am to 4am daily and all are non-
smoking. Admission is free to all facilities and
the minimum gambling age is 18 for playing
VGM's, as well as for pari-mutuel betting.

Aqueduct
110-00 Rockaway Boulevard
Jamaica, New York 11417
(718) 641-4700
Website: www.nyra.com/index_aqueduct.html
Map: **#5** (15 miles E. of Manhattan)

Admission: Free   Clubhouse: $5
Valet: $5
Restaurants: 2
Buffet: B/L/D- $20/$30 (Sat/Sun)
Special Features: Live thoroughbred racing
Wed-Sun. Daily simulcasting of thoroughbred
racing.

Batavia Downs Gaming
8315 Park Road
Batavia, New York 14020
(585) 343-3750
Website: www.batavia-downs.com
Map: **#7** (35 miles E. of Buffalo)

Toll-Free: (800) 724-2000
Restaurants: 2   Valet Parking: No
Buffets: B- $9.95 (Sun) D-$13.95/
          $21.95 (Fri/Sat)
Overnight RV Parking: No
Special Features: Live harness racing Tue/
Wed/Fri/Sat from early August through
early December. Daily simulcasting of
thoroughbred and harness racing.

Empire City at Yonkers Raceway
8100 Central Avenue
Yonkers, New York 10704
(914) 968-4200
Website: www.yonkersraceway.com
Map: **#11** (20 miles N. of Manhattan)

Restaurants: 3
Valet: $10
Special Features: Year-round live harness racing Mon/Tue/Thu-Sat evenings. Daily simulcasting of thoroughbred and harness racing.

Fairgrounds Gaming & Raceway
5600 McKinley Parkway
Hamburg Fairgrounds
Hamburg, New York 14075
(716) 649-1280
Website: www.buffaloraceway.com
Map: **#8** (15 miles S. of Buffalo)

Toll-Free: (800) 237-1205
Restaurants: 2   Valet Parking: No
Casino Size: 27,000 Square Feet
Overnight RV Parking: Yes
Special Features: Live harness racing Wed/Fri-Sun from January through July. Simulcasting Wed-Sun of thoroughbred and harness racing. Admission and parking are Free.

Finger Lakes Gaming & Racetrack
5857 Route 96
Farmington, NY 14425
(585) 924-3232
Website: www.fingerlakesgaming.com
Map: **#6** (25 miles S. of Rochester)

Restaurants: 3   Valet Parking: $3
Buffets: B-$15.95 (Sun) L-$15.95 D-$19.95
Casino Size: 28,267 Square Feet
Overnight RV Parking: Call for permission
Senior Discount: Various Mon-Thu if 60+
Special Features: Live thoroughbred horse racing (Fri-Tue) mid-April through December. Daily simulcasting of harness and thoroughbred racing.

Monticello Gaming & Raceway
204 Route 17B
Monticello, New York 12701
(845) 794-4100
Website: www.monticelloraceway.com
Map: **#9** (50 miles W. of Newburgh)

Toll-Free: (866) 777-4263
Admission: Free   Self-Parking: Free
Restaurants: 1   Valet Parking: $2
Buffets: L/D-$13.95/$19.95 (Fri/Sat)
Overnight RV Parking: Free/RV Dump: No
Senior Discount: Buffet discount Tue if 55+
Special Features: Year-round live harness racing Mon-Thu. Daily simulcast of thoroughbred and harness racing.

Saratoga Gaming and Raceway
342 Jefferson Street
Saratoga Springs, New York 12866
(518) 584-2110
Website: www.saratogaraceway.com
Map: **#10** (25 miles N. of Schenectady)

Toll-Free: (800) 727-2990
Restaurants: 5   Valet Parking: $3
Buffets: L-$12.95 D-$14.95
Casino Size: 55,000 Square Feet
Overnight RV Parking: Free
Special Features: Live harness racing Thu-Sat evenings from March through mid-December. Daily simulcasting of thoroughbred and harness racing. Wed Senior buffet for $6.95

Tioga Downs
2384 West River Road
Nichols, New York 13812
Website: www.tiogadowns.com
Map: **#14** (30 miles W. of Binghamton)

Toll-Free: (888) 946-8464
Restaurants: 2   Valet Parking: $3
Buffets: B-$12.99 (Sun) L-$11.99/$13.99 (Sun)
    D-$13.99/$17.99 (Fri/Sat)
Casino Size: 19,000 Square Feet
Overnight RV Parking: Free
Special Features: Live harness racing on Fri-Sun from May through mid-September. Daily simulcasting of thoroughbred and harness racing.

Vernon Downs
4229 Stuhlman Rd
Vernon, New York 13476
(315) 829-2201
Website: www.vernondowns.com
Map: #1 (30 miles E. of Syracuse)

Toll-Free Number: (877) 888-3766
Room Reservations: (866) 829-3400
Suites: 175 Price Range: $59-$159
Restaurants: 1   Valet Parking: $2
Buffets: L- $10.99 D- $13.99
Casino Size: 28,000 Square Feet
Overnight RV Parking: Free/RV Dump: No
Special Features: Live harness racing Thu-Sat
evenings late mid-April through early-November. Daily simulcasting of thoroughbred and
harness racing.

Canadian Casinos

If you are traveling to the Buffalo area there
are two nearby Canadian casinos just across
the border in Niagara Falls, Ontario.

All winnings are paid in Canadian currency
and the minimum gambling age is 19. Both
casinos are open 24 hours and offer the
following games: blackjack, Spanish 21,
craps, baccarat, mini-baccarat, pai-gow poker,
Caribbean stud poker, three-card poker and
let it ride.

Casino Niagara
5705 Falls Avenue
Niagara Falls, Ontario L2G 3K6
(905) 374-3589
Website: www.casinoniagara.com/
Map: #4

PRICES ARE IN CANADIAN DOLLARS
Toll-Free Number: (888) 946-3255
Restaurants: 6   Valet Parking: $5
Buffets: L-$11.95 D-$16.95
Casino Size: 100,000 Square Feet
Other games: Poker
Overnight RV Parking: Free/RV Dump: No
Senior Discount: Various Tue if 55 or older
Special Features: Free shuttle to/from Niagara
Fallsview Casino.

Niagara Fallsview Casino Resort
6380 Fallsview Boulevard
Niagara, Ontario L2G 7X5
(905) 358-3255
Website: wwwfallsviewcasinoresort.com
Map: #4

PRICES ARE IN CANADIAN DOLLARS
Toll-Free Number: (888) 325-5788
Room Reservations: (888) 888-1089
Rooms: 340 Price Range: $249-$350
Suites: 28 Price Range: $359-$559
Restaurants: 10   Valet Parking: $20
Buffets: B-$12 L/D-$20
Other Games: Pai Gow (tiles), Casino War,
      Big 6 Wheel, Sic Bo, Poker
Casino Size: 180,000 Square Feet
Overnight RV Parking: No
Special Features: Spa/fitness center. 1,500-
seat theatre. Free shuttle to/from Casino
Niagara. Additional Hilton hotel connected
by walkway.

NORTH CAROLINA

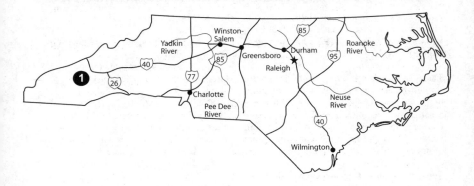

North Carolina has one Indian casino. In August, 1994 the state's Eastern Band of Cherokee Indians signed a compact with the governor to allow forms of video gambling. According to the terms of the compact, the video machines must be games of skill and they are required to return a minimum of 83% and a maximum of 98%.

No live table games are offered at the Cherokee Casino, only video slots, video poker, and digital verisons of poker, blackjack, and baccarat.

The slots are different than slots you will find in other casinos because of the required "skill" factor. With these "skill" slots you have two opportunities to spin the reels. The "skill" factor comes into play because after seeing the results of your first spin you then have to decide whether to keep none, one, two, or all three of the symbols on each reel before you spin them again.

The casino is open 24 hours and the minimum gambling age is 21.

For more information on visiting North Carolina call the state's division of travel & tourism at (800) 847-4862 or go to: www.visitnc.com.

Harrah's Cherokee Casino
777 Casino Drive
Cherokee, North Carolina 28719
(828) 497-7777
Website: www.harrahs.com
Map: **#1** (55 miles S.W. of Asheville)

Toll-Free Number: (800) HARRAHS
Rooms 555 Price Range: $129-$199
Suites: 21 Price Range: Casino Use Only
Restaurants: 5   Liquor: No
Valet Parking: $8
Buffets: B-$9.50 (Sat/Sun)
L-$12.50/$18.00 (Sat/Sun)
D-$18.00/$22.00 (Fri)/ $26.00 (Sun)
Overnight RV Parking: No
Special Features: 1,500-seat entertainment pavilion.

NORTH DAKOTA

North Dakota has more than 800 sites throughout the state that offer blackjack, with betting limits of $1-$25, for the benefit of charities.

There are also six Indian casinos which are limited by law to the following maximum bet limits: blackjack-$100 (two tables in a casino may have limits up to $250), craps-$60, roulette-$50, slots/video poker-$25 and poker-$50 per bet, per round with a maximum of three rounds.

The terms of the state's compact with the tribes require gaming machines to return a minimum of 80% and a maximum of 100%. However, if a machine is affected by skill, such as video poker or video blackjack, the machines must return a minimum of 83%.

All casinos are open 24 hours and offer: blackjack, craps, roulette, slots, video poker and video keno. Optional games include: Spanish 21 (S21), Caribbean stud poker (CSP), let it ride (LIR), poker (P), three-card poker (TCP), keno (K), bingo (BG), big-6 wheel (B6) and off-track betting (OTB). The minimum age requirement is 21 for casino gambling and 18 for bingo.

For information on visiting North Dakota call the state's tourism office at (800) 435-5663 or go to: www.ndtourism.com.

Dakota Magic Casino & Hotel
16849 102nd Street SE
Hankinson, North Dakota 58041
(701) 634-3000
Website: www.dakotamagic.com
Map: #5 (50 miles S. of Fargo)

Toll-Free Number: (800) 325-6825
Rooms: 111 Price Range: $70-$110
Suites: 8 Price Range: $150-$240
Restaurants: 1 Liquor: Yes Valet Parking: No
Buffets: Brunch-$9.95 (Sat/Sun) L-$9.95
       D-$14.34/$19.95 (Fri/Sat)
Casino Size: 24,000 Square Feet
Other Games: P
Overnight RV Parking: Free/RV Dump: Fee
Senior Discount: Various on Mon if 55+
Special Features: 25-space RV park ($10 summer/$5 winter). 10% off rooms for seniors.

Four Bears Casino & Lodge
202 Frontage Rd
New Town, North Dakota 58763
(701) 627-4018
Website: www.4bearscasino.com
Map: #1 (150 miles N.W. of Bismarck)

Toll-Free Number: (800) 294-5454
Rooms: 97 Price Range: $74
Suites: 3 Price Range: $105
Restaurants: 2 Liquor: Yes Valet Parking: No
Buffets: B-$7.95 L-$8.95
       D-$15.95/$19.95 (Wed)
Other Games: P, TCP, LIR
Overnight RV Parking: Free/RV Dump: No
Senior Discount: Various Tue/Thu if 55+
Special Features: 85-space RV park ($25 per night). Nearby marina. 1,000-seat event center.

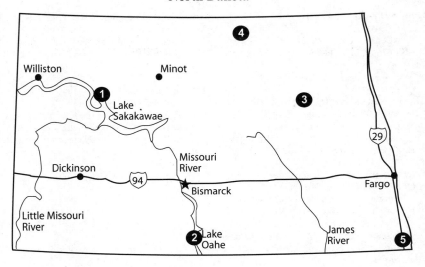

Prairie Knights Casino & Resort
7932 Highway 24
Fort Yates, North Dakota 58538
(701) 854-7777
Website: www.prairieknights.com
Map: **#2** (60 miles S. of Bismarck)

Toll-Free Number: (800) 425-8277
Rooms: 92 Price Range: $65-$75
Suites: 4 Price Range: $90-$135
Restaurants: 2 Liquor: Yes Valet Parking: No
Buffets: L/D-$9.95
Casino Size: 42,000 Square Feet
Other Games: TCP, LIR, No Roulette
Overnight RV Parking: Free/RV Dump: Free
Senior Discount: $7.95 buffet 11am -2pm
              (Mon-Fri) if 55+
Special Features: 12-space RV park ($5 per
night) at casino. 32-space RV park ($10 per
night) at marina. Free RV dump at marina. $50
rooms for slot club members. Convenience
store.

Sky Dancer Hotel & Casino
Highway 5 West
Belcourt, North Dakota 58316
(701) 244-2400
Website: www.skydancercasino.com
Map: **#4** (120 miles N.E. of Minot)

Toll-Free Number: (866) 244-9467
Rooms: 70 Price Range: $65-$90
Suites: 27 Price Range: $65-$90
Restaurants: 2 Liquor: Yes Valet Parking: No
Buffets: B-$7.95 (Sat/Sun) L-$6.95 (Mon-Fri)
D-$8.95/$9.95 (Mon)/$16.95 (Fri)/$15.95 (Sat)
Casino Size: 25,000 Square Feet
Other Games: P, LIR, BG, OTB (Tue-Sun),
              FCP,No Craps
Overnight RV Parking: Free/RV Dump: Free
Special Features: Gift shop.

Spirit Lake Casino & Resort
Highway 57
Spirit Lake, North Dakota 58370
(701) 766-4747
Website: www.spiritlakecasino.com
Map: **#3** (6 miles S. of Devil's Lake)

Toll-Free Number: (800) WIN-U-BET
Rooms: 108 Price Range: $50-$75
Suites: 16 Price Range: $79-$149
Restaurants: 3 Liquor: No Valet Parking: Free
Buffets: B-$5.50/$9.95 (Sun) L-$6.50
　　　　D-$10.95/$20.00 (Wed)
Casino Size: 45,000 Square Feet
Other Games: P, BG, No roulette
Overnight RV Parking: Must use RV park
Senior Discount: Various on Monday if 55+
Special Features: 15-space RV park ($18
per night). Gift shop. Discount smoke shop.
32-slip marina. Slot club members get 10%
off rooms.

Turtle Mountain Chippewa Mini-Casino
1 Sailor Ave
Belcourt, North Dakota 58316
(701) 477-6438
Map: **#4** (120 miles N.E. of Minot)

Restaurants: 1 Liquor: Yes Valet Parking: No
Other Games: Only Machines
Overnight RV Parking: Free/RV Dump: No
Special Features: Affiliated with and located
four miles east of Sky Dancer Hotel and
Casino.

OHIO

Ohio voters passed a statewide referendum in November 2009 to allow one casino in four major cities: Cleveland, Cincinnati, Columbus and Toledo.

The 96,000-square-foot Horseshoe Casino Cleveland is expected to open by early 2012 and more information can be found on their web site at horseshoe.com/info/cleveland

The Hollywood Casino Toledo will feature 119,000 square feet of gaming space and it is expected to open by mid-2012. Their web site is hollywoodcasinotoledo.com

The Horseshoe Casino Cincinatti is expected to open by spring 2013. More current information can be found on their horseshoe. com/info/cincinnati web site.

The Hollywood Casino Columbus will feature 130,000 square feet of gaming space and it is expected to open by mid-2012. Their web site is hollywoodcasinocolumbus.com

In July 2009 Ohio Governor Ted Strickland signed an executive order authorizing video lottery terminals to be allowed at seven horse tracks throughout the state. The VLTs will be regulated by the Ohio Lottery Commission and the earliest they are expected to be in operation is early 2012.

Following are the seven horse tracks that are eligible to have the VLTs. Call ahead to each track before visiting to be sure they have their VLTs in operation.

For tourism information, call the Ohio Division of Travel and Tourism at (800) BUCK-EYE, or visit their web site at www. discoverohio.com

Beulah Park
2811 SouthWest Boulevard
Grove City, Ohio 43123-2561
(614) 871-9600
Website: www.beulahpark.com
Map: **#1** (10 miles SW. of Columbus)

Restaurants: 1
Special Features: Live horse racing October-April. Daily simulcast.

Lebanon Raceway
665 North Broadway Street
Lebanon, Ohio 45036-1753
(513) 932-4936
Website: www.lebanonraceway.com
Map: **#2** (28 miles NE. of Cincinnatti)

Restaurants: 1 Snack Bar Admission: Free
Special Features: Live Harness racing February-May. Daily simulcast.

Northfield Park Racetrack
10705 Northfield Road
Northfield, Ohio 44067-1236
(330) 467-4101
Website: www.northfieldpark.com
Map: **#3** (10 miles SE. of Clevland)

Restaurants: 2
Admission: Free/$1.75 (Fri/Sat)
Clubhouse: $1.25 (Mon/Wed)/$3 (Fri/Sat)
Special Features:Daily Simulcast. Live racing Mon/Tue/Fri/Sat.

Raceway Park
5700 Telegraph Road
Toledo, Ohio 43612-3691
(419) 476-7751
Website: www.racewayparktoledo.com
Map: **#4**

Restaurants:1 Admission: $2.50
Special Features: Live racing mid-April-early-October Fri/Sat/Sun.

River Downs
6301 Kellogg Avenue
Cincinnati, Ohio 45230
(513) 232-8000
Website: www.riverdowns.com
Map: **#5**

Restaurants: 1 Admission: Free
Special Features: Live racing Mid-April-early-September. No races Mon/Wed. Daily simulcast.

Scioto Downs
6000 S High Street
Columbus, OH 43207
(614) 491-2515
Website: www.sciotodowns.com
Map: **#6**

Restaurants: 1
Admission: Free/$2 (Thu-Sat)
Special Features: Daily simulcast. Live Racing May-September Thu-Sat.

Thistledown
21501 Emery Road
N Randall, OH 44128
(216) 662-8600
Website: www.thistledown.com
Map: **#7** (16 miles SE. of Clevland)

Toll-free Number: (800) 289-9956
Restaurants: 1 Admission: Free
Special Features: Live Racing May-October. No races Sun/Wed. Daily simulcast.

OKLAHOMA

All Oklahoma Indian casinos are allowed to offer both Class II and Class III gaming machines.

Most casinos offer only Class II machines which look like slot machines, but are actually games of bingo and the spinning video reels are for "entertainment purposes only." Some casinos also offer traditional Class III slots.

In either case, the gaming machines are not allowed to accept or payout in coins. All payouts must be done by a printed receipt or via an electronic debit card. No public information is available concerning the payback percentages on gaming machines in Oklahoma.

Most, but not all, casinos with card games such as blackjack, let it ride or three-card poker, etc., offer a player-banked version where players must pay a commission to the house on every hand they play. The amount of the commission charged varies, depending on the rules of each casino, but it's usually 50 cents to $1 per hand played. Call the casino to see if they charge a commission. Roulette and dice games are not permitted in Oklahoma.

There are also two horse racing facilities in Oklahoma which feature Class II gaming machines.

All Oklahoma Indian casinos offer gaming machines. Other games include: blackjack (BJ), mini-baccarat (MB), poker (P), three-card poker (TCP), pai gow poker (PGP), let it ride (LIR), bingo (BG) and off-track betting (OTB).

Not all Oklahoma Indian casinos serve alcoholic beverages and the individual listings note which casinos do serve it. Unless otherwise noted, all casinos are open 24 hours. The minimum gambling age is 18 at some casinos and 21 at others.

For more information on visiting Oklahoma call the Oklahoma Tourism Department at (800) 652-6552 or go to: www.travelok.com

Ada Gaming Center
1500 North Country Club Road
Ada, Oklahoma 74820
Website: www.chickasaw.net
(580) 436-3740
Map: **#2** (85 miles S.E. of Oklahoma City)

Restaurants: 1 Liquor: No
Hours: 9:00am-7:00am Daily
Casino Size: 22,482 Square Feet
Other Games: BJ, P, OTB
Overnight RV Parking: No
Special Features: Located in travel plaza with gas station and convenience store.

Ada Travel Plaza
201 Latta Road
Ada, Oklahoma 74820
(580) 310-0900
Website: www.chickasaw.net
Map: **#2** (85 miles S.E. of Oklahoma City)

Restaurants: 1 Snack Bar Liquor: No
Overnight RV Parking: No
Special Features: Located in travel plaza with gas station and convenience store.

Black Gold Casino
288 Mulberry Lane (on Route 70)
Wilson, Oklahoma 73463
(580) 668-9248
Website: www.chickasaw.net
Map: **#39** (112 miles S. of Oklahoma City)

Casino Size: 3,744 Square Feet
Restaurants: 1 Snack Bar Liquor: No
Overnight RV Parking: Free/RV Dump: No
Special Features: Located in travel plaza with gas station and convenience store.

Bordertown Bingo and Casino
130 W. Oneida Street
Seneca, Missouri 64865
Website: www.bordertownbingo.com
(918) 666-1126
Map: **#42** (90 miles N.E. of Tulsa)

Toll-Free Number: (800) 957-2435
Restaurants: 1   Liquor: Yes
Other Games: BJ, P, TCP, BG, OTB
Overnight RV Parking: Must use RV park
Special Features: 30-space RV park ($9 night).
Casino is located directly on the Oklahoma/
Missouri border near Wyandotte.

Bordertown Outpost Casino
67901 East 100 Rd
Wyandotte, OK 74370
(918) 666-6770
store.bordertownbingo.com
Map: **#42** (90 miles N.E. of Tulsa)

Overnight RV Parking: Free/RV Dump: No

Buffalo Run Casino
1000 Buffalo Run Boulevard
Miami, Oklahoma 74354
(918) 542-7140
Website: www.buffalorun.com
Map: **#33** (89 miles N.E. of Tulsa)

Restaurants: 1   Liquor: Yes
Other Games: BJ, TCP, FCP, OTB
Overnight RV Parking: Free/RV Dump: No
Special Features: 2,000-seat showroom.

Cash Springs Gaming Center
West First and Muskogee Streets
Sulphur, Oklahoma 73086
(580) 622-2156
Map: **#35** (84 miles S. of Oklahoma City)

Toll-Free Number: (866) 622-2156
Restaurants: 1   Liquor: No
Overnight RV Parking: Free

Checotah Indian Community Bingo
830 North Broadway
Checotah, Oklahoma 74426
(918) 473-5200
Map: **#6** (120 miles E. of Oklahoma City)

Restaurants: 1
Hours: 8am-6am
Casino Size: 8,000 Square Feet
Other Games: BG
Overnight RV Parking: No

Cherokee Casino - Ft. Gibson
US Highway 62
Ft. Gibson, Oklahoma 74338
(918) 207-3593
Website: www.cherokeestarrewards.com
Map: **#54** (80 miles E. of Tulsa)

Restaurants: 1 Deli   Liquor: No
Overnight RV Parking: No
Senior Discount: various Thu if 55+

Cherokee Casino - Ramona
31501 US 75 Hwy
Ramona, OK 74061
(918) 535-3800
Website: www.cherokeestarrewards.com
Map: **#60** (30 miles N. of Tulsa)

Restaurants: 1

Cherokee Casino & Inn - Roland
Interstate 40 and Highway 64
Roland, Oklahoma 74954
(918) 427-7491
Website: www.cherokeestarrewards.com
Map: **#8** (175 miles E. of Oklahoma City)

Toll-Free Number: (800) 256-2338
Rooms: 45 Room Rates: $59-$119
Suites: 12 Room Rates: $89-$179
Restaurants: 1 Deli   Liquor: Beer Only
Casino Size: 28,000 Square Feet
Other Games: P, BJ, TCP
Overnight RV Parking: Free/RV Dump: No

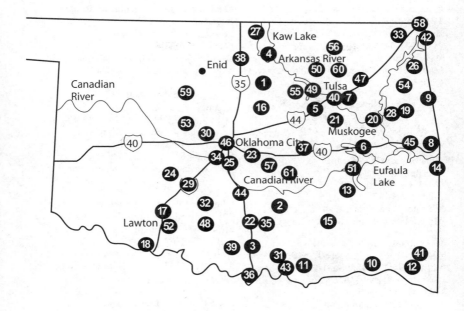

Cherokee Casino - Sallisaw
1621 West Ruth Avenue
Sallisaw, OK 74955
(918) 774-1600
Website: www.cherokeestarrewards.com
Map: **#45** (160 miles E. of Oklahoma City)

Toll-Free Number: (800) 256-2338
Restaurants: 1   Liquor: Beer only
Casino Size: 22,000 Square Feet
Other Games: BJ, P
Overnight RV Parking: Free/RV Dump: No

Cherokee Casino - Tahlequah
16489 Highway 62
Tahlequah, Oklahoma 74464
(918) 207-3600
Website: www.cherokeestarrewards.com
Map: **#19** (83 miles S.E. of Tulsa)

Restaurants: 1 Snack Bar   Liquor: No
Other Games: BJ, P, TCP
Overnight RV Parking: Free/RV Dump: No

Cherokee Casino - West Siloam Springs
7300 West US Highway 412
W. Siloam Springs, Oklahoma 74338
(918) 422-6301
Website: www.cherokeestarrewards.com
Map: **#9** (85 miles E. of Tulsa)

Toll-Free Number: (800) 754-4111
Restaurants: 2   Liquor: Yes
Other Games: BJ, P
Overnight RV Parking: Free/RV Dump: No

Chisholm Trail Casino
7807 N. Highway 81
Duncan, Oklahoma 73533
(580) 255-1668
Website: www.chilsomtrailcasino.com
Map: **#48** (79 miles S. of Oklahoma City)

Casino Size: 22,000 Square Feet
Restaurants: 1   Liquor: No
Overnight RV Parking: Free/RV Dump: No
Other Games: BJ, TCP

Choctaw Casino - Broken Bow
1790 South Park Drive
Broken Bow, Oklahoma 74728
(580) 584-5450
Website: www.choctawcasinos.com
Map: **#41** (235 miles S.E. of Oklahoma City)

Restaurants: 1 Snack Bar   Liquor: No
Hours: 10am-2am/5am (Fri/Sat)
Overnight RV Parking: Free/ RV Dump: No

Choctaw Casino - Grant
US Highway 271
Grant, Oklahoma 74738
(580) 326-8397
Website: www.choctawcasinos.com
Map: **#10** (200 miles S. of Oklahoma City)

Restaurants: 1 Deli   Liquor: No
Rooms: 40 Price Range: $72-$102
Buffets: B- $8.99 (Sat/Sun) L-$8.99
     D-$11.99/$19.99 (Fri/Sat)
Other Games: BJ, P
Overnight RV Parking: No

Choctaw Casino - Idabel
1425 Southeast Washington
Idabel, Oklahoma 74745
(580) 286-5710
Website: www.choctawcasinos.com
Map: **#12** (240 miles S.E. of Oklahoma City)

Toll-Free Number: (800) 634-2582
Restaurants: 1   Liquor: No
Casino Size: 11,000 Square Feet
Overnight RV Parking: Must check-in at front desk/RV Dump: No

Choctaw Casino - McAlester
1638 South George Nigh Expressway
McAlester, Oklahoma 74501-7411
(918) 423-8161
Website: www.choctawcasinos.com
Map: **#13** (130 miles S.E. of Oklahoma City)

Toll-Free Number: (877) 904-8444
Restaurants: 1   Liquor: No
Other Games: BJ, P, TCP
Casino Size: 17,500 Square Feet
Overnight RV Parking: Free/RV Dump: No
Special Features: Blackjack games open at 2pm

Choctaw Casino - Pocola
Interstate 540
Pocola, Oklahoma 74902
(918) 436-7761
Website: www.choctawcasinos.com
Map: **#14** (195 miles E. of Oklahoma City)

Toll-Free Number: (800) 590-5825
Restaurants: 2   Liquor: No
Buffets: L-$8.99 (Mon)/$10.99 (Sat/Sun)
     D-$10.99/$14.99 (Fri/Sat)
Other Games: BJ, OTB, P
Overnight RV Parking: Free/RV Dump: No
Special Features: Card-based roulette.

Choctaw Casino - Stringtown
895 North Highway 69
Stringtown, Oklahoma 74569
(580) 346-7862
Website: www.choctawcasinos.com
Map: **#15** (163 miles S.E. of Oklahoma City)

Restaurants: 2   Liquor: No
Hours: 10am-1am/4am (Thu-Sat)/1am (Sun)
Overnight RV Parking: Free/RV Dump: No

Choctaw Casino Resort
4418 South Highway 69/75
Durant, Oklahoma 74701
(580) 920-0160
Website: www.choctawcasinos.com
Map: **#11** (150 miles S.E. of Oklahoma City)

Toll-Free Number: (800) 788-2464
Room Reservations: (580) 931-8340
Rooms: 40 Price Range: $69-$99
Suites: 4 Price Range: $99-$129
Restaurants: 2   Liquor: No
Buffets: B-$11.99 (Sun) L- $8.99
     D-$14.99/$19.99 (Fri/Sat)
Casino Size: 36,000 Square Feet
Other Games: BJ, P, BG (Thu-Sun)
Senior Discount: various Thu if 55+
Overnight RV Parking: Must use RV Park/
     RV Dump: No
Special Features: Free shuttle buses from Dallas and Fort Worth. 75-space RV park ($30-$50 nightly).

Cimarron Casino
821 W. Freeman Avenue
Perkins, Oklahoma 74059
(405) 547-5352
Website: www.cimarroncasino.com
Map: **#16** (60 miles N. of Oklahoma City)

Restaurants: 1 Snack Bar   Liquor: Yes
Other Games: P
Overnight RV Parking: No

Comanche Nation Casino
402 South East Interstate Drive
Lawton, Oklahoma 73502
(580) 354-2000
Website: www.comanchenationcasino.com
Map: **#17** (86 miles S.W. of Oklahoma City)

Toll-Free Number: (866) 354-2500
Restaurants: 1   Liquor: Yes
Other Games: BJ, TCP, P, OTB
Senior Special: Various on Wed if 55+
Overnight RV Parking: Free, must get pass from front desk first (With Hook Ups)/RV Dump: No

Comanche Red River Casino
Highway 36 and Highway 70
Devol, Oklahoma 73531
(580) 299-3378
Website: www.comancheredrivercasino.com
Map: **#18** (125 miles S.W. of Oklahoma City)

Toll-Free Number: (866) 280-3261
Restaurants: 1   Liquor: Yes
Casino Size: 52,500 Square Feet
Other Games: BJ, P, TCP
Overnight RV Parking: Check-in at front desk (With Hook Ups)/RV Dump: No
Senior Special: Various on Mon if 55+
Special Features: Drive-thru smoke shop.

Comanche Spur Casino
9047 US Highway 62
Eldon, Oklahoma 73538
(580) 492-5502
Website: www.comanchespur.com
Map: **#29** (75 miles S.W. of Oklahoma City)

Restaurants: 1   Liquor: No
Hours: 11am-12am/2am (Fri/Sat)
Senior Special: Various on Wed if 55+
Overnight RV Parking: No
Special features: Smoke shop. Convenience store.

Comanche Star Casino
Rt 3 and Hwy 53
Walters, Oklahoma 73572
(580) 875-2092
Map: **#52** (25 miles S.E. of Lawton)

Restaurants: 1   Liquor: No
Hours: 12pm-11pm/1am (Fri/Sat)
Casino Size: 7,000 Square Feet
Overnight RV Parking: No

Creek Nation Casino - Bristow
121 West Lincoln
Bristow, Oklahoma 74010
(918) 367-9168
Website: www.creeknationbristow.com
Map: **#5** (60 miles N.E. of Oklahoma City)

Restaurants: 1 Snack Bar   Liquor: No
Hours: 8am-6am
Overnight RV Parking: No

Creek Nation Casino - Eufaula
806 Forest Avenue
Eufaula, Oklahoma 74432
(918) 689-9191
Map: **#51** (135 miles E. of Oklahoma City)

Restaurants: 1 Snack Bar   Liquor: No
Hours: 10am-3am/4am (Fri/Sat)
Overnight RV Parking: No

Creek Nation Casino - Holdenville
221 East Willow St.
Holdenville, OK 74848
(405) 379-3321
Map: **#61** (75 miles S.E. of Oklahoma City)

Hours: 12pm-12am/2am (Fri/Sat)/10pm (Sun)
Overnight RV Parking: No

Creek Nation Casino - Muscogee
3420 West Peak Boulevard
Muskogee, Oklahoma 74403
(918) 683-1825
Website: www.creeknationcasino.net
Map: **#20** (50 miles S.E. of Tulsa)

Restaurants: 1   Liquor: No
Other Games: BJ, P, TCP, BG
Casino Size: 22,500 Square Feet
Senior Discount: Various Mon if 55+
Overnight RV Parking: Free/RV Dump: No

Creek Nation Casino - Okemah
1100 S. Woodie Guthrie
Okemah, Oklahoma 74859
(918) 623-0051
Map: **#37** (72 miles E. of Oklahoma City)

Hours: 8am-6am Daily
Restaurants: 1   Liquor: No
Other Games: BG
Overnight RV Parking: Free/RV Dump: No

Creek Nation Casino - Okmulgee
1901 North Wood Drive
Okmulgee, Oklahoma 74447
(918) 756-8400
Website: www.cncokmulgee.com
Map: **#21** (45 miles S. of Tulsa)

Restaurants: 1   Liquor: No
Casino Size: 10,000 Square Feet
Overnight RV Parking: Free/RV Dump: No

Creek Nation Travel Plaza
Highway 75 and 56 Loop
Okmulgee, Oklahoma 74447
(918) 752-0090
Map: **#21** (45 miles S. of Tulsa)

Restaurants: 1 Snack Bar   Liquor: No
Overnight RV Parking: Free/RV Dump: No
Special Features: Gas station and convenience
store. Burger King.

Davis Trading Post
Interstate 35 and Highway 7
Davis, Oklahoma 73030
(580) 369-5360
Website: www.chickasaw.net
Map: **#22** (75 miles S. of Oklahoma City)

Restaurants: 1   Liquor: No
Overnight RV Parking: Free/RV Dump: No

Downstream Casino Resort
69300 East Nee Road
Quapaw, Oklahoma 74363
(918) 919-6000
Website: downstreamcasino.com
Map: **#58** (On the border of OK, MO, and KS)

Toll-Free Number: (888) 396-7876
Rooms: 200 Price Range: $99-$199
Suites: 22 Price Range: $199-$399
Restaurants:5   Liquor: Yes
Buffet: B-$8.95 (Sun) L-$9.95/$10.95 (Sun)
          D-$16.95/19.95(Fri/Sat)
Casino size: 70,000 Square feet
Other Games: P, FCP, OTB, TCP, MB, PGP
Special Features: Only Casino/Hotel in the
country located in three States: Oklahoma,
Missouri, and Kansas. Gambling Age: 18

Duck Creek Casino
10085 Ferguson Road
Beggs, Oklahoma 74421
(918) 267-3468
Map: **#21** (35 miles S. of Tulsa)

Restaurants: 1 Snack Bar   Liquor: No
Hours: 9am-7am Daily
Casino Size: 5,000 Square Feet
Overnight RV Parking: No

Feather Warrior Casino - Canton
301 NW Lake Road
Canton, Oklahoma 73724
(580) 886-2490
Website: web-featherwarrior.com
Map: **#59** (60 miles N. W. of Okla. City)

Restaurants: 1 Snack Bar   Liquor: No
Hours: 11am-2am/10am-2am (Fri-Sun)
Casino Size: 2,200 Square Feet
Overnight RV Parking: Free/RV Dump: No

Feather Warrior Casino - Watonga
1407 S. Clarence Nash Boulevard
Watonga, Oklahoma 73772
(580) 623-7333
Website: web-featherwarrior.com
Map: **#53** (70 miles N. W. of Okla. City)

Restaurants: 1 Snack Bar   Liquor: No
Hours: 11am-2am/10am-2am (Fri-Sun)
Casino Size: 2,200 Square Feet
Overnight RV Parking: Free/RV Dump: No

Fire Lake Casino
41207 Hardesty Road
Shawnee, Oklahoma 74801
(405) 273-2242
Website: www.winatfirelake.com
Map: **#23** (38 miles E. of Oklahoma City)

Restaurants: 1   Liquor: Yes
Buffets: B-$4.99 (Sat/Sun) L-$6.99/$8.99 (Fri)
          D- $8.99/$14.99 (Fri)
Other Games: BJ, P, BG, OTB, TCP
Overnight RV Parking: Free/RV Dump: No
Senior Discount: Various Sun if 55+

Fire Lake Grand Casino
777 Grand Casino Boulevard
Shawnee, Oklahoma 74851
Website: www.firelakegrand.com
(405) 964-7263
Map: **#23** (38 miles E. of Oklahoma City)

Restaurants: 3   Liquor: Yes
Buffets: B-$9.95 (Sat)/12.95 (Sun) L-$7.95
          D-$9.95/ $21.95 (Fri)
Casino Size: 125,000 Square Feet
Other Games: BJ, P, K
Overnight RV Parking: Free/RV Dump: No
Special Features: 3,000-seat event center.

First Council Casino
12875 North Highway 77
Newkrik, Oklahoma 74647
Website: www.myfirstwin.com
(580) 448-3015
Map: **#27** (Just south of the Kansas State line)

Toll-Free: (877) 725-2670
Restaurants: 3   Liquor: Yes
Casino Size: 125,000 Square Feet
Other Games: BJ, P
Overnight RV Parking: Free/RV Dump: No
Special Features: 3,000-seat event center.

Fort Sill Apache Casino
2315 East Gore Boulevard
Lawton, Oklahoma 73502
(580) 248-5905
Website: www.Fortsillapachecasino.com
Map: **#17** (86 miles S.W. of Oklahoma City)

Restaurants: 1 (2 snack bars)   Liquor: Yes
Casino Size: 7,700 Square Feet
Other games: BJ, TCP, C
Overnight RV Parking: Free/RV Dump: No
Special Features: Offers card versions of
craps.

Gold Mountain Casino
1410 Sam Noble Parkway
Ardmore, Oklahoma 73401
(580) 223-3301
Website: www.chickasaw.net
Map: **#3** (100 miles S. of Oklahoma City)

Restaurants: 1   Liquor: No
Casino Size: 8,620 Square Feet
Overnight RV Parking: Free/RV Dump: No
Special Features: Tobacco shop.

Gold River Casino
Highway 281
Anadarko, Oklahoma 73005
(405) 247-6979
Website: www.goldriverok.com
Map: **#24** (60 miles S.W. of Oklahoma City)

Toll-Free Number: (800) 280-1018
Restaurants: 1   Liquor: No
Casino Size: 12,000 Square Feet
Other Games: BJ, P
Senior Discount: Various Tue if 55+
Overnight RV Parking: Free/RV Dump: No

Golden Pony Casino
Hwy. I-40, Exit 227 Clearview Rd.
Okemah, Oklahoma 74859
(918) 623-2620
Map: **#37** (72 miles E. of Oklahoma City)

Toll-free Number: (877) 623-0072
Restaurants: Snack Bar   Liquor: No
Overnight RV Parking: Free/RV Dump: No

Goldsby Gaming Center
1038 West Sycamore Road
Norman, Oklahoma 73072
(405) 329-5447
Website: www.chickasaw.net
Map: **#25** (21 miles S. of Oklahoma City)

Restaurants: 1   Liquor: No
Other Games: BG
Casino Size: 23,007 Square Feet
Overnight RV Parking: No

Grand Lake Casino
24701 S. 655th Road
Grove, Oklahoma 74344
(918) 786-8528
Website: grandlakecasino.com
Map: **#26** (80 miles N.E. of Tulsa)

Toll-Free Number: (800) 426-4640
Restaurants: 1   Liquor: Yes
Other Games: BJ, P, TCP
Casino Size: 45,000 Square Feet
Overnight RV Parking: No

Hard Rock Hotel & Casino Tulsa
770 W Cherokee Street
Catoosa, Oklahoma 74015
(918) 384-7800
Website: www.cherokeecasino.com
Map: **#7** (a suburb of Tulsa)

Toll-Free Number: (800) 760-6700
Rooms: 130   Price Range: $59-$149
Suites: 20   Price Range: $160-$515
Restaurants: 4   Liquor: Yes
Buffets: B-$6.99   L-$8.99
      D-$13.99/$22.99 (Fri/Sat)
Casino Size: 80,000 Square Feet
Other Games: BJ, P, TCP
Overnight RV Parking: Free/RV Dump: No

High Winds Casino
61475 E. 100 Road
Miami, Oklahoma 74354
(918) 541-9463
Website: highwindscasino.com
Map: **#33** (89 miles N.E. of Tulsa)

Restaurants: 1   Liquor: Yes
Overnight RV Parking: Free/RV Dump: No

Kaw Southwind Casino
5640 North LaCann Drive
Newkirk, Oklahoma 74647
(580) 362-2578
Website: www.southwindcasino.com
Map: **#27** (106 miles N. of Oklahoma City)

Toll-Free Number: (866) KAW-BINGO
Restaurants: 1   Liquor: No
Other Games: BJ, BG, P
Senior Discount: Various Mon if 55+
Overnight RV Parking: Free/RV Dump: No

Keetoowah Casino
2450 South Muskogee
Tahlequah, Oklahoma 74464
 (918) 456-6131
Website: keetoowahcherokeecasino.com
Map: **#28** (15 miles S.E. of Tulsa)

Restaurants: 1   Liquor: No
Casino Hours: 8am-2am/ 24 hours (Thu-Sat)/
          10am-2am (Sun)
Overnight RV Parking: Yes

Kickapoo Casino
25230 East Highway 62
Harrah, Oklahoma 73045
(405) 964-4444
Website: kickapoo-casino.com
Map: **#23** (31 miles E. of Oklahoma City)

Restaurants: 1   Liquor: No
Other Games: BJ
Senior Special: Various on Tue if 55+
Overnight RV Parking: Free/RV Dump: No

Kiowa Casino
County Road 1980
Devol, Oklahoma 73531
(580)299-3333
Website:www.kiowacasino.com
Map: **#18** (125 miles S.W. of Oklahoma
City)

Toll-Free Number: (866)370-4077
Restaurants: 3   Liquor: Beer Only
Buffets: B-$11.50 (Sun)
          L-$9.50/$11.50 (Sat)
          D-$11.50/$21.00 (Fri/Sat)
Other Games: BJ, TCP,
Overnight RV Parking: Free/RV Dump: No

Little Bit of Paradise Casino
12901 N. Highway 77
New Kirk, OK 74647
(580) 448-3201
Map: **#27** (Just south of the Kansas State line)

Overnight RV Parking: Free/RV Dump: No

Lucky Star Casino - Clinton
101 N. Indian Hospital Road
Clinton, Oklahoma 73601
(580) 323-6599
Website: www.luckystarcasino.org
Map: **#29** (85 miles W. of Oklahoma City)

Restaurants: 1   Liquor: No
Other Games: P, BJ
Overnight RV Parking: Free/RV Dump: No

Lucky Star Casino - Concho
7777 North Highway 81
Concho, Oklahoma 73022
(405) 262-7612
Website: www.luckystarcasino.org
Map: **#30** (35 miles N.W. of Oklahoma City)

Restaurants: 1   Liquor: Yes
Other Games: BJ, P
Casino Size: 40,000 Square Feet
Overnight RV Parking: Free/RV Dump: Free
Special features: Free RV hookups (must
register first).

Lucky Turtle Casino
64499 East Highway 60
Wyandotte, Oklahoma 74370
(918) 678-3767
Map: **#42** (90 miles N.E. of Tulsa)

Restaurants: 1   Liquor: No
Casino Size: 4,000 Square Feet
Overnight RV Parking: No
Special Features: Convenience store.

Madill Gaming Center
902 South First Street
Madill, Oklahoma 73446
(580) 795-7301
website: www.chickasaw.net
Map: **#31** (122 miles S. of Oklahoma City)

Restaurants: 1   Liquor: No
Hours: 8am-8pm/10am-8pm (Sun)
Casino Size: 2,071 Square Feet
Overnight RV Parking: No

Marlow Gaming Center
Route 3
Marlow, Oklahoma 73055
(580) 255-1668
Map: **#32** (79 miles S. of Oklahoma City)

Restaurants: 1   Liquor: No
Hours: 9am-7am Daily
Overnight RV Parking: Free/RV Dump: No

Miami Tribe Entertainment
202 South 8 Tribes Trail
Miami, Oklahoma 74354
(918) 542-8670
Map: **#33** (89 miles N.E. of Tulsa)

Restaurants: 1   Liquor: No
Overnight RV Parking: No

Native Lights Casino
12375 N. Highway 77
Newkirk, Oklahoma 74647
(580) 448-3100
Website: www.nativelightscasino.com
Map: **#27** (106 miles N. of Oklahoma City)

Toll-Free Number: (877)468-3100
Restaurants: 1   Liquor: Yes
Other Games: BJ, TCP, LIR
Overnight RV Parking: Free/RV Dump: No

Newcastle Gaming Center
2457 Highway 62 Service Road
Newcastle, Oklahoma 73065
(405) 387-6013
Website: www.chickasaw.net
Map: **#34** (19 miles S. of Oklahoma City)

Restaurants: 1   Liquor: Yes
Casino Size: 44,622 Sqaure Feet
Other Games: BJ, OTB, TCP
Overnight RV Parking: Free/RV Dump: No

Osage Casino - Bartlesville
222 Allen Rd.
Bartlesville, Oklahoma 74003
(918) 335-7519
Website: www.milliondollarelm.com
Map: **#56** (50 miles N. of Tulsa)

Restaurants: 2   Liquor: No
Buffet: D-$12.00/$18.99 (Fri)
Other Games: BJ, P
Senior Discount: Various Mon-Wed if 50+
Overnight RV Parking: No

Osage Casino - Hominy
Highway 99
Hominy, Oklahoma 74035
(918) 885-2990
Website: www.milliondollarelm.com
Map: **#49** (44 miles N.W. of Tulsa)

Restaurants: 1   Liquor: No
Hours: 10am-12:00am/ 2:00am (Thurs)/
3:00am (Fri/Sat)
Other Games: BJ, P
Senior Discount: Various Sun/Wed/Thu if 50+
Overnight RV Parking: Free/RV Dump:No

Osage Casino - Pawhuska
201 N.W. 15th Street (at Highway 99)
Pawhuska, Oklahoma 74056
(918) 287-1072
Website: www.milliondollarelm.com
Map: **#50** (a suburb of Tulsa)

Restaurants: 1   Liquor: No
Hours: 10am-12:00am / 2:00am (Thurs)/
10:00am-3:00am (Fri/Sat)
Senior Discount: Various Sun/Wed if 50+
Overnight RV Parking: Free/RV Dump: No

Osage Casino - Ponca City
73 N City View Road
Ponca City, Oklahoma 74601
(918) 335-7519
Website: www.milliondollarelm.com
Map: **#5** (50 miles N.W. of Tulsa)

Restaurants: 2   Liquor: No
Hours: 10am-3am/4am(Thu-Sun)
Senior Discount: Various Mon-Thu if 50+
Overnight RV Parking: No

Osage Casino - Sand Springs
301 Blackjack Drive (on Highway 97T)
Sand Springs, Oklahoma 74063
(918) 699-7727
Website: www.milliondollarelm.com
Map: **#40** (a suburb of Tulsa)

Toll-Free Number: (877) 246-8777
Restaurants: 2   Liquor: Yes
Other Games: BJ, P, TCP
Senior Discount: Various Mon-Thu if 50+
Overnight RV Parking: No

Osage Casino - Tulsa
951 W. 36th Street North
Tulsa, Oklahoma 74127
(918) 699-7740
Website: www.milliondollarelm.com
Map: **#40**

Toll-Free Number: (877) 246-8777
Restaurants: 1   Liquor: Yes
Casino Size: 47,000 Square Feet
Other Games: BJ, P, TCP
Senior Discount: Various Mon-Thu if 50+
Overnight RV Parking: Free/RV Dump: No

Peoria Gaming Center
8520 S. Hwy 69A
Miami, Oklahoma 74354
(918) 540-0303
Map: **#33** (89 miles N.E. of Tulsa)

Restaurants: 1 Snack Bar Liquor: No
Hours: 10am-Midnight/2am (Fri-Sat)
Overnight RV Parking: No
Special features: Adjacent to Buffalo Run
Casino which allows overnight RV parking.

Quapaw Casino
58100 E. 66th Road
Miami, Oklahoma 74355
(918) 540-9100
Website: www.quapawcasino.com
Map: **#33** (89 miles N.E. of Tulsa)

Restaurants: 1   Liquor: Yes
Other Games: BJ, TCP, FCP
Overnight RV Parking: Free up to 3 days/
RV Dump: No
Special Features: Senior specials on Wed.

Rivermist Casino
Hwy 65 and Hwy 99
Konowa, OK 74849
(580) 925-3994
Map: **#2** (75 miles S.E. of Oklahoma City)

Restaurants: 1
Hours: 10am-12am/2am (Thu-Sat)

River Spirit Casino
1616 East 81st Street
Tulsa, Oklahoma 74137
(918) 299-8518
Website: www.creeknationcasino.com
Map: **#40**

Toll-Free Number: (800) 299-2738
Restaurants: 5   Liquor: No
Buffets: B-$9.95/$21.95 (Sun) L-$9.99
          D-$12.49/$27.49 (Thu/Sat)/$24.99 (Fri)
Casino Size: 81,000 Square Feet
Other Games: BJ, P, TCP, BG
Senior Disc: Buffet discount Mon/Tue if 50+
Overnight RV Parking: Free/RV Dump: No
Special Features: Separate nonsmoking
casino. Free shuttle to/from local hotels.

Riverwind Casino
1544 W. State Highway 9
Norman, Oklahoma 73072
(405) 364-7171
Website: www.riverwind.com
Map: **#25** (21 miles S. of Oklahoma City)

Toll-Free Number: (888) 440-1880
Restaurants: 2   Liquor: No
Buffets: L-$12.00/$14.00 (Sat)/$16.00 (Sun)
          D-$14.00/$9.00 (Tue)/
          $23.99 (Fri)/$16.00 (Sun)
Casino Size: 60,000 Square Feet
Other Games: BJ, P, OTB
Overnight RV Parking: Free/RV Dump: No
Special Features: 1,500-seat showroom.
Senior Breakfast special Wednesdays.

Sac and Fox Casino
42008 Westech Road
Shawnee, Oklahoma 74804
(405)275-4700
Web Site: www.sacandfoxcasino.com
Map: **#23** (40 Miles E. of Okalhoma City)

Restaurants: 1   Liquor: Yes
Casino Size: 8,600 Sqaure Feet
Other Games: P, BJ, C, TCP
Overnight RV Parking: No

Sac and Fox Casino - Stroud
356120 E 926 Road
Stroud, Oklahoma 74079
(918) 968-2540
Web Site: www.sacandfoxcasino.com
Map: **#5** (60 miles N.E. of Oklahoma City)

Restaurants: 1   Liquor: Yes
Casino Size: 8,600 Sqaure Feet
Other Games: P, BJ, C, TCP
Overnight RV Parking: No

Sac and Fox Sports Center
42008 Westech Road
Shawnee, Oklahoma 74804
(405)273-0409
Web Site: www.sacandfoxcasino.com
Map: **#23** (40 Miles E. of Okalhoma City)

Restaurants: 1   Liquor: Yes
Casino Size: 8,600 Square Feet
Overnight RV Parking: No

Seminole Nation Casino
11277 Hwy 99
Seminole, OK 74868
(405) 382-3218
Map: **#57** (60 miles S.E of Oklahoma City)

Restaurants: 1 Snack Bar   Liquor:No
Other Games: BG
Overnight RV Parking: No

Seminole Nation Trading Post
US 59 and US 270
Wewoka, Oklahoma 74884
(405) 257-2010
Map: **#57** (60 miles E. of Oklahoma City)

Toll-Free Number: (866) 723-4005
Restaurants: 1   Liquor: Yes
Casino Size: 3,424 Square Feet
Overnight RV Parking: No
Special Features: Convenience store.

Seven Clans Paradise Casino
7500 Highway 177
Red Rock, Oklahoma 74651
(580) 723-4005
Website: okparadisecasino.com
Map: **#1** (82 miles N. of Oklahoma City)

Toll-Free Number: (866) 723-4005
Restaurants: 1   Liquor: Yes
Casino Size: 23,000 Square Feet
Other Games: BJ
Overnight RV Parking: Must use RV park
Senior Discount: Various Thu if 55+
Special Features: 7-space RV park ($10 per night). Convenience store and gas station.

Silver Buffalo Casino
620 East Colorado Drive
Anadarko, Oklahoma 73005
(405) 247-5471
Website: www.silverbuffalocasino.com
Map: **#24** (60 miles S.W. of Oklahoma City)

Restaurants: 1   Liquor: Beer Only
Hours: 9am-5am/6am (Fri/Sat)
Overnight RV Parking: Free/RV Dump: No

Stone Wolf Casino & Grill
54251 S 349 Rd
Pawnee, OK 74058
(918) 454-7777
www.stonewolfcasino.com
Map: **#55** (57 miles N.W. of Tulsa)

Hours: 8am-2am/7am-2am (Thu)/24hrs (Fri-Sun)
Buffet: B-$7.00 (Thu-Sun)
Senior discount: Various Thu if 55+

Sugar Creek Casino
4200 N. Broadway
Hinton, OK 73047
(405) 542-2946
Website: www.Sugarcreekcasino.net

Buffet: L-$6.99 D-$7.99/$9.99 (Wed)/
     $9.99 (Fri/Sat)
Overnight RV Parking: No

The Stables Casino
530 H Street Southeast
Miami, Oklahoma 74354
(918) 542-7884
Website: www.the-stables.com
Map: **#33** (89 miles N.E. of Tulsa)

Toll-Free Number: (877) 774-7884
Restaurants: 1   Liquor: Yes
Other Games: BJ, OTB
Overnight RV Parking: No

Texoma Gaming Center
HC 68 Box 13
Kingston, OK 73439
(580) 564-6000
Website: www.chickasaw.net
Map: **#43** (130 miles S. of Oklahoma City)

Restaurants: 1   Liquor: No
Overnight RV Parking: No
Special Features: Convenience store and KFC.

Thackerville Gaming Center
I-35 exit 1
Thackerville, OK 73459
(580)276-1727
Map: **#36** (124 miles S. of Oklahoma City)

Overnight RV Parking: Free/RV Dump: No

Thackerville Travel Gaming
Interstate 35, Exit 1
Thackerville, Oklahoma 73459
(580) 276-4706
Website: www.chickasaw.net
Map: **#36** (124 miles S. of Oklahoma City)

Restaurants: 1 Snack Bar   Liquor: No
Casino Hours: 9am - 6am
Overnight RV Parking: Free/RV Dump: No

Thunderbird Casino - Norman
15700 East State Highway 9
Norman, Oklahoma 73026
(405) 360-9270
Website: thunderbirdcasino.net
Map: **#25** (21 miles S. of Oklahoma City)

Toll-Free Number: (800) 259-5825
Restaurants: 1   Liquor: Yes
Other Games: BJ, TCP
Casino Size: 40,000 Square Feet
Overnight RV Parking: Free

Thunderbird Casino - Shawnee
2051 S. Gordon Cooper Dr
Shawnee, OK 74801
(405) 360-9270
Website: thunderbirdcasino.net
Map: **#23** (38 miles E. of Oklahoma City)

Toll-Free Number: (800) 259-5825
Hours: 9am-2am/24 hours (Fri/Sat)

Tonkawa Casino
1000 Allen Drive
Tonkawa, Oklahoma 74653
(580) 628-2624
Website: www.tonkawacasino.com
Map: **#38** (91 miles N. of Oklahoma City)

Restaurants: 1 Snack Bar   Liquor: No
Other Games: BJ, LIR
Hours: 10am-2am/ 24 hours (Fri/Sat)
Overnight RV Parking: Free/RV Dump: No

Trading Post Casino
291 Agency Road
Pawnee, Oklahoma 74058
(918) 762-4466
Website: www.tradingpostcasino.com
Map: **#55** (57 miles N.W. of Tulsa)

Restaurants: 1   Liquor: No
Casino Size: 3,600 Square Feet
Overnight RV Parking: No
Special Features: Convenience store/gas station.

Treasure Valley Casino
I-35, Exit 55 (Highway 7)
Davis, Oklahoma 73030
(580) 369-2895
Website: www.chickasaw.net
Map: **#22** (75 miles S. of Oklahoma City)

Rooms: 59 Price Range: $69-$89
Suites: 2 Price Range: $95-$129
Restaurants: 2   Liquor: No
Casino Size: 19,666 Square Feet
Other Games: BJ, P, TCP
Overnight RV Parking: Free/RV Dump: No

Two Rivers Casino
20 White Eagle Dr
Ponca City, OK 74601
(580)762-5444
Map: **#5** (50 miles N.W. of Tulsa)

Restaurants: 1
Hours: 12pm-12am/2am (Fri/Sat)
Other Games: BG
Overnight RV Parking: Free/RV Dump: No

Washita Gaming Center
P.O. Box 307
Paoli, Oklahoma 73074
(405) 484-7777
Website: www.chickasaw.net
Map: **#44** (52 miles S. of Oklahoma City)

Restaurants: 1   Liquor: No
Casino Size: 6,335 Square Feet
Overnight RV Parking: No
Special Features: Convenience store.

Wilson Travel Plaza
354 Route 1
Wilson, Oklahoma 73463
(580) 668-9248
Map: **#39** (112 miles S. of Oklahoma City)

Restaurants: 1   Liquor: No
Overnight RV Parking: Free/RV Dump: No

WinStar Casino
Interstate 35, Exit 1
Thackerville, Oklahoma 73459
(580) 276-4229
Website: www.winstarworldcasino.com
Map: **#36** (124 miles S. of Oklahoma City)

Toll-Free Number: (800) 622-6317
Rooms: 395 price range: $79-$109
Suites: 40 price range:$89-$179
Restaurants: 5   Liquor: No
Buffet: B-$10.99 L-$14.99 D-$18.99
Other Games: BJ, P, BG,
          MB, TCP, PGP, OTB
Casino Size: 169,824 Square Feet
Overnight RV Parking: Free/RV Dump: No
Senior Discount: $1 off buffets and
                various Wed if 55+
Special Features: 152-space RV ($25 per
night)

Wyandotte Nation Casino
100 Jackpot Place
Wyandotte, Oklahoma 74370
(918) 678-4946
Website: www.wyandottecasinos.com
Map: **#26** (90 miles N.E. of Tulsa)

Toll-Free Number: (866) 447-4946
Restaurants: 2   Liquor: Yes
Other Games: BJ, TCP
Overnight RV Parking: No

Pari-Mutuels

Oklahoma has two horse tracks which offer Class II electronic video gaming machines as well as pari-mutuel betting on horse races. Admission is free to the casinos, but there is an admission charge for horse racing. The minimum gambling age is 18.

Cherokee Casino Will Rogers Downs
20900 S. 4200 Road
Claremore, Oklahoma 74017
(918) 283-8800
Map: **#47** (30 miles N.E. of Tulsa)
Website: www.cherokeestarrewards.com

Hours: 11am-1am/4am (Fri)/
       10am-4am(Sat)/ 1am (Sun)
Self-Parking: Free
Restaurants: 1
Overnight RV Parking: Must use RV park
Special Features: Live horse racing Feb-May.
Daily simulcasting of horse racing. 400-space
RV park ($32 per night/$10 without hookups).

Remington Park Racing • Casino
One Remington Place
Oklahoma City, Oklahoma 73111
(405) 424-1000
Website: www.remingtonpark.com
Map: **#46**

Toll-Free Number: (800) 456-4244
Hours: 10am-12am/2am (Thu)/3am (Fri/Sat)
Self-Parking: Free   Valet Parking: Free
Restaurants: 2
Buffet: L-$7.99/$8.99 (Fri)/
        $12.99 (Sat)/$9.99 (Sun)
        D-$9.99/$8.99 (Mon)/$16.99 (Thu)/
        $10.99 (Fri)/$12.99 (Sat)
Overnight RV Parking: No
Senior Discount: various Tue if 55+
Special Features: Live horse racing Thu-Sun.
Daily simulcasting of horse racing. Buffet
dicount for slot club members.

OREGON

Oregon law permits bars and taverns to have up to six video lottery terminals that offer various versions of video poker. Racetracks are allowed to have no more than 10 machines. The maximum bet allowed is $2 and the maximum payout on any machine is capped at $600.

These machines are the same as regular video gaming devices but are called lottery terminals because they are regulated by the state's lottery commission which receives a share of each machine's revenue. The machines accept cash but do not pay out in cash; instead, they print out a receipt which must be taken to a cashier.

According to figures from the Oregon Lottery, during its fiscal year from July 1, 2010 through June 30, 2011, the VLT's had an approximate return of 92.46%.

There are nine Indian casinos in operation in Oregon. According to the governor's office which regulates the Tribe's compacts, "there is no minimum payback percentage required on the Tribe's machines. Each Tribe is free to set their own limits on their machines."

All casinos offer blackjack, slots and video poker. Some casinos also offer: craps (C), roulette (R), poker (P), Pai Gow Poker (PGP), let it ride (LIR), three card poker (TCP), four card poker (FCP), big 6 wheel (B6), bingo (BG), keno (K) and off track betting (OTB). Unless otherwise noted, all casinos are open 24 hours and the minimum gambling age is 21 (18 for bingo).

For Oregon tourism information call (800) 547-7842 or go to: www.traveloregon.com.

Chinook Winds Casino Resort
1777 N.W. 44th Street
Lincoln City, Oregon 97367
(541) 996-5825
Website: www.chinookwindscasino.com
Map: **#4** (45 miles W. of Salem)

Toll-Free Number: (888) CHINOOK
RV Reservations: (877) 564-2678
Room Reservations: (877) 423-2241
Rooms: 227 Price Range: $89-$184
Suites: 81 Price Range: $184-$264
Restaurants: 4   Liquor: Yes
Buffets: B-$7.95 L-$8.95
        D-$12.95/$15.95 (Fri/Sat)
Other Games: C, R, P, LIR, TCP, PGP, K, BG
Overnight RV Parking: Free/RV Dump: No
Senior Discount: Meal discounts if 55+
Special Features: 51-space RV Park ($35/$45 per night). Childcare center. Video arcade. 18-hole golf course.

Kah-Nee-Ta High Desert Resort & Casino
6823 Highway 8
Warm Springs, Oregon 97761
(541) 553-1112
Website: www.kahneeta.com
Map: **#5** (100 miles E. of Portland)

Toll-Free Number: (800) 554-4786
Rooms: 109 Price Range: $149-$199
Suites: 30 Price Range: $179-$269
Restaurants: 2   Liquor: Yes
Casino Size: 25,000 Square Feet
Hours: 8:30am-2am/ 4am (Fri/Sat)
Overnight RV Parking: Free/RV Dump: No
Special Features: 51-space RV park ($50 per night). 18-hole golf course. Horseback riding. European spa.

Kla-Mo-Ya Casino
34333 Hwy 97 North
Chiloquin, Oregon 97624
(541) 783-7529
Website: www.klamoyacasino.com
Map: #7 (20 miles N. of Klamath Falls)

Toll-Free Number: (888) 552-6692
Restaurants: 2   Liquor: No
Overnight RV Parking: Free/RV Dump: No
Senior Discount: Various on Mondays if 55+
Special Features: Buffet discounts for slot club members and seniors.

The Mill Casino Hotel
3201 Tremont Avenue
North Bend, Oregon 97459
(541) 756-8800
Website: www.themillcasino.com
Map: #6 (75 miles S.W. of Eugene)

Toll-Free Number: (800) 953-4800
Rooms: 109 Price Range: $89-$136
Suites: 3 Price Range: $149-$239
Restaurants: 4 Liquor: Yes
Buffets: D-$24.95 (Fri/Sat)
Other Games: C, R
Overnight RV Parking: Free/RV Dump: No
Senior Discount: 10% off food if 55+
Special Features: 65-space RV park ($37-$72 per night spring/summer; $25-$35 fall/winter). Free local shuttle. Room and food discounts for slot club members.

The Old Camp Casino
2205 W. Monroe Street
Burns, Oregon 97720
(541) 573-1500
Website: www.oldcampcasino.com
Map: #8 (250 miles S. of Pendleton)

Toll-Free Number: (888) 343-7568
Restaurants: 1   Liquor: Yes
Summer Hours: 9am-11pm
                    9am-2am (Fri)
                    8am-2am (Sat)
                    8am-11pm (Sun)
Winter Hours: 10am-10pm (Wed/Thu)
                    10am-Midnight (Fri)
                    9am-Midnight (Sat)
                    9am-10pm (Fri)
Other Games: P (Fri-Sun), BG (Sun/Wed/Fri)
Overnight RV Parking: Must use RV park
Special Features: Liquor sold in lounge and restaurant only. 15-space RV park ($6 per night/$15 w/hookups). BJ only played Fri-Sun.

Seven Feathers Hotel & Casino Resort
146 Chief Miwaleta Lane
Canyonville, Oregon 97417
(541) 839-1111
Website: www.sevenfeathers.com
Map: #1 (80 miles S. of Eugene)

Toll-Free Number: (800) 548-8461
Room Reservations: (888) 677-7771
Rooms: 146 Price Range: $69-$109
Restaurants: 4 Liquor: Yes
Buffets: B-$20.00 (Sun)
D-$21.99 (Thu)/$17.99 (Fri/Sat)/ $15.99 (Sun)
Casino Size: 27,300 Square Feet
Other Games: C, R, P, LIR, PGP,
         TCP, FCP, K, BG
Senior Discount: $2 off buffet if 50+
Overnight RV Parking: Free/RV Dump: No
Special Features: 191-space RV park ($36-$44 per night). 18-hole golf course.

Spirit Mountain Casino
P.O. Box 39
Grand Ronde, Oregon 97347
(503) 879-2350
Website: www.spiritmountain.com
Map: #2 (85 miles S.W. of Portland)

Toll-Free Number: (800) 760-7977
Reservation Number: (888) 668-7366
Rooms: 94 Price Range: $89-$169
Suites: 6 Price Range: $169-$219
Restaurants: 5 Liquor: Yes
Buffets: B-$8.95 L-$9.95/$11.95 (Sat/Sun)
        D-$14.95/$18.95 (Fri/Sat)
Other Games: C, R, P, PGP, LIR, TCP, K, BG
Overnight RV Parking: Free/RV Dump: Free
Special Features: Childcare center. Video arcade. Slot club members receive a $20 room discount.

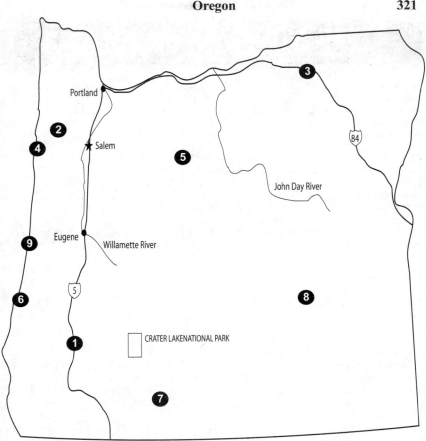

Three Rivers Casino & Hotel
5647 US Highway 126
Florence, Oregon 97439
(541) 997-7529
Website: www.threeriverscasino.com
Map: **#9** (61 miles W. of Eugene)

Toll-Free Number: (877) 374-8377
Rooms: 75 Price Range: $99-$149
Suites: 18 Price Range: $139- $279
Restaurants: 5 Liquor: Yes
Buffets: B-$9.99 (Sun) L-$9.99
　　　　D-$14.99/$18.99 (Fri)/$12.99 (Sun)
Other Games: C, R, P, K, BG
Overnight RV Parking: Free/RV Dump: No
Senior Discount: $1 off buffet if 55+

Wildhorse Resort & Casino
72777 Highway 331
Pendleton, Oregon 97801
(541) 278-2274
Website: www.wildhorseresort.com
Map: **#3** (211 miles E. of Portland)

Toll-Free Number: (800) 654-9453
Rooms: 100 Price Range: $70-$100
Suites: 5 Price Range: $129- $149
Restaurants: 4 Liquor: Yes
Buffets: B-$4.95/$11.95 (Sun)
　　　　L-$9.95 D-$14.95/$16.95 (mon)/
　　　　$21.95 (Thu)
Casino Size: 80,000 Square Feet
Other Games: C, R, P, TCP, K, BG
Overnight RV Parking: Free/RV Dump: No
Senior Discount: Various on Tuesdays if 55+
Special Features: 100-space RV park ($20/$29
per night). Cultural Institute. 18-hole golf
course. Health spa. Child care center.

PENNSYLVANIA

In July 2004 the Pennsylvania legislature authorized the legalization of slot machines at 14 locations throughout the state: seven racinos, five stand-alone casinos, and two hotel resorts.

All casinos can have up to 5,000 machines, except the resort licensees, which are allowed up to 600. As of August 2011, 12 of the licenses had been awarded. One license for a racino had not yet been awarded, plus a license which originally been awarded to Foxwoods Casino in Philadelphia was revoked in December 2010.

In January 2010 the Pennsylvania legislature approved the addition of table games, including live poker, for all casinos. The first casinos began offering tables games in July 2010.

Pennsylvania gaming regulations require that gaming machines return a minimum of 85%. All casinos are open 24 hours and admission is free. However, the casinos at the two hotel resorts are not open to the general public. You must be a guest of the resort in order to play at their casinos.

The minimum gambling age is 18 for pari-mutuel betting and 21 for gaming machines.

Unless otherwise noted, all casinos offer: slots, video poker, craps, blackjack, roulette, three card poker, mini-baccarat and Pai-gow Poker. Optional games include: baccarat (B), poker (P), let it ride (LIR), Pai Gow (PG), Big 6 Wheel (B6), Spanish 21 (S21), four card poker (FCP) and Casino War (CW).

Following is information from the Pennsylvania Gaming Control Board regarding average slot payout percentages for the one-year period from July 1, 2010 through June 30, 2011:

CASINO	PAYBACK %
Mount Airy	91.37
Parx Casino	91.26
Presque Isle	90.89
Hollywood Casino at PN	90.81
Sands Bethelem	90.79
The Meadows	90.72
Mohegan Sun at PD	90.61
Harrah's Chester	90.55
The Rivers	90.54
Sugar House	89.87

For more information on visiting Pennsylvania call their Office of Tourism at (800) 237-4363 or visit their website at www.visitpa.com.

Lady Luck Nemacolin
1001 Lafayette Drive
Farmington, PA 15437
724.329.8555
Website: www.nemacolin.com/

EXPECTED TO OPEN BY LATE 2012
Room Reservations: (800) 422.2736
Rooms: 300 Price Range: $255-$789
Suites: 27 Price Range: $359-$2,999
Restaurants:
Special Features: Located at Nemacolin Woodlands Resort. Casino is affiliated with Isle of Capri Casinos. 20-space RV park open 4/27 through 11/26 with nightly rate of $150/$160 (Fri/Sat). All room/RV rates do not include $15 daily resort fee. You must be a guest of the resort for admittance to the casino.

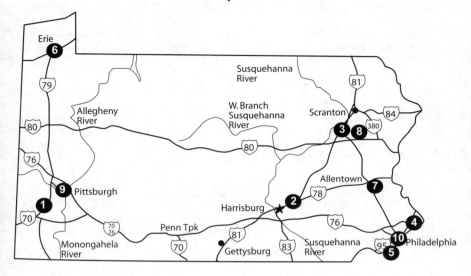

Mount Airy Resort & Casino
44 Woodland Road
Mount Pocono, Pennsylvania 18344
(570) 243-4800
Website: www.mounttairycasino.com
Map: **#8** (30 miles S.E. of Scranton)

Toll-Free Number: (877) 682-4791
Rooms: 175 Price Range: $159-$269
Suites: 25 Price Range: $259-$349
Restaurants: 3
Buffets: B-$24.95 (Sun) L/D-$15.99
Casino Size: 68,000 Square Feet
Other Games: P, LIR, B, PG
Special Features: 18-hole golf course. Spa.

Presque Isle Downs & Casino
8199 Perry Highway
Erie, Pennsylvania 16509
Website: www.presqueisledowns.com
Map: **#6**

Toll-Free Number: (866) 374-3386
Valet Parking: $3
Restaurants: 4
Buffets: B-$8.95 L-$13.95
D-$16.95/$19.95 (Fri/Sat)
Other Games: FCP, LIR
Special Features: Live thoroughbred horse
racing Wed-Sun May-September. Daily
simulcast of harness and thoroughbred racing.

Rivers Casino
777 Casino Dr.
Pittsburgh, PA 15212
(412) 231-7777
Website: www.theriverscasino.com
Map: **#9**

Toll-free Number: (877) 558-0777
Parking: $3 Valet Parking: $6/$12 (Fri-Sun)
Restaurants: 4
Buffets: L-$13.95/$19.95 (Sun)
          D-$19.95/$27.95 (Fri)/$21.95 (Sat)
Other Games: P, CW
Special Features: Free parking for player's
club members who play and put points on
card.

Sugar House Casino
1080 N Delaware Ave
Philadelphia, PA 19125
(267) 232-2000
Website: www.sugarhousecasino.com
Map: **#10**

Restaurants: 1
Casino Size: 45,000 Square Feet
Other Games: P, B, PG

Sands Casino Resort Bethlehem
77 Sands Blvd
Bethlehem, Pennsylvania 18015
Website: www.pasands.com
Map: **#7** (60 miles N of Philadelphia)

Toll-Free number: (877) SANDS-77
Rooms: 288 Price Range: $129-$239
Suites: 22 Price Range: $249-$349
Restaurants: 2
Other Games: B, PG, P, B6, LIR,
                CSP, TCP, CW
Special Features: Food court with Nathan's
Hot Dogs.

Valley Forge Convention Center Casino
1210 First Avenue
King of Prussia, PA 19406
(610) 354-8212
Website: www.vfconventioncenter.com

EXPECTED TO OPEN BY MID-2012
Room Reservations: Radisson Hotel Valley
Forge, (800) 395-7046
Room Reservations: Valley Forge Scanticon
Hotel (610) 265-1500
Restaurants: 3
Casino Size: 33,000 Square Feet
Special Features: Two hotels attached to
convention center: Radisson Hotel Valley
Forge www.radissonvalleyforge.com and
the Valley Forge Scanticon Hotel www.
scanticonvalleyforge.com You must be a
guest of one of the hotels for admittance to
the casino.

Pari-Mutuels

Harrah's Chester Casino & Racetrack
35 E. 5th Street
Chester, Pennsylvania 19013
(484) 490-2207
Website: www.harrahs.com
Map: **#5** (8 miles S. of Philadelphia airport)

Toll-Free Number: (800) 480-8020
Valet Parking: $10
Restaurants: 6
Buffets: L-$15.99/$24.99 (Sat/Sun)
         D-$19.99/$24.99 (Sat/Sun)
Other Games: P, PG, FCP, LIR, B, B6
Special Features: Live harness racing from
mid-April through November. Daily simulcast
of harness and thoroughbred racing. No lunch
buffet Mon/Tue.

Hollywood Casino at Penn National
720 Bow Creek Road
Grantville, Pennsylvania 17028
(717) 469-2211
Website: www.pennnational.com
Map: #2 (16 miles N.E. of Harrisburg)

Restaurants: 1
Buffets: L-$14.99
         D-$14.99/$21.99 (Fri/Sat)
Casino Size: 45,000 Square Feet
Other Games: LIR, FCP, P, S21
Special Features: Live thoroughbred horse
racing Wed-Sat evenings all year long. Daily
simulcast of harness and thoroughbred racing.

The Meadows
210 Racetrack Rd
Washington, Pennsylvania 15301
(724) 225-9300
Website: www.meadowsgaming.com
Map: **#1** (25 miles S.W. of Pittsburgh)

Valet Parking: $3
Restaurants: 3
Other Games: P, LIR, FCP, B, B6
Special Features: Live harness racing various
evenings all year long. Daily simulcast of
harness and thoroughbred racing.

Mohegan Sun at Pocono Downs
1280 Highway 315
Wilkes-Barre, Pennsylvania 18702
(570) 831-2100
Website: www.poconodowns.com
Map: **#3** (20 miles S.W. of Scranton)

Valet Parking: Not Offered
Restaurants: 11
Buffets: B-$16.99 (Sun) L-$12.99
        D-$16.99/$21.99 (Fri)
Other Games: LIR, S21, P
Special Features: Live harness racing various evenings early April through mid-November Daily simulcast of harness and thoroughbred racing.

Parx Casino and Racing
3001 Street Road
Bensalem, Pennsylvania 19020
(215) 639-9000
Website: www.philadelphiapark.com
Map: **#4** (18 miles N.E. of Philadelphia)

Toll-Free Number; (888) 588-PARX
Valet Parking: $5
Restaurants: 3
Other Games: P
Special Features: Thoroughbred horse racing Sat-Tue afternoons all year long. Friday racing added January and February. Daily simulcast of harness and thoroughbred racing.

RHODE ISLAND

Rhode Island has two pari-mutuel facilities which both feature video lottery terminals (VLT's). These machines are the same as regular video gaming devices but are called lottery terminals because they are regulated by the state's lottery commission which receives a share of each machine's revenue. The machines accept cash but don't pay out in cash; instead, they print out a receipt which must be taken to a cashier.

All VLT's are programmed to play at least six different games: blackjack, keno, slots and three versions of poker (jacks or better, joker poker and deuces wild).

According to figures from the Rhode Island Lottery for the one-year period from August 1, 2010 through July 30, 2011 the average VLT return at Twin River was 91.36%, at Newport Grand it was 90.86%

The minimum gambling age in Rhode Island is 18. For information on visiting Rhode Island call the state's tourism division at (800) 556-2484 or go to: www.visitrhodeisland.com.

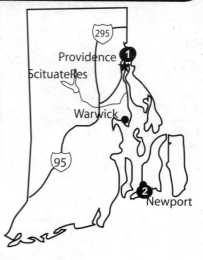

Newport Grand
150 Admiral Kalbfus Road
Newport, Rhode Island 02840
(401) 849-5000
Web Site: www.newportgrand.com
Map: **#2**

Toll-Free Number: (800) 451-2500
Restaurants: 1   Valet Parking: $2.50
Buffet: D - $17.95 (Fri-Sat)
Hours: 10am-1am/ 2am (Fri/Sat)
Admission: Free
Overnight RV Parking: No
Special Features: Daily simulcasting of horse racing, dog racing and jai-alai.

Twin River
1600 Louisquisset Pike
Lincoln, Rhode Island 02865
(401) 723-3200
Web Site: www.twinriver.com
Map: **#1** (10 miles N. of Providence)

Toll-Free Number: (877) 827-4837
Restaurants: 4   Valet Parking: Free
Admission: Free
Overnight RV Parking: No
Special Features: Live dog racing (Mon/Wed/Fri/Sat) throughout the year. Daily (except Tuesday and Sunday) simulcasting of horse and dog racing.

SOUTH CAROLINA

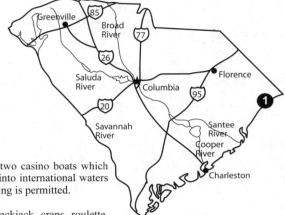

South Carolina has two casino boats which sail three miles out into international waters where casino gambling is permitted.

Both boats offer: blackjack, craps, roulette, three card poker, slots and video poker. Due to security restrictions, you must present a photo ID or you will not be allowed to board.

For more information on visiting South Carolina go to: www.discoversouthcarolina.com or call their tourism department at (800) 872-3505

The Big "M" Casino
4491 Waterfront Avenue
Little River, South Carolina 29566
(843) 249-9811
Website: www.bigmcasino.com
Map Location: **#1** (35 miles N. of Myrtle Beach)

Reservation Number: (877) 250-5825
Ship's Registry: U.S.   Gambling Age: 21
Buffet: $10 am cruise/ $15 pm cruise
Schedule:
   10:45am - 4:00pm   (Tue-Fri)
   11:45am - 5:00pm   (Sat/Sun)
   6:45pm - 11:45pm   (Sun-Thu)
   6:45pm - 12:00am   (Fri/Sat)
Price: $20
Port Charges: None   Parking: Free
Other Games: Poker, Craps, Let it Ride
Special Features: 600-passenger *Diamond Girl II* sails from Little River waterfront. Free shuttle available from Myrtle Beach. Must be 18 or older to board. No cruises Monday.

SunCruz Aquasino
4495 Mineola Avenue
Little River, South Carolina 29566
(843) 280-2933
Website: www.suncruzaquasino.com
Map Location: **#1** (35 miles N. of Myrtle Beach)

Ship's Registry: U.S.   Gambling Age: 18
Buffets: L/D-$10
Schedule:
   11:00am - 4:15pm (Tue-Fri)
   Noon - 5:15pm (Sat/Sun/Holidays)
   7:00pm - 12:15am (Sun-Thu)
   7:00pm - 12:30am (Fri/Sat)
Price: $10
Port Charges: Included   Parking: Free
Other Games: Let It Ride
Senior Discount: Free buffet and boarding
               Wed/Fri if 55+
Special Features: 600-passenger *Aquasino* sails from Little River waterfront. Must be 18 or older to board.

SOUTH DAKOTA

South Dakota's bars and taverns are allowed to have up to 10 video lottery terminals (VLT's) that offer the following games: poker, keno, blackjack and bingo.

These machines are the same as regular video gaming devices but are called lottery terminals because they are regulated by the state's lottery commission which receives a share of each machine's revenue.

The machines accept cash but don't pay out in cash; instead, they print out a receipt which must be taken to a cashier. The maximum bet is $2 and the maximum payout allowed is $1,000.

Slot machines, as well as blackjack and poker are only permitted at Indian casinos and in Deadwood.

Deadwood was once most famous for being the home of Wild Bill Hickok who was shot to death while playing cards in the No. 10 Saloon. The hand he held was two pairs: black aces and black eights, which is now commonly referred to as a "dead man's hand." Wild Bill is buried in the local cemetery along with another local celebrity: Calamity Jane.

The first casinos in Deadwood opened on November 1, 1989. All of the buildings in the downtown area are required to conform with the city's authentic 1880's architecture. Many of the casinos are located in historic structures but there are also some new structures which were designed to be compatible with the historic theme of the town. The old No. 10 Saloon is still operating and you can actually gamble in the same spot where old Wild Bill bit the dust!

South Dakota law limits each casino licensee to a maximum of 30 slot machines and no one person is allowed to hold more than three licenses. Some operators combine licenses with other operators to form a cooperative which may look like one casino but in reality it's actually several licensees operating under one name.

The state's gaming laws originally limited blackjack, poker, let it ride and three-card poker bets to a maximum of $5, however, in late 2000 the law was changed to allow maximum bets of $100.

In addition to the Deadwood casinos, there are also nine Indian casinos in South Dakota. These casinos are also subject to the $100 maximum bet restrictions.

Here are statistics from the South Dakota Commission on Gaming for the payback percentages on all of Deadwood's slot machines for the one-year period from July 1, 2010 through June 30, 2011:

Denomination	Payback %
1¢ Slots	90.66
5¢ Slots	91.31
25¢ Slots	90.88
$1 Slots	92.05
$5 Slots	91.78
Average	90.99

Some of the larger casinos are open 24 hours but most of the smaller ones are open from 8 a.m. until midnight Sunday through Thursday and 8 a.m. until 2 a.m. on the weekends.

The Deadwood Trolly runs a scheduled shuttle service to all of the casinos that operates from 8 a.m. to midnight weekdays and 7 a.m. to 3 a.m. on weekends. During the summer months the weekday hours are extended until 1:30 a.m. The cost is $1 per ride.

Unless otherwise noted, all casinos offer slot machines and video poker. Some casinos also offer: blackjack (BJ), let it ride (LIR), three-card poker (TCP), Caribbean stud poker (CSP) and poker (P). Most of the Indian casinos also offer bingo (BG).

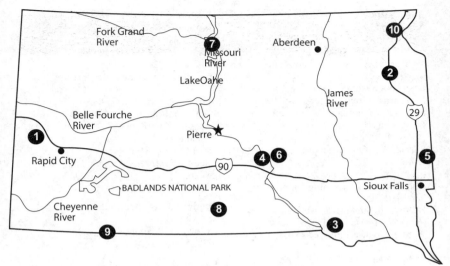

The minimum gambling age is 21 at all Deadwood and Indian casinos (18 for bingo at Indian casinos). South Dakota's casinos have very liberal rules about allowing minors in casinos and virtually all of the casinos will allow children to enter with their parents until about 8 p.m. Additionally, South Dakota is the only jurisdiction that will allow children to stand next to their parents while they are gambling.

For South Dakota tourism information call (800) 732-5682. For information on visiting Deadwood call the city's Chamber of Commerce at (800) 999-1876, or visit their website at www.deadwood.org.

Deadwood

Map: **#1** (in the Black Hills, 41 miles N.W. of Rapid City. Take I-90 W. Get off at the second Sturges exit and take Hwy. 14-A into Deadwood)

Best Western Hickok House
137 Charles Street
Deadwood, South Dakota 57732
(605) 578-1611
Website: www.bestwestern.com

Best Western Reservations: 800-837-8174
Rooms: 38   Price Range: $50-$120
Restaurants: 1
Special Features: Hot tub and sauna.

Bourbon Street
667 Main Street
Deadwood, South Dakota 57732
(605) 578-1297

Restaurants: 1
Special Features: Free mardi gras beads and dirty rice daily.

Buffalo-Bodega Gaming Complex
658 Main Street
Deadwood, South Dakota 57732
Website: buffalo-bodega.com
(605) 578-1162

Restaurants: 1
Other games: BJ
Special Features: Oldest bar in Deadwood. Steakhouse restaurant. Ice cream parlor.

Bullock Express
68 Main Street
Deadwood, South Dakota 57732
(605) 578-3476
Website: www.historicbullock.com

Reservation Number: 800-526-8277
Rooms: 38   Price Range: $40-$65
Restaurants: 1
Casino Hours: 7am-12am

Bullock Hotel
633 Main Street
Deadwood, South Dakota 57732
(605) 578-1745
Website: www.historicbullock.com

Reservation Number: 800-336-1876
Rooms: 26   Price Range: $75-$100
Suites: 2 Price Range: $130-$160
Restaurants: 1
Hours: 24 Hours Daily
Special Features: Deadwood's oldest hotel.

Cadillac Jacks's Gaming Resort
360 Main Street
Deadwood, South Dakota 57732
(605) 578-1500
Website: www.cadillacjacksgaming.com

Toll Free Number: (866) 332-3966
Rooms: 92 Price Range: $75-$175
Suites: 11 Price Range: $199-$309
Restaurants: 1
Hours: 24 Hours Daily
Casino Size: 10,000 Square Feet
Other Games: BJ, P
Special Features: Hotel is AmericInn. 15% off rooms for slot club members. Free valet parking.

Celebrity Hotel & Casino
629 Main Street
Deadwood, South Dakota 57732
(605) 578-1909
Website: www.celebritycasinos.com

Toll-Free Number: (888) 399-1886
Rooms: 9 Price Range: $69-$129
Suites: 3 Price Range: $99-$159
Hours: 24 Hours Daily
Special Features: Car and motorcycle museum. Free to hotel guests, otherwise admission charge. Includes the **Mint Casino.**

Deadwood Dick's Saloon and Gaming Hall
51 Sherman Street
Deadwood, South Dakota 57732
(605) 578-3224
Website: www.deadwooddicks.com

Toll Free Number: (877) 882-4990
Rooms: 5 Price Range: $80-$125
Suites: 6 Price Range: $125-$450
Restaurants: 1
Other Games: BJ, P
Special Features: Antique mall with 30 dealers.

Deadwood Frontier Club
681 Main Street
Deadwood, South Dakota 57732
(605) 578-3430

Restaurants: 1
Other Games: BJ
Special Features: Video arcade.

Deadwood Gulch Resort
304 Cliff Street
Deadwood, South Dakota 57732
(605) 578-1294
Website: www.deadwoodgulch.com

Reservation Number: (800) 695-1876
Rooms: 95   Price Range: $79-$119
Restaurants: 1
Hours: 24 Hours Daily
Casino Size: 7,500 Square Feet
Other Games: BJ
Special Features: Free breakfast for hotel guests.

Deadwood Gulch Saloon
560 Main Street
Deadwood, South Dakota 57732
(605) 578-1207

Nestled in the Black Hills of South Dakota, the entire city of Deadwood has been designated a national historic landmark. Free historic walking tours are offered daily.

Deadwood Mountain Grand
1906 Deadwood Mountain Dr.
Deadwood, South Dakota 57732
(605) 559-0386
Website: www.deadwoodmountaingrand.com

Hotel Expected to Open Late 2011
Toll-free Number: (877) 907-4726
Rooms: 90 Price Range: Not set at Press time
Suites: 8   Price Range: Not set at Press time
Restaurants: 3
Hours: 24 Hours Daily
Casino Size: 7,500 Square Feet
Other Games: BJ
Special Features: 2,500-seat entertainment center.

First Gold Hotel & Gaming
270 Main Street
Deadwood, South Dakota 57732
(605) 578-9777
Website: www.firstgold.com

Reservation Number: (800) 274-1876
Rooms: 101   Price Range: $59-$119
Suites: 1   Price Range: $99-$219
Restaurants: 2
Buffets: B- $6.95 L- $7.95
        D- $12.95/ $19.95 (Fri/Sat)
Hours: 24 Hours Daily
Casino Size: 11,000 Square Feet
Other Games: BJ, TCP
Senior Discount: 10% off room if 55+
Special Features: RV park located next door.
Includes **Blackjack** and **Horseshoe** casinos.

Four Aces
531 Main Street
Deadwood, South Dakota 57732
(605) 578-2323
Website: www.fouracesdeadwood.com

Toll Free Number: (800) 834-4384
Rooms: 59 Price Range: $55-$109
Suites: 5 Price Range: $89-$199
Restaurants: 1
Buffets: B/L-$9.99 D-$11.99/$19.99 (Fri/Sat)
Hours: 24 Hours Daily
Casino Size: 24,000 Square Feet
Other Games: BJ, TCP
Senior Discount: room/food discounts if 55+
Special Features: Hotel is Hampton Inn.

Gold Country Inn
801 Main Street
Deadwood, South Dakota 57732
(605) 578-2393

Reservation Number: (800) 287-1251
Rooms: 53   Price Range: $59-$89
Restaurants: 1

Gold Dust Gaming & Entertainment Complex
688 Main Street
Deadwood, South Dakota 57732
(605) 578-2100
Website: www.golddustgaming.com

Toll-Free Number: (800) 456-0533
Rooms: 56 Price Range: $149-$209
Suites: 22 Price Range: $159-$219
Restaurants: 1
Buffets: B/L-$9.99
       D-$11.99/$21.99 (Fri/Sat)
Hours: 24 Hours Daily
Casino Size: 30,000 Square Feet
Other Games: BJ, P, TCP
Senior Discount: $1 off buffets if 55 or older
Special Features: Hotel is Holiday Inn Express. Largest gaming complex in Deadwood with eleven casinos. Free continental breakfast for hotel guests, indoor pool, gym, whirlpool, arcade. Includes **French Quarter**, **Legends** and **Silver Dollar** casinos.

Gulches of Fun
225 Cliff Street
Deadwood, South Dakota 57732
(605) 578-7550
Website: www.gulchesoffun.com

Reservation Number: (800) 961-3096
Rooms: 66 Price Range: $80-$130
Suites: 5 Price Range: $90-$149
Restaurants: 1
Hours: 24 Hours Daily
Special Features: Hotel is Comfort Inn. Family amusement center with rides and mini-golf.

Hickok's Iron Horse
27 Deadwood Street
Deadwood, South Dakota 57732
(605) 578-7700

Toll Free Number: (877) 815-7974
Rooms: 19 Price Range: $89-$159
Suites: 4 Price Range: $149-$209
Casino Size: 1,000 Square Feet
Hours: 24 Hours Daily

Hickok's Saloon
685 Main Street
Deadwood, South Dakota 57732
(605) 578-2222
Website: www.hickoks.com

Other Games: BJ, TCP
Special Features: Video arcade.

The Lodge at Deadwood
100 Pince Crest Ln
Deadwood, South Dakota 57732
(605) 571-2132
Website: www.deadwoodlodge.com

Toll-Free Number: (877) 393-5634
Rooms: 100 Price Range: $89-$165
Suites: 40 Price Range: $99-$219
Restaurants: 2
Hours: 24 Hours Daily
Casino Size: 11,000 Square Feet
Other Games: BJ, TCP, P, FCP

Lucky 8 Gaming Hall/Super 8 Motel
196 Cliff Street
Deadwood, South Dakota 57732
(605) 578-2535
Website: www.deadwoodsuper8.com

Reservation Number: (800) 800-8000
Rooms: 47 Price Range: $40-$75
Suites: 4 Price Range: $95-$135
Restaurants: 1
Hours: 24 Hours Daily
Special Features: Video arcade. Free continental breakfast for hotel guests.

McKenna's Gold
470 Main Street
Deadwood, South Dakota 57732
(605) 578-3207

Special Features: Includes **The Chase** casino.

Midnight Star
677 Main Street
Deadwood, South Dakota 57732
(605) 578-1555
Website: www.themidnightstar.com

Toll-Free Number: (800) 999-6482
Restaurants: 2
Other Games: BJ, TCP, LIR
Special Features: Sports Bar & Grill.

Mineral Palace Hotel & Gaming Complex
601 Main Street
Deadwood, South Dakota 57732
(605) 578-2036
Website: www.mineralpalace.com

Reservation Number: (800) 84-PALACE
Rooms: 63 Price Range: $109-$179
Suites: 4 Price Range: $129-$389
Restaurants: 1
Hours: 24 Hours Daily
Other Games: BJ, TCP
Special Features: Cappuccino/espresso bar.
Liquor store. Includes **Union Palace** casino.

Miss Kitty's Gaming Emporium
647 Main Street
Deadwood, South Dakota 57732
(605) 578-1811
Website: www.historicbullock.com/mk.htm

Restaurants: 2
Hours: 24 Hours Daily
Special Features: Chinese restaurant. Includes
Green Door Club Casino

Mustang Sally's
634 Main Street
Deadwood, South Dakota 57732
(605) 578-2025

Old Style Saloon #10
657 Main Street
Deadwood, South Dakota 57732
(605) 578-3346
Website: www.saloon10.com

Toll-Free Number: (800) 952-9398
Restaurants: 1
Casino Size: 4,000 Square Feet
Other Games: BJ, P
Special Features: August-September there
is a reenactment of the "Shooting of Wild
Bill Hickok" at 1, 3, 5 and 7 p.m. Wild Bill's
chair and other Old West artifacts on display.
Italian restaurant. Includes **The Utter Place**
card room.

Oyster Bay/Fairmont Hotel
628 Main Street
Deadwood, South Dakota 57732
(605) 578-2205

Restaurants: 1
Special Features: Historic restoration of
1895 brothel, spa and underground jail cell.
Oyster bar.

Silverado - Franklin Historic Hotel &
 Gaming Complex
700-709 Main Street
Deadwood, South Dakota 57732
(605) 578-3670
Website: www.silveradocasino.com

Toll-Free Number: (800) 584-7005
Reservation Number: (800) 688-1876
Rooms: 80 Price Range: $89-$129
Suites: 15 Price Range: $159-$209
Restaurants: 1
Buffets: B-$10.95/$9.95 (Sun) L- $12.95
              D-$17.95/$21.95 (Fri/Sat)
Hours: 24 Hours Daily
Casino Size: 20,000 Square Feet
Other Games: BJ, P, LIR, TCP, CSP
Senior Discount: 30% off buffet if 50+

Tin Lizzie Gaming
555 Main Street
Deadwood, South Dakota 57732
(605) 578-1715
Web Sit: www.tinlizzie.com

Toll-Free Number: (800) 643-4490
Restaurants: 1
Buffets: B-$4.99
Hours: 24 Hours Daily
Casino Size: 8,300 Square Feet
Other Games: BJ
Senior Discount: Various if 50+

Veterans Of Foreign War
10 Pine Street
Deadwood, South Dakota 57732
(605) 722-9914

Hours: 9:30am-12am Daily

Wooden Nickel
9 Lee Street
Deadwood, South Dakota 57732
(605) 578-1952

Special Features: Includes **Martin Mason** and
Lee Street Station casinos.

Indian Casinos

Dakota Connection
RR 1, Box 177-B
Sisseton, South Dakota 57262
(605) 698-4273
Website: www.dakotanationgaming.com
Map: **#10** (165 miles N. of Sioux Falls)

Toll-Free Number: (800) 542-2876
Restaurants: 1   Liquor: No
Buffets: B-$8.95 (Sat/Sun) L-$9.50 (Sun)
Hours: 24 Hours Daily
Other Games: BG
Overnight RV Parking: Free must register at
                     players club/RV Dump: No

Dakota Sioux Casino
16415 Sioux Conifer Road
Watertown, South Dakota 57201
(605) 882-2051
Website: www.dakotanationgaming.com
Map: **#2** (104 miles N. of Sioux Falls)

Toll-Free Number: (800) 658-4717
Rooms: 88 Price Range: $69-$99
Suites: 12 Price Range: $109-$199
Restaurants: 1   Liquor: Yes
Buffets: B-$4.95 (Mon)/ $7.95 (Sat/Sun)
       D-$9.95/$7.95 (Tue/Wed)/$14.95 (Fri/Sat)
Hours: 24 Hours Daily
Other Games: BJ, P
Overnight RV Parking: Free/RV Dump: Free
Senior Discount: Specials on Mon if 55+
Special Features: 9-space RV park (Free,
including hookups). $10 room discount for
slot club members.

Fort Randall Casino Hotel
East Highway 46
Pickstown, South Dakota 57367
(605) 487-7871
Website: www.ftrandallcasino.com
Map: **#3** (100 miles S.W. of Sioux Falls)

Room Reservations: (800) 362-6333
Rooms: 57 Price Range: $59-$89
Suites: 2 Price Range: $79-$109
Restaurants: 1 Liquor: Yes
Buffets: B-$9.95 (Sat/Sun) L-$5.95/
          $8.95 (Fri/Sat)
       D-$9.95/$5.95 (Mon)/$19.95 (Sat)
Hours: 24 Hours Daily
Other Games: BJ, P, BG (Wed-Sun)
Overnight RV Parking: Free/RV Dump: Free
Senior Discount: Specials on Wed if 50+
Special Features: 20-space RV park (Free,
including hookups).

Golden Buffalo Casino
321 Sitting Bull Street
Lower Brule, South Dakota 57548
(605) 473-5577
Website: www.lbst.org/casino.htm
Map: **#4** (45 miles S.E. of Pierre)

Room Reservations: (605) 473-5506
Rooms: 38 Price Range: $39-$54
Restaurants: 1 Liquor: Yes
Buffets B-$6.95 (Sat/Sun) D-$6.95
Hours: 8am-12:30am/1:30am (Fri/Sat)
Casino Size: 9,000 Square Feet
Other Games: BG (Wed), No blackjack
Overnight RV Parking: Free/RV Dump: Free
Senior Discount: Specials on Mon if 50+

Grand River Casino and Resort
P.O. Box 639
Mobridge, South Dakota 57601
(605) 845-7104
Website: www.grandrivercasino.com
Map: **#7** (240 miles N.E. of Rapid City)

Toll-Free Number: (800) 475-3321
Rooms: 38 Price Range: $65-$110
Suites: 2 Price Range: $90-$135
Restaurants: 1 Liquor: Yes
Buffets: B-$6.95 (Sun)
       D-$9.50/$7.50 (Tue)/$14.95 (Sun)
Hours: 24 Hours Daily
Other Games: BJ, P (Sat/Sun)
Overnight RV Parking: Free/RV Dump: No
Special Features: 10-space RV park ($10 per
night).

Lode Star Casino & Hotel
P.O. Box 140
Fort Thompson, South Dakota 57339
(605) 245-6000
Website: www.lodestarcasino.com
Map: **#6** (150 miles N.W. of Sioux Falls)

Room Reservations: (888) 268-1360
Restaurants: 1 Liquor: Yes
Rooms: 50 Price Range: $50-$75
Hours: 7am-2am/4am (Fri/Sat)
Other Games: BJ, P (Mon/Thu/Sat)
Overnight RV Parking: Free/RV Dump: No

Prairie Wind Casino & Hotel
HC 49, Box 10
Pine Ridge, South Dakota 57770
(605) 867-6300
Website: www.prairiewindcasino.com
Map: **#9** (85 miles S.E. of Rapid City)

Toll-Free Number: (800) 705-9463
Rooms: 78 Price Range: $60-$99
Suites: 6 Price Range: $116-$156
Restaurants: 1 Liquor: No
Buffets: B-$7.95
D-$11.95/$12.95 (Wed/Sat)/$13.95 (Thu/Fri)
Hours: 24 Hours Daily
Other Games: BJ, TCP
Overnight RV Parking: Free/RV Dump: No
Special Features: Casino is located 12 miles
East of Oelrichs off Hwy. 385 and 8 miles
West of Oglala on Hwy. 18.

Rosebud Casino
Highway 83 (on SD/NE stateline)
Mission, South Dakota 57555
(605) 378-3800
Website: www.rosebudcasino.com
Map: **#8** (22 miles S. of Mission)

Toll-Free Number: (800) 786-7673
Room Reservations: (877) 521-9913
Rooms: 58 Price Range: $89-$109
Suites: 2 Price Range: $99-$129
Restaurants: 2 Liquor: Yes
Buffets: Brunch-$11.99 (Sun) D-$11.99
Hours: 24 Hours Daily
Other Games: BJ, P (Fri-Tue), BG
Overnight RV Parking: Free/RV Dump: No
Senior Discount: Various if 55+
Special Features: Hotel is Quality Inn. Located
22 miles S. of Mission, SD and 9 miles N. of
Valentine, NE.

Royal River Casino & Hotel
607 S. Veterans Street
Flandreau, South Dakota 57028
(605) 997-3746
Website: www.royalrivercasino.com
Map: **#5** (35 miles N. of Sioux Falls on I-29)

Toll-Free Number: (800) 833-8666
Rooms: 108 Price Range: $60-$80
Suites: 12 Price Range: $90-$105
Restaurants: 2   Liquor: Yes
Buffets: B-$9.99 (Sun)
         L-$7.99/$13.99 (Sun)
         D-$13.95(Sat/Sun)/$15.95 (Fri)
Hours: 24 Hours Daily
Casino Size: 17,000 Square Feet
Other Games: BJ, P (Thu-Sun), LIR, OTB
Overnight RV Parking: Free/RV Dump: No
Special Features: 21-space RV park ($10 per night).

Visit our website:
americancasinoguide.com

• Casino News
• Casino Travel Info
• Casino Promotions
• U.S. Casino Directory
• Casino Discussion Forum
• Money-saving Casino Offers
• FREE Educational Gambling Videos

TEXAS

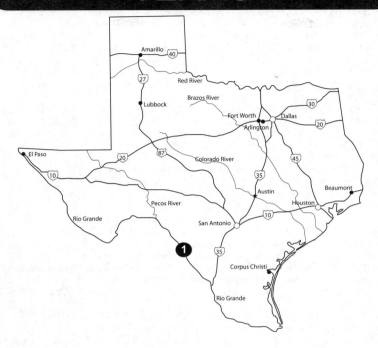

Texas has one Indian casino which offers class II gaming machines based on bingo. It also offers pull tab machines, bingo, poker and a player-banked blackjack game where each player must pay a commission to the house for each bet that is made. The commission is 50¢ for $3-$50 bets and $1 for bets over $50. The minimum gambling age is 21 and the casino is open 24 hours daily.

Class II video gaming devices look like slot machines, but are actually bingo games and the spinning reels are for "entertainment purposes only." No public information is available concerning the payback percentages on any gaming machines in Texas' Indian casino.

For more information on visiting Texas call (800) 888-8TEX or go to: www.traveltex.com.

Kickapoo Lucky Eagle Casino
Lucky Eagle Drive
Eagle Pass, Texas 78852
(830) 758-1995
Website: kickapooluckyeaglecasino.com
Map: **#1** (140 miles S.W. of San Antonio)

Toll-Free Number: (888) 255-8259
Restaurants: 1 Liquor: Yes Valet Parking: No
Buffets: L-$4.99/$8.99 (Sun) D-$8.99
Casino Size: 16,000 Square Feet
Overnight RV Parking: Free/RV Dump: Free
Special Features: 20-space RV park (Free, including hookups).

WASHINGTON

All Indian casinos operating in Washington have compacts with the state allowing them to offer table games, as well as electronic 'scratch' ticket games which use a finite number of tickets with a predetermined number of winners and losers.

These video gaming machines have a maximum bet of $5 and aren't allowed to accept cash. Instead, a cashless system is used whereby you have to go to a cashier cage, or a kiosk, get a "smart" card and deposit money to that card's account. The machines will then deducts losses from, or credit wins to, your account. Ticket-in ticket-out (TITO) receipts are also used in some casinos.

All of the state's Tribes are not required to release information on their slot machine percentage paybacks. However, according to the terms of the compact between the Tribes and the state, the minimum prize payout for electronic 'scratch' ticket games is 75%.

Most Washington casinos are not open on a 24-hour basis and the hours of operation are noted in each casino's listing.

All casinos offer blackjack, craps, roulette, slots, video poker and pull tabs. Optional games offered include: baccarat (B), mini-baccarat (MB), poker (P), pai gow poker (PGP), Caribbean stud poker (CSP), three-card poker (TCP), Spanish 21 (S21), big 6 wheel (B6), keno (K), Off-Track Betting (OTB) and bingo (BG). The minimum gambling age is 21 at most casinos (at some it's 18) and 18 for bingo or pari-mutuel betting. Look in the "Special Features" listing for each casino to see which allow gambling at 18 years of age.

Although most of the casinos have toll-free numbers be aware that some of these numbers will only work for calls made within Washington.

For more information on visiting Washington call their tourism department at (800) 544-1800 or go to: www.experiencewashington.com.

Angel of the Winds Casino
3438 Stoluckquamish Lane
Arlington, Washington 98223
(360) 474-9740
Website: www.angelofthewinds.com
Map: **#22** (50 miles N. of Seattle)

Restaurants: 1 Liquor: Yes Valet Parking: Free
Other Games: P, TCP, FCP, PGP, S21, K
Overnight RV Parking: Free/RV Dump: No

Chewelah Casino
2555 Smith Road
Chewelah, Washington 99109
(509) 935-6167
Website: www.chewelahcasino.com
Map: **#13** (50 miles N. of Spokane)

Toll-Free Number: (800) 322-2788
Restaurants: 1 Liquor: No Valet Parking: No
Buffets: B- $6.45 (Sat)/$10.95 (Sun)
          L-$8.45 D-$10.49 (Thu)/$25.99 (Fri)
Hours: 8:30am-2am
Casino Size: 22,000 Square Feet
Other Games: S21, P
Overnight RV Parking: Free/RV Dump: No
Senior Discount: Various Wed if 55+
Special Features: One block from Double Eagle Casino. 20-space RV park ($10 per night). Gambling age is 18.

Coulee Dam Casino
515 Birch Street
Coulee Dam, Washington 99155
(509) 633-0766
Website: www.colvillecasinos.com
Map: **#11** (190 miles E. of Seattle)

Toll-Free Number: (800) 556-7492
Restaurants: 1 Deli Liquor: Yes
Hours: 9am-2am/24 Hours (Fri/Sat)
Other Games: Only gaming machines
Overnight RV Parking: Free/RV Dump: No
Special Features: Gambling age is 18.

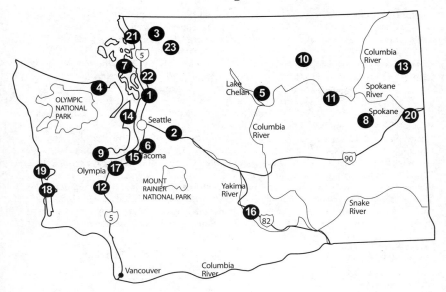

Emerald Queen Hotel & Casino at Fife
5700 Pacific Highway East
Fife, Washington 98424
(206) 594-7777
Website: www.emeraldqueen.com
Map: **#15** (a suburb of Tacoma)

Toll-Free Number: (888) 820-3555
Rooms: 130 Price Range: $89-$109
Suites: 10 Price Range: $179-$229
Restaurants: 1 Liquor: Yes Valet Parking: No
Buffets: B-$19.95 (Sun) L-$12.95 D-$19.95
Other Games: Only gaming machines/keno
Overnight RV Parking: No

Emerald Queen Casino at I-5
2024 East 29th Street
Tacoma, Washington 98404
(206) 383-1572
Website: www.emeraldqueen.com
Map: **#15** (a suburb of Tacoma)

Toll-Free Number: (888) 831-7655
Restaurants: 3 Liquor: Yes Valet: Free
Buffets: L-$12.95 D-$24.95
Other Games: S21, PGP, CSP, LIR
Overnight RV Parking: Free/RV Dump: No
Special Features: Sports bar.

Little Creek Casino Resort
91 West Highway 108
Shelton, Washington 98584
(360) 427-7711
Website: www.little-creek.com
Map: **#9** (23 miles N. of Olympia off Hwy
101/108 interchange)

Toll-Free Number: (800) 667-7711
Rooms: 92 Price Range: $95-$219
Suites: 6 Price Range: $219-$575
Restaurants: 2 Liquor: Yes Valet Parking: Free
Buffets: B-$8.95/$15.95 (Sun) L-$10.95/
$12.95 (Sat)
D-$15.95/$23.95 (Fri/Sat)
Hours: 9am-4am/5am (Fri/Sat)
Casino Size: 30,000 Square Feet
Other Games: S21, P, PGP, K, BG
Overnight RV Parking: Free/RV Dump: No
Senior Discount: Various Mon-Wed if 50+
Special Features: Indoor pool. Gift shop.

Lucky Dog Casino
19330 N. Highway 101
Shelton, Washington 98584
(360) 877-5656
Website: www.myluckydogcasino.com
Map: **#9** (23 miles N. of Olympia)

Toll-Free Number: (877) LUCKY-4-U
Restaurants: 1 Liquor: Yes Valet Parking: No
Hours: 10am-12:00am/2am (Fri-Sat)
Casino Size: 2,500 Square Feet
Other Games: S21, PGP, P
Overnight RV Parking: Call Ahead/RV Dump: No
Senior Discount: Various Mon-Thu if 50+
Special Features: Will reimburse up to two
days of RV parking fees at participating RV
parks. Call for details.

Lucky Eagle Casino
12888 188th Avenue SW
Rochester, Washington 98579
(360) 273-2000
Website: www.luckyeagle.com
Map: **#12** (26 miles S. of Olympia)

Toll-Free Number: (800) 720-1788
Rooms: 65 Price Range: $99-$135
Suites: 4 Price Range: $138-$265
Restaurants: 5 Liquor: Yes Valet Parking: No
Buffets: L-$9.95/$13.95 (Sun)
          D-$13.95/$20.95 (Fri/Sat)
Hours: 9am-4am/6am (Fri/Sat)
Casino Size: 75,000 Square Feet
Other Games: S21, P, PGP, TCP, K, BG
Overnight RV Parking: Free/RV Dump: No
Senior Discount: Various specials Mon if 55+
Special Features: 20-space RV park ($20-$25
per night).

Mill Bay Casino
455 Wapato Lake Road
Manson, Washington 98841
(509) 687-2102
Website: www.colvillecasinos.com
Map: **#5** (200 miles N.E. of Seattle on the N.
shore of Lake Chelan)

Toll-Free Number: (800) 648-2946
Restaurants: 1 Liquor: Yes Valet Parking: No
Other Games: S21, PGP, P
Overnight RV Parking: Free/RV Dump: No
Senior Discount: Various Tuesdays if 55+
Special Features: Gambling age is 18.

Muckleshoot Casino
2402 Auburn Way South
Auburn, Washington 98002
(253) 804-4444
Website: www.muckleshootcasino.com
Map: **#6** (20 miles S. of Seattle)

Toll-Free Number (800) 804-4944
Restaurants: 5 Liquor: Yes Valet Parking:
Free
Buffets: B-$9.95 L-$14.95/$17.95 (Sat/Sun)
          D-$19.95/$24.95 (Fri/Sat/Sun)
Other Games: S21, B, MB, P, PGP, CSP,
          TCP, K, BG
Overnight RV Parking: Free/RV Dump: No
Senior Discount: Various on Tue if 55+
Special Features: Two casinos in separate
buildings, one is non-smoking.

Nooksack Northwood Casino
9750 Northwood Road
Lynden, Washington 98264
(360) 734-5101
Website: www.northwood-casino.com
Map: **#3** (14 miles N. of Bellingham)

Toll-Free Number (877) 777-9847
Restaurants: 2 Liquor: Yes Valet Parking: No
Buffets: B-$7.95 (Sat/Sun) L-$7.95 (Fri/Sat)
D-$12.95/$13.95 (Thu)/$11.95 (Tue/Fri/Sat)
Hours: 9am-4am
Casino Size: 20,000 Square Feet
Other Games: Only Gaming Machines
Overnight RV Parking: Free/RV Dump: No
Senior Discount: Various Wed/Thu if 50+
Special Features: RV hook-ups available for
$15 per night.

Nooksack River Casino
5048 Mt. Baker Highway
Deming, Washington 98244
(360) 592-5472
Website: www.nooksackcasino.com
Map: **#23** (14 miles E. of Bellingham)

Toll-Free Number (877) 935-9300
Restaurants: 4 Liquor: Yes Valet: Free
Hours: 10am-1am/3am (Fri/Sat)
Casino Size: 21,500 Square Feet
Other Games: S21, MB, P, PGP, TCP, K
Overnight RV Parking: Free/RV Dump: No
Senior Discount: Various on Wed/Thu if 55+
Special Features: 6-space RV park ($10 per
night).

Northern Quest Casino
N. 100 Hayford Road
Airway Heights, Washington 99001
(509) 242-7000
Website: www.northernquest.com
Map: **#20** (10 miles W. of Spokane)

Toll-Free Number (888) 603-7051
Rooms: 200 Prices $149-$199
Suites: 50 Prices: $239-$539
Restaurants: 4 Liquor: Yes Valet: Free
Buffets: B-$9.95/$15.95 (Sun) L-$11.45
 D-$9.95 (Mon)/21.95 (Tue/Fri)/
 $15.95 (Wed/Thu/Sat/Sun)
Casino Size: 21,500 Square Feet
Other Games: S21, PGP, TCP, K, OTB, P
Overnight RV Parking: Free/RV Dump: No
Senior Discount: $2 Buffet discounts if 55+

Okanogan Bingo Casino
41 Appleway Road
Okanogan, Washington 98840
Website: www.colvillecasinos.com
(509) 422-4646
Map: **#10** (165 miles E. of Seattle)

Toll-Free Number: (800) 559-4643
Restaurants: 1 Snack Bar Liquor: Yes
Hours: 8am-4am/24 Hours (Fri/Sat)
Other Games: Only machines,
 Poker & bingo (Fri-Tue)
Overnight RV Parking: Free/RV Dump: No
Senior Discount: Discount breakfast & lunch if 55+
Special Features: Gambling age is 18.

The Point Casino
7989 Salish Lane NE
Kingston, Washington 98346
(360) 297-0070
Website: www.the-point-casino.com
Map: **#14** (18 miles W. of Seattle via
Bainbridge Ferry)

Toll-Free Number (866) 547-6468
Restaurants: 1 Liquor: Yes Valet Parking: No
Buffets: L-$10.95 (Sun)
 D-$15.95/$19.75 (Sat)
Casino Size: 18,500 Square Feet
Other Games: S21, PGP, P
Overnight RV Parking: Free/RV Dump: No
Senior Discount: Various on Tue if 55+
Special Features: $15 off Seattle and Edmonds
Ferry fees reimbursed after one hour of play.

Quil Ceda Creek Nightclub & Casino
6410 33rd Avenue N.E.
Tulalip, Washington 98271
(360) 551-1111
Website: www.quilcedacreekcasino.com
Map: **#1** (30 miles N. of Seattle)

Toll-Free Number: (888) 272-1111
Restaurants: 1 Liquor: Yes Valet Parking: No
Casino Size: 52,000 Square Feet
Other Games: S21, PGP, TCP
Overnight RV Parking: Free/RV Dump: No
Special Features: One mile from Tulalip
Casino.

Quinault Beach Resort and Casino
78 Route 115
Ocean Shores, Washington 98569
(360) 289-9466
Website: www.quinaultbeachresort.com
Map: **#19** (90 miles W. of Tacoma)

Toll-Free Number: (888) 461-2214
Rooms: 159 Price Range: $116-$189
Suite: 9 Price Range: $289-$449
Restaurants: 2 Liquor: Yes Valet Parking: Free
Buffets: B-$12.95 (Sun)
 D-$15.95 (Wed)/$24.95 (Fri)
Casino Size: 16,000 Square Feet
Hours: 9am-5am/6am (Fri/Sat)
Other Games: S21, P, PGP, LIR, TCP, K
Overnight RV Parking: Free (must register
first at front desk)/RV Dump: No
Senior Discount: Various if 55+

Red Wind Casino
12819 Yelm Highway
Olympia, Washington 98513
(360) 412-5000
Website: www.redwindcasino.net
Map: **#17**

Toll-Free Number: (866) 946-2444
Restaurants: 1 Liquor: Yes
Buffets: B-$8.00 L-$13.00/$18.00 (Sun)
 D-$17.00/$22.00 (Fri/Sat)
Hours: 8am-5am/24 hrs (Fri/Sat/Sun)
Casino Size: 12,000 Square Feet
Other Games: S21, P, PGP, TCP, LIR, K
Overnight RV Parking: Free/RV Dump: No
Senior Discount: Various Mon-Fri if 55+

7 Cedars Casino
270756 Highway 101
Sequim, Washington 98382
(360) 683-7777
Website: www.7cedarscasino.com
Map: **#4** (70 miles N.W. of Seattle via ferry)

Toll-Free Number: (800) 4-LUCKY-7
Restaurants: 2 Liquor: Yes
Buffets: L-$10.95/$11.95 (Sun)
        D-$9.95/$10.95 (Mon)/
        $12.95 (Tue)/$16.95 (Fri/Sat)
Hours: 9am-3am/4am (Fri/Sat)
Other Games: S21, P, PGP, LIR, TCP, K,
        BG, OTB (Wed-Mon)
Overnight RV Parking: Free (Must check-in
        first)/RV Dump: No

Shoalwater Bay Casino
4112 Highway 105
Tokeland, Washington 98590
(360) 267-2048
www.shoalwaterbaycasino.com
Map: **#18** (75 miles S.W. of Olympia)

Toll-Free Number: (888) 332-2048
Restaurants: 1 Liquor: No Valet Parking: No
Buffets: L-$3.99 D-$3.99/
        $5.99 (Wed/Sun)/$9.99 (Fri/Sat)
Hours: 10am-Midnight/2am (Fri/Sat)
Casino Size: 10,000 Square Feet
Other Games: S21, PGP, TCP, No Craps/Roulette
Overnight RV Parking: No
Senior Discount: Various on Tue if 55 or older
Special Features: 15-space RV park across
the street ($7/$15 with hook ups per night).

Silver Reef Hotel • Casino • Spa
4876 Haxton Way
Ferndale, Washington 98248
(360) 383-0777
Website: www.silverreefcasino.com
Map: **#21** (7 miles N. of Bellingham)

Toll-Free Number: (866) 383-0777
Rooms: 105 Price Range: $129-$169
Suites: 4 Price Range: $279-$299
Restaurants: 4 Liquor: Yes Valet Parking: No
Buffets: L-$9.95/$12.95 (Thu/Fri)/
        $13.95 (Sat/Sun)
        D-$15.95/$23.95 (Thu/Fri)/$21.95(Sat)
Casino Size: 48,000 Square Feet
Other Games: S21, PGP, TCP, FCP
Overnight RV Parking: Free/RV Dump: No

Skagit Valley Casino Resort
5984 N. Darrk Lane
Bow, Washington 98232
(360) 724-7777
Website: www.theskagit.com
Map: **#7** (75 miles N. of Seattle)

Toll-Free Number: (877) 275-2448
Room Reservations: (800) 895-3423
Rooms: 74 Price Range: $99-$139
Suites: 29 Price Range: $179-$219
Restaurants: 3 Liquor: Yes Valet Parking: No
Buffets: B-$14.95 (Sun)
        L-$7.95/$9.95 (Mon)/ $8.95(Sat)
        D-$15.95/$17.95 (Fri/Sat)
Hours: 9am-3am/5am (Fri/Sat)
Casino Size: 26,075 Square Feet
Other Games: P, PGP, FCP, K
Overnight RV Parking: No
Senior Discount: Various on Mon if 55 or older
Special Features: Two 18-hole golf courses.
2,700-seat outdoor events center. Health spa.

Snoqualmie Casino
37500 SE North Bend Way
Snoqualmie, WA 98065
(425) 888-1234
Website: www.snocasino.com
Map: **#2** (30 miles E. of Seattle)

Restaurants: 5 Liquor: Yes
Buffets: L-$14.95/$16.95 (Sat/Sun)
        D-$14.95/$23.95 (Tue/Sat)/
        $25.95 (Thu)/$26.95 (Fri)/$29.95 (Sun)
Hours: 24 Hours Daily
Other Games: S21, B, PGP, P, TCP

Suquamish Clearwater Casino Resort
15347 Suquamish Way N.E
Suquamish, Washington 98392
(360) 598-8700
Website: www.clearwatercasino.com
Map: **#14** (15 miles W. of Seattle via Bainbridge Ferry)

Toll-Free Number: (800) 375-6073
Room Reservations: (866) 609-8700
Rooms:70 Room Rates: $79-$139
Suites: 15 Room Rates: $109-$169
Restaurants: 4 Liquor: Yes Valet Parking: Free
Buffets: B-$13.95 (Sat/Sun) L-$9.95
D-$14.95/$23.95 (Fri/Sat)
Hours: 9am-5am/24 Hours (Fri/Sat)
Casino Size: 22,000 Square Feet
Other Games: S21, P, PGP, TCP, LIR, K
Overnight RV Parking: Free/RV Dump: No
Senior Discount: Various first Mon of month if 55+
Special features: Seattle and Edmonds Ferries fee reimbursed with qualified play. Gambling age is 18.

Swinomish Casino
12885 Casino Drive
Anacortes, Washington 98221
(360) 293-2691
Website: www.swinomishcasino.com
Map: **#7** (70 miles N. of Seattle, between I-5 and Anacortes on Hwy. 20)

Toll-Free Number: (888) 288-8883
Restaurants: 2 Liquor: Yes Valet: Free
Buffets: L-$15.99 (Sun)
D-$14.95/$25 (Fri)/$18.95 (Sat)
Hours: 8am-4am/24 hours (Fri/Sat)
Casino Size: 23,000 Square Feet
Other Games: P, PGP, TCP, FCP, BG, K, OTB
Overnight RV Parking: Must use RV park
Senior Discount: Buffet discount if 55+
Special Features: 35-space RV park ($22/$25 per night). Gift shop.

Tulalip Casino
10200 Quil Ceda Boulevard
Tulalip, Washington 98271
(360) 651-1111
Website: www.tulalipcasino.com
Map: **#1** (30 miles N. of Seattle)

Toll-Free Number: (888) 272-1111
Rooms: 370 Room Rates: $105-$195
Suites: 23 Room Rates: $235-$325
Restaurants: 4 Liquor: Yes Valet Parking: Free
Buffets: B-$9.95 L-$11.95
D-$18.95
Hours: 10am-6am/24 Hours (Thurs-Sat)
Casino Size: 45,000 Square Feet
Other Games: S21, B, MB, P, PGP, CSP, TCP, FCP LIR, K, BG
Overnight RV Parking: Free/RV Dump: No
Senior Discount: Various on Tue if 50+
Special Features: 2,300-seat amphitheatre. One mile from Quil Ceda Creek Casino.

Two Rivers Casino & Resort
6828-B Highway 25 South
Davenport, Washington 99122
(509) 722-4000
Website: www.two-rivers-casino.com
Map: **#8** (60 miles W. of Spokane)

Toll-Free Number: (800) 722-4031
Restaurants: 1 Liquor: No Valet Parking: No
Hours: 8am-10pm/12am (Fri/Sat)
Casino Size: 10,000 Square Feet
Overnight RV Parking: Must use RV park
Special Features: Regular slots. 100-space RV park ($35 per night). 260-slip marina and beach. Gambling age is 18.

Yakama Nation Legends Casino
580 Fort Road
Toppenish, Washington 98948
(509) 865-8800
Website: www.yakamalegends.com
Map: **#16** (20 miles S. of Yakima)

Toll-Free Number: (877) 7-COME-11
Restaurants: 2 Liquor: No Valet Parking: No
Buffets: L-$8.99/$12.99 (Thu/Sun)
          D-$12.99/$18.99 (Thu)
Hours: 9am-4am/5am (Sat/Sun)
Casino Size: 45,000 Square Feet
Other Games: S21, P, PGP, TCP, LIR, K
Overnight RV Parking: Free/RV Dump: No
Senior Discount: Various on Tue if 55 or older
Special Features: Childcare center. Indoor
waterfall. Gambling age is 18.

Card Rooms

Card rooms have been legal in Washington since 1974. Initially limited to just five tables per location, the law was changed in 1996 to allow up to 15 tables. One year later, a provision was added to allow house-banked games. Permissible games include: blackjack, Caribbean stud poker, pai gow poker, let it ride, casino war and numerous other card games. Baccarat, craps, roulette and keno are not allowed.

The maximum bet at each card room is dependant on certain licensing requirements and is capped at either $25 or $100. Additionally, the rooms can be open no more than 20 hours per day. These card rooms are now commonly called "mini-casinos." The minimum gambling age in a card room is 18.

Each city and county has the option to ban the card rooms so they are not found in every major city (Seattle has none). Due to space limitations we don't list all of the Washington card rooms in this book.

For a list of card rooms, we suggest that you contact the Washington State Gambling Commission at (360) 486-3581, or visit their website at: www.wsgc.wa.gov

WEST VIRGINA

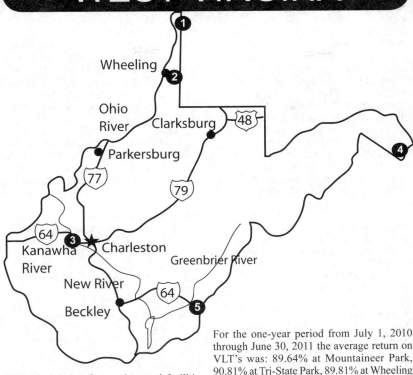

Wheeling

Ohio
River   Clarksburg   48

Parkersburg

77

79

64

Kanawha   Charleston
River
Greenbrier River

New River   64

Beckley

West Virginia has four pari-mutuel facilities and one resort hotel that feature video lottery terminals. The VLT's are the same as regular video gaming devices but are called lottery terminals because they are regulated by the state's lottery commission which receives a share of each machine's revenue.

The maximum allowable bet on a machine is $5 and there is no limit on the prize payouts. Most of the gaming machines pay out coins or tokens, but there are also some machines which will only print out a receipt which must be taken to a cashier.

West Virginia law requires that VLT's return a minimum of 80% to a maximum of 95%. VLT games include: slots, blackjack, keno and numerous versions of poker. The minimum gambling age is 18.

For the one-year period from July 1, 2010 through June 30, 2011 the average return on VLT's was: 89.64% at Mountaineer Park, 90.81% at Tri-State Park, 89.81% at Wheeling Island and 89.75% at Charles Town Races.

West Virginia law also allows bars, as well as restaurants that serve alcohol, to have up to five VLT's. Fraternal organizations are also allowed to have up to 10 VLT's. All of these machines are identical to the machines found at the racetracks, except they only print out tickets and do not pay out in cash.

All West Virgina casinos also offer the following table games: blackjack, craps, roulette, three-card poker, four-card poker and Let It Ride. Optional games offered include: poker (P), pai gow poker (PGP), Caribbean stud poker (CSP), Spanish 21 (S21) and big 6 wheel (B6).

For West Virginia tourism information call (800) 225-5982 or go to: www.callwva.com.

Charles Town Races & Slots
P.O. Box 551
Charles Town, West Virginia 25414
(304) 725-7001
Website: www.ctownraces.com
Map: **#4** (320 miles N.E. of Charleston, on the Virginia border)

Toll-Free Number: (800) 795-7001
Rooms: 132 Price Range: $109-$189
Suites: 18 Price Range: $134-$289
Restaurants: 4 Valet Parking: $4/$6 (Fri-Sun)
Buffets: L-$12.99/$16.99 (Sun)
        D-$16.99/$26.99 (Tue)/
        $19.99 (Fri)/$21.99 (Sat)
Overnight RV Parking: Free/RV Dump: No
Special Features: Live thoroughbred racing Wed-Sun. Daily simulcasting of horse and dog racing. Food court with five fast-food outlets.

The Greenbrier
300 W. Main Street
White Sulphur Springs, WV 24986
(304) 536-1110
www.greenbrier.com
Map: **#5** (120 miles S.E. of Charleston)

Toll-free Number: (800) 453-4858
Rooms: 238 Price Range: $319-$545
Casino Hours: 11am-3am (Mon-Thu)
        11am-4am (Fri/Sat)
        1pm-3am (Sun)
Casino Size: 75,000 square Feet
Other Games: P, B
Special Features: Casino open to hotel guests only. Dress code strictly enforced.

Mardi Gras Casino & Resort
1 Greyhound Drive
Cross Lanes, West Virginia 25313
(304) 776-1000
Website: www.tristateracetrack.com
Map: **#3** (10 miles N.W. of Charleston)

Toll-Free Number: (800) 224-9683
Restaurants: 5 Valet Parking: $3
Casino Size: 30,000 Square Feet
Other Games: B6
Overnight RV Parking: Free/RV Dump: No
Special Features: Live dog racing Wed-Mon. Daily simulcasting of horse and dog racing. Hotel expected to open late 2011

Mountaineer Casino Racetrack & Resort
State Route #2
Chester, West Virginia 26034
(304) 387-2400
Website: www.mtrgaming.com
Map: **#1** (35 miles N. of Wheeling)

Toll-Free Number: (800) 804-0468
Room Reservations: (800) 489-8192
Rooms: 238 Price Range: $117-$179
Suites: 20 Price Range: $165-$229
Restaurants: 8 Valet Parking: $5
Hours: 24 Hours Daily
Other Games: P, B6
Overnight RV Parking: Free/RV Dump: No
Special Features: 18-hole golf course. Spa and fitness center. Live thoroughbred racing Sat-Tue. Daily simulcasting of horse/dog racing.

Wheeling Island
Racetrack & Gaming Center
1 S. Stone Street
Wheeling, West Virginia 26003
(304) 232-5050
Website: www.wheelingisland.com
Map: **#2**

Toll-Free Number: (877) 946-4373
Room Reservations: (877) 943-3546
Rooms: 142 Price Range: $135-$165
Suites: 9 Price Range: $169-$250
Restaurants: 4 Valet Parking: $5
Buffets: L-$12.95/$13.49 (Sun)
        D-$15.95/$19.95 (Fri)/$17.95 (Sat)
Hours: 24 Hours Daily
Casino Size: 50,000 Square Feet
Other Games: CSP, P
Overnight RV Parking: Free/RV Dump: No
Senior Discount: Various on Wed if 55+
Special Features: Live dog racing daily except Tue/Thu. Daily simulcasting of horse and dog racing.

WISCONSIN

All Wisconsin casinos are located on Indian reservations.

The Tribes are not required to release information on their slot machine percentage paybacks, but according to the terms of the compact between the state and the tribes "for games not affected by player skill, such as slot machines, the machine is required to return a minimum of 80% and a maximum of 100% of the amount wagered."

All casinos offer blackjack, slots and video poker. Some casinos also offer: craps (C), roulette (R), mini baccarat (MB), poker (P), Pai Gow Poker (PGP), let it ride (LIR), big 6 wheel (B6), bingo (BG), keno (K) and off-track betting (OTB). Unless otherwise noted, all casinos are open 24 hours and the minimum gambling age is 21 (18 for bingo).

For visitor information contact the state's department of tourism at (800) 432-8747 or their web site at: www.travelwisconsin.com.

Bad River Lodge Casino
U.S. Highway 2
Odanah, Wisconsin 54861
(715) 682-7121
Website: www.badriver.com
Map: **#1** (halfway between Ironwood, MI and Ashland, WI; 45 miles east of Duluth, MN on US 2)

Toll-Free Number: (800) 777-7449
Lodge Reservations: (800) 795-7121
Rooms: 42 Price Range: $40-$65
Suites: 8 Price Range: $60-$75
Restaurants: 2 Liquor: Yes
Casino Size: 19,200 Square Feet
Hours: 8am-2am Daily
Other Games: C, R, P, TCP, LIR
Overnight RV Parking: Free/RV Dump: Free
Senior Discount: Various dining specials throughout the week if 55+.
Special Features: 20-space RV park (Free). Gas station. Grocery store.

Ho-Chunk Gaming Black River Falls
W9010 Highway 54 East
Black River Falls, Wisconsin 54615
(715) 284-9098
Website: www.mpcwin.com
Map: **#8** (110 miles M.W. of Madison on Hwy. 54, 4 miles E. of I-94)

Toll-Free Number: (800) 657-4621
Rooms: 60 Price Range: $49-$88
Suites: 6 Price Range: $88-$125
Restaurants: 2 Liquor: Yes
Buffets: L-$7.99/$10.99 (Fri/Sat)/$11.95 (Sun)
    D-$12.99/$14.99 (Fri-Sun)
Open 24 hours daily Memorial to Labor Day
Size: 35,000 Square Feet
Other Games: BG, TCP, FCP, LIR
Overnight RV Parking: Free/RV Dump: No
Senior Discount: $5 off bingo Sundays if 55+
Special Features: 10% off food/hotel for slot club members.

Ho-Chunk Gaming Madison
4002 Evan Acres Rd.
Madison, WI 53718
(608)223-9576
Website: www.dejope.com
Map: **#17**

Toll-Free Number: (888)248-1777
Restaurants: 1 Liquor: No
Hours: 7am-4am Daily
Casino Size: 22,000 Square Feet
Other Games: Only Gaming Machines
Senior Discount: $5 free play on Wed if 55+

Ho-Chunk Gaming Nekoosa
949 County Road G
Nekoosa, Wisconsin 54457
(715) 886-4560
Website: www.rbcwin.com
Map: **#15** (50 miles S. of Wausau)

Toll-Free Number: (800) 782-4560
Restaurants: 2 Liquor: Yes
Other Games: R, P, LIR, TCP
Overnight RV Parking: Free (must check-in
      first with security)/RV Dump: No
Senior Discount: Specials on Thu if 55+
Special Features: Smoke and gift shop.
Convenience store.

Ho-Chunk Gaming Tomah
27867 Highway 21
Tomah, Wisconsin 54660
(608) 372-3721
Map: **#16** (3 miles E. of Tomah on Hwy 21)

Restaurants: 1 Snack Bar Liquor: No
Hours: 8am-Midnight/2am (Fri/Sat)
Casino Size: 2,000 Square Feet
Other Games: Only Gaming Machines
Special Features: Convenience store. Open
24 hours Fri-Sat during the summer.

Ho Chunk Gaming Wisconsin Dells
S3214 Highway 12
Baraboo, Wisconsin 53913
(608) 356-6210
Website: www.ho-chunk.com
Map: **#4** (40 miles N. of Madison. On Hwy.
12 just S. of Delton)

Toll-Free Number: (800) 746-2486
Room Reservations: (800) 446-5550
Rooms: 295 Price Range: $79-$140
Suites: 20 Price Range: $130-$240
Restaurants: 4 Liquor: Yes
Buffets: B-$7.99 (Sat-Sun) L-$9.99
      D-$12.99/$24.99 (Wed) $14.99 (Fri)/
      $15.99 (Sat)
Casino Size: 90,000 Square Feet
Other Games: C, R, P, TCP,
            OTB, BG (Tue-Sun)
Overnight RV Parking: Free/RV Dump: No
Special Features: Smoke shop. Free local
shuttle. Kid's Quest childcare center.

Ho-Chunk Gaming Whittenberg
N7214 US Hwy 45
Wittenberg, WI 54499
(608) 372-3721
Map: **#16** (3 miles E. of Tomah on Hwy 21)

Restaurants: 1 Snack Bar Liquor: No
Casino Size: 2,000 Square Feet
Other Games: Only Gaming Machines
Special Features: Convenience store. Open
24 hours Fri-Sat during the summer.

Lake of the Torches Resort Casino
510 Old Abe Road
Lac du Flambeau, Wisconsin 54538
(715) 588-7070
Website: www.lakeofthetorches.com
Map: **#7** (160 miles N.W. of Green Bay.
Heading N. on Hwy. 51, go left on Hwy. 47,
12 miles to casino)

Toll-Free Number: (800) 25-TORCH
Room Reservations: (888) 599-9200
Rooms: 88 Price Range: $95-$155
Suites: 13 Price Range: $150-$195
Restaurants: 2 Liquor: Yes
Buffets: B-$6.50 L-$8.75/$12.95 (Sat/Sun)
      D-$13.95/$15.95 (Sat)/$24.50 (Fri)
Other Games: P, BG (Wed-Sun)
Overnight RV Parking: Free/RV Dump: No
Special Features: Slot club members get 20%
off room and other discounts.

Legendary Waters Resort & Casino
Highway 13 North, Box 1167
Bayfield, Wisconsin 54814
(715) 779-3712
Website: www.legendarywaters.com
Map: **#6** (70 miles E. of Duluth, MN on Hwy.
13, 3 miles N. of Bayfield)

Toll-Free Number: (800) 226-8478
RV Reservations: (715) 779-3743
Rooms: 50 Price Range: $75-$99
Suites: 7 Price Range: $109-$199
Restaurants: 1 Liquor: Yes
Hours: 10am-2am Daily
Other Games: BG (Fri/Sat/Sun), P
Overnight RV Parking: Must use RV park
Special Features: Campground and 30-space
RV park ($25-$30 per night). 34-slip marina.

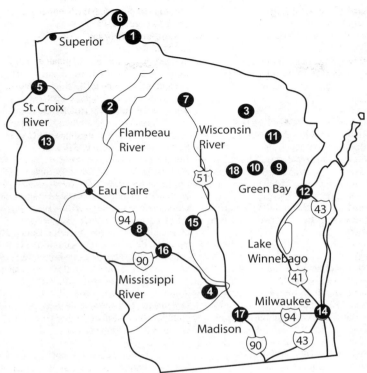

Superior
St. Croix River
Flambeau River
Wisconsin River
Eau Claire
Green Bay
51
94
Lake Winnebago
Mississippi River
43
41
Milwaukee
94
Madison
90
43

LCO Casino, Lodge & Convention Center
13767 W County Road B
Hayward, Wisconsin 54843
(715) 634-5643
Website: www.lcocasino.com
Map: **#2** (55 miles S.E. of Duluth, MN. 3 miles
N.E. of Hayward on county trunk B)

Toll-Free Number: (800) 526-2274
Room Reservations: (800) LCO-LODGE
Rooms: 53 Price Range: $59-$89
Suites: 22 Price Range: $80-$130
Restaurants: 2 Liquor: Yes
Buffets:B-$6.95 (Sat) L-$8.95//$12.95 (Sun)
    D-$8.95/$10.95 (Fri/Sat)/$12.95 (Sun)
Casino Size: 35,000 Square Feet
Other Games: C, R, P, LIR, BG
Overnight RV Parking: Free (must register
first at customer service)/RV Dump: No
Special Features: Nearby 8-space RV park
(Free). Sports lounge. Gift shop. No bingo
Mon/Sat.

Menominee Casino Resort
P.O. Box 760, Highways 47 & 55
Keshena, Wisconsin 54135
(715) 799-3600
Website: www.menomineecasinoresort.com
Map: **#9** (40 miles N.W. of Green Bay on Hwy.
47, 7 miles N. of Shawano)

Toll-Free Number: (800) 343-7778
Rooms: 100 Price Range: $60-$90
Suites: 8 Price Range: $100-$145
Restaurants: 1 Liquor: Yes
Buffets: B-$12.99 (Sun)
    D-$15.99 (Fri)/$17.99 (Sat)/$12.99 (Sun)
Casino Size: 33,000 Square Feet
Other Games: C, R, P, LIR, TCP, BG, B6
Overnight RV Parking: Free/RV Dump: No
Special Features: 60-space RV park ($15 per
night). Gift shop. Smoke shop.

Mole Lake Casino & Lodge
Highway 55
Mole Lake, Wisconsin 54520
(715) 478-5290
Website: www.molelake.com
Map: **#3** (100 miles N.W. of Green Bay on
Hwy. 55, 7 miles S. of Crandon)

Toll-Free Number: (800) 236-9466
Motel Reservations: (800) 457-4312
Motel Rooms: 25 Rates: $55-$75
Lodge Rooms: 65 Price Range: $71-$93
Lodge Suites: 10 Price Range: $81-$136
Restaurants: 2 Liquor: Yes
Hours: 7am-2am/3am (Fri-Sat)
Other Games: BG (Fri-Tue)
Overnight RV Parking: Free/RV Dump: No
Special Features: Motel is two blocks from
casino.

North Star Mohican Casino
W12180A County Road Af
Bowler, Wisconsin 54416
(715) 787-3110
Website: www.northstarcasinoresort.com
Map: **#10** (50 miles N.W. of Green Bay)

Toll-Free Number: (800) 775-2274
Restaurants: 2 Liquor: Yes
Casino Size: 66,000 square Feet
Other Games: C, R, LIR, TCP, P,
        BG (Sun-Fri)
Overnight RV Parking: Free/RV Dump: Fee
Special Features: 57-space RV park ($25/$28
per night). Smoke shop. $10 freeplay with
stay at RV park.

Oneida Bingo & Casino
2020 Airport Drive
Green Bay, Wisconsin 54313
(920) 494-4500
Website: www.oneidacasino.net
Map: **#12** (across from Austin Straubel
Airport, take Interstate 43 to Highway 172)

Toll-Free Number: (800) 238-4263
Reservation Number: (800) 333-3333
Rooms: 408 Price Range: $105-$159
Suites: 40 Price Range: $195-$449
Restaurants: 3 Liquor: Yes
Buffets: L-$11.99/$13.99 (Sat/Sun)
        D-$16.99/$19.99 (Wed)
Hours: 10am-4am (Tables)/24 Hours (Slots)
Other Games: C, R, P, LIR, MB,
        TCP, FCP, BG, OTB
Overnight RV Parking: Free/RV Dump: No
Special Features: Two casinos. One is
connected to Radisson Inn where hotel rooms
are located. Free local shuttle. Smoke shop.

Oneida Casino - Mason Street
2522 W. Mason Street
Green Bay, Wisconsin 54313
(920) 494-4500
Website: www.oneidacasino.net
Map: **#12**

Restaurant: 1
Casino Size: 38,000 square feet
Overnight RV Parking: Free/RV Dump: No

Oneida Casino Travel Center
5939 Old 29 Drive
Green Bay, Wisconsin 54313
(920) 865-7919
Website: www.oneidacasino.net
Map: **#12**

Restaurant: 1
Casino Size 5,800 square feet
Overnight RV Parking: Free/RV Dump: No

Potawatomi Bingo Casino
1721 W. Canal Street
Milwaukee, Wisconsin 53233
(414) 645-6888
Website: www.paysbig.com
Map: **#14**

Toll-Free Number: (800) PAYS-BIG
Restaurants: 6　Liquor: Yes
Buffets: B-$18.00 (Sun)　L-$13.00
　　　　　D-$17.00/$13 (Tue/Thu)/
　　　　　$29.00 (Wed)/$24.00 (Fri/Sat)
Casino Size: 38,400 Square Feet
Other Games: S21, C, R, P, PGP, TCP,
　　　　　CW, B, LIR, FCP, BG, OTB
Overnight RV Parking: Free/RV Dump: No
Special Features: Smoke-free casino on 2nd
floor.

Potawatomi Carter Casino Hotel
Highway 32
Carter, Wisconsin 54566
(715) 473-2021
Website: www.cartercasino.com
Map: **#11** (85 miles N. of Green Bay on
Hwy. 32)

Toll-Free Number: (800) 487-9522
Lodge Reservations: (800) 777-1640
Rooms: 70　Price Range: $75-$95
Suites: 29　Price Range: $85-$150
Restaurants: 2　Liquor: Yes
Casino Size: 25,000 Square Feet
Other Games: C, LIR, TCP, BG (Wed-Sun)
Overnight RV Parking: Must use RV park
Senior Discount: Specials on Thu if 55+
Special Features: 10-space RV park ($15 per
night). 24-hour gas station and convenience
store.

St. Croix Casino Danbury
P.O. Box 98, Highways 35 & 77
Danbury, Wisconsin 54830
(715) 656-3444
Website: www.holeinthewallcasino.com
Map: **#5** (26 miles E. of Hinckley, MN)

Toll-Free Number: (800) 238-8946
Rooms: 45　Price Range: $60-$65
Suites: 1　Price Range: $80
Restaurants: 1　Liquor: Yes
Hours: 8am-2am/4am (Fri/Sat)
Casino Size: 22,500 Square Feet
Other Games: C, R, TCP
Overnight RV Parking: Must use RV park
Special Features: Craps and Roulette only
offered on weekends. 35-space RV park ($15
per night). $10 off room for slot club members.

St. Croix Casino & Hotel
777 US Highway 8
Turtle Lake, Wisconsin 54889
(715) 986-4777
Website: www.stcroixcasino.com
Map: **#13** (105 miles S. of Duluth, MN on
Hwy. 8)

Toll-Free Number: (800) 846-8946
Room Reservations: (800) 782-9987
Rooms: 145　Price Range: $55-$73
Suites: 8　Price Range: $95-$135
Restaurants: 2　　Liquor: Yes
Buffets: B-$6.99 (Sun)　L-$7.99
　　　　　D-$10.99/$24.99(Thu)
Casino Size: 95,000 Square Feet
Other Games: MB, C, R, P
Overnight RV Parking: Must use RV park
Special Features: 20% off rooms for slot
club member. 18-space RV park ($20/$25 for
electricity & water per night).

WYOMING

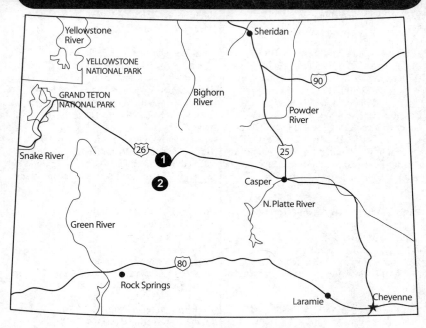

Wyoming's Indian casinos offer Class II bingo-type gaming machines, plus traditional Class III slot machines. Two of the casinos also offers some card-based table games.

The machines don't pay out in cash. Instead they print out a receipt which must be cashed by a floor attendant or taken to the cashier's cage. You can also make bets via a cashless system whereby you get a "smart" card and deposit money to that card's account. The machines will then deducts losses from, or credit wins to, your account.

No public information is available regarding the payback percentages on Wyoming's gaming machines. Unless otherwise noted, the casinos are open 24 hours and the minimum gambling age is 18.

For Wyoming tourism information call (800) 225-5996 or visit their web site at: www. wyomingtourism.org

Little Wind Casino
693 Blue Sky Highway 132
Ethete, Wyoming 82520
(307) 438-7000
Website: www.windrivercasino.com/info/lwc.php
Map: **#2** (140 miles W. of Casper)

Restaurants: 1 Liquor: No Valet Parking: No
Casino Size: 1,920 Square Feet
Other Games: Blackjack (Thu-Sun), Three Card Poker
Overnight RV Parking: Free/RV Dump: No
Senior Discount: Various on Tue if 55+
Special Features: Convenience store. Gas station.

Shoshone Rose Casino
5690 U.S. Highway 287
Lander, Wyoming 82520
(307) 335-7529
Website: www.thesrcasino.com
Map: **#2** (140 miles W. of Casper)

Restaurants: 1 Liquor: No Valet Parking: No
Casino Size: 7,000 Square Feet
Overnight RV Parking: No

Wind River Casino
10269 Highway 789
Riverton, Wyoming 82501
(307) 856-3964
Website: www.windrivercasino.com
Map: **#1** (125 miles W. of Casper)

Toll-Free Number: (866) 657-1604
Restaurants: 2 Liquor: No Valet Parking: No
Other Games: Blackjack, Three Card Poker
Casino Size: 8,000 Square Feet
Overnight RV Parking: Free/RV Dump: No
Senior Discount: Various on Tue if 55+
Special Features: Smoke shop with 80 slot
machines. Gas station.

Casino Index

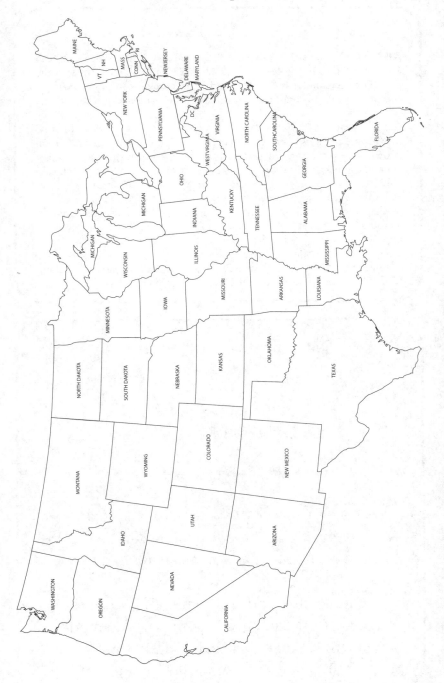

<u>Notice</u>

All copyrights of Casino Vacations Press, Inc., publisher of the American Casino Guide, are protected by federal law. **The barter, trade, sale, purchase or transfer for compensation, in whole or in part, of any of the coupons in this book, is strictly prohibited and makes them void.**

Casino Vacations Press, Inc. and/or its parent or subsidiaries, will not be responsible if a participating merchant refuses to honor a coupon offer in this book. However, we will try to secure compliance. Additionally, Casino Vacations Press, Inc. and/or its parent or subsidiaries, disclaims all alleged liability, for bodily injury or property damage resulting from any accident, event or occurrence on, or resulting from the use of the premises of the participating merchants. Casino Vacations Press, Inc. and/or its parent or subsidiaries, disclaims all warranties, expressed or implied, or otherwise imposed by law, regarding the condition of those premises or the safety of same. Casino Vacations Press, Inc. and/or its parent or subsidiaries, disclaims all alleged vicarious liability for bodily injury or property damage resulting from the acts or ommissions of the participating merchants.

Don't miss the 2013 edition of
the American Casino Guide

Completely Updated
More Casinos! • More Coupons!

On Sale - November 1, 2012

Ask for ISBN #978-1-883768-22-5 at
your favorite bookstore or call (800) 741-1596
or order online at: americancasinoguide.com

Be sure to sign up for our monthly newsletter
at americancasinoguide.com/newsletter and
we will send you a special offer to buy the
2013 Guide at a pre-publication price!

Coupon Directory

COUPON CHANGES

Coupon offers can change without notice.
To see a list of any coupon changes, go to:
americancasinoguide.com/coupon-changes.html

We will list any coupon changes on that page.

AMERICAN CASINO GUIDE

$20 Off.

- Reserve any size car, minivan, or SUV in the United States, Latin America, Caribbean or Asia Pacific.
- Valid for a rental of at least 4 days.
- Valid through 12/31/12.
- Saturday-overnight keep required.
- Book online at alamo.com or call 1-800-462-5266. Be sure to request Contract ID 7015000 and Coupon Code AD7779SDW at time of reservation.

See terms and conditions on reverse side of this coupon.

CASINO COUPON

AMERICAN CASINO GUIDE

One FREE Day.

- Reserve a compact through fullsize car in the United States, Latin America, Caribbean or Asia Pacific.
- Valid for a rental of at least 5 days.
- Valid through 12/31/12.
- Saturday-overnight keep required.
- Book online at alamo.com or call 1-800-462-5266. Be sure to request Contract ID 7015000 and Coupon Code AF4172SDW at time of reservation.

See terms and conditions on reverse side of this coupon.

CASINO COUPON

AMERICAN CASINO GUIDE

Save Up to 20%.

Going somewhere? Drive Happy® and save up to 20% each time you rent with Alamo®.

Book online at alamo.com or call 1-800-462-5266 and be sure to request Contract ID 7015000 at the time of reservation.

See terms and conditions on reverse side.

CASINO COUPON

Terms and Conditions

To save $20 off your rental, rent a compact through fullsize car, minivan or SUV for at least four days and get behind the wheel before December 31, 2012.Keeping the rental for a Saturday night and no longer than 28 days is a must. This offer is good at any US, Latin America, Caribbean or Asia Pacific Alamo location. Make your reservation 24 hours ahead of time. This offer can't be combined with another. Renter must meet standard rental qualifications. Drivers under age 25 may have to pay higher rates. The dollars off is prorated against the base rate for the length of your rental. axes, government charges of up to 23%, recoupment fees of up to $2US per day or $3US per rental, airport fees of up to $6 US per day or $19 US per rental, refueling, additional driver fee, one-way rental charge and optional items [i.e. CDW Waiver Savers® up to $30 US per day] are extra. Remember to check your insurance policy and/or credit card for rental vehicle coverage. Availability is limited. This offer may change without notice. Blackout dates may apply and this offer is void where prohibited. Bring this coupon to the rental counter when you pick up your car. It only works once. We can't accept this coupon if it has been purchased, sold or bartered for cash. In some countries, the value may be converted to local currency. There is no cash refund for the part you haven't used.

Terms and Conditions

To get a free day, simply rent a compact through fullsize car for at least four days and get behind the wheel before December 31, 2012. Keeping the rental for a Saturday night and no longer than 28 days is a must. This offer is good at participating US, Latin America, Caribbean or Asia Pacific Alamo location, except for one, Manhattan N.Y. Make your reservation 24 hours ahead of time. This offer can't be combined with another. Renter must meet standard rental qualifications. The free day is prorated against the base rate for the length of your rental. Taxes, government charges, recoupment fees, multiple airport fees, refueling, additional driver fee, drivers under age 25, one-way rental charge, and optional items [i.e. CDW Waiver Savers® up to $30 US per day] are extra. Remember to check your insurance policy and/or credit card for rental vehicle coverage. Availability is limited. This offer may change without notice. Blackout dates may apply and this offer is void where prohibited. Bring this coupon to the rental counter when you pick up your car. It only works once. We can't accept this coupon if it has been purchased, sold or bartereded for cash. In some countries, the value may be converted to local currency. There is no cash refund for the part you haven't used.

Terms and Conditions

To save up to 20 % off your rental, rent any size car get behind the wheel before December 31, 2012. This offer is good at participating US and Canada Alamo locations. Make your reservation 24 hours ahead of time. This offer can't be combined with another. Renter must meet standard rental qualifications. Drivers under age 25 may have to pay higher rates. This 20% discount is only good on your base rate. Taxes, government charges of up to 23%, recoupment fees of up to $2US per day or $3US per rental, airport fees of up to $6 US per day or $19 US per rental, refueling, additional driver fee, one-way rental charge and optional items [i.e. CDW Waiver Savers® up to $30 US per day] are extra. Remember to check your insurance policy and/or credit card for rental vehicle coverage. Don't forget, availability is limited. This offer may change without notice. And, unfortunately, blackout dates may apply and this offer is void where prohibited. In some countries, the value may be converted to local currency.

AMERICAN CASINO GUIDE

 **Save $20 off a weekly rental.**

- Reserve any size car, minivan or SUV in the United States, Latin America, Caribbean or Asia Pacific.
- Requires a 5-day minimum rental and a Saturday overnight.
- Valid through 12/31/12.
- Reserve online at nationalcar.com or call 1.800.CAR.RENT® and reference Contract ID 5028092 and Coupon Code ND4410JDAF.

Subject to terms and conditions on reverse side.

CASINO COUPON

AMERICAN CASINO GUIDE

 **One car class upgrade.**

- Reserve a compact through midsize car in the United States or Canada.
- Valid through 12/31/12.
- Book online at nationalcar.com or call 1-800-CAR-RENT®. (800-227-7368)
- Reserve online at nationalcar.com or call 1.800.CAR.RENT® and reference Contract ID 5028092 and Coupon Code NU25093JDB.

Subject to terms and conditions on reverse side.

CASINO COUPON

AMERICAN CASINO GUIDE

 **Save up to 20%.**

You drive a hard bargain. Save up to 20% on rentals at National Car Rental®.

Reserve online at nationalcar.com or call 1.800.CAR.RENT® and reference Contract ID 5028092. Go National. Go Like a Pro.

Subject to terms and conditions on reverse side.

CASINO COUPON

Terms and Conditions

To receive $20 off the weekly rate, rent a compact through fullsize car, Minivan or SUV for at least five days, starting before December 31, 2012. To take advantage of this offer, make a reservation at least 24 hours in advance. Please note that a Saturday overnight is required and a 28-day maximum rental applies. Unfortunately, we cannot combine this offer with any other discount and cannot apply the offer to a previous or existing reservation. All standard rental qualifications apply. This discount is applied directly to your base rate and unlimited mileage charges only. Be aware that taxes, surcharges, recovery and recoupment fees and other charges may apply, and that optional products and services (such as damage waiver and additional drivers fees) are extra charges. Please check your auto insurance policy and/or credit card agreement for rental vehicle coverage. Regrettably, the availability of this offer is limited to participating U.S., Latin America, Caribbean and Asia Pacific locations and is subject to change without notice. Blackout dates may also apply. Please present the original coupon at time of rental. We cannot accept the coupon if it has been purchased, bartered or sold for cash. International customers should be advised that some countries may convert the value of the offer into local currency.

Terms and Conditions

To receive a free upgrade to the next available car class, rent a compact through midsize vehicle before December 31, 2012. To take advantage of this offer, make a reservation at least 24 hours] in advance. Unfortunately, we cannot combine this offer with any other discount and cannot apply the offer to a previous or existing reservation. We can only accept one coupon per rental. All standard rental qualifications apply. Be aware that taxes, surcharges, recovery and recoupment fees and other charges may apply, and that optional products and services (such as damage waivers and additional drivers fees) are extra charges. Please check your auto insurance policy and/or credit card agreement for rental vehicle coverage. Regrettably, the availability of this offer is limited to participating U.S. and Canada locations and is subject to change without notice. Vehicle upgrade is limited to availability at time of pick up. Blackout dates may also apply. Please present the original coupon at time of rental. We cannot accept the coupon if it has been purchased, bartered or sold for cash. International customers should be advised that some countries may convert the value of the offer into local currency.

Terms and Conditions

To receive 20% off the rate, rent any size car starting before December 31, 2012. To take advantage of this offer, make a reservation at least 24 hours in advance. Please note that a 28-day maximum rental applies. Unfortunately, we cannot combine this offer with any other discount and cannot apply the offer to a previous or existing reservation. All standard rental qualifications apply. This discount is applied directly to your base rate only. Be aware that taxes, surcharges, recovery and recoupment fees and other charges may apply, and that optional products and services (such as damage waivers and additional drivers fees) are extra charges. Please check your auto insurance policy and/or credit card agreement for rental vehicle coverage. Regrettably, the availability of this offer is limited to participating U.S. and Canada locations and is subject to change without notice. Blackout dates may also apply. International customers should be advised that some countries may convert the value of the offer into local currency.

kidsquest.com

Buy 1 Hour, Get 1 Hour FREE

Hourly child care activity center
Caring for children 6 weeks to 12 years old.

Kids Quest activity center offers infant and toddler care, a Techno Quest video and arcade games area, a Karaoke Star Stage, gym, quiet play zone, and an indoor playground, Cosmic Club, and Sparkle Salon (activities vary by center). Shoe-free, socks required.

A current American Casino Guide Discount Card must be presented when redeeming this coupon, or offer is void

---

Play $30 Get $10 FREE!

Play $30 and receive $10 on your Premier Club Card. Must be a Premier Club member. Offer expires December 31, 2012. See reverse for full details.

A current American Casino Guide Discount Card must be presented when redeeming this coupon, or offer is void

---

Veranda CAFÉ

Free Appetizer with the Purchase of Two Entrées
(Excluding Seafood Appetizers)

Present this coupon to your server at the Veranda Cafe before ordering to receive one FREE appetizer with the purchase of two Entrées. Valid Sunday-Thursday. See reverse for more details.

A current American Casino Guide Discount Card must be presented when redeeming this coupon, or offer is void

americancasinoguide.com

Present this coupon when you check in at any Kids Quest and receive the second hour of child care FREE with any purchase of the first hour. A photo ID required. Limit one coupon per family per visit. Not valid with any other offer. Non-transferable. Management reserves all rights. No cash value. No money back for unused time. Offer expires 12/31/12.

Valid at all Kids Quest locations. Las Vegas centers include Boulder Station, The Palms, Red Rock Casino, Santa Fe Station, Sunset Station and Texas Station.

For additional locations visit: www.kidsquest.com

Am Cas Guide

Offer void if coupon is copied or sold

---

americancasinoguide.com

Gold Creek Casino
400 E. Bennett Avenue
Cripple Creek, CO 80813

Double Eagle Casino
442 E. Bennett Avenue
Cripple Creek, CO 80813

(800) 711-7234
(719) 689-5000
www.decasino.com

Must present coupon. Limit one coupon per customer per day. Not valid for use with any other coupons, ads or promotions. Must be 21 years of age and a Premier Club Member. Membership in Premier Club is free. Management reserves the right to cancel or change this promotion at any time. Valid through December 31, 2012

Offer void if coupon is copied or sold

---

americancasinoguide.com

Veranda
C A F E

Veranda Cafe
at Foxwoods Resort Casino
Open Daily at 7 a.m.
www.foxwoods.com

Prices do not include tax or gratuity. Valid Sunday – Thursday. Not valid on holidays. Only one coupon per person allowed. Management reserves all rights. Offer valid through December 30, 2012.

Offer void if coupon is copied or sold

CEDARS STEAK HOUSE

2-For-1 Soup or Salad

Present this coupon to your server at Cedars Steak House before ordering to receive two soups or salads for the price of one. Valid Sunday-Thursday. See reverse for more details.

A current American Casino Guide Discount Card must be presented when redeeming this coupon, or offer is void

FOXWOODS

Free Appetizer with the Purchase of Two Entrees
(Excluding the Jumbo Combo)

Present this coupon to your server at The Hard Rock Cafe before ordering to receive one FREE appetizer with the purchase of two entrees. See reverse for more details.

A current American Casino Guide Discount Card must be presented when redeeming this coupon, or offer is void

GET $25 FREE SLOT PLAY
SIGN UP TODAY!

Offer good for new IsleOne® club members only.
Valid November 1, 2011 – December 30, 2012

A current American Casino Guide Discount Card must be presented when redeeming this coupon, or offer is void

americancasinoguide.com

**Cedars Steak House
at Foxwoods Resort Casino
Open Daily at 11:30 a.m.
www.foxwoods.com**

Prices do not include tax or gratuity. Valid Sunday – Thursday. Not valid on holidays. Only one coupon per person allowed. The higher priced item will be charged. Management reserves all rights. Offer valid through December 30, 2012.

Offer void if coupon is copied or sold

americancasinoguide.com

FOXWOODS

**Hard Rock Cafe
at Foxwoods Resort Casino
Open Daily at 11 a.m.
www.foxwoods.com**

Prices do not include tax or gratuity. Not valid on holidays. Only one coupon per person allowed. Management reserves all rights. Offer valid through December 30, 2012.

Offer void if coupon is copied or sold

americancasinoguide.com

CONNECT WITH US **@IsleCasinoPP**

**777 ISLE OF CAPRI CIRCLE
POMPANO BEACH, FL 33069**

1-877-ISLE-2WIN
www.theislepompanopark.com

© 2011 Isle of Capri Casinos, Inc. Excluding holidays. Cannot be combined with any offer. Must be 21. Gambling problem? Call 1-888-ADMIT-IT.

POMPANO PARK

Offer void if coupon is copied or sold

FREE Dessert
with the purchase
of an Entrée

MARDI GRAS CASINO

Present this coupon at The French Quarter Restaurant located on the 3rd floor to receive one dessert free when an entrée is purchased at regular menu price. See reverse for details.

A current American Casino Guide Discount Card must be presented when redeeming this coupon, or offer is void

Buy One Entrée,
Receive One FREE

MARDI GRAS CASINO

Present this coupon at The Dawg House Bar and Grill or the French Quarter Restaurant and Bar to receive one entrée free when an entrée is purchased at regular menu price. See reverse for details.

A current American Casino Guide Discount Card must be presented when redeeming this coupon, or offer is void

JOLIET CASINO & HOTEL

Buy One Entrée
Get One FREE

Present this coupon at Mosaic or The Reserve Steakhouse, along with your Total Rewards card, to receive one FREE entrée (of equal or lesser value) with the purchase of one entrée. All ages welcome. See reverse for full details.

A current American Casino Guide Discount Card must be presented when redeeming this coupon, or offer is void

MARDI GRAS CASINO

831 N. Federal Highway
Hallandale Beach, FL 33009
(877) 557-5687
(954) 924-3200

Must be 21 years of age to purchase & consume alcohol. Not valid on any other offer or special. Limit one coupon per person.

Original coupon must be presented (no photocopies). Tax and gratuity not included. Management reserves the right to cancel or alter this coupon without prior notice. Offer expires 12/30/12.

When gambling is no longer a game…call 1-888-ADMIT-IT.

Offer void if coupon is copied or sold

MARDI GRAS CASINO

831 N. Federal Highway
Hallandale Beach, FL 33009
(877) 557-5687
(954) 924-3200

Must be 21 years of age to purchase & consume alcohol. Free entrée must be of equal or lesser value than purchased entrée. Not valid on any other offer or special.

Limit one coupon per person. Original coupon must be presented (no photocopies). Tax and gratuity not included. Management reserves the right to cancel or alter this coupon without prior notice. Offer expires 12/30/12.

When gambling is no longer a game… call 1-888-ADMIT-IT.

Offer void if coupon is copied or sold

JOLIET CASINO & HOTEL

151 N. Joliet Street
Joliet, IL 60432
(815) 740-7800
harrahsjoliet.com

Maximum value in Mosaic is $20.00. Maximum value in The Reserve Steakhouse is $40.00. Valid for cash sales only. Valid for dine in only. Alcohol and gratuity not included. Some restrictions apply. Not valid at our buffet or Ace's diner. See Total Rewards for complete details. Valid Total Rewards card required. In some cases a valid government issued picture ID may also be required. Subject to rules available at venue. This offer is non-transferable, non-negotiable, subject to availability, cannot be combined with any other offer or complimentary. Must be 21 years of age or older to gamble. Alteration, duplication or unauthorized use voids this offer. Some blackout dates may apply. Harrah's reserves the right to change or cancel this program at any time upon IGB approval. Harrah's employees and their immediate families are not eligible. Know When To Stop Before You Start. Gambling Problem? Call 1-800-GAMBLER. ©2011, Caesars License Company, LLC. All rights reserved. Offer expires 12/30/12.

Offer void if coupon is copied or sold

AMERICAN CASINO GUIDE

BUY ONE MEAL, GET ONE FREE
AT PASSPORTS BUFFET

OFFER VALID SUNDAY - THURSDAY ONLY

Present this coupon to the cashier at Passports Buffet
to receive your buy one meal, get one free. Excludes
alcohol and gratuity. No cash value.
Valid through December 30, 2012.
See back for complete details. CASINOG

Majestic®
Star
CASINO & HOTEL

Player Account Number _____

A current American Casino Guide Discount Card must be
presented when redeeming this coupon, or offer is void

AMERICAN CASINO GUIDE

FREE REGULAR CUP OF COFFEE
AT JACKPOT JAVA

Present this coupon to the cashier at Jackpot Java for a
free regular cup of coffee. Excludes alcohol and gratuity.
No cash value. Valid through December 30, 2012.
See back for complete details. CASINOG

Majestic®
Star
CASINO & HOTEL

Player Account Number _____

A current American Casino Guide Discount Card must be
presented when redeeming this coupon, or offer is void

AMERICAN CASINO GUIDE

ALL THRILLS! ALL THE TIME!
$5 Free PLAY WITH NEW CARD SIGN UP!

ARGOSY®
CASINO
SIOUX CITY

A current American Casino Guide Discount Card must be
presented when redeeming this coupon, or offer is void

**5000 South Beach Blvd.
Bay St. Louis, MS 39520
www.silverslipper-ms.com
1-866-SLIPPER**

Present this coupon to the Players Club to redeem offer. Must be a Silver Slipper Casino Players Club member to participate. Membership is free; must be 21 years or older. Not valid on holidays or holiday weekends.

Limit one coupon, per person for the duration of the promotion. Not valid with any other offer. Management reserves all rights. Offer expires 12/24/12.

ACG12

Offer void if coupon is copied or sold

RESORT & CASINO • BILOXI

**875 Beach Boulevard
Biloxi, MS 39530
(228) 386-7111 • (888) 595-2534
www.beaurivage.com**

Coupon must be presented at Memphis Q Smokehouse in the Beau Rivage. Must be 21 years of age. May not be used in conjunction with any other offers. Memphis Q closed Sunday and Monday.

Not valid at any other outlet when Memphis Q is closed. Limit one coupon per guest check. Offer subject to change or cancellation without notice. Valid through December 30, 2012.

Offer void if coupon is copied or sold

HOLLYWOOD
Casino®
TUNICA, MS

Buy One
Epic Buffet and
Get One Free!

Enjoy two buffets for the price of one at Hollywood's Epic Buffet!
Dine and play among movie memorabilia in an authentic
Hollywood atmosphere 7 days a week! See reverse for details.

HOLLYWOOD
Casino®
TUNICA, MS

Room Rates
From $59
(Sun-Thu)

Special packages available! Call 1-800-871-0711
for reservations. See reverse for details.

ARGOSY®
CASINO
HOTEL & SPA

Buy One
Terrace Buffet
Get One FREE!

Present this coupon to buffet cashier to receive two buffets
for the price of one! Valid any day, except holidays, for
breakfast, lunch or dinner. Offer expires 12/18/12.

Comp Code #108

americancasinoguide.com

US Hwy 93
Boulder City, NV. 89005
(702) 293-5000
(800) 245-6380
www.haciendaonline.com

HOTEL & CASINO "A FUN PLACE!"

Overlooking Beautiful Lake Mead, Near Hoover Dam

One Coupon Per Party Of Two. May not be combined with any other offer or discount.
Cannot be redeemed as cash. Management reserves the right to cancel or modify this at
any time without notice. Tax and gratuity not included. Expires 12/31/12.

Offer void if coupon is copied or sold

---

americancasinoguide.com

US Hwy 93
Boulder City, NV. 89005
(702) 293-5000
(800) 245-6380
www.haciendaonline.com

HOTEL & CASINO "A FUN PLACE!"

Overlooking Beautiful Lake Mead, Near Hoover Dam

Present this coupon, pay for one night stay and receive a second night FREE.
Must be 21 years of age. Excludes weekends, holidays, and special events.
Cannot be redeemed for cash. Management reserves the right to cancel this offer
at any time without notice. Expires 12/31/12

Offer void if coupon is copied or sold

---

americancasinoguide.com

1 Main Street
Jean, NV 89019
(800) 634-1359
www.stopatjean.com

To Redeem: 1) Present this coupon with club card (or join club) at the Gold Strike club booth to
receive a validation slip. 2) Present this coupon and your validation slip to server before ordering
entree or to cashier as you enter buffet.

Must be at least 21 years of age and a member of, or join, Gold Strike's Cash & Comp Club.
Offer may not be combined with any other offers or programs. Limit one redemption per club
account. Offer not valid to employees of Gold Strike. Management reserves all rights. Offer
expires 12/30/12.

Jean is located at Exit 12 off I-15
Just 20 minutes south of the world famous Las Vegas Strip.

Offer void if coupon is copied or sold

$10 FREE Slot Play or $10 Matchplay!

New members only, present this coupon at the
Players Advantage Club® booth, sign up for card and receive
$10 in FREE slot play or a $10 table games matchplay.
See reverse for more details.

A current American Casino Guide Discount Card must be
presented when redeeming this coupon, or offer is void

2-For-1 Breakfast or Lunch Buffet

Present this coupon to the **ace** | PLAY™ Center at Arizona Charlie's Boulder
to receive one FREE breakfast or lunch buffet when you purchase one buffet at the
regular price. Not valid on Saturday, Sunday or holidays. See reverse for details.

ace | PLAY card #_____

A current American Casino Guide Discount Card must be
presented when redeeming this coupon, or offer is void

2-For-1 Breakfast or Lunch Buffet

Present this coupon to the **ace** | PLAY™ Center at Arizona Charlie's Decatur
to receive one FREE breakfast or lunch buffet when you purchase one buffet at the
regular price. Not valid on Saturday, Sunday or holidays. See reverse for details.

ace | PLAY card #_____

A current American Casino Guide Discount Card must be
presented when redeeming this coupon, or offer is void

americancasinoguide.com

 **GRAND LODGE CASINO**

AT HYATT REGENCY LAKE TAHOE

111 Country Club Drive
Incline Village, NV 89451
(775) 832-1234
(800) 327-3910

Must be 21 years of age, or older. New accounts only. One offer per account. Management reserves the right to alter or change promotion at any time. Expires 12/31/12.

Offer void if coupon is copied or sold

americancasinoguide.com

4575 Boulder Highway
Las Vegas, NV 89121
702-951-5800
800-362-4040
ArizonaCharliesBoulder.com

Must be 21 years of age or older. Must present **ace** | PLAY™ card and surrender this original coupon (no photocopies) to the **ace** | PLAY Center representative for a voucher. Resale prohibited. Maximum two people per coupon. Tax and tip are not included. Not valid for takeout. Management reserves the right to change or cancel this promotion at any time without notice. Valid through December 21, 2012.

Offer void if coupon is copied or sold

americancasinoguide.com

740 S. Decatur Boulevard
Las Vegas, NV 89107
702-258-5200
800-342-2695
ArizonaCharliesDecatur.com

Must be 21 years of age or older. Must present **ace** | PLAY™ card and surrender this original coupon (no photocopies) to the **ace** | PLAY Center representative for a voucher. Resale prohibited. Maximum two people per coupon. Tax and tip are not included. Not valid for takeout. Management reserves the right to change or cancel this promotion at any time without notice. Valid through December 21, 2012.

Offer void if coupon is copied or sold

2-For-1 Admission Tickets

Present this coupon to the Atomic Testing Museum Box Office
to receive two tickets to the museum for the price of one.
See reverse for details.

SKU# 566

A current American Casino Guide Discount Card must be
presented when redeeming this coupon, or offer is void

20% OFF

Redeem at the Bally's Spa for 20% off any spa treatment.
See reverse for details.

Offer code: 20SPA

A current American Casino Guide Discount Card must be
presented when redeeming this coupon, or offer is void

BALLY'S
LAS VEGAS

20% OFF PURCHASE

Redeem at select Bally's stores for 20% off your
purchase. See reverse for details.

Offer code: GUIDE CPN

A current American Casino Guide Discount Card must be
presented when redeeming this coupon, or offer is void

755 East Flamingo Road
Las Vegas, Nevada
(702) 589-9450
atomictestingmuseum.org

Offer valid for one free ticket to The Atomic Testing Museum with the purchase of a second ticket of equal or greater value. This offer is based on availability, has no cash value and cannot be combined with any other offer, promotion or discount. Management reserves all rights and may change or cancel this promotion at any time without notice. Offer is valid through December 28, 2012.

3645 Las Vegas Blvd. S.
Las Vegas, NV 89109
702-967-4111
BallysLasVegas.com

Limit 1 coupon per guest. Subject to availability. No cash value. Not valid on previously purchased services. Cannot be combined with any other offer. Subject to availability. Blackout dates may apply. Management reserves all rights. Offer subject to change or cancellation without notification. Offer expires 12/31/12

3645 Las Vegas Blvd. S.
Las Vegas, NV 89109
702-967-4111
BallysLasVegas.com

Valid at Bally's Avenue Shop, Signatures Shop, Park Place Jewelers, Le Menagerie, & Les Elements Shop. Excludes Pandora in Park Place Jewelers. Not valid on previous purchases. Limit 1 coupon per guest. Subject to availability. No cash value. Not valid on previously purchased tickets. Cannot be combined with any other offer. Subject to availability. Blackout dates may apply. Management reserves all rights. Offer subject to change or cancellation without notification. Offer Expires 12/31/12

$10 Blackjack Matchplay

Present this coupon at any blackjack table, along with your Bigshot Players Club card, prior to the start of a hand and we'll match your bet of $10 if you win. See reverse for details.

2-for-1 Lunch or Dinner Entrée

Buy one lunch or dinner entrée in our restaurant and get one entrée of equal or lesser value FREE! Present to server before ordering. See reverse for more details.

2,500 Slot Club Points For New Members

Present this coupon at the Bigshot Players Club booth to receive 2,500 FREE slot club points when you join as a new member. See reverse for more details.

**3016 E. Lake Mead Blvd.
N. Las Vegas, NV 89030
(702) 642-1940**

Limit: one coupon per person, per month. Cannot be redeemed for cash. Must be 21 or older. Cannot be combined with any other offer or promotion. Non-transferable. Offer void if sold.

Must present original coupon (no photocopies). Not responsible for lost or stolen coupon. Management reserves all rights. Offer may be changed or discontinued at anytime at the discretion of management. Offer expires December 30, 2012.

Offer void if coupon is copied or sold

**3016 E. Lake Mead Blvd.
N. Las Vegas, NV 89030
(702) 642-1940**

Limit one coupon per person. Must be 21 years or older. Purchase one lunch or dinner entrée to receive the second one of equal or lesser value free. Not valid on take out orders.Coupon is void if altered or duplicated. Must present original coupon (no photocopies).

Tax, beverages and gratuity are not included. Not valid with any other offers or discounts. Management reserves the right to cancel or modify offer at any time. Coupon has no cash value. Offer expires December 30, 2012.

Offer void if coupon is copied or sold

**3016 E. Lake Mead Blvd.
N. Las Vegas, NV 89030
(702) 642-1940**

Valid for new accounts only. Must be 21 or older. Cannot be combined with any other offer or promotion. Non-transferable. Offer void if sold. Please allow up to 48 hours for points to reflect on account balance.

Must present original coupon (no photocopies). Not responsible for lost or stolen coupon. Management reserves all rights. Offer may be changed or discontinued at anytime at the discretion of management. Offer expires December 30, 2012.

Offer void if coupon is copied or sold

CHAPEL OF THE FLOWERS

Intimate. Elegant. Legendary.

www.littlechapel.com

Wedding Package Bonus

Purchase a Traditional wedding package or larger and get a free 8x10 photograph and an additional two weeks of Internet ceremony viewing time. See reverse for details.

A current American Casino Guide Discount Card must be presented when redeeming this coupon, or offer is void

---

Clarion

20% Off Best Available Room Rate

Call 1-800-633-1777 and request group code: LCAS. Certain blackout dates may apply. Must present coupon upon check-in. See reverse for details.

A current American Casino Guide Discount Card must be presented when redeeming this coupon, or offer is void

---

Clarion

20% Off at The Bistro Restaurant

Present this coupon to your server before ordering at the Bistro Restaurant to receive 20% off your check, including wine and/or cocktails. See reverse for more details.

A current American Casino Guide Discount Card must be presented when redeeming this coupon, or offer is void

Intimate. Elegant. Legendary.

1717 Las Vegas Blvd. S.
Las Vegas, NV 89104
(800) 843-2410
www.littlechapel.com

Coupon must be redeemed at the Chapel of the Flowers. Limit one coupon per couple. Not valid with any other offer. Based on availability. No cash value. Management reserves the right to alter or cancel this promotion at any time. Expires 12/30/12.

Clarion Hotel and Casino
305 Convention Center Drive
Las Vegas, NV 89109
(702) 952-8000
www.clarionhotelvegas.com

Rate is subject to 12% tax. Must present coupon upon check-in. Subject to availabililty. Management reserves all rights to alter or discontinue this offer at any time without prior notice. Not valid with any other offer. Limit one coupon per room. Valid through 12/23/12.

Clarion Hotel and Casino
305 Convention Center Drive
Las Vegas, NV 89109
(702) 952-8000
www.clarionhotelvegas.com

Present this original coupon (no photocopies) to your server in the Bistro restaurant to receive 20% off your check, including wine and/or cocktails. Limit: one coupon per check. No cash value. Must be 21 years of age or older. Tax and gratuity not included. Resale prohibited. Management reserves all rights. Offer expires 12/23/12.

50% off at the Flame Steakhouse

Redeem this coupon for a 50% discount on your total bill, up to a maximum of $25 at the Flame Steakhouse. Coupon valid Sunday-Thursday only. Reservations recommended.

A current American Casino Guide Discount Card must be presented when redeeming this coupon, or offer is void

Play $10 and get $10 free play

(with your Passport Players Club Card)

Play $10 on slots or video poker and get $10 free play. Upon playing $10 through any Ellis Island slot or video poker machine, you will be credited with $10 in free-play. See reverse for details.

Name_____PPC_____

A current American Casino Guide Discount Card must be presented when redeeming this coupon, or offer is void

2-For-1 Menu Item

(or 50% off one item when dining alone).

Present this coupon, along with your Passport Players Club Card, at the Restaurant or BBQ in Ellis Island Casino & Brewery to receive one FREE menu item when you purchase one item at the regular price, or 50% off one item when dining alone. Not valid on daily specials. See reverse for more details.

A current American Casino Guide Discount Card must be presented when redeeming this coupon, or offer is void

americancasinoguide.com

600 E. Fremont Street
Las Vegas, NV 89101
(702) 385-5200
(800) 634-6703
www.ECVegas.com

Coupon must be surrendered to the server at the Flame Steakhouse before ordering. Must be 21 years or older to participate. Excludes holiday periods. Gratuities not included. Offer is non transferable and cannot be combined with any other offer. Limit: one coupon per person, per year. Management reserves all rights. Offer expires 12/27/12.

Offer void if coupon is copied or sold

americancasinoguide.com

4178 Koval Lane
Las Vegas, NV 89169
(702) 733-8901
www.ellisislandscasino.com

Must be playing with Passport Player's Club card, membership is free. Upon playing $10 through any slot or video poker machine, present this coupon at the Passport Players Club and you will be credited with $10 in free-play. Allow 24 hours for free-play to post to your account. Free-play must be played through once to cash out. Limit one voucher per customer. One time only. No cash value. Not valid in conjunction with any other offer. Must be 21 years or older to redeem. Management reserves the right to cancel or change this offer at any time. Offer expires December 30, 2012.

Offer void if coupon is copied or sold

americancasinoguide.com

4178 Koval Lane
Las Vegas, NV 89169
(702) 733-8901
www.ellisislandscasino.com

Present this original coupon (no photocopies) to the hostess in the restaurant or the BBQ, along with your Passport Players Club Card, to receive one FREE menu item from the regular menu with the purchase of another menu item at the regular price (or 50% off one item if dining alone). The FREE item must be of equal or lesser value. Limit: one coupon per customer. No cash value. Must be 21 years of age or older. Tax and gratuity not included. Membership in Passport Players Club must be in good standing. Resale prohibited. Management reserves all rights. Offer expires 12/30/12.

Offer void if coupon is copied or sold

4 FREE Cocktails
at the Casino Bar!

Present this coupon, along with your Passport Players Club Card,
at the Casino Bar inside Ellis Island Casino & Brewery to receive
four FREE cocktails of your choice. See reverse for more details.

A current American Casino Guide Discount Card must be
presented when redeeming this coupon, or offer is void

2 FOR 1
ENTRÉE

Emerald Island Grille

Come in and enjoy the luck of the Irish! Buy one entree
and get the second entree of equal or lesser value of FREE!*

A current American Casino Guide Discount Card must be
presented when redeeming this coupon, or offer is void

Settle to #635

FREE DESSERT
SPECIAL!

Emerald Island Grille

Purchase an entree at regular price & receive
a menu item dessert FREE!*

A current American Casino Guide Discount Card must be
presented when redeeming this coupon, or offer is void

Settle to #912

americancasinoguide.com

4178 Koval Lane
Las Vegas, NV 89169
(702) 733-8901
www.ellisislandcasino.com

Must be 21 years of age or older. No restrictions on brands. Gratuity not included. Please present before ordering. Original coupon must be presented (no photocopies) along with your Passport Players Club Card. Membership in Passport Players Club must be in good standing. Resale prohibited. Management reserves the right to cancel or alter this coupon without prior notice. Offer expires 12/30/12.

americancasinoguide.com

120 Market Street
Henderson, NV 89015
(702) 567-9160
The *Jewel* of Henderson

NEVADA'S *ONLY* ALL PENNY CASINO!

Redeem this coupon at Emerald Rewards Center prior to dining. Must be 21 years of age and an Emerald Rewards Member. Limit one coupon per member. Steak Entrees & Daily Specials Excluded. Coupon has no cash value. Copies are not accepted Offer Valid to December 31, 2012.

emeraldislandcasino.com

americancasinoguide.com

120 Market Street
Henderson, NV 89015
(702) 567-9160
The *Jewel* of Henderson

NEVADA'S *ONLY* ALL PENNY CASINO!

Redeem this coupon at Emerald Rewards Center prior to dining. Must be 21 years of age and an Emerald Rewards Member. Limit one coupon per member. Not Valid With Any Other Offer, Tier Meals, Coupon, or Promotions. Entree must be paid with, cash, credit, or points. Coupon has no cash value. Copies are not accepted. Offer Valid to December 31, 2012.

emeraldislandcasino.com

FREE GIFT
FOR NEW SIGN-UPS!

Sign Up At Emerald Rewards Center &
Receive A Free Gift! See Reverse For Details.

Settle to #934

A current American Casino Guide Discount Card must be
presented when redeeming this coupon, or offer is void

2-For-1
Erotic Heritage Museum
Admission Tickets

Present this coupon at time of purchase at the Erotic Heritage
Museum to receive two admission tickets for the price of one.
See reverse for details.

A current American Casino Guide Discount Card must be
presented when redeeming this coupon, or offer is void

One Complimentary Appetizer
or Dessert with the purchase of
two entrées at Don B's Steakhouse

Present this coupon to your server before ordering to
receive one complimentary appetizer or dessert with the
purchase of two entrées at Don B's Steakhouse
See reverse for more details.

ACG0112

A current American Casino Guide Discount Card must be
presented when redeeming this coupon, or offer is void

120 Market Street
Henderson, NV 89015
(702) 567-9160
The *Jewel* of Henderson

Redeem this coupon at Emerald Rewards Center . Must be 21 years of age and a New Sign Up. Limit one coupon per person. Not Valid With Any Other Offer. While Supplies Last. Copies are not accepted. Offer expires December 31, 2012.

emeraldislandcasino.com

Erotic Heritage Museum
3275 Industrial Road
Las Vegas, NV 89109
(702) 369-6442

The Las Vegas Erotic Heritage Museum is a 17,0000-square-foot facility dedicated to the preservation of erotic artifacts, fine art and film.

Present this coupon at time of purchase at the Erotic Heritage Museum to receive two admission tickets for the price of one. Save $15. No cash value.

Must be at least 18 years of age. Management reserves all rights and may change or cancel this promotion at any time without notice. Offer is valid through December 28, 2012.

301 Fremont St.
Las Vegas, NV 89101
(702) 388-2400
1-800-274-LUCK
fitzgeraldslasvegas.com

Must be 21 years of age or older. Tax and gratuity not included. Reservations recommended. Please call (702) 388-2460. Coupon has no cash value and may be revoked/cancelled at anytime. Employees of Fitzgeralds are not eligible. Not valid with any other offer. Management reserves all rights. Offer valid through 12/30/12.

2-For-1 Burger in the Courtyard Grill

Present this coupon to your server in the Courtyard Grill to receive one FREE burger with the purchase of one burger of equal or greater value. See reverse for more details.

ACG0212

A current American Casino Guide Discount Card must be presented when redeeming this coupon, or offer is void

---

Get a Free Fitz Keychain With a New Club Fitz Sign-Up

Present this coupon at the Club Fitz Card Center to receive one free keychain when you first sign up for a Club Fitz Card. Only Valid for New Members.

ACG0312

A current American Casino Guide Discount Card must be presented when redeeming this coupon, or offer is void

---

2-for-1 VIP Tickets

Buy one VIP ticket to Fitz of Laughter at Fitzgeralds Casino and get a second ticket FREE. See reverse for more details.

A current American Casino Guide Discount Card must be presented when redeeming this coupon, or offer is void

**301 Fremont St.
Las Vegas, NV 89101
(702) 388-2400
1-800-274-LUCK**
fitzgeraldslasvegas.com

Present this original coupon to your server at the Courtyard Grill to receive one FREE burger with the purchase of another burger at the regular price. The FREE burger must be of equal or lesser value. Limit: one coupon per customer. No cash value. Must be 21 years of age or older. Tax and gratuity not included. Resale prohibited. Management reserves all rights. Offer valid through 12/30/12.

**301 Fremont St.
Las Vegas, NV 89101
(702) 388-2400
1-800-274-LUCK**
fitzgeraldslasvegas.com

Present this coupon at the Club Fitz Card Center to receive your one FREE keychain. Must be a new Club Fitz member. Limit: one coupon per new account. Non-transferable. No cash value. Must be 21 years of age or older. Management reserves the right to modify, change or cancel this offer at any time without prior notice. Offer valid through 12/30/12.

**301 Fremont Street
Las Vegas, NV 89101
(702) 388-2111**
www.fitzgeraldslasvegas.com

Coupon must be redeemed at the Fitz Las Vegas Box Office. Limit one coupon per party. Not valid with any other offer. Based on availability. No cash value. Management reserves the right to alter or cancel this promotion at any time. Expires 12/30/12.

KEVIN BURKE
Fitz of Laughter
handcrafted comedy

Feast of Laughter
Dinner Package for $21.95

Get the Feast of Laughter dinner package for $21.95. Includes Rib-eye dinner and taxes. See reverse for more details.

$10 Off Regular or VIP Tickets

Receive $10 off regular or VIP tickets to Marriage Can Be Murder at Fitzgeralds Casino. See reverse for more details.

2-FOR-1
TICKETS

Redeem at the Flamingo Box Office for 2-for-1 tickets to X-Burlesque. See reverse for details.

Offer code: XBACG241

americancasinoguide.com

301 Fremont Street
Las Vegas, NV 89101
(702) 388-2111
www.fitzgeraldslasvegas.com

Coupon must be redeemed at the Fitz Las Vegas Box Office. Limit two tickets per coupon. Not valid with any other offer. Based on availability. No cash value. Box office fee not included. Management reserves the right to alter or cancel this promotion at any time. Expires 12/30/12.

Offer void if coupon is copied or sold

americancasinoguide.com

301 Fremont Street
Las Vegas, NV 89101
(702) 388-2111
www.fitzgeraldslasvegas.com

Coupon must be redeemed at the Fitz Las Vegas Box Office. Offer valid for up to four discounted tickets. Not valid with any other offer. Based on availability. No cash value. Management reserves the right to alter or cancel this promotion at any time. Expires 12/30/12.

Offer void if coupon is copied or sold

americancasinoguide.com

Flamingo

3555 Las Vegas Blvd. S.
Las Vegas, NV 89109
702-733-3111
Flamingo.com

Present coupon at time of purchase to redeem. Must be 18. Limit 4 per coupon. Subject to availability. No cash value. Not valid on previously purchased tickets. Cannot be combined with any other offer. Subject to availability. Blackout dates may apply. Management reserves all rights. Offer subject to change or cancellation without notification. Offer expires 12/31/12.

Offer void if coupon is copied or sold

AMERICAN CASINO GUIDE

2-FOR-1 CLASSES

Redeem at the Flamingo Box Office for 2-for-1 admission to X-Burlesque University. See reverse for details.

Offer code: XBUACG

A current American Casino Guide Discount Card must be presented when redeeming this coupon, or offer is void

---

AMERICAN CASINO GUIDE

FREE SPA PASS

Redeem at the Flamingo Spa for a free spa day pass. See reverse for details.

Offer code: RFDM3

A current American Casino Guide Discount Card must be presented when redeeming this coupon, or offer is void

---

AMERICAN CASINO GUIDE

20% OFF BREAKFAST

Redeem at Margaritaville at Flamingo and receive 20% off breakfast. See reverse for details.

Offer code: JBMTT3

A current American Casino Guide Discount Card must be presented when redeeming this coupon, or offer is void

Flamingo

3555 Las Vegas Blvd. S.
Las Vegas, NV 89109
702-733-3111
Flamingo.com

Present coupon at time of purchase to redeem. Limit 4 per coupon. Subject to availability. No cash value. Not valid on previously purchased tickets. Cannot be combined with any other offer. Subject to availability. Blackout dates may apply. Management reserves all rights. Offer subject to change or cancellation without notification. Offer Expires 12/31/12.

Flamingo

3555 Las Vegas Blvd. S.
Las Vegas, NV 89109
702-733-3111
Flamingo.com

Limit 1 pass per coupon. Spa pass is valid for 1 day. Pass provides access to the Fitness Facility, Steam Room, Sauna, Whirlpools and lounge area. Subject to availability. No cash value. Not valid on previously purchased passes. Cannot be combined with any other offer. Subject to availability. Blackout dates may apply. Management reserves all rights. Offer subject to change or cancellation without notification. Offer expires 12/31/12.

Flamingo

3555 Las Vegas Blvd. S.
Las Vegas, NV 89109
702-733-3111
Flamingo.com

Breakfast served from 8am - 10:30am. Limit 4 per coupon. Valid at the Margaritaville location at Flamingo Las Vegas only. Subject to availability. No cash value. Must be presented at time of purchase to redeem. Tax & gratuity not included. Cannot be combined with any other offer. Subject to availability. Blackout dates may apply. Management reserves all rights. Offer subject to change or cancellation without notification. Offer expires 12/31/12.

15% OFF

Redeem at Hamada at Flamingo and receive 15% off your
dinner bill of $40 or more. See reverse for details.

Offer code: HOJFLV

HOTEL • CASINO
LAS VEGAS

Double Points (Up to 500) for members of the Royal Players Club™

Double your Royal Players Club™ points (up to 500)
with this coupon! See reverse for more details.

HOTEL • CASINO
LAS VEGAS

2-for-1 Lunch or Dinner Entrée in Magnolia's

Buy one lunch or dinner entrée in Magnolia's and
get one entrée FREE! See reverse for more details.

3555 Las Vegas Blvd. S.
Las Vegas, NV 89109
702-733-3111
Flamingo.com

Limit 4 per coupon. Minimum bill of $40 before tax & gratuity. Valid at the Hamada of Japan location at Flamingo Las Vegas only.Subject to availability. No cash value. Must be presented at time of purchase to redeem. Tax & gratuity not included. Cannot be combined with any other offer. Subject to availability. Blackout dates may apply. Management reserves all rights. Offer subject to change or cancellation without notification. Offer expires 12/31/12.

202 Fremont Street
Las Vegas, NV 89101
(702) 385-4011
(800) 634-6045
www.fourqueens.com

Strictly limited to one coupon per person per 12 month period. Coupon has no cash value. Must be 21 years or older. Points must be earned on day of redemption. Offer valid for Royal Players Club™ members only. Double points will be added to account within 48 hours. Management reserves the right to cancel or modify offer at any time without notice. Coupon is void if altered or duplicated. Offer expires December 30, 2012.

202 Fremont Street
Las Vegas, NV 89101
(702) 385-4011
(800) 634-6045
www.fourqueens.com

Strictly limited to one coupon per person per 12 month period. Must be 21 years or older. Must redeem coupon at the Royal Players Club to receive voucher for Magnolia's. Purchase one lunch or dinner entrée (equal or greater value) to receive the second one free. Offer valid only in Magnolia's. Coupon is void if altered or duplicated. Tax, alcoholic beverages and gratuity are not included. Not valid with any other offers or discounts. Management reserves the right to cancel or modify offer at any time. Coupon has no cash value. Offer expires December 30, 2012.

Mike **Hammer**
-comedy magic show
2-for-1 Show Tickets
**Buy one ticket to the Mike Hammer Comedy Magic
Show and receive a second one FREE. See reverse
for more details.**

A current American Casino Guide Discount Card must be
presented when redeeming this coupon, or offer is void

$10 Off
Tickets

Get $10 off any general or VIP ticket (before taxes and fees). Wed - Sun,
9pm in the Canyon Club. Coupon must be presented at the Four Queens
box office. Good for up to four tickets. See back for details.

A current American Casino Guide Discount Card must be
presented when redeeming this coupon, or offer is void

GOLD COAST.
HOTEL & CASINO · LAS VEGAS

Earn 200 points,
Get Free Buffet
(Keep the points)

Earn 200 points playing slots then present this original coupon and
B Connected Card to the B Connected Club, and receive a voucher that
will entitle bearer to one FREE breakfast, lunch or regular dinner buffet.
See reverse side for details.

A current American Casino Guide Discount Card must be
presented when redeeming this coupon, or offer is void

americancasinoguide.com

HOTEL • CASINO
LAS VEGAS
202 Fremont Street
Las Vegas, NV 89101
(702) 385-4011
(800) 634-6045
www.fourqueens.com

Show open to all ages. Must be 21 to redeem coupon.Must redeem coupon at the Four Queens Box Office to receive second ticket for free with purchase of one at full price. Coupon is void if altered or duplicated. Tax and box office fees are not included. Not valid with any other offers or discounts. Show times: 7pm Tuesday-Saturday. Subject to availability. Management reserves the right to cancel or modify offer at any time. Coupon has no cash value. Offer expires December 29, 2012.

Offer void if coupon is copied or sold

americancasinoguide.com

HOTEL • CASINO
LAS VEGAS
202 Fremont Street
Las Vegas, NV 89101
(702) 385-4011
(800) 634-6045
www.fourqueens.com
www.lacagefourqueens.com

Subject to availability. Show times subject to change. Offers cannot be combined. Coupon is void if altered or duplicated. Management reserves all rights. Not for resale. Valid through December 29, 2012.

Offer void if coupon is copied or sold

americancasinoguide.com

GOLD COAST
HOTEL & CASINO · LAS VEGAS

Gold Coast Hotel & Casino
4000 W. Flamingo Road
Las Vegas, NV 89103
(702) 367-7111 • (800) 331-5334
www.goldcoastcasino.com

Must be 21 or older and have an active B Connected Card. Not valid on Holidays. Earn 200 points playing slots on same day original coupon is presented to B Connected Club to obtain voucher. Limit one coupon per person. Excludes specialty night dinners. This coupon has no cash value, cannot be combined with any other offer or used more than once. Reproduction, sale, barter or transfer are prohibited and render this coupon void. Management reserves the right to change or discontinue this offer without notice. Expires 12/30/12.

Offer void if coupon is copied or sold

GOLD COAST

HOTEL & CASINO · LAS VEGAS

$5 in Slot Dollars (With new enrollment)

Present this original coupon and a valid government issued photo ID to the B Connected Club when enrolling as a new member of the B Connected Club and receive $5 worth of slot play. Downloadable slot play will be added to new account. Offer limited to new members. Not valid with any other offer or promotion. See reverse side for details.

A current American Casino Guide Discount Card must be presented when redeeming this coupon, or offer is void

GOLD COAST

HOTEL & CASINO · LAS VEGAS

$5 Match Play

Present this original coupon and B Connected Card to the B Connected Club for a match play voucher. Voucher and equal wager of real chips or cash should be presented to the dealer. See reverse side for details.

A current American Casino Guide Discount Card must be presented when redeeming this coupon, or offer is void

$25 FREE PLAY for earning 200 points, or $5 FREE PLAY for 50 points

Earn 200 points while playing with your Club 1906 card and receive $25 FREE slot play, or earn 50 points and receive $5 FREE slot play. Offer valid for new members only. See reverse side for full details.

A current American Casino Guide Discount Card must be presented when redeeming this coupon, or offer is void

americancasinoguide.com

GOLD COAST®

HOTEL & CASINO · LAS VEGAS

Gold Coast Hotel & Casino
4000 W. Flamingo Road
Las Vegas, NV 89103
(702) 367-7111 • (800) 331-5334
www.goldcoastcasino.com

Must be 21 or older present a valid government issued photo ID. Limit one coupon per person. Valid for new members in B Connected club (formerly known as Club Coast who are not considered as new members.) This coupon has no cash value, cannot be combined with any other offer or used more than once. Reproduction, sale, barter or transfer are prohibited and render this coupon void. Management reserves the right to change or discontinue this offer without notice. Expires 12/30/12

Offer void if coupon is copied or sold

americancasinoguide.com

GOLD COAST®

HOTEL & CASINO · LAS VEGAS

Gold Coast Hotel & Casino
4000 W. Flamingo Road
Las Vegas, NV 89103
(702) 367-7111 • (800) 331-5334
www.goldcoastcasino.com

Must be 21 or older and have an active B Connected Card. Limit one coupon per person and limit one coupon per wager. Coupon good for play on any Gold Coast casino table game but excludes live poker. Good for one decision on even-money bets only. Win or lose, coupon is claimed by the house. If you tie then the coupon may be re-bet. This coupon has no cash value, cannot be combined with any other offer or used more than once. Reproduction, sale, barter or transfer are prohibited and render this coupon void. Management reserves the right to change or discontinue this offer without notice. Expires 12/30/12.

Offer void if coupon is copied or sold

americancasinoguide.com

GOLDEN GATE
HOTEL & CASINO
ONE FREMONT STREET · LAS VEGAS

One Fremont Street
Las Vegas, NV 89101
(702) 385-1906
Reservations (800) 426-1906

Offer valid for new members only. Coupon must be surrendered to Club 1906 at the time of sign-up and required points must be earned the same day. Limit one coupon per account.

Must provide government issued ID to join Club 1906. Must be 21 or older.

Club hours are 9am-1am daily. Offer expires December 30, 2012.

Offer void if coupon is copied or sold

Buy One Get One 50% Off

Present this coupon at any Haagen Dazs shop listed on the back, purchase your choice of any menu item and receive your choice of a second menu item of equal or lesser value at half price!

$10 Free Slot Play for New Sign Ups

Present this coupon at the Rockstar Players Club to receive $10 in Free Slot Play. Valid for new members only.
See reverse for more details.

$10 Matchplay on any Table Game

For Match Play offer, place a $10 even-money minimum bet with this voucher at any participating table game, along with your Rockstar Players Club card, and get an extra $10 if you win! See reverse for more details.

americancasinoguide.com

MGM Grand Hotel - Star Lane Mall
MGM Grand Hotel - Food Court
New York New York Hotel • Bally's Hotel
The Venetian Hotel • Fashion Show Mall
Monte Carlo Hotel

Must present coupon to cashier prior to ordering. Offer has no cash value. Not valid with any other offer. One coupon per person. Subject to change or cancellation without prior notice. Offer valid through December 31, 2012.

americancasinoguide.com

HARD ROCK HOTEL & CASINO
LAS VEGAS
4455 Paradise Road, Las Vegas, NV 89169
(702) 693-5000
hardrockhotel.com

Valid for new Rockstar Players Club members only. Limit one coupon per account. Cannot be redeemed for cash. Non-negotiable. Not valid with any other offer. Must be 21 years of age or older, with valid ID, to redeem. No photocopies accepted. Management reserves all rights. Offer expires December 30, 2012.

americancasinoguide.com

HARD ROCK HOTEL & CASINO
LAS VEGAS
4455 Paradise Road, Las Vegas, NV 89169
(702) 693-5000
hardrockhotel.com

Limit one coupon per account per 12-month period. For Match Play offer, place a $10 minimum bet with voucher at any participating table game, along with your Rockstar Players Club card, and you will receive an extra $10 if you win! Even money bets only. Cannot be redeemed for cash. Non-negotiable. Not valid with any other offer. Must be 21 years of age or older, with valid ID, to redeem. No photocopies accepted. Management reserves all rights. Offer expires December 30, 2012.

HARD ROCK HOTEL & CASINO
LAS VEGAS
4455 Paradise Road, Las Vegas, NV 89169
(702) 693-5000
hardrockhotel.com

Call (800) 343-4346 and ask for offer 'HACG12'. Subject to availability. Taxes and resort fees may apply. May not be combined with any other offer. Management reserves the right to change or cancel this promotion at any time. Complete details are available by phone at the number listed above. Offer expires December 30, 2012.

Offer void if coupon is copied or sold

Harrah's

3475 Las Vegas Blvd. S.
Las Vegas, NV 89109
702-369-5000
harrahs.com

Valid at The Spa at Harrah's Las Vegas only. Limit 1 treatment per coupon. Subject to availability. No cash value. Not valid on previously purchased services. Cannot be combined with any other offer. Subject to availability. Blackout dates may apply. Management reserves all rights. Offer subject to change or cancellation without notification. Offer expires 12/31/12

Offer void if coupon is copied or sold

Harrah's

3475 Las Vegas Blvd. S.
Las Vegas, NV 89109
702-369-5000
harrahs.com

Valid at Flavors Buffet at Harrah's Las Vegas only. Present coupon at time of purchase to redeem. Limit 4 per coupon. Excludes Buffet of Buffets passes. Subject to availability. No cash value. Not valid on previously purchased tickets. Cannot be combined with any other offer. Subject to availability. Blackout dates may apply. Management reserves all rights. Offer subject to change or cancellation without notification. Offer Expires 12/31/12

Offer void if coupon is copied or sold

HOOTERS
Casino Hotel ◆ Las Vegas

**115 East Tropicana Avenue
Las Vegas, Nevada 89109
(702) 739-9000
(800) 235-5987
www.hooterscasinohotel.com**

Must be 21 years of age or older and a new member of the Owl Rewards Club to redeem. Membership is always free. Original coupons (no photocopies) must be presented at the Owl Rewards Club during operational hours. This offer can only be redeemed on designated Free Slot Play Machines. Cash prizes are awarded only for Top Prize. For official rules, please see the Owl Rewards Club. Only one coupon per person. Not valid with any other offer or promotion. No cash value and non-transferable. Not for resale. Management reserves the right to alter or cancel this promotion at any time. Voucher is valid through December 28, 2012.

Offer void if coupon is copied or sold

This voucher must be redeemed at least one hour prior to show time at the Hooters Box Office. Must be 21 years of age or older. Show tickets are only issued on the day of redemption. No cash value, non-transferable and based on availability. Blackout dates may apply. Not for resale. Gratuity and LET not included. Management reserves all rights. Expires 12/28/12.

HOOTERS
Casino Hotel ◆ Las Vegas

115 East Tropicana Avenue, Las Vegas, NV 89109
866-LVHoots · www.hooterscasinohotel.com

Offer void if coupon is copied or sold

IMPERIAL® PALACE

**3535 Las Vegas Blvd. S
Las Vegas, NV 89109
800-351-7400
ImperialPalace.com**

Limit 1 treatment per coupon. Subject to availability. No cash value. Not valid on previously purchased services. Cannot be combined with any other offer. Subject to availability. Blackout dates may apply. Management reserves all rights. Offer subject to change or cancellation without notification. Offer expires 12/31/12

Offer void if coupon is copied or sold

EMPEROR'S 25%
B U F F E T OFF

Redeem this coupon at the Emperor's Buffet at Imperial Palace
and receive 25% off buffet admission. See reverse for details.

Offer code: ACGE1

2-FOR-1
TICKETS

Redeem at the Imperial Palace Box Office for 2-for-1
tickets to Frank Marino's Divas. See reverse for details.

Offer code: FMACG

$5 Table Games
Match Play

Redeem at The MoreClub and receive a $5 table games
match play. See reverse for details.

IMPERIAL® PALACE

3535 Las Vegas Blvd. S
Las Vegas, NV 89109
800-351-7400
ImperialPalace.com

Present coupon at time of purchase to redeem. Limit 4 per coupon. Excludes Buffet of Buffets passes. Subject to availability. No cash value. Not valid on previously purchased tickets. Cannot be combined with any other offer. Subject to availability. Blackout dates may apply. Management reserves all rights. Offer subject to change or cancellation without notification. Offer Expires 12/31/12

Offer void if coupon is copied or sold

IMPERIAL® PALACE

3535 Las Vegas Blvd. S
Las Vegas, NV 89109
800-351-7400
ImperialPalace.com

Present coupon at time of purchase to redeem. Limit 4 per coupon. Subject to availability. No cash value. Not valid on previously purchased tickets. Cannot be combined with any other offer. Subject to availability. Blackout dates may apply. Management reserves all rights. Offer subject to change or cancellation without notification. Offer expires 12/31/12

Offer void if coupon is copied or sold

1821 Las Vegas Boulevard North
N. Las Vegas, NV 89030
(702) 399-3000 • www.jerrysnugget.com

Limit one coupon per customer per month. Must be a MoreClub member. MoreClub membership is free. Present original coupon to The MoreClub and receive a $5 table games match play issued from The MoreClub Kiosk. No photocopies will be honored. Table games match play kiosk ticket good for 24 hours after issuance. A $5 minimum bet is required. Voucher surrendered after first hand. Good for one hand, one wager. Player rating required at time of play. Cannot be redeemed for cash. Not valid with any other offer. Must be 21 years of age or older to redeem. Management reserves all rights. Offer expires December 31, 2012.

Offer void if coupon is copied or sold

$25 Towards the Purchase of Two Entrées at TJ's Steakhouse!

Serving prime steaks broiled over mesquite charcoal, succulent chops and fresh fish in a cozy atmosphere. Open daily 5:30 p.m. to 10:30 p.m. See reverse for more details.

$10 Blackjack Matchplay

Present this coupon at any blackjack table, along with your Bigshot Players Club card, prior to the start of a hand and we'll match your bet of $10 if you win. See reverse for details.

2-for-1 Lunch or Dinner Entrée

Buy one lunch or dinner entrée in our restaurant and get one entrée of equal or lesser value FREE! Present to server before ordering. See reverse for more details.

americancasinoguide.com

Las Vegas

Hilton

3000 Paradise Road
Las Vegas, NV 89109
(702) 732-5755
(800) 732-7117
www.lvhilton.com

Present this coupon to your server when ordering. Must surrender coupon. Not valid with any other offers. Not valid on holidays. Maximum credit $12.50 per person. Nontransferable. Nonredeemable for cash. Las Vegas Hilton management reserves the right to change or cancel this promotion at any time. Restaurant hours/days subject to change. Must be 21 years of age or older to gamble or consume alcohol. Expires 12/28/12. c/l #19412.

americancasinoguide.com

5288 Boulder Highway
Las Vegas, Nevada 89122
(702) 435-9170
(800) 825-0880

Limit: one coupon per person, per month. Cannot be redeemed for cash. Must be 21 or older. Cannot be combined with any other offer or promotion. Nontransferable. Offer void if sold.

Must present original coupon (no photocopies). Not responsible for lost or stolen coupon. Management reserves all rights. Offer may be changed or discontinued at anytime at the discretion of management. Offer expires December 30, 2012.

americancasinoguide.com

5288 Boulder Highway
Las Vegas, Nevada 89122
(702) 435-9170
(800) 825-0880

Limit one coupon per person. Must be 21 years or older. Purchase one lunch or dinner entrée to receive the second one of equal or lesser value free. Not valid on take out orders. Coupon is void if altered or duplicated. Must present original coupon (no photocopies).

Tax, beverages and gratuity are not included. Not valid with any other offers or discounts. Management reserves the right to cancel or modify offer at any time. Coupon has no cash value. Offer expires December 30, 2012.

AMERICAN CASINO GUIDE

2,500 Slot Club Points
For New Members

Present this coupon at the Bigshot Players Club booth to receive
2,500 FREE slot club points when you join as a new member.
See reverse for more details.

A current American Casino Guide Discount Card must be
presented when redeeming this coupon, or offer is void

AMERICAN CASINO GUIDE

$5 in FREE
Slot Play

(When you Earn 10 points)

New members only, present this coupon at the Player's Club
booth when you sign up for our slot club and receive
$5 in FREE slot play. See reverse for more details.

A current American Casino Guide Discount Card must be
presented when redeeming this coupon, or offer is void

AMERICAN CASINO GUIDE

FREE Drink at
Lucy's Bar & Grill

Present this coupon to your server at Lucy's Bar &
Grill to receive one FREE draft beer, or one FREE well
drink. See reverse for more details.

A current American Casino Guide Discount Card must be
presented when redeeming this coupon, or offer is void

5288 Boulder Highway
Las Vegas, Nevada 89122
(702) 435-9170
(800) 825-0880

Valid for new accounts only. Must be 21 or older. Cannot be combined with any other offer or promotion. Non-transferable. Offer void if sold. Please allow up to 48 hours for points to reflect on account balance.

Must present original coupon (no photocopies). Not responsible for lost or stolen coupon. Management reserves all rights. Offer may be changed or discontinued at anytime at the discretion of management. Offer expires December 30, 2012.

(702) 399-3297 • (877) 333-9291
3227 Civic Center Drive
N. Las Vegas, NV 89030
www.luckyclubcasino.com

Restrictions apply. See Players' club for complete rules. Limit one coupon per customer. Must be a new member. Free Play expires one month after coupon redemption date. This offer is non-transferable, non refundable and has no cash value. MUST mention ACG. Must present and surrender this coupon upon use. No exceptions. Not available in conjunction with any other offer, Management reserves all rights. Must be 21 or older. Offer subject to change or cancellation at any time without notice. Offer expires December 30, 2012.

(702) 399-3297 • (877) 333-9291
3227 Civic Center Drive
N. Las Vegas, NV 89030
www.luckyclubcasino.com

Restrictions apply. Limit one coupon per customer. Good for one free draft or well drink. This offer is non-transferable, non refundable and has no cash value. MUST mention ACG. Must present and surrender this coupon upon use. Gratuity not included. No exceptions. Not available in conjunction with any other offer. Management reserves all rights. Must be 21 or older. Offer subject to change or cancellation at any time without notice. Offer expires December 30, 2012.

$10 Blackjack Matchplay
(New Members Only)

Make a $10 bet and we will match your bet at the blackjack tables. See reverse for more details.

A current American Casino Guide Discount Card must be presented when redeeming this coupon, or offer is void

---

BODIES
THE EXHIBITION
$5 off Admission

Located inside the Luxor Resort, this exhibition showcases real full-bodies and organs, providing a detailed, three-dimensional vision of the human form rarely seen outside of an anatomy lab, or a morgue. Present this coupon at the admission booth to receive $5 off each admission for up to 4 people.

A current American Casino Guide Discount Card must be presented when redeeming this coupon, or offer is void

---

TITANIC
THE ARTIFACT EXHIBITION
$5 off Admission

Located inside the Luxor Resort, the epic story of the "ship of dreams" is revived through Titanic: The Artifact Exhibition. Present this coupon at the admission booth to receive $5 off each admission for up to 4 people.

A current American Casino Guide Discount Card must be presented when redeeming this coupon, or offer is void

CASINO

(702) 399-3297 • (877) 333-9291
3227 Civic Center Drive
N. Las Vegas, NV 89030
www.luckyclubcasino.com

Restrictions apply. Limit one coupon per customer. Must place $10 bet on top of Match Play Coupon in betting space. Good for one play: win or lose. Blackjack pays even money. Valid only on standard Blackjack table. This offer is non-transferable, non refundable and has no cash value. MUST mention ACG. Must present and surrender this coupon upon use. Not available in conjunction with any other offer, Management reserves all rights. Must be 21 or older. Offer subject to change or cancellation at any time without notice. Offer expires December 30, 2012.

BODIES
THE EXHIBITION

The Bodies exhibition is open daily at 10 a.m. with the last admission at 9 p.m For more information and pricing, please call (800) 557-7428 or visit www.bodiestickets.com. Located in the Luxor Resort on Las Vegas Boulevard (The Strip). Maximum discount is $20. Not valid with any other discount. Expires December 31, 2012.

TITANIC
THE ARTIFACT EXHIBITION

The Titanic exhibition is open daily at 10 a.m. with the last admission at 9 p.m For more information and pricing, please call (800) 557-7428 or visit www.titanictix.com. Located in the Luxor Resort on Las Vegas Boulevard (The Strip). Maximum discount is $20. Not valid with any other discount. Expires December 31, 2012.

Madame Tussauds
LAS VEGAS

2-For-1 General Admission
Sunday through Thursday

Receive one FREE ticket with the purchase of a full-price adult general admission ticket at Madame Tussauds Interactive Wax Attraction located in front of the Venetian Resort on Las Vegas Boulevard. Only valid Sunday through Thursday.

5106

A current American Casino Guide Discount Card must be presented when redeeming this coupon, or offer is void

---

Buy One Drink and Get One FREE, Plus No Cover Charge

Present this coupon before ordering to receive one free drink with the purchase of another at regular price, plus no cover charge. See reverse for more details.

LAS VEGAS

A current American Casino Guide Discount Card must be presented when redeeming this coupon, or offer is void

---

Buy One Get One 50% Off

Present this coupon at any Nathan's listed on the back, purchase your choice of any menu item and receive your choice of a second menu item of equal or lesser value at half price!

A current American Casino Guide Discount Card must be presented when redeeming this coupon, or offer is void

Who would you like to meet at the World Famous Madame Tussauds Las Vegas? Featuring life like wax creations of your favorite celebrities, Madame Tussauds lets you "grab hold" of your favorite stars.

Madame Tussauds Las Vegas is open daily at 10 a.m. For more information and pricing, please call (866) 841-3739 or visit madametussauds.com. Located in front of the Venetian Resort on Las Vegas Blvd (The Strip). Not valid with any other discount promotion. Expires December 31, 2012.

Offer void if coupon is copied or sold

**3400 Las Vegas Blvd S
Las Vegas, NV 89109
(702) 242-KING (5464)
bbkingclubs.com**

Must be 21 years of age or older. Tax and gratuity not included. One coupon per visit. House wine, well liquor or domestic beer only. Free drink is lowest priced drink. Coupon has no cash value and may be revoked/cancelled at anytime. Not valid with any other offers. Offer valid through 12/30/12.

Offer void if coupon is copied or sold

MGM Grand Hotel • Palms Hotel and Casino
New York New York Hotel
Venetian Hotel Grand Canal Shops • Bally's Hotel
Luxor Hotel • Fashion Show Mall Food Court

Must present coupon to cashier prior to ordering. Offer has no cash value. Not valid with any other offer. One coupon per person. Subject to change or cancellation without prior notice. Offer valid through December 31, 2012.

Offer void if coupon is copied or sold

AMERICAN CASINO GUIDE

FREE Fish Fillet or Hushpuppies

Receive an additional fish fillet or order of hushpuppies with any meal purchase at Fulton's Fish Frye in the Village Streets at the New York-New York Hotel and Casino. Valid Monday through Friday. See reverse for more details.

A current American Casino Guide Discount Card must be presented when redeeming this coupon, or offer is void

AMERICAN CASINO GUIDE

GONZALEZ GONZALEZ

FREE Frozen Margarita

Receive one free frozen house margarita with the purchase of any entrée at Gonzalez Y Gonzalez at the New York-New York Hotel and Casino in Las Vegas. Valid every day. See reverse for more details.

A current American Casino Guide Discount Card must be presented when redeeming this coupon, or offer is void

AMERICAN CASINO GUIDE

GREENBERG & SONS
EST. 1923
Delicatessen

10% Off

Present this coupon to receive 10% off your entire order at Greenberg & Sons Delicatessen in the Village Streets at the New York-New York Hotel and Casino. Valid Monday through Friday. See reverse for more details.

A current American Casino Guide Discount Card must be presented when redeeming this coupon, or offer is void

New York-New York Hotel & Casino
3790 Las Vegas Blvd S
Las Vegas, NV 89109
Open Daily From 11am

Present this original coupon to the server when placing your order at Fulton's Fish Frye in the Village Streets to redeem. Valid Monday through Friday. Limit one coupon per customer. Offer may not be used in conjunction with any other offer or promotion and has no cash value. Management reserves all rights. Offer expires 12/30/12.

New York-New York Hotel & Casino
3790 Las Vegas Blvd S
Las Vegas, NV
Open daily at 11am

Present this original coupon to the server <u>WHEN PLACING YOUR ORDER</u> at Gonzalez Y Gonzalez Dining and Tequila Bar to redeem. Valid every day. Limit one coupon per customer. Offer may not be used in conjunction with any other offer or promotion and has no cash value. Management reserves all rights. Must be 21 years of age or older, with a valid form of ID. Offer does not include gratuity. Offer void if sold. Offer expires 12/30/12.

New York-New York Hotel & Casino
3790 Las Vegas Blvd S
Las Vegas, NV
Open Daily From 10am

Present this original coupon to the server when placing your order at Greenberg & Sons Delicatessen in the Village Streets to redeem. Valid Monday through Friday. Limit one coupon per customer. Offer may not be used in conjunction with any other offer or promotion and has no cash value. Management reserves all rights. Offer void if sold. Offer expires 12/30/12.

50% Off
Beverage

Present this coupon to receive 50% off a beverage with the purchase of two slices at Sirrico's Pizza in the Village Streets at the New York-New York Hotel and Casino. Valid Monday through Friday, 2pm – 6pm only. See reverse for more details.

2-for-1 Admission

**Have a scream!
Ride The Roller Coaster
at New York-New York.**

**Purchase one Roller Coaster Pass
at regular price and receive one
free ride ticket.**

Auth #199108869

Buy One
Get One
50% Off

Present this coupon at any New York Pretzel listed on the back, purchase your choice of any menu item and receive your choice of a second menu item of equal or lesser value at half price!

New York-New York Hotel & Casino
3790 Las Vegas Blvd S
Las Vegas, NV
Open Daily From 10am

Present this original coupon to the server when placing your order at Sirrico's Pizza in the Village Streets to redeem. Valid Monday through Friday, 2pm until 6pm only. Limit one coupon per customer. Offer may not be used in conjunction with any other offer or promotion and has no cash value. Management reserves all rights. Offer void if sold. Expires December 30, 2012.

Offer void if coupon is copied or sold

3790 Las Vegas Boulevard South
Las Vegas, NV 89109
(866) 815-4365

Height Restrictions apply. Hours of operation subject to weather conditions and other circumstances which may suspend service. Coupon is void if altered or duplicated. Must present original coupon (no photocopies). Not Valid for re-rides. Expires 12/30/12.

Offer void if coupon is copied or sold

Venetian Hotel Grand Canal Shops
MGM Grand Hotel - Star Lane Mall
New York New York Hotel - MGM Entrance
Bally's Hotel

Must present coupon to cashier prior to ordering. Offer has no cash value. Not valid with any other offer. One coupon per person. Subject to change or cancellation without prior notice. Offer valid through December 31, 2012.

Offer void if coupon is copied or sold

THE OPERA HOUSE
CASINO

40 Credit Bonus on Four-of-a-Kind

Present this coupon to the floorperson when you win a four-of-a-kind (no wild cards) on any denomination up to and including $1 video poker machines at the Opera House Casino and receive a 40-coin credit. You must present a valid ID and you must be playing maximim coins in order to receive this bonus. See reverse for more details.

A current American Casino Guide Discount Card must be presented when redeeming this coupon, or offer is void

---

THE OPERA HOUSE
CASINO

Buy One Entrée Get One Free
(or 50% one entrée when dining alone)

Purchase one entrée in Cadillac Joe's Restaurant and get a second entrée for FREE, or get 50% off one entrée when dining alone. See reverse for details.

A current American Casino Guide Discount Card must be presented when redeeming this coupon, or offer is void

---

The ORLEANS℠
HOTEL & CASINO · LAS VEGAS

$10 Table Games Match Play

This coupon entitles the bearer to $10 in match play on any casino table game at The Orleans (except live poker). Present to your casino dealer. Good for one decision on even-money bets only. An equal wager of real chips or cash must accompany this coupon. See reverse side for details.

A current American Casino Guide Discount Card must be presented when redeeming this coupon, or offer is void

THE OPERA HOUSE CASINO

2542 Las Vegas Blvd. N.
N. Las Vegas, Nevada 89030
(702) 649-8801

Must be 21 or older to redeem. Natural four-of-a-kind only. Maximum coins bet. Must present valid ID. Floor person must verify. Valid on any denomination up to and including $1. Management reserves the right to cancel, alter or discontinue promotion at any time. Original coupon (no photocopies) must be presented. Limit one coupon per person, per year. Valid through 12/30/12.

Date_____

Name_____

Signature_____

THE OPERA HOUSE CASINO

2542 Las Vegas Blvd. N.
N. Las Vegas, Nevada 89030
(702) 649-8801

Present this original coupon to your server in the restaurant, along with your Silver Rewards Club card, to receive one FREE entree with the purchase of another entree at the regular price, or 50% off a single entree when dining alone. The FREE entree must be of equal or lesser value. Not valid for to-go orders. Limit: one coupon per customer, per month. No cash value. Must be 21 years of age or older. Tax and gratuity not included. Management reserves all rights. Offer expires 12/30/12.

The ORLEANS
HOTEL & CASINO · LAS VEGAS

4500 W. Tropicana Ave.
Las Vegas, NV 89103
(702) 365-7111
(800) ORLEANS
www.orleanscasino.com

When using this promotional coupon, if you lose your wager the coupon will be claimed by the house. If you win your bet, your winnings will be paid in live gaming chips and the coupon wagered will be claimed by the house. Live gaming chips may be re-bet or exchanged for cash. If your bet is a tie, you may re-bet your coupon.

Bearer must be at least 21 years of age and prepared to present a photo ID. Limit one coupon per person per 30-day period. Coupon has no cash value and cannot be combined with any other offer or used more than once. Reproduction, sale, barter and transfer are prohibited and render this coupon void. Management reserves all rights. Offer expires December 31, 2012.

The ORLEANS℠

HOTEL & CASINO · LAS VEGAS

Two Showroom Tickets For The Price of One

This coupon entitles the bearer to one free ticket of equal value for purchase of one ticket to any show in The Orleans Showroom. Present coupon at The Orleans Showroom box office. See reverse side for details.

The ORLEANS℠

HOTEL & CASINO · LAS VEGAS

Two Tickets to Big Al's Comedy Club For the Price of One

This coupon entitles the bearer to one free ticket of equal value for purchase of one ticket to any show in Big Al's Comedy Club at The Orleans. Present coupon at The Orleans Showroom box office. See reverse side for details.

2-For-1 Show Tickets

Present this coupon at time of purchase at the Louie Anderson Theater box office at the Palace Station Hotel to receive two-for-one show tickets.

americancasinoguide.com

4500 W. Tropicana Ave.
Las Vegas, NV 89103
(702) 365-7111
(800) ORLEANS
www.orleanscasino.com

HOTEL & CASINO · LAS VEGAS

Bearer must be at least 21 years of age and prepared to present a photo ID. Limit one coupon per person. Coupon has no cash value and cannot be combined with any other offer or used more than once.

Reproduction, sale, barter and transfer are prohibited and render this coupon void. Management reserves all rights. Offer expires December 31, 2012.

---

americancasinoguide.com

BIG AL'S COMEDY CLUB

4500 W. Tropicana Ave.
Las Vegas, NV 89103
(702) 365-7111
(800) ORLEANS
www.orleanscasino.com

Bearer must be at least 21 years of age and prepared to present a photo ID. Limit one coupon per person. Coupon has no cash value and cannot be combined with any other offer or used more than once.

Reproduction, sale, barter and transfer are prohibited and render this coupon void. Management reserves all rights. Offer expires December 31, 2012.

---

americancasinoguide.com

AT THE
LOUIE ANDERSON THEATER

Palace Station Casino
2411 Sahara Ave.
Las Vegas, NV 89102
(702) 221-6567

Present this coupon at time of purchase at the Louie Anderson Theater box office at the Palace Station Hotel to receive two-for-one show tickets. No cash value.

Show times are 8:30 pm Tuesdays through Saturdays (dark Sunday and Monday). Doors open at 8:00 pm. May not be used with any other offers. All ages welcome - under 21 years of age must be accompanied by an adult 21 years of age or older. Management reserves all rights and may change or cancel this promotion at any time without notice. Offer is valid through December 28, 2012.

$10 in FREE Slot Play!

Earn 500 base points in one day on slots or 2,000 base points in one day on video poker and receive $10 in Free Slot Play. See reverse for complete details.

3X Points!

Present this coupon at the Club Palms booth and receive 3X points for one day's play from 12:01am to 11:59pm. See reverse for more details.

$10 Match Play for Any Even-Money Table Game Bet

Make a $10 even-money bet at blackjack, craps or roulette with this coupon and your Club Palms Card and receive a FREE $10 Match Bet!

Present this coupon along with your Club Palms card to the Club Palms booth to redeem. Points must be earned in one 24-hour period from 12:01am– 11:59 pm. Offer must be redeemed on day points are earned. Not valid on manual adjustments or bonus points. Limit one coupon per customer. No cash value. Not valid in conjunction with any other offer. Must be 21 years of age or older. Expires Dec. 31, 2012.

Offer void if coupon is copied or sold

Must present Club Palms card with coupon. Not valid with any other promotion or point offer. 400,000 point maximum adjustment. Must be 21 years of age or older. Management reserves the right to change or cancel this offer at any time. Not valid on designated machines. Limit: one coupon per person, per year. Offer expires 12/31/12.

Offer void if coupon is copied or sold

Must be 21 years of age or older and a Club Palms member. Make a $10 minimum even-money bet at any blackjack, craps or roulette game, along with this original coupon (no photocopies), and receive a $10 Match Bet. Good for one decision on even money bets only. Win or lose, coupon is claimed by the house. If you tie, then coupon may be re-bet. No cash value. Limit: one coupon per customer, per year. Not valid with any other offer. Management reserves all rights. Offer expires 12/31/12.

Offer void if coupon is copied or sold

20% Off

Redeem at select Paris Las Vegas stores for
20% off your purchase. See reverse for details.

Offer code: GUIDE CPN

A current American Casino Guide Discount Card must be
presented when redeeming this coupon, or offer is void

Eiffel Tower Ride
2-FOR-1 TICKETS

Redeem at the Paris Box Office for 2-for-1 admission to
the Eiffel Tower Ride. See reverse for details.

Offer code: AMCAS2012

A current American Casino Guide Discount Card must be
presented when redeeming this coupon, or offer is void

Anthony Cools   Free Upgrade to VIP Seating

Get a FREE upgrade to VIP seating with the purchase of a regular price
ticket to the Anthony Cools Hypnotism show. Valid for up to two tickets.
Coupon must be presented at the box office. See back for full details.

A current American Casino Guide Discount Card must be
presented when redeeming this coupon, or offer is void

American Casino Guide - 2012

**3655 Las Vegas Blvd. S
Las Vegas, NV 89109
702-946-7000
ParisLasVegas.com**

Valid at Paris Le Journal Shop, Eiffel Tour Shop, Les Enfants Shop, & La Vogue Bridal & Bachelorette Boutique. Not valid on previous purchases. Limit 1 coupon per guest. Subject to availability. No cash value. Not valid on previously purchased tickets. Cannot be combined with any other offer. Subject to availability. Blackout dates may apply. Management reserves all rights. Offer subject to change or cancellation without notification. Offer expires 12/31/12

Offer void if coupon is copied or sold

**3655 Las Vegas Blvd. S
Las Vegas, NV 89109
702-946-7000
ParisLasVegas.com**

Present coupon at time of purchase to redeem. Limit 4 per coupon. Subject to availability. No cash value. Not valid on previously purchased tickets. Cannot be combined with any other offer. Subject to availability. Blackout dates may apply. Management reserves all rights. Offer subject to change or cancellation without notification. Offer expires 12/31/12

Offer void if coupon is copied or sold

**Paris Las Vegas Casino & Hotel
3655 Las Vegas Boulevard S.
Las Vegas, NV 89109
(702) 946-7000 or visit
www.parislasvegas.com**

Subject to availability. Show times subject to change. Offers cannot be combined. Coupon must be presented at time of purchase and is only available through the box office. Management reserves all rights. Not for resale. Valid through December 31, 2012. Offer Code: AMCAS2012

Offer void if coupon is copied or sold

10% Off

Redeem this coupon at Pink's to receive 10% OFF
of any food purchase. See reverse for details.

A current American Casino Guide Discount Card must be
presented when redeeming this coupon, or offer is void

---

spice market buffet

25% OFF

Redeem at the Spice Market Buffet to receive
25% OFF admission. See reverse for details.

Offer code: 25BUF

A current American Casino Guide Discount Card must be
presented when redeeming this coupon, or offer is void

ph planet hollywood
RESORT & CASINO · LAS VEGAS

2-FOR-1 DRINKS

Redeem at the Extra Bar or Playing Field Lounge at
Planet Hollywood Resort & Casino to get two drinks
for the price of one. See reverse for details.

PFL Offer code: ACG1B   EB Offer code: ACG2B

A current American Casino Guide Discount Card must be
presented when redeeming this coupon, or offer is void

3667 Las Vegas Blvd S
Las Vegas, NV 89109
702-785-5555
planethollywoodresort.com

Present coupon at time of purchase to redeem. Valid at the Pink's in the Miracle Mile Shops at Planet Hollywood Resort & Casino only. Limit 1 coupon per guest. Subject to availability. No cash value. Cannot be combined with any other offer. Blackout dates may apply. Management reserves all rights. Offer subject to change or cancellation without notification. Offer expires 12/31/12

3667 Las Vegas Blvd S
Las Vegas, NV 89109
702-785-5555
planethollywoodresort.com

Present coupon at time of purchase to redeem. Limit 4 per coupon. Excludes Buffet of Buffets passes. Subject to availability. No cash value. Not valid on previously purchased tickets. Cannot be combined with any other offer. Subject to availability. Blackout dates may apply. Management reserves all rights. Offer subject to change or cancellation without notification.Offer Expires 12/31/12

3667 Las Vegas Blvd S
Las Vegas, NV 89109
702-785-5555
planethollywoodresort.com

Must be 21 with valid ID. Present coupon at time of purchase to redeem. Second drink must be of equal or lesser value. Subject to availability. No cash value. Cannot be combined with any other offer. Subject to availability. Blackout dates may apply. Management reserves all rights. Offer subject to change or cancellation without notification. Offer expires 12/31/12

FREE Frozen Margarita

Receive one free frozen margarita with purchase of any entrée at Yolos Mexican Grill at Planet Hollywood Resort & Casino. Valid Monday through Friday from 11:30am until 6pm. See reverse for more details.

V THEATER
In the Miracle Mile Shops at Planet Hollywood

2-for-1 Show Tickets
Your choice of
- *V - The Ultimate Variety Show*
- *The Mentalist*
- *Or any Other V Theater Show*

Present this coupon to the V Theater Box Office when you purchase a full price adult show ticket and receive a second show ticket free OR purchase a single full price adult show ticket and get 50% off. See back for full details.

SAXE THEATER
2-for-1 Show Tickets
Your choice of
VEGAS! The Show | BeatleShow! | Or any Other Saxe Theater Show!

Present this coupon to the Saxe Theater Box Office when you purchase a full price adult show ticket and receive a second show ticket free OR purchase a single full price adult show ticket and get 50% off. See back for full details.

americancasinoguide.com

Planet Hollywood Resort & Casino
3667 Las Vegas Blvd S
Las Vegas, NV
Open Daily From 11:30am

Present this original coupon to the server when placing your order at Yolos Mexican Grill to redeem. Valid Monday through Friday, from 11:30am until 6pm. Limit one coupon per customer. Offer may not be used in conjunction with any other offer or promotion and has no cash value. Management reserves all rights. Must be 21 years of age or older, with a valid form of ID. Offer does not include gratuity. Offer void if sold. Expires December 30, 2012.

Offer void if coupon is copied or sold

americancasinoguide.com

V THEATER

In the Miracle Mile Shops
at Planet Hollywood
Las Vegas, Nevada
866-932-1818

This coupon has no cash value, cannot be combined with any other offer or applied to prior purchase. Restrictions apply. Management reserves all rights. Expires 12/30/12.

Code: Promo14

Offer void if coupon is copied or sold

americancasinoguide.com

In the Miracle Mile Shops
at Planet Hollywood

In the Miracle Mile Shops
at Planet Hollywood
Las Vegas, Nevada
866-932-1818

This coupon has no cash value, cannot be combined with any other offer or applied to prior purchase. Restrictions apply. Management reserves all rights. Expires 12/30/12.

Code: Promo15

Offer void if coupon is copied or sold

2-for-1
Pole Dancing
Class

Buy one admission to a pole dancing class at Pole Fitness Studio
and get a second one FREE. First time customers only.
See reverse for more details.

CARNIVAL
W**O**RL**D**
BUFFET

$5
Off

Redeem at the Carnival World Buffet® at Rio Las Vegas
for $5 off buffet admission. See reverse for details.

Offer code: CB5TZ

VILLAGE
SEAFOOD BUFFET

$10
Off

Redeem at the Village Seafood Buffet® at Rio Las Vegas
for $10 off buffet admission. See reverse for details.

Offer code: 10VSB

americancasinoguide.com

4265 S Arville St Suite A
Las Vegas, NV 89103
(702) 878-7653
www.PoleFitnessStudio.com

Coupon must be redeemed with the receptionist at Pole Fitness Studio. Limit one coupon per party of two. Not valid with any other offer. Based on availability. First time customers only. No cash value. Management reserves the right to alter or cancel this promotion at any time. Expires 12/30/12.

americancasinoguide.com

3700 W. Flamingo Rd.
Las Vegas, NV 89103
702-777-7777
RioLasVegas.com

Present coupon at time of purchase to redeem. Limit 4 per coupon. Excludes Buffet of Buffets passes. Subject to availability. No cash value. Not valid on previously purchased tickets. Cannot be combined with any other offer. Subject to availability. Blackout dates may apply. Management reserves all rights. Offer subject to change or cancellation without notification. Offer expires 12/31/12

americancasinoguide.com

3700 W. Flamingo Rd.
Las Vegas, NV 89103
702-777-7777
RioLasVegas.com

Present coupon at time of purchase to redeem. Limit 4 per coupon. Excludes Buffet of Buffets passes. Subject to availability. No cash value. Not valid on previously purchased tickets. Cannot be combined with any other offer. Subject to availability. Blackout dates may apply. Management reserves all rights. Offer subject to change or cancellation without notification. Offer Expires 12/31/12

VOODOO
STEAK
$10 Off Entrée

Redeem at Voodoo Steak at Rio Las Vegas for
$10 off your entrée. See reverse for details.

Offer code: ACGR1

RIVIERA
HOTEL · CASINO · LAS VEGAS
www.rivierahotel.com

2 Free
Comedy Club
Tickets

Redeem at the Riviera Box Office for 2 Free Comedy Club
tickets. See reverse for details.

RIVIERA
HOTEL · CASINO · LAS VEGAS
www.rivierahotel.com

$10 Match Play for
Any Even-Money
Table Game Bet

Make a $10 even-money bet at blackjack, craps or
roulette with this coupon and your Club Riviera Card
and receive a FREE $10 Match Bet!

**3700 W. Flamingo Rd.
Las Vegas, NV 89103
702-777-7777
RioLasVegas.com**

Minimum purchase of 2 entrees. Tax & gratuity not included. Subject to availability. No cash value. Not valid on previously purchased services. Cannot be combined with any other offer. Subject to availability. Blackout dates may apply. Management reserves all rights. Offer subject to change or cancellation without notification. Offer expires 12/31/12

**2901 Las Vegas Blvd. S.
Las Vegas, NV 89109
(800) 634-3420
rivierahotel.com**

Valid at the Comedy Club at the Riviera Las Vegas only. Present coupon at time of purchase to redeem. Limit 1 coupon per party. No cash value. Cannot be combined with any other offer. Subject to availability. Blackout dates may apply. Management reserves all rights. Offer subject to change or cancellation without notification. Offer expires December 30, 2012.

**2901 Las Vegas Blvd. S.
Las Vegas, NV 89109
(800) 634-3420
rivierahotel.com**

Must be 21 years of age or older and a Club Riviera member. Make a $10 minimum even-money bet at any blackjack, craps or roulette game, along with this original coupon (no photocopies), and receive a $10 Match Bet. Good for one decision on even money bets only. Win or lose, coupon is claimed by the house. If you tie, then coupon may be re-bet. No cash value. Limit: one coupon per customer, per 12-month period. Not valid with any other offer. Management reserves all rights. Offer expires December 30, 2012.

SAM'S TOWN®

Earn 200 points, Get Free Buffet
(Keep the points)

Earn 200 points playing slots then present this original coupon and B Connected Card to the B Connected Club, and receive a voucher that will entitle bearer to one FREE breakfast, lunch or regular dinner buffet. See reverse side for details.

A current American Casino Guide Discount Card must be presented when redeeming this coupon, or offer is void

SAM'S TOWN®

Two FREE Drinks at any Casino Bar For NEW Members

Present this coupon when signing up for a new B Connected Card to receive two FREE well, call or draft beers at any casino bar. See reverse for more details.

Offer Validation
Stamp
Here

A current American Casino Guide Discount Card must be presented when redeeming this coupon, or offer is void

SAM'S TOWN®

One FREE Room Night

Pay for two nights and get a third night FREE! Good Sunday through Thursday. Holidays and convention periods excluded. Blackout dates may apply. Subject to availability. For reservations call 1-800-897-8696 and ask for offer "ACG12"

A current American Casino Guide Discount Card must be presented when redeeming this coupon, or offer is void

americancasinoguide.com

SAM'S TOWN®

Sam's Town Hotel & Gambling Hall
5111 Boulder Highway
Las Vegas, NV 89122
(702) 456-7777 • (800) 897-8696
www.samstownlv.com

Must be 21 or older and have an active B Connected Card. Not valid on Holidays. Earn 200 points playing slots on same day original coupon is presented to B Connected Club to obtain voucher. Limit one coupon per person. Excludes specialty night dinners. This coupon has no cash value, cannot be combined with any other offer or used more than once. Reproduction, sale, barter or transfer are prohibited and render this coupon void. Management reserves the right to change or discontinue this offer without notice. Expires 12/30/12.

americancasinoguide.com

SAM'S TOWN®

Sam's Town Hotel & Gambling Hall
5111 Boulder Highway
Las Vegas, NV 89122
(702) 456-7777 • (800) 897-8696
www.samstownlv.com

Present this coupon when signing up for a new B Connected card to receive two free well, call or draft beers at any casino bar. Must be 21 years of age or older. Coupon cannot be used in conjunction with any other offer. Management reserves right to change or cancel offer at any time. Must present B Connected Card with coupon for redemption. Coupon has no cash value. Expires 12/30/12. One per customer.

AM85999

americancasinoguide.com

SAM'S TOWN®

Sam's Town Hotel & Gambling Hall
5111 Boulder Highway
Las Vegas, NV 89122
(702) 456-7777 • (800) 897-8696
www.samstownlv.com

This voucher entitles the bearer to one free room night at Sam's Town Hotel & Casino, with the purchase of two nights at the prevailing rate. Must have advance reservations. Must present voucher upon check-in. Not valid in conjunction with any other offer. Management reserves the right to cancel this promotion at any time. Credit card or cash deposit required. Guest is responsible for all incidental charges. Must be 21 or older. Limit one free room per person. Offer expires 12/28/12.

SILVER NUGGET
CASINO

$10 Blackjack Matchplay

Present this coupon at any blackjack table, along with your Silver Rewards card, prior to the start of a hand and we'll match your bet of $10 if you win. See reverse for details.

SILVER NUGGET
CASINO

$50 Bingo Matchplay

Purchase $50 in Bingo cards and receive two $25 matchplay vouchers for bingo, must be used in two different sessions. See reverse for full details.

SILVERTON
Casino • Hotel • Las Vegas

2-For-1 Seasons Buffet
(or 50% off when dining alone)

Must redeem at Silverton Rewards Loyalty Club to receive actual voucher. Must purchase one Seasons buffet at regular price, to receive a second buffet, of equal or lesser value, for free. Good for one time use only. Expires December 30, 2012.

CASINO

2140 Las Vegas Blvd. N.
N. Las Vegas, Nevada 89030
(702) 399-1111

Limit one offer per person, per month. Must enroll in Silver Rewards Club, or be a current member. Coupon must be surrendered after bet wins or loses. If you tie, then coupon may be re-bet. Cannot be redeemed for cash. Not valid with any other offer. Must be 21or older to redeem.No photocopies accepted. Management reserves all rights. Offer expires12/31/12.

Offer void if coupon is copied or sold

CASINO

2140 Las Vegas Blvd. N.
N. Las Vegas, Nevada 89030
(702) 399-1111

Limit one offer per person, per month. Must enroll in Silver Rewards Club, or be a current member. Cannot be redeemed for cash. Not valid with any other offer. Must be 21or older to redeem. No photocopies accepted. Management reserves all rights. Offer expires12/31/12.

Offer void if coupon is copied or sold

Casino • Hotel • Las Vegas

Silverton Hotel and Casino
3333 Blue Diamond Road
Las Vegas, NV 89139
www.silvertoncasino.com
702-263-7777 • 866-946-4373

Present this original coupon to the Silverton Rewards Loyalty Club. Must be a Player's Club member, or sign up as a new club member to receive the offer. Player's Club membership is free. Limit one per customer. Offer is non-transferable, may not be used in conjunction with any other offer or promotion and has no cash value. Management reserves all rights. Must be 21 years of age or older, with a valid form of ID. Offer does not include gratuity. Offer void if sold. Expires 12/30/12.

Offer void if coupon is copied or sold

SILVERTON
Casino • Hotel • Las Vegas

Join the Silverton Rewards Loyalty Club and receive $10 in FREE Slot Play!

New Silverton Rewards Loyalty Club members only. Must redeem at the Silverton Rewards Club and sign up as a new Club member. Good for one time use only. See reverse for more details.

A current American Casino Guide Discount Card must be presented when redeeming this coupon, or offer is void

---

SILVERTON
Casino • Hotel • Las Vegas

20% Off Hotel Stay

Please mention "American Casino Guide" at time of reservation and present coupon at check-in to receive discount. See reverse for more details.

A current American Casino Guide Discount Card must be presented when redeeming this coupon, or offer is void

---

STRATOSPHERE
HOTEL | **CASINO** | TOWER

Two-For-One Tower Admission Tickets

Get one FREE Tower admission ticket with the purchase of one Tower admission ticket at full price. Coupon must be presented at the Stratosphere Ticket Center. See back for details.

A current American Casino Guide Discount Card must be presented when redeeming this coupon, or offer is void

americancasinoguide.com

SILVERTON
Casino • Hotel • Las Vegas

Silverton Hotel and Casino
3333 Blue Diamond Road
Las Vegas, NV 89139
www.silvertoncasino.com
702-263-7777 • 866-946-4373

Present this original coupon to the Silverton Rewards Loyalty Club. Must sign up as a new club member to receive the offer. Free slot play will be expired one year from being issued. Offer is non-transferable, may not be used in conjunction with any other offer or promotion and has no cash value. Management reserves all rights. Must be 21 years of age or older, with a valid form of ID. Offer void if sold. Offer expires 12/30/12.

Offer void if coupon is copied or sold

americancasinoguide.com

SILVERTON
Casino • Hotel • Las Vegas

Silverton Hotel and Casino
3333 Blue Diamond Road
Las Vegas, NV 89139
www.silvertoncasino.com
702-263-7777 • 866-946-4373

This voucher entitles bearer to 20% off rack room rate at Silverton Casino Hotel. Must have advance reservations. Subject to availability. Must present voucher upon check-in. Not valid in conjunction with any other offer. Management reserves all rights to cancel this promotion at any time. Credit card required. Guest is responsible for tax, telephone, room service and all other additional charges. Black out dates are March 9 - 11, 2012 and November 29 - December 9, 2012. Must be 21 years or older. Limit one discounted room per person. Offer expires December 30, 2012. Settle to Marketing #148.

Offer void if coupon is copied or sold

americancasinoguide.com

STRATOSPHERE
HOTEL | **CASINO** | TOWER

2000 Las Vegas Blvd. S. • Las Vegas, NV 89104
800-99-TOWER • 702-380-7777

Management reserves all rights. Not for resale. Offers cannot be combined. Valid through December 30, 2012. **OFFER CODE: ACGTA (Coupon must be presented at the Stratosphere Ticket Center.)**

Offer void if coupon is copied or sold

Two-For-One
Show Tickets

**Get one FREE BITE LAS VEGAS
ticket with the purchase of one
BITE LAS VEGAS ticket at full price.
Coupon must be presented at the Stratosphere
Ticket Center. See back for details.**

A MOLYNEUX CREATION ®

HOTEL & CASINO · LAS VEGAS

2-For-1
Breakfast or
Lunch Buffet
(or 50% off when dining alone)

Buy one breakfast or lunch buffet and get a second one FREE (or 50% off
when dining alone). Offer valid Monday–Saturday. Coupon has no cash
value, must be 21 years of age or older. Must be a B Connected member
to redeem. See reverse for full details.

HOTEL & CASINO · LAS VEGAS

5X
Points!

Present this coupon to the B Connected Club and receive
5X points for one day's play from 12:01am-11:59pm.
See reverse for more details.

STRATOSPHERE

HOTEL | **CASINO** | TOWER

2000 Las Vegas Blvd. S. • Las Vegas, NV 89104
800-99-TOWER • 702-380-7777

Must be at least 18 years of age to attend the show. Subject to availability. Show times subject to change. Offers cannot be combined. Management reserves all rights. Not for resale. Valid through December 30, 2012. **OFFER CODE: ACGBT (Coupon must be presented at the Stratosphere Ticket Center.)**

HOTEL & CASINO · LAS VEGAS

(702) 636-7111 • 1-877-677-7111
9090 Alta Dr
www.suncoastcasino.com

Present this coupon to St. Tropez Buffet cashier. Tax and Gratuity is not included Original coupon (no photocopies) must be presented at the time of purchase. This offer is not valid with any other offer or promotion and is not valid on holidays. This offer is void if sold. Management reserves the right to change or cancel this offer at anytime. Offer expires 12/20/12

Offer Code: SBFAOPZ67

B Connected Membership # _____

HOTEL & CASINO · LAS VEGAS

(702) 636-7111 • 1-877-677-7111
9090 Alta Dr
www.suncoastcasino.com

Present this coupon to the B Connected Club with your B Connected Membership card. This offer is not cannot be used with any other offer or point multiplier offer. Must be 21 years of age. Management reserves the right to change or cancel this offer at any time. Limit one coupon per person. Offer Expires 12/20/12

Group Codes: 5XAMER11R 5XAMERIIS 5XAMERIIE

call1.800.640.9777
for **RESERVATIONS**
4100 Paradise Rd.
Las Vegas, NV • 89109

Call 1-800-640-9777 to make your reservation. Offer is good only after purchasing first night's stay at $49. This offer is valid for a Sunday through Wednesday arrival only during the months of June, July, August or December. Not valid Holidays. No cash value. One coupon per customer. Must be 21 years of age or older. Based on availability. Management reserves the right to modify, change or cancel this offer at anytime without prior notice. Offer expires 12/30/12.

www.terriblescasinos.com

Offer void if coupon is copied or sold

733.7000
4100 Paradise Rd.
Las Vegas, NV • 89109
www.terriblescasinos.com

Present this coupon, along with your Terrible's Player Card, to the Cashier at the Buffet when paying for your meal. Receive one FREE buffet with the purchase of one buffet at the regular price, or receive 50% off when dining alone. Does not apply to Thursday night seafood buffet. Must be a Players Club member. Limit: one coupon per person. Non-transferable. No cash value. Must be 21 years of age or older. Tax and gratuity not included. Management reserves the right to modify, change or cancel this offer at anytime without prior notice. Offer expires 12/30/12.

Offer void if coupon is copied or sold

733.7000
4100 Paradise Rd.
Las Vegas, NV • 89109
www.terriblescasinos.com

Must be 21 years of age or older and also be a Terrible's Players Club member. Make a $10 minimum even-money bet at any craps, blackjack or roulette game, along with this coupon (no photocopies), and receive a $10 Matching Bet. Valid for one bet only and original coupon must be surrendered after play. Offer void if sold. No Cash Value. Limit: one coupon per customer. Not valid with any other offer. Management reserves all rights. Offer expires 12/30/12.

Offer void if coupon is copied or sold

TUSCANY
SUITES & CASINO

2-For-1
Menu Item at
The Cantina
(or 50% off one item when dining alone)

Present this coupon, along with your Tuscany Player's Club Card, to your server at The Cantina to receive one FREE menu item when you purchase one item at the regular price, or receive 50% off one item when dining alone. See reverse for more details.

TUSCANY
SUITES & CASINO

$5 Table Games Match Play

This coupon entitles the bearer to $5 in match play on any even-money bet. Present to your casino dealer. Good for one decision on even-money bets only. An equal wager of real chips or cash must accompany this coupon. See reverse side for details.

Bella Panini

Buy One Get One 50% Off

Present this coupon at Bella Panini in the Venetian Hotel Grand Canal Shops, purchase your choice of any menu item and receive your choice of a second menu item of equal or lesser value at half price!

americancasinoguide.com

255 E Flamingo Road
Las Vegas, NV 89169
(702) 893-8933 • (877) 887-2261
www.tuscanylv.com

Present this original coupon to your server, along with your Tuscany Player's Club Card, to receive one FREE menu item from the regular menu with the purchase of another menu item at the regular price (or 50% off one item if dining alone). The FREE item must be of equal or lesser value. Limit: one coupon per customer, per calendar month. No cash value. Must be 21 years of age or older. Tax and gratuity not included. Resale prohibited. Management reserves all rights. Offer expires 12/30/12.

Offer void if coupon is copied or sold

americancasinoguide.com

255 E Flamingo Road
Las Vegas, NV 89169
(702) 893-8933 • (877) 887-2261
www.tuscanylv.com

When using this promotional coupon, if you lose your wager the coupon will be claimed by the house. If you win your bet, your winnings will be paid in live gaming chips and the coupon wagered will be claimed by the house. Live gaming chips may be re-bet or exchanged for cash. If your bet is a tie, you may re-bet your coupon.

Bearer must be at least 21 years of age and prepared to present a photo ID. Limit one coupon per person per 30-day period. Coupon has no cash value and cannot be combined with any other offer or used more than once. Reproduction, sale, barter and transfer are prohibited and render this coupon void. Management reserves all rights. Offer expires 12/30/12.

Offer void if coupon is copied or sold

americancasinoguide.com

Bella Panini

Venetian Hotel Grand Canal Shops

Must present coupon to cashier prior to ordering. Offer has no cash value. Not valid with any other offer. One coupon per person. Subject to change or cancellation without prior notice. Offer valid through December 31, 2012.

Offer void if coupon is copied or sold

THE GRAND CANAL SHOPPES
AT THE VENETIAN®

FASHION SHOW
LAS VEGAS

FREE Premier Passport

Please redeem this voucher at Fashion Show Concierge, lower level near Macy's or at Brighton or Welcome to Las Vegas at The Grand Canal Shoppes to receive your complimentary Premier Passport! While supplies last. Expires 12/31/12.

A current American Casino Guide Discount Card must be presented when redeeming this coupon, or offer is void

FREE Milkshake

Present this coupon at any Johnny Rocket's listed on the back, purchase any burger and fries and receive a milkshake FREE! See reverse for details.

A current American Casino Guide Discount Card must be presented when redeeming this coupon, or offer is void

Rialto Deli

20% Off

Present this coupon to receive 20% off your entire order at Rialto Deli at the Venetian Resort Hotel Casino. Valid every day after 2 pm. See reverse for more details.

A current American Casino Guide Discount Card must be presented when redeeming this coupon, or offer is void

THE GRAND CANAL SHOPPES
AT THE VENETIAN®

Adjacent to The Palazzo across
from Fashion Show and TI
24-Hour Shopping Line
(702) 414-4500
www.thegrandcanalshoppes.com

GGP

FASHION SHOW
LAS VEGAS

Located on the Strip across
from Wynn Las Vegas,
The Palazzo and TI
Concierge (702) 369-8382
www.thefashionshow.com

SHOPLV3

Venetian Hotel Grand Canal Shops
Fashion Show Mall
Meadows Mall Food Court
Flamingo Hotel Food Court

Must present coupon to cashier prior to ordering. Offer has no cash value. Not valid
with any other offer. One coupon per person. Subject to change or cancellation
without prior notice. Offer valid through December 31, 2012.

Rialto Deli

at the Venetian Resort Hotel Casino
3355 Las Vegas Blvd S • Las Vegas, NV
Open Daily From 8am

Present this original coupon to the server when placing your order at Rialto
Deli to redeem. Valid every day after 2 pm. Limit one coupon per customer.
Offer may not be used in conjunction with any other offer or promotion
and has no cash value. Management reserves all rights. Offer void if sold.
Expires December 30, 2012.

San Gennaro Grill
Buy One Get One 50% Off

Present this coupon at the San Gennaro Grill in the Venetian Hotel Grand Canal Shops, purchase your choice of any menu item and receive your choice of a second menu item of equal or lesser value at half price!

A current American Casino Guide Discount Card must be presented when redeeming this coupon, or offer is void

 **20% Off**

Present this coupon to receive 20% off your entire order at Shake 'N Burger in the Grand Canal Shoppes at the Venetian Resort Hotel Casino. Valid every day after 2 pm. See reverse for more details.

A current American Casino Guide Discount Card must be presented when redeeming this coupon, or offer is void

TOWERS DELICATESSEN
SINCE 1915

20% Off

Present this coupon to receive 20% off your entire order at Towers Deli in the Grand Canal Shoppes at the Venetian Resort Hotel Casino. Valid every day after 2 pm. See reverse for more details.

A current American Casino Guide Discount Card must be presented when redeeming this coupon, or offer is void

San Gennaro Grill
Venetian Hotel Casino Floor

Must present coupon to cashier prior to ordering. Offer has no cash value. Not valid with any other offer. One coupon per person. Subject to change or cancellation without prior notice. Offer valid through December 31, 2012.

Venetian Resort Hotel Casino
3355 Las Vegas Blvd S
Las Vegas, NV 89109
Open Daily From 8am

Present this original coupon to the server when placing your order at Shake 'N Burger to redeem. Valid every day after 2 pm. Limit one coupon per customer. Offer may not be used in conjunction with any other offer or promotion and has no cash value. Management reserves all rights. Offer void if sold. Expires December 30, 2012.

TOWERS DELICATESSEN

in the Grand Canal Shoppes at the Venetian Resort Hotel Casino
3355 Las Vegas Blvd S • Las Vegas, NV
Open Daily From 10am

Present this original coupon to the server when placing your order at Towers Deli to redeem. Valid every day after 2 pm. Limit one coupon per customer. Offer may not be used in conjunction with any other offer or promotion and has no cash value. Management reserves all rights. Offer void if sold. Expires December 30, 2012.

FREE Cocktail
and Line Pass

Present this coupon to your server to receive one free wine,
house cocktail or draft with the purchase of same. Guest may
also present this coupon to the VIP host for immediate entry
to V Bar at the Venetian Resort Hotel Casino.

$5 Matchplay
on any Even
Money Bet

Present this coupon at any blackjack table prior to the start of play
and we'll match your bet of $5 if you win. See reverse for details.

10% off any
menu item at
the Western Cafè

Present this coupon at the Western Cafè at the Western Casino
at time of ordering to receive 10% off any one menu item.
See reverse for details.

Venetian Resort Hotel Casino
3355 Las Vegas Blvd S
Las Vegas, NV
Open Daily From 5pm

Present this original coupon to the server when placing your order and/or to the doorperson to gain immediate entry. Valid every day. Limit one coupon per customer. Offer may not be used in conjunction with any other offer or promotion and has no cash value. Management reserves all rights. Must be 21 years of age or older, with a valid form of ID. Offer does not include gratuity. Offer void if sold. Expires December 30, 2012.

899 E Fremont Street
Las Vegas, NV 89101
(702) 384-4620

Limit: one coupon per person, per calendar month. Cannot be redeemed for cash. Must be 21 or older. Cannot be combined with any other offer or promotion. Good for one decision on even-money bet only. Win or lose, coupon is claimed by the house. If you tie, then coupon may be re-bet.

Must present original coupon (no photocopies). Management reserves all rights. Offer may be changed or discontinued at anytime at the discretion of management. Offer expires 12/29/12.

899 E Fremont Street
Las Vegas, NV 89101
(702) 384-4620

Management reserves the right to modify this offer at any time without prior notice. Original coupon must be presented (no photocopies).

Cannot be combined with any other offer, advertisement or mailing. Must be 21 years of age or older. Limit one coupon per person per visit. Subject to availability. Gratuity not included. Offer valid through 12/29/12.

Two-For-One
Show Tickets

Get one FREE "Remembering Red: A Tribute to Red Skelton" ticket
with the purchase of one ticket at full price. Coupon must be presented
at the box office. See back for full details.

A current American Casino Guide Discount Card must be
presented when redeeming this coupon, or offer is void

$45 Off Sunset
Dinner Ride

Present this coupon at time of purchase to receive $45 off the
regular price of the sunset dinner ride. See reverse for details.

A current American Casino Guide Discount Card must be
presented when redeeming this coupon, or offer is void

COLORADO BELLE
CASINO · RESORT · LAUGHLIN

One
FREE
Night!

Buy one night at $39 and get your second night FREE!
Advance reservations required. Call (702) 298-2453 ext. 3338
Monday to Friday 9am – 4:30pm. Mention Code ACGCB.

A current American Casino Guide Discount Card must be
presented when redeeming this coupon, or offer is void

americancasinoguide.com

Westin Casuarina
160 E Flamingo Rd
Las Vegas, NV 89109
(724) 513-4031 or visit
www.redskeltoncomedyshow.com

Subject to availability. Shows 2 P.M. Monday and Tuesday. Show times subject to change. Offers cannot be combined. Children 12 and under free with ticketed adult. Management reserves all rights. Not for resale. Valid through December 27, 2012.

Offer void if coupon is copied or sold

americancasinoguide.com

2470 Chandler Ave Suite 11
Las Vegas, NV 89120
(702) 792-5050
wildwesthorsebackadventures.com

Present this coupon at time of purchase to receive $45 off the regular price of the sunset dinner ride. No cash value. Offer valid for all party members.

This adventure includes roundtrip transportation, a 1.5 hour trail ride in beautiful Glendale, a mouthwatering steak BBQ dinner, spectacular views, and memories that will last a lifetime. Management reserves all rights and may change or cancel this promotion at any time without notice. Offer is valid through December 23, 2012.

Offer void if coupon is copied or sold

americancasinoguide.com

COLORADO BELLE
CASINO · RESORT · LAUGHLIN

2100 S Casino Dr
Laughlin, NV 89029
(702) 298-4000
(800) 477-4837
www.coloradobelle.com

Must be at least 21 with valid photo ID. Subject to availability. Credit Card required to reserve room. Rate based on standard room. Valid Sunday – Wednesday. Excludes holidays and special events. Subject to change/cancellation. Limit one coupon per stay. Non-negotiable. No cash value. May not be redeemed by Edgewater or Colorado Belle employees. Management reserves all rights. Valid through 12/29/2012.

Offer void if coupon is copied or sold

COLORADO BELLE
CASINO · RESORT · LAUGHLIN

FREE Buffet!

Buy one buffet and receive the second buffet FREE!
Redeem this coupon at Colorado Belle's Captain's Buffet.
Must be at least 21. Comp # 63150

COLORADO BELLE
CASINO · RESORT · LAUGHLIN

$5 FREE Slot Play!

Join the ACCESS Club and receive $5 in Free Slot Play! For new member
sign-up's only. Redeem at the Colorado Belle's ACCESS Club booth.
See reverse for details.

EDGEWATER
CASINO · RESORT · LAUGHLIN

One FREE Night!

Buy one night at $39 and get your second night FREE!
Advance reservations required.Call 702-298-2453 ext. 3338
Mon-Fri 9am – 4:30pm. Mention Code ACGEW.

americancasinoguide.com

COLORADO BELLE
CASINO · RESORT · LAUGHLIN

2100 S Casino Dr
Laughlin, NV 89029
(702) 298-4000
(800) 477-4837
www.coloradobelle.com

Gratuity not included. Must be at least 21. Subject to change/cancellation. No cash value, non-refundable, non-negotiable. Only original coupons accepted. May not be redeemed by Edgewater/Colorado Belle employees. May not be combined with any other offer/discount. Valid through 12/29/2012. Comp # 63150

Offer void if coupon is copied or sold

---

americancasinoguide.com

COLORADO BELLE
CASINO · RESORT · LAUGHLIN

2100 S Casino Dr
Laughlin, NV 89029
(702) 298-4000
(800) 477-4837
www.coloradobelle.com

Must be at least 21 to sign up. Management reserves all rights. Receive a free hat or t-shirt with 100 points on the first day. Offer expires 12/29/12.

Name: _____

Address: _____

City: _____ State: _____ Zip: _____

ACCESS Clerk: _____ Valid: _____

Offer void if coupon is copied or sold

---

americancasinoguide.com

CASINO · RESORT · LAUGHLIN

2020 S Casino Dr
Laughlin, NV 89029
(702) 298-2453
(800) 667-4837
www.edgewater-casino.com

Must be at least 21 with valid photo ID. Subject to availability. Credit Card required to reserve room. Rate based on standard room. Valid Sunday – Wednesday. Excludes holidays and special events. Subject to change/cancellation. Limit one coupon per stay. Non-negotiable. No cash value. May not be redeemed by Edgewater or Colorado Belle employees. Management reserves all rights. Valid through 12/29/2012.

Offer void if coupon is copied or sold

AMERICAN CASINO GUIDE

EDGEWATER
CASINO • RESORT • LAUGHLIN

FREE Buffet!

Buy one buffet and receive the second buffet FREE!
Redeem this coupon at Edgewater's Grand Buffet.
Must be at least 21. Comp # 63025

A current American Casino Guide Discount Card must be
presented when redeeming this coupon, or offer is void

AMERICAN CASINO GUIDE

EDGEWATER
CASINO • RESORT • LAUGHLIN

$5 FREE Slot Play!

Join the ACCESS Club and receive $5 in Free Slot Play! For new member
sign-up's only. Redeem at the Edgewater's ACCESS Club booth.
See reverse for details.

A current American Casino Guide Discount Card must be
presented when redeeming this coupon, or offer is void

AMERICAN CASINO GUIDE

Buy One Buffet - Get One FREE!

Present this coupon at the Fresh Market Square Buffet at Harrah's Laughlin
at time of purchase. Buy one buffet (brunch or dinner) and receive one buffet
free! Valid at Harrah's Laughlin only. Offer code: 176

A current American Casino Guide Discount Card must be
presented when redeeming this coupon, or offer is void

americancasinoguide.com

CASINO • RESORT • LAUGHLIN

2020 S Casino Dr
Laughlin, NV 89029
(702) 298-2453
(800) 667-4837
www.edgewater-casino.com

Gratuity not included. Must be at least 21. Subject to change/cancellation. No cash value, non-refundable, non-negotiable. Only original coupons accepted. May not be redeemed by Edgewater/Colorado Belle employees. May not be combined with any other offer/discount. Valid through 12/29/2012. Comp # 63025

Offer void if coupon is copied or sold

americancasinoguide.com

EDGEWATER

CASINO • RESORT • LAUGHLIN

2020 S Casino Dr
Laughlin, NV 89029
(702) 298-2453
(800) 667-4837
www.edgewater-casino.com

Must be at least 21 to sign up. Management reserves all rights. Receive a free hat or t-shirt with 100 points on the first day. Offer expires 12/29/2012.

Name: _____
Address: _____
City: _____ State: _____ Zip: _____
ACCESS Clerk: _____ Valid: _____

Offer void if coupon is copied or sold

americancasinoguide.com

LAUGHLIN

2900 South Casino Drive
Laughlin, Nevada 89029
(702) 298-4600 • (800) HARRAHS
www.harrahs.com

Management reserves the right to modify this offer at any time without prior notice. Original coupon must be presented (no photocopies). Not valid on weekends (Friday/Saturday) or holidays. Cannot be used in conjunction with any other offer. Must be 21 or older to redeem. Coupon has no cash value. Limit one coupon per person per visit. Subject to availability. Gratuity not included. Offer valid through 12/15/12. Must be 21 years or older to gamble. Know When To Stop Before You Start.® Gambling Problem? Call 1-800-522-4700. ©2011, Caesars License Company, LLC. Know When To Stop Before You Start.® Gambling Problem? Call 1-800-522-4700. ©2011, Caesars License Company, LLC.

Offer void if coupon is copied or sold

Buy One Entree - Get One FREE!

Present this coupon at the Beach Cafe at Harrah's Laughlin at time of seating.
Buy one entree at the Beach Cafe and receive one entree of equal
or lesser value FREE! Valid at Harrah's Laughlin only. Offer code: 176

A current American Casino Guide Discount Card must be
presented when redeeming this coupon, or offer is void

PAHRUMP NUGGET HOTEL • CASINO

$5 Match Play for Any Even-Money Table Game Bet
(with your Club Nugget Card)

Make a $5 even-money bet at blackjack, craps or roulette
with this coupon and your Club Nugget Card and receive a
FREE $5 Match Bet! See reverse for more details.

A current American Casino Guide Discount Card must be
presented when redeeming this coupon, or offer is void

PAHRUMP NUGGET HOTEL • CASINO

$5 in FREE Slot Play Guaranteed!

New members only, present this coupon at the Club Nugget Booth,
sign up for a Club Nugget card and receive at least $5 in FREE slot
play with a chance to win up to $500! See reverse for more details.

A current American Casino Guide Discount Card must be
presented when redeeming this coupon, or offer is void

americancasinoguide.com

2900 South Casino Drive
Laughlin, Nevada 89029
(702) 298-4600 • (800) HARRAHS
www.harrahs.com

Management reserves the right to modify this offer at any time without prior notice. Original coupon must be presented (no photocopies). Not valid on weekends (Friday/Saturday) or holidays. Cannot be used in conjunction with any other offer. Must be 21 or older to redeem. Limit one coupon per person per visit. Subject to availability. Gratuity not included. Offer valid through 12/15/12. Must be 21 years or older to gamble. Know When To Stop Before You Start.® Gambling Problem? Call 1-800-522-4700. ©2011, Caesars License Company, LLC.

americancasinoguide.com

681 S. Highway 160
Pahrump, NV 89048
(775) 751-6500
(866) 751-6500
www.pahrumpnugget.com

Must be 21 years of age or older and a Club Nugget member. Make a $5 minimum even-money bet at any blackjack, craps or roulette game, along with this original coupon (no photocopies), and receive a $5 Match Bet. Valid for one bet only and coupon must be surrendered after play. If you tie, then coupon can be re-bet. No Cash Value. Limit: one coupon per customer. Not valid with any other offer. Resale prohibited. Management reserves all rights. Offer expires 12/30/12.

americancasinoguide.com

681 S. Highway 160
Pahrump, NV 89048
(775) 751-6500
(866) 751-6500
www.pahrumpnugget.com

Must be 21 years or older. Not valid with any other offers or discounts. Management reserves the right to cancel or modify this offer at any time. Limit one coupon per account. Must show valid I.D. Coupon has no cash value. Free play must be played on a slot machine and cannot be cashed out. May not be combined with any other offer or promotion. Offer expires 12/30/12.

PAHRUMP NUGGET
HOTEL • CASINO

One FREE Hotel Night Stay!

Pay for one room night at the full rate and receive the second room night FREE. See reverse side for more details.

A current American Casino Guide Discount Card must be presented when redeeming this coupon, or offer is void

Harrah's
RENO

Buy One Carvings® Buffet Get One FREE!

Receive one Carvings Buffet FREE with the purchase of a full price Carvings Buffet. Present this coupon and Total Rewards® card to the Carvings Buffet cashier at Harrah's Reno prior to seating. Valid at Harrah's Reno only. See reverse for details. Coupon code: CG2F1

A current American Casino Guide Discount Card must be presented when redeeming this coupon, or offer is void

GOLD RANCH
CASINO & RV RESORT

$10 in FREE Slot Play

Valid with new membership only. One coupon per account. Redeem at Ranch Rewards Club from 10am until 10pm. No cash value. Management reserves all rights. See reverse for details.

#16010

A current American Casino Guide Discount Card must be presented when redeeming this coupon, or offer is void

PAHRUMP NUGGET
HOTEL • CASINO

681 S. Highway 160
Pahrump, NV 89048
(775) 751-6500
(866) 751-6500
www.pahrumpnugget.com

Valid Sunday through Thursday for consecutive night stays in the same room. Holidays and special events excluded. Subject to availability. Must have advance reservations by calling 866-751-6500 and must advise the Pahrump Nugget Hotel agent that you are calling for the *American Casino Guide offer.* Must present and surrender this coupon upon check-in. No exceptions.

Management reserves the right to modify or cancel this promotion at any time. Not valid with any other offer. Customer required to place credit card on file at check-in. Customer responsible for all other additional charges. Must be 21 or older. Limit one free room night per coupon. Offer expires 12/30/12.

Harrah's
RENO

219 North Center Street
Reno, Nevada 89501
(775) 786-3232 • (800) HARRAHS
www.harrahs.com

Cannot be combined with any other offer. Gratuity not included. Management reserves the right to change or discontinue offer without notice. Restrictions apply. Must be 21 or older to gamble. Know When To Stop Before You Start. ® Gambling Problem? Call 1-800-522-4700. ©2011, Caesars License Company, LLC. Offer valid through December 30, 2012.

GOLD RANCH
CASINO & RV RESORT

Exit #2 I-80 West
Verdi, NV 89439
(775) 345-6789
(877) 927-6789
www.goldranchrvcasino.com

- Offer valid for adults 21 years of age or older.
- Present original coupon (no photocopies).
- Limit one coupon per account.
- Management reserves the right to cancel or alter this coupon without prior notice.
- Not valid with any other offer.
- Offer expires 12/30/12.

GOLD RANCH
CASINO & RV RESORT

$5 in FREE Food at Sierra Café

Present this coupon at the Ranch Rewards Club for $5 in FREE food at the Sierra Café. See reverse for more details.

#16011

A current American Casino Guide Discount Card must be presented when redeeming this coupon, or offer is void

---

GOLD RANCH
CASINO & RV RESORT

FREE Drink at Kantina Bar

Present this coupon to your server at the Kantina Bar for one FREE domestic beer or well drink. See reverse for more details.

A current American Casino Guide Discount Card must be presented when redeeming this coupon, or offer is void

---

Two-For-One Admission

Present this coupon and get one free admission with the purchase of one adult admission at Ripley's Believe It or Not.® Located on the famous Atlantic City Boardwalk. See back for full details.

A current American Casino Guide Discount Card must be presented when redeeming this coupon, or offer is void

GOLD RANCH
CASINO & RV RESORT

Exit #2 I-80 West
Verdi, NV 89439
(775) 345-6789
(877) 927-6789
www.goldranchrvcasino.com

- Offer valid for adults 21 years of age or older.
- Present original coupon (no photocopies) to Ranch Rewards Center.
- Limit one coupon per person.
- Management reserves the right to cancel or alter this coupon without prior notice.
- Dine-in only.
- Gratuity not included.
- Offer expires 12/30/12.

GOLD RANCH
CASINO & RV RESORT

Exit #2 I-80 West
Verdi, NV 89439
(775) 345-6789
(877) 927-6789
www.goldranchrvcasino.com

- Offer valid for adults 21 years of age or older.
- Present original coupon (no photocopies) to server prior to ordering.
- Limit one coupon per person.
- Management reserves the right to cancel or alter this coupon without prior notice.
- Gratuity not included.
- Offer expires 12/30/12.

Ripley's Believe It or Not!®

On the Boardwalk at
New York Avenue
Atlantic City, NJ 08401
(609) 347-2001

Open year 'round
Call for operating hours

Adults: $15.99
Children (5-12) $9.99
4 and under Free
Prices subject to change

Not valid with any other offer. Limit: one free ticket per coupon. Expires December 30, 2012.